THE RIGHTS OF THE CHILD AND THE CHANGING IMAGE OF CHILDHOOD

International Studies in Human Rights

VOLUME 18

For a list of titles published in this series, see final page of this volume.

The Rights of the Child
and
the Changing Image of Childhood

by

PHILIP E. VEERMAN

MARTINUS NIJHOFF PUBLISHERS
DORDRECHT / BOSTON / LONDON

Library of Congress Cataloging-in-Publication Data

```
Veerman, Philip E.
   The rights of the child and the changing image of childhood / by
Philip E. Veerman.
      p.   cm. -- (International studies in human rights ; v. 18)
   Includes bibliographical references (p.    ) and index.
   ISBN 0-7923-1250-3 (HB)
   1. Children's rights.  2. Children--Legal status, laws, etc.
I. Title.  II. Series.
HQ789.V44  1991
305.23--dc20                                                  91-19966
```

ISBN 0-7923-1250-3

Cover photo: "The Youngest Breaker Boys", by Lewis Hines. Reproduced courtesy of George Eastman House, International Museum of Photography, Rochester, NY, USA.

Published by Martinus Nijhoff Publishers,
P.O. Box 163, 3300 AD Dordrecht, The Netherlands.

Sold and distributed in the U.S.A. and Canada
by Kluwer Academic Publishers,
101 Philip Drive, Norwell, MA 02061, U.S.A.

In all other countries, sold and distributed
by Kluwer Academic Publishers Group,
P.O. Box 322, 3300 AH Dordrecht, The Netherlands.

Printed on acid-free paper

All Rights Reserved
© 1992 Kluwer Academic Publishers
Kluwer Academic Publishers incorporates the publishing programmes of Martinus Nijhoff Publishers.
No part of the material protected by this copyright notice may be reproduced or utilized in any form or by any means, electronic or mechanical, including photocopying, recording or by any information storage and retrieval system, without written permission from the copyright owners.

Printed in the Netherlands.

*This book is dedicated to
the memory of my familymember
Ina Clara Blom, born
9.7.1925 in Amsterdam
murdered on 22.10.1943
in Auschwitz*

Contents

Acknowledgements	xi
Introduction	xv

PART A: DEFINING 'CHILDREN' AND THEIR 'RIGHTS'

I. To What Extent Did the 'Image of Childhood' Change?	3
II. In Search of Workable Definitions	13

PART B: THE ANALYSIS OF CHILDREN'S RIGHTS – A CONCEPTUAL FRAMEWORK

III. Shye's 'Systemic Quality of Life Model'	39
IV. From Basing Children's Rights on Needs to Basing Them on Effective Functioning	57

PART C: THE PIONEERS

V. Ellen Key and the Right of the Child to Choose Its Own Parents Wisely	75
VI. Eglantyne Jebb: The World Is My Country	87
VII. Janusz Korczak and the Right of the Child to Respect	93
VIII. Modern Pioneers	113
IX. The Children's Liberation Movement	133

PART D: DECLARATIONS AND CONVENTIONS: PAST AND PRESENT — 153

X. The International Consensus	
1. The Declaration of Geneva (1924)	155
2. The United Nations Declaration on the Rights of the Child (1959)	159

3. The United Nations Convention on the Rights of the Child (1989) ... 181
4. The World Declaration on the Survival, Protection and Development of Children (1990) ... 209

XI. National and Regional Declarations
1. The Children's Charter of President Hoover's White House Conference on Child Health and Protection (1930) ... 231
2. A Children's Charter in Wartime of the United States Department of Labor Children's Bureau (1942) ... 237
3. The Declaration of Opportunities for Children (Adopted by the Eighth Pan American Child Congress, May 1942) ... 243
4. The Children's Bill of Rights of the New York State Youth Commission (1949) ... 247
5. The Pledge to Children: Mid-Century White House Conference on Children and Youth (1950) ... 250
6. The Children's Charter, Japan (1950) ... 254
7. The Children's Bill of Rights of the White House Conference on Children (1970) ... 254
8. Rights of Youth, Formulated by the White House Conference on Youth (1971) ... 259
9. The Charter of the Rights of the Arab Child of the League of Arab States ... 260
10. Declaration of the Rights of the Child in Israel (1989) ... 263
11. Declaration of the Rights of Mozambican Children (1979) ... 267
12. Towards New Regional Charters ... 270
13. The Charter on the Rights and Welfare of the African Child ... 271

XII. Ideological Declarations
1. The Declaration of the Rights of the Child, Proposed to 'Prolet'cult' (Moscow, 1918) ... 281
2. The Children's Charter for the Post-War World, Proclaimed by a Conference of the New Education Fellowship in London, 1942 ... 285
3. The Draft-Charter of Children's Rights of the British Magazine 'Where' (1971) ... 287
4. The Ten Commandments for Adults of Leonhard Froese, (Marburg, Germany, 1979) ... 292
5. The Youth Charter-Act Proposed by Professor James Wallace, M.P. (1985) ... 295
6. The Labour Party Charter for Young People (London, 1985) ... 297
7. The Children's Legal Centre Manifesto for Children (London, 1987) ... 299
8. 'Childrens and Young People's Charter' (Labour Party, London, 1990) ... 304

Contents

XIII. Specified and Sectarian Declarations and Conventions
  1. International Labour Legislation — 309
  2. Concerning the Minimum Age for Admission to Employment, ILO Convention No. 138 (1973) — 314
  3. The Declaration of the Rights of the Adolescent (1922) — 318
  4. The Youth Charter (Adopted in Oslo at the Thirteenth World Congress of the International Confederation of Free Trade Unions, ICFTU, in 1983) — 319
  5. International Agreements Relating to the Traffic of Women and Children (1904, 1910, 1921) — 323
  6. The Children's Charter of the International Council of Women (1922). — 325
  7. A Bill of Rights for Children, Proposed by Henry Foster and Doris Freed (1972). — 328
  8. The Rights of Children in Divorce Actions (Wisconsin, U.S.A., 1966) — 332
  9. A Bill of Rights for Foster Children (1973). — 338
  10. The U.N. Declaration Relating to Foster Placement and Adoption (1986) — 341
  11. The Charter of Rights for Children in Care of the London Borough's Children's Regional Planning Committee (August, 1986) — 346
  12. A Bill of Rights for Juveniles (New York State, Division for Youth, 1973) — 351
  13. Charters for Children in Hospital — 354
  14. Rights of Children Formulated by the Joint Commission on Mental Health of Children (USA, 1969) — 359
  15. The Children and Youth Bill of Rights of the National Association of Social Workers, NASW (USA, 1975) — 363
  16. The Declaration of the Psychological Rights of the Child of the International Association of School Psychologists (1979) — 366
  17. The Malta Declaration of the Child's Right to Play (of the International Playground Association, November 1977) — 369

XIV. Summary and Conclusions — 395

Suggestions for Further Research — 401

Appendices — 413

Bibliography — 604

About the Author — 625

Index of Subjects — 626

Index of Children's Rights — 638

Index of Names   642
Index of Cases   650
Index of Documents   651

Acknowledgements

During the many years that it took me to write this book I was assisted by a great many persons and institutions to whom I want to extend my thanks.

The Netherlands-America Commission for Educational Exchange who nominated me for a grant under the Fulbright Research Scholar Programme made it possible for me to collect an important part of the material. Columbia University in the City of New York and its School of Social Work received me as a Visiting Scholar and provided office space. UNICEF also provided office space at UNICEF House in New York. I am especially grateful to Mr. Jack Charnow of UNICEF's History-Project for his encouragements and suggestions. The Council for International Exchange of Scholars in Washington D.C. was also very helpful during my stay in the United States.

The board of the 'Weeshuis der Hervormden' in Schiedam, the Netherlands, provided financial support for this part of the project. My stay as a Visiting Fellow at the University of London Institute of Education was made possible by the British Council Fellowship and enabled me to collect another major part of information. The Netherlands Organisation for Scientific Research (NWO) also helped me with a travel grant.

Support for my research in Israel, where I collected material about Janusz Korczak, came from the 'Memorial Foundation for Jewish Culture' in New York, the 'Stichting R.C. Maagdenhuis' in Amsterdam, the 'Goudse Stichting voor Joodse Sociale Arbeid' in Voorburg, The Netherlands, the 'Amsterdamse Universiteits Vereniging', the 'Fronica Sanders Foundation' in Amsterdam, the M.A.O.C. Gravin van Bylandt Foundation in the Hague, the Foundation 'Witte Bedjes' of the Parool Newspaper in Amsterdam, the Stichting Steunfonds in Dordrecht, the Clara Mendes Foundation in Amsterdam, the 'Centraal Israelietisch Wees- en Doorgangshuis Machseh Lajesoumem' in The Hague, and the 'Maatschappij tot Nut der Israelieten in Nederland', Amsterdam. In 1982 the Max and Bernard Meyers Foundation in Amsterdam gave me a travel grant for some first investigations. Thanks to the constant financial support of my parents, Paul Veerman and Willy Veerman-Blom, this project could be brought to a successful end.

Mr. Reuven Yatziv of the Korczak Archives (the Ghetto Fighters House, Kibbutz Lohamei Haghetaot, Israel) and Mrs. Alla Raviv in Jerusalem helped me read Polish texts and letters.

I am very grateful that many former pupils and former co-workers of Janusz Korczak agreed to share with me their memories of the vanished world of Jewish Warsaw and of life in the orphanage of Janusz Korczak and

Stefania Wilszynska. I am already using this rich oral history material for other studies.

Professor Lea Dasberg (Emerita of the History and Theory of Education Chair at the University of Amsterdam), the supervisor of the thesis on which this study is based, was always available for advice and suggestions. I owe her special thanks, not only for her careful final reading of the manuscript but also for the many stimulating conversations we had.

Professor Jan van der Ploeg (State University, Leyden), co-supervisor of my thesis, helped shape this study by some essential suggestions.

I am happy that a committee of prominent scientists approved the study: Professors E.A. Alkema (Faculty of Laws of the University of Amsterdam and the State University, Leyden, The Netherlands), Th. van Boven (Faculty of Law, State University, Maastricht, The Netherlands), Th. Dibbits (Emeritus, Pedagogics, Didaktisch Instituut, University of Amsterdam, The Netherlands), M.C. de Langen (Faculty of Law, University of Amsterdam, The Netherlands) and E. Verhellen (State University, Gent, Belgium).

Dr. Samuel Shye (Research-Director of the Louis Guttman Institute of Applied Social Research in Jerusalem), taught me the language of his 'Systemic Quality of Life Model' during many interesting sessions.

I am grateful to Professor Albert J. Solnit (Sterling Emeritus of the Pediatrics and Psychiatry Chair of Yale University) for our many stimulating meetings.

I thank Professor Stephen Goldstein (former Dean of the Faculty of Law of the Hebrew University in Jerusalem) for his careful comments on Chapter II. Dr Malfrid Grude Flekkøy (Oslo) read Chapter VIII.

My friend Klaas Groen (former Director-General of Special Youth Care of the Dutch Ministry of Social Welfare, Health and Culture) wrote me many letters and gave helpful advice.

Mr. Kees Nederlof of the Dutch Ministry of Foreign Affairs gave me his word processor. Jossi Miller (legal intern DCI-Isreal) helped to make the index.

Simone Ek of Rädda Barnen (Swedish Save the Children) allowed me to make use of her *Compilation of the on-going work of the drafting of the United Nations Convention on the Rights of the Child*.

Without the translating and editorial work of Mrs. Hannah Yakin this manuscript would never have reached the offices of Martinus Nijhoff. Dr. Anita Weiner (Senior Lecturer at the School of Social Work of Haifa University) helped me tremendously by her final editing of the text. Ms. Maja Landau also edited several chapters. Graphic designer Edna Eisenberg spent many hours with me thinking how to visualise ideas and analytic work.

Professor J.C. Hudig (former Juvenile Judge in Rotterdam) suggested the general approach to my subject. Dr. D.Q.R. Mulock Houwer (former Secretary-General of the International Union for Child Welfare) drew my attention to the importance of pioneers in this field.

My wife Lea shared the journey of this study with me. My deepest thanks for her support, her patience and her co-operation all along the way.

Picture 1. The Voyage of Life: Childhood (Thomas Cole, dated 1842; canvas. National Gallery of Art, Washington D.C., U.S.A.).

Picture 2. The Voyage of Life: Youth (Thomas Cole, dated 1842; canvas. National Gallery of Art, Washington D.C., U.S.A.).

Introduction

The Declaration of Independence of the United States, adopted on July 1776, formulates "that all men are created equal" and "that they are endowed by their Creator with certain inalienable Rights" – not a self-evident thought in those days.

In 1779 Hannah More, fearing that the new ideas about the rights of men would find their way from America and France to good old England, wrote disdainfully that "the logical next step of our benefactors would be to enlighten the world with thoughts about the rights of youngsters, children and babies."[1]

Two Centuries after Hannah More's bantering remarks, the rights of the child were already nothing to sneer at, and if she could read what was written about the subject in 1979, 'the International Year of the Child', she would be very upset. During that year plans were revealed in the United Kingdom to found a *Children's Legal Centre* in London, the object of which was "to promote the acknowledgement that children and youngsters must be allowed to participate as independent human beings in all decisions concerning their lives."[2]

"Not long ago," writes Barbara Chrisholm, "it was absurd to talk about the rights of the child, but today it is a serious social issue."[3]

In this study an attempt will be made to answer the following two questions:

1. *Did the Image of Childhood change during our century and how?*
2. *Is it possible to study Children's Rights systematically in different parts of the world and in different periods of this century?*

In order to answer these questions, we shall study some developments in the field of the rights of the child, the work of pioneers in children's rights, and Declarations and Conventions during the Twentieth Century.

Throughout this study the author assumes that

- ideas on children's rights are expressions of an image of childhood of the beholder;

- children's rights are formulated with the intention of promoting the interests of children;
- rights may be cast in a quality of life scheme, provided that such a scheme is sufficiently comprehensive.

NOTES

1. More, Hannah, *Strictures on the Modern System of Female Education; with a view of the Principles and conduct among women of rank and fortune*, Vol. 1, London, 1799.
2. *The Children's Legal Centre*, London, brochure. Although the initiative was first taken in 1979, the centre opened its doors only in 1981.
3. Chrisholm, Barbara, 'Children's Rights', in: *Perception, Canadian Journal of Social Comment*, Vol. 1, No. 2, Nov./Dec. 1977, pp. 22–27.

PART A

Defining 'Children' and Their 'Rights'

CHAPTER I

To What Extent Did the Image of Childhood Change?

"Possibly not," said the Time Traveller. "But now you begin to see the object of my investigations into the geometry of Four Dimensions. Long ago I had a vague inkling of a machine..."

"To travel through Time!" exclaimed the Very Young Man. "That shall travel indifferently in any direction of Space and Time, as the driver determines."

Filby contented himself with laughter.

"But I have experimental verification," said the Time Traveller.

"It would be remarkably convenient for the Historian," the Psychologist suggested. "One might travel back and verify the accepted account of the Battle of Hastings, for instance!"

H.G. Wells in *The Time Machine*, published in London in 1895.

In 1960 Philippe Ariès published his book *L'Enfant et la Vie Familiale sous l'Ancien Régime*. Until then concepts like 'child', 'youth' and 'adolescence' were considered to be invariable and of all times.[1]

Kruithof, Noordman and De Rooy write[2] "Rather polemically, he (Ariès) stated for instance, that the concept 'child' did not exist in the Middle Ages and that puberty was an invention of the Eighteenth Century."

Ariès, in the English translation by Robert Baldick[3] writes: "In medieval society the idea of childhood did not exist; this is not to suggest that children were neglected, forsaken or despised. The idea of childhood is not to be confused with affection for children: it corresponds to an awareness of the particular nature which distinguishes the child from the adult, even the young adult. In medieval society this awareness was lacking. That is why, as soon as the child could live without the constant solicitude of his mother, his nanny or his cradle rocker, he belonged to adult society."

This English translation is, according to Adrian Wilson[4], not reliable. Baldick translates the French word *sentiment* as 'idea' and elsewhere sometimes as 'concept', retaining only one aspect of its meaning, although Ariès never uses *notion* and *idée* as equivalents. '*Sentiment*' as Ariès uses it, says Wilson, is not easily translated into English, for it carries both 'conceptual' and 'sentimental' connotations. 'Awareness of childhood' is, according to Wilson, perhaps the least clumsy rendition of *sentiment de l'enfance*.

Adrian Wilson mostly uses the term *sentiment de l'enfant* without translating it. Although I agree with Wilson that the term *concept of childhood* is not exact, I shall not, in the present work, follow his example; we cannot altogether avoid the term *concept of childhood* since it has by now become firmly rooted in the Anglo-Saxon literature from which I shall quote.

The publication of Ariès' book initiated a real polemic, which is sometimes called 'the Ariès discussion'. The crux of this discussion is the following: Is the image we have about the specific nature of children consistent over time, or was Ariès right when he concluded that the image of childhood has radically changed since the Middle Ages? Clearly this question cannot be avoided in a study about the rights of the child, because if the concept of childhood is subject to change, ideas on rights of the child will change with it.

According to Wilson, Ariès' work is a vigorous attack on the conservative notion that the family has undergone a long decline. Ariès deals mainly with the *attitudes* of adults towards children, not with children themselves. These attitudes are studied in the same way as other cultural attitudes (towards love, death etc.) are studied. Ariès explains that in the Middle Ages children were treated like adults. Medieval man's life was short and preparation for adulthood was not an essential requirement. He attacks the idealisation of family life in 'the good old days'. According to him, people lived differently and the family life style was in no way better than today, as is often claimed by historians who say that the family is in decline.

Says Patrick H. Hutton: "It was not that medieval man had no conception of childhood. Rather he had no idea of the developmental link between the child's and the adult's mentality". The passage between the developmental stages was conceived to be a matter of initiation, not of formation. "The stages of life were recognised, but subsumed under the general conception of life as a microcosm of the cosmic cycle of repetition. The recognition of childhood as a special time of life, separate from adulthood and a preparation for it, emerged gradually from the end of the Middle Ages to enter the consciousness of all strata of Western society only in the eighteenth century."[5]

Friend and foe seem to agree that the French cultural-historian Ariès has provided an extremely important scientific contribution.

Adrian Wilson[6] who is otherwise quite critical about Ariès, nonetheless claims that his oeuvre is the first stage in the historical investigation of a new field.

In addition Mark C. Yudof, who is also unmistakably critical of Ariès, even says that "Ariès' thinking is, in its generality and novelty, reminiscent of that of Freud, Darwin, Einstein, and others – those who have given us entirely new structures for considering the human condition, and that for those who tend to view history in terms of 'great' events, persons and ideas, his writing and research demonstrate the importance and fascination of applying the historical method to the social minutiae of past generations."[7]

The methods Ariès used in his research have often been criticised. Wilson, for instance[8], talks about "primitive research methods".

Stone[9] calls the book "badly flawed in both its methodology and its conclusions." The fact that much of Ariès' work is based on the study of paintings from the Middle Ages, has been especially criticised.

For our purpose Wilson's criticism of Ariès' 'fundamental argument', that traditional French society lacked an *awareness of the particular nature of childhood*, is more important. Wilson argues that, although that particular society lacked *our* awareness, it definitely had *an* awareness of childhood.

Mark Yudof attacks Ariès thesis even more strongly: "There is every reason to believe, given what we know of child development, that parents in earlier centuries were perfectly aware of the special nature of childhood and recognised it as a definite time of life."[10] He agrees that children were for much less time in a position of dependence, but argues that this is a far cry from the proposition that children were perceived as mini-adults from the moment they left their mother's breast. He states that there is no reason to suppose that even seven-year-olds participated in adult society, undifferentiated from those who were older, bigger, and presumably wiser.

Another criticism, often voiced against the work of Ariès is that his book professes to deal with 'the' child in general, whereas in reality it deals only with children of the higher classes. He completely ignores the influence of economic change, class differences and the birth of capitalism on the image of childhood.

Lea Dasberg[11] is one of the authors who attacks Ariès for his tendency to generalise. She writes that we cannot speak about 'the' developmental phases of the child, unless we ignore the fact that children are socially, economically and historically defined.

Does Change Imply Progress?

Ariès' conception of the historical process, characterised by inevitability and chronological continuity, has been attacked by those who do not favour an exclusively linear interpretation of the historical process.

Probably in order to prove that there has been no decline of the family, Ariès points out that the idea of *progress* has strongly influenced Western thought. On the other hand he challenges the notion of a golden age in the future.[12]

Ariès linear view of history gave way to the thought that children have

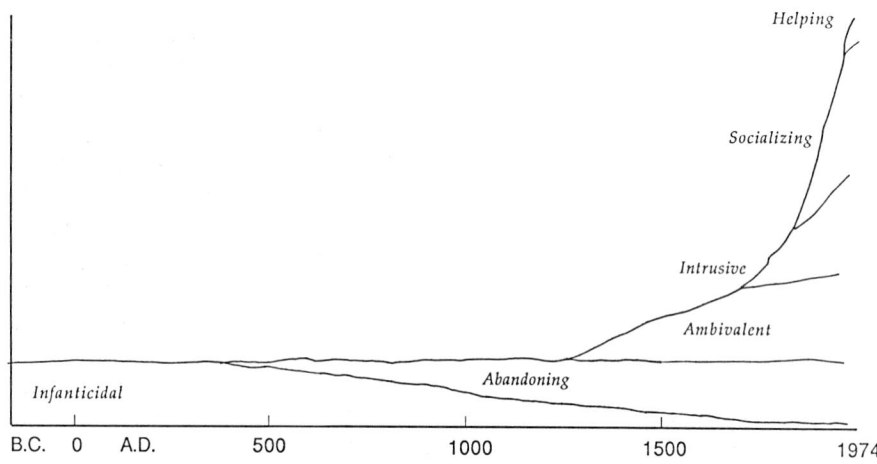

Fig. 1.1. The evolution of the parent-child relationship according to DeMause.

gradually acquired more and more rights, received more enlightened rearing and are served by better agencies and professions than has been the case in the past.

DeMause goes much further than Ariès. In his paper 'The Evolution of Childhood', he specifies a sequential progression from bad to better, and thus attaches a value judgement to the thoughts of Ariès, never intended by Ariès himself.

In the following pages of this chapter we shall talk about the work of some very influential writers who have dealt with the history of childhood and who based their views of linear development, change and progress on Ariès' work.

"The history of childhood is a nightmare from which we have only begun to awaken" writes Lloyd DeMause. His 'psychogenic theory of social change' points neither to the technological nor to the economic but rather to the 'psychogenic' changes in personality. These changes occur due to successive generations of parent-child interactions, which are *the* central force of change in history. According to DeMause the evolution of the parent-child relationship constitutes an independent source of historical change.[13]

The farther we go back in history, says DeMause, the lower the level of child care and the more likely children were to be killed, abandoned, beaten, terrorised, and sexually abused. DeMause explains these changes as follows: "The origin of this evolution lies in the ability of successive generations of parents to regress to the psychic age of their children and work through the anxieties of that age in a better manner the second time they encounter them than they did during their own childhood." DeMause also believes that, by dividing time, from antiquity till today, in six phases, he can point out how this evolution of 'child-rearing modes' has come about. The fifth phase, for instance (the Nineteenth and the first half of the Twentieth Century) distinguishes itself, according to DeMause, from the others, in that the raising of the child became less a process of conquering the will than of training it. From the middle of the Twentieth Century till today the so-called 'helping mode' came into being: this implies an enormous investment of time and energy by the parents, in order to help the child, at least until the age of six, to reach his or her daily goals. This means, according to DeMause, that the parents have to put up with a great deal of trouble. They must deal with the regressions of the child, the intensity of games, their own attempts to interpret the child's emotional conflicts, and their efforts to produce objects that may be of interest to the child. If the hand of the parent dashes out in a stress situation, he subsequently apologises.

DeMause does not provide statistical evidence to support his judgement that our ancestors were more cruel to their children, and loved them less than we do today. We often find a similar attitude among people who claim that parents in the Third World love their children less and that in those parts of the world 'life is cheap'.

Third World parents love their children as much as others, but it is not within their power to withhold the suffering of hunger and epidemics from them.[14]

Emmanuel LeRoy Ladurie made a study of the French village of Montaillou in the period of 1294–1324. He concludes that although some writers have said that love of children is a comparatively recent phenomenon, there was then undeniably an ambience of affection, and the death, illness or separation from a young child could be a source of sorrow or real suffering for parents.[15] Joseph E. Illick says: "Such a statement seemed to demand a response from the author of *The Evolution of Childhood*, but none was forthcoming."[16]

One gets the impression, when reading DeMause, that children all over Europe were raised in exactly the same way, without regional differences! The dangers of overrating the developments in one's own time and country should be obvious, and DeMause is a clear example of a scientist who fell into exactly such a trap.

Although the concept of progress had always been important in Western Society, it reached its peak between 1750 and 1900. According to Nisbet it became the dominant idea, despite the rising importance of other ideas such as equality, social justice, and popular sovereignty – each of which was without question a beacon light in this period.[17] He continues: "All of the social sciences without exception – political economy, sociology, anthropology, social psychology, cultural geography, and others – were almost literally founded upon the rock of faith in human progress from Turgot and Adam Smith on through Compte, Marx, Tylor, Spencer, and a host of others. (. . .) In historiography the idea of progress became with rarest exceptions the very foundation of the field."

Today we make a distinction between the concepts 'progress', 'evolution' and 'development', but in the eighteenth and nineteenth century these words were synonyms. Nisbet mentions that the theories of *social* evolution from the nineteenth century till today, as conceived by Talcott Parsons, Leslie White and others, have their origin in what Compte referred to in the 1830s as his 'law of progress'.[18] DeMause, as we see, is in extremely good company!

Two groups of authors often call on Ariès for the support of their own – opposing – theories about the rights of the child.

The first group claims that children and adolescents have received less and less rights over time. They place the blame on the development of the idea of childhood as a separate status.[19]

The second group, which usually refers to DeMause as well, claims that children have acquired more and more rights.[20]

Both points of view are, in my opinion, strongly biased in favour of the ultimate goal.

Thus there are two camps: those who plead for the abolishment of childhood – the sooner the better – and those who defend from assault what Lea Dasberg[21] has called 'youth-land', i.e. a 'land-in-time where the child can ripen in a community of peers who are in the same phase of development'.

Edna J. LeShan, for instance, quotes in her book *The Conspiracy Against Childhood*[22] the words of Winfred E. Bain: "It is well known (. . .) that life expectancy is longer than ever before in history. Despite this vista of longevity, there is a rift among many who 'really want the best' for children. Many want to curtail the period of childhood, not by denial of vitamins and tender loving care, but by haste toward getting them into adult patterns."

LeShan says about the assaults on the fortress of childhood: "It is my belief that we are trying to eliminate childhood and *that* is what is so terrible about being a child today. Whatever agonies children have ever lived before, it was never so clearly childhood itself that was felt to be the enemy (. . .) I am concerned that as we attempt to eliminate childhood, we will destroy ourselves as well as our children. Any society that looks with suspicion, impatience or hostility on childhood, has within it a deep and awful sickness that infects adult and child alike."

Others believe we should raise our children by getting them out of the special protected area and giving them responsibilities as soon as possible.

Tribe[23] states that perceiving childhood as a cultural artifact, an invention of the cultural revolution, is often connected with a notion that treating children as 'special' tends to oppress them. He is in favour of abandoning our fixation on age as an independent significant variable.

John Clarke of the Centre for Contemporary Studies in Birmingham, U.K., thinks that the 'image of childhood' and the 'image of juvenile delinquency' are two sides of the same coin. The latter side is the image of everything the child must *not* be. He connects these dominant ideologies directly with the "apparatus of social control developed by the dominant class." And all this he connects with the need in the Capitalist Society to ensure an uninterrupted and stable reproduction of the labour force. According to Clarke such concepts as family, work, child and youth have deliberately been kept as undefined as possible, in order to create a deep and pervasive non-political consensus.[24] Children who do not conform to this ideal image must be rescued and restored to their proper child-like nature (and coincidentally, to a life of industriousness, sobriety, thrift and morality). As Clarke puts it, there is a genuine conspiracy against youth. However unfairly children of the working class have been and are still treated, Clarke's reasoning is over-simplified.

The most important criticism of Ariès' work comes from Linda A. Pollock[25] who dismisses his "linear concept of history"[26] altogether. In her book *Forgotten Children: Parent-Child Relationships* 1500–1900, Pollock writes that, as far as the history of childhood is concerned, continuity far outweighs change.

Referring to this statement, J.R. Gillis concludes: "The works of Ariès, Stone, Shorter, DeMause, and almost everyone else who has written on the subject, are shown to be inadequate, not only in their use of evidence, but also in their overall conclusions."[27] Gillis finds that the emphasis on change can be explained by the ethos of the 1960s and early 1970s, decades obsessed with change.[28]

Historians have not only grossly exaggerated the aspect of change, says Gillis, but what's worse, they have also distorted both past and present. Gillis believes that we have now come to a certain rest and that therefore the contrast between the present and the distant past is less pronounced. Therefore continuity of human behaviour rather than change has now again come into the focus of attention.[29] Gillis agrees with the central theme of Pollock's thesis and states that the previous conception of the history of childhood no longer stands, and that the task of reconstructing the past has only begun.

It is interesting to note that in other fields similar discussions are taking place. In developmental psychology there is now a debate about the thesis that change (as reflected in different developmental stages) is too much stressed while elements of continuity are neglected.

Taking into account all arguments, it is my opinion that there are not only changes but also continuity. We must not overstress the changes that have taken place, and we must not take for granted that every change is also an improvement[30], as DeMause does. It is nevertheless wrong to view every change à priori as unfavourable, as Naherny and Rosario[31] do.

Changes that did occur were not necessarily the same for all children and youngsters. In this respect one can mention the differences between boys and girls. Boys were often longer allowed to stay children while girls married earlier. Other differences include regional variations as well as ethnic, cultural and class differences. Although we must be careful not to stereotype cultural groups, we are entitled to draw conclusions, based on research, that cultures do vary on attitudes and values pertinent to children's rights. What a 'good' parent does, varies from culture to culture, as does the role of the child and the relative priority of various rights.[32] Socio-economic and demographic variables (and consequent fertility variables) have their influence.[33]

It is dangerous to view everything in the light of change because it can lead to simplification.

Interesting is that authors who support more rights for children (mainly psychologists, educators and lawyers) often bring the theories of Ariès, and DeMause etc. to bear. Eugeen Verhellen[34], for instance, writes: "Historians show that only during the last centuries are certain social developments responsible for the fact that 'children' are separated from the rest of society in a harsh way. In other words until a certain period in Western history, 'children' did not exist as a 'separate social category'." Verhellen, it seems, does not realise that there are many other interpretations of history.

I would like to finish this chapter with a note on the adult-centred attitude of most researchers who tend to concentrate their thoughts only on attitudes *towards* and *of* children[35], as if children are passive entities and not, by their own right, important social factors.

This Chapter has dealt with the concept of childhood. We have tried to explain the relativity of this concept. How children are viewed in society creates what we call the 'image of childhood' in that particular society. Our thesis is that ideas concerning the rights of children are dependent on the prevailing image of childhood, and that when that image changes the ideas about the rights of the child also change.[36]

NOTES

1. Kruithof, Bernard, Noordman, Jan and Rooy, de, Piet, *Geschiedenis van Opvoeding en Onderwijs*, Nijmegen, 1982, SUN, Socialistische Uitgeverij Nijmegen, p. 7.
2. idem.
3. Ariès, Philippe, *l'Enfant et la Vie Familiale sous l'Ancien Régime*, Paris 1960, in the English translation by Robert Baldick, *Centuries of Childhood, A Social History of Family Life*, New York, 1962, Vintage Books, and London, Jonathan Cape Ltd., p. 128.
4. Wilson, Adrian, 'The Infancy of the History of Childhood: An Appraisal of Philippe Ariès' in: *History and Theory*, Vol. XIX, No. 2, 1980, pp.132 and 134, Note 13.
5. Hutton, Patrick, H., 'The History of Mentalities: The New Map of Cultural History', in: *History and Theory*, No. 20, 1981, Vol. XX, p. 239. See also: Hoyles, M. *Changing Childhood*, London, 1979, Writers and Readers; Plumb, I.H., 'Children: The victims of time'. In Plumb, I.H. (ed.), *The Light of History*, London, 1972, Allen Lane; Wong, B., 'Children's Rights: A contemporary historical perspective' in: *Educational Perspectives*, 1980, 19(3), pp. 3–7.
6. Wilson, Adrian, op. cit., p. 152.
7. Yudof, Mark, G., 'The Dilemma of Children's Autonomy', in: *Policy Analysis*, Vol. 2, No. 3, summer 1978, p. 391.
8. Wilson, Adrian, op. cit., p. 149.
9. Stone, Lawrence, 'The Massacre of the Innocents' in : *New York Review of Books*, Vol. XXI, No. 18, 14 Nov. 1974, p. 28.
10. Yudof, Mark, G., op. cit., p. 391.

11. Dasberg, Lea, *Grootbrengen door Kleinhouden, als Historisch Verschijnsel*, Meppel, 1975, Boom, p. 25 and in the 10th, enlarged edition, 1984, p. 32.
12. Hutton, op. cit., p. 246.
13. DeMause, Lloyd, 'The Evolution of Childhood', in: Jenks, Chris, *The Sociology of Childhood, Essential Readings*, London, 1982, Baksford Academic and Educational Ltd. pp.48–59; this quote on p. 49.
14. Vittachi, Tarzie, V. *Children's Rights: A Question of Obligation*, New York, January 27th, 1986, UNICEF, No. 8481 G.
15. LeRoy Ladurie, Emmanuel, *Montaillou, Cathans and Catholics in a French Village*, 1294–1324, New York, 1980, quoted in: Illick, Joseph, E., 'Does the History of Childhood have a Future?' (See under 16).
16. Illick, Joseph, E., 'Does the History of Childhood have a Future?', in: *The Journal of Psycho-History*, Fall 1985, Vol.13, No.2, p. 169.
17. Nisbet, Robert, *History of the Idea of Progress*, New York, 1980, Basic Books, pp. 171,175 and 176.
18. idem, p. 175.
19. Freeman, Bonnie Cook, 'Trends, Conflicts and Implications in Student Rights', in: Haubrich, Vernon, F., and Apple, Michael, W., eds., *Schooling and the Rights of Children*, Berkeley Call. 1974, McCutchan Publ. Corporation, pp.159–197.
20. Fox, Vivian, C., 'Historical Perspectives on Children's Rights', in Verhellen, E. and Spiesschaert, F., *Ombudswork for Children*, Leuven, Acco 1989, p. 297.
21. Dasberg, Lea, op.cit, p. 19 (in the 10th edition, pp. 16–17).
22. Leshan, Edna, J., *The Conspiracy Against Childhood*, New York, 1968, Athenaeum, p. 6. Also: Winfred E. Bain: 'With Life So Long, Why Shorten Childhood?' in: *Childhood Education*, Sept.1961. Also: LeShan continues on p. 9: "If there are those among us who despair about childhood today, it is not because we long for something in the past, but rather that we had hoped for much in our own time." See also: Freud-Loewenstein, Sophie, 'Children without Childhood', in *Jewish Spectator*, Winter 1984, pp. 33–36. Also: Edwards Newton ('Youth as a Population Element', in *The Annals of the American Academy of Political and Social Science*, CXCIV, 1937 pp. 7–8) writes about the changing age structure of the population, which affected the status of youth in American life: "Having proportionately fewer young dependents to care for, society is able to take a new attitude toward childhood and youth as a period of development and growth, and it is able to supply the financial resources necessary to support an expanded and enriched educational program."
23. Tribe, Laurence, H., 'Childhood, Suspect Classifications and Conclusive Presumptions: Three Linked Riddles' in: *Law and Contemporary Problems*, Summer 1975, Vol. 39, No. 3, p. 8.
24. Clarke, John, *The three R's – Repression, Rescue and Rehabilitation: Ideologies of Control for Working Class Youth*, Birmingham, Centre for Contemporary Cultural Studies, The University of Birmingham, Sub and Popular Culture Series: SP No. 41, p. 4.
25. Pollock, Linda, A., *Forgotten Children: Parent-Child Relations 1500–1900*, Cambridge 1983, Cambridge University Press.
26. Takanishi, Ruby, 'Childhood as a Social Issue: Historical Roots of the Contemporary Child Advocacy Movement' in: *Journal of Social Issues*, Vol. 34, No.2, 1978, p. 9.
27. Gillis, John, R., Review of *Forgotten Children: Parent-Child Relations 1500–1900*, in: *Journal of Interdisciplinary History*, Vol. XVI, No. 1, 1985, pp. 142–144.
28. idem, p. 143.
29. idem, p. 144.
30. Rothman, David, I., 'Documents in Search of a Historian: Toward a History of Childhood and Youth in America', in: *Journal of Interdisciplinary History*, Vol.II, No.2, Autumn 1971, pp. 367–377.
31. Naherny, Patricia, K. and Rosario, José, 'Morality, Science and the Use of the Child in History', in: Haubrich, Vernon, F. and Apple, Michael, W., eds. *Schooling and the Rights of Children*, Berkeley, Call., 1974, McCutchan Publishing Comp. pp. 1–40.

32. Morton, T, L., Dubanoski, Richard, A. and Blaine, Daniel, D., 'Cross-Cultural Perceptions of Children's Rights', in: Henning, James, S., *The Rights of Children, Legal and Psychological Perspectives*, Springfield, Ill., 1982, Charles C. Thomas Publishers, pp. 141–160; Also: Barry, H., Baron, K. and Child, L. 'Cross-Cultural Survey of Some Sex Differences in Socialisation' in: *Journal of Abnormal and Social Psychology*, 1975, 55, pp. 327–332 and: Thomas, D.R., 'Authoritarianism, Child Rearing Practices, and Ethno-centrism in Seven Pacific Islands Groups', in: *International Journal of Psychology*, 1975, 10, pp. 235–246.

    An interesting example of how concepts about the rights of the child sometimes vary, is given by Aref Abu-Rabia, who is an anthropologist and the inspector of Bedouin education in Beer-Sheva, Israel: "First of all, against the law of Islam, the Bedouin custom is, that a girl has no right to any heritage. Instead, when she marries, her father or brother give her some gifts. She also has the right to go back and live indefinitely with her family, if she is divorced from her husband. The rights, therefore, belong only to the sons and not to the daughters.

    Usually, the eldest brother has more rights. The Bedouin do it in a simple way: when the mother gives birth to a child, the father and mother give the child a gift of a sheep or a goat or even a she-camel: at the circumcision they also give the boy a sheep or a goat. By the time he is 20 or 30, he has more sheep and goats than his younger brothers.

    There are also common sheep and goats, which belong to the whole family, and which the brothers have to divide among themselves. However, before dividing, they take all the gifts and put them aside. Now, a sheep or a goat which you have had for maybe 20 years, may now have 15, 20 or even 30 descendants, all of which are first put aside before dividing the rest. So, if you ask the fathers, they will say: all children have the same rights."

    From: Abu-Rabia, Aref, *Education Development Among Bedouin Tribes of the Negev Desert*, paper delivered at the Bi-National (The Netherlands and Israel) Conference on education, Yeroham, Dec. 14–19, 1986.
33. A study by Cigdem Kagitcibasi (*The Changing value of children in Turkey*, Honolulu, Hawaii, 1982, East-West Population Institute, No. 60 E, revealed significant and consistent inter-relations among the socio-economic background variables, values of children, and fertility, pointing to the key role of the value of children in explaining fertility. With increased education, children's economic value decreases whereas their psychological value increases.
34. Verhellen, E., 'De Conventie voor de Rechten van het Kind; Een strategische stap naar respectvolle omgang met het kind', in: Verhellen, E., Spiesschaert, F. and Cattrijse, L., editors, *Rechten van kinderen, Een tekstbundel van de Rijksuniversiteit Gent naar aanleiding van de UNO Conventie van de Rechten van het kind*, Antwerpen/Arnhem, 1989, Kluwer Rechtswetenschappen and Gouda Quint B.V., p. 11.
35. See: Demos, John, 'Developmental Perspectives on the History of Childhood' in: *Journal of Interdisciplinary History*, Vol. II, No. 2, Autumn 1971 p. 315.
36. James Faubion and Gary B. Melton conclude "that the concept of childhood is both historically and culturally relative, and that it is deeply embedded in broader authority relations within a society." They think that "childhood has a largely symbolic character which shifts with major changes in social organisation more than with changes in the repertoire of knowledge about child development." See: Melton, Gary, B., *Child Advocacy, Psychological Issues and Interventions*, New York (London, 1983, Plenum Press, p. 200).

CHAPTER II

In Search of Workable Definitions

In books on children's rights, definitions often have to be accepted at face value, since no information is supplied about the professional theories leading to these definitions. We shall try to avoid such an approach.

Most of the definitions we shall use in this study come from the philosophy of law and the philosophy of education.

In this chapter we shall throw some light on key concepts we intend to use in our study. First, however, we must keep in mind that there is a real 'watershed' between the Anglo-American and the European theoreticians, and that the legal philosophers of both groups have had little influence on one another. There are, nevertheless, some scientists[1] who manage to bridge the gap. The 'continental' Hans Kelsen[2], for instance, is also read in the Anglo-American scientific community, but he mainly deals with the justification of the legal structure and the laws. Second, there are authors quoted by colleagues in the field of children's rights, who have never dealt explicitly with the rights of children. Thus, John Rawls' book *A Theory of Justice*[3] is often quoted in articles and books about the rights of the child.[4] Rawls, however, does not pay any special attention to children. All he does is mention the fact that his theories apply also to children.

Right, No-right, Duty, Privilege

The concept 'right' can be approached from different directions. The American legal philosopher Wesley N. Hohfeld (1919) has shown how complex this concept is, from which other concepts it has to be differentiated, and to which other concepts it is related. Hohfeld's work has greatly influenced jurisprudence in general. According to Walter K. Kamba there is hardly a book about rights which does not refer to Hohfeld's analysis scheme and terminology. It has, among other things, been adopted in the American *Restatement of the Law*.[5] The 'pure analytical legal theorist' Hohfeld[6] criticises the fact that many key words are used by different authors with different

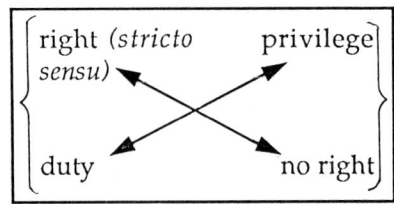

Fig. 2.1. Wesley N. Hohfeld's scheme of analysis. (The related concepts are indicated by brackets, and the opposites by arrows.)

meanings. He tries to put order in this chaos and describes eight fundamental concepts.

Right in the strict sense of the word (not including moral rights) is the correlative of *duty* and the opposite of *no-right*.[7] If a person knows that he has a certain *right*, he can ask: What *must the other* do for me? Thus, *right* is, according to Hohfeld, synonymous with *claim*.[8] A person has a right to do an act if others are under a correlative duty to permit the act or to forbear from preventing it.

Duty is the correlative of the concept *right*, above defined, and the opposite of *privilege*. A person or organisation, having a particular *duty*, should answer the question: What *must I do* for that other person?[9] This is often a 'tripartite' situation such as one doesn't normally encounter.

Example: It is not only a *child's* duty to go to school, it is also a right. This right implies a duty for the *State* and the municipalities. Moreover it is also a duty of the *parents* to send their child to school.

Privilege is the correlative of the legal concept *no-right* and the opposite of *duty*. A person may do an act in the sense that he is not under a duty to forbear from it, but others are free to prevent him. A person, knowing that he has a particular *privilege*, can answer the question: What *may* I do?[10]

To be *without right* is the correlative of *privilege* and the opposite of *right*. A person, knowing that he has *no-right* against another, can ask: What *may* another person do?

According to Max Radin[11] most fundamental rights are actually privileges, but the term 'right' has become an integral part of the English literature.[12] Nevertheless Radin finds Hohfeld's distinction between privilege and right of prime importance, and he proposes to maintain it.

Radin henceforth talks about *demand-rights* and *privilege-rights*. Demand-right, according to Radin, confirms the duty of the other, whereas privilege-right is absence of duty.

Twenty-five years after Hohfeld published his views about legal concepts[13] Radin suggested that they needed a revision because the rigid distinction between rights and duties also permitted a false emphasis to be placed on duties as against rights. He proposed to replace Hohfeld's diagram by the following classification:

demand-right * right
no demand-right * privilege

When we talk about privilege, the main point is the absence of legal duties. According to Radin there are nevertheless some privileges that cannot be separated from the concept duty: he considers it for instance a privilege-right to bear a child and consequently have custody of the child.

When we shall, in this study, use the word *privilege*, we shall adhere to Hohfeld's view relating to an absence of legal duties. Hohfeld's analytical approach is especially useful in our study about children's *rights* because it pinpoints the strong relationship between rights and duties.

Example: On Mount Kamon (Jabel-al-Kamane) in the Galilee in Israel, Bedouins have built their houses since the Ottoman Empire. In the 1960s the Israeli government decided to concentrate the Bedouins in certain areas. The Kammana Bedouins living on Mount Kamon, were ordered to move to Wadi Salamah (in Hebrew Nahal Tzalmon). Most of them (some eight hundred) refused. For them a difficult period began. They cannot obtain permits to build houses, and neither water nor electricity are supplied. The Bedouins bring their water up the hill in containers and have generators for their electricity.[14] The Israeli Ministry of Education and Culture refused to give their kindergarten either a permit to operate or financial support, despite the fact that, according to Israeli Law, all children are obliged to go to school when they are five years old. The Ministry of Interior refuses to give Kammana the status of a village which means that officially it does not exist. The Israel-Section of Defence for Children International (DCI) was of the opinion that whether or not Kammana exists officially, the government has the duty to provide education to which these Israeli Bedouin children have a right.

An author who shows us the strong relationship between duties and rights, is Simone Weil in a book she wrote during the last year of her life (1943) while she worked at the headquarters of the free Frenchmen in London. Her book *L'Enracinement* was published in 1949. In 1952 it appeared in English under the title *The Need for Roots*.[15] Already on the first page she describes duties as follows: "The notion of obligations comes before that of rights, which is sub-ordinate and relative to the former. A right is not effectual by itself, but only in relation to the obligation to which it corresponds, the effective exercise of a right springing not from the individual who possesses it, but from other men who consider themselves as being under a certain obligation towards him. Recognition of an obligation makes it effectual.... It is nonsense to say that men have, on the one hand rights, and on the other obligations. Such words only express differences in point of view. The actual relationship between the two is as between object and subject.... Obligations alone remain independent of conditions. They belong to a realm situated above all conditions, because it is situated above this world.... Obligations, whether unconditional or relative, eternal or changing, direct

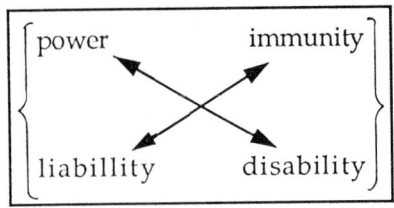

Fig. 2.2.

or indirect with regard to human affairs, all stem, without exception, from the vital needs of the human being."[16]

Criticism on this very individualistic opinion about rights is of a recent date. Michael Sandel[17], for instance, stresses the fact that our starting point towards the well-being of citizens should be the well-being of the community as a whole. According to Sandel[18] we cannot regard ourselves as independent. We are members of this family or community or nation or people, as bearers of this history, as sons and daughters of that revolution, as citizens of this republic. "To imagine a person incapable of constitutive attachments such as these is not to conceive an ideally free and rational agent, but to imagine a person wholly without character, without moral depth.... While the contours of my identity will in some ways be open and subject to revision, they are not wholly without shape. And the fact that they are not, enables me to discriminate among my more immediate wants and desires.... As the independent self finds its limits in those aims and attachments from which it cannot stand apart, so justice finds its limits in those forms of community that engage the identity as well as the interests of the participants."

According to Lomasky[19], morality is the main condition for a community wherein the rights of each individual can be safeguarded. He opposes placing autonomy too central in the rights-theories. Therefore he builds his theory around the concept of community.

Power, Liability, Immunity, Disability

Hohfeld also describes four other basic concepts: power, liability, immunity and disability. When we talk about power, we always mean legal power and not physical or other powers of the kind described by Mauk Mulder.[20]

The correlative of *a legal power* is, according to Hohfeld, *legal liability*. The person with the power is in a position to affect the legal relations of the other, in particular by placing him or her under a duty.[21] The opposite of legal power is legal *disability* (to have no power).

George W. Goble[22] considers power to be the basic legal concept. All legal concepts are derivatives of this one. The term power indicates that somebody has the means to change an other person's legal status.

Example: In many countries the court has the power to terminate parental rights. In other words: the parents are *liable* to be divested of authority, for instance 'parental rights' can be transferred to social-welfare authorities. To be liable is in the terminology of George Goble "the other end of the *power* relation."[23]

Liability is the correlative of power and the opposite of immunity.[24] A person who is dependent on the legal measures which someone else or a social institution like the court can impose on him, is in a position of dependency. A person who cannot be affected by legal measures possesses *immunity*.

The correlative of *immunity*, in Hohfeld's classification[25], is *disability* (no power).

Kamba: The term *unqualified* indicates that someone is not competent to alter the legal relations of another.[26] He therefore prefers the term *non-power*. As Hohfeld talks about *legal relations*, and *incapacity* falls outside his focus of attention, it seems a good idea to use the term *no-power* for disability. "But," opposes Goble[27], "one doesn't use the term 'not-light' when one means 'dark'. It must be remembered that after all, words are but labels for conceptions, or mental pictures. What particular characters are used as the labels is not a matter of great importance, but it is of great importance to know what mental picture a particular character stands for."[28]

The above were basic concepts as defined by Hohfeld and elaborated upon by others. We shall now discuss relevant concepts he did not touch upon.

Incompetence

Hohfeld's concepts *disability* and *no-power* are related to the concept *incompetence*. Says Skolnick[29]: "Although childhood is subdivided into different age-linked stages, the distinguishing feature of all childhood is incompetence." This point of view can be found in many theories of developmental psychology and also in legislation where it is even known as a formal category. Children are considered to be (still) incompetent to bear responsibility.

Emancipated Minor

An important question in the discussion about the rights of the child is to what extent children and youngsters are capable of taking decisions. In a legal sense adults are considered to be capable of acting but children and youngsters are not. A distinction must be made between *de facto* and *de jure* competence.[30] Many minors are in fact (de facto) capable of acting, but do not have the right to do so according to the law (de jure). Occasionally the special rights and duties belonging to 'being a minor' can be removed. Nevertheless, Goldstein, Anna Freud and Albert Solnit[31] explain, it is not possible to make an exception for each and every case, so that somewhere an age limit must be drawn. In many countries this limit which has long been 21 has in the course of time become 18 years.

In some countries the law allows some youngsters to take certain steps without asking their parents. In American professional literature the term *partial emancipation* is used in this respect. In such cases youngsters receive one or more rights, which are in general reserved to adults, while the parents are not released from their duties. Since the second half of the sixties, partially emancipated youngsters have received rights that up till that time were privileges.[32]

Thus, in some Western countries youngsters do not need their parents' consent for consultation about venereal diseases, alcohol and drug problems, and, in the case of girls, for abortions.

Autonomy

A basic concept, important for the study of children's rights, which we want to touch upon in this chapter, is personal *autonomy*[33] as against *heteronomy* (the absence of autonomy). This concept relates to the exertion of power over the person in question. A person who possesses autonomy can weigh his or her decisions in great moral freedom. In the American and English Philosophy of Education literature wherein autonomy is discussed, the concept of *freedom* is central.

It is the belief of most authors that education must create the conditions for (later) autonomic functioning (as little involvement by third parties as possible) in a democratic society, because under those circumstances education should have an intellectually liberating effect. Others believe that education does not have a liberating effect in the intellectual sense. Michel Foucault[34], for instance, believes that education produces people according to qualification and social norms, that it has a repressive nature, and that it amounts to nothing but exertion and restriction.

John Holt, the pioneer of the *children's liberation movement*, is in agreement with the liberal American tradition when he says that *freedom* is a very important aim of education and that children can and should be allowed to act in an autonomous way.

In this study the word autonomy will stand for the ability of people to choose whether to act or not.

Much of the discussion about the granting of rights to children evolves around the question to what extent children already have autonomy. Ivan Illich[35] thinks that children are born with autonomy and that compulsory education infringes on their rights. Personally I agree with R.F. Dearden that education can and should contribute to the obtaining of autonomy. Indeed, I believe that this is true for everything that has to do with raising children (e.g. family, community centres, etc.) Says Dearden: "The development of *personal autonomy* was an aim of increasing prominence in education.[36] But to set up something as an aim implies that a certain value is placed upon it. A final question which therefore clearly deserves to be asked concerns this value. What, then, is the value of autonomy?"[37] Autonomy, says Dearden, gives us self-respect, but that is not the only value we must pursue. Dearden: "Without morality, for instance, the more autonomous an agent is, the worse he is likely to be. Great criminals are markedly autonomous men. . . . The rise of autonomy to prominence in education certainly does not mark the eclipse of such other values as morality and truth. Acceptable processes in education always have a variety of claims to satisfy."[38]

To acquire autonomy is, according to Dearden, not something that comes automatically with age. It is a learning task set by a particular ideal of human development. However, this creates a dilemma for adults and it will probably always be a strong temptation to save children from mistakes and misjudgments. "Information and skills will often need to be supplied or taught by others if self-determination is not self-frustration."

Active and Passive, Positive and Negative Rights

The distinction between active and passive rights is an old one.[39] Under *active rights* we usually assume those rights that indicate the *power to choose or do something*: sign or not sign a contract, vote or not vote, undergo an abortion or not. In short, the possibility to decide about one's actions and occupations, and to determine what to do with one's life.

Under *passive rights* we understand being allowed to do or receive certain things.

The distinction between positive and negative rights is best explained with the words 'freedom to' and 'freedom from'.

Passive negative rights are the rights of freedom from interference.

Passive positive rights are the rights to receive material things such as food and toys, or immaterial things such as education, care etc.

Example: In December 1965 John and Mary Beth Tinker (aged fifteen and thirteen) and Christopher Eckhardt (aged sixteen) took part in a meeting where it was decided to demonstrate against the war in Vietnam by wearing a black armband until New Year. The headmasters of the schools in their home town, Des Moins, got wind of this plan and decreed that they would not admit children with black armbands into their schools. On December 16th, Mary Beth and Christopher wore black armbands, the next day John wore one, too. The three pupils were sent home and not allowed to attend school until after New Year, when the period designated for their demonstration was over. The fathers of the children petitioned the United States Supreme Court. They won the case which has sometimes been called 'the landmark case concerning Pupils' Rights.[40] Never before had a Supreme Court in the U.S. explicitly mentioned the fact that minors, too, fell under the Constitution and have, therefore, the *active right* to freedom of speech and the *passive negative right* to freedom from intervention.

Traditionally, legal rights did not deal with welfare, which is a *passive positive right* of rather recent date. The Universal Declaration of Human Rights evolves mainly around *passive negative rights*, assuring that the State will not interfere with a citizen's pursuit of goods, nor deprive him of what he has won by his efforts.

Henry Shue[41] argues that, instead of dividing rights into positive and negative, it is more sensible to examine the relatively positive duties (to aid the deprived), the relatively negative duties (to avoid depriving), and the intermediate duties (to protect from deprivation). These elements are mixed together in various proportions in the implementation of every right. In order to demonstrate how certain rights are related to certain duties, Shue adds that a complete account of a human right must specify the correlative duties and the relevant agents: what needs to be done in order to fulfil the right and who ought to do it. According to Shue, if a right is considered positive, the duties related to it are only positive.

Having explained the difference between positive and negative rights, we shall now connect these concepts to the *two concepts of liberty* espoused by the English philosopher Isaiah Berlin.[42]

Negative liberty, according to Isaiah Berlin, is *liberty from*, or absence of interference. In Chapter X we shall see that the ideas about the Children's Liberation Movement sprang originally from this negative concept of liberty. Says Isaiah Berlin: "Every plea for civil liberties and individualistic rights . . . springs from this individualistic, and much disputed, conception of man.[43] . . . But individualistic freedom is not the sole criterion of social action.[44] We compel children to be educated and we forbid public executions. These are certainly curbs of freedom. We justify them on the ground that ignorance, or a barbarian upbringing, or cruel pleasures and the excitements are worse for us than the amount of restraint needed to repress them. This judgement in turn depends on how we determine good and evil . . . which are, in their turn, bound up with our conception of man."

The *positive meaning* of the word 'liberty' stems, according to Berlin[45], from the wish on the part of the individual to be his own master. I wish my life and decisions to depend on myself, not on external forces of whatever kind. I wish to be an instrument of my own, not of other men's acts of will. I wish to be subject, not an object. Berlin has tried to demonstrate that this positive meaning of the word *freedom* has been the driving force behind many nationalistic and socialistic claims to self-determination. It is his opinion that the liberty of people or peoples to live as they deem best, must be weighed against other values, such as equality, justice, happiness, security or public order.

Welfare rights

Hohfeld points out the concepts from which the concept 'right' should be distinguished. It is a subject of discussion in the Philosophy of Law whether or not the concept right should be broadened and made to include welfare rights. The following will hopefully throw some light on the discussion: The so-called welfare rights belong to the *positive rights*. Something is claimed from the authorities. According to M. Friedman[46] there is no agreement yet as to what exactly is meant by welfare rights as formulated in *social welfare legislation*. Friedman claims that the term indicates provisions that meet three standards: First, the state defines or implies a minimum standard of living or some minimum aspect of the standard of living. Second, it asserts or implies that there is a group that falls below the minimum and one may tell how this group is to be identified. Third, it sets up or implies some program to help all or part of that group in order to reach or approach the minimum standard.[47] If we look, for instance, at the Dutch 'Law of Income Support Benefits' (A.B.W.) we shall see that with its introduction, social assistance was no longer considered within the field of charity but became a (positive) right instead.

International standards[48] determine what exactly is the minimum level of social protection and welfare, the attainment of which must be sought by all States.

Every welfare legislation must determine who is eligible.[49] Before a child can receive an orphan's allowance, it must be proven that he or she is indeed an orphan. A person who applies for social assistance, must show his financial data, and prove clearly that he belongs to the entitled group. This can be stigmatising but not as badly as in the times of charity. Sometimes a selection must be made in order to determine whose claims to public housing are more valid. We are then not dealing with the right to public housing, but to a specific treatment under specific conditions.[50]

Marxists have argued that welfare legislation as a whole has only one goal: to preserve the capitalistic system. According to this view capitalist welfare is not a matter of relief of need for its own sake, but rather a means for controlling and moulding the population to suit the requirements of the free market economy.[51]

Be that as it may, it is only recently that lawyers and educators have begun to deal with the quality of welfare services and education. The right to education for instance has been extended: initially it implied only access to education, now the discussion is about the right to quality education.[52]

Many welfare rights are also tested for quality. In case of disagreement this can be a problem for a judge. More and more often they must appeal to expert witnesses, which means that more inter-disciplinary co-operation becomes necessary.

Legal Rights, Constitutional Rights and Moral Rights

When we speak of *legal rights*, we shall henceforth follow Wringe's definition.[53] He claims that if A has a right to X, that right is legal if A can appeal to a rule, established by law, stating that all people belonging to a certain category have a right to X and if A can claim that he or she belongs to the category in question.

The American professional literature sometimes deals with *constitutional rights* concerning children. It often refers to cases that have appeared before the Supreme Court where constitutional rights have sometimes been declared applicable to children.[54]

Wringe[55]: "Sometimes it is suggested that a moral right is simply something that ought to be a legal right." But to pretend that legal rights are the only rights would be too simple. It is a view which could easily be used to negate claims that are not (yet) classified within a legal framework.

According to Wringe moral and legal rights may be characterised and justified independently. Robert Young argues that where the rights invoked are moral ones, there is a loss of definiteness or determinateness in legal talk. Young also raises the problem of the justification of moral rights. There has undoubtedly been a far more thorough mapping of legal than of moral rights. Young is sceptical about community acceptance of children's moral rights.[56] In his opinion we have the moral right to have our legal rights honoured, and one valid reason for saying that a certain interest should be protected by law, is precisely because this interest corresponds to a moral right. We may also think we have many moral rights to which the protection of the law would be quite inappropriate. Young moreover argues that when something has been legally determined, it means that it is also a moral right.

Contrary to Feinberg's classification[57] of moral rights, we shall, in this study, understand that A has a moral right to X if this right is not yet legally determined, but A can, by virtue of ethical, historical or ideological reasons, argue that the right should be legalised. The above does not imply that all moral rights are rightly formulated and must therefore be legalised.

In a broader and more controversial view about rights, Martha Minow[58] says that rights are not limited to those rules formally announced and enforced by public authorities. Instead, rights represent articulations – public or private, formal or informal – of claims that people use in order to persuade others (and themselves), as to how they should be treated, and as to what they should be granted.[59]

Minow[60], therefore, supports an extension of the concept 'rights' to include those claims that have not been recognised (by Parliament for instance) but that keep popping up as regularly as clockwork to give us hope and encourage us to try and convince others of their importance. The opposition against all sorts of 'new' rights indicates that Minow's views are not commonly accepted. Iredell Jenkins, emeritus professor of philosophy in Alabama, writes for instance[61]: "Obviously the basic issue is the status of rights – of what a right is – for on this hinges the identification of rights. Without becoming superficial or simplistic, I believe it is fair to say that disputes on this issue have centred on two broad views. One of these holds that rights have a metaphysical and moral status: they are extra- and supra-legal. Rights derive directly from God or Nature – from the ultimate structure of things – and they belong to man as part of his intrinsic nature, as much as his body, his mind, and his various powers. Law merely recognises these rights and enforces respect for them. This is the classical view, as expressed in the doctrines of natural law and natural rights, and it was the dominant influence for centuries. The other view holds that rights are strictly legal entities or notions. They owe their being and their nature exclusively to law – to the substantive and procedural apparatus of a legal system – whose creatures they are. Law literally creates rights: the legislative or juridical act accords certain privileges and protection to some persons and imposes corresponding duties on other persons, and it is this act that brings the right into being and constitutes its content. This is the view made famous by Holmes and Cray, and it is associated with the schools of legal positivism, formalism, and analytical jurisprudence."

"We must differentiate," says Jenkins, "between metaphysical, moral, political, legal, social and rhetorical rights." He himself would like to reserve the term 'rights' to the legal context, and is against broadening it to include welfare or moral rights, which is very much the practice nowadays.

Since, however, many formulated 'rights' of the child do not fit into Hohfeld's scheme, we shall, in the present study, not limit ourselves to his definitions but also study the formulated 'Moral Rights' of children. Often authors on children's rights differentiate between 'hard rights' (rights as interpreted by the law) and 'soft rights' (the social and personal needs of children which, when fulfilled, allow children to develop their personality and talents to the fullest capacity).[62] Child psychiatrist Irvin Berlin even calls these rights 'guideposts for parenting.'

Rights are now also formulated not only for individuals, but also for collectives, such as for instance *the right to development*.

The Scandinavian School of Legal Realism

Jenkins wants to limit the concept of 'rights' whereas Hagerström, Olivecrona and others[63] relativize the concept of rights even further. In their opinion 'rights' are merely beliefs of people and expressions of feelings. Olivecrona distinguishes between language which describes facts and language which performs some other function, such as to induce people to behave in particular ways or to express or arouse emotions.[64] "A directive which makes use of an emotionally charged word, for example 'right' or 'duty', is a powerful instrument of persuasion," writes Ross. For Olivecrona the word 'right' is hollow. Geoffrey MacCormack who made a study of this school of realism, explains that the word 'right' "is used in sentences which look as though they are descriptions of fact." Cultural anthropologists[65] are interested in questions this school raises because it treats the word 'right' as an expression of modern man about an invisible and mystical power. Modern man looks upon rights differently than primitive man, but he "nevertheless retains the form of structure which primitive man had given them."[66]

Human Rights, Natural Rights

The concept of *human rights* is anchored in *natural rights*, a term we use to indicate that there exist eternal rights derived from human nature and not dependent on human acknowledgement.[67] These rights are not a gift from society or from any government. They do not derive from the Constitution; they antecede the Constitution.[68] Since the concept *natural law* became a matter of great controversy, and the term *natural rights* fell into disfavour, we have increasingly become used to talking about *human rights*, especially since the Second World War.[69]

The term *human rights*, just like *rights*, has been much discussed and broadened in the course of the years. In a publication by the Dutch Ministry of Foreign Affairs[70] we read, for instance, that by constantly broadening the concept 'human rights' we have much reduced the keenness of the qualification: 'violation of human rights'. It appears that there was a need for terms, the meaning of which had not yet been broadened – or, as some prefer to say, hollowed out. Thus we speak today about 'elementary' or 'fundamental' human rights in order to indicate such rights as the right to live and the inviolability of the person.[71]

By *human rights* we understand, with Henkin, those moral-political claims that, by contemporary consensus, every human being has, or is deemed to have, on his society and on his government, and that are considered indispensable for the development of the individual.

"International Human Rights are recognised as inherent," says Henkin, "but it is not necessarily assumed that man is in principle autonomous, that rights antecede government."

Human Rights are enumerated in Declarations (such as the *Universal Declaration of Human Rights* of December 10th, 1948[72]) and in international agreements such as Conventions.

International human rights drew heavily on American constitutionalism (and on related constitutional developments in Europe and Latin America), but also on various ideologies such as socialism and other commitments to the welfare state. According to Marxists, it *should not necessarily be assumed that man is, in principle, autonomous.*[73]

'Orthodox' Marxists are of the opinion that the institution of human rights and freedoms has a clearly defined class nature. They stress the *obligations* of citizens rather than the aspect of autonomy.[74]

When, in 1985, I investigated the problem of truancy in what was then East and West Berlin[75], I observed very different approaches. In East Berlin youngsters of the 'pioneers movement' immediately fetched the truant and brought him to school. A representative of the parents' association also visited the father at work to discuss the problem. On the other hand, in West Berlin truancy was not seen as a responsibility of the community.

Even the United States Government, which often claims to be the pioneer of human rights, has problems with adherence to international human rights conventions. Indeed, it is often only prepared to adhere if this requires no change in the pursuit of its relevant policies. This, of course, is also true in respect to other countries. However, the United States must deal with the problem that its Constitution was especially drafted to create workable ties between the States of the Union, and, therefore, the Federal Government has little power to meddle in the internal affairs of the various States. International Human Rights Conventions are based on a different conception of Government.

According to Louis Henkin[76], *International Human Rights* were born after various socialisms were established and spreading and the idea of 'the welfare state' became nearly universal. This implies a certain conception of government. This concept includes not only freedoms which governments must not invade, but also rights to what is essential for human well-being, which governments must actively provide or promote. They imply a government that is activist, intervening, and committed to economic-social planning for the society, in order to satisfy economic-social rights of the individual. This was not the concept of government held in the United States. The United States Constitution was especially liberty-oriented. Allowing freedom of speech, for instance, was more important than forbidding racist speech. Against the background of these different values it becomes comprehensible that the United States did not ratify several international conventions, such as the 1919 I.L.O.-Convention fixing the Minimum Age for Admission of Children to Industrial Employment. Only in 1986 did the United States accede to the 1948 Convention on the Prevention and Punishment of the Crime of Genocide.

Prominent Americans like Henkin argue that the United States should no longer hesitate and should accede to other International Human Rights Conventions as soon as possible.

Civil Rights and Political Rights; Economic, Social and Cultural Rights

A further subdivision of the term *human rights*, is in *civil and political rights* on the one hand and *economic, social and cultural rights* on the other.

Under *civil rights* we generally classify[77] those rights that: safeguard our lives, and protect our bodies from torture and from contact with harmful materials (forced upon us by the authorities); that protect us from arbitrary arrest, detention and expulsion; that are against slavery, slander, interference with our personal life styles, and intrusion in our privacy; against limiting our freedom of movement, infringement on our ownership's rights and violation of our freedom of thought, conscience and religion. Also under *civil rights* fall the right to equal treatment and protection under the law, the right to a fair trial of one's case by an independent Court, and the right not to be treated as guilty before being convicted. In the United States there is a further distinction between the terms *civil rights* stressing the positive aspect, and *civil liberties* stressing the negative aspect (freedom from interference.) In the age of the Welfare State, positive rights are very important, especially for minority groups (for instance the Blacks and Hispanics in the United States) and thus the term 'civil rights' is used a great deal.

Under *political rights* we include freedom of speech, press, the right to vote, to be chosen, and freedom of association..

Economic and social rights deal with the minimum conditions for welfare and well-being. These include, among other things, freely chosen employment, fair payment for labour, reasonably limited working hours, and a certain minimal standard of living including social services, and education.[78]

Cultural rights are the right to freely take part (actively and passively) in cultural life, to participate in and benefit from scientific progress, and the right to protection of one's scientific, literary and artistic work. 'Cultural rights' also often refer to the rights of minorities to preserve their distinctive culture.[79]

Human rights have been proclaimed in Declarations and recorded in International Conventions. The two most important International Conventions in the field of human rights, adopted in 1966, are the *International Covenant on Civil and Political Rights* and the *International Covenant on Economic, Social and Cultural Rights*.[80] Children's rights are an integral part of human rights, but it was felt that, in view of the vulnerable position of children, special Declarations and Conventions were necessary.

Freedom Rights – Social Rights

Theodoor C. Van Boven[81] is of the opinion that the concept of human rights is the product of history and of civilisation and, as such, subject to evolution. "In fact," writes Van Boven, "the development of human rights has gone through various stages and the concept of human rights started off as a political concept, i.e. it meant respect for a sphere of freedom of the human person from the State." The State was bound not to intervene in the sphere of 'civil rights' or 'freedom rights'. The next stage was, according to Van Boven, not placed in opposition to the State. "He (who exerts his political rights) is the person who takes part in the political structuring of society of which he is a member."[82] Finally the idea of economic, social and cultural rights emerged. "These rights are to be realised through or by means of the State."[83]

Controversies about classical rights such as freedom rights are easy to deal with in court. As for social rights, many lawyers considered them for a long time to be political, maybe because *social* had for them the connotation of *socialistic*. Aalt Heringa[84] explains that "unlike the freedom rights, the implementation of social rights takes place on the basis of trust in the State- (organs)." The state has *to do* something (give subsidy for instance). According to Alkema[85] "the borderline between civil and fundamental rights is not sharp. Civil rights often contain social elements and there is a tendency in jurisprudence to give those elements more profile."

In the case of children[86] the borderline is even more blurred because of the adults' duty to care for the children and to give them things.

Declarations and Conventions

A *Declaration* is the statement of principles.[87] It is not considered to be a binding document. Because of it, however, certain norms may be taken into consideration, followed up and be more explicitly formulated.

A *Convention* is a treaty between States, endorsed and recommended by several States acting together[88] or by one or several organisations. It differs from a Declaration in that it carries specific obligations. Conventions are binding and can be considered 'hard' law as compared to the 'soft' law of Declarations. Conventions require the active decision of individual States in order to be ratified. The first step is for States to mark the text of a Convention as authentic and definitive through the signature of their representatives. The final confirmation given by parties to a Convention is a ratification. By the act of ratification the State in question accepts the obligations of the Convention. The time between signature and ratification gives the government of the State the opportunity to study the Convention and to decide if and where reservations should be made and where the domestic law must be adapted.

A Convention dating from 1973 (see Chapter XIII), concerning the minimum age for admission to employment, was, after ten years, ratified by only twenty-six States Parties. The reason for this was that in the Third World States, poverty stricken families continued to depend on their children's work to stay afloat. In these countries there were many second thoughts about the feasibility of abrupt legislation against all labour below a minimum age. Ratification of the Convention was thus postponed.

The term ratification applies to States that have been present during or involved in the drafting of the Convention. Accession applies to States that come into the picture at a later stage. It is the act with which such a State accepts the opportunity to become a party to a Convention signed by other States. After accession that State is equally bound by the Convention.

According to the Constitution of some States the joining of a Convention must be approved by Parliament and sometimes legislation must be passed especially for such ratification. A Convention can include a clause to the effect that it will come into force only after a certain number of States have ratified it. For a contracting Party, the Convention normally comes into force after it deposits an instrument of ratification. The *United Nations Convention on the Rights of the Child of* 1989, for instance, entered into force on September 2, 1990, the thirteenth day after the twentieth State deposited its instrument of ratification with the Secretary-General of the United Nations. From then on it was considered to be binding for the contracting States. Unless a Convention provides otherwise, a State can join the group of parties after the Convention has already come into force. New terminology has also recently been introduced, such as, 'acceptance' which indicates a trend towards less formality.

A Protocol is a treaty that amends or supplements another treaty. Such a protocol extends the right defined in a specific treaty and has the same legal consequences as a Convention.

Codes of Conduct – Standards

Beside legal rules there are codes of conduct that groups impose on themselves. In the United States, for instance, the Child Welfare League of America sets standards for the major child-welfare services.[89]

Various professional groups have their specific codes, according to which members are expected to act.

Courts can demand that *standards* be adhered to. In fact, as a rule they attempt to enforce standards related to quantity, such as the relationship between the number of doctors and nurses to the number of patients. These standards are easy to control. It is Goldstein's opinion, however, that they are second in importance to standards relating to quality, and that quantity standards should never be a goal but only a means by which quality is realised.

In the case *G.L. versus Zumwalt*[90], a Federal court in the U.S. established that the policy on foster children in Jackson County, Missouri should be improved by enforcing standards used by the Child Welfare League of America. The court succeeded in convincing parties to accept a so-called *consent decree*, meaning that it was achieved through mutual consent. Five months after the three-year old boy G.L. had been placed in a foster family, he was admitted into a hospital where child abuse by the foster parents was diagnosed. Before abusing the child, however, the foster parents had in vain asked the local authorities for help. *G.L. versus Zumwalt* marks the first time in the United States that high quality standards of foster care administration were mandated by federal court order. Much that appeared in the consent decree had earlier been presented in the *Standards for Foster Family*

Picture II.1. March 1988. Protest demonstration in New York City against violence applied by the teachers in an elementary school on 182nd Street and Amsterdam Avenue. 'Education is a right, not a privilege', is the slogan carried by parents and children. (Photo: Francisco Gonzalez.)

Care of the Child Welfare League of America and in the *Standards for Foster Family Systems for Public Agencies*[91] of the American Public Welfare Association. However, the nature of these standards, codes and norms was only advisory. That a federal court declared them binding was therefore an important step forward.

A landmark was the *International Code for the Marketing of Substitute Mothermilk*[92] by the World Health Organisation (WHO) on May 21st, 1981. Since the various action groups found the proposal for the code too weak, and the industries found it too strong, a compromise had to be reached. As it is, the code forbids the promotion of substitute mothermilk among the public in general and among pregnant women and new mothers in particular. It prohibits advertising except in nutritional and medical literature and bans distribution of samples, especially by ladies dressed in nurses' uniforms, paid by the industries, who called themselves milk-nurses, and who visited new mothers and presented them with baby food and nursing bottles. The spreading of promotional material through health organisations is forbidden.[93] Information from workers in these organisations may only be factual and scientific. Stickers on tins of substitute mother milk must carry sentences like: 'breast is best' and 'consult your doctor before use'. Moreover, to prevent idealisation of bottle feeding, pictures of babies may not appear on the wrappers.[94]

Such a code, however, has no legal power and is, like a Declaration, only a recommendation. Only Sri Lanka, Toga, Guatemala and Peru have so far transformed the discussed WHO-code into a law.

From reports of the International Baby Food Action Network (IBFAN) called *Breaking the Rules*, we can learn how often the code is neglected.

An important new instrument (1990), the *United Nations Rules on the Protection of Juveniles Deprived of Their Liberty*, also does not set out legally-binding standards. Nonetheless it is important because it provides guidelines which administrators, planners and policy makers can use as a point of reference in developing guidelines adapted to the economic and social realities of their countries. It sets goals for nations to aim at and constitutes a form of technical assistance.[95]

Summarizing, we can say that the concept 'rights' has been subject to a great deal of change during our century.

Some authors would like to keep it exclusively related to legal matters, but the reality is that our discussion about the rights of the child has left the legal area far behind. It has even been suggested that 'rights' nowadays have become synonymous with 'social goals'.

Instead of determining a single definition of 'rights', we shall discuss if and how the definition of rights has changed, especially in connection with children.

Rodham wrote [96]: "The phrase 'children's rights' is a slogan in search of a definition." In Chapter I we studied the image of childhood. The different notions of childhood[97] "add to the inherent difficulty of defining rights." In this chapter we have searched for possible building blocks, particularly in the Philosophy of Law, that may contribute to a better phrasing of workable definitions. We were able to find some important building blocks, but not one that will provide us with *the* only definition of 'rights' or even better 'children's rights'. Nevertheless, the search has widened our outlook, and the limitations and relativity of some common definitions and concepts have been brought into perspective.

Closer to pedagogics we found the basic concept of autonomy. Understanding this concept has implications for the rights of the child. We accept that education must create the conditions for later autonomous and responsible functioning. The major implication for us is that children and youngsters must be allowed to *learn* how to handle autonomous responsibility. The ability to handle rights does not come naturally with age. Children must therefore have the chance to familiarize with this skill at an early stage. The 'Rights of the Child' thus becomes a real *educational* issue.

Notes

1. Based on communication with Prof. Stephen Goldstein, former Dean of the Faculty of Law of the Hebrew University, Jerusalem, October 1989.

2. Idem.
3. Rawls, John, *A Theory of Justice*, Cambridge, Mass., 1971, Harvard University Press.
4. For Instance Worsfold, V.L., 'A Philosophical Justification for Children's Rights' in: *Harvard Educational Review*, 44, 1974, No. 1, February, pp. 142–157, also reprinted in *The Rights of Children*, reprint series No. 9, Harvard Educational Review, pp. 29–48. Also: Freeman, M.P.A. *The Rights and the Wrongs of Children*, London and Dover N.H. 1983, Frances Pinter Publishers, p. 5.
5. American Law Institute, *Restatement of the Law of Property*, St. Paul, 1936, American Law Institute Publishers, Vol. I, pp. 3–13, "The object of the Institute in proposing the Restatement is to present an orderly statement of the general common law of the United States." Also: Freeman, Michael 'Children's rights, some unanswered questions and some unquestioned answers' in: *Poly Law Review*, Vol. 5, No. 1. pp. 9–17. However, Freeman notices that demands for children's rights go far beyond Hohfeld's classification. Lord Lloyd of Hampstead and M.D.A. Freeman write in *Lloyd's Introduction to Jurisprudence* (London, 1985, Stevens & Sons) that "Hohfeld's account... remains today, despite its faults, the source to which most (and not just jurists) return".
6. Corbin, Arthur L., 'Legal Analysis and Terminology' in: *Yale Law Journal*, Vol. XXIX, 1919–1920, pp. 163–173. The diagrams of Fig. 1, are copied from Kemba, Walter, I. 'Legal Theory and Hohfeld's Analysis of a Legal Right' in: *The Juridical Review*, 1974, part 3, December, p. 2249.
7. Hohfeld, Wesley, N., 'Some Fundamental Legal Conceptions as Applied in Judicial Reasoning', 1917, 23 *Yale Law Journal*, 26, pp. 710–770, and *Fundamental Legal Conceptions as Applied in Judicial Reasoning*, New Haven, Conn., 1919, Yale University Press.
8. Bertram Bardman, in his article 'Rights and Claims' in the *Journal of Value Inquiry*, 7, 1973, pp. 204–213, argues that the concept of claims is primary and that the concept of rights is secondary. "Without claims there would be no rights. Rights are not *sui generis*. They come from claims. Claims make rights possible." Also: C.A. Wringe (in his book *Children's Rights, a Philosophical Study*, 1981) refers to what he calls "three traditional attempts to account for the concept of rights which, if valid, would importantly affect the way we approach the justification of rights claims in general, and those made on behalf of children in particular. The first is the tendency to identify rights with powers, the second defines rights as the correlatives of duties, and the last assumes that rights are some form of claim. Wringe argues that rights are not powers, nor can they adequately be accounted for as correlatives of duties, nor as claims. He made an attempt to provide "a positive account of what it is to have a right," but since his attempt is not widely accepted, we only mention it here in the footnote.
9. Corbin, op. cit., p. 107.
   Shlomo Nahmias writes that "it is interesting to note that Jewish Law from the very outset did not recognize parents' rights in the ordinary meaning of 'rights' but rather as obligations, i.e. obligations to perform *mitzva* (an act of loving kindness)." See: Nahmias, Shlomo, 'Laws of Education and Freedom of the Individual', in: *Educational Administration and Policy Making, the Case of Israel*, Herzliya, Unipress, 1982.
10. Idem.
11. Radin, Max, A. 'A Restatement of Hohfeld', in: *Harvard Law Review*, 1938, Vol. 51, p. 1.
12. Idem.
13. Idem.
14. Veerman, Philip E., 'Right to Education: A village that "does not exist" ' in: *The International Children's Rights Monitor*, Special Issue 1989, Vol. 6, pp. 18–19. The Israel Section of Defence for Children International could obtain a temporary permit for the village's kindergarten.
15. Weil, Simone, *The Need for Roots, Prelude to a Declaration of Duties towards Mankind*, London, Henley and Boston, 1952, Routledge and Kegan Paul, (first French edition published in 1949 under the title L'Enracinement).

16. Idem, pp. 3-7.
17. Sandel, Michael, I., *Liberalism and the Limits of Justice*, Cambridge, 1982, Cambridge University Press.
18. Idem, pp. 181-183.
19. Lomasky, Loren, E., *Persons, Rights and the Moral Community*, New York and Oxford, 1987, Oxford University Press. "From one perspective," says Lee Teitelbaum, "the demand for autonomy reflects a loss of sense of community." In: New Mexico Law Review, Vol. 10, summer 1980, p. 252.
20. Mulder, Mauk, *Omgaan met Macht*, Amsterdam, 1977, Elseviers Publ. House.
21. See: Eekelaar, J.M., 'What are Parental Rights' in: *Law Quarterly Review*, 89, 1973, p. 212.
22. Goble, George, W., 'A Redefinition of Basic Legal Terms' in: *Columbia Law Review*, 1935, Vol. 35, pp. 535-547.
23. Goble, George, W. Op.cit., p. 535.
24. Corbin, Arthur, C., Op.cit., p. 109.
25. Kamba, Walter, J., 'Legal Theory and Hohfeld's Analysis of a Legal Right' in: *The Juridical Review*, December 1974, p. 49.
26. Idem, p. 257.
27. Goble, George, W., 'A Redefinition of Basic Legal Terms' Op.cit.
28. Idem.
29. Skolnick, Arlene, 'The Limits of Childhood: Conceptions of Child Development and Social Context', in: *Law and Contemporary Problems*, Summer 1975, Vol. 39, No. 3, pp. 38-77.
30. Melton, Gary, B., *Reforming the Law Impact of Child Development Research*, New York/-London, 1987, The Guildford Press.
31. Goldstein, Joseph, Freud, Anna en Solnit, Albert, I., *Before the Best Interests of the Child*, New York, 1979, The Free Press.
32. Guggenheim, Martin and Sussman, Alan, *The Rights of Young People*, New York, 1985, Bantam Books. Also: Katz, Sanford, N., Shroeder, William, A., Sidman, Lawrence, R., 'Emancipating our Children – Coming of Legal Age in America', in: *The Youngest Minority*, Lawyers in Defense of Children, 1974, ABA Press, pp. 291-2-2.
33. Robert, P., 'Historique du droit des Mineurs ou la Conquète de l'Autonomie à travers l'Histoire', in: *Reéducation*, 23, 1968, 07/08, No. 203. Also: Freeman, M.D.A., in his article 'Taking Children's Rights Seriously', in *Children and Society*, No. 4, 1987-1988, p. 307, writes that R. Dworkin (*Taking Rights Seriously*) "seems to be defining rights in terms of duties... Equality by itself cannot explain what Dworkin is trying to explain, namely that rights as such *trump* (his word) countervailing utilitarian considerations. Something more is needed. I suggest that this additional concept is autonomy. A plausibly theory of rights may take account not just of rights but of the normative value of autonomy, the idea that persons as such have a set of capacities that enables them to make independent decisions regarding appropriate life choices."
34. Foucault, Michel, *Discipline and Punish; the Birth of the Prison*, New York, 1977, Pantheon Books, published in French under the title *Surveiller et Punir*.
35. Illich, Ivan, *Deschooling Society*, New York, 1970.
36. Dearden, R.F., 'Autonomy and Education', in: Dearden, R.F., Hirst, P.H. and Peters, R.S., *Education and the Development of Reason*, London, 1972, Routledge and Kegan Paul, p. 58.
37. Dearden, R.F., Op.cit.
38. Idem, p. 71.
39. Tuck: Already in the beginning of the sixteenth century we seem to have an argument which has recurred repeatedly in the history of rights theories: the question of the relationship between... 'active' and 'passive' rights. Richard Tuck in *Natural Rights Theories*, Cambridge, 1970, Cambridge University Press extensively dwells on the work of the Dominican theologian Silvestro Mazzolini da Prierio, who in 1515 took part in an age-old discussion about the relationship between two Latin concepts: 'dominium', which meant possession,

and 'ius', which meant right. Some people claimed that the two concepts meant the same. This is of interest for us because in those times the authorities considered children to be the possession of their fathers. The French still talk about the *code paternel*. The term reminds us of the time that only those who possessed, had rights, and someone who had a right to something, also possessed it. But, says Mazzolini da Prierio in 1515, according to other people, it is not identical, for an inferior does not have *dominium* over a superior, but he may have a *ius* against him. Thus for example a son has a *ius* to be fed by his father. To have a *dominium* implies that one has a *ius*, but not vice versa, for in addition to a *ius* one must have superiority.

40. Goldstein, Stephen R. and Gee, E. Gordon, *Law and Public Education, Cases and Materials*, second edition, Indianapolis, New York, Charlottesville, Virginia, 1980, The Bobbs-Merrill Camp. Inc., p. 219, for an extensive description of this case. Also: Koenings, Sharon, L. and Ober, Steven, L. 'Legal Precedents in Student Rights Cases' in, Haubrich, Vernon, F. and Apple, Michael, W., *Schooling and the Rights of Children*, Op.cit., p. 144. Koenings and Ober call it a landmark case. See for the Supreme Court decision itself: 393 U.S. 503.
41. Shue, Henry, 'The Interdependence of Duties' in : Alston, P. and Tomasevski, K., editors, *The Right to Food*, Dordrecht, 1987, Martinus Nijhoff Publishers/Utrecht, Stichting Studieen Informatiecentrum Mensenrechten (SIM), pp. 83–97.
42. Berlin, Isaiah, *Two Concepts of Liberty*, Oxford, 1958, Clarendon Press, pp. 7–15.
43. Idem, p. 12.
44. Idem, p. 54.
45. Idem, p. 16.
46. Friedman, Lawrence, M., 'Social Welfare Legislation: An Introduction', in: *Stanford Law Review* 21, 1969, pp. 217–226, idem, p. 220, Kartashkin, Vladimir 'Economic, Social and Cultural Rights', in: Vasak, Karel, ed. *The International Dimensions of Human Rights*, Westport, Conn., 1982, UNESCO and Greenwood Press, p. 113. Also: Friedman, Lawrence, 'Education as a Form of Welfare, Legal and Social Problems' in: Goldstein, Stephen, ed., *Law and Equality in Education*, Jerusalem, The Jerusalem Van Leer Institute p. 168.
47. Friedman, Lawrence, in the *Stanford Law Review*, Op.cit., p. 220.
48. Kartashkin, Vladimir 'Economic, Social and Cultural Rights', in: Vasak, Karel, ed. *The International Dimensions of Human Rights*, Westport, Conn., 1982, UNESCO and Greenwood Press, p. 113.
49. Friedman, Lawrence, in : Law and Equality in Education, Op. cit., p. 168.
50. Friedman, Lawrence, 'Social Welfare Legislation: An Introduction', Op. cit., p. 231. Catherine I. Ross quotes in her article 'Children and Liberty' in *The American Journal of Orthopsychiatry*, 1982, p. 478, Walter Rauschenbusch (author of *The Rights of the Child in the Community*, published in 1915): "Rights have to be fought for and won. They have to be wrested by agitation, by political organisation, often by physical force, from hostile classes and interests. The child can maintain nothing, not even itself." It seems that this definition of children (powerless beings) is changing fast. This, according to Ross, is connected to the fact that questions about the entitlement of minors to standard political and civil rights are being seriously debated.
51. Campbell, Tom, *The Left and Rights, a Conceptual Analysis of the Idea of Socialist Rights*, London, 1983, Routledge and Kegan Paul, pp. 202–203.
52. Friedman, Lawrence, 'Education as a Form of Welfare', Op.cit., p. 174.
53. Wringe, Colin A., *Children's Rights, A Philosophical Study*, London, 1981, Routledge and Kegan Paul, p. 42, "to assert that A. has a right to X where the right is a legal right is to claim that there is a rule, typically to be found in written form (statute, charter, regulation, etc.) to the effect that all persons of a certain category may do or have X, and also to claim that A. is a person of that category."
54. Burt, Robert, A., 'Developing Constitutional Rights of, in, and for Children', in: *Law and Contemporary Problems*, Vol. 39, No. 3, Summer 1975, pp. 118–143.
55. Wringe, Op.cit., p. 43.

56. Young, Robert, "Education and the 'Rights' of Children and Adolescents", in: *Edu. Phil. and Theory*, Vol. 8, No. 1, pp. 17-31.
57. Feinberg, I., *Social Philosophy*, Englewood Cliffs, N.J., 1973.
58. Minow, Martha, 'Interpreting Rights: An Essay for Robert Cover', in: *The Yale Law Journal*, July 1987, No. 8, Vol. 96, pp. 1860-1915.
59. Idem.
60. Minow, Martha, 'Are Rights Rights for Children?' in *Am. Bar. Found. Res. J.*, 1987.
61. Jenkins, Iredell, *Social Order and Limits of Law, a Theoretical Essay*, Princeton, New Jersey, 1980, Princeton Univ. Press, p. 242.
62. Berlin, Irving, N., et al. (Group for the Advancement of Psychiatry), *How Old is Old Enough? The Ages of Rights and Responsibilities*, 1989, p. 75, Ch. 5, *"The Moral Imperative: Social and Personal "Rights" of Children and Adolescents"*.
63. Hagerström, Axel, Inquiries into the Nature of Law and Morals. Olivecrona, Karel, *Law as Facts*, 1939.
64. MacCormack, Geoffrey, 'Scandinavian Realism', in: *The Juridical Review, The Law Journal of Scottish Universities*, 1970, Vol. 15, pp. 33-53.
65. I am grateful to anthropologist Mike Soltman of Haifa University for his suggestions.
66. MacCormack, Op.cit., p. 50.
67. Ministry of Foreign Affairs of the Netherlands, *Vademecum Mensenrechten*, 's-Gravenhage, 1987.
68. Henkin, Louis, 'Rights: American and Human', in: *Colombia University Law Review*, 1979, No. 3, Vol. 79, pp. 405-425.
69. Idem.
70. Ministry of Foreign Affairs of the Netherlands, 1987, Op.cit. "When we speak about fundamental rights, we mean such rights as the right to live and the inviolability of human beings.
71. Idem.
72. *Universal Declaration of Human Rights*, G.A. Res. 217, U.N. Doc. A/810, 1948.
73. Morsink, Johannes, 'The Philosophy of the Universal Declaration', in: *Human Rights Quarterly*, Vol. 6, No. 3, August 1984, pp. 316 & 333. Also: Weston, Burns, H., 'Human Rights', in: *Human Rights Quarterly*, Vol. 6, No. 3, August 1984, pp. 257-258.
74. Kartashkin, Vladimir, 'The Socialist Countries and Human Rights', Op.cit., p. 631.
75. Veerman, Philip E., 'Spijbelen in Grote Steden', in: *Welzijnsmaandblad*, April 1985.
76. Based on conversation with Prof. Louis Henkin, Professor of Constitutional Law, at Columbia University in New York, May 1988.
77. Ministry of Foreign Affairs of the Netherlands, *Vademecum Mensenrechten*, Op.cit.
78. Idem.
79. Donnelly, Jack, *Universal Human Rights in Theory and Practice*, New York, 1984, Cornell University Press, p. 156.
80. Idem.
81. Boven, Theodoor C. van, 'Distinguishing Criteria of Human Rights', in: Vasak, Karel, *The International Dimensions of Human Rights*, Op.cit., p. 49.
82. Idem.
83. Idem.
84. Heringa, A.W., *Sociale Grondrechten, Hun plaats in de gereedschapskist van de rechter*, Proefschrift, The Hague, 1989, T.M.C. Asser Instituut, p. 402.
85. Alkema, Evert A., *Studies over Europese Grondrechten, De invloed van de Europese Conventie op het Nederlandse Recht*, Proefschrift, 1978, Deventer, Kluwer, p. 277.
86. Alkema, Prof. E.A., in a personal communication with the author, June 1990. This is also the case with various groups, such as prisoners, Alkema explained.
87. Ressler, Everett, M., Boothby, Neil and Steinbock, Daniel, J., *Unaccompanied Children, Care and Protection in Wars, Natural Disasters, and Refugee Movements*, New York and Oxford, 1988, Oxford University Press, p. 210.
88. DCI/UNICEF, *Briefing kit on the United Nations Convention on the Rights of the Child*,

Geneva and New York, 1989. Two very important Conventions are: *International Covenant on Civil and Political Rights*, G.A., Res. 2200, 21 U.N. GAOR, Supp. (No.16)52, U.N.Doc. A/6316(1966), and *International Covenant on Economic, Social and Cultural Rights*, G.A., Res. 2200, 21 U.N., GAOR, Supp. No. 16, U.N. Doc. A/6316(1966).

89. The Child Welfare League of America (CWLA) undertook in 1955 to formulate a series of Standards. In 1964 they published *Standards for Child Welfare Institutions*. Since then they published *Standards for Adoption Service, Standards for Child Protective Service, Standards for Day Care Service, Standards for Foster Family Care, Standards for Group Home Services for Children, Standards for Homemaker Service for Children, Standards for Services for Unmarried Parents and Standards for Residential Centers for Children*.

    The Ontario Ministry of Community and Social Services (Canada), published: *Foster Care: Proposed Standards and Guidelines for Agencies Placing Children*, Toronto, October 1981.

90. G.L. against Zumwalt; see Mushlin, Michael, B., Levitt, Louis and Anderson, Lauren, 'Court-ordered Foster Family Care Reform: A Case Study', in *Child Welfare*, Vol. LXV, No. 2, March 1986, pp. 141–154. Idem, p. 144.

91. American Public Welfare Association, *Standards for Foster Family Services Systems for Public Agencies*, Washington D.C., 1979, Department of Health, Education and Welfare.

92. The legal implications of the acceptance of a behaviour code in the form of a recommendation or a guideline are discussed in a report by the director-general of the World Health Organisation to the thirty-fourth World Health Assembly (see document WHA 34/1981/REL/1, addendum 3 and World Health Organisation, *International Code of Marketing of Breast-Milk Substitutes*, Geneva, 1981).

93. Sikkink, Kathryn, 'Codes of Conduct for Transnational Corporations: The Case of the WHO/UNICEF Code' in: *International Organisation*, Vol. 40, Autumn 1986, No. 4.

94. IBFAN (International Baby Food Action Network), *Breaking the Rules, 1988–1989, A Report of the International Marketing Practices of the Infant Food and Feeding Bottles Industry*, Geneva, Minneapolis and Penang. Rachid, Rosalind, 'Switzerland's Nestlé Nurses Its Sullied Baby Food Image', in: *The Journal of Commerce*, August 7, 1989. Also: Kasteren, van, Ineke, *Het Probleem van de Kunstmatige Babyvoeding is de (derde) Wereld nog niet uit*, Soest, Vereniging Borstvoeding Natuurlijk Afdeling, Soest.

    It is interesting that Marie Parent, the editor of the Belgian periodical *Le Journal des Mères* in 1925 pleads that every child has the right to his mother's milk. (see *The World's Children*, Vol. 5, No. 6, p. 85 (March 1925).

95. Samaan, George, Defence for Children International (DCI), *Statement on the Draft United Nations Standard Minimum Rules for the Protection of Juveniles Deprived of their Liberty*, given at the Western Asia Preparatory Meeting for the Eighth U.N. Conference on Prevention of Crime and Treatment of Offenders. Statement delivered in Cairo, May, 1989. For the standards see: *Eighth United Nations Congress on the Prevention of Crime and the Treatment of Offenders, Havana, Cuba, 27 August to 7 September* 1990, A/Conf. 144/28, 5 October 1990.

96. Rodham, H., 'Children Under the Law', in: *Harvard Educational Review*, Vol. 43, No. 4, Nov. 1973, pp. 487–514.

97. Bevan, H.K., *Child Law*, London, 1989, Buttersworth, p. 11.

PART B

The Analysis of Childrens Rights –
A Conceptual Framework

CHAPTER III

Shye's 'Systemic Quality of Life Model'

In this chapter we shall introduce a model which was especially developed for the evaluation of the well-being of human beings. It can easily be adapted to the well-being of children and will serve as a guide for the systematic identification of children's rights.

With the help of the 'Systemic Quality of Life Model' developed by Samuel Shye, we can successfully separate the various claims that are made on behalf of children.[1] Since this model has been tested empirically and since its internal structure has been validated[2], this model has advantages over other frameworks for analysis. It is a practical tool which provides us with a uniform, rational set of criteria by which very rich and intricate material can be analysed, compared and evaluated.

It is not only a model derived from the abstract system-approach[3], but its criteria refer to contents from the fields of welfare, social psychology, education, organisational systems, and so forth.[4] Moreover, with Shye's 'Systemic Quality of Life Model' we can classify the various models for analysis of children's rights, described at the end of this chapter.

In this study we shall always use the 'Systemic Quality of Life Model' to map and analyse developments in the field of the rights of the child during the twentieth century. We shall use the term 'quality of life' when talking about the rights of the child, since this term does not have the standard connotation that other concepts, such as 'happiness', and 'good life', have.

According to William J. Overholt and Herman Kahn[5], 'the concept 'quality of life' represents to some extent an evolution from earlier concepts (such as standard of living, good life, and a good place to raise children), because they are either crude and materialistic or passé and moralistic.

Later in this study[6] we shall draw a connection between the concepts 'quality of life' and 'self-determination'.

The view a child has of his or her rights depends on the developmental phase of that particular child, and on past experiences, at home and in school, concerning rights. Melton[7] points out that according to research poor children are relatively slow in acquiring the view that rights have any relevance to them. There is also evidence that adults of low socio-economic

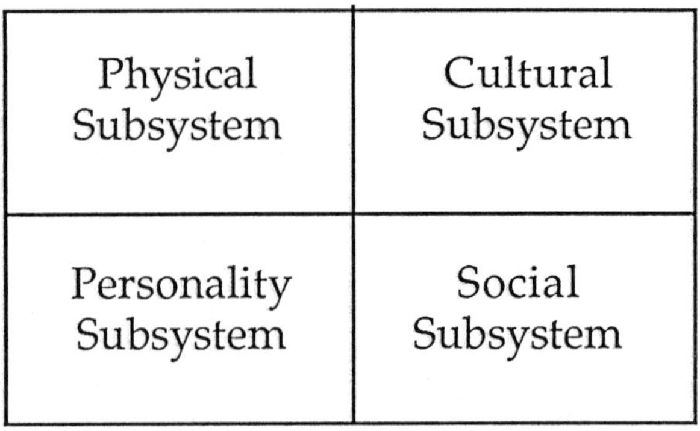

Physical Subsystem	Cultural Subsystem
Personality Subsystem	Social Subsystem

Fig. 3.1. The General Human System. The four subsystems and their interrelationships. (Shye's faceted conceptualization permits testing the validity of the model by multidimensional scaling.)

status, particularly those who belong to minority groups, are relatively ignorant of their legal rights and of the legal and moral means to social change. Such ignorance has the effect of reinforcing discrimination. A belief in their own limited rights may reflect the social, legal and ethical reality of life for disadvantaged groups in our society.

Prosperity can but does not always influence the quality of life. In affluent Sweden, for instance, the Social-Democratic politician Olaf Palme once said that industrialisation and technological growth have reached a point where Sweden must cope with those large enterprises and organisations that give its citizens a feeling of powerlessness and anonimity.

The term 'quality of life' indicates not only 'the degree of satisfaction one has with one's life'[10], but also 'to what extent one has the means to increase the possibility of realising one's 'life plan'.[11] The rights of the child are those aspects that help children and youngsters realise their potential.

We shall give a very concise description of the sixteen item matrices in Shye's 'Systemic Quality of Life Model' and show in nine examples how it can be used as a classification model. The examples will gradually become more complex.

Shye: "The human condition has been conceptualised as an action system of four *subsystems*: the personality manifestations, the cultural commitments, the physical-biological interactions and the social interactions."[12] Schematically we can render these four subsystems as follows:

Every human being, in particular every child or youngster, encapsulates the General Human System and functions in each of the four subsystems:

The Personality Subsystem comprising individual and general personality features of the General Human System.

The Physical Subsystem comprising the material aspects of the General Human System.

The Social Subsystem comprising social aspects of the General Human System.

The Cultural Subsystem comprising values and norms.
Furthermore, within each of the four subsystems the human individual functions in four modes.

The four *modes*, also called 'functioning modes', require additional clarification: The *expressive mode* constitutes the universe of the living subsystem's exercise of power and ability to control. Within each subsystem the power and control are an expression of those internal forces and pressures directed toward the creation of a reality which reflects the subsystem's own characteristics.[13] We thus have the expressive mode of the personality subsystem, the expressive mode of the physical subsystem, the expressive mode of the social subsystem and the expressive mode of the cultural subsystem.

The *adaptive mode* comprises the accommodation between the subsystem and its environment. Shye: "Effective adaptability contributes to the maintenance and growth of the system itself."[14] According to certain attachment theories even babies negotiate, which would mean that they come into the world with the capacity to influence the behaviour of adults. Jannie Sanders-Woudstra: "The view that new-born babies are psychologically undifferentiated and only gradually become socialised by parents and society, has been rejected. Babies are endowed with a biological equipment that enables them to seek stimulation and to interact with their caretakers".[15] We thus have the adaptive mode of the personality subsystem, the adaptive mode of the physical subsystem, the adaptive mode of the social subsystem and the adaptive mode of the cultural subsystem.

The *integrative mode* is the universe of internal events which occur fully within the subsystem such as ongoing health. A dynamic balance within the system is all the time maintained. Often it is conflict management. Events are subject to ongoing internal adjustments which take place by compensatory or complementary processes.[16] Again we have the integrative mode of the personality subsystem, the integrative mode of the physical subsystem, the integrative mode of the social subsystem and the integrative mode of the cultural subsystem.

The *conservative mode* refers to an adherence to structural patterns that have been internalised by the subsystem. This can be a genetic code, a cultural code, a social fibre or identity of the subsystem. These are the relatively permanent, inherent characteristics which the system acquired from outside at the time of its creation. The need for stability, safety and a stable social environment can be classified in this mode. The subsystem's functioning in the conservative mode is more effective when the system adheres to the various aspects of its structure.[17] We have the conservative mode of the personality subsystem, the conservative mode of the physical subsystem, the conservative mode of the social subsystem and the conservative mode of the cultural subsystem.

Shye defines 'quality of life' as the universe of items which ask about the individual's functioning in each of the four modes and in each of the four subsystems. Webster's Dictionary defines 'mode' as 'particular functioning arrangement or condition'. Shye defines his four modes: the *expressive mode* (exercise of power), the *adaptive mode* (external interactions), the *integrative mode* (internal harmony) and the *conservative mode* (adherence to structure).[18]

On the basis of reasonable, fundamental axioms Shye demonstrates that the four subsystems are exhaustive and mutually exclusive. The same is true for the four functioning modes within each subsystem. (See notes 4 and 14.)

Fig. 3.2. on page 43 describes the content of each of the modes within each of the subsystems.

Analytically the model can be further detailed by regarding each of the sixteen modes as a sub-subsystem in its own right. For example the conservative mode of the social subsystem can be looked upon as a sub-subsystem. As such it has its own expressive, adaptive, integrative and conservative modes. Consider for example the illustration that Shye gives: 'The Constitution of a State determines the governing structure of the State. Adherence to the Constitution pertains to the conservative mode and the social subsystem. But the Constitution itself may be changed or amended. How such changes can take place in the Constitution pertain to the expressive mode of the Constitution and hence, to the expressive mode of the sub-subsystem of the conservative functioning of the social subsystem.

We shall on page 44 introduce the graphical rendition of the 'Systemic Quality of Life Model' which will be shown throughout the present work whenever we want to analyse a situation.

This model will immediately show us the differences and analogies of, for instance, the various Declarations of the Rights of the Child. Figure 3.3 also represents a hypothesis for further empirical research, since it makes the correlation between various elements within the whole system visible.

The hypothesis is that in the centre of the 'Systemic Quality of Life Model' there is little or no differentiation. The greater the distance from the centre, the more differentiation there is. A child is born into a specific cultural environment with its own code, and also into a specific social network and with certain physical endowments and a budding self-identity. The conservative mode concerns the system's adherence to the essentials of these features, that is: it is concerned with stability and continuity.

As is shown in Figure 3.3, on page 44 the conservative modes of the four subsystems lie in the centre of the map, and the expressive modes at the outer border. The integrative and adaptive modes of each subsystem occupy an intermediate region, but lie opposite each other on different planes.

In the graphic representation (see Fig. 3.3) the colour black means that a certain right, classified in that mode, is explicitly mentioned in a text. Dots are used to indicate that the right is implied rather than mentioned. White means no mentioning whatsoever. Sometimes a bolder black is used to emphasise that a specific mode in a subsystem is especially emphasised.

Ideally, Figure 3.3. should be three-dimensional as shown in Figure 3.4,

Subsystem and Mode	Occurrences related to
Personality Subsystem	
Expressive Mode	The emergence of specific behaviours (actions, perceptions, emotions, beliefs), peculiar to the individual.
Adaptive Mode	Interactional process between the personality and its environment (including the individual's other three subsystems as well as environment external to the individual).
Integrative Mode	Interactions among personality characteristics.
Conservative Mode	The basic structure of (set of relationships among) personality components.
Physical Subsystem	
Expressive Mode	Exerting physical energy upon the subsystem's environment
Adaptive Mode	Interactional processes between the individual's body (bodily needs) and the environment. (The 'environment' of the individual's physical existence includes the other three subsystems as well as the environment external to the individual.)
Integrative Mode	Interactions among the individual's various physical characteristics.
Conservative Mode	The basic physical constitution.
Social Subsystem	
Expressive Mode	The exertion of social influence, including interpersonal influence and societal power (political activity.)
Adaptive Mode	Interactional processes between the individual as a carrier of social roles and the environment (including the other three subsystems.)
Integrative Mode	Interactions among the individual's various social roles.
Conservative Mode	Social structure of the community of the individual.
Cultural (value) Subsystem.	
Expressive Mode	The assertion and upholding of values, the exertion of moral influence.
Adaptive Mode	Interactional processes between the individual as a carrier of values, and the environment (including the other three subsystems.)
Integrative Mode	Interactions among the values held by the individuals.
Conservative Mode	The value structure of the community of the individual.

Fig. 3.2. The four modes of the four subsystems of individual human functioning: explications. *Note:* S. Shye, the 'Systemic Quality of Life Model' (abridged), reprinted with permission from *Social Indicators Research* (Wolters-Noordhoff-Kluwer Academic Publishers) 21: 343–378, 1989.

with the adaptive and integrative modes above, rather than beside each other.

Sometimes we are concerned with eliminating distress rather than with facilitating a child's full potential. Consequently we may classify something in a particular mode, not in order to emphasise the right to development in

Chapter III

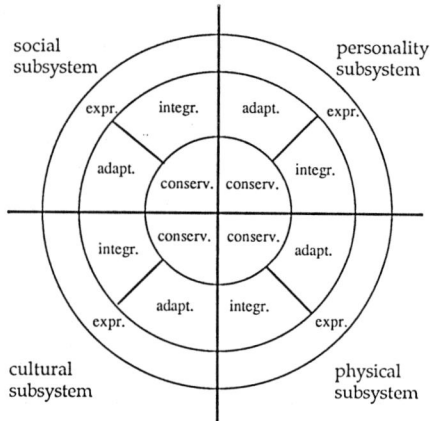

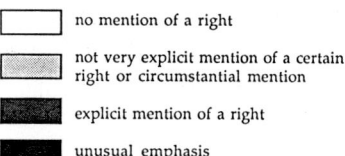
no mention of a right

not very explicit mention of a certain right or circumstantial mention

explicit mention of a right

unusual emphasis

Fig. 3.3.

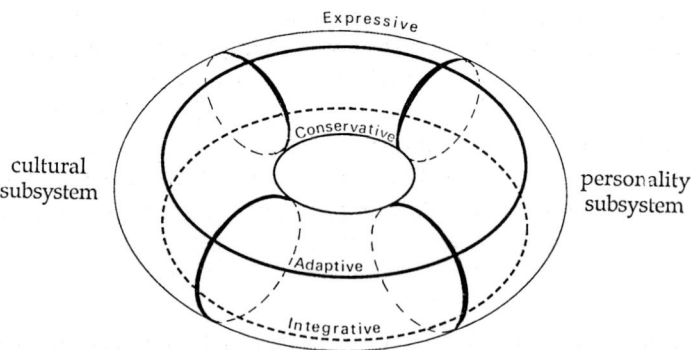

Fig. 3.4.

that mode, but in order to avoid distressful conditions. For example, the right of the child to explore the environment and the right of the child not to be put in jail are both classified in the *expressive mode* of the *physical subsystem*.

In order that the reader may become acquainted with the way we intend to use Shye's 'Systemic Quality of Life Model', we shall give a number of examples. The first and second examples are rather 'pure'; the others are chosen to show how we shall analyse more complex situations.

Example 1
In the *Declaration of Geneva* of 1924 we read in Principle 2: "The child that is hungry must be fed." This passive positive right refers, of course, to physical food and not to cultural symbolical food like the unleavened bread the Jews 'need' during Passover, or the consecrated wafers the Catholics 'need' during certain church services. We are therefore dealing with the physical subsystem. Food is part of the interaction between the physical subsystem and the environment, or as Shye puts it: "Obtaining resources from the environment for the system is part of negotiating with it."[19] Thus the relationship between the system (child) and its environment can be classified in the *adaptive mode* of the *physical subsystem*.

Example 2
In the United Nations Convention on the Rights of the Child of 1989 we read in Article 14(1): "States Parties shall respect the right of the child to freedom of thought, conscience and religion." The context of this Article indicates that it refers mainly to the religious values of the child. It would have been clearer if it had explicitly mentioned the right of the child to *expression* of religious beliefs and values, because as long as beliefs are not expressed, they cannot be regulated by law. If any law can be applied to religion, it is only to its manifestation. Article 14(1) can, therefore, be classified in the *expressive mode* of the *cultural subsystem*.

Fear how far the expression of beliefs can be taken has led many states to make reservations. The Jordanian representative in the U.N. General Assembly on November 20th, 1989: "Jordan interprets Article 14 on religion, as meaning that the child has the right to practice, not choose, his or her religion."

Example 3
And how shall we use the 'Systemic Quality of Life Model' to analyse the *right to recreation* as mentioned in Principle 7 of the United Nations Declaration of the Rights of the Child?

To the extent that recreation means 'recharging one's batteries' for the provision of mental nourishment, it can be classified in the *adaptive mode* of the *personality subsystem*.

Example 4
In the Preamble of the United Nations Declaration on the Rights of the Child of 1959 we read in paragraph five that the child "shall be entitled to grow and develop in health." The Dutch delegation to the United Nations proposed in vain to change the text, on the grounds that it is not possible to guarantee health. The proposed text ran: "He shall be entitled to grow and develop under conditions conductive to his health."[20]

Tarzie Vittachie[21] points out that the circumstances of millions of people are certainly no guarantee for health. Medical care for the poor, unfortunately, is still widely regarded as a concession by the State rather than a Right.

Shye: "If, as a consequence of the penetration of a virus into the live body, the suitable antibodies multiply sufficiently, they will restore the body's balance and thus maintain its health and wholesomeness. The antibody differs from the virus in an essential way and compensates for the existence of the virus. . . . From the system's point of view, such events are subject to ongoing internal adjustments which take place by compensatory and complementary processes. The manner in which the system relates to such events we shall term the *integrative mode*."[22] As we are dealing with health, we can classify this example in the *integrative mode* of the *physical subsystem*.

Example 5
Article 12(1) of the United Nations Convention on the Rights of the Child says that "States Parties shall assure to the child who is capable of forming his or her own views, the right to express those views freely in all matters affecting the child, the views of the child being given due weight in accordance with the age and maturity of the child."

This Article can, for instance, be understood as referring to political expression of opinions by youngsters. In Chapter II we mentioned the case of *Tinker v. Des Moines Independent Community School District*. We spoke about it as a case wherein a negative right was acknowledged, namely the right to be protected from interference (freedom from interference). But the case also is concerned with expressing one's political views and having power over one's social environment, and hence it can also be classified in the *expressive mode* of the *social subsystem*. To the extent that value preferences are reflected the *expressive mode* of the *cultural subsystem* is also involved.

Moreover we can view this case as an example of a positive right, namely freedom of speech. Michael J. Dale writes: "The Warren Court upheld the constitutional rights of juveniles, finding that the suspension of students in public schools for wearing armbands as a symbolic protest against foreign policy in the Vietnam War, violated the students personal rights to freedom of speech."[23]

It is important to keep in mind that the decision in the case Tinker v. Des Moines was taken by the American Supreme Court presided by Chief Justice

Earl Warren. His successor, Chief Justice Warren Burger was appointed by President Nixon and assumed the office in June 1969. He and 'his' Supreme Court cancelled much of the expansion of juvenile rights that took place during the 1960s and early 1970s.

If we consider how many countries forbid even adults to express their (political) opinions, we should not be surprised that Article 12(1) of the United Nations Convention on the Rights of the Child has been kept deliberately vague.

Example 6
Janusz Korczak formulated 'the right of the child to have secrets'. This can be viewed as an extension of the 'right to privacy'. In his children's book 'The Bankruptcy of Little Jack'[24], Korczak describes how Jack hides all sorts of things in boxes, and how nobody knows this. Secrets do not have to be things, though. Thus Matt, in *King Matt on the deserted island*[25] tells nobody about his adventures.

Lax et al.[26] wrote about this: "He spoke to no one about his adventures because it would have been unpleasant if people did not believe him." Korczak was irritated to see how adults sometimes put children to shame with degrading remarks about their thoughts, stories or adventures.

The Ombudsman for Children of the 'Jerusalem Council on Children and Youth'[27] gave a good example of the right to have secrets. A teacher had confiscated a note on a pupil's desk. "Please don't read it," the child had asked. However, the teacher read the note and also read it out loud in class! The Ombudsman wrote to the Organisation of Teachers about this case and pointed out that a 'code of ethics' of teachers was badly needed.

To the extent that the secrets Korczak was concerned with express something of the child's inner personality, personal secrets may be regarded as pertaining to the *expressive mode* of the *personality subsystem*. The secrecy is then but a manifestation of a need to control and shape such expression without interference. From the point of view of the system, secrecy in this case is serving the purpose of free and accurate 'effective' expression.[28]

Example 7
The 'right to have a name' is mentioned in Principle 3 of the Declaration of the Rights of the Child, and in Article 7(1) of the United Nations Convention on the Rights of the Child.

How shall we classify this right? A name is an institutional aspect of one's identity. Therefore the right to have a name can be classified in the *conservative mode* of the *personality subsystem*. However, it is also a social institution. It gives a person a social status and is important for legal transactions. We can therefore classify it in the *adaptive mode* of the *social subsystem*. Since the drafters' intention is hard to deduce from the text of the Declaration, I asked Mrs. Dr. F.T. Diemer-Lindeboom who had been a member of the Dutch delegation to the United Nations and who had attended the discussion in 1959, what this intention had been. Mrs. Diemer said[29]: "Concerning the right to have a name, we should be careful not to look at, and search for answers in the Declaration from the viewpoint of later developments in the West, such as Erik Erikson's psychosocial stages of development in which identity is so central in adolescence. It is more basic. To bear a name is often essential to our existence."

Dr. Haim H. Cohn, who represented Israel between 1957 and 1967 in the 'Human Rights Commission' of the United Nations, told me in March 1989, that "there were several holocaust survivors who did not know their names or their parents' names. The Commission wanted to determine that in the case of these child-refugees it was necessary to express the legal right to a name, so that no child could be rejected for the lack of a name."

The Declaration of the Rights of the Child rectifies the omission in the 'Universal Declaration of Human Rights' with respect to a name. From the context we understand that the intention was to grant children the right to belong to a social institution, which is required for admission to many countries. In view of the above we can classify the right to have a name in the *adaptive mode* of the *social subsystem*.

Example 8
Principle 2 of the Declaration of the Rights of the Child also deals with the right to have a nationality. How shall we classify this? If we had not studied the discussion that led to the inclusion of this right in the Declaration, we would classify it in the *adaptive mode* of the *social subsystem*, since nationality can be defined as a social convention among people.

Haim Cohn: "Many human rights are not immediately enforceable rights of children. Since a child is not a qualified petitioner, somebody must claim the right for him. But if the legal guardian does not claim that right for him, it is quite irrelevant. We, in the Human Rights Commission, wanted to make clear in the Declaration that whether anybody claims this right or not, or whether any State grants children a nationality or not, the child enjoys the right to a nationality. (The Nazi's for instance took away the German nationality from Jewish children)."

However, we can also classify the right to a nationality in the *conservative mode* of the *physical subsystem*, for according to Mrs. Diemer the intention was the right of children to dwell within the boundaries of a country without being expelled (physical security).

After the Second World War there were large groups of refugees. This was also the case in 1956 when events in Hungary and the Near East constituted a fresh source of alarm about the well-being of children. Mrs. Diemer: "The right to a nationality was of course very important because of the many displaced persons after the war. To be deprived of this right is a great social handicap. The child, in such a case, has the status of an outcast. As the child is part of the fibre of the country, the right to a nationality can be classified in the *adaptive mode* of the *social subsystem*, as well as in the *conservative mode* of the *physical subsystem* (e.g. refugees in wartime).

Example 9
The last example concerns sex education and is a little more challenging.

Michael Schofield formulated 'the right to know' for adolescents. "Adolescents are fed up hearing about the wonder of childbirth.... Many sex education books today still tell children that masturbating is harmful."[30]

What Schofield wants to say is that adolescents often worry a great deal about sexuality and that nobody talks to them about it. The issue is not simple curiosity, like when a child is interested in history or mathematics. Schofield argues that all questions adolescents may have about sex should be answered and that there should be no restrictions.

The right to know, interpretable as the right to a certain kind of behaviour (i.e. cognitive), belongs in the *expressive mode* of the *personality subsystem*. *What* the adolescent wants to know in this case, belongs in the *integrative mode* of the *physical subsystem* (sex as internal balancing) and the *integrative mode* of the *social subsystem* (interpersonal intimacy). The 'right to know' as formulated by Schofield, belongs in the *integrative mode* of the *personality* and of the *social subsystems*.

The cultural subsystem guides the flow of information when it comes to defining what is good for children and youngsters. Van Ussel[31] describes for instance how, in early days, Bibles for children in the Netherlands were purified of everything sexual. As a result of this and similar actions Dutch youngsters were more childish and psychologically backward than their peers across the cultural border. The *cultural subsystem* is therefore also circumstantially involved through its *adaptive mode* which screens, shapes and interprets all information.

In connection with the right to know, a very instructive letter to the editor was published in the English periodical 'Childright'.[32]

> Dear Childright,
> Recently I received a letter from my son's school (*Mornington Road High School, Hindeley, Wigan*) informing me that during March they had planned a five week programme to cover subjects such as AIDS and other sexual-transmitted diseases and that, if I had any objections, alternative arrangements could be made for my child.
> I was very pleased at the school's initiative towards AIDS but I was horrified when I realised the letter's implications – that parents apparently have the right to withhold their consent and deprive their children of such vital information.
> I feel strongly that parents' rights are too heavily weighed and that children should have their rights too, independently of their parents – and that such rights should be enshrined in the statute books. Children who do not receive

information about AIDS and other sexually-transmitted diseases, jeopardise the informed.

Chris Hesford

Formulated Right and Intention

From most of the above examples we can deduce that we must differentiate between a formulated right and its intention. To gain some insight into the purpose of a specific right, we must refer to the context, mentioned in reports of meetings and other documents. Unfortunately very often no such reports can be found, whereas the articles themselves, as Freeman[33] notices, are deliberately vague.

In the 1959 Yearbook of the United Nations we find only the following sentence concerning the right of the child to recreation and play: "On the initiative of Mexico, Peru and Rumania, it was agreed to add a paragraph to Principle 7 – setting forth the right of the child to receive education – proclaiming that the child shall have full opportunity for play and recreation, *directed to the same purposes of education*." About the purpose of such education the Declaration does not elaborate. All we read is: "He (the child) shall be given an education which will promote his general culture, and enable him on a basis of equal opportunity to develop his abilities, his individual judgment, and his sense of moral and social responsibility, and to become a useful member of society."

Another way to discover the purpose of a right, is to consider its historical context. This is why the present study sometimes reads like a history of ideas.

Shye's 'Systemic Quality of Life Model' provides us with the tools to go beyond the history of ideas and to map the 'quality of life' of children today, so that we may know in which fields it needs to be improved.[34]

Shye's model offers many advantages over other models[35] used to analyse the Rights of the Child. Well-known models have been published by Rogers and Wrightsman and by Wald. We shall show that these models are less differentiated than Shye's 'Systemic Quality of Life Model' and that their theoretical basis is not as sound.

Rogers and Wrightsman

Rogers and Wrightsman have developed a classification framework consisting of two important conceptual orientations which they cut across five different content areas. These two conceptual orientations are *nurturance* and *self-determination*.

In their taxonomy they focus attention upon the potential rather than the legally recognised rights of children. Under nurturance orientation they

| | Conceptual Dimension | |
Content Area	Nurturance	Self-Determination
Health	Free health care	Choice to refuse or accept treatment
Education-Information	Quality education	Choice not to attend school
Economic	Equal pay for equal work	Right to enter into binding contracts
Safety-Care	Products safely designed	Choice of where to live
Legal-Judicial-political	Due process	Choice of legal counsel

Fig. 3.5. The framework for analysis of Rogers and Wrightsman.

understand 'the provision by society of supposedly beneficial objects, environments, services, experiences etc. for the child'. The nurturance orientation is essentially paternalistic (or maternalistic).[36]

Under the *self-determination orientation* the authors include 'those potential rights that would allow children to exercise control over their environments, to make decisions about what they want, to have autonomous control over various facets of their lives'.[37] Well-meaning adults with a nurturance orientation decide for the children what is good for them. Adults with a self-determination orientation let children mind their own business. These two very important categories might be interpreted as basic attitudes of the adults. But the authors point out that reactions of the adults often depend on the subject. "Conceivably a person might be supportive of giving children the right to make choices in the area of education, yet at the same time be strongly opposed to giving children the right to make their own choices regarding health care."[38]

Rogers and Wrightsman have examined which of the two adult attitudes was dominant in five content areas they designated as: Health, Education-Information, Economic, Safety-Care, and Legal-Judicial-Political. Thus they simplify this very complex material by dividing it into two categories. Our objection to this model is that it maps *only* basic attitudes and leaves us with the problem that parents are inconsistent.

Another shortcoming is that this model suggests sometimes contrasts where there are none. There is no real contrast between 'equal pay for equal work' and 'the right to enter into binding contracts'. It would be preferable to find

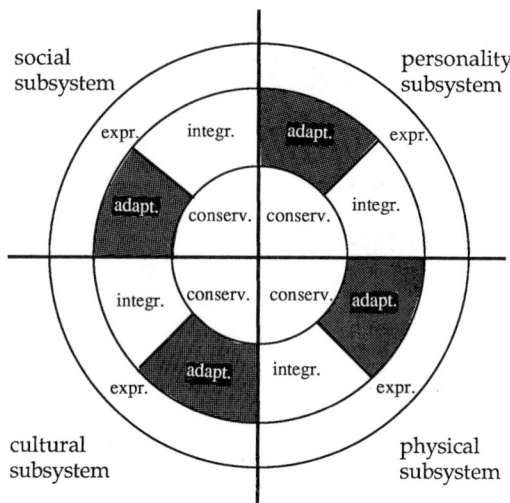

Fig. 3.6. Rogers and Wrightsman's "Nurturance". Interpreted by the Systemic Quality of Life Model.

under 'Nurturance' in this Content Area the 'protection against participation in the labour market'.

According to Rogers and Wrightsman the Nurturance Orientation is paternalistic (or maternalistic). What is good or desirable for the child is determined for the child by society or some subject of society.[39] However, it is our opinion that this is not necessarily a one-way track and that Shye's 'Systemic Quality of Life Model' is better equipped for mapping such interaction.

Example
If a child is allergic to milk or does not like it, the educator will most probably try to find some substitute food. In Shye's terms there is question of negotiating even in cases where the nurturance-oriented voice of the adult is dominant. That is why we classify the *nurturance orientation* in the *adaptive mode* of the four subsystems.

The self-determination orientation as described by Rogers and Wrightsman, means giving the child the political power to choose. In Shye's 'Systemic Quality of Life Model' it is classifiable in the *expressive mode* of the *social subsystem*. Since there is an element of negotiating with social institutions (like the right to enter binding contracts), we also classify the self-determination orientation in the *adaptive mode* of the *social subsystem*. A concern with the *expressive mode* of the *personality and physical subsystems* can also be found.

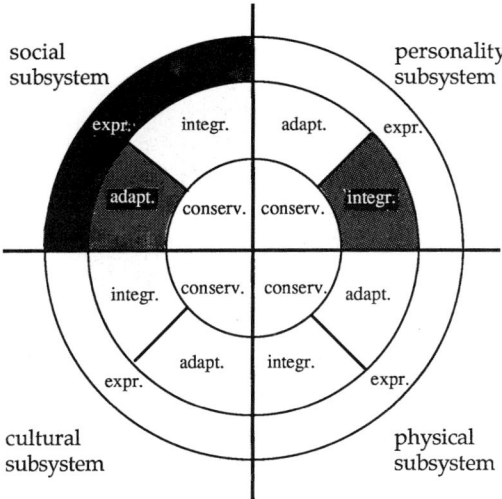

Fig. 3.7. "Self-determination" as described by Rogers and Wrightsman. Interpreted by the Systemic Quality of Life Model.

Example

A young person decides to quit school to spend his or her time painting and drawing.

(A) Generalized claims against the world

(B) The right to greater protection from abuse, neglect and exploitation by adults

(C) The right to be treated in the same manner as an adult, with the same constitutional protections, in relationship to State actions

(D) The right to act independently of parental control and/or guidance

---

Fig. 3.8. Michael Wald's framework for analysis.

Michael Wald

Michael Wald distinguishes four categories of claims under the general rubric of children's rights (as rendered in Fig. 3.8.).

Michael Freeman[40] uses these same categories in his important book *The Rights and Wrongs of Children*.

 A. In the first category are, for instance, the right to adequate health care; the right to adequate housing; the right to live in a safe community;[41] "In many respects," says Wald, "these types of claims are the most important 'rights' that could be given to children. They lie at the heart of a child's well-being." This category of rights do not apply only to children but to all people. Freeman calls them Welfare Rights.

Says Wald: "Demands for such rights recognise that children cannot provide for themselves and need the care and guidance of adults."[42] According to Freeman all ten issues of the *Declaration of the Rights of the Child* of the United Nations (1959) fall under this category.[43] He calls them the clearest statement of children's rights in the sense of right to welfare.

B. The second category aims at a better protection of children against activities of adults. It stresses the vulnerability of children, particularly babies and the very young, and it imposes a caretaker role upon parents. This approach to the Rights of the Child is the oldest and the most firmly entrenched. Says Freeman[44] "When rights are spoken of within this framework, the attention is on certain freedoms that we believe children should have: freedom *from* abuse and neglect can also be looked at in terms of a parent's lack of rights. Hohfeld would have called this parental lack of rights a no-right."

Wald stresses that we often disregard children's views when we give them more protection.[45] As an example he mentions the pleas for less violence on TV.

C. It is in the third category that, according to Wald, children's advocates make their strongest claim.[46] Their point of departure is often a protest against special treatment for children. One example is the lowering of the age at which children reach legal majority. Others are the right to have a lawyer when appearing in Juvenile Court; the right to use contraceptives or have an abortion; the right to sign a contract and the right to speak one's mind.

D. The fourth category is called by Freeman "rights against parents" because this is the claim that children should be free to act independently from their parents even before reaching majority.[47] The most important issues in this category are whether or not parents can decide to what school their children should go, and what medical care they should receive.

This fourth category is very undifferentiated. Moreover the boundaries between the third and the fourth category are often unclear. In cases like this the superiority of Shye's 'Systemic Quality of Life Model' can be demonstrated. Here the components do not overlap. It is a comprehensive model which classifies 'rights' and 'proposed rights' in terms of what is good for the 'system' (i.e. the child).

The above having been stated, we must keep in mind that, no matter how functional a classification model may be, it can only pinpoint problems, never solve them.

NOTES

1. Michael Wald wrote: "It is first necessary to separate the various types of claims being made on behalf of children." See: Wald, Michael, 'Children's Rights', in: *University of California at Davis Law Review*, Vol. 12, 1979, p. 259:
2. Shye, Samuel, *A systemic Facet Theoretic Approach to the Study of Quality of Life*, Jerusalem, Israel, Institute of Applied Social Research, 1979. Also: Shye, S., The Systemic Life Quality Model: A Basis for Urban Renewal Evaluation. *Social Indication Research*, 1989.
3. Shye, S., 'Nonmetric Multivariate Models for Behavioral Action Systems', in Canter, David, editor, *Facet Theory, Approaches to Social Research*, New York/Berlin, 1985, Springer Verlag, p. 101.
4. Shye, S., 'The Systemic Life Quality Model: A Basis for Urban Renewal Evaluation', in: *Social Indicators Research*, 21: pp. 343–378, 1989. Also: Worner, Yochanan, *People Care in Institutions*, Binghamton, N.Y., 1990, The Haworth Press.
5. Overholt, William, I. and Kahn, Herman, 'Perceptions of Quality of Life: Some Effects of Social Strata and Social Change. The Erosion of Social Levels' in: Baron, William, Z., *Quality of Life*, Lexington, Mass., Lexington Body, pp. 163–187.
6. In Chapter IV, pages 64 and 65.
7. Melton, Gary, 'Teaching Children About Their Rights', in: Henning, James S., editor, *The Rights of Children, Legal and Psychological Perspectives*; Springfield, Illinois, 1982, Charles C. Thomas.
8. Morris, David and McAlpin, Michelle Bl, *Measuring the Condition of India's Poor, The Physical Quality of Life Index*, New Delhi, 1982, Promilla & Co., Publishers, p. 88.
9. Board, Joseph, B., 'Only Human: The Quality of Life Debate in Sweden', in: *Social Change in Sweden*, No. 17, March 1980, Swedish Information Service.
10. Musschenga, A.W., *Kwaliteit van Leven, Criterium voor het Medisch Handelen?*, Baarn, 1987, Ambo Books, p. 23.
11. Idem.
12. Shye, S., 'Human Life Quality: An Action System', in: Shye, S., *Multiple Scaling, The Theory and Application of Partial Order Scalogram Analysis*, Amsterdam/New York/Oxford, 1985, North-Holland, pp. 245–246.
13. Shye, S., 'Nonmetric Multivariate Models for Behavioral Action Systems', in: Canter, David, ed., *Facet Theory, Approaches to Social Research*, New York/Berlin, 1985, Springer Verlag, p. 102.
14. Idem, p. 103.
15. Sanders-Woudstra, J.A.R., 'Opgroeien in een gezin, is dat nou zo leuk?', in Lieshout, Jan van, ed. *Opgroeien in gezin... leuk?*, Rotterdam, 1988, Stichting Therapeutische Gezinsverpleging, p. 13.
16. Shye, S., 1985, op. cit., p. 104.
17. Idem, pp. 104–105.
18. Shye, S., 'Human Life Quality: An Action System', in: Shye, S., *Multiple Scaling, The Theory and Application of Partial Order Scalogram Analysis*, Amsterdam/New York/Oxford, 1985, North-Holland, pp. 246–247.
19. Shye, S., Personal communication.
20. Netherlands Ministry of Foreign Affairs, *Verslag over de Veertiende Algemene Vergadering van de Verenigde Naties, New York*, 15 September – 2 December 1959.

21. Vittachi, V., Tarzie, *Children's Rights: A Question of Obligations*, UNICEF – Internal Report, New York, January 27th, 1986.
22. Shye, S., 1985, op. cit., p. 104.
23. Dale, Michael, J., 'The Burger Court and Children's Rights – A Trend Toward Retribution' in: *Youth Law News*, Vol. VIII, No. 1, Jan./Feb. 1987, p. 25.
24. Korczak, Janusz, *Bankructwo Malego Dzeka*, Warsaw, 1924.
25. Korczak, Janusz, *Król Macius Na Wyspie Bezludnej*, Warsaw, 1923.
26. Lax, Elisabeth, Kirchhoff, Hella and Beiner, Friedhelm, 'Die Rechte des Kindes im Spiegel der Kinderbücher Korczaks' in beiner, F. ed., *Janusz Korczak, Zeugnisse einer Lebendiger Pädagogik*, Heinsberg, 1982, Agentur Dieck, p. 123.
27. Personal communication by Dr. Menachem Horovitz, Ombudsman for Children of the Jerusalem Council on Children and Youth, Sept. 1989. Dr. Horovitz retired in January 1990.
28. Personal communication by Prof. Shye.
29. Letter from Mrs. Dr. F.T. Diemer-Lindeboom to the author, dated May 5th, 1987.
30. Schofield, Michael: 'Sex Education Now and Then: The Right of Children to Know' in: Vaughon, Mark, editor, *Rights of Children*, Report of the First National Conference on Children's Rights, held in London, March 11–12, 1974, London, National Council for Civil Liberties, pp. 16–19.
 Except for the 'right to know' formulated by Schofield, there are many other such rights. Another important 'right to know' is, for instance, the right of adopted children to know who their biological parents are.
31. Ussel, van, Jos 'Wie houdt er niet van kinderen?' Bespiegelingen over de ontwikkeling van de Westerse houding tegenover het kind, in: *De Gids*, No. 7, 1976, Vol. 139, pp. 443–454.
32. Hesford, Chris, 'Sex education: whose right?', in *Childright*, April 1987, p. 19.
33. Freeman, M.D.A., *The Rights and Wrongs of Children*, London and Dover NH, 1983, Frances Pinter Publishers.
34. Shye, S, 'Nonmetric Multivariate Models for Behavioral Action Systems', op. cit., p. 105.
35. Boli-Bennett, John and Meyer, John, W., 'The Ideology of Childhood and the State: Rules Distinguishing Children in National Constitutions, 1870–1970', in: *Am. Sociol. Review*, Dec. 1987, pp. 797–812. Also Cohen, Morris, L., Lee, Luke, T. and Stepan, Jan, *The Rights of the Child: A Classification Plan*, A Guide to the Compilation and Review of Laws Affecting the Rights of the Child in Each Country in Observance of the International Year of the Child, Medford, Mass., Law and Population Programme, The Fletcher School of Law and Diplomacy, 1987, Law and Population Monograph Series No. 46. Also: Minow, Martha, 'The Public Duties of Families and Children', in: Hartmann, T., ed., *From Children to Citizens: The Role of the Juvenile Court*, Springer Verlag, 1987, p. 1315, (Conceptions of Children's Rights). Also: Rogers, Carl M. and Wrightsman, Lawrence S., 'Attitudes Toward Children's Rights: Nurturance of Self-Determination?', in *Journal of Social Issues*, 34, No. 2, 1987, pp. 59–68. Also: Wald, Michael, 'Children's Rights: A Framework for Analysis', in *University of California at Davis Law Review*, Vol. 12, 1979, pp. 256–280.
36. Rogers and Wrightsman, op. cit.
37. Idem.
38. Idem.
39. Idem.
40. Freeman, M., op. cit.
41. Wald, M., op. cit., p. 260.
42. Idem.
43. Freeman, M., op. cit., p.40.
44. Idem, p. 43.
45. Wald, M., op. cit., p. 263.
46. Wald, M., op. cit., p. 266.
47. Freeman, M., op. cit., p. 48.

CHAPTER IV

From Basing Children's Rights on Needs to Basing Them on Effective Functioning

During the course of the twentieth century psychologists, social workers and educators have learned to describe their goals more and more in terms of *rights*. They claim that the concept of 'human rights' is synonymous with the concept of 'needs' or 'basic needs'.[1] "This is no coincidence," says the Belgian philosopher L. Apostel[2] "because there is a remarkable similarity between basic needs and human rights."

The *Social Commission of the United Nations*, for instance, decided to support the idea of a 'United Nations Declaration on the Rights of the Child', because "the needs of the child justified an instrument in addition to the Universal Declaration of Human Rights."[3] The Committee ('Forum') on Children's Rights of the *White House Conference on Children* was of the same opinion. In the introduction to its 1970 report we read: "Our consideration of children's rights is based on a knowledge of their developmental needs and characteristics. When defining a child's rights in a series of entitlements, it must be recognized that as a child grows, many of his developmental needs and characteristics change, including his capacity for mastering certain tasks. Children in the same developmental phase can have differing needs depending upon many factors either within them or in their environment. Public policy and action – Federal, State, and local – must rest upon this knowledge if it is to provide our children with the opportunities for healthy growth, internal well-being, and fulfilment."[4]

Rights are based on some 'quality of life' notion conceptualised in different terms, such as lists of needs or end results. In this Chapter we shall first look at the 'needs model' and then propose to base rights on effective functioning.

Needs

Feshbach and Feshbach[5] believe that needs are more universal than rights and less subject to negotiating. According to the philosopher Kahtchadourian[6] someone can need something in a subjective sense (e.g. 'I need a drink, now that I have finished this book.'), while the non-subjective sense of 'needs' refers to what a person needs for his or her general well-being. Sometimes people are aware of what they need, but often, according to Kahtchadourian, (especially if they are children) they are not. It might well be in the child's 'best interests' that such needs be fulfilled. Thus, having interests becomes a condition for having rights.

"In psychology the term 'needs' denotes whatever is required for the health or well-being of a person. If certain commodities or conditions are lacking, the result will be an internal disturbance which generates a drive. Examples are the need for oxygen, for food, for stimulation, or for love. A wider use of this term is sometimes found in personality theory, where it refers to anything a person wants with sufficient consistency over time to be treated as a feature of his personality."[7]

The term 'needs' is, however, often avoided by psychologists and others who are concerned with the development of children. Senn and Solnit,[8] for instance, talk about *tasks in progress*, meaning tasks a child has to fulfil during its development. Solnit[9] finds this a more positive approach because it emphasises less that the child is 'needy'. Other authors do not use 'needs' as a technical term, but write about *opportunities, how children become more competent, or ways in which a child acquires a new (adult) status*. Most psychologists use the word *drive* in preference to *need*, when referring to the particular objects of the drive or need, such as food, sex or prestige.

There are exceptions, such as social workers or UNICEF staff members who refer to children's needs when confronted with needy children. The American psychologist Henry A. Murray[10] also uses the word *need* rather than *drive*, and dismisses the term *instinct* because "it limits one to needs which can be proved innate."[11] Murray: "Most of the primary viscerogenic needs, such as hunger and thirst, seem to be innate in the usual sense of the term. Presumably they are provoked by internal conditions regardless of the environment. Other needs, called by us 'psychogenic needs,' though found to operate without obvious dependence upon the viscerogenic needs, were perhaps once subsidiary to the latter. Furthermore, though their manifestations have been observed in all peoples, they are influenced to a great extent by cultural forms, particularly when the latter are represented by the parents."[12]

The viscerogenic needs (which have to do with physical satisfactions) are less influenced by the social cultural environment than the psychogenic needs. To equate such viscerogenic needs with rights is, therefore, not a problem. Psychogenic, or secondary, needs (according to Murray, dependent upon and derived from primary needs) are more influenced by the (trends in the) social-cultural environment.

For example, in the 1920s the psychologist Watson pointed out that it might be better not to kiss and hug children. In 1943 Margaret Ribble[13] wrote in her book *The Rights of Infants* that "the newborn baby ... needs to be rocked gently ... he needs to be carried about at regular intervals, until such time as he can move and co-ordinate his own body ... he needs frequent periods of close contact with the mother." She drew the attention to the fact that the child has not only a need for physical care and food but also an inborn need for love. In 1975 Psychoanalyst Selma Freiberg published an article in the same spirit titled 'The Right to Know Love'.[14] The term *need* may also be used, as Hartung[15] explains, "to denote requirements of which the person becomes aware when he requires values that demand that he should strive for a certain end or comfort himself in a given fashion in a given situation. This usage is found in sociology, anthropology and social psychology.

Goulet differentiates between *needs of the first degree, needs of importance for personal development (so-called enhancement needs) and needs for luxury*. Under needs of the first degree Goulet reckons not only things like food, clothing and lodging, but also protection from nature and outside dangers. Indeed, says Goulet, people have to lessen their vulnerability with respect to events that threaten to overwhelm them. As an example he mentions the need to build rooms to store the harvest. It is clear that, before other needs can be fulfilled, energy must be spent on the needs of the first degree. Only thereafter does it become relevant for man to actualise his or her latent possibilities. But to do this man must have the opportunity to discover what his or her potentials are. "Such needs are called enhancement needs because they are not so directly ordered to utilitarian functions except insofar as they contribute to expression and creation. Ultimately, of course, creation and expression are themselves *useful* (indeed necessary) to health, growth, and maturity. Nevertheless, they are self-validating ends: it is good for its own sake to be healthy or proficient."[16]

Although important civilisations have contributed to man's taste for luxury, this does not, according to Goulet, justify the *need* for such things. He calls these needs a sign of "puberty", because in such cases man bases his identity and his feeling of belonging on the possession of luxuries rather than on the searching for his or her own actualization. I saw, for instance, a shop in the New York Soho ('Think Big') where only needless objects are sold, such as thirty-inch long toothbrushes and fifteen-inches tall cognac glasses. Is buying such things based on a 'need'?

Goulet looks at things against the background of the great opposites in the world: "in real life, massive wastefulness and luxurious display coexist alongside monumental needs. Otherwise stated, a relative superfluity of goods is enjoyed by a minority while the majority suffers from an absolute insufficiency of goods. Political realism and moral objectivity alike dictate new producer priorities. There is no justification for allowing a few wealthy societies to use a disproportionate share of world resources for the satisfaction of luxury needs while the basic needs of the masses are left unmet."[17]

Vittachi refers mainly to humanistic psychologists such as Avraham Maslow, when he describes a spectrum of needs: "In considering children's needs it would be telling to look at hierarchy horizontally, as a spectrum nuanced in terms of urgency. *Survival and life sustaining needs* would stand on the left end of the spectrum: air, water, food, warmth, tenderness, physical and mental safety." Next come *life protecting needs*: "shelter, security, hygiene, preventive health care; *life enriching needs*: education, spiritual 'food', a knowledge of moral, aesthetic and social values and duties, a sense of self-respect, identity, an assurance of belonging, companionship"; *life embellishing needs*: music, toys, pictures, stories, fantasy; *life 'development' needs*: functional training of innate talents, and vocational education to go hand in hand with general education appropriate to their future." These five categories of needs may be further subdivided and extended to include *life enhancing needs*.[18]

The question remains whether 'wants' should be included at the right end of the spectrum, and where in the spectrum 'needs' become 'wants'. At the right side of Vittachi's spectrum *needs* and *wants* mingle. What is the need of a young person and when should we call it a want? Lester Rand of the *Youth Research Institute* in New York[19] (an organisation which researches *product ownership* for industry and publicity purposes) interviews through his office every year some 2400 youngsters between the ages 13 and 20, in order to establish what young people want and how they spend their money. He found that in 1977 fourteen percent of the interviewees had their own telephone, and in 1987 thirty-one percent. In 1977 sixty percent of the youngsters had their own stereo set, in 1987 seventy-one percent. In 1977 twenty-three percent owned a TV set, in 1987 forty-five percent. In 1987 seventeen percent of the American teenagers had their personal stereo cassette recorder. Pocket calculators were in 1977 owned by twenty-two percent of the youngsters, in 1987 by forty-four percent. Americans often measure quality of life in terms of material wealth.

Policies of production should, according to Goulet, be geared to the fact that luxury needs are less important than first degree needs or enhancement needs. To the question *what kind of (economic) development* must be aimed for, Goulet answers: "The development must be conform to the most important needs, characterised by moderation and wise use of materials, especially those that are scarce.

Vittachi, who was born in what was at the time Ceylon, told me how he was in his youth received in India by Mahatma Ghandi. "What is your message for the countries that have just achieved independence and those that will soon achieve it?" asked Vittachi. Ghandi answered: "Fulfil your needs and reduce your wants."[20]

We shall now analyse one particular *need* that is generally considered equal to a *right*, even a basic right. It is the need for survival or the life sustaining need.

The Basic Needs Strategy of UNICEF

We shall see that the fulfilment of a particular need/right such as the need/right to food is connected with many other issues. "Land rights, labour rights and the right to food are conceptually and pragmatically linked," writes Roger Plant.[21] "As food is generally produced on the land, access to the land or its products is a prerequisite for survival."[22] If reforms relating to the ownership of land are not proposed, it is at least our *duty* to follow a policy (for instance by subsidising food) that would realise this right for all citizens.

The World Health Organisation (WHO) reports "that the first and most essential need of the child is adequate food. There is little purpose in planning to safeguard his birth and to protect him from disease and accident if he is to succumb to malnutrition; there is no point in providing for his education if he is too hungry to learn."[23]

UNICEF was founded by a resolution of the General Assembly of the United Nations on December 11, 1946 as the United Nations International Children's Emergency Fund.[24] Most governments had never considered the possibility that UNICEF would become a permanent organisation of the United Nations. Since it was only meant to help children in countries that suffered from food shortage and were plagued by disease in the aftermath of the Second World War, there surely would be no reason for it to exist after those problems were solved. UNICEF, however, was there to stay. It became the leading organisation in the struggle against world-wide poverty and under-development.[25] In light of its search for a more permanent function, its Executive Board decided in March 1960, "to undertake consultations with beneficiary countries and the technical agencies concerned for the purpose of ascertaining the priority needs of children in these countries and identifying the fields in which UNICEF might assist in order to contribute to the greatest possible extent to their present and future welfare."[26]

UNICEF's new activities were not isolated. During the 1976 *World Employment Conference* organised by the *International Labour Organisation* (ILO), the Member States decided, for instance, that "strategies, national development plans and policies should explicitly include as a priority objective the promotion of employment and the satisfaction of the basic needs of each country's population."[27] An action programme was adopted which provided a set of measures for the implementation of the so-called *basic needs strategy*. It called on governments to change their development policies so that enough jobs, food, lodging, schools, drinking water, medical provisions and other essentials for their population were guaranteed. Although such claims had been voiced earlier,[28] this was the first time that nearly all international organisations participating in the World Employment Conference of the ILO adopted the term *basic human needs* or *basic needs* and pledged to work for a *basic needs strategy*. "Although some established elites saw the new code word as a threat to existing patterns of wealth and power, the term 'basic needs' has nevertheless crowded its way into the vocabulary of development planners and policy-makers."[29] The World Bank, for instance, "has overcome an earlier reluctance to support rural reforms, health, education and family planning."[30] The call to meet the basic human needs, especially in the less developed 'South' became, according to Cleveland and Wilson[31] a "code-word for economic justice, for fairness, for equity in the distribution of the benefits of growth, not just among nations but among people within nations." Thus the World Bank stated that the "economical growth was of little use for the (fast-growing) poorest population in the Third World. The great emphasis we have always put on economy, overshadowed the aim and the policy . . . the new demand is, therefore, to put man and his needs in the centre of development."[32] That man has to be put central, is not a controversial issue; the question is: how do we do it?

A valuable view is that of Denis Goulet[33] who tries to determine which development is 'human'. The vital necessities of traditional society are, according to Goulet, often considered to be mainly material, and whether they are physical objects or services, need priorities are simply those demands which effectively motivate suppliers to keep supplying."[34] It is Goulet's opinion, however, that the vital necessities consist of more than only food, lodging etc. However limited a community budget, it always spends part on artistic expression, and indeed, "no society would be advised to pursue the satisfaction of survival needs to the exclusion of others." Goulet's point of departure is that the development of *each* human being is connected with the development of the *whole* of humanity. No theory about needs, says Goulet, can oversee the existence of super-abundance alongside total lack. He finds, therefore, that any theory about needs must not try to stay objective but should take a stand on injustice and on how the great differences in opportunities to fulfil needs, can be overcome. Goulet criticises Maslow's theory that a person does not reach maturity before all his basic needs have been fulfilled.[35]

The emphasis which UNICEF and similar organisations put on basic needs and rights, such as the right to food and the right to survival, shows that every assistance, except in emergencies, must be geared to a policy of development. sadly, a new and more just economic order, on which such development will be based, is still far away.

Needs Approach Versus 'Quality of Life' Approach

The Director of the Centre for the Appraisal of Social Reality and the Quality of Life in Calcutta, India, Professor Ramkrishna Mukherjee[36] examined two ways to research the 'Quality of Life':

1. Social indicators research which considers the elites' valuation of what the people need in order to attain a better quality of life;
2. what he calls 'conventional quality of life research' which ascertains what people want in order to improve their quality of life.

Mukherjee points out that need items, basic or otherwise, are culture-bound. "Even in the case of food, any standardised quantitative measure of nutrition cannot override the determining role of culture-specific food intake, which is no less marked in the U.S.A., the U.S.S.R., France and China than, for example, in Japan, India, Iran and Nigeria. The impact of culture on the formulation of people's basic needs of people is perhaps more pronounced with respect to clothing, housing, health, education, leisure, security, etc. as suggested by 'poverty studies'".[37] This variability of quality cannot be ignored, according to Mukherjee. In the 'need-based quality of life research' there are many attempts to list all the human needs. Norman C. Dalkey[38] offers, for instance, a list of such needs.[39]

In 1976 a meeting of experts dealing with indicators of social and economic change, took place. A paper presented during that conference by Johan Galtung and Aners Wirak is of special importance for our study. Galtung and Wirak[40] deal with human needs and human rights.[41] They recognise the shortcoming of this image of Man: "It is analytical, fragmentary, chopping Man into a set of needs rather than trying to develop a holistic conception of Man."

They thought that a 'solution' could be found, and presented an indicative long list of agreed-upon needs. Two criteria were formulated to designate a need:

1. "*If it is a necessary condition for a human being to exist, it is a need.* In other words, if non-satisfaction leads to the disintegration, destruction, non-existence of the *human* being."
2. "*If it is a necessary condition for a society to exist over longer time, then it is a need.* In other words, if the non-satisfaction leads to disruption, disintegration, or non-existence of the society, such as through revolt or non-participation, apathy, anomie."

The authors[42] formulated "a list that gives some indication of what has to be produced, as a minimum for need satisfaction at a basic level to take place."

Mukherjee points out[43] that although such research aims at changing society in order to meet the needs of the masses and to improve their quality of life, it is often done by experts who advise the elites. He describes what he calls "want-based quality of life research" which is concerned with eliciting what people want and how their wants are realised. Johansson's[44] criticism of such research is that it often functions as a 'pseudo-plebiscite'.

In this study we have opted for a 'Systematic Quality of Life Model' based on *effectiveness* of the human individual and not on 'needs' or 'wants of the people'. This model, described in Chapter III, hypothesises an interlocking network of functioning (in subsystems and modes) in which each part enhances the others.

The Need for Self-Determination – The Right to Self-Determination

The Kiddie-Libber Richard Farson,[45] with whom we shall extensively deal in Chapter IX wrote "that children, like adults, should have the right to decide the matters which affect them most directly. The issue of self-determination is at the heart of children's liberation. The acceptance of the child's right to self-determination is fundamental to all the rights to which children are entitled." Although the author of this study does not agree with the implications of the Kiddie-Libbers theories, we cannot deny that 'self-determination' is one of the most important needs of children.[46]

The approach of the motivation psychologists Deci and Ryan[47] is more fruitful. Their definition of the concept self-determination is "a quality of human functioning that involves the experience of choice to self-determination." According to Deci and Ryan this capacity to make choices is also a *need*.[48]

Deci[49] takes the stand that the child is from the earliest age, intrinsically motivated to acquire *self-determination*. For adults this implies that we must encourage the process towards self-determination. In this connection Deci points out how important it is that teachers create a learning climate wherein children can discover and experiment. "When the environments become more controlling, children lose intrinsic motivation and self-esteem."[50]

Contrary to the Kiddie-Libbers, Deci and Ryan do not jump to the conclusion that every toddler is capable of taking responsibilities, but point out that children – if they develop satisfactorily – have a gradually increasing need to be responsible for the contents of their own lives and that they will want to implement their rights. We consider Deci and Ryan's self-determination as a so-called *developmental line*.[51]

Piaget,[52] Elkind,[53] Kohlberg[54] and others have shown that cognitive and emotional changes take place. For Deci and Ryan self-determination is the driving force for such development. For other authors different functioning modes are important. For us self-determined behaviour is just one component of the sixteen functioning modes (in this case it is the *expressive mode of the personality subsystem*). But one of the manifestations of the expressive mode in the personality subsystem is the way in which the individual decides to strike a balance between the various other modes.

It is possible that by promoting a right in one functioning mode, a right belonging in another functioning mode can be reduced.[55] If we are aware of this pattern of inter-dependencies, it will help us to formulate and evaluate rights. It is the built-in sensitivity for the totality[56] that distinguishes the 'Systematic Quality of Life Model' from the other models discussed in this chapter.

'Effective Functioning' Instead of 'Needs'

We propose that rights should be formulated by functioning modes[57], whereby each society, culture and particular set of circumstances should offer its particular repertoire. Our thesis is that the child has the right to function effectively in all sixteen functioning modes of the 'Systemic Quality of Life Model'. To promote this thesis the present author and Samuel Shye have formulated a *Declaration on the Rights of the Child based on the Systemic Quality of Life Model*. Our Declaration (Appendix XLV) portrays the entire array of relationships between functioning modes and rights.

NOTES

1. Apostel, L. 'De rechten en noden van het kind en/of de rechten en noden van de mens, open vragen en persoonlijke overtuigingen', in: Verhellen, E., Spiesschaert, F. en Cattrijse, L., *Rechten van het kind, Een tekstbundel van de Rijksuniversiteit Gent naar aanleiding van de UNO-Conventie voor Rechten van het Kind*, Antwerpen/Arnhem, 1989, Kluwer Rechtswetenschappen Gouda and Quint B, pp. 54–59.
2. Idem.
3. U.N. Document E/CN.4/512, p. 4.
4. White House Conference on Children, 1970, The Rights of Children, Report of Forum 22, pp. 345–346.
5. Feshbach, Norma Deitch and Feshbach, Seymour, 'Toward an Historical, Social and Developmental Perspective on Children's Rights', in *Journal of Social Issues*, 1978, Vol. 34, No. 2, p. 6.
6. Katchadourian, Haig, 'Toward a Foundation for Human Rights', in: *Man and World, an International Philosophical Review*, 1985, Vol. 18, No. 2, pp. 219–239.
7. Hotopf, W.H.N., in: Gould, Julius, Kalb, William, L., *A Dictionary of the Social Sciences*, 1964, The Free Press of Glencoe, compiled under the auspices of the UNESCO, p. 462.
8. Senn, Milton, J.E. and Solnit, Albert, J., *Problems in Child Behaviour and Development*, Philadelphia, 1968, Lea & Febiger.
9. Interview with Albert Solnit on May 6, 1988, in New York.
10. Murray, Henry, A., *Explorations in Personality, A Clinical and Experimental Study of Fifty Men of College Age*, New York, 1938, Oxford University Press, p. 73.

    Murray's definition of a need is: "A need is a construct (a convenient fiction or hypothetical concept) which stands for a force (the physico-chemical nature of which is unknown) in the brain region, a force which organizes perception, apperception, intellection and action in such a way as to transform in a certain direction an existing, unsatisfying situation. A need is sometimes provoked directly by internal processes of a certain kind (viscerogenic, endocrinogenic, thalamicogenic) arising in the course of vital sequences, but, more frequently (when in a state of readiness) by the occurrence of one of a few commonly effective press (or by anticipatory images of such press).
11. Idem, p. 74.
12. Idem, p. 75. Murray used the word *need*, in the same way as psychologists today use the word *motive*.
13. Ribble, Margaret, A., *The Rights of Infants*, New York and London, 1965, Columbia University Press, p. 3.
14. Freiberg, Selma, 'The Right to Know Love' in: *Redbook Magazine*, February 1975.
15. Hartung, Frank, E.K., in: Gould, Julius, and Kolb, William, L., *A Dictionary of the Social Sciences*, The Free Press of Glencoe, published under the auspices of the UNESCO, 1964, p. 463.

    Hartung: "Thus when need is used in this manner it is understood that *human* needs are not homologous with the hierarchy of needs that have been established for animals. One's human needs, being derived from socio-cultural experience, are qualitatively different in three respects from the organic necessities for physical existence. First, the locus of existence of human needs is the culture and society in which the person lives. Second, the person develops needs that are appropriate to the general values by which he lives. Third, the

person is able to have needs because he becomes able to think through the use of symbols. Through symbols he can organize and comprehend his experience, and through the use of language can infer the existence of his needs or motives, and learn to interpret certain situations as calling for the expression of a certain kind and degree of action and perhaps also of emotion."
16. Goulet, Dennis, *The Cruel Choice, A New Concept in the Theory of Development*, New York, 1971, Atheneum, p. 247.
17. Idem, p. 246.
18. Vittachi, V. Tarzie, *Children's Rights: A Question of Obligations*, New York & Geneva, UNICEF, 1987, brochure.
19. Interview by telephone with Lesler Rand in New York, June 1988.
20. Interview with Tarzie Vittachi, former Deputy Executive Director for External Relations, UNICEF, in New York, March 4, 1988.
21. Plant, Roger, 'The Right to Food and Agrarian Systems: Law and Practice in Latin America', in Alton, P., and Tomasevski, *The Right to Food*, Dordrecht and Utrecht, 1987, Stichting Studie en Informatiecentrum Mensenrechten (SIM) and Martinus Nijhoff Publishers, p. 200.

Between 400 and 500 million people in the world are chronically under-nourished (see: European Communities, European Parliament, *Report drawn up on behalf of the Committee on Development and Co-operation on the fight against hunger*, Medeiros Ferreira, reporter, 1986–1987, Series A, Document A 2–193/86, December 19, 1986, p. 9.
22. Idem.
23. World Health Organisation, 'The Health Needs of Children', in: Sicault Georges, editor, *The Needs of Children*, Op. cit., pp. 73–103. As a report of the U.N. No: E/ICEF/415.
24. A number of countries did not believe in assistance by international organisations like the United Nations, and rather favoured bilateral assistance since this would put them in a position to influence the policies of those countries they were assisting. According to Professor Harold Fruchtbaum whom I interviewed in New York on March 18, 1988, the United States government killed the United Nations Relief and Rehabilitation Administration (UNRRA) (which began operations in 1944) in 1946, when it insisted that UNRRA was not longer needed.. UNICEF was only perceived as a temporary phenomenon, as could be understood from the name: United Nations Children's *Emergency* Fund. Sir Robert Jackson: 'Foreword', in: Black, Maggie, *The Children and the Nations, The Story of UNICEF*, Sydney, 1986, Australia, p. 8) wrote: "The word 'emergency' was of vital importance in securing the support of some governments that were not keen to see any new institution established which resembled even part of the UNRRA's work." Sir Robert Jackson: "UNICEF developed a very distinct character of its own. It was most fortunate that this was the case, for in 1950 the U.S. – incredible as it may seem today – led a campaign to terminate UNICEF's existence. This action, of course, reflected the same attitude that had brought an end to UNRRA's invaluable work. Fortunately, this attack was repulsed, and UNICEF was able to survive, thus enabling innumerable children all over the world to benefit from its aid in the years to come." (p.9).

The Swedes (especially the president of the Swedish National Committee for UNICEF, Nils Thedin) firmly supported the proposal to research the needs of children. We read in *Sweden and UNICEF* 1955–1985, a study by Ulla Wickbom, that in the *executive board* of UNICEF of 1960 not all the delegates were in favour of such research. "But a larger group, favoured the idea and it was suggested that a survey be undertaken by a small group of independent and impartial experts who would visit a number of countries where the conditions were representative for the general situation of children in the Third World." In June 1961 Nils Thedin underwrote Sicault's conclusions. (See note 23).

Wickbom: "Although the survey to a great extent was of a preliminary nature it covered such a large field and presented such important results that there was no urgent need for an extended global survey. The evaluation of the needs of children could very well serve as a starting point for the reorientation of UNICEF's policy." According to Wickbom the

following prediction of Thedin's came true: "The survey provided UNICEF with a basis for a broadening of the range of aid and became the introduction to a new approach.
25. See Chapter 8 in Maggie Black's book, Op. cit. The change of name shows a change of intention: the words 'International' and 'Emergency' were taken away and the name became: *United Nations Children's Fund.*
26. *Official Records of the Economic and Social Council*, Twenty-ninth Session, Supplement No. 2A (E/3336–E/ICEF/398), para 46.
27. Quoted by Ghai, Dharam, 'Basic Needs and its Critics', in: *IDS Bulletin*, Institute of Development Studies at the University of Sussex, Brighton, England, June 1978, Vol. 9, No. 4, p. 16. See also: International Labour Organisation (I.L.O.), *Employment, Growth and Basic Needs*, Geneva, 1976.
28. See: Ghai, Dharam, Op. cit.
29. Cleveland, Harlan and Wilson, Thomas, W., *Human Growth, An Essay on Growth, Values and the Quality of Life*, Princeton, New Jersey, 1978, the Aspen Institute for Humanistic Studies, pp. 15–16.
30. Idem.
31. Idem, p. 11.
32. World Bank staff paper, quoted in Cleveland and Wilson, Op. cit., p. 17. Recommended literature on the subject of *basic human needs* is the article in the *IDS Bulletin*, June 1978, Vol. 9, No. 4, pp. 7–11: Green, Reginald Herbold, 'Basic Human Needs: Concept or Slogan, Synthesis or Smokescreen?'

The United Nations Development Program (UNDP) proposed to use a *Human Development Index (HDI)*, to indicate the percentage of people that have clean drinking water, have the means to see a doctor, have education etc. as is done by the World Bank in regard to income. See: Human Development Report, 1990.
33. Goulet, Denis, *The Cruel Choice, A New Concept in the Theory of Development*, New York, 1971, Atheneum.
34. Idem, pp. 237–239.
35. The most important hypotheses in Maslow's motivation-theory is the *hierarchy hypothesis*: people are motivated by a system of needs that is of a hierarchic nature. The hierarchy-pyramid of needs consists of the *physical needs* on the bottom and then, piled on top of each other in the following order: the need for safety, the *affiliative needs, the esteem-needs and the self-actualization needs*. This last group of needs also comprises the need for creativity, for knowledge and understanding and the 'aesthetic needs'. In this building a difference is made between 'lower' and 'higher' needs. Self-realisation demands, according to Maslow, fulfilment of the lower needs. A higher need can dominate after a lower need has been fulfilled. Higher needs appear later in a person's development. Physical needs (hunger, thirst etc.) and the need for safety dominate the life of a baby. For school-age children the *affiliative needs* and the *esteem needs* are central. The need for self-actualization is first faced in adolescence but dominates the life of certain individuals only in adulthood.
36. Mukherjee, Ramkrishna, *The Quality of Life, Valuation in Social Research*, New Delhi/Newbury Park/London, 1989, Sage Publications.
37. Idem, pp. 38–39.
38. Dalkey, Norman, C., Lewis, Ralph and Snyder, David, 'Measurement and Analysis of the Quality of Life', in: Dalkey, Norman, C., *Studies in the Quality of Life*, Lexington (Massachusetts), Toronto and London, 1972, pp. 85–100.
39. Idem. Here needs are called 'characteristics'. Dalkey asked students to answer the following: (a) Drawing on both your own experience and your experience with other people, give a list of those characteristics of events that you believe to have the strongest influence on the quality of life of an adult American. (For this exercise we will not raise the issue of whether or not the factors are strongly culture-dependent.) Accompany each characteristic with a short definition or set of synonyms. List at least five such characteristics, but no more than ten. (b) For each characteristic, indicate whether it can generate both positive and negative effects, or only one of these.

Dalkey's thirty-eight needs/characteristics:
   Relaxation-easing, recreation, leisure, rest;
   Playfulness-fun;
   Humorous;
   Satisfying to the senses-warm, physical pleasure;
   Privacy-withdrawn from social visibility;
   Intimacy-affection, friendship, closeness, tenderness;
   Comfort;
   Physical well-being-health, feeling good and "alive";
   Pleasurable-satisfying, feeling of contentment;
   Depression-sorrow, grief, tragedy;
   Marital satisfaction;
   Aesthetic surroundings;
   Personal-the event is shared by a few people;
   Spiritual serenity-inspiration, oneness with God;
   Novelty-surprising, unanticipated, unexpected;
   Exciting-stimulating, arousing;
   Freedom-lack of restraints, lack of compulsion;
   Aggression-interpersonal conflict, blowing off steam;
   Security-safety, as opposed to anxious or threatened;
   New-unfamiliar, strange;
   Innovative-creative;
   Meaningfulness-importance, sincerity, genuineness, usefulness;
   Material well-being-affluence, material comforts;
   Educational-one learns something from the event;
   Planned for-anticipated, scheduled;
   Charity-humanitarian, satisfaction of helping others;
   Self-esteem-ego satisfying, pride, self-image;
   Job satisfaction-job motivation, enjoyment of work;
   Equality-justice;
   Evaluative-brings feedback or environmental awareness;
   Control-directness, under one's own power;
   Business esteem-job progress, success in work;
   Accomplishment-achievement, meeting goals, success;
   Social acceptance-belonging, recognition by peer group;
   Dominance-one-upmanship, superiority, competition;
   Historical import-event's identification with stream of humanity;
   Status-prestige, position, external image;
   Sexual fulfilment-sex life or love life.
The above list is in our opinion typically the product of an affluent society. Moreover it is too long and not systematical enough to be useful.
40. Galtung, Johan and Wirak, Anders 'Human Needs, Human Rights and the Theories of Development', paper presented at the United Nations Education, Scientific and Cultural Organisation (UNESCO) Workshop on Applicability of Social Indicators to National Planning, held in Bangkok, Thailand, January 23, 1976, in: UNESCO, (editors and publisher), *Indicators of Social and Economic Change and Their Applications*, Paris, 1977, pp. 20–21.
41. Idem, p. 21.
42. Values: Basic Needs, Material and Non-Material.

Security
Category: Security
Needs and/or rights: Individual: against accident, homicide
                                Collective: against attack, war
Goods/services: Security

Welfare
Category: Physiological
Needs and/or rights: Input: nutrition, air, water, sleep
 Output: movement, excretion
Goods/services: Food, water
Category: Ecological
Needs and/or rights: Climatic: protection, privacy
 Somatic: protection against disease, health
Goods/Services: Clothes, shelter, medical treatment
Category: Socio-cultural
Needs and/or rights: Culture: self-expression, dialogue, education
Goods/services: Schooling

Freedom
Category: Mobility
Needs and/or rights: Right to travel and be travelled to
 Rights to expression and impression
Goods/services: Transportation, communication
Category: Politics
Needs and/or rights: Rights of consciousness-formation
 Rights of mobilization
 Rights of confrontation
Goods/services: Meetings, media, parties, elections
Category: Legal
Needs and/or rights: Rights of due process of law
Goods/services: Courts, etc.
Category: Work
Needs and/or rights: Right to work
Goods/services: Jobs
Category: Choice
Needs and/or rights: Right to choose occupation
 Right to choose spouse
 Right to choose place to live

Identity
Category: Relation to self (individual needs)
Needs and/or rights: Need of self-expression, praxis, creativity
Goods/services: Hobbies, leisure
Needs and/or rights: Need for self-actuation, realizing potentials synchronically and diachronically
Goods/services: Leisure, vacation
Needs and/or rights: Need for well-being, happiness, joy
Goods/services: Vacation
Needs and/or rights: Need for a sense of purpose, a sense of meaning with life
Goods/services: Religion, ideology
Category: Relation to others (collective needs)
Needs and/or rights: Need for affection, love, sex, spouse, offspring
Goods/services: Primary groups
Needs and/or rights: Need for roots, belongingness, support, association with similar humans
Goods/services: Secondary groups
Category: Relation to society (social needs)
Needs and/or rights: Need to be active, to be subject, not passive, client, object
Category: Relation to society (social needs)
Needs and/or rights: Need to understand what conditions one's life, for social transparency

	Need for challenge, new experience – also intellectual and aesthetic
Category:	Relation to nature
Needs and/or rights:	Need of some kind of partnership with nature

Source: Galtung, Johan and Wirak, Anders in: UNESCO, 1977, *Indicators of Social and Economic Change and Their Applications*.

43. Mukherjee, Ramkrishna, *The Quality of Life, Valuation in Social Research*, Op. cit., p. 45.
44. Johansson, S., The level of living survey: A Presentation, *Sartyck ur Acta Sociologica*, 1973, 3, pp. 211–219.
45. Farson, Richard: *Birthrights*, pp. 26–27.
46. A point for criticism might be (see: Kagan, Jerome, *Unstable Ideas: Temperament, Cognition, and Self*, Cambridge, Mass., 1989, Harvard University Press) "observers ... unconsciously confuse ... political and psychological definitions," as Kagan explains relating to the concept *freedom*.
47. Deci, Edward and Ryan, Richard, M., *Intrinsic Motivation and Self-determination in Human Behaviour*, New York and London, 1985, Plenum Press, p. 38.
48. Idem.
49. Interview with Edward Deci in New York on June 13, 1988.
50. Deci: "Increasingly with intrinsic motivation as with drives and emotions, the behaviour becomes cognitively mediated and takes on a structure that could probably be called purposive, decided or self-determined."
    It is jour opinion tat the intrinsic motivation for self-determination (Deci and Ryan) is a 'developmental line' (Anna Freud).
51. Freud, Anna, *Normality and Pathology in Childhood*, London, 1966, The Hogarth Press. Anna Freud described here her concept of *a developmental line*.
52. Piaget, Jean, *Logic and Psychology*, New York, 1957, Basic Books.
53. Elkind, D., *Cognitive Development in Adolescence*, in Adams, F. Understanding Adolescence: Current development in adolescent psychology, pp. 128–158, Boston, 1968, Allyn and Bacon.
54. Kohlberg, L., *Assessing Moral Judgment Stages*, New York, 1977, Humanities Press.
55. Example: Often the need/right of the child to physical safety is described (which we classify in the *conservative mode* of the *physical subsystem*) Also the need/right to physical activity is described (which we classify in the *expressive mode* of the *physical subsystem*). These two functioning modes have to be balanced for each child.
56. Foss, Laurence and Rothenberg, Kenneth, *The Second Medical Revolution, From Biomedicine to Infomedicine*, Boston/Shaftesbury, 1988, New Science Library, Shambhala. In other fields than children's rights such as medicine and psychiatry, the colleagues are moving away from the 'atomic paradigm' "in which a given stimulus has a predictable response, to a mutual causal, paradigm." The new models incorporate "mutual causal processes that are characteristic of complex systems.
57. The four modes of the four subsystems of individual human functioning: further explanations.

Subsystem and Mode	Criterion for effective functioning
Personality Subsystem	
Expressive mode	Behaviours that faithfully reflect ('similar to') the personality system. Such concerted behaviours can become viable and lead to growth (self realization or the evolution, over time, of structural differentiation).
Adaptive mode	Compatibility based on mutual compensations and complementations between personality and its environment. These include the availability of mental-recreational resources, accepting and being accepted by others, as well as establishing

	and maintaining agreement between the personality and the individual's own social, cultural and physical fields.
Integrative mode	Compatibility based on mutual complementation, agreement and balance among individual's personality traits. This includes peace of mind, and those aspects of mental health that can be defined in terms of balance, or lack of conflict, among personality components.
Conservative mode	Adherence to a personality structure; maintaining the degree of stability and continuity needed to affirm personality identity. These include fundamental sense of personal confidence and those aspects of mental health that can be defined in terms of structural stability and identity.
Physical subsystem	
Expressive mode	Physical exertions that faithfully reflect the subsystem's capability and potential. If well co-ordinated they can lead to growth, physical development and structural differentiation in the individual's physique. Physical exertions, and growth, can be manifested in the other three subsystems as well as in the environment external to the individual.
Adaptive mode	Compatibility based on mutual compensations. These include the availability of physical resources for the individual (air, food, shelter, energy) as well as the individual's body adjustment to uncontrollable conditions.
Integrative mode	Compatibility based on complementation, agreement and balance among individual physical traits. This includes feeling physically well and those aspects of physical health that can be defined in terms of balance, or lack of conflict, among the various bodily parts and processes.
Conservative mode	Continuity of physical structure including fundamental sense of bodily confidence, freedom from violence and accidents, and those aspects of physical health that can be defined in terms of genetic regularity and irrevocable bodily damage.
Social subsystem	
Expressive mode	Social activities that faithfully reflect the inner characteristics of the social subsystem (the individual's social base). If well co-ordinated they can lead to growth in the sphere of social relations and (if growth is experienced by many in the community) to societal evolution and structural differentiation.
Adaptive mode	Compatibility based on mutual complementation and need fulfilment between the individual's social roles and all aspects of their environment. This includes valuable and profitable relations that stem from roles such as family member, employee or employer, citizen, consumer of goods and services. Maintenance of good relations with all social institutions.
Integrative mode	Compatibility based on mutual complementation, agreement and balance among the individual's social roles. This includes a sense of being socially wholesome. Those aspects of social affinity (non-alienation) including inter-personal intimacy, that can be defined in terms of balance and agreement (no conflict) among social roles, belong here.
Conservative mode	Stability in the social structure, experienced as a fundamental sense of belonging and trust, including those aspects of social

affinity (non-alienation) that can be defined in terms of social identity.

Cultural (value) subsystem

Expressive mode	'Convincing' activities, faithfully reflecting value commitments, ideology or religion. If well co-ordinated they can lead to growth and refinement in the sphere of values and (if growth is shared by many in the community) to evolution and differentiation in the structure of value commitments.
Adaptive mode	Compatibility based on mutual complementation between values held by the individual and all aspects his or her environment. The environment includes, in particular, values held by others as well as external social and physical conditions. The individual's other three subsystems are also part of his or her value-environment.
Integrative mode	Compatibility based on mutual complementation, agreement and balance among the individual's value commitments. This includes a sense of being morally and culturally wholesome and those aspects of moral integrity that can be defined in terms of balance among values.
Conservative mode	Stability in the value structure experienced as a fundamental sense of commitment to a set of values or a culture. This defines the individual cultural identity.

Reprinted with permission from Samuel Shye: *Social Indicators Research*; 21:364–366, 1989, Wolters-Noordhoff-Kluwer, Academic Publishers.

PART C

The Pioneers

CHAPTER V

Ellen Key and the Right of the Child to Choose Its Own Parents Wisely

Ellen Key, one of the first authors who wrote about the Rights of the Child, was born on December 11th, 1848, in Sundsholm, Sweden. She grew up on her parents' idyllic rural estate by a lake and throughout her youth hardly met any children except her five younger brothers and sisters.

Her parents were Emil Key and the countess Sophie Passe. According to 't Hart[1] they were both typical representatives of the Swedish rural aristocracy who had nevertheless liberal ideas and a strong democratic orientation. Ellen's father was a land owner and from 1867 till 1883 he was a member of the Swedish Parliament, the Rikstag, where he caused some turmoil by proposing to abolish capital punishment. At home, he tried to educate his children to have respect for others by instructing his servants to send the children out of the kitchen with a wet rag around their necks, if the children tried to order the servants about. But, he did not allow his children to talk during meals until they had reached the age of sixteen.[2]

When Ellen was nineteen she studied at the Art Academy in Stockholm. During the following years she wrote some essays on art history and travelled to Berlin, Vienna, Florence, Rome, Paris, Amsterdam and Cambridge. In the late 1870s a family misfortune obliged her to take up teaching in Stockholm.

Although Ellen Key never married she became well-known as an author of books about marriage and motherhood. At a time when husbands were the legal guardians not only of their children but also of their wives, Key advocated settling disputes about guardianship in the mother's favour. Moreover she recommended that the institute 'marriage' should be fully reformed, and that it should rest on a foundation of economic independence and easy access to divorce, without which "many children were yet born in legalised prostitution, through legalised rape."[3] Marriage without love was, according to Key, immoral, while cohabitation with love needed no further sanction.[4] "It was the right to love which Key would have us cherish, rather than the right to own another person – the beauty of singleness of devotion rather than the cruel habit of trying to force people to carry out rash promises made in moments of exaltation".[5] She pleaded[6] for a new idealistic marriage and a new love ethic, based on loyalty and self-discipline. She was for a 'trial marriage' which, according to her, should be "the bulwark against the corruption of prostitution."

Key's concept of love contains an element of emancipation: women must be liberated in order to fulfil a marriage based on love.[7] Key's ideas must be seen in the context of the changed function of the family. As in most European countries, the inception of a women's rights movement in Sweden was closely related to the disintegration of a traditional agricultural society with its estates, rigid family structure and clearly defined political corporations and interest groups.[8] An expanding market economy and a more flexible capital formation were accompanied by new demands which were irreconcilable with the laws and precepts of traditional society.[9] The more the production methods in society changed, the more it became necessary to find arguments that would justify the institution 'marriage'. More and more authors tried to define the essence of love which they claimed was a condition for marrying and the mortar for keeping a couple together. This was the general atmosphere when Key formulated the rights of the child who was to be conceived and born in true love.[10]

Key pointed out that as long as Society did not provide optimal day care facilities for very young children, the need of women to work must remain second to the need of children for care. The most important task of women was, according to Key, the education of the new generation. This opinion was not appreciated by the majority of the feminist movement.

Key was pleased with the developments in the natural sciences and the new theories of medical sciences and genetics, because these sciences enabled many questions to be viewed independently from religious ethics. She wished to see religious ethics replaced by secular ethics. Her opinions were very much coloured by Social Darwinism. She believed that by consciously applying the evolutionist theories on natural selection and the struggle for survival, the development of humanity could be influenced and eventually a 'higher type' of man could be created.

Key:[11] "He who knows that man has become what he now is under constant transformations, recognises the possibility of so influencing his future development that a higher type of man will be produced.... With what concerns our own race, the improvement of the type of man, the ennobling of the human race, the accidental still prevails in both exalted and lower forms. But civilisation should make man conscious of an end and responsible in all these spheres where up to the present he has acted only by impulse, without responsibility. In no respect has culture remained more backward than in those things which are decisive for the formation of a new and higher race of mankind. It will take the thorough influence of the scientific view of humanity to restore the full naive conviction, belonging to the ancient world, of the significance of the body".

In historiography a great deal of attention has been paid to a right-wing interpretation of these theories. 'Struggle' and 'selection' were considered unavoidable and even worthy of glorification. Today, however, more historians, such as Piet de Rooy[12] take an interest in the different interpretation of the same theories, which deny that natural selection can – let alone, must – be applied to humanity.

When Ellen Key had read the works of Herbert Spencer (1820–1903), who introduced evolutionism into the social sciences, she thought that now religious morality could be replaced by the dogma of evolution "which offered the solution of the problem of problems: the place of man in nature and his coming into being."[13]

According to Spencer's philosophy, the individual's aspirations must be judged after taking into consideration the effects they will have on the lives of future generations. The possibility exists that life-styles chosen by individuals will be inherited by their offspring as acquired characteristics.[14]

Ellen Key's very personal ideas about these matters are not easy to classify. She was a supporter of individualism, but she was also charmed by the rising star of socialism. It was, however, a particular brand of socialism which interested her: an evolutionist-humanist-oriented brand.[15] In her publications Key mentions such socialists as the social-democratic politician from Bavaria Georg Vollmar, the English art historian, architect and utopian-socialist William Morris, and Alfred Russel Wallace (the British zoologist best known for his theory of the origin of species through natural selection, independent of Charles Darwin). Thorbjörn Lengborn,[16] with whom I corresponded about Key's work, wrote that according to one of her nephews, she voted for the Social Democrats. She was not privileged to do this often, since the Swedish Parliament did not enfranchise women before 1921.

It is with reference to A.R. Wallace that Key unfolds her ideas about a society, free from exploitation, wherein marriages will be concluded in order to give two mature personalities a chance to unite in their efforts to raise the next generation.

In 1900 Ellen Key published her 'bestseller' *The Century of the Child*.[17] This book has been translated into Dutch, French, English, German, Italian, Danish, Latvian, Polish, Russian etc.

The fact that a Swedish author became so famous showed that it was no longer possible to solve problems exclusively on a national level.[18] Ellen Key sensed that she stood on the verge of a new cultural phase,[19] during which important shifts would take place in various fields of the human mind. If we read *The Century of the Child* today, it is like leafing through a medieval manuscript. The social situation has been irreversibly changed. Many rights Key formulated are already forgotten,[20] and countless changes suggested by Key have been imperceptibly accepted. Some ideas, of which we have experienced the disastrous results, have become totally unacceptable.

The opening chapter of *The Century of the Child* deals with what Key calls: the child's 'first right', namely 'the right to choose its parents wisely.'

Key: "In a much-discussed play: *The Lion's Whelp*[21] we read the following conversation between an old and a young man:

The Older Man: 'The next century will be the century of the child, just as this century has been the woman's century. When the child gets his rights, morality will be perfected. Then every man will know that he is bound to the life which he has produced with other bonds than those imposed by society and the laws. You understand that a man cannot be released from his duty as father even if he travels around the world; a kingdom can be given and taken away, but not fatherhood.'

The Youth: 'I know this.'

The Older Man: 'But in this all righteousness is still not fulfilled – in man's carefully preserving the life which he has called into existence. No man can early enough think over the other question, whether and when he has the right to call life into existence."

"This dialogue," says Ellen Key, "has supplied me with a title for my book. It is the point of departure of my assertion, that the first right of the child is to select its own parents."[22]

To understand this better, we shall quote some passages of *The Century of the Child*.

"What here must be first considered is the thought constantly being brought out by Darwinian writers, that the natural sciences, in which must now be numbered psychology, should be the basis of juristic science as well as of pedagogy. Man must come to learn the laws of natural selection and act in the spirit of these laws. Man must arrange the punishments of society in the service of development; they must be protective measures for natural selection. In the first place this must be secured by hindering the criminal type from perpetuating itself. The characteristics of this type can only be determined by specialists. But the criminal must be prevented from handing on his characteristics to his posterity. So the human race will be gradually freed from atavisms which reproduce lower and preceding stages of development. . . . Then comes the requirement that those with inherited physical or psychical diseases shall not transmit them to an offspring. . . . There is an old axiom that we are obliged to thank our parents for life. Our parents, I know from my own experience, can themselves have been the heirs of bodily and mental health, resulting from the fact that maternal and paternal ancestors all made early, right, and happy marriages. But generally, parents must on their part, ask the children's pardon for the children's existence."[23]

We are immediately struck, says Jansen,[24] by the strange heading of Key's first chapter, which states that the child has the right to choose his parents wisely. Strange, because the unborn child is not able to choose and take a 'decision'. What Key had in mind with this rather unusual sounding right was that a man and a woman, about to conclude a union that could result in the birth of a child, must ask themselves seriously whether their own physical and spiritual constitution gave them the right to suppose that such a child would be physically and spiritually healthy.

Ellen Key's oeuvre has become very famous, but other authors have, in fact, formulated similar thoughts, some even before she did. Frances S.

Hallowes, for instance, wrote in 1896: "The children's rights are: to be born into the world in a healthy condition. Parents are guilty of wilfully disregarding the laws of God who deny the power of pre-natal influences. The wrongs of children begin before birth. The weak body and weaker will, the diseases engendered by drink and impurity, are handicapping tens of thousands of lives for joyousness and usefulness in our land."[25]

A great concern of Ellen Key was that many children were born with handicaps as a result of their parents' venereal diseases. Looking back to the beginning of the century, the German writer Stephan Zweig (1881–1942) wrote about forty years later in *The World of Yesterday*:[26] "Whereas today, thanks to Paul Ehrlich's therapy, in the clinics of the small and medium-sized universities weeks often pass by in which the professor is unable to show his students a freshly infected case of syphilis, the statistics of those days show that in the army and in the big cities at least one or two out of every ten young men had fallen victim to infection. Youth was reminded incessantly of the danger. Going through the streets of Vienna, one could read on the door of every sixth or seventh house, *Specialist for Skin and Venereal Diseases*, and to the fear of infection was added the horror of the disgusting and degrading forms of the erstwhile cures, of which the world of today also knows nothing. For weeks on end the entire body of anyone infected with syphilis was rubbed with mercury, the effect of which was that the teeth fell out and other injuries to health ensued. The unhappy victim of a severe encounter felt himself not only physically but spiritually spotted, and even after so horrible a cure, he could never be certain that the cunning virus might not at any moment awake from its captivity and paralyse the limbs from the spine, or soften the brain." Also many children were born with handicaps as a result of these venereal diseases.

It was Key's particular merit that in a time when family planning was not even considered to be a right of the parents, she already formulated this right as belonging to *the child*. The right of the child to choose its parents can be re-formulated as the right of the child not to be born. We are dealing with the question of the right to exist, or rather the right 'not to exist'. This 'to be or not to be' question is so central that we can place it in the centre of the 'Systemic Quality of Life Model', right in the heart of the *conservative modes* of *all four subsystems*.

This brings us to modern so-called *wrongful life* – cases, in which the plaintiffs argue that it would have been better if they had not been born.[27] Peter Procarnik, whose mother contracted German measles while pregnant, was born with multiple defects, including eye lesions, heart disease and hearing loss. In the case against the doctor in 1984 (*Procarnik v. Cillo*) before the Supreme Court of New Jersey, the essence of the claim was that the child's *very life* was wrongful.

Although the court allowed here a cause of action for wrongful life, it decided to evade the problem of comparing non-life to impaired life: "Our decision to allow the recovery of extraordinary medical expenses is not

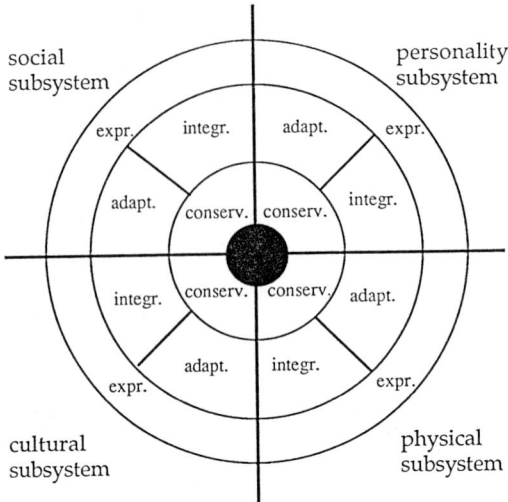

Fig. 5.1. Ellen Key's "Right of the Child to choose his own parents". Interpreted by the Systemic Quality of Life Model.

premised on the concept that non-life is preferable to an impaired life, but is predicated on the needs of the living."

In another famous case Joy Turpin charged that she would not have been conceived if the defendant, a licensed speech and hearing specialist, had correctly diagnosed the hereditary deafness of her older sister (*Turpin v. Sortini*).[28] The court denied payment of general damages here because it could not determine whether Joy Turpin had suffered an injury by being born deaf rather than by not being born at all. The court said: "Even if it were possible to overcome the first hurdle it would be impossible to assess general damage in any fair, non-speculative manner." Irwin Saltz:[29] "In fact, these are twin problems, both stemming from the difficulty of placing a value on human life. The choice is not between being born with health or without it. The choice is between life and non-existence."

The fundamental question raised by Ellen Key pops up, without her name being attached to it, not only in the modern *wrongful life* torts, but also in the growing problem of children born with AIDS. In 1988 Dr. Stephen Joseph, Commissioner of Health of New York City told a UNICEF meeting:[30] "We will see this year in New York City 1,000 infants born infected with the AIDS virus." The Minister of Health of Zaire, Nganbu Kabéya, told a reporter in 1987 that nine percent of the babies under nine months of age in Zaire were carriers of AIDS.[31] Thus we are faced with the dilemma that on the one hand 'the right of the child to choose its own parents' has lost much of its impact and seems to be out-dated, while on the other hand this right, as formulated by Key, is more relevant than ever.

Key, who died on April 25th 1926, is considered to be the 'Mother of the New Education Movement (Reformpädagogik). More and more educators became convinced that *man is intrinsically good*. The consequence is that the educators do not have the right to interfere with the development of the child, as opposed to the former educational principles whereby the teachers' instruction was central.

Education, it is today argued, must not hamper the child, but liberate it to follow its own natural development.[32] The spontaneous, natural interests of the child are to be stimulated. The child must be forced as little as possible.

Key in *The Century of the Child*: "The desire for knowledge, the capacity for acting by oneself, the gift of observation, all qualities children bring with them to school, have, as a rule, at the close of the school period disappeared. They have not been transformed into actual knowledge or interests." She talked, therefore, about 'soul murder in the schools'.[33] The 'new belief' she pleaded for in 1900 was that "almost every fault is but a hard shell enclosing the germ of virtue. Even men of modern times still follow in education the old rule of medicine, that evil must be driven out by evil, instead of the new method, the system of allowing nature quietly and slowly to help itself, taking care only that the surrounding conditions help the work of nature. This is education." And she continued to point out that it was a pedagogical crime to suppress the real personality of the child and to supplant it with another personality.[34] "The only correct starting point, so far as a child's education in becoming a social human being is concerned, is to treat him as such, while strengthening his natural disposition to become an individual human being . . . None of the individual characteristics of the child expressive of his life will be suppressed." The child, according to Key, has a right to be naughty and a right to have his or her feelings, his or her likes and dislikes. She revolts against drilling children and fears that this will suppress their personality. Key: "Only during the first few years of life is a kind of drill necessary, as a precondition to a higher training. The child is then in such a high degree controlled by sensation, that a slight physical pain or pleasure is often the only language he fully understands. Consequently for some children discipline is an indispensable means of enforcing the practice of certain habits. For other children, the stricter methods are entirely unnecessary even at this early age, and as soon as the child can remember a blow, he is too old to receive one."[35]

It became increasingly fashionable to regard education as *Hilfe zur Selbsterziehung* (Friedrich Wilhelm Foerster 1869–1966).[36] The educational task no longer consists of influencing the child by force, authority and disciplinary measures, but of strengthening the child's positive qualities so much that they will help him conquer his own 'lower self'. Self-constraint should be used instead of external constraint, self-discipline instead of external discipline. What modern educators like Foerster want to achieve is a voluntary discipline rooted in the child's own understanding and sustained by the

Picture V.1. Ellen Key at the time her *Century of the Child* became a bestseller.

strength of his own free will. Freedom and discipline reconciled. Foerster pleads for some sort of self-government by students as a means of acquiring discipline.

The New Education ('vom Kinde aus') Movement of which Ellen Key was one of the most important founders, took as a starting point the needs and the life-world of the child. Standards should not be rooted in the world of adults but extracted from the 'asking' child. This required new methods in the schools. Key pleaded for these changes.

The new educators view the child as a 'species sui generis'. The child is not a human being in the making whose worth increases as it comes closer to maturity, but, instead, he derives his worth from what he is at any given moment.

The German pedagogue Berthold Otto (1859–1933) argued that we must follow the signals sent out by the child. He was convinced that the only way to maturity lead through communication. In his oeuvre, the 'interaction with children' had, therefore, a central place. "Through question and answer, through conversation, the child learns to understand, and as his command of language grows, so does his mental strength."[37]

In the beginning of our century many children were, just like Ellen Key herself, not allowed to talk when the adults were speaking, and if no one asked them anything, they were supposed to keep silent. Otto wanted to promote the children's 'desire to ask questions'.

By mental interaction with children, by the game of questions and answers, emotional maturity was reached in a natural way. By asking questions, says Otto, the emotional curiosity is expressed; by asking, the child tries to fill in gaps in his or her knowledge. Otto, therefore, formulated *the child's unlimited right to question*. Questions posed by children should no longer be seen as troublesome.

The Italian physician and pedagogue Maria Montessori (1870–1952) expressed the opinion that educators must not offer children a certain subject matter before they were ready to accept it, and that each child had the right to work in his own tempo adjusted to his needs. Montessori[38] claimed that the aims of education had all too often been the disciplining of the child.

Many pedagogical historians of education, among them Wolfgang Scheibe,[39] call Ellen Key the initiator of the new pedagogical movement, which tries to extract its standards from the needs of the child. This changed conception led to the formulation of new rights for children such as, for instance, the *right to optimal development*, the *right to ask questions*, and the *right to respect*. About this last right we shall have more to say in chapter VII dealing with Janusz Korczak.

Notes

1. Hart, 't, Willem Anne, *Ellen Key*, Leyden, 1948, Doctoral Dissertation, State University Leyden, p. 23.
2. Idem, p. 25, see also: Nyström – Hamilton, Louise, *Ellen Key: Her Life and Work*, New York, 1913, Putnöm (translated from the Swedish).
3. Register, Cheri, 'Motherhood at Centre: Ellen Key's social vision', in *Women's Studies Int. Forum*, Vol. 5, No. 6, p. 607.
4. Idem.
5. Dell, Floyd, *Women as World Builders; Studies in Modern Feminism*, Chicago, 1913, Forbes and Comp., p. 83.
6. Idem, p. 84.
7. Ambjörnsson, Ronny, *Samhällsmodern, Ellen Keys kvinnouppfatting till och med 1896*, Göteborg, 1974, Göteburg Universitet, Institutionen för idé – ooh Lördumshistoria pp. 262–281. I wish to thank Prof. Ranny Ambjörnsson of the University of Umea for our correspondence about this part of the present study.
8. Idem, p. 262.
9. Idem, p. 264.
10. Jansen, W., *Ellen Key en Hare Paedagogische Idealen*, Utrecht, 1905, C.H.E.Breyer, p. 94.
11. Key, Ellen, *Barnets ärhundrade* (2 Volumes), Stockholm, 1900, Albert Bonniers Förlag, in translation: *The Century of the Child*, New York and London, 1909, G.P.Putnam's Sons, pp. 5–6.
12. Rooy, de, Piet, *Darwin en de Strijd langs Vaste Lijnen*, Nijmegen, 1987, Sun-Publishing House, p. 9.
13. Haeckel, Ernst, *De Wereldraadselen, Populaire Studië over Montessorische Philosophie*, Baarn, (1913), originally published in German in 1894.

14. Ambjörnsson, Ronny, op. cit., p. 275.
15. Idem, p. 279.
16. Letter from Thorbjörn Lengborn, Litteraturveten Skapliga Institutionen, Stockholm, dated November 11th, 1986. Thorbjön Lengorn published a book in Swedish about Key: *En Studie i Ellen Key Pedagogiska tänkande främst med Utgangspunkt fran 'Barnets ärhundrade'*, (A study about Ellen Key's educational thought with 'the Century of the Child' as point of departure), Stockholm, 1977, with a summary in German.
17. Key, Ellen, *Barnets ärhundrade*, Stockholm, 1900, Albert Bonniers Förlag.
18. Anweiler, Oskar, 'Der Internationale Zusammenhang der Reformpädagogik zu Beginn des 20. Jahrhunderts', in: *Bildung und Erziehung*, 14(1961), 7(1), p. 285.
19. Hart, 't, Willem Anne, op. cit., p. 136.
20. Luke T. Lee of the *International Advisory Committee on Population and Law* told the UNICEF Executive Board Meeting on May 28th, 1975: "Forgotten are the rights of the child – to be born wanted – wanted in the sense that the parents indeed want the child to be born, and not just by accident; wanted in the sense that the society wants the child to be born as evidenced by the availability of adequate health care, food, housing, education and job opportunities which the society can provide to each and every child; and above all, wantedness in the sense that the child, if it had the choice, would have wanted to be born, especially if neither the parents nor the society really wants it." See E./ICEF/N60/166/9 June 1975, Appendix B.
21. Gote, Harold, pen-name used by Steenhoff, Helga Frideborg Maria (Frida), born Wadström (1865–1945). Her play *Lejonets Unge* (The Lion's Whelp) was, according to the Kungl. Bitlioteket in Stockholm in a letter to me, published in 1896.

In a discussion about the play in a periodical *Ord och Bild* in 1896, we read that a young sculptress, Saga Leire (the Lion's whelp), visits a village to make a bust of the mayor. She stays with a (Lutheran) bishop, Manfred Vik and his wife Odegard. The bishop pleads for "freedom without prejudices, and tolerance," which appear to be rare commodities among his colleagues. Mrs Vik, too, is described as a liberal person. In the same house lives Adil Barfot, the bastard son of Odegard Vik, "the result of a youthful lapse devoid of love." Adil falls in love with Saga, but he is poor and will not be able to marry her for years to come. Adil therefore will depart for London to study journalism while Saga will go to Paris to improve her sculpting skills. Adil is very sad because his first love is thus coming to grief. His mother is of the opinion that a man must marry for love because "otherwise he takes refuge to something not quite pure." The two young people discuss their impending separation and here it is that Saga shows herself to be 'the lion's whelp'. Like a young lion she brandishes her claw and opposes herself against social conventions. Whereupon Adil and Saga depart for Paris without having the intention to get married for the time being. Manfred Vik must, in his quality of bishop, denounce their behaviour, but does not for so much withhold them his personal sympathy.
22. Key, Ellen, *The Century of the Child*, op. cit., p. 45.
23. Idem, p. 46.
24. Jansen, W., *Ellen Key en Hare Paedagogische Idealen*,Utrecht, 1905, C.H.Breyer, p. 48.
25. Hallowes, Frances, S., *The Rights of Children in Spirit,Mind and Body; Thoughts for Parents*, London, 1896, S.W.Partridge & Co., pp. 7 and 8.
26. Zweig, Stefan, *The World of Yesterday, An Autobiography*, New York, 1943, The Viking Press,p.88; in German: *Die Welt von gestern; Erinnerungen eines Europäers*, Stockholm, 1944, Bermann-Fisher Verlag.
27. Procarnik v. Cillo, 97, *N.J.* 478 A.2d.755, 1984. The term 'wrongful life' was first used in 1963 when an illegitimate child sued his father for causing him to be stigmatised as illegitimate. The court was afraid that encouragement would extend "to all others born into the world under conditions they might regard as adverse. One might seek damages for being born of a certain colour, another because of race; one for being born with a hereditary disease, another for inheriting unfortunate family characteristics. . . . The present case could be just a forerunner of those which may confront the courts in the future. . . ." *Joseph*

Dennis Zepeda v. Louis Roul Zepeda, 190 *North Eastern Reporter*, 2nd series, pp. 849–859.
28. Turpin v. Sortini, 31 Cal.3d 220, 643 p. 2d 954(1982).
29. Saltz, Irwin, 'Better Off Never Born?' in *ABA Journal*(American Bar Association) Chicago, April 1, 1986, Vol. 72, pp. 46–49. Also: Andrews, Lori, B., *Medical Genetics: A Legal Frontier*, Chicago, 1987, American Bar Foundation. Also: Zelizer Viviana, A., *Pricing the Priceless Child*, New York, 1985, Basic Books, pp. 138–168, and: Note,'Wrongful Birth: A Child of Tort Comes of Age', in: 50 *U.Cin.L.Rev.* 65, 1981.
30. Joseph, Stephen, C.,'*The Common Challenge to Humanity: AIDS and Children and the Implications for a Global Future*'. Keynote address to the 1988 Non Governmental Organisations Committee on UNICEF Forum 'Children's Rights an Agenda for Action', April 15, 1988, New York.
31. Danois, Jacques, interview with the Minister of Health of Zaire: 'Een seropositieve moeder kan haar kind in de baarmoeder met AIDS besmetten', in: *UNICEF Nieuws*, the Netherlands, October 1987, No. 206, p. 18.
32. Dietrich, Th., *Die pädagogische Bewegung 'Vom Kinde aus'*,Bad Heilbrunn, 1973.
33. Key, Ellen, New York and London, 1909, op. cit. pp. 108 and 124.
34. Idem.
35. Idem.
36. Foerster, Friedrich Wilhelm, *Erziehung und Selbsterziehung; Hauptgeschichtspunkte für Eltern und Lehrer, Seelsorger und Jugendpfleger*, Zurich, 1919, Schulthess.
37. Otto, Berthod, *Die Reformation der Schule*, Gross-Lichterfelt, 1912, Verlag des Hauslehrers.
38. Standing, E.M., *Maria Montessori: Her Life and Work*, Fresno,Calif. 1959, Academy Guild Press.
39. Scheibe, Wolfgang, *Die Reformpädagogische Bewegung*, 1900–1932, Eine einführende Darstellung, Weinheim/Basel, 1969,1974. See also: Flitner, Wilhelm and Kudritzki, Gerhard, *Die deutsche Reformpädagogik* Part I: Die Pioniere der Pägagogischen Bewegung, Dusseldorf and Munich, 1961, and Reble, Albert, *Geschichte der Pädagogik*, Stuttgart, 1951, 1975, Ernst Klett Verlag, pp. 272–274. See also: Rang, Adalbert, 'Zum Bildungskonzept der Reformpädagogik' in: Hansmann, Otto and Marotzki, Winfried, Eds. Diskurs Bildungstheorie II: Problemgeschichtliche Orientierungen, Weinheim, 1989, Deutscher Studien Verlag, pp. 273–304.

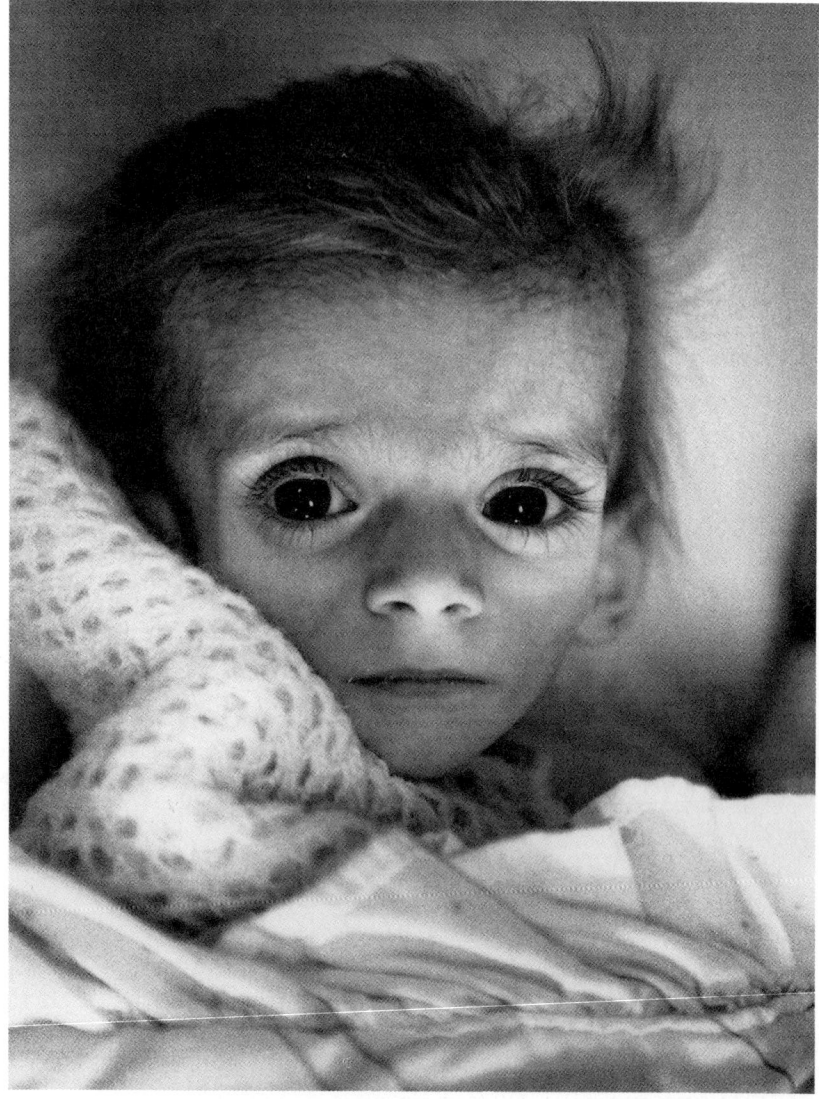

Picture V.2. AIDS patient, one and a half year old, in the Colentina Hospital in Bucharest, Rumania. Till the revolution of 1989, AIDS was a state secret. (Photo: Vincent Mentzel.)

CHAPTER VI

Eglantyne Jebb: The World Is My Country

During the First World War, an important strategy of both sides was to lower the morale of the enemy by reducing his food supply.[1] After September 16th, 1918, when the Austrians asked for peace negotiations and the Bulgarians for a cease-fire, the food blockade was not called off. Even after October 3rd, when the German Emperor had fled to the Netherlands, and October 6th, when the new German government had asked for an armistice, it was still maintained. Only on March 14th, 1919, was it finally lifted.

Herbert Hoover, the coordinator for food assistance in Europe (who later would become President of the U.S.) wrote in his memoirs[2] that the continuation of the food blockade during the four months after the armistice was a sin against statesmanship and the whole of humanity. Hoover: "Nations can take philosophically the hardships of war; when the fighting is over, they begin to bury the past as part of the fight. But when they lay down their arms and surrender upon promises and assurances that they will be no longer attacked and that they may have food for their women and children, and then find the worst instrument of attack upon them is maintained – then hate never dies."[3]

Hoover[4] tells how in March 1919 he met the British head of the 'Big Four' delegation Admiral Rosslyn Wemyss, in a Brussels hotel where the negotiations with the Germans were taking place. "Young man," said Wemyss to Hoover. "I don't see why you Americans want to feed these Germans." Hoover answered: "Old man, I don't understand why you British want to starve women and children after they are licked."

The reasons for the allied continuation of the food blockade were political and economic: a dash for power in the post-war economic sector, and a way to influence world food prices.[5] Hoover: "Neither the British nor the French wanted Germany to get into the export business before they had recovered their own markets. Britain, France and Italy wanted to control German economic life for some years after peace. They had the blockade working."[6]

After the war child mortality in Germany rose, according to Hoover[7], by thirty percent, while one third of the children were ill owing to undernourishment. Towards the end of the First World War, some thirteen million children urgently needed help and more than four million children in Central and East Europe were dying.[8]

Already before the war Eglantyne Jebb (1876-1928), the daughter of a wealthy Englishman who owned an estate in Shropshire[9], showed an interest in social issues. She was the fourth child in a family of six, and educated by French and German governesses. In 1895 she went to Oxford to study history, but later switched to education and became a primary school teacher for children of poor families in a Malborough *church school*. Not very ladylike, said her contemporaries. Miss Jebb had to give up teaching, however, due to poor health.[10] She went to live with her mother who was, by now, a widow and had moved to Cambridge.

According to Fuller[11] the war made it impossible for citizens like Eglantyne Jebb to work behind the front line and extend help to the victims. From behind her desk in Cambridge, she maintained contacts she had made with influential Red Cross officials[12], during her pre-war visit to Macedonia.[13] Thus she obtained information about the horrors of the war and the fate of the children. Together with her sister, who was married to the politician Charles Buxton, she collected facts about civilian victims of the war and published them in the Cambridge Magazine. After the war, while the food blockade still prevailed, the two sisters, together with some friends, founded the *Fight the Famine Council*. The group, consisting of very respectable Englishmen and women, including Lady Courtney of Penwith and Lord Parmoor, organised a number of meetings in order to influence public opinion in favour of lifting the food blockade. However, this was not enough for Eglantyne Jebb. According to Fuller[14] she wanted to do something more drastic to save the children, of whose terrible plight she had learned in the course of her researches during the war.[15] On April 15th the idea was first mentioned to appoint a committee, the *Save the Children Fund*, which would undertake to offer actual assistance. Two days later the board of directors of the *Save the Children Fund* convened for the first time. On May 19th, 1919, the first public meeting of the *Fund* took place in the *Royal Albert Hall* in London. Gillian Wilson[16] writes in an article about Eglantyne Jebb, that the kind of relief planned by the *Save the Children Fund* was, in those days, by no means self-evident. Wilson: "They were accused by some of a camouflage attempt to support foreigners and the Bolsheviks, or of giving money to foreign children 'who will rise up and fight you in twenty-five years.'[17]

When Bernard Shaw, who supported the *Save the Children Fund*, was asked why he helped 'enemy children', he answered: "I have no enemies under seven."[18]

On May 15th, 1919, a few days before the meeting in the *Royal Albert Hall*, Eglantyne Jebb was called before the Lord Mayor[19], and accused of having published a pamphlet featuring the picture of a starving Austrian baby, without having previously submitted the pamphlet to the censor. Except for a symbolic fine of five English Pounds, this brought her a great deal

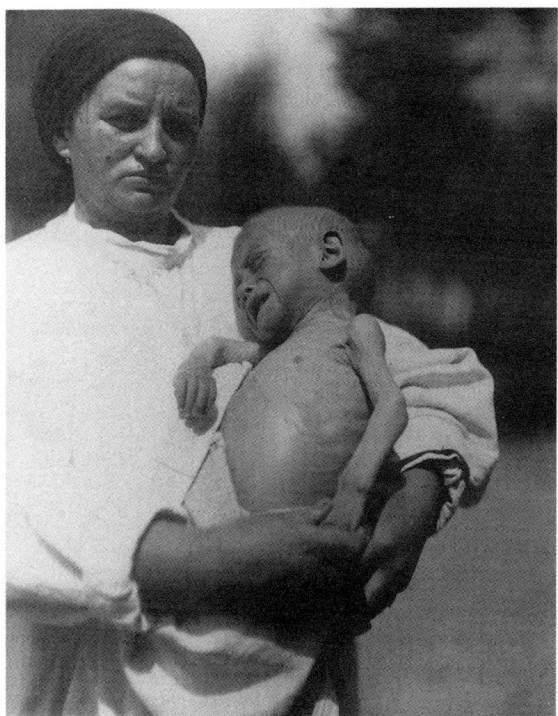

Picture VI.1. An Austrian baby in the arms of a nurse, 1919. (Photo by the American Relief Administration. Courtesy: Herbert Hoover Presidential Library.)

of publicity, which was, no doubt, one of the reasons why the meeting at the *Albert Hall* was so well attended. Lord Parmoor presided over the meeting and Robert Smillie, chairman of the *Miners' Federation of Great Britain*, was one of the speakers. He proposed to vote for the following resolution: "This meeting urges the necessity of pressing forward every measure of effective relief to meet the appalling conditions of the famine districts, and especially to stay the mortality among the children." A few days later Smillie suited his actions to his words and sent the *Save the Children Fund* a cheque for ten thousand English Pounds.

According to Jebb the *Save the Children Fund* owed its existence to the fact that common people could not bear to see children die without at least trying to help – to save as many as possible. The *Save the Children Fund* had a golden rule: Nationality, religion or race of children who needed to be saved were of no consideration whatsoever.[20]

"After the war," wrote Jebb[21], "when the fighting was finished, the enemy was disarmed, his submarines surrendered, his aeroplanes destroyed, his soldiers dispersed; months afterwards we kept a weapon which was for use first and mainly against the children, the weak, the sick, the old, the women, the mothers, the decrepit: starvation and disease. Our papers told us –

Picture VI.2. Eglantyne Jebb on the SS Trocillo, 1921. (Courtesy of the Save the Children Fund.)

our patriotic papers – how well it was succeeding. Correspondents wrote complacently, sometimes exultingly, of how thin and pinched were all children, how defective the next generation would be; and how the younger children, those of seven and eight, looked like children of three or four; and how those beneath this age simply did not live. Either they were born dead, or if they were born alive – what was there to give them? Milk? An unheard-of luxury... It was this situation which called the 'Save the Children' Movement into being."

The work of the *Save the Children Fund* would expand so much that it soon became one of the most important relief organisations of the United Kingdom. When in 1921 a harvest in Soviet Russia failed, Eglantyne Jebb's *Save the Children Fund* was one of the first to collect money for the children who were the victims of famine in the Soviet Union.[22] When the *SS Torcillo* left the port of London with food for the children in Russia, this was a national event in the United Kingdom.

In 1922 the Fund extended help to thousands of Armenian orphans many of whom had seen their parents murdered by the Turks. Many more groups of needy children were helped in the course of the years. In 1979 the Fund was the largest *International Children's Charity* of the United Kingdom. It had a budget of six million English Pounds and projects in fifty countries.

Jebb had a knack for involving the right people, such as leaders of various church societies whom she recruited as patrons of her organisation, as well as prominent members and ex-members of parliament, like Mr. Percy Alden[23] and Lord Weardale.[24]

In 1919 Marion Chadwick, as a representative of the *Save the Children Fund*, helped to found its Swedish counterpart: Rädda Barnen.[25]

Most important were the connections Eglantyne Jebb had established with the International Committee of the Red Cross in Geneva. With the help of the Red Cross, she founded in Geneva on January 6th, 1920, the *Save the Children International Union*, which would be joined by many national relief organisations. Alice Salomon states that this International Organisation compelled its member organisations to think international. Salomon: "Because assistance to needy children is a world responsibility."[26]

Notwithstanding the assistance of the *International Union* and the member organisations, Miss Jebb decided that the plight of children should be brought to a higher level of attention. She wrote: "The world's children stand in urgent need of better protection, because it is they who pay the heaviest price for our short-sighted economic policies, our political blunders, our wars. Adults can pass through a period of stress and strain and perhaps be none the worse for it, once it is over, but if we fail to give children their physical requirements and we restrict their educational advantages, they may well be handicapped in consequence for the rest of their lives."[27]

In 1924 Jebb scored her most important achievement, the *Declaration of the Rights of the Child*, or the *Declaration of Geneva*. We shall deal extensively with this declaration in part D, Chapter X, where many such declarations are analysed.

Eglantyne Jebb died in December 1928 in Geneva. A friend who attended her funeral wrote: "I thought it was an enormous tribute to Eglantyne that a fanatical Papist and a fanatical (protestant) Ulsterman could arrange that funeral together!"[28]

Jebb's major concern is with the *principle of universality*, according to which *all* children, regardless of nationality, race, or faith etc., are entitled to their rights. This message, at a time when one could be convicted for 'antipatriotic activities', is outstanding. It is echoed in some of the other Declarations on the rights of the child that we shall analyse, but in Jebb's work it is the central theme.

NOTES

1. Hoover, Herbert, *The Memoirs of Herbert Hoover, Years of Adventure* 1874–1920, New York, 1951, The MacMillan Company, p. 257. Hoover himself did not consider this an

effective strategy. "I did not believe in starving women and children. And above all, I did not believe that stunted bodies and deformed minds in the next generation were secure foundations upon which to rebuild civilisation. The facts were that soldiers, government officials, munition workers and farmers in enemy countries would always be fed; that the impact of blockade was upon the weak and the women and children. . . . I insisted that the war would not be won by the blockade on food for women and children, but by the blockade on military supplies and by military action.

2. Hoover, Herbert, idem, p. 352.
3. Idem. Unfortunately we did not learn much: for instance in the summer of 1990 food was used as a weapon. Lieut. Col. Mengistu Haile Mariam of Ethiopia did not allow food to enter Tigre and Eritrea. On the other hand the Eritrean Peoples Liberation Front, which was fighting the Mengistu, said (according to the New York Times of June 10, 1990) "that Soviet planes trying to bring in American wheat would fly into Asmara at their own peril".
4. Idem, p. 345.
5. Idem, p. 335.
6. Idem, and p. 336.
7. Idem p. 337.
8. Fuller, Edward, *She Championed Children*, London, 1953, Edinburgh Howe Press, p. 13.
9. Through her sister, Eglantyne Jebb was invited, in 1913, to travel to Macedonia, and supervise the assistance to refugees. In Monastir (today Yugoslavia), she found many thousands of refugees as a result of the war in the Balkans. Many children were starving to death.
10. According to Graham, (see note 13), the beginning of an ailment of the thyroid gland that would in the course of time made her almost an invalid.
11. Fuller, Edward, *The Right of the Child, A Chapter in Social History*, London, 1951, Victor Gollancz Ltd., pp. 22 and 23.
12. Eglantyne Jebb corresponded mainly with Dr. Frédéric Ferrière, one of the members of the Red Cross Committee.
13. Graham, Janet, "Saviour to the World's Children", in: *The World's Children*, March 1979, pp. 9–11. Also: Bruce Glacier, Katharine, *Eglantyne Jebb and the World's Children*, Manchester, The Northern Voice and Solomon, Alice, *Eglantyne Jebb* 1876–1928, Geneva, 1936.
14. Fuller, Edward, *The Right of the Child*, op. cit.,p. 25.
15. Idem, p. 26.
16. Wilson, Gillian, "The White Flame", in: *World's Children*, September 1976, p. 6. The title of the article refers to a name of honour her fellow workers in war-stricken Hungary gave her. Julia Vajaki wrote in 1928 also "Her greatness was the greatness of the spirit, that apostolic spirit which has lighted our path for us; the 'white flame' we used to call her".
17. Idem, p. 6.
18. Idem.
19. Fuller, Edward, *The Right of the Child*, Op. cit., p. 26. This happened, according to Fuller, because of a law concerning the defence of the United Kingdom, *The Defence of the Realm Act*.
20. Jebb, Eglantyne, quoted in: Tomlinson, Rederick, "Jubilee Year of 'Save the Children Fund' " in: *International Child Welfare Review*, May 1969, No. 2, p. 38.
21. Jebb, Eglantyne, *The Real Enemy*, London 1928, The Weardale Press, p. 29.
22. Save the Children Fund, *The History of the Save the Children Fund*, London, June 1985.
23. Later: Sir Percy Alden. Alden was one of the pioneers of a *voluntary social service*.
24. Lord Weardale was one of the pioneers of the *Inter-Parliamentary Union*.
25. Fuller, Edward, *the Right of the Child*, Op. cit., p. 33.
26. Salomon, Alice, *Eglantyne Jebb* 1876–1928, Op. cit., p. 28.
27. Eglantyne Jebb quoted by Gillian Wilson in his article 'The White Flame' in: *The World's Children*, September 1976, p. 7.
28. Letter from E.M. to Mabel Few (in London), December 21, 1928. Found in the archives of the *Save the Children Fund* in London.

CHAPTER VII

Janusz Korczak and the Right of the Child to Respect

The Polish pediatrician Henryk Goldszmit (1878–1942)[1] was in his early thirties when he visited Forest Hill[2] in London. He was, at that time, already a well-known author who wrote under the pen-name of Janusz Korczak. In the Polish journal *Swiatlo*[3], he expresses his envy of the lovely twin houses, one for girls and one for boys, the lawn, the workshop, the animals and the small museum, and his astonishment when asked: 'What is so interesting about it?' Indeed, for a Jewish pediatrician who knew the terrible conditions of Warsaw's orphanages, the two children's homes in Forest Hill[4] must have been a revelation.

During his visit to London Korczak made the crucial decision never to have children. *The Century of the Child* had been translated into Polish and Korczak must have read Ellen Key's words: "Conscientious young people see it nowadays as their duty to miss the pleasure of parenthood, rather than to pass on an unhappy heritage."

When Korczak was eleven his father became mentally ill and died in a psychiatric hospital. In those days psychiatrists believed that such diseases were inherited.

"Instead of having a son I chose the idea of serving the child and his rights", Korczak wrote many years later about this decision.[5] Those moments in a London park were the turning point[6] in his life.

Korczak served the child and his rights as no one else in history did. Not only did he formulate ideas about the rights of the child, but he put them into practice for more than thirty years.

From 1912 till 1942 he was the Director of a Jewish Orphanage *Dom Sierot*, (the House of Orphans). During many of those years he was also involved in the non-Jewish Warsaw orphanage *Nasz Dom*, (Our Home).

Korczak's Ideas

In 1929 Korczak published *The Right of the Child to Respect*,[7] wherein he protests against the attitude of many educators who behave "as if there were

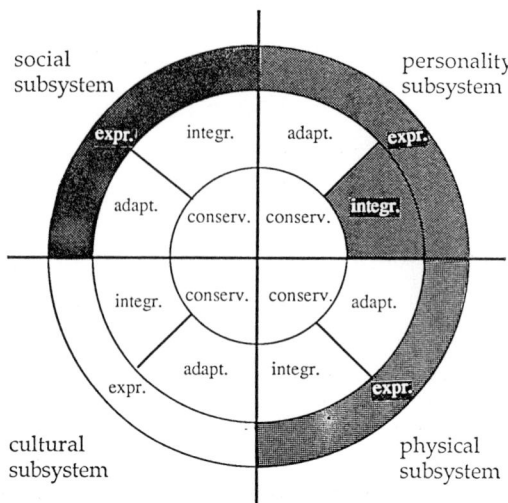

Fig. 7.1. Rights formulated by Janusz Korczak. Interpreted by the Systemic Quality of Life Model.

two lives, one serious and respectable for adults and the other indulgently tolerated and less valuable for children."

"There are no children as such," says Korczak. "There are only men. Men with different experiences, different drives and different reactions."[8] Child-innocence he calls a sweet illusion. In his book *How to Love a Child*[9] we read: "One the worst blunders is to think that pedagogy is the science of the child, when in reality it is the science of men."

What Korczak means by *the right of the child to respect*, is clarified when he writes about respect for failure and respect for the child's tears. "Even the tears of a child are treated like a joke, made to seem less important, irksome," he bitterly remarks.[10] Respect should also be shown for the labour of developing knowledge. "We are constantly at odds with the children.... We nag, admonish, scold and punish them, but we don't inform kindly. How poor would the child's knowledge be if he didn't have his peers to rely upon, and if he didn't eavesdrop and pick up scraps of adult conversation."[11]

"The child is a foreigner who does not understand the language of the street plan, who is ignorant of the laws and customs. Occasionally, he likes to go sight-seeing on his own. When he encounters a difficulty, he asks for information and advice. Wanted: a guide to answer questions politely!"[12]

"Unintelligently we divide years into less and more mature ones. There is no such thing as present immaturity, no hierarchy of age, no higher and lower grades of pain and joy, hopes and disappointments."[13]

Korczak often expresses his wish to give children a higher status in society. With empathy he quotes a child: "When Father spills the tea, Mother says: 'Never mind.' But she always makes a fuss when it's me."[14]

"Let us demand respect for the clear eyes, smooth foreheads, youthful effort and confidence," he recommends. "Why should dulled eyes, a furrowed brow, untidy grey hair, or bent resignation command greater respect?"[15]

Since Korczak's intention was to give children more influence and a higher social status, we classify his *right of the child to respect* in the *expressive mode* of the *social subsystem* of Shye's 'Systemic Quality of Life Model'.

Korczak's viewed society as consisting of two classes, one with the adults who had all the rights, and one with children who depended upon the adults.[16] He demanded respect for the child's belongings and his or her own budget. "Everyone has the right to property, no matter how insignificant or worthless. Whatever property the child has, chestnuts, earrings or chocolate wrappings, they must be dealt with as if they were a file with secret documents." In his children's book *The Bankruptcy of Little Jack*[17], the boy Jack asks the Minister of Finance to found a bank for children. This 'right to respect for the child's belongings and budget' can be classified in the *expressive mode* of the *physical subsystem* (more control over the physical environment).[18]

Elsewhere Korczak pleads for the right to privacy. This we classify in the *expressive mode* of the *physical subsystem* (privacy in a room or a corner of a room) and also in the *expressive mode* of the *personality subsystem*, (for instance to keep a diary which is not read by the parents). This right overlaps with *the right of the child to have secrets*, (already discussed as Example Six in Chapter III) which we have classified in the *expressive mode* of the *personality subsystem*.

In his book *The Child's Right to Respect*, Korczak formulates 'the child's right to be himself'. "We foolishly desire that no one should ever be out of place, that not one of the ten thousand seconds of the school hour (count them!) should raise difficulties. We demand uniformity of virtues and moments and, in addition, that they all suit our tastes and patterns. Can a case of similar tyranny be found in history? A generation of Neros has proliferated."[19] The 'right to be oneself' belongs in the (*expressive mode* of the *personality subsystem*). In as much as it allows the child to act according to his or her essential characteristics, it also belongs in the *integrative mode* of the *personality subsystem*.

Closely connected with the 'right to be oneself' is 'the child's right to the present day'. "Children are not people of tomorrow, they are people today," says Korczak. "The child lives today. He has value as an individual today. Because we think of the child as 'a citizen in embryo' or 'a future man' valuable years are lost."[20] We can interpret this 'right to the present day' as a means for giving the child a higher status. It is classifiable in the *expressive mode* of the *social subsystem*.

Korczak warned against over-protection of children by adults. Provocatively he formulated 'the child's right to his or her own death'.[21] This was not a plea for euthanasia but an explanation that risks should be taken in education. Korczak thought that we should not be too anxious that a child might hurt himself. He did, however, not advocate a *laissez-faire*-education in which too much freedom is allowed. In his children's book *King Matt the First*[22] he warned that a Children's Parliament might well turn into chaos.

According to Korczak, the child has *the right to express his or her feelings and thoughts, to ask questions, but also not to express him- or herself*.[23] This we classify in the *expressive mode* of the *personality subsystem*.

Korczak and the Declaration of Geneva

In 1929 Korczak wrote in *The Rights of the Child to Respect*: "The authors of the Declaration of Geneva have mistaken duties for rights. Instead of making demands they try to persuade. The Declaration is only an appeal for good-will, a request for more understanding."

Korczak himself wrote a great deal about the right of the child, but never formulated a *Declaration*.

Patricia Piziali[24] tried to answer the question whether there was a difference between Janusz Korczak's child advocacy concepts and documented historical public Declarations. She prepared a so-called 'Child Right Comparative Matrix', consisting of the ten Principles of the 1959 United Nations *Declaration on the Rights of the Child*, listed horizontally, and national and international selected contributors including Janusz Korczak, listed vertically. If a 'child advocacy concept', or 'right' had been publicly advocated by a certain contributor, the appropriate box was marked with an 'X'. The same was done for Janusz Korczak through an examination of his literary and educational works.[25] The child advocacy concepts were tabulated, analysed, and interpreted. In order to compare Korczak with contemporary contributors (selected by Piziali according to criteria she does not explain) Piziali formulates a *Declaration of the Rights of the Child of Janusz Korczak*, and concludes that in his book on children's rights Korczak does not place priority on any one of his declared rights, but that they all have equal value. According to Piziali, Korczak acknowledges that the child always has a right, simply because the child is a person with dignity and respect. "He considers the spiritual, physical, social, emotional, cultural, and intellectual needs of each child, as set forth in *Korczak's unique Declaration*,[26]" which in reality is only Piziali's selection and interpretation of Korczak's *work*.

Our interpretations (see Figure 7.1) of the rights formulated by Korczak, lead to different conclusions. We think that Korczak especially emphasised the *expressive mode* of the *social subsystem* (higher status for children), as well as the expressive modes of the *personality and physical subsystem*.

Betty Jean Lifton, could also not resist the temptation of formulating "Janusz Korczak's Declaration of Children's Rights"[27] in her excellent biography of Korczak.[28] These attempts to formulate Janusz Korczak's Declar-

Picture VII.1. Korczak with children of the Jewish orphanage, c. 1935. Playing the violin (in the middle) is Samuel Gogol, who was interviewed for this study. (Courtesy: Ghetto Fighters House, Israel.)

ation on the Rights of the Child are like playing all the melodies of a certain composer at once, and claiming the Maestro has composed a symphony.

Realisation of Korczak's Ideas in the Orphanage

Korczak never belonged to or tried to create a 'school'. He had no dogmas and he did not write in professional jargon. From his works we distil, in addition to a plea for respect for the child, also a romantic image of the child (although we agree with Kurzweil[29] that this image was not dominant). For instance, in *How to Love a Child* we find the following passage: "When I perceive in the child an eternal flame taken from the fire stolen by a god, a spark of critical thought, righteous anger, a fit of enthusiasm, autumnal sadness, the sweetness of self-sacrifice, energetic searchings which are cheerful and full of trust, relentless questioning of causes and aims, wearying endeavours, awful pangs of conscience, then I fall on my knees before the child because I am inferior to him, weak and cowardly."

According to Stefan Woloszyn[30] Korczak believed that the child would save the world. In Korczak's play (*Senate of Madmen*)[31] God dies, but not the need for God. God changes himself to small pearls that fall into the hearts of children like rain.[32]

Between 1898 and 1903, when Korczak studied medicine and pediatrics, he became influenced by Polish progressive intellectuals[33], such as the experimental psychologist Jan Wladyslaw Dawid and his wife Jadwiga, the activist behind the *Flying University*.[34] In those days Korczak used to fantasise about an inter-professional perspective on child study and even an integrative science *pedology* combining developmental psychology, psychiatry, pediatrics and other behavioural sciences. Although his work carried him away from the medical profession, he remained dedicated to it. He kept statistical data and charts about his children and used to weigh and measure them every week.[35]

Like every educator of those days Korczak was also influenced by Rousseau[36] and Pestalozzi.[37] His dedication to the children resembles, in our opinion,[38] that of Pestalozzi who had written: "Their happiness was mine, their soup was mine. I slept in their midst..."

In December 1907 the Russians permitted the founding of a new organisation for Jewish children in Warsaw. A group of Jewish philanthropists raised 118.000 Roubles to build a modern Children's Home on Krochmalnastreet. In the 1910 Annual Report of the *Association for Help to Orphans*, we read that "a new period has started in the history of the Association. What was only a dream, will soon be reality: a Home for the Orphans."[39]

The year 1910 was an important year for the organisation in yet another way: The chairman of the building-commission, Dr. Eliasberg persuaded his colleague Dr. Goldszmit (Korczak) to join *Dom Sierot*. Dr. Goldszmit who was already a well-known pediatrician and author[40] stopped his practice and became the director. However, he could not have fulfilled this task without his loyal assistant Stefania Wilczynska.[41]

Between 1906 and 1908 Stefania studied natural sciences in Liège, Belgium. We also discovered that during the summer of 1906 she was registered at the Faculty of Sciences of Geneva University.[42] Above wealth and education, however, Stefa preferred a life of hard work. Her parents lived near a small orphanage, a forerunner of *Dom Sierot*, operated by the Association for Help to Orphans. She decided that with her great talents for organising, she could contribute a great deal to this poorly run program. When the new orphanage in Krochmalnastreet was opened Stefania Wilczynska became the manager of Korczak's Home.

Korczak and Stefa both chose to set aside their private lives in order to dedicate their lives to the children. They both lived among the children. Korczak's room was situated between the boys' and the girls' dormitories. Stefa's room was on the far side of the girls' dormitory. Although the director and the manager of *Dom Sierot* addressed each other as 'Doctor' and 'Mrs. Stefa,' there were, between them, some elements of a husband-wife relationship. They shared the care for the children and Stefa mothered the absent-minded writer.

Ida Merzan[43] remembers how Korczak once hurried through the dining hall on his way to a meeting. Stefa came running from the other side and shouted 'Mister Doctor, Mister Doctor'. The Doctor headed for the door. When Stefa caught up with him, he stopped impatiently. 'Did you take your handkerchief?' asked Stefa. Korczak had to admit that he had not. Mrs. Stefa gave him one. Korczak continued on his way. Stefa shook her head and muttered: 'Just like a child, forgetting his handkerchief, while he has a cold.'

In 1914 the war took Korczak to Kiev, away from the children and his writings. Stefania Wilczynska ran the Home alone. From a letter she wrote eleven years later, reflecting upon this period[44], we understand how difficult the work in *Dom Sierot* was: "It was so terribly lonely when Dr. Goldszmit went to the war in 1914. My circumstances were better than yours, because Korczak had already created a valuable educational system in the House. On the other hand this was an enormous responsibility. God helped me, and this valuable educational system was not destroyed."

In June 1918 Korczak returned to Warsaw, bringing with him the manuscript of *How to Love a Child*. "I wrote this in a field hospital under the sound of cannon fire," he commented.

In November 1918 Poland became again independent and Josef Pilsudski became its Chief of State. Richard Watt describes that "of the many 'new' nations that were born or reborn in the wake of World War I, none was faced with the variety and enormity of problems that Poland encountered during the first months of its existence."[45] According to Watt only about fifteen percent of the Polish industrial workers were employed. Nearly half a million Poles had been killed while serving in the Austrian, Russian or German armies. Another million had been wounded. Spanish influenza was sweeping through the country and there were serious outbreaks of typhus. Starvation was widespread."[46]

There was much work for Korczak in his Jewish orphanage with its hundred children between five and fourteen. Nevertheless he made time available for *Nasz Dom*, the orphanage for children of Polish workers who had been imprisoned and persecuted.[47] This Home was managed by Maria Falska, an active member of the Polish Socialist Party. She, too, devoted her life to the orphans and implemented many of Korczak's ideas.

In *Dom Sierot*, meanwhile, the system of self-government became better established. At a time when methods in many schools were authoritarian, and warm relationships between pupils and educators were often unthinkable, Korczak wrote about the despotism of educators. He devoted a great deal of thought to methods for preventing the adults in *Dom Sierot* from being authoritative and unjust. In order to ensure fair treatment for the children he established a court and a 'code of law' or *codex* for all the pupils, independently of age or status. The court, consisting of five children, held weekly sessions.[48] Stefa was the court's secretary.

According to Korczak's one-time secretary Igor Newerly,[49] when Korczak created the court of peers, he had been inspired by Bronislaw Trentowski's book *Chowanna* (1842), and by the 1783 report by the National Educational Committee which nobody had ever studied as seriously as Korczak.

"The court must defend the vulnerable," writes Korczak, "so that they will not be bothered by the strong. It must defend the conscientious and the hard-working, so that they will not be annoyed by the careless and idle."

Korczak himself was several times summoned before the court. Many former pupils remember that he was once brought to court by a small and shy girl for putting her on a high bureau and leaving her there as a practical joke. The satisfaction was visible when the court announced its verdict: "The defendant guilty as charged, according to paragraph 100 of the codex ("the court declares that the charge is justified")". From then on the children sometimes called Korczak 'Setka' (one hundred in Polish).

Frost[50] calls the codex an approach of graded social engineering ranging from persuasion and guidance through reprimand to sanction vis-à-vis the offender. Thus the Court could ask individual A 'to forgive individual B'. However, the Court could also render the verdict: 'We do not forgive'. The Court could recommend expulsion of the offender from the Institution. Expulsion, although hardly ever used, was not a hollow threat. It actually figures a number of times in the annals of the Orphanage.[51]

The codex had one thousand paragraphs. The first ninety-nine paragraphs provided for dismissal of a charge or for a statement that the court did not try the case. For example:

§4 The Court declares itself satisfied that nothing of the kind will ever happen again. Case dismissed.
§10 The Court finds in the act committed by A not guilt but an example of civic courage (gallantry, uprightness, honesty, lofty impulse, sincerity, good-heartedness).
§11 The Court expresses thanks to A for notifying it of his guilt.
§13 The Court, expressing regret for what has happened, is of the opinion that A is not guilty.
§53 The Court pardons A since there was no intention on his part to offend B (infliction of mental pain).
§54 The Court pardons A on the ground that it was a joke (a silly joke).

Minimum punishment starts at paragraph 100.

§200 The court rules that A acted incorrectly.
§300 The Court rules that A acted wrongly.
§400 The Court rules that A acted very wrongly.
§700 Rules that the text of the judgement must be sent to the family.
§800 Summons the family to the orphanage to discuss the situation. Paragraph 900 seeks a 'guardian' (another child) for the child in question to help him or her behave well. All children had such a

guardian or *apotropos*) during the first few months of their stay in *Dom Sierot*.

§1000 Gives the Court (of peers) the power to expel the child from the Home. However the expelled child has the right to apply for readmission after three months.

Former pupil Ignacy Cukierman[52] wrote me: "Before I was admitted to *Dom Sierot* at the age of 11, I lived on Ostrowska Street among thieves, prostitutes, pimps, and an extremely poor Jewish population that supported itself by peddling rags for paper mills, and potato peels for cow food. I was proud to be a pupil of *Dom Sierot*. Sometimes there were small incidents such as children's reaction to what they perceived as unreasonable demands by staff members. The offended child usually summoned the offender to Court where the dispute was resolved by ruling who was at fault. There was no appeal to the ruling."

Jacques Dodiuk[53] remembers that Korczak even tried to extend jurisdiction for his pupils into the schools they attended in Warsaw. Often the schools were unwilling to co-operate on this point. "Once I took action against a school teacher who had slapped my hand with a ruler. I was outraged because in the orphanage the educators never touched us. After my complaint Mrs. Stefa talked with the headmaster of the school who made me come into his office with the teacher who subsequently disappeared from the school. At another time I was a judge. This was a great distinction. But I have also often been judged and once I was even punished according to Article 800."

Simona Kowal[54] tells that she once had to appear before the court: "Yes, for coming late or for having been at odds with a girl-friend. Example of a punishment: to clean up some mess with a broom."

Arie Sadè[55] relates how once, when he was a judge, Stefa incriminated herself because she had screamed outrageously at a child.

Srulek Szwarzberg[56] remembers the responsibility of being a guardian. "If the other boy was again summoned in Court, they would put the blame on me, the guardian." Proudly he adds that the behaviour of the other boy improved so much that he subsequently became a guardian himself.

All my interviewees confirm that the Court was a very important social institution in *Dom Sierot*. Less clear is the function of the Home's Parliament. According to Hanna Mortkowicz-Olczakowa[57] this Parliament had twenty-two elected deputies who met once a year. Korczak himself writes: "The Parliament is composed of twenty deputies. Five children are a constituency. Any candidate receiving four votes is elected. The Parliament endorses or rejects laws drafted by the Judicial Board."[58] It seems that during the years Korczak experimented with the Parliament it was sometimes more and sometimes less important. Most of the former residents I interviewed hardly remember the Parliament. However, Izak Skalka[59] who was one of its members recalls that the Home's Parliament mainly enquired into the fairness of requests made by children.

Former pupil G. Mandelblatt[60] found Parliament too preposterous a name for a commission which mainly handed out tasks and rewards for having done them properly.

Most former pupils of *Dom Sierot* with whom I spoke, did not appreciate the *plebiscite*, introduced by Korczak. A child was voted into one of several categories. In *Mister Doktor*[61] by Hanna Mortkowicz-Olczakowa, the Polish names of the categories are translated as 'difficult new-comer', 'indifferent inhabitant', 'pleased companion', 'citizen', 'king and friend of the children.'

Votes, giving each resident, child or worker, an evaluation, were regularly taken. The evaluation was either expressed by a *plus*, which meant that one was a much liked person, or a *minus*, which meant that one was not appreciated as an resident, or a *plus-minus*. A former co-worker[62] of Korczak told me that she thought the system was a progressive, educational one, since a child was placed in a category according to his or behaviour rather than according to intelligence. Some former pupils told me, however, that, since belonging to the highest categories carried certain privileges, they used to 'lobby' before the vote was taken.

Korczak the Educator

Korczak was a charismatic educator. He greatly inspired the twenty students or *bourgists* who, in exchange for room and board, worked four hours a day with the children. The idea of educating educators was introduced into the Home in 1920. "We lived on the first floor of *Dom Sierot*," says former *bourgist* Jochevet Cuk.[63] Every evening the *bourgists* recorded their observations. In the same notebook Stefa added her comments in red ink. These observations were discussed with Korczak once a week.[64]

With Korczak the children felt more relaxed than with the serious Stefa whose role was to demand things. Korczak was the one who gave warmth and joy.

Ignacy Cukierman, now living in Montreal, wrote to me that he remembers how the Doctor took part in the children's games, something Stefa never did. Children climbed on the Doctor or sat on his lap. He often looked like a tree with many small birds in it.

Stefa had excellent assets for running a home with more than hundred children and very little help. Some former pupils[65] speak highly about her, but others remember that she did not hide her preferences for children who looked pretty, were intelligent and behaved well, thus causing jealousy and grief.

Stefa's task was difficult. With the help of a housekeeper, a cook, twenty *bourgists* and two paid educators, she managed a Home for hundred destitute children. In 1925 she wrote: "I am so tired, although I do not have physical complaints . . .I never tried to pity myself. . . You did not know me in the past. But now I have become so one-track-minded. It is so difficult to go away from the Children's Home even for a few hours."[66]

All the children had duties, such as helping to clean, wash and cook. Some children would wake up others. As a reward they received 'work credits' with which a postcard or 'commemorative card' could be earned.

Shlomo Nadel[67] described the home as "a place so organised that it ran like a Swiss watch." Another pupil who wants to stay anonymous, relates how, during the Second World War, when she was living in Siberia and had to use the lavatory outside the house, she used to dream of the clean bathrooms of *Dom Sierot*. While Stefa saw to it that everything functioned well, Korczak sometimes broke the rules by making jokes or behaving like a naughty boy himself.

Was Korczak's Self-Government System Unique?

Korczak was not the only educator in his time who experimented with self-government. Dan Mulock Houwer[68] tells us about what he called the *Socio-Educational System* in residential care. In this system the individual needs of the child are second to the effort of building an ideal community.

In the village of Freeville in New York State 'Daddy' William R. George created a private residential community, the *George Junior Republic*, with self-government by the adolescents or *citizens*. David and Roxa van Dyck report: "Modeled after the American republic, it includes: the legislative branch, the monthly town meeting of all free voting citizens (an earned distinction), the executive branch, a President, Vice-President, Secretaries of State and Treasuries, all elected, plus the Attorney General and other appointments. The judicial branch has seven court levels and requires citizens to study authority, have a degree of self-control and a basically sound mental state as well as a willingness to leave an unhealthy past."[69] Punishments in the *George Junior Republic* were stricter than in *Dom Sierot*. Among the major negative sanctions were fines and expulsion.

In Poland the *Medem Sanatorium* near Warsaw, also experimented with self-government.[70] However, no contact was maintained between Korczak and the *Medem Sanatorium* group. The educators in the Medem Sanatorium raised the children in Yiddish while the pupils of *Dom Sierot* had to speak Polish from the day they entered the Home. Moreover their surnames were often changed into Polish names. The Medem Sanatorium became especially known for its children's parliament, the 'Kinderkreis'.

In 1910 Paul Geheeb started his Odenwaldschule for an elite population in Hessen. In this *New School* pupils, teachers and the director had the same rights.[71] The children were responsible for keeping order, but there was no *Court of Peers*.

Of all the pioneers Korczak stands out because he not only formulated

Picture VII.2. 'Mister Doctor', some staff and children of Dom Sierot. (Courtesy: Sz. Nadel.)

ideas on children's rights, but also dedicated his life to trying them out. Korczak's ideas are often misunderstood.[72] He claimed that *respect for the child* was the basic requirement of an educator. A novelty was that he formulated this as a *Right*.[73]

The Last March

On September 1st, 1939, the Germans invaded Poland. On February 15th, 1940, Stefa who had in 1936 visited some former pupils in Israel, wrote them through the International Committee of the Red Cross: "We are healthy. I work a little in the orphanage but Korczak works very much. I did not come, because I could not come without the children. Yours Stefa."[74]

On August 6th, 1942, the Germans liquidated Dom Sierot. Among those who saw the children march to the train for Treblinka, was the social worker N. Remba.[75] "This was no march to the train," he writes. "It was a silent protest against banditry! All the children were lined up in fours. Leading the procession was Korczak, his eyes fixed ahead, holding a child with each hand. A second group was headed by Stefania Wilczynska." Regina Itkin-Arzylewicz says that Korczak held the hand of three-year old Romca Sztokman, the child of her sister Rozka, a worker and former pupil of Dom Sierot.[76] Chawa Kempinski-Hurowitz, who also witnessed Korczak's last march wrote me: "I remember seeing Janusz Korczak walking with the children and many other people. There were many Germans around them. When I came home and saw my dear parents, I cried because I knew this would probably be the end for all of us."[77]

NOTES

1. In *A Chronology of the Life, Activities, and Works of Janusz Korczak* (prepared by Maria Falkowska, Maria Bronikowska and Alexander Lewin of the Instytut Badan Pedagogicznych in Warsaw in 1978 and translated into English by Edwin P. Kulawiec in 1980 and published by The Kosciuszko Foundation in New York) we read that "In 1911 Korczak was *in all likelihood* in London, where he visits various educational centres, among others, a school and a home for orphans in Forest Hill near London." Since Korczak never mentioned when he was in London, we shall probably never know the exact year.
2. Józef Goldszmit, Korczak's father (a well-known lawyer in Warsaw), kept putting off the official registration of Korczak's birth for a number of years.
3. Korczak, J., 'Forest Hill', in: *Swietlo*, 1912, No. 2, pp. 30–32.
4. After a *tour de force* (the Royal Commission on Historical Manuscripts, the Greater London Record Office and Historical Library, the Public Record Office, the Social Care Association, the University of Essex (Oral History Department), the National Children's Home, the Library of the Department of Education and Science, the Library of the Home Office, London Boroughs of Greenwich) I turned to *The Times* Newspaper who mentioned *The London Borough of Lewisham*. Their archivist Carl Harrison finally sent me *the Annual Report of the Boys and Girls Industrial Homes, Forest Hill* (1910). We read in this Annual Report that the aim of the Boys and Girls Industrial Homes was "to give the children a fair start in life, in the hope that they will become capable and honest and God-fearing men and women." Described are what kind of children were admitted:

   * Mother dead; Father, a carman, left with nine children under 15 years of age.
   * Father too ill to work; Mother delicate; ten other children, three only earning, therefore, eight under 14 years to be supported.
   * Mother in an asylum; Father nearly blind, earning 5 to 7 shillings a week; another child with grandmother.
   * Father and Mother both dead; five children, two eldest earning a few shillings each.
   * Father, a sailor, signed off at Sydney, has not been heard of since; Mother left with five children under 11 years.
   * Father dead; Mother, in domestic service, contributes a little towards boy's maintenance.
   * Father suffering from consumption; Mother can hardly earn anything; seven children under the age of 14.

   Mr. Harrison wrote me in a letter dated October 22nd, 1985: "The Forest Hill Industrial Homes were *Homes*, not Schools. At Shaftesbury House and Louise House the children did work (shoemaking and gardening for the boys, laundry work for the girls) which earned money for the Homes, and which might help them to find employment when they left. But for their academic education the children went daily to a school unconnected with the Homes. In the 1870s this was the Christ Church National (that is Church of England) School in Church Vale, Forest Hill. In 1911 it was the Rathfern Road London County Council School in Catford, not far from Shaftesbury House. The teacher who received Korczak was presumably at Rathfern Road School. The Homes were in no way connected with the School Boards, or the Education Act of 1870. They were charitable foundations, supported entirely by private donations, and the income from the work done by the children." In the *Directory of Child Saving Institutions* of these days two homes in the Forest Hill neighbourhood are mentioned: *Shaftesbury House*, a home for boys, founded in 1873, with 40 boys (from 7–10 years of age) and *Louise House*, a girls home, founded in 1881 for 30 girls (age 6–10 years) Both homes were called 'industrial schools'. Korczak mentions a workshop in his article.

Middleton, N. *When Family Failed, The Treatment of Children in the Care of the Community during the First Half of the Twentieth Century*, London, 1971, Victor Gollancz Ltd. Here we read "The staff who stood *in loco parentis* were singularly reluctant to take up any role other than that of the authoritarian. Yet, these were the key people in dealing with children in institutions." See also: Veerman, Philip, E., 'Janusz Korczak and the rights of the child', in: *Concern* (magazine of the National Children's Bureau, London) spring 1987, No. 62, pp. 7–9.

5. Letter to Mieczyclaw Zylbertal, March 30, 1937, in Korczak Archives, Kibbutz Lohamei Haghetaot, Ghetto Fighters House, Israel.
6. These turning points are often called 'epiphanies'. See: Denzin, Norman, K., *Interpretive Interactionism*, Newbury Park, CA, 1989, Sage. Also: Denzin, Norman, K., Interpretive Biography, Newbury Park, CA, 1989, Sage, p. 70. "In epiphanies personal character is manifested. They are often moments of crisis. They alter the fundamental structures in a person's life. Their effects may be positive or negative."
7. This book is not yet published in English. There is a German translation available: Korczak, Janusz. *Das Recht des Kindes auf Achtung*, published by Van Den Hoeck & Ruprecht in Gottingen and Zurich. Parts of this book are also in: Korczak, Janusz, *Selected Works* (edited by Martin Wolins). Warsaw 1967, published for the National Science Foundation in Washington D.C.
8. Korczak, Janusz, *How to Love a Child*, published in Warsaw in 1920. It is not available in English, but is published in Gottingen as *Wie Man ein Kind lieben soll*, 1979.
9. Korczak, Janusz, *If I were young again*. Also not translated in English. There is a German translation: *Wenn Ich Wieder Klein Bin*, published by Van Den Hoeck & Ruprecht.
10. 'The Right to Respect', in: *Selected Works of Janusz Korczak*, Op. cit., p. 487.
11. Idem.
12. Idem, p. 486.
13. Idem, p. 489.
14. Idem, p. 487.
15. Idem, p. 499.
16. Lewin, Aleksander, *Système Moderne de l'éducation et la patrimoine des pédagogues-novateurs*: J. Korczak, A. Makarenko and C. Freivet, Warsaw, 1976, Institut des Recherches Pédagogiques.
17. Korczak, Janusz, *Bankructwo Malego Dzeka*, Warsaw, 1924.
18. *Selected Work of Janusz Korczak*, Op. cit., p. 487.
19. The Right to Respect in: *Selected Works of Janusz Korczak*, Op. cit., p. 493.
20. Idem, p. 471.
21. I do not agree with F.H.O, Rest's interpretation, ('Das Recht des Kindes auf seinen Tod, Die Bedeutung Janusz Korczaks für die Erziehung in der Sterblichkeit', in: Beiner, Friedhelm, *Janusz Korczak, Zweites Wuppertaler Korczak-Kolloquium*, Wuppertal, 1984, Universität-Druck, pp. 221–236). Rest: "Die Kindesrechte sind als Menschenrechte zu verstehen; eine Sterbeerziehung muss wie eine Pädagogik 'zum Tode', zur Erziehung in der Sterblichkeit erweitert, zuendegedacht werden, weil das Sterben nicht Leben beendet, sondern ein Teil des Lebens ist, jener Teil, der dem Leben gehört, seitdem es sich anschickte, Individualität und Geistigkeit hervorzubringen.
22. Korczak, Janusz. *Krol Macius Pierwszy*, Warsaw, 1922. In English: *King Matt the First*, New York, 1986, Farrar, Straus and Giroux. Bettelheim considered the book a Bildungsroman wherein we are told about the emotional, moral and personal development of a hero like Goethe's Wilhelm Meister or Tolland's Jean Christophe.
23. Kahn, Gerard, 'Das Recht des Kindes auf Achtung', in *Schweizer Lehrerzeiting*, 3, February 1988, pp. 5–10.

24. Piziali, Patricia Anne, *A Historical Study of the Origin and Current Status of Child Advocacy Concepts with Particular Attention to the Contributions of Janusz Korczak*, doctoral dissertation, Washington, 1981, The Faculty of the Graduate School of Education and Human Development, the George Washington University.
25. Not many of Korczak's works were available in the English translation in 1980 and 1981.
26. The so-called "Janusz Korczak Declaration of a Child's Rights" (by Miss P. Piziali, 1981):

   * A child has a right to his and her own identity as a person, as a child – a right for the present moment, a right to the present day, and a right to be what he/she is.
   * Any infant, any child born alive has the right to live.
   * A child has a right to a premature death and has a right to die after birth.
   * A child has a right to a family who wants him/her – the child's own family, if possible.
   * A child has a right to the basics of life itself, enough good food and water, clothing, shelter, medical care, love, security.
   * A child has a right to the kind of physical safety and health care for growth and development before and after birth.
   * A child had a right to learn, to be educated about him/herself, the human race, the world – in order to find ways for self-protection, self-support, and ways to live with others in a spirit of peace and universal brotherhood.
   * A child has a right to grow and ripen, to dream and labour at developing knowledge, toil of growth and youthful effort.
   * A child had a right to err, to fail, to criticize, to make demands, to make conditions, to demand respect for grief and tears, to be respected as a child.
   * A child has a right to enjoyment, a right to play, a right to active participation, a right to joy, a right to sorrow, a right to be a child.
   * A child has a right to a name and a nationality from his birth, a right to a caring community and country.
   * A child has a right to a family and friends who can help his/her life and growth.
   * A child has a right to a belief, to truth, to a secret, to a mystery, to justice, freedom, dignity, and equality.
   * A child has a right to professional help for himself/herself and for his/her family to stay and grow together.
   * A child has a right to rehabilitation, if handicapped.
   * A child has a right to a government that protects him/her from neglect, cruelty, and exploitation of any kind.
   * A child has a right to be independent as well as dependent and to become a responsible citizen of his/her community and country.
   * A child has a right to constitutional protection, a right to juvenile justice, a right to speak up, to make complaint, a right to childhood and to respect for the child's intellect.
   * A child has a right to understanding, tolerance, acceptance on the part of all adults and to respect for what the child can become.
   * A child has a right to adult models who demonstrate consideration for others, integrity in living, a desire to work out problems and offenses, a sense of ethical values and most especially compassion and empathy.
   * A child has a right to a peaceful, non-racist world where violence and wars are considered obsolete.
   * A child has a right to enjoy these rights regardless of race, colour, sex, religion, national, and social origin.

27. "Janusz Korczak's Declaration of Children's Rights," (by Betty Jean Lifton, 1988).

   * The child has the right to love. ("Love *the* child, not just your own.")
   * The child has the right to respect. ("Let us demand respect for shining eyes, smooth

foreheads, youthful effort and confidence. Why should dulled eyes, a wrinkled brow, untidy grey hair, or tired resignation command greater respect?")
* The child has the right to optimal conditions in which to grow and develop. ("We demand: do away with hunger, cold, dampness, stench, over-crowding, over-population.")
* The child has the right to live in the present ("Children are not people of tomorrow; they are people today.")
* The child has the right to be himself or herself. ("A child is not a lottery ticket, marked to win the main prize.")
* The child has the right to make mistakes. ("There are no more fools among children than among adults.")
* The child has the right to fail. ("We renounce the deceptive longing for perfect children.")
* The child has the right to be taken seriously. ("Who asks the child for his opinion and consent?")
* The child has the right to be appreciated for what he is. ("The child, being small, has little market value.")
* The child has the right to desire, to claim, to ask. ("As the years pass, the gap between adult demands and children's desires becomes progressively wider.")
* The child has the right to have secrets. ("Respect their secrets.")
* The child has the right to "*a* lie, *a* deception, *a* theft." (He does not have the right to lie, deceive, steal.")
* The child has the right to respect for his possessions and budget. ("Everyone has the right to his property, no matter how insignificant or valueless.")
* The child has the right to education.
* The child has the right to resist educational influence that conflicts with his or her own beliefs. ("It is fortunate for mankind that we are unable to force children to yield to assaults upon their common sense and humanity.")
* The child has the right to protest an injustice. ("We must end despotism.")
* The child has the right to a Children's Court where he can judge and be judged by his peers. ("We are the sole judges of the child's actions, movements, thoughts, and plans . . .I know that a Children's Court is essential, that in fifty years there will not be a single school, not a single institution without one.")
* The child has the right to be defended in the juvenile-justice court system. ("The delinquent child is still a child . . . Unfortunately, suffering bred of poverty spreads like lice: sadism, crime, uncouthness, and brutality are nurtured on it.")
* The child has the right to respect for his grief. ("Even though it be for the loss of a pebble.")
* The child has the right to commune with God.
* The child has the right to die prematurely. ("The mother's profound love for her child must give him the right to premature death, to ending his life cycle in only one or two springs . . .Not every bush grows into a tree.")

28. Lifton, Betty Jean, *The King of Children, A Biography of Janusz Korczak*, New York, 1988, Farrar, Straus and Giroux.
29. Kurzweil, Zvi, Erich, 'Korczak's Educational Writings and the Image of the Child', in *Jewish Education*, Vol. 38, No. 1, January 1968, pp. 19–28.
30. Woloszyn, Stefan, *Korczak*, Warsaw, 1978.
31. *Senat Szalencow*, Warsaw, 1931.
32. I thank Betty Jean Lifton for sharing the transcript of her interview with Professor Woloszyn with me.
33. Szalazakowa, Alicja, *Janusz Korczak*, Warsaw, 1978, Wydawnictwa Szkolne i pedagogicne, p. 30.
34. The *Flying University* was an underground College offering lectures on Polish Culture. Since the Czar considered this to be a danger, the location had to be changed for each lecture.
35. See: Kulawiec, Edwin, P., 'Janusz Korczak Physician -Humanitarian', in: *JAMA, Journal*

of the American Medical Association, May 10, 1979, Vol.241, No. 20, pp. 2165-2166, and: Ströder, I., 'Der Arzt als Erzieher des Kindes': zur Verleihung des Korczak – Preises an Professor Halikowski', in *Pädagogische Rundschau*, 34, 1980, No. 7, July, pp. 437-443.

36. Bellerate, Bruno, 'Janusz Korczak e Jean Jacques Rousseau: Punti di Convergenza e Motivi di un Rifiuto', in: Universita degli studi di Roma 'La Spienza', *Annali del Dipartimento di Scienze dell'Educazione*, 5, 1983, pp. 259-271. I thank Professor Bellerate for our interesting discussion in Rome at the Salesiano University in June 1984.
37. Cornaz-Besson, Jacqueline, 'Les Affinités entre Korczak it Pestalozzi', in: Actes du Colloque de Geneva, *Janusz Korczak l'homme, le médecin, l'éducateur, le poète*, Geneva, 1982, A la Bacconière, pp. 65-76.
38. Veerman, Philip, E. 'Het Weeshuis van Korczak, een oase in Warsaw, in *Sjow-Tijdschrift voor Jeugdbescherming en Jeugdwelzijn*, 1983, No. 1/2, Vol. 11, pp. 38-42. Pestalozzi wrote this in the letter from Stanz. Published in: *Pestalozzi über seine Anstalt in Stanz*, Weinheim/Berlin/Basel, 1971, Verlag Julius Beltz, mit einer Interpretation von Wolfgang Klafki.
39. In the Korczak Archives of Kibbutz Lohamei Haghetaot in Israel. I thank Mr. Reuven Jatziv for helping me with the translation from the Polish.
40. His *Children of the Street* (Warsaw, 1901) and the *Child of the Drawing Room* (Warsaw, 1906) was already a success.
41. Veerman, Philip, E. 'In the Shadow of Janusz Korczak; The Story of Stefania Wilczynska', in *The Melton Journal*, No. 23, Spring 1990, pp. 8-9.
42. Letter to the author of Claire-Lise L'homme, of the *Université de Geneva*, February 4, 1986. I thank Mrs. L'homme and the rector of the University for their help.
43. Merzan, Ida, *Pan Doktór i Pani Stefa*, Warsaw, 1979. I thank Mrs. Alla Raviv in Jerusalem for translating most of this book from the Polish for me.
44. Letter of Stefania Wilczynska to Feiga Lipshitz (in Archives of Kibbutz Lohamei Haghetaot). Feiga Lipshitz worked at the time in a Children's Home in Bialystok under very difficult circumstances.
45. Watt, Richard, M., *Bitter Glory, Poland and Its Fate* 1918 *to* 1939, New York 1979, Simon and Schuster, pp. 60-61.
46. During a typhus epidemic in 1920 Korczak works in an isolation hospital on Kamiona Street. There he contracts the disease. His mother takes care of him. She also contracts the disease and dies. Korczak becomes very depressed.
47. Szlazakowa, Alicja, *Janusz Korczak*, Op. cit., p. 46.
48. Korczak, Janusz, How to Love a Child, in: *Selected Works of Janusz Korczak*, Op. cit., p. 405.
49. Newerly, Igor, *Zywe Wiczanie*, Warsaw, 1978.
50. Frost, Shimon, 'Janusz Korczak: Friend of Children', in: *Moral Education Forum*, Vol. 8, No. 1, Spring 1983, p. 14.
51. The policy of *Dom Sierot* was to admit half-orphans if, for instance their mother had five other children at home, or if the mother was sick and could not take care of her children. Korczak, however, hardly ever admitted children with severe behavioural disturbances.
52. Letter (dated December 8, 1985) to the author by Mr. Ignacy Cukierman in Montreal, Quebec, Canada. I thank the Canadian Jewish Congress for contacting Mr. Cukierman for me.
53. Dodiuk, Jacques, 'Les Années Heureuses dans la Maison de l'Orphelin' in: *Informations UNESCO*, No. 734/735, Paris, 1978 (in English published in: *UNESCO Features*, 1978, No. 734/735). I thank Mr. Dodiuk for the interview in Paris on October 24, 1982.
54. Interview with Simone Kowal in Paris, held for the author by Salomè Cahen-Burckhardt on August 15, 1987.
55. Interview by the author with Arie Sadè in Beersheva, Israel, 1985.
56. Interview by the author with Israel (Srulek) Szwarzberg in Rechovot, Israel, September 2, 1985.
57. Mortkowicz-Olczakowa, Hanna, *Janusz Korczak, Artz und Pädagoge*, Weimar, 1961, Mun-

ich and Salzburg, 1967, Anton Pustet Verlag, p. 127; in English: *Mister Doctor, The Life of Janusz Korczak*, London, 1965, p. 112.
58. Korczak, Janusz, 'The Child's Right to Respect' in: *Selected Works of Janusz Korczak*, Op. cit., p. 458.
59. Interview with Izak Skalka, in Tel Aviv on September 23, 1985. Mr. Skalka showed me a photography of ten children. It was glued to a piece of cardboard. On the back were stamped the words "Samorzad Domu Sierot", Self-government of Dom Sierot. It was a momentum of his participation in the self-government in 1934 and 1935.
60. Interview by the author with G. Mandelblatt on July 18, 1988, in Brighton Beach (New York City).
61. Mortkowicz-Olczakowa, Hanna, *Mister Doctor*, Op. cit. Alicja Szlazakowa (*Janusz Korczak*, Warsaw, 1978, p. 74) gives as the *civic categories* in *Our Home* comrade, inhabitant, indifferent inhabitant and difficult newcomer.
62. Interview with Ada Hagari-Poznanska in 1985 in Kibbutz Giv'at Haim.
63. Interview with Jochevet Cuk on August 26, 1985, in Rehovot, Israel.
64. There are several such notebooks in the Archives of Kibbutz Lohamei Haghetaot.
65. Sachs, Shimon and Plotkin, Ronit, Stefa, *The Woman behind Korczak*, (in Hebrew), Tel Aviv, 1988, Papyrus.
66. Letter to Feiga Lipshitz (in the Archives of Lohamei Haghetaot).
67. Interview with Shlomo Nadel on July 29, 1982, in Ramle, Israel.
68. Hellinckx, W. and Pauwels, I., *Orthopedagogische Ontwikkelingen in de Kinderbescherming; Leven en Werk van Dr. D.Q.R. Mulock Houwer*, Louvain/Amersfoort, 1984, Acco. Interview of Dr. Mulock Houwer by the author on October 30, 1982, and second interview on June 20, 1984. Dr. Mulock Houwer was from 1957–1967 Secretary General of the World Union for Child Welfare in Geneva. In the 1920s Mulock Houwer also experimented with self-government and court systems. He gives a nice example (in *Het Tijdschrift voor Ervaringsopvoedkunde*, 1928, Vol. 7, pp. 329–330 in his article 'rechtsspraak door kinderen'). "A judge between 9 and 12 years of age who addresses a furiously stampeding accused with: "In this place you are expected to behave. Go outside and calm yourself," shows an amazingly relaxed and assertive behaviour which may make many an adult envious.
69. Dyck, Van, David and Cyck, Van, Roxa, 'George Junior Republic; A Fresh Start for Troubled Teens', in *A Journal of the New York State School Boards Association, Inc.*, November 1983, pp. 16–17. Also: Engelen, Clara, (Jonkvrouw), 'An American Children's Republic', in: *Tijdschrift voor Armenzorg en Kinderbescherming*, 1908, pp. 170–172 and pp. 174–176. Also Know, William, E., *Notes on Social Life in the George Junior Republic*, 1967, found in the William R. George and George Junior Republic Papers, Department of Manuscripts and University Archives, Cornell University Libraries, Ithaca, New York).
70. Letter to the author from Luba Gilinsky (former co-worker of the Medem Sanatorium), now living in Los Angeles, CA. Also interview with Mr. Luden, former pupil of the Medem Sanatorium, made in Tel Aviv on September 26, 1985.
71. Schäfer, Walter, *Paul Geheeb, Aus den Deutschen Landerziehungsheimen*, Stuttgart, sine anno, Ernst Klett Verlag. Also Popta, Van, W.M., *De Landerziehungsheime (New Schools), Geschiedenis, Ontwikkeling en Betekenis*, Amsterdam, 1929, H.I. Paris. Interview with Dr. Erich Steinitz on June 10, 1987, in Jerusalem. Dr. Steinitz worked as a chemistry teacher in the Odenwaldschule from 1926 till 1929. He tells about the beautiful surroundings and the ski hikes. A regular topic was whether or not the beautiful surroundings would spoil the children. See also: Kurzweil, Zvi Erich, *Vorläufer Progressiver Erziehung*, Ratingen/Kastellaun/ Dusseldorf, 1974, A. Henn Verlag. Chapter 6 describes the Odenwaldschule and Chapter 8 the work of Korczak.
72. Bruno Bettelheim was right when he pointed out in the introduction to the English translation of *King Matt the First*, that the pediatrician Goldszmit (Korczak) was convinced that children must have the right to govern themselves, and that he was an ardent pleader for children's rights. But he was wrong when he added that 'liberation' (in the modern sense of John Holt and Richard Farson) was one of Korczak's goals. Also René Görtzen (*Weg*

met de Opvoeding, Meppel/Amsterdam, 1984, Boom) only distils those elements out of Korczak's work which create the impression that he was a *Kiddie Libber*. This was definitely not the case.

73. Dietz, Gerhard, 'Kinder und Erwachsene als Partner; Eine Darstellung das besonderen erzieherischen Verhältnisses bei Janusz Korczak', in: *Vierteljahrsschrift für Wiss. Pädagogik*, No. 61, 1985, pp. 242–263.
74. In the Archives of Kibbutz Lohamei Haghetaot.
75. In the underground archives of the Warsaw Ghetto (Emmanuel Ringelblum, *Ksovim fun getto*) in the Archives of Yad Vashem (The Holocaust Martyrs and Heroes Remembrance Authority in Jerusalem).
76. Interview by the author with Regina Itkin (born Arzylewicz), sister of Rozka, in Akko, Israel, on September 2, 1985. Rozka worked in Dom Sierot.
77. Testimony sent to me by Mrs. Chava Kempinski (born Hurowitz). This letter is now in the archives of Yad Vashem.

CHAPTER VIII

Modern Pioneers

By the late 1960s the time was ripe for new organisations which aimed at child advocacy. In their 1972 report on *Child Advocacy*[1] by Kahn and others, the following claim was made: "Child advocacy appeared during such an era of social reform.... The concept was attractive because it combined the promise of needed change with a lack of specificity; i.e., it represented a kind of social venture capital. It was soon identified as an activity that might be financed. Thus child advocacy understandably took many forms and had many sponsors. It was a banner behind which to rally, a funding bandwagon on which to ride, and a gimmick to exploit. But it also represented a series of efforts to cope with children's unmet needs in the following ways: affirming new concepts of legal entitlements; offering needed services in areas where none existed; persisting in the provision of services when other more conventional programs dropped cases; assuring access to entitlements and help; mediating between children or families and institutions such as schools, health facilities and courts; and facilitating self-organization among deprived community groups, adolescents, parents, or parents of handicapped children.... A new development such as child-advocacy focuses on goals and structure before it specifies techniques."[2]

Some of the projects researched by Kahn and his colleagues have in the meantime disappeared. Today, less than twenty years after the book was published, it looks remarkably old-fashioned.

In Europe new organisations and institutions (such as Ombudsmen)-emerged. Miek de Langen says that "the central and new approach at the end of this Century of the Child is to regard children as people with their own thoughts, wishes, potentials and experiences rather than as not-yet-grown-ups, which has been the dominant view in this century, where the emphasis was often put on dependence, vulnerability and inexperience, or briefly the aspect of 'not-yet-hood'."[3]

In this chapter we shall discuss five new strategies in working for children's rights:

* Creating an official spokes-person for children;
* Class action suits;
* Providing information about the legal position of children and trying to improve it;
* Lobbying for children;
* Building an international movement.

1. *An Official Spokes-Person for Children*

A strategy that has proven effective in the fight against bureaucracy is the appointment of an *Ombudsman*. The concept 'Ombudsman' is of Scandinavian origin. However, in this particular work for children the title 'Ombudsman for Children' is not used in Norway.[4] It is officially translated as 'Commissioner for Children'.

In Norway there are four million inhabitants including one million children and adolescents. Bratholm and Matheson[5], both Norwegians, are of the opinion that "although the Norwegian welfare state has taken giant steps forward during the last decades, children seem in some respects to have become the victims of the welfare state and the adult portion of the population appears to have gained many of its benefits at the expense of children." This explained the urgency of a 'Commissioner for Children'.[6] The first Ombudsperson, Malfrid Grude Flekkøy, a child psychologist, was appointed in 1981. The present Ombudsman is a young physician, Trond Viggo Torgersen, who appears often on television in a special program.

In the *Norway Information*[7] we read that "the task of the Commissioner for Children is to assess the impact of the societal situation on the conditions under which children grow up, and promote the interests of children both in the public and the private sectors."

The 'Commissioner for Children' in Norway can build on democratic values[8] and has the following tasks:

a) To initiate or to hear instances involving the protection of the rights and interests of children in connection with planning and study-reports in all fields;
b) To ensure that legislation relating to the protection of children's interests is observed;
c) To propose measures which can strengthen children's safety under the law;
d) To put forward proposals for measures which can solve or prevent conflicts between children and society;
e) To ensure that sufficient information is given to the public and private sectors concerning children's rights and measures required for children.

The most important feature of the Norwegian Commissioner for Children is political independence. He or she has the right and the obligation to criticise any administrative level, any group, organisation or person who disregards the interests of children, regardless of political or other considerations. When, for instance, Mrs. Flekkøy opposed new regulations for nursery schools and kindergartens, many municipalities based their decisions on her informative statement.[9]

The Office receives approximately 2000 requests, inquiries, and complaints per year. Some of the problems are raised more than once. The number of unduplicated cases, over six years, including those raised by the Ombudsperson herself, totals approximately 4500. Ten percent of the cases were referred by children.[10]

Some of the matters that bother children would never have been noticed by adults. As a simple example Mrs Flekkøy mentions in a letter to me that she pleaded for more respect for children by shop keepers. No shop keeper would offer an adult chocolate instead of money as a refund for empty bottles, but this happens regularly to children.[11]

In Finland and Sweden there is no legislation concerning a Children's Ombudsman. In Helsinki, Finland, the work is carried out by a lawyer at the Mannerheim League for Child Welfare. There are some 300-400 cases yearly.[12] His task is not to be an official spokesman for children, but to give children free legal information and legal aid.

Marten Stenberg[13] of the Swedish Children's Rights Committee wrote me that Sweden does not have State employed Children's Ombudsmen. However, two Non-Governmental Organisations, Rädda Barnen and BRIS[14] employ Ombudsmen to whom a child can phone or write if he or she is unhappy in a particular situation or if there are problems in the relations with his or her guardian. In 1970 Rigmor von Euler became the first 'Children's Ombudsman' in Sweden. Mrs Von Euler had been a school counsellor and was particularly interested in the problems of child abuse and neglect. She has taken up issues such as abuse and neglect, children in hospitals, and violence in the mass media. Today there are four children's Ombudsmen on Rädda Barnen's staff, each specialising in a different area: (1) child abuse and neglect, (2) problems of immigrant children, (3) problems of refugee children, and (4) problems of children in hospitals, the handicapped, and issues in parenthood education. The Ombudsmen focus on public awareness campaigns, education and financial support for research on children[15], and also act as a link between ordinary people and the 'bureaucrats'. A successor to Mrs. Von Euler, Ombudsman Bo Carlsson, explains that his work is less focused on raising the position of children in general, and more on specific issues: "If someone knows a neighbour is beating his child, but is reluctant to contact the authorities, he will come to me and I act as an intermediary."[16]

From Scandinavia the concept 'Ombudsman' has travelled to other parts of the world. In 1984 the *Minister of Community and Social Services* of the Province Ontario in Canada proposed an Act in the Ontario Legislature. According to the Minister himself this proposal for the *Child and Family*

Services Act was "one of the finest pieces of social legislation in North America."[17] The *Child and Family Services Act* gave the Minister the opportunity officially to establish an *Office of Child and Family Service Advocacy*. The office had already been in operation on an experimental base since 1978, with the goal of protecting the rights and interests of children in Ontario.[18]

The 1984 law[19] mentions that the tasks of this office are, among others, "to co-ordinate and administer a system of advocacy, except for advocacy before a court, on behalf of children and families who receive or seek approved services or services purchased by approved agencies; and to advise the Minister on matters and issues concerning the interests of those children and families."

Les Horne who manages the small office in Toronto says: "*Rights of the Child* is a broad concept. By occupying ourselves mainly with child protection-children's law we could at least be effective in a certain sector. Thus we can at least see to it that in a certain institution the mail of the pupils is not opened any more."[20]

Elsewhere in the *Ontario Child and Family Services Act*[21] the task of the office in relation to the *children in care* is even more detailed. It is stated that children in care have, for instance, the right to receive visitors privately. Besides the right to receive relatives on a regular base the child may also receive a member of the Canadian Parliament, the legislature of Ontario, the child's lawyer or someone else who represents the child.

In a brochure for young people, Les Horne's *Office of Child and Family Service Advocacy* explains what his office can do for children and adolescents.[22]

"*There is an office at Queen's Park in Toronto called 'The Office of Child and Family Advocacy'. In that office, we can't care for you like the people you live with care for you. We can't listen to complaints about the things that worry you like they can. If you don't like supper, think that your bed is too hard, or haven't been able to visit your family lately, there are ways to complain and to be heard in the place where you live. But . . . sometimes very bad things happen and it is impossible to get help by the usual methods of dealing with complaints. That is when you should write them down or have someone do it for you, and send them to us at the Office of Child and Family Advocacy.*"

Every month at least twenty-five complaints reach the office. All the complaints are dealt with. Horne and his staff approach every complaint as realistically as possible. "We have trained ourselves to listen well," says Horne[23] "We see it as our task to make people elsewhere in the system react to what we throw in their laps. We want to work as little bureaucratically as possible.[24] We are a small group and instead of sending letters and writing reports we travel all over Ontario."

"Are you not afraid," we asked Les Horne, "that the only function of your office is to make the government institutions run more smoothly?"

"We have been created to that end," he said. "But we do not smooth out things if we think that in the interest of children they deserve the attention of the opposition in parliament. I do not exist to make life easier for the Minister."

Says the journalist Prudence Whiddington: "Les Horne's effective but quiet success in his role as Ontario's child and family advocate can be attributed in part to his personality, and in part to his years of experience with all sorts of conditions and people. It is not easy to fool Les Horne. Nor is it easy to argue against the carefully weighed suggestions and comments that are his way of unfurling the safety net of child and family advocacy."[25]

In another part of Canada, British Columbia, the Provincial Ombudsman Stephen Owen announced in 1987 the appointment of Brent Parfitt as a special Deputy Ombudsman for Children and Youth. "This new position represents a recognition of the special vulnerabilities and needs of children in our society," wrote Owen.[26]

Les Horne works in a Ministry, but in British Columbia the Ombudsman for Children is politically independent like his model in Norway.[27] Brent Parfitt[28] thinks that "co-ordination is the key to success in helping young people in their dealings with the government... and that youngsters have to learn how to complain." However, a pamphlet published by his office[29] warns youngsters: "We will not automatically take your side of the issue, but we shall try to make sure that you are being treated fairly. So, if you have a problem and you can't find a solution, maybe we can help."

Co-ordination is also one of the most important tasks of the *Defensor de la Infancia*[30] in Costa Rica. In September 1988 Mario A. Viquez Jimenez, appointed by decree[31], took the oath before the President of Costa Rica, Dr. Oscar Arias Sánchez. Unfortunately, the Ombudsman for Children of Costa Rica ran into some problems and the office lost some independence.

Between September 1986 and December 1989 Dr. Menachem Horovitz worked as the Ombudsman of the Jerusalem Council for Children and Youth.[32] However, he did not limit his work to Jerusalem. This experimental project was made possible by the Dutch philanthropist Oscar van Leer. The project had three objectives.[33]

a) To receive complaints/requests from children, youth, parents, institutions and the general public in any area that affects the rights of children.
b) To expose problem areas in legislation, welfare services and other institutions which have a negative effect on the interests and rights of children and youth.
c) To publicize information on the rights of children and youth.

Dr. Horovitz considered it most important to work less bureaucratically than most offices. Within 24 hours of receiving a letter he would take up contact, report on findings and sometimes receive clients personally. This was quite different from the proceedings in many government offices. Indeed,

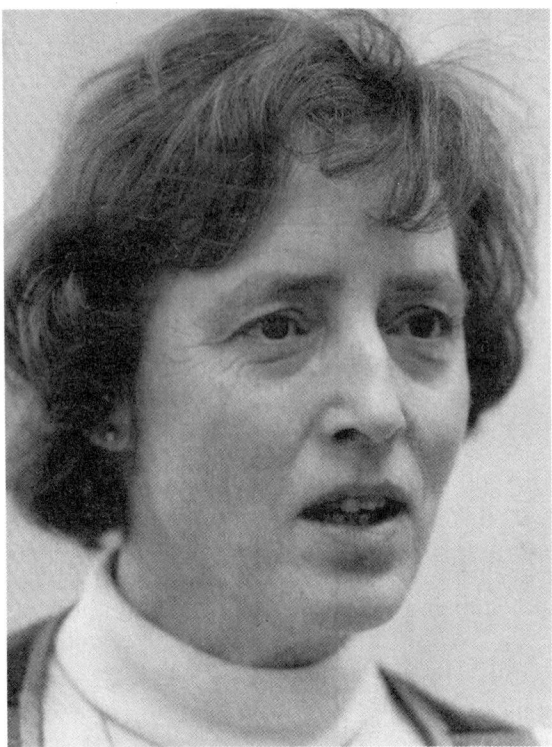

Picture VIII.1. Malfrid Grude Flekkøy, Norwegian Ombudsman for Children 1981–1989.
(Photo: Rolf Soler/Nationen.)

many complaints Dr. Horovitz received dealt with letters unanswered by officials. The Ombudsman of Jerusalem made a point of taking *every* complaint seriously. Thus a patient in a mental hospital once drew his attention to the fact that a certain factory employed children in the evenings. The complaint proved to be fully justified and the Ministry of Labour and Social Affairs sued the factory.[34]

Forty percent of the cases that reached Dr. Horovitz related to child welfare, thirty percent to education. Many schools broke the rules, for instance by suspending pupils without conforming to the official proceedings. Dr. Horovitz urged the Teachers' Unions to establish a *Code of Ethics for Teachers*. However, thus far nothing has been done in this field.

Although an Ombudsman for Children was obviously needed, the Jerusalem Pilot Project ended in December 1989[35]. The *Ministry of Education and Culture*[36] and the *Council for the Child in Placement*[37] have both appointed their own Ombudsperson.

Mr. Avraham Ben-Hador, a retired Juvenile Judge, investigates complaints made by children and child-care workers about problems in children's residential institutions, ranging from improper placement to sexual abuse. It seems the foundations are being laid for an official and politically independent

Picture VIII. 2. Menachem Horovitz, Ombudsman for Children in Jerusalem from 1986–December 1989.

Ombudsman for Children in Israel. To this purpose Parliament Member Dedi Zucker presented a Private Member's Bill.[38]

In other countries, too, initiatives to establish Ombudsmen for Children are being developed.[39] In the state South Australia a Children's Interests Bureau has been established in Adelaide. In 1990 the Province of Vienna in Austria appointed a social worker and a psychologist to work as Ombudsmen. The German State North-Rhine Westphalia appointed an Ombudsman for children (who is a civil servant of the Ministry of Social Affairs in Dusseldorf). In New Zealand, an Ombudsman, Ian Hassall, the *Commissioner for Children*, started his work recently too.

It appears that "people have become more and more aware that if there is no one to whom the citizen can turn with feelings of injustice, the gap between the government and the governed is likely to grow. This may create a build-up of sullen resentment of authority which is detrimental to progress and development in society."[40] Ombudsmen for Children can represent a 'human element' in our ever-growing bureaucracies and complex organisations.[41] It is our opinion that their effectiveness will increase as they become more independent without, however, losing their official status. To make an ombudsman's office part of a Ministry is therefore against the idea of the ombudsman's office.

All Ombudsmen are trying to strike a balance between the child and the social-institutional environment. We can, therefore, classify Ombudswork for children's rights in the *adaptive mode* of the *social subsystem*.

2. *Class Action Suits*

A strategy which is well developed in the United States is 'class advocacy'. Although a 'class' is represented by an individual case, the outcome of the court's decision creates precedents of which other individuals belonging to that 'class', will benefit.[42] The Masters of this art are the staff-members of the San Francisco based Youth Law Center. The story of the Center shows how in the United States litigation can bring about changes.

The Youth Law Center is a private, non-profit, public-interest law office, headed by attorney Mark Soler, and dedicated to the protection of the rights of minors. Since 1978 the Center has provided legal education, advice, counsel, representation, and technical assistance all over the United States. Staffed by seven attorneys, the Center is equipped to respond quickly and effectively to requests for assistance from state and local officials, community groups, parents and attorneys. The Center has brought successful litigation on behalf of children. In addition these activities "raise the level of public awareness of the vulnerable status of children and the need for constant vigilance for their protection"[43] Mark Soler told me[44] that the threat of litigation is so powerful that changes are often made immediately after the Youth Law Center takes its first steps in that direction. The fact that changes can be accomplished out of fear of being sued is probably unique to the judicial system of the United States. Authorities often agree to implement the changes proposed by experts, if the Youth Law Center agrees not to sue. Class action suits, although an 'American speciality', are not popular with the judges. The Youth Law Center therefore often demands that a judge visit a controversial facility and inspect the conditions in person.

The Youth Law Center publishes[45] the results so that all parties concerned and the public at large will know the decision of the court. Thus chances are high that people will turn to the Youth Law Center if the decisions are not implemented.

When we look at some of the class action cases, we see that the Center has been most successful in cases concerning jails.

In the case of *Hunt v. County of Los Angeles*, for instance, a lawsuit was brought against the County of Los Angeles and the Los Angeles Sheriff's Department for locking up children in the Lennox Sheriff's Sub-Station where there was sight and sound contact with adult inmates.

The Youth Law Center has brought similar suits to the courts: in *Baumgartner v. City of Long Beach*[46] a lawsuit was brought against the County of Los Angeles, the City of Long Beach, and the Los Angeles Department of Children's Services for allowing the incarceration of thousands of children each year in the Long Beach Adult Jail.

Another lawsuit, filed in May 1989, charged that the State Youth Authority failed to provide adequate services for handicapped youths confined at the Northern Reception Center-Clinic in Sacramento. The lawsuit, *Nick O. v.Terhune*, was filed as a class action by the Youth Law Center of San Francisco on behalf of a Bay Area youth in the United States District Court of Sacramento.[47] The suit[48] alleges that the California Youth Authority is violating federal law by routinely failing to assess special education needs and failing to develop and implement individualised education plans for youth confined at home.

Largely because of the Youth Law Center's efforts things are beginning to change for the 479,000 children who, according to the United States Department of Justice, are held in adult jails each year.[49] Soler's top priority is to put an end to unnecessary incarcerations. He is also interested in abuses at State-run Reform schools and in foster-care.

Since the intention of class action suits is to improve conditions of youth in general, we cannot classify them in Shye's 'Systemic Quality of Life Model'.

3. Providing information about the legal position of children and working for improvement

In the Netherlands a unique approach was developed by the so-called 'Children's Law Shops'. The first such center of legal aid for children opened in Amsterdam in 1985 in an old shop, with the intention to create a low threshold for children and youngsters. 'Law Shops' for adults have existed in the Netherlands since the sixties. In these offices people of the lower income classes who are sometimes afraid to enter a law firm, can receive help with problems such as writing an official letter etc. A brochure explains the idea behind such a 'shop' for children:

"The 'Children's Law Shop" is not just another shop where you can buy all kind of things. It is an office where children can talk to adults who are familiar with the laws children sometimes have to deal with. There are many rules for children, their parents or guardians and family. Children may want to know things about divorce, guardianship, adoption, somebody's will etc."

The brochure further explains to youngsters what it has to offer. *"Perhaps you are the victim or the cause of a traffic accident. What should you do in case of damage. Or maybe your ball has hit a window. When you go to school there are certain rules. What about compulsory education? Punishment, suspension, expulsion? What is possible and what is allowed? Is there some-*

Picture VIII. 3. Elisabeth Jameson and Mark Soler of the Youth Law Center in San Francisco. (Photo: Susan Gilbert.)

thing you would like to know about children's homes, running away, obtaining a residence permit (for foreign children), maltreatment, scholarships? In the Children's Law Shop you can ask whatever you want to know about law."[50]

The brochure further explains:

* by telling you exactly what the situation is and how the law applies to your case;
* by writing, together with you, a letter, to a family member, the school, the police, a store or firm, in order to explain a case clearly and tell those concerned your opinion;
* by accompanying you to, for instance, the police, a family member, a Juvenile Court's Magistrate, a school or a children's home and, together with you, explain a case or clear up a situation;
* by helping you, if legally possible, to submit your case before the judge. Usually, however, this is very complicated;
* The 'Children's Law Shop' will see to it that you receive the rights you are entitled to.
* The 'Children's Law Shop' can assist in questions about rights and laws.

Poublon and Kloosterboer[51] give a nice example of the way these people work with youngsters: "Frank has secured a temporary job for three weeks in a store during the school holidays. On the Friday before he is due to begin, the store owner phones and says that his store will be closed for renovations and Frank will not be able to start work until a week later. Thus he will work only two weeks. Frank goes to the 'Children's Law Shop'. The assistant on duty helps Frank to write a letter to the store owner, wherein he points out that, since he knew only on Friday that he could not start working on Monday as planned, he did not have the time to find another job. The Children's Law Shop requested compensation. Within a week Frank received a letter wherein the store owner offered his excuses and promised to comply."

Today five *Children's Law Shops* are operating in the Netherlands and one in Belgium. Since their aim is to improve the social status of youngsters, we classify their work in the *adaptive mode* of the *social subsystem*.

4. *Lobbying for Children*

The most successful children's lobby at a national level is, in our opinion, the American *Children's Defense Fund* (CDF) in Washington D.C. Many interest groups have their lobbies as close as possible to Capitol Hill.[52] Since children cannot lobby for themselves the CDF has taken this task upon itself.

According to its president, Marian Wright Edelman, the CDF was formed "in order to help policy makers, other adults and social agencies understand and better serve the needs of all children."[53] The CDF is a non-profit organisation of lawyers, federal policy monitors, researchers, and community liaison people dedicated to long-range systematic advocacy and reform on behalf of children. The CDF seeks to improve the conditions of children through public information, research, administrative agency monitoring, litigation, and through technical back-up to local groups working with children.

The CDF is in some respects doing the same work as the Youth Law Center (litigation), but the CDF specialisation is their combination of different strategies: They use not only litigation, but also monitoring, proposing model legislation, making publicity which may provoke congressional hearings, organising local efforts and providing other actions that may lead to change. The CDF staff is of the opinion that "many of the changes that are required are matters of data collection."[54] Another method of the CDF is asking the right questions, for instance why existing policies on a certain subject are not enforced.

Staff member of the CDF James D. Weill[55] writes: "We are working to make sure that all American children get the basic food, shelter, health care, education, child care and parenting they need to grow up healthy and with full development of their potential."

From its start in 1973 the CDF focused on

1. the exclusion of children from school;
2. the classification and treatment of children with special needs;
3. the use of children in medical (particularly drug) research and experimentation;
4. the child's right to privacy in the face of growing computerisation and data banks;
5. a reform of the juvenile justice system;
6. child development and day care.

More recently the CDF is trying to develop long-term media campaigns run by hired media specialists.

The United States federal investment in areas of health, family income, homelessness and housing, nutrition, education, child care, etc. are yearly examined by the CDF. The results are published.[56]

When I visited the CDF in Washington D.C. in May 1988, I understood that adolescent pregnancy and homelessness are new areas of special concern. All in all the most important task of the CDF is to put pressure on members of the United States Federal Congress, the Senate and State Legislations, so that laws are made and enforced that will promote the quality of life of children.

Since the CDF is trying to improve the quality of life for all children in the United States in general, its work cannot be classified in the 'Systemic Quality of Life Model'.

5. Building an International Movement for Children's Rights

In 1979 Nigel Cantwell, a former English probation-officer, tried to interest the International Union for Child Welfare (IUCW) in Geneva in undertaking activities related to children's rights. The IUCW, however, told Mr. Cantwell that it could not take a stand on children's rights issues.[57] Human Rights Organisations did not want to become more involved with children's rights either, not even after activities preparing the International Year of the Child (1979) showed that in addition to the well-known tragedies of famine, malnutrition and related maladies, children are often detained arbitrarily or in deplorable conditions, tortured, arbitrarily separated from their families, and discriminated against by reason of race, sex, colour or religion.[58]

In order to promote and protect the rights of children Nigel Cantwell organised a group of founders of the *Defence for Children*. He obtained the co-operation of such influential people as Canon Joseph Moerman (Secretary General of the International Catholic Child Bureau and 'father' of the International Year of the Child) and André Dunant (Vice-President of the International Association of Family Court Magistrates).

On July 5, 1979, *Defence for Children* was constituted in Geneva as a

Picture VIII.4. Marian Wright Edelman of the Children's Defense Fund (1987). (Photo: Rick Reinhard.)

Non-Profit Association under the Swiss Civil Code. Its founding committee consisted of thirteen members from eleven countries.

In the first years of its existence *Defence for Children* focused mainly on individual cases, such as child abduction by one parent to another country. The new human rights group for children also campaigned for the release of a mother in the Philippines, detained together with her two children (aged eighteen months and three years). The mother had been arrested for political reasons without being charged. As a result of this campaign the mother was acquitted by the court and released with her children.

While *Defence for Children* (since 1982 called *Defence for Children International* or DCI) was working on the case of the two Philippine children, it emerged that practically no literature was available on children in prison, written from the point of view of the best interests of the child.[59] The DCI General Assembly therefore decided to undertake a world-wide study on the situation of children incarcerated with adults. Besides collecting information on the subject DCI asked forty individuals in different countries to carry out in-depth investigations and provide national reports. The DCI Exploratory Study on children in Adult Prisons was the first world-wide attempt at a systematic analysis of the fate of children imprisoned with adults. Research and information-gathering activities confirmed the initial assumption: imprisonment of children in adult prisons is a universal phenomenon. A book

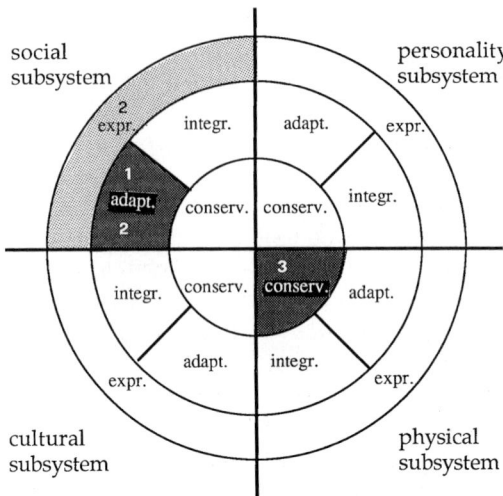

Fig. 8.1. The work of Ombudsmen (1), the Children's Law centers (2), and Defence for Children International (3), interpreted by the Systemic Quality of Life Model.

edited by Katarina Tomasevski[60], based on this material, was published in 1986.

In 1983, after the formation of the Working Group of Non-Governmental Organisations for the United Nations Convention on the Rights of the Child, DCI established a secretariat for the N.G.O.-group.

In June 1984 *Amnesty International* (British Section) sponsored a meeting of organisations interested in discussing the need for establishing *rules* for the treatment of children deprived of their liberty. This subject fell within the field of concern of the new organisation.[61] Thus DCI became more and more involved in setting standards and less and less in individual cases.

Since DCI's participation in the meetings of a special Commission of the Hague Conference on Private International Law in June 1990, DCI is pressing for a new Convention on inter-country adoption.[62]

Among the concerns of DCI are child labour, trafficking and sale of children for prostitution, the rights of abandoned children, the rights of refugee children, the rights of children of indigenous peoples, involuntary 'disappearances', extra-judicial executions, slavery, arbitrary detention. It appears that children are spared none of these violations of human rights. However, attention was all too often reserved for adult victims. A major component of DCI's mandate[63], is to reveal the specific nature of the violation of children's rights, wherever they occur.

Members of DCI are entitled to participate in activities, such as group work and letter-writing campaigns, and to attend the movement's International General Assembly (held once every three years). DCI has today about one thousand members (as compared to *Amnesty International* with 200,000 members).[64]

Although DCI has not yet found a formula to 'exploit' the fact that it is a world-wide movement, it has created many national sections and has a great potential towards becoming a powerful lobby-group for children's rights.

The structure of DCI is more complicated than that of *Amnesty International* (where sections only work for other countries, never for their own). DCI sections will have to choose between playing the part of action groups (and not being taken very seriously by authorities), or attracting 'establishment figures' in their boards who can influence governments but will tone down the critical voice of the section itself.

DCI writes reports and undertakes missions, such as investigating the situation of children deprived of their liberty in Turkey.[65] Unfortunately the International Secretariat of DCI in Geneva as well as its Sections operate on a weak financial basis.

Since it is still a relatively small movement, the importance of work of its Sections remains often unnoticed.

Most of DCI's main concerns deal with extreme child maltreatment and the safety of the child. They belong in the *conservative mode* of the *physical subsystem*.

Conclusion

The future will show whether or not the five strategies[66] described in this Chapter are examples of new social developments. It is my impression that the work of the modern pioneers is striking roots. However, much will depend on the seriousness of their commitments.

NOTES

1. Kahn, Alfred, J., Kamerman, Sheila, B., McGowan, Brenda,G., *Child Advocacy, Report of a national baseline study*, New York, 1972, Columbia University School of Social Work, p. 9.
2. Idem, p. 122.
3. Langen, de, Mieke, 'Children's Rights', in: Verhellen, E. and Spiesschaert, F., eds. Ombudswork for Children, A way of *Improving the Position of Children in Society*, Louvain/Amersfoort, 1989, Acco, pp. 481–493.
4. Flekkøy, Malfrid Grude: 'The *Ombudsman* for Children: The needs of young consumers – information, communication, legislation,', Oslo, report, sine anno, p. 2.
5. Bratholm, Anders and Matheson, Wilhelm, 'The Rights of the Child in Norway', in: Pappas, Anna Mamalakis, *Law and the Status of the Child*, New York, 1979, UNITAR (United Nations Institute for Training and Research), Vol.2, p. 537.
6. Barne ombudet (Commissioner for Children), *Working for the Rights of the Child*, report, Oslo, sine anno, p. 9.

7. The Royal Norwegian Ministry of Foreign Affairs, 'Commissioner for Children in Norway', *Norway Information*, Oslo, UDA/141/83/ENG, September 1983. See also: Flekkøy, Malfrid, Grude; The Norwegian Commissioner ('Ombudsman') for Children: Practical Experiences and Future Goals', in: Verhellen, E. and Spiesschaert, F., eds., *Ombudswork for Children*, Op. cit., p. 122.
8. There is a consensus about these and other social democratic values in Norway, which makes things easy. Metze, Marcel 'De Noorse ziekte' in: *Intermediair*, Vol.21, August 30, 1985, No. 35, pp. 1–9, quotes a research: "The three most important issues that have priority with the Norwegians are pensions, health care and assistance to the rather few unemployed. The Norwegians, even those who belong to the right-wing political parties, are impregnated with social-democratic values." The author also quotes Andreas Hompland who worked in the 1970s as a journalist for the daily newspaper *Dagbladet*: "The social-democratic policy of re-dividing had reached its end. Contra-effects began to develop. The care-state has originated a disgust with bureaucracy.
9. Flekkøy, Malfrid, Grude, 'Child Advocacy in Norway', in: *Children and Society*, 4, 1988–1989, pp. 307–318; See also: Flekkøy, Malfrid, 'Speaking for Children', in: *Childright*, February, 1985, No. 14, p. 20. Also: Ryan, Michael, 'Who Speaks for Children?' in: *Parade Magazine*, July 8, 1990, p. 8. See also: Flekkøy, Malfrid, Grude, *Working for the Rights of Children*, Florence, 1990, UNICEF/International Child Development Centre, Innocenti, Essays, No. 1. See also: Flekkøy, Malfrid, *A Voice for Children, Speaking Out as Their Ombudsman*, London, 1991, UNICEF and Jessica Kingsley Publishers.
10. Flekkøy, Malfrid, Grude, 'Child Advocacy in Norway: The Ombudsman', in: *Child Welfare*, Vol.LXVIII, No. 2, March-April 1989, pp. 113–122.
11. Letter of Mrs. Flekkøy to the author (November 14, 1985, Ref.111 6/85 MGF/AIR).
12. Molander, Helena, *The Work of the Children's Ombudsman in Finland*, presentation at the Andra Nordiska Seminariet, 1985.
13. Letter from Märten Stenberg of Gothenburg, Secretary of Utredningen om Barnens Rätt, to the author, December 5, 1985.
14. BRIS is a grass-roots organisation, founded in 1971, providing support for victims of abuse.
15. Rädda Barnen, *The Spokesman for Children*, *Rädda Barnen's Advocacy Role*, Fact Street, Ministry of Foreign Affairs of Norway, Oslo, No. 4, sine anno.
16. Mosey, Chris, 'Sweden's New Children's Ombudsman: Children are people, too!', in: *Sweden Now*, 1, 1980, p. 16. See also: Ronstrom, Anitha, 'Sweden's Children's Ombudsman: A Spokesperson for Children', in: *Child Welfare*, Vol.LXVIII, No. 2, 1989, March/April, pp. 123–128.
17. Speech by the *Honorary Mr. Drea* in the *Legislative Assembly of Ontario*, to be found in: *Debates with Session, 32nd Parliament, 1984, Ontario*, p. 2314. Not everybody agreed with the Minister. Opposition Delegate R.F. Johnston of the New Democratic Party said: "I do not think we are quite at a stage yet to say 'this is the best piece of legislation that has been developed in North America!'" It was Mr. Johnston's opinion that the Act should start with a *Charter of the Rights of the Child in Ontario*. He had drafted a concept for such a Charter which he read in the House. Contrary to what Mr. Johnston had hoped, however, this improvement was not included in the Act.
    a) The right to food, clothing and housing in order to ensure good health and personal development." Anybody who knows anything about families on waiting lists for housing at the moment and about the kinds of choices some single mothers are making in giving up their children because they do not want them to live in unsanitary conditions while they wait nine months to get into Ontario Housing Corp. accommodations will know that if this were a fundamental right here, we would be talking about a very different kind of act, something that would force this government to produce proper sanitary housing for those families.
    b) The right to an environment free from physical abuse, exploitation and degrading treatment.
    c) The right to health care necessary to promote physical and mental health and to remedy

illness." Again, the causes of kids' entry into care can often be found in these areas and not in the actual reasons given at the time with respect to acts of physical abuse that might have taken place.

d) The right to reside with parents and siblings except where it is in the best interest of the child for the child to reside elsewhere.
e) The right to parental and adult support, guidance and continuity in the child's life.
f) The right to an education which will ensure every child the opportunity to reach and exercise his or her full potential." That supposedly is now enshrined in Bill 82. I say "supposedly" because I am not convinced we have done that.
g) The right to play and recreation.
h) The right to have his or her opinions heard and to be included to the greatest extent possible when any decisions are being made affecting his or her life." That right is recognized in a fashion in this act, but it is an area of concern because of the definitions of "consent" and of what is the proper involvement of children in major decisions affecting their lives.
i) the right to independent adult counselling and legal assistance in relation to all decisions affecting guardianship, custody or a determination of status." I am not sure this right is there for children who are put into children's mental health centres until they have already been in those centres for 90 days.
j) The right to a competent interpreter where language or a disability is a barrier in relation to all decisions affecting guardianship, custody or a determination of status.
k) The right to an explanation of all decisions affecting guardianship, custody or a determination of status." That matter is addressed more in this act than it has been in the past.
l) The right to be informed of the rights of children and to have them applied and enforced." It is interesting that we will find this dealt with only with respect to the rights of children in institutions in this act; we will not find it anywhere else.

See R.F. Johnston, *Debates 4th Session, 32nd Parliament*, 1984, Ontario, p. 2324 and 2328. I thank the staff of the Legislative Library of the Legislature of the Province of Ontario in Toronto.

18. Ontario Ministry of Community and Social Services, *Office of Child and Family Service Advocacy*, brochure, Toronto, October 13, 1987.
19. In the *Child and Family Services Act* 1984, Statutes of Ontario, 1984, published by the Ministry of the Attorney General), p. 182.
20. Ontario Ministry of Community and Social Services, *Someone who Listens, when should I write to the Advocate?* Toronto, Ontario, 1986, Queens Printer for Ontario.
21. This means:

   a) a child who is in the care of a foster parent;
   b) a child who is detained in a place of temporary detention, committed to secure or open custody under the *Young Offenders Act*, Canada, or held in a place of open custody under section 91 or Part IV (Young Offenders).

22. *Someone who Listens*, brochure, Toronto, Ont., Op. cit.
23. Les Horne, personal information, June 1988.
24. This may be the reason that so little has been put on paper by the office. There are, for instance, no annual reports.
25. Whiddington, Prudence, "When it is serious you can let us know; Les Horne, Child and Family Advocate," in: *Dialogue*, April-May 1986, p. 3.
26. Correspondence (July 4, 1988) with Mr. Brent Parfitt, Deputy Ombudsman in Victoria, B.C., Canada.
27. Kelk, Doug, 'Ombudsman for B.C. Children', in: *The Times Colonist* (Victoria, B.C.), September 2, 1987.
28. Baldrey, Keith, 'Deputy battles bureaucratic teen trap', in: *The Vancouver Sun*, October

28. 30, 1987. See also: Office of the Ombudsman, 1987 *Annual Report to the Legislative Assembly of British Columbia*, Vancouver, 1988.
29. Ombudsman, British Columbia, *The Ombudsman and Youth*, Vancouver, sine anno.
30. Ministerio de Justicia y Gracia Defensoria de la Infancia, *El Defensor de la Infancia en Costa Rica*, San José, 1988.
31. Decreto No. 17733 – J del 9 de Setiembre de 1987.
32. The Jerusalem Council for Children and Youth, *Summary of Activities*, Jerusalem, 1987. The Council was created in December 1984. The Council did set itself five main goals:

    (1) public education;
    (2) lobbying appropriate bodies for changes and improvements in services for children;
    (3) Upgrading and strengthening existing organizations presently serving children in the city;
    (4) facilitating and encouraging integrated planning of children's services; and
    (5) establishing selected pilot projects in areas currently not being served.

33. The Jerusalem Council for Children and Youth, *Annual Report*, October 1988. See also: Rauche-Elnekave, Helen, 'Advocacy and Ombudswork for Children: Implications of the Israeli Experience', in: *Child Welfare*, Vol. LXVIII, No. 2, March-April 1989, pp. 101–102.
34. Conversation with Dr. Menachem Horovitz in December 1989.
35. Pressure from the National Council for the Child on the Jerusalem Council for Children and Youth which operated the Ombudsman project was an important factor in the decision process that lead to the termination by the Jerusalem Council of the project. The National Council for the Child has appointed a new Ombudsman, Dr. Aahron Langerman (a former Director-General of the Ministry of Labour and Social Affairs). However, it is my impression that Dr. Horovitz, will not be easily replaced.
36. Since August 1990 Mrs. Bilha Noi works as an Ombudsperson for children within the Israeli Ministry of Education and Culture. Since December 1990 her office is called 'open line' of the Ministry of Education and Culture. Since she is a civil servant, it will be difficult for her to express criticism on policies of her Ministry.
37. Interview with Mr. Avraham Ben-Hador, lawyer, on December 19, 1989.
38. Proposal by Member of Parliament Dedi Zucker, No. 03/0976/A/024 of November 23, 1987. In December 1991 member of Parliament Edna Solodar promised to take it up.
39. 'Inner London Education Authority (ILEA) draws up an Ombudsman scheme', in: *The Times Educational Supplement*, November 28, 1986, p. 17. See also: Hodges, Lucy, 'Child Ombudsman to investigate State education grievances', in: *The Times*, February 11, 1986. Unfortunately Mrs. Thatcher disbanded the Inner London Education Authority (ILEA), thus putting an end to the plans for appointing an Ombudsman. Now a study funded by the Gulbenkian Trust is pleading to appoint an Ombudsman in the U.K. In the Netherlands a pilot study has been carried out. However, it did not lead to concrete results. See: Stichting voor het Kind, *Kinder-Ombudsman, werkverslag van een onderzoeksproject*, Amsterdam, May 1982. In the former Federal Republic of Germany a 'Children's Commission' was established in the National Parliament in Bonn. The Committee of four Members of Parliament of the four political parties has undertaken some of the tasks which in Norway are carried out by the Commissioner for Children. See: Kommission zur Wahrnehmung der Belange der Kinder im Deutschen Bundestag *Zwischenbericht, über die Tätigkeit der Kommission* von Mai 1988 bis Juni 1989, Bonn, 1989. For a local Ombudsman for Children, See: Lindsay, Mike, 'Promoting Children's Rights – by appointment', in: *Childright*, 1988, July/August, No. 49, pp. 16–19.
40. MacDermot, Niall, 'The Ombudsman Institution', in: *The Review, International Commission of Jurists*, December 1978, No. 21, pp. 37–38.

41. Longford, Michael, D., 'Can Bureaucracies Become More Flexible and Responsive?' in: *Long Range Planning*, Vol. 19, No. 1, pp. 99–104, 1986.
42. Melton, Gary, B., *Child Advocacy, Psychological Issues and Interventions*, New York and London, 1983, Plenum Press, pp. 95–96.
43. Soler, Mark, 'Effective Legal Advocacy for Children', in: *San Francisco Barrister*, Vol. 8, No. 4, April, 1984, pp. 3–5.
44. Interview with Mark Soler in June 1988.
45. Youth Law Center, *Program Description*, San Francisco, CA, 1989.
46. *Los Angeles Herald Examiner*, 'Long Beach agrees to stop putting kids in adults jails', February 14, 1987. Soler, Mark, 'Our Delinquency on Juvenile Justice; Locking up Children in Adult Jails is a National Disgrace', in: *Los Angeles Times*, January 20, 1984. See also: Perl, Peter, 'Suits Filed on Behalf of Youths Jailed in D.C.; Actions Seek to Separate Juveniles and Adults and to Obtain Damages for Assaulted Boy', in: *Washington Post*, November 26, 1985.
47. Dorfman, Anne, 'Youth Prisons Face Lawsuit on Conditions', in: *San Francisco Banner Daily Journal*, May 26, 1989.
48. Peters, Alexander, 'CYA Center Neglects Learning – Disabled Youth, Suit Alleges', in: *The Recorder*, May 26, 1989.
49. Hall, Michael, I., 'Profile' (of Mark Soler), in: *San Francisco Banner Daily Journal*, September 28, 1987.
50. *Kinderrechtswinkel*, brochure, (authors of brochure not mentioned), Amsterdam, sine anno.
51. Poublon, Guus and Kloosterboer, Karin, 'Wat heeft jeugd met recht te maken? Drie jaar Kinderrechtswinkel Amsterdam', in: *Jeugd en Samenleving*, July/August, 1988, No. 7/8, pp. 385–394. Also: Moll, Hans, 'Winkel etaleert de rechten van het kind', in *Folia Civitatis*, April 19, 1985, p. 7. Also: Kinderrechtswinkel Utrecht, *Jaarverslag* 1988, *Utrecht*, 1989. This part of Chapter VIII is also based on an interview with Monique van der Zouw (lawyer) and Karien Smits (pedagogue). Interview with the author on June 4, 1986, in the 'Children's Law Shop', Amsterdam.
52. There is also a small political action committee in Washington D.C., Kidspac, which supports political candidates who in turn support programmes and policies that founder and president William Harris considers to be good for America's children.
53. Wright Edelman, Marian, *Children Out of School in America*, A report, Washington D.C., 1974, CDF. See also: Children's Defense Fund, *The Children's Defense Fund Looks at America from a Special Point of View*, Washington D.C., sine anno, CDF.
54. Beck, Rochelle and Butler, John, An Interview with Marian Wright Edelman, in: *The Harvard Educational Review*, Vol. 44, No. 1, February, 1974, pp. 53–73.
55. Weill, James, D., *The Children's Defense Fund: Aims, Procedures and Results*, Paper presented at the International Congress of Ombudswork for Children, December 16, 1987, Gent, Belgium.
56. Children's Defense Budget, *A Children's Defense Budget*, Washington D.C., 1988, CDF.
57. Interview by the author with Nigel Cantwell of Defence for Children International on April 21, 1988 in New York.
58. Defence for Children International (DCI), *Information Paper related to Agenda Item 5: Protection of the Rights of Children*, Budapest, 81st Inter-Parliamentarian Conference (13–18 March 1989).
59. Interview with Mr. Cantwell.
60. Tomasevski, Katarina, editor, *Children in Adult Prisons, An International Perspective*, London, 1986, Frances Pinter Publishers.
61. The Standard Rules have since been adopted. Effective lobbying led to the decision to prepare draft standard minimum rules on the protection of juveniles deprived of their liberty. The idea that such rules should be prepared was adopted by the 7th U.N. Congress

on the Prevention of Crime and Treatment of Offenders in 1985. (Resolution 21, A/CONF.121/22/Rev.1.) The draft rules were submitted to the 8th Congress (in Cuba in the summer of 1990) where they were accepted. (See: United Nations, *Eighth U.N. Congress on the Prevention of Crime and the Treatment of Offenders*, Havana, Cuba, 27 August to 7 September 1990, A/Conf.144./28, 5 October 1990).

62. Cantwell, Nigel, 'A flying start – a Convention on inter-country adoption proposed by the Hague Conference', in: *International Children's Rights Monitor*, 1990, Vol. 7, Nos.1–2.
63. See for changing ideas about DCI's mandate: Defence for Children, *The First Year July 1979–July 1980*, Geneva, 1981. Defence for Children International (DCI), *Report on Activities of the Secretary General for the Period September 1982–July 1984*, Geneva, 1984.
64. Swan, van der, José, 'Vijfentwintig jaar Amnesty International; Steek liever een kaars aan dan de duisternis te vervloeken', in *Intermediair*, Vol.22, No. 19, May 9, 1986, pp. 51–61.
65. Defence for Children International, *Children in Prison in Turkey*, Geneva, 1988.
66. The Spokesman for Children – approach has been evaluated in 1989–1990. See for instance: Melton, Gary, B., 'Lessons from Norway: The Children's Ombudsman as a Voice for Children', in: *Case Western Reserve Journal of International Law*, Spring, 1991, no. 2, vol. 23, pp. 197–254. The Spokesman for children-approach is also spreading in its original and in modified forms. A public opinion poll carried out in Norway in 1989 showed that 74 per cent of a random population sample (all over 15 years of age) knew about the office of the ombudsman. Over the years the Swedish Parliament and Government have increased the budget of the Ombudsman for Children. All this and more is a strong sign that the ombudsman's office in Norway is considered as permanent (see: Flekkøy, *Working for the Rights of the Child*, Florence, 1990, p. 19).

The Norwegian ombudsman for Children has already left her mark on legislation. For instance the ombudsman pushed an already existing proposal prohibiting physical punishment through Parliament. She was also instrumental in raising the age at which young people can be tried and sentenced by adult courts. She was also successful in pointing out that regulations concerning the rights of hospitalised children had to be changed.

CHAPTER IX

The Children's Liberation Movement

The authors who stand in the spotlight in this chapter do not only want to grant children more rights; they want to wipe out all borders between childhood and adulthood. "The conception 'child'," says Farson,[1] founding his thesis on the work of Ariès, "is but a myth."

John Holt, whom we consider to be one of the most important exponents of the *Children's Liberation Movement*, argued that he did not belong to this group since he did not want to *liberate* children but only to remove the obstacles that impeded their liberty.[2] He wrote that if certain children decided that they were satisfied with the existing situation, he would not like to liberate them. If we nevertheless place Holt in the *Children's Liberation Movement*, it is because he insisted, like the other pioneers of the movement, that the need for *self-determination* had nothing to do with age.

The term *Toward the Liberation of the Child* appeared for the first time as a sub-title of the book *Children's Rights*,[3] published in 1971. In this book the English pedagogue A.S. Neill wrote that educators must not be afraid to grant children a great deal of freedom. In the same book Leila Berg wrote an interesting article on self-government, in which she described a number of experiments. However, in this book only the American child psychiatrist Robert Ollendorff deals explicitly with children's rights. He states that the first basic right of the adolescent is *self-determination*.[4]

Some younger authors also contributed to this anthology. A group from Ann Arbor (Michigan, USA), calling itself *The Youth Liberation Program*[5] described their demands for, among other things, the power to determine their own destiny and the immediate abolishment of 'adult chauvinism'.

In 1973 David Gottlieb and some other authors[6] published another book, *Children's Liberation*, in which they tried to show that being a child increases the probability of unfair, unconstitutional and inhumane treatment.[7] The authors, however, did not offer solutions toward 'child liberation' or formulate specific rights for children and adolescents. A year later this was done by Richard Farson and John Holt, unquestionably the two most important exponents of the *Children's Liberation Movement*, in their books *Birthrights*[8] and *Escape from Childhood*.⁹ Both books were intensively reviewed[10] and are always included in bibliographies about the rights of the child.

In this chapter we shall also analyse the book *Equal Rights for Children* by the philosopher Howard Cohen, and the 1988 plea for 'children's suffrage' by Ian Hunter of the C.B.S. radio station in Canada.

Farson's Ten Rights

Richard Farson's point of departure is that children's right to self-determination is fundamental to all other rights they are entitled to claim.[11] In his opinion children, like adults, must have the right to decide about everything that concerns them. Self-determination is the heart of the matter. It will prevent the adherence to different standards for children and adults. What is good for adults, says Farson, is good for children. To the question whether children's rights should be geared to the needs of any specific age, Farson answers: " . . . asking what is good for children is beside the point. We will grant children rights for the same reason we grant rights to adults, not because we are sure that children will then become better people, but more for ideological reasons, because we believe that expanding freedom as a way of life is worthwhile in itself. And freedom, we have found, is a difficult burden for adults as well as for children."[12]

According to Farson the same rights must prevail for children and adults: "The achievement of children's rights must apply to children of all ages, from birth to adulthood. Some of the rights may seem inappropriate to apply to the very young because of the obvious incapacities of small children. But rights cannot be withheld from the very young solely on the basis of age any more than they can be withheld from the very old who may be similarly incapacitated."[13]

Farson tries to avoid the question of moulding rights according to needs by an ethical point: "The fact is that we know very little about the necessary ingredients to make a good human being. There simply are no experts in this field."[14] He thus simply ignores the vast literature on the cognitive and emotional changes during the different stages of development.

Farson, a psychologist, was many years president of the *Esalen Institute* in California, (an Institute for *educational seminars* on various psychological issues). When *Birthrights* was published, Farson was not working with children but was Dean of the *School of Environmental Design* of the *California Institute of Arts*.

Farson formulates nine rights, all derived from the right to self-determination. We have, in the present study, somewhat changed the order of Farson's rights, in order to group together the rights that are, in our opinion, characteristic for the *Children's Liberation Movement*. Three additional rights, mentioned by many authors outside the *Children's Liberation Movement*[15] and therefore not exclusively belonging to that movement, are: *the Right to*

Responsive Design (according to which houses and schools are adapted to the child, and city planners consider the need of children to play safely),[16] *the Right to Freedom from Physical Punishment*,[17] and *the Right to Justice*.[18]

The following rights, typical for the Children's Liberation Movement, were proposed by Farson:

1. *The Right of the Child to Alternative Home Environments.* Farson pleads for moving toward an acceptance of pluralism in child rearing.[19] In addition to the family we must create as many alternate living groups as possible (communes, projects for adolescents who want to live independently, etc.) Farson: "The main objective of all these alternatives is to make it possible for the child to exercise choice in his own living arrangements."[20]
2. *The Right to Information* that is accessible to adults. Farson: ". . . children are denied information by being denied access to adult life, and in turn are denied access to adult life by being denied information."[21] Challenging censorship in general, Farson opposes the practice of libraries to withhold certain books from children, and denounces television channels who schedule certain movies, considered 'unsuitable' for children, only late at night. He also argues that children must give their consent to authorities who want to keep records of them, and pleads for the right of children to inspect all such records.
3. *The Right to Educate Oneself.* According to Farson children must have the right to determine which kind of education they want, if any. "If education is truly self-determined, then the child has a better chance to grow into maturity, having developed his values on the basis of personal experience rather than as a result of adult indoctrination."[22] Farson, who on the whole is no great believer in the possibilities to reform education,[23] says: "It can only change as a result of action from those who are exploited and oppressed by it – the children."[24] To accomplish this, Farson proposes to abolish compulsory education. He thinks that this may give children and adolescents the power to help determine their own schooling. This will perhaps lead to less indoctrination. Children are now more or less imprisoned, says Farson, since they do not go to school by their own free will. We must acknowledge the fundamental right of children to leave this (indoctrinating) environment if they wish.

    Adults must also point out to children the alternatives of those values that are taught in school, so that the children can choose for themselves. Farson[25]: "Freedom from indoctrination means that children choose whatever belief system comforts and inspires them, not necessarily the systems that adults would have them choose."
4. *The Right to Sexual Freedom.*[26] Children and adults should, according to Farson, have the same right to information about sex.[27] This would mean the end of censorship. Children would be allowed to read every-

thing adults can read.[28] According to Farson, this would also mean that children should be able to express their sexuality in the same way (and with the same restrictions) as adults. They must be allowed to experiment with their sexuality, provided that both partners agree, without fearing punishment.[29]

5. *The Right to Economic Power*. Children must have "the right to work, to acquire and manage money, to receive equal pay for equal work, to gain promotions to leadership positions, to own property, to develop a credit record, to enter into binding contracts, to engage in enterprise, to obtain guaranteed support apart from family, and to achieve financial independence."[30] Farson thinks that by allowing children to be financially independent, we shall drop many of the ways in which we control them.

6. *The Right to Political Power*. Student government, says Farson,[31] is still a joke in most schools and colleges, and within the family the adult usually dictates the activities of the child. Thus children have no opportunity in our society to see self-government in action and gain experience with democracy. In order to put an end to this situation, he proposes that all children and adolescents receive the right to vote and to participate in the political process. Dramatically, he states that eighty million citizens of the United States do not have the basic rights of democratic citizenship and the right to participate in the political process, only because they are children.[32]

We have already lowered the voting age from twenty-one to eighteen. In most countries this has been accepted as a wise decision. However, politicians refuse to take the needs of children into consideration before they become a constituency. Children must therefore receive the right to vote, not just at eighteen, but at any age.[33] The argument that children are not competent to vote is not relevant for Farson. Children should have the right to vote because they are members of our society and because without the vote, they are deprived of the necessary attention that is given to those who have it.[34]

"We are afraid," Farson writes in 1974, "that if we give children the vote, they will use it irresponsibly. But nothing indicates that they will vote less responsibly than adults." Must children have the right to hold high office, too? "Yes," says Farson, even though he admits[35] that the physical, emotional and cognitive limitations of early childhood will always restrict very young children to some extent.

Today Farson still believes in these theories. He told me: "Nobody believes that one-year old children will vote, but that does not mean we must deprive them of the *right* to vote. How many elderly people in our society are (almost) senile? Do we take away their right to vote? The granting of rights is not based on developmental-psychological phases or on age. I know many a ten-year old child who could vote much more intelligently than certain adults. Therefore: *forget about age*."[36]

Birthrights, says Farson[37] has been ridiculed, just like Holt's *Escape from Childhood*. He told me: "I believe this happens to all liberation movements in the beginning. Look at what happened to Blacks and women. Nevertheless, these two groups have improved their position in society a great deal. Children have not reached this phase yet. I think discrimination against them is too great and prejudices are too deeply rooted."

The Eleven Rights of John Holt

In 1964 John Caldwell Holt sounded an alarm concerning the American school system in his first book *How Children Fail*.[38] At first the book by the school teacher from Boston was ignored and thus practically reduced to nonexistence. However, after Holt wrote to *The New York Times* book reviewer Fremont-Smith: "I don't like to be ignored because what I have to say is unique", Fremont Smith responded in the same year by writing a review in which he called the book "possibly the most penetrating and probably the most eloquent book on education to be published in recent years."

In this book Holt describes how children are often paralysed by the fear to fail, how they spend most of their energy trying to please the teacher, to discover what sort of answer he likes best, and to formulate just such an answer. According to Mel Allen[39], it was Holt's book that in fact launched the *Educational Reform Movement* in the mid-sixties.

In 1967 Holt's second book, *How Children Learn* was published by Pikman. From this moment he became, according to Allen, something of a celebrity. He crisscrossed the country giving speeches[40] and wrote six other books. In *Escape from Childhood*, published in 1974, he describes eleven rights of the child, and in *Freedom and Beyond*, published in 1972, he describes the idea that it is not only possible to learn outside the school, but that education should be synonymous with real, non-school life. He imagines a time machine which projects him into a future society. "Where are your schools?" he asks, and the inhabitants of Future-Land have no idea what he is talking about. "We learn all the time," they answer. "We don't need any special buildings for it."

In *The Underachieving School* (1969) Holt proposes to let every child be the planner, director and assessor of his own education. He proposes to encourage children with the inspiration and guidance of more experienced and expert people. The child "should receive as much help as he asks for in order to decide what he is to learn, when he is to learn it, how he is to learn it, and how well he is learning it." Holt argues that this will change our schools from prisons into educational centres where everybody can acquire knowledge into an independent way.

In 1969 Holt still believed that changes in the existing school system were possible. In 1974, however, after the publication of *Escape from Childhood*, he said, according to Susannah Sheffer (who continues Holt's work[41]), that "he had been cured forever from being sentimental about childhood."

Although Holt's voice sounds somewhat more sensitive than Farson's, their points of departure are similar. Holt argues, for instance, that the same rights, duties and responsibilities adults have, must also be *available* to children.[42] Whether or not a child will want to make use of such a right, if ever he receives it, is optional. A good example of Holt's approach is his argument about *the right of the child to vote*. He differentiates between the needs of a six- and a ten-year old. He sees, for instance, that a six-year old girl who has helped her mother with an electoral campaign, might want to vote although she would probably not give up anything more immediately exciting in order to do so. "But I have known more than a few ten-year-olds who seem to understand at least as much about the world and its problems as I or most of my friends did when we left college."[43]

We shall now summarise the eleven 'rights', Holt describes in *Escape from Childhood*.

1. *The Right of the Child to Vote*. Holt thinks it unjust that children cannot vote. Decisions of politicians influence the lives of children as well. To have no say in these decisions gives children the minds and souls of slaves, he says. It makes them indifferent, lazy, cynical, irresponsible, and above all, stupid.[44] "If what I think does not make a difference, why think?" is the reasoning Holt attributes to children.
2. *The Right to Work*. Holt argues that the laws, formulated in the beginning of our Century to prohibit child labour, are not doing today's children a great favour. The exploitation of children at the time did not differ much from the exploitation of their parents who were also suffering in the mines, the mills and the sweatshops. "What made child labour in the Nineteenth Century so horrible was, in the first place, that children did not choose and could not refuse to do it."[45] Holt does not mention that the parents, too, had no choice! "Now that the economical situation has been improved for all of us, it is time to review the prohibition to work."[46] Children of any age should have the right to work for money, says Holt. They should have the right to save their earnings and spend their money according to their own judgement.[47] Work for them might be novel, adventurous, another way of exploring the world.
3. *The Right to Own Property* Children should have the right to own at least *some* property: if the child earns money it must belong to him or her. If a child receives a gift, that, too, must be *his* property, and he should have the right to use and/or dispose of it as he sees fit.[48]
4. *The Right to a Guaranteed Income*. To make children less dependent on the breadwinner, Holt proposes that a minimum income should be

guaranteed to everyone who chooses to be independent, including all children "down to an early age – as early as the child wants to receive it."[49] This right must help the child to exercise a number of other rights[50] such as the right to leave home, to travel and to seek alternate guardians.
5. *The Right to Choose One's Guardian.* The author wants to give children and adolescents three options. One: to stay with the biological or adoptive parents and be dependent on them. Two: to become legally and financially independent. Three: (the compromise) to live as dependents but under the care and control of people *of the child's own choosing.*[51] They will be the child's guardians until one or both parties decide to end this guardianship-agreement.
6. *The Right to Travel.* Just like adults, children should be able to travel without parents' permission, says Holt. But what if a child gets lost? If he knows how to get in touch with his home or with friends, or if he has with him his name and address, being lost or confused for a while will do him no harm.[52] What keeps children from travelling is chiefly lack of funds, but a guaranteed minimum-income would solve that problem.
7. *The Right to Drive.* In many States of the United States adolescents are allowed to drive. If youngsters drive unwisely or drink, they do this more out of bravado than out of ignorance. It is their way to act 'grown-up'. "This is all pretence, as it has to be in a society that allows no real way to be grown-up." Although the age limit for being allowed to drive is much lower in the U.S. than in many other places, Holt would like to see such a minimum age completely abolished in the United States. According to him, anyone, at whatever age, who can prove that he or she has the knowledge and skills to drive a car safely and well, ought to be allowed to do so.
8. *The Right to Control One's Sex Life.* Holt pictures a society[53] wherein sex is much less perilous for children than it is in reality. We should not view children as innocent and a-sexual beings, says Holt, but acknowledge and respect their feelings in this regard as well as in all others, including a possible refusal of sex.
9. *The Right to Use Drugs.* We have already seen that the word *protection* does not figure in the vocabulary of the 'kiddie libbers'. This becomes even more evident in Holt's chapter on drugs. In his own home the adult should be in a position to lay down the rules – for instance if he does not want smoking. But outside the home, the child's choice should prevail. "On the whole I believe," says Holt[54] "that people ought to be able to use the drugs they want. I don't think we should 'protect' children against whatever drugs their elders use, and in a society in which most of their elders do use drugs and many use them excessively and unwisely, I don't see how we can".
Holt thinks that adolescents drink and smoke too much in order to *look*

grown-up in a society in which there is no real and serious way *to be* grown-up. He admits that they are often driven to do this by social pressure from peer groups, but in his opinion this is a way to show their courage in a society in which there is no serious and authentic way to do so.

Escape from Childhood was written in 1972, at a time when people were less aware of some characteristics of drugs, the problems with heroin and cocaine had not yet reached today's proportions, and crack was not yet on the market. Many people were more worried about marijuana smoking, which, according to Holt, is less dangerous than our tendencies to imprison children in special children's world.

10. *The Right to Total Legal and Financial Responsibility.* This right is one of the 'escape routes' Holt wants to establish for children, in order to give them the opportunity to live and work (if they wish) as fully legally and financially responsible citizens.[55] Children and adolescents should have the right to apply for citizenship, and if they can show that they understand the responsibilities and obligations they are undertaking, they should be allowed to be accountable to their fellow citizens and the law for what they do. Holt:[56] "But what I want more for the child than the right, in spite of being a child, to have all the protection that the law grants to adults. I want in addition the right to decide *not* to be a child, not to be dependent any longer on guardians of any kind, but to live as an independent financially and legally responsible citizen. I want the right, in all respects, to escape from childhood.

11. *The Right to Control one's Learning.* In *the Underachieving School* (1969), John Holt had already touched upon this subject. In *Escape from Childhood* he formulates it again[57] – this time in the terms of rights. "I want them to have the right ... to decide whether they want to learn in a school and if so which one and for how much of the time." The right to give meaning to one's own learning is very important for Holt. According to him "no human right, except the right to life itself, is more fundamental than this.[58] ... If we take from someone the right to decide what he will be curious about, we destroy his freedom of thought."[59] What we should give children, he explains, is the right *to learn* instead of the right to *being forced to learn*. Although children should have the final say in these matters, Holt does not minimise the influence of parents and other adults, if their relationship with the child is good. He only wants to abolish the element of compulsion.

Holt does not present the rights he has formulated as a package deal that Society can take or leave; he suggests that we start by granting one or more rights to children without waiting until all the others have been accepted. The rights of the child should not be of overriding importance in *all* our decisions. The right, for instance, to possess a drum, may in certain cases be second to the right of another member of the child's household. The rights of others are for Holt also important.

When in 1964 *How Children Fail* was published, Holt tried to launch an educational reform movement, but in the mid-seventies he decided that meaningful school reform was impossible. Susannah Sheffer of Holt Associates Inc., whom I saw in Boston, told me[60] that he had lost his belief in positive changes in the school system. He reached the conclusion that "school was not a good idea gone wrong, but a wrong idea from the word go." In 1971 *Instead of Education* appeared and a year later he started his own periodical *Growing Without Schooling* wherein he argues that children must not be sent to school at all.

John Holt died of cancer on September 15th, 1985 in his home in Boston. He was sixty-two years old.[61]

Susannah Sheffer who works with *Holt Associates Inc.*, continues his work and publishes the periodical. She says: "It was very painful for him to realise that people do not at all want to change schools. He started to look for other solutions." He said that the best learning environment for a child was not school, no matter how humane, but a supportive home.[62] The movement, says Sheffer, has now some tens of thousands of adherents. A 10-year old home scholar writes in *Growing without Schooling*[63] "I never had any grown-up tell me I should be in school. When I tell grown-ups I am home-schooled they are shocked. They are speechless... When I first moved here, the school kids kept telling me I would grow up stupid, and I should be in school to be smart. I thought they were right and kept begging my mother to send me to school. Mom said no. Mom thought I would understand that school can be very boring sometimes. Sometimes I would have to do things I didn't want to do just because I was in school, and I wouldn't be able to do the things I wanted to because they wouldn't be on the schedule. Then I would have to go to the principal's office or something." Noteworthy is that in this case the mother discourages the free choice of her child (a kiddie-libbers principle). Here 'freedom' becomes compulsory!

In most other countries such a *home-schoolers*-movement could never exist. It shows how free people in the United States are supposed to interpret the concept *freedom*.[64]

How Howard Cohen elaborated the ideas of Holt and Farson

The philosopher Howard Cohen[65] objects to *protection* as the foundation of the relationship between adults and children. In his book *Equal Rights for Children*[66], he wonders why a child should not be able to make decisions and vote. Are their lives not equally influenced by decisions the chosen politicians make? Some children and adolescents, thinks Cohen, have a great interest in politics. Why should they not be allowed to have their say?[67] In seeking a practical application for the theories of Holt and Farson, Howard

Cohen argues that equal rights for children is a policy, rooted in the dictates of social justice, which we would be better off adopting.[68]

In the *Philosophy of Law* it is generally accepted that in order to exercise one's rights, a person must be a free, *moral agent*, and it is often brought to the fore that children have not yet reached the crucial stage in their intellectual and moral development that makes them into such *moral agents*. Cohen introduces a new element which he calls a *child agent*: an adult who advises children how to use their rights. According to Cohen the prevailing assumption is that in order to have a right, a person must be able to initiate the exercise of it on her or his own.[69] However, this is not true. If children were able to borrow the capacities they lack from those who have them, the fact that some children do not have full capacities would no longer be a relevant reason to impose a double standard of rights.[70] What the child needs is an adult whom he or she can ask for advise when signing a contract, opening a bank account, receiving credit, managing property, etc. Cohen: "A seven-year-old could probably not keep a budget or buy or sell a car without assistance. But this does not mean that these children could not make financial decisions... There is no reason to think that they could not make these decisions with the help of a financial advisor... The point here is that by relying on the capacities of agents children could exercise their rights without doing harm to themselves or others, without interfering with the obligations their parents or guardians might have to society at large, and without doing much harm to the system of rights and liberties."[71]

It is Cohen's opinion that equal rights for children will depend on the workability of a system of children's agents.[72] The task of these agents is not to protect children or keep them from making mistakes, but only to provide those capacities which would be necessary in order for the child to exercise his or her rights. Thus, by taking into account that children cannot do everything completely on their own, Cohen first somewhat weakens the impact of Farson's and Holt's propositions that children must have all the rights available to adults. He tries to bring them a little closer to reality, but stops halfway by refusing to specify the qualifications for being such a *child agent*.[73] He limits himself to a few superficial remarks about the *child agent's* need to be trustworthy and easy to reach, and alludes at the danger that if all child agents would be professionals, a new bureaucracy would be created (organisations of child agents), especially if every *child agent* also had a *supervisor*.[74] Some supervision over the work of child agents is, nevertheless, desirable so that 'advisors' who do not take their assignment seriously can be fired. The main reason why Cohen refuses to present an exhaustive plan is that he fears that such a plan might be dismissed because of its details.

He explains that we must not fear that children will become a powerful force for social change since it is highly unlikely that children, as a group, would have the time, energy, interest or sophistication to organise themselves for concerted action.[75] The real question, he argues, is not whether children are able to participate, but whether in doing so they would undermine the working of the democratic system. He believes that this would not be the case. Cohen thinks[76] that the participation of adults has been idealised, and that if children can vote and be elected, things will at worst go on largely as they do now. They may, however, improve somewhat since in the long run Society can only gain by introducing participation in democratic decision making at an early age.[77]

Children's Suffrage
Howard Cohen's ideas about *children's suffrage* were enthusiastically received by Bob Franklin of Leeds University[78] in Great Britain, and by the Canadian author and radio producer Ian Hunter. Franklin edited a book *The Rights of Children*.[79] The chapter he wrote about 'Children's Political Rights' is clearly cast in the liberationist mould. Not to grant children political rights, says Franklin[80], equals violating fundamental democratic principles. The fact that children do not have those rights, stems chiefly from the unwillingness of adults to relinquish some of their own political power and abandon their paternalistic attitude.[81] When children will be in a position to vote for whom they think will best promote their interests, the political parties will suddenly want to do more for children and adolescents. Franklin views children as a minority group suffering from discrimination.

Hunter argues that "Young people are ... in effect non-persons ... The laws reflect society's attitude and what these laws say about society is that the adult population does not respect underage people as they now do women, Blacks, native Indians and others who have been in the same segregated state youth are in now, but who fought to get out of it. Their fight began with getting the right to vote."[82]

Franklin was on the air in a radio program produced by Ian Hunter for the C.B.S. in Canada on May 30th, 1988. In Canada the *Canadian Council on Children and Youth* had already pleaded in favour of children's suffrage[83] but this was the first time that the issue was seriously discussed in a radio program.

Ian Hunter, with whom I corresponded extensively,[84] does not doubt that children must receive the vote: "But will the kids buy it? That's the crucial question with youth suffrage. If they don't want it, no one will give it to them."[85] He recommends that, at the next elections, they bring their lunch and perhaps a sleeping bag. If they don't get to vote they should explain Section Three of the *Canadian Charter of Rights and Freedoms* to the poll clerks[86] and if that doesn't help, they should do what Ghandi did and sit down in the polling station. "If every citizen can't vote, then no one can vote."[87]

Hunter wrote me also that he hopes to dedicate himself in the coming years to the launching of a *Youth Suffrage Movement*. "If it succeeds in Canada," wrote Hunter, "world-wide consequences may be expected!"

Chapter IX

Evaluation of the Children's Liberation Movement

When I asked Tarzie Vittachi, a former UNICEF official born in Sri Lanka, what he thought about the 'Children's Liberation Movement', he commented: "These are the problems of the 'People of Plenty'."[88]

Robert Mnookin[89] who also views the 'kiddie libbers' rather sceptically, nevertheless warns us not to reject their ideas too quickly, because buried in their rhetoric are important questions. Although an element of domination of children by adults is inevitable, this gives no license to ignore the moral dimension implicit in the liberators challenge: What are the justifications for giving one human being power over the nature, training and experience of another? Other questions that are raised[90] are, for instance: Who is a citizen? Who is excluded from the making of laws? Who must be included in the conception 'equality'? How mature must a person be to make decisions? Is age a just criterion for the granting of autonomy?[91]

The 'kiddie libbers' want to treat children as undersized adults and thus make education superfluous. Snik[92] denies the fact that children are born helpless and need time to grow up. The Dutch author René Görtzen says in his book *Away with Education* that "autonomy lies in the cradle"[93] and the Dutch writer of children's books Guus Kuijer believes that "people, and therefore also children, have the right to physical protection and, apart from that, the right to as much neglect as possible."[94]

The Children's Liberation Movement brings us face to face with some important points of discussion concerning the rights of the child: When is a child capable of assuming the responsibility attached to a certain right? Is it not sometimes more important for a child or adolescent that the adult person assumes his own responsibilities instead of escaping from them?[95]

According to Robert Mnookin[96] the 'kiddie libbers'' claim that children should have more legal autonomy (to decide things for themselves) can be best evaluated in the light of the ongoing contributions of developmental psychology. Research should yield important insights concerning the relationship between age and the range of cognitive and emotional capabilities of young people.

We shall now map the Children's Liberation Movement's most characteristic claims with the help of the 'Systemic Quality of Life Model'.

Farson's first right ("the right of the child to choose or be assisted in finding alternative living quarters") belongs in the *expressive mode* of the *physical subsystem* (changing places is something physical). Farson stresses, however, that the aim of this right of the child is to exercise choice in the selection of his or her social environment. Social power and social freedom are the most important elements of this right. We can, therefore, also classify it in the *expressive mode* of the *social subsystem*.

"The right to receive all available information" concerns individual behaviour in the realm of knowledge and cognitive behaviour and essentially pertains to the *expressive mode* of the *personality subsystem*. To the extent

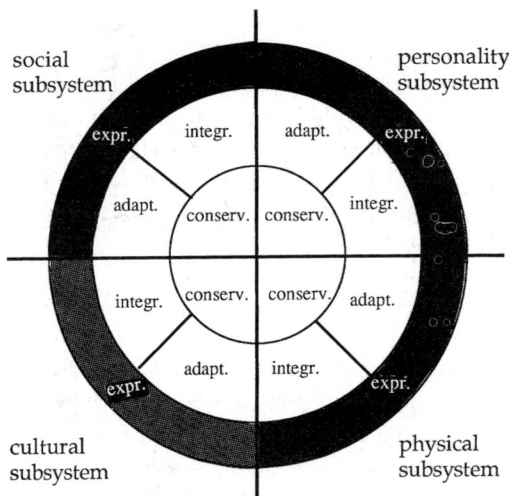

Fig. 9.1. Rights formulated by Richard Farson. Interpreted by the Systemic Quality of Life Model.

that individual choices reflect one's value preferences, this right also concerns *the expressive mode* of the *cultural subsystem*.

Farson's third right ("to educate oneself, to determine which kind of education they want, if any") is not concerned with adapting school systems to individual children, but is rather an issue of 'kidpower'. Whatever the child chooses, let him do his thing! Although education belongs in the adaptive mode of the cultural subsystem, we classify it in this case in the *expressive mode* of the *social subsystem*, since the stress is on choice.

Farson's fourth right, dealing with 'sexual freedom', is an *expression of power of the physical type*. This classification, which minimises the interpersonal aspects (social subsystem) of sex, is made because it seems that the spirit of the article is directed to the physical aspect of sexual freedom ("they must be allowed to experiment with their sexuality"), rather than to its interpersonal aspect.

Farson's "right to economic power" aims at liberating the children from oppression by the parents. This right belongs in the *expressive mode* of the *social subsystem*.

Farson's "right to political power" has little to do with the expression of personal- or value-preferences of the child or adolescent but again with social power. It belongs in the *expressive mode* of the *social subsystem*.

John Holt's "right of the child to vote" belongs, like many of Farson's rights, in the *expressive mode* of the *social subsystem*.

The "right to work", is not classifiable in the adaptive mode of the social subsystem, since work, in this case, is not merely a means for interacting with social institutions. The "right to work" aims, in Holt's own words, at "another way of exploring the world." It belongs in the *expressive mode* of the *personality subsystem*..

Holt's "right to own property" is the expression of physical power. It belongs in the *expressive mode* of the *physical subsystem*.

The "right to a guaranteed minimum income" expresses Holt's concern with children's right to act in the physical environment according to their own will. It belongs in the *expressive mode* of the *physical subsystem*. This classification is confirmed by Holt's remark that this right aims at "making children less dependent on the breadwinner."

Normally parents or guardians constitute the primary social environment from which the individual child derives his or her sense of social belonging. Hence the general concern is with the *conservative mode* of the *social subsystem*. However, Holt's "right to choose one's guardian" definitely involves the *expressive mode* of the *social subsystem*. Central here is the claim that the child has the right to initiate changes in the conservative mode. This shows the author's concern with (freedom of) expression in every subsystem.

Holt's "right to travel" is the right to roam around in the physical environment. This is classifiable in the *expressive mode* of the *physical subsystem*. The "right to drive" also belongs in the *expressive mode* of the *physical subsystem*. However, it also means the possession of a driving licence (which raises the child or adolescent's social status and makes this right classifiable in the *expressive mode* of the *social subsystem*.)

Holt's "right to control one's sex life" is primarily concerned with the child's control over his own life. This suggests the *expressive mode*. However, the expressive mode of what system? The domain of concern is sex which primarily resides in the *integrative modes* of the *social and physical subsystems* (for instance 'interpersonal intimacy' and 'biological balances'). These two modes themselves can therefore, be considered the sub-subsystems in which Holt recommends that children should receive the right to exercise power.

Farson, when dealing with the same issue, relates to the physical subsystem as such. Holt's recurrent concern is with the children's control over their own lives. This is manifested by his tendency to specify the expressive mode in many subsystems and sub-subsystems.

Holt's right to "total legal and financial responsibility" belongs analytically in the adaptive mode of the social subsystem. However, it is more specific and advocates that power be given to the individual child beyond the present level. Hence it is further classifiable as pertaining to the *expressive mode* of the *sub-subsystem of social-adaptability*.

The right of the child "to control his or her own learning" can be classified in the *expressive mode* of the *personality subsystem* since Holt stresses the importance of curiosity. It is also affiliated with the *adaptive mode* of the *social subsystem* since it Holt mentions explicitly that these preferences will be acted upon through the nature of school attendance.

We shall now look at the rights formulated by Howard Cohen who writes: "Children should have the right to vote in elections at all levels of govern-

Children's Liberation Movement

Picture IX.1. John Holt visiting a school. (Photo: John Walmsley.)

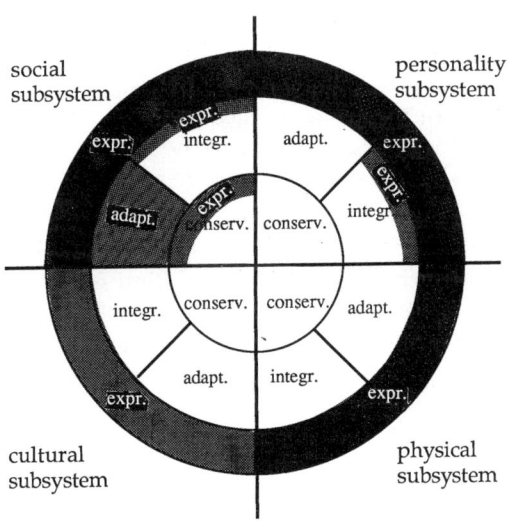

Fig. 9.2. Rights formulated by John Holt. Interpreted by the Systemic Quality of Life Model.

ment; the right to run for elective offices which do not have special constitutional age requirements over and above the age of majority; the right to initiate petitions, referenda, and recall elections; the right to organise into legitimate political parties or join already existing ones as full members; and the right of access to all lobbying channels now open to adults... When I say that children should have these rights, I mean that all children should have them. There should be no barrier to political participation which is established solely on the basis of age."

Cohen claims that even if children cannot take part in the political game, they understand its rules much earlier than the adults are prepared to acknowledge.

An important factor in the work of all members of the children's liberation movement, is the right of children to participate in the political process, which, as we have seen, belongs in the *expressive mode* of the *social subsystem*. All the 'kiddie libbers' claim that children should receive this right in order to have influence in the social context.

Typical of Cohen's contribution is his proposal to appoint *child agents*. He wanted to create a mechanism to achieve *social adaptability*.

Cohen's elaboration of Holt's and Farson's thoughts, that children must have the right "to dispose of their own money" can be classified in both the *social* and the *physical subsystems*. His explanation[97] makes clear why this right belongs in two subsystems. The aim of the right is "to limit parental control... Parents have presently the right to their children's income and children may not do anything with their money that requires a legal contract (except through their parents)". The key word here is 'legal contract', which would make it possible to sue children in court if they did not keep these contracts. Money itself is a 'social institution' and has legal consequences. We classify this right in the *adaptive mode* of the *social subsystem*. However, since it has to do with the child's right to determine for himself whether his business is sound or not[98], Cohen's concern is also with the *expressive mode* of the *adaptive-social sub-subsystem*.

In Chapter III we said we would try to avoid considering the mode of a subsystem as a sub-subsystem. When analyzing Farson's 'rights' we did not have to go to a deeper level of analysis, since he was only concerned with the expressive mode. When analyzing Holt's and Cohen's work, however, we were sometimes forced to employ a deeper level of analysis of the 'Systemic Quality of Life Model'. We had to consider several modes of a subsystem as sub-subsystems. Holt's and Cohen's ubiquitous concern with *kid power* stressed the expressive mode within these sub-subsystems.

Notes

1. Farson, Richard, *Birthrights: A Bill of Rights for Children*, New York, 1974, Macmillan, p. 17–25, Chapter 'The Invention of Children'.
2. John Holt on a tape *The Rights of Children*, conversation between Richard Farson and John Holt, Jeffrey Norton Publishers Tape Library, 1974, Guildford, CT., Number 40067, Audio-Forum, Sound Seminars.
   Confusingly many 'kiddie libbers' declare that they belong to the *Children's Rights Movement* without further differentiation. Even worse is that some social scientists do not differentiate between the Children's Rights Movement and the Children's Liberation Movement. This is

the case, for instance, in Pennink, E., 'The Children's Rights Movement' in Langen, M. de, Graaf, J.H. de, and Kunneman, F.B.M., *Kinderen en Recht*, Deventer/Gouda, 1989.

Eugeen Verhellen (in: Verhellen, E., Spiesschaert, F., and Cattrijse, L., *Rechten van Kinderen*, 1989 *pp.* 17–18) *mentions three mainstreams in this so-called 'Children's Rights Movement'*: *the reform stream* (who claims that our society underrates the ability of children to make rational decisions; the *radical stream* (the 'kiddie libbers'); the *pragmatic stream* (who has doubts about the practical consequences of giving children all the rights adults have except if competence to exert a right can be proven. Verhellen: "It is my objection that it brings some adults in a judging position.

3. Adams, Paul; Berg, Leila; Berger, Nan; Duane, Michael; Neill, A.S.; Ollendorff, Robert, with an introduction by Goodman, Paul, *Children's Rights, toward the Liberation of the Child*, New York and Washington D.C., 1971, Praeger Publisher. Mark Gerzon (in: *A Childhood for every child; the politics of parenthood*, New York, 1973: Outerbridge and Lazare write: "The oppression of children by adults has continued after every previous revolution that adults have engineered.
4. Ollendorff, Robert, 'The Rights of Adolescents', in: *Children's Rights, toward the Liberation of the Child*, Op. cit., p. 120.
5. Youth Liberation of Ann Arbor, 'Youth Liberation Program', 1972, reprinted in: Gross, Beatrice and Gross, Ronald, *The Children's Rights Movement, Overcoming the Repression of Young People*, Garden City, N.Y , 1977, Anchor Books ,Anchor Press/Doubleday, pp. 329–333. The book, edited by Gross and Gross, is a reader with many short articles.
6. Gottlieb, David, editor, *Children's Liberation*, Englewood Cliffs, N.J., 1973, Prentice Hall, Inc., with contributions by Peter B. Meyer, Daniel Katkin, Thomas I. Cottle, Paul Lerman, Norman K. Denzin and George B. Leonard.
7. Idem, p. 4.
8. Farson, op. cit. (Note 1).
9. Holt, John, *Escape From Childhood, The Needs and Rights of Children*, New York, 1974, Ballantine Books (Division of Random House).
10. Levine, George, Review of both books in *The New York Times* of May 19th, 1974.
   Holt's book was later reviewed, for instance, in *Newsweek*, September 2nd, 1974, p. 27, by Shana Alexander, and in *Compact* (publication of the Educational Committee of the United States), November/December 1974, p. 28, by Sandra Jackson.
11. Farson, Op. cit., p. 27.
12. Idem, p. 31.
13. Idem, pp. 31–32.
14. Idem, p. 31.
15. Jobling, Megan, 'Children in Flats, an Abstract of Research Findings', in *Highlights*, No. 4., London, June 1973, National Children's Bureau. In Dutch: (a) Bladergroen, W.J., 'Kind en Leefmilieu', in Schoefen, I., and others, *Wonen tussen Utopie en Werkelijkheid*, Nijkerk, 1980, Info Uitgeverij, pp. 84–92. Also: Ackermans, E., *De Woonomgeving als Speelgelegenheid*, Leyden/Groningen, 1970, Nederlands Instituut voor Praeventieve Geneeskunde TNO/'Wolters-Noordhoff'.
16. Various action groups outside the Children's Liberation Movement have worked toward a safe environment. In the Netherlands the 'Stop the Murder of Children on the Road' 'pressure group' is very active. In the United Kingdom the group *Kids Alive* is active.
17. In the United Kingdom *STOPP* (Society of Teachers Opposed to Physical Punishment) has been instrumental in forbidding spanking in the classroom. In the United States there is a *National Committee to Abolish Corporal Punishment in Schools*, and a *Committee to End Violence Against the Next Generation*.
18. See: *In Re Gault*, 387, *U.S.* 1, 1967.
19. Farson, Op. cit., p. 62.
20. Idem.
21. Idem, p. 84.
22. Idem, p. 111. Farson (p.97): "The manner in which subjects are taught derives its power

not from its intrinsic appeal to children, but more from the fact that they are compelled to sit through it.
23. Farson: "The educational system functions not to educate children, but to maintain the system.... School serves that custodial function extremely well by incarcerating children all day, every day.... "School is the place where we want children to be; we don't want them anywhere else." (p.105).
24. Farson, Op. cit., p. 112.
25. Idem, p. 110.
26. Idem, pp. 129–153.
27. According to Farson this cannot be left to school teachers who have a tendency to present sexuality in the light of a Walt Disney world, and who, moreover, do not present the complete spectrum of human sexuality. What he means is that the accent lies on heterosexuality.
28. Farson: "No one has yet determined whether or not such material is harmful to either adults or children, or whether or not it precipitates sex crimes. The question of whether or not pornography is harmful is, again, beside the point. If it is information available to adults, it must be available to children." (p.135.)
29. Farson, Op. cit., p. 153.
30. Idem, p. 154.
31. Idem, p. 180.
32 dem, p. 175.
33. Idem, pp. 176–177.
34. Idem, p. 182.
35. Idem, p. 185.
36. In a long telephone interview on June 27th 1988.
37. Idem. Farson is nowadays occupied with *communications* and *computers*. He is the President of the *Western Behavioral Sciences Institute* in La Jolla, California. This organisation offers leadership training to people in the industries and also gives them the opportunity to make use of a computer network wherein business people exchange experience through computers. He left the children's field completely.
38. Holt, John, *How Children Fail*, Dell, 1964, Pitman Publishing Company.
39. Allen, Mel, 'The Education of John Holt', in *Yankee*, December, 1981, pp. 1–7.
40. Idem.
41. Conversation in Boston with Susannah Sheffer of *Holt Associates Inc.*, on May 30th, 1988, in Boston.
42. Holt, John, *Escape from Childhood, The Needs and Rights of Children*, New York, 1974, E.P. Dutton & Co., Inc.
43. Idem, p. 118.
44. Idem, p. 115.
45. Idem, Op. cit., p. 141.
46. Holt doesn't deny that poverty still exists today: "But though we have far more and worse poverty than a rich nation should, we do not have much of the poverty common in the nineteenth-century industrial towns. And, as I have pointed out, we are not likely to give children the right to work unless and until we find ways to have much less poverty than we do now. In such a society, in which none would fear the desperate poverty that created child labour, no one would be compelled to work long hours at degrading, destructive, and dangerous work or try to force children into it." (p.142)
47. Holt, John, *Escape from Childhood*, Op. cit., p. 128.
48. Holt does not, however, consider the clothes a child wears to be his or her possession, unless the child has paid for these clothes with his own money. For do not younger children in the same family often need the clothes that were originally bought by their parents for an older sibling? And if a child receives a bicycle for which his parents have painfully saved the money, it would, according to Holt, be *wrong* if he sold it to use the money otherwise.
49. Holt, John, *Escape from Childhood*, Op. cit., pp. 168–171.

50. Holt, John, *Escape from Childhood*, Op. cit., p. 169. I have somewhat changed the order in which Holt has mentioned the rights in this book.
51. Idem, pp. 156-167.
52. Holt (p.151) "Someone might ask, suppose we didn't know how to get in touch with home or friends, then what? We can only say that a child who would travel far without that much information is so reckless and foolish that even now the law and his parents can probably not keep him out of trouble."
53. Holt (p.213): "Some people have voiced to me the fear that if it were legal for an adult to have sex with a consenting child, many young people would be exploited by unscrupulous older ones. The image here is of the innocent young girl and the dirty old man Here, too, we are caught with the remains of old myths." Holt does not seem to acknowledge that children might nevertheless become the victims of adults. Farson in his article *Child Protection that Backfires*, argues that parents rather than strangers exploit and mistreat the children. Holt and Farson do not fear that adults who seek the friendship of children may want to abuse them. "The best way to protect children," says Farson, "is by giving them the same legal rights we give to adults.
54. Holt, John, *Escape from Childhood*, Op. cit., pp. 194 and 201.
55. Idem, p. 172.
56. Idem, p. 183.
57. Idem, p. 186.
58. Idem.
59. Idem.
60. Interview in Boston, May 30, 1988.
61. Coughlin, W.P., 'Educator John Holt, author who advocated radical education reforms at 62' in: *The Boston Globe*, September 15th, 1985, p. 1.
62. Allen, Mel, 'The Education of John Holt' in: *Yankee*, December 1981, p. 2.
63. Olson, Rachel, 'Telling about Home-Schooling' in: *Growing Without Schooling*, 1988, No. 61, pp. 20-21.
64. Henkin, Louis, 'Rights: American and Human', in: *Columbia University Law Review*, Vol. 79, April 1979, No. 3, pp. 405-425
65. Conversation with Howard Cohen in Boston on May 30, 1988. Prof. Cohen is now the dean of the *College of Arts and Sciences* of the University of Massachusetts in Boston. In 1979, when Prof. Cohen wrote *Equal Rights for Children*, he worked in the *Philosophy Department* of the same University. For the last five years he has been the dean of the University and the consultant for the police force. He considers this to be the other side of the same unity, the powerful as opposed to the powerless children.
66. Cohen, Howard, *Equal Rights for Children*, Littlefield, 1980, Adams & Co.
67. Conversation with Prof. Cohen in May 1988 in Boston.
68. Cohen, Howard, *Equal Rights for Children*, p. 101.
69. Idem, p. 56.
70. Idem, p. 57.
71. Idem, pp. 59-60.
72. Idem, p. 73.
73. Idem, Chapter VI.
74. Idem, p. 89.
75. Idem, p. 106.
76. Idem, p. 114.
77. Sometimes, however, reality proves to be different because young people are attracted to 'easy solutions' as was the case in 1984 in Israel where an opinion poll showed that 40 to 50 % of the adolescents openly supported the 'solution' of the racist Meir Kahane, whereupon the Ministry of Education and Culture developed a curriculum geared to the promoting of tolerance and coexistence. Also: Bradly Burston in his article *The Sweet Noise of Democracy; Freedom of Expression is the Basis of a Just Society - High-school Students Think Otherwise, and Somebody's Doing Something About It*, in *Spectrum*, March 1986, pp. 18-

19. A recent study by Prof. Kalman Benyamini of the Hebrew University in Jerusalem showed that the vast majority of Israeli teenagers believe that there is nothing wrong with transferring Palestinians out of the territories!
78. Franklin, Bob, editor, *The Rights of Children*, London, 1986, Basil Blackwell.
79. Idem, 'introduction, p. 18.
80. There were other enthusiast reactions. An article in the *San Francisco Chronicle*, November, 23rd, 1976, was for instance titled: 'Youngsters – the last minority?'.
81. Franklin, Bob, 'Children's Political Rights', in: Franklin, Bob, *The Rights of Children*, p. 49.
82. *Giving kids the vote*, Canadian Broadcasting Corporation, an 'ideas documentary', broadcast on Monday, May 30, 1988, by the CBS-AM radio station.
83. Canadian Council on Children and Youth, *Admittance Restricted: The Child as Citizen in Canada*, Ottawa, 1978, CCCY.
84. Ian Hunter sent me a tape of his show, broadcast of May 30, 1988 on CBS. Others can also order this by writing to No. 303–152, West Hastings Street, Vancouver, B.C., Canada V6B 1G8.
85. Hunter, Ian: '"When you're older' is no reason to deny young people their rights. The fight for those rights begins with the right to vote. NOW!
Until 1920 the Canadian *Federal Elections Act* stated that 'women, madmen and criminals' could not vote. Canadian citizens of Chinese origin did not get the vote before 1948; Canadian citizens of Japanese and Indian origin received it in 1949.
86. Hunter, Ian, *Universal Suffrage Tour*, description of a project, July 20th, 1988, not published.
87. Idem, p. 2.
88. Interview with Tarzie Vittachi in 1988 in New York. He referred to a book by David Plotter 'People of Plenty'.
89. Mnookin, Robert, 'Children's Rights: Beyond Kiddie Libbers and Child Savers' in *Journal of Clinical Child Psychology*, Fall 1978, p. 164. According to Mnookin the same is true for those who stand at the other side of the spectrum: the 'protectors'.
90. Reed, T.M. and Johnston, P., 'Children's Liberation', in: *Philosophy*, 55, 1980, pp. 2263–266.
91. Mnookin, Robert, Op. cit., p. 164.
92. Snik observed that the image of the child here leads to inadequate practices: "we view the child ... as a pre-rational being, subjected to the laws of nature, who, through a metamorphosis of sorts, all of a sudden changes into a rational, self-determined person. Seen in this light, children and adults are each other's opposites." Snik, G., 'Ontwikkeling en Opvoeding', in: Haaften, A.W. van, *Ontwikkelingsfilosofie*, Muiderberg, 1986, Coutinho, pp. 175–187.
93. Görtzen, René, *Weg met de Opvoeding*, Amsterdam/Meppel, 1984, Boom Pers. Görtzen mentions that in the Federal Republic of Germany the *Freundschaft mit Kinder-Förderkreis* group under the chairmanship of Hubertus von Schoenebeck pleads for self-determination for children, and for equal rights without age boundaries.
94. Kuijer, Guus, *Het Geminachte Kind*, Amsterdam, 1980, De Arbeiders Pers.
95. My paraphrase of the title of Holt's book 'Escape from Childhood': 'Escape from Responsibilities?'
96. Mnookin, Robert, 'Children's Rights: Beyond Kiddie Libbers and Child Lovers' in: *Journal of Clinical Child Psychology*, Fall 1976, p. 167. See also: Baumrind, D., 'Reciprocal Rights and Responsibilities in Parent-Child Relations', in: Journal of Social Issues, 1978, 34(2), pp. 179–196.
97. Cohen, Howard, Op. cit., p. 93.
98. With the help of a child agent if necessary.

PART D

Declarations and Conventions: Past and Present

In Part B we have seen how the pioneers in the field tried out new possibilities and formulated important ideas. *Declarations* and *Conventions*, however, provide us with more tangible evidence of changing ideas on children's rights. They often come into existence through consensus and are milestones in the history of the rights of the child. They provide us with concrete material for comparisons.

Declarations of the rights of the child often summarise those principles that have a special connection with child welfare. They can be used as guidelines for actions. They also offer us a framework for the interpretation of these actions. According to P. van Dijk they are guidelines for policy and instruments of public opinion rather than standards to be used by national and international judges.[1]

Although certain aspects of the rights of the child have been regulated in Conventions since the beginning of the Twentieth Century, it is only since November 1989 that a true *Convention on the Rights of the Child* has aimed to harmonise the different human rights standards relating to children.

Forty-five such Declarations have been included in this study as appendices. In the following chapters we shall analyse them all.

Chapter X deals with Declarations reached by international consensus in the League of Nations and the United Nations.

Chapter XI deals with national and regional Declarations.

In Chapter XII we shall analyse ideological statements disguised as *Declarations on the Rights of the Child*.

In Chapter XIII we shall analyse the so-called special or sectarian Declarations and Conventions. These are the concerns of specific interest groups, such as women, social workers, lobbyists for the welfare of children in hospital etc.

Note

1. Dijk, van, P., 'De Internationale Bescherming van Rechten van het Kind', in: *Familie- en Jeugdrecht*, Vol. 1,6, 1979, pp. 165–180.

CHAPTER X

The International Consensus

1. THE DECLARATION OF GENEVA (1924)[1]

See Appendix IX

On March 16th, 1922, Eglantyne Jebb pleaded in a memorandum[2] for the creation of a *Code for Children*[3] Such a code should "not be a piece of legislation but rather a document defining the duties of adults towards children, which each country should recognise either by means of State intervention or by private action."

Discussions by the *Socialist Youth International* and the *International Council of Women*, (*I.C.W.*) which led to the formulation of the *Declaration of the Rights of the Adolescent* and the *Children's Charter of the I.C.W.* (see Chapter XIII) had been followed with great interest by the *Save the Children International Union*[4] in Geneva. Although the founder of this Union, Eglantyne Jebb, acknowledged the importance of these 'Children's Charters', they were, in her opinion, too detailed and resembled a list of standard minimum rules rather than a declaration of fundamental principles.[5]

A Committee of the British *Save the Children Fund*, founded by Miss Jebb (see Chapter VI), was already working on a declaration of those needs of children that must be satisfied under all circumstances, even in times of great economic pressure.[6] However, this effort was no more than a finger-exercise before the concert.

Miss Jebb told her friends in London that she wanted the *Save the Children International Union*[7] to issue a short declaration that would be easy to translate and easy to understand.

To accomplish this, she travelled from London to Geneva where she whisked Etienne Clouzot, the Secretary General of the *Save the Children International Union*, out of his office and into a quiet restaurant on top of Mount Salève overlooking Lac Léman, where she disclosed her plans. The declaration she had in mind would have a short catchy title and a brief introduction followed by a few clear-cut statements. Clouzot was convinced. There and then they sat down to draft the text of the proposed declaration.

It was Clouzot who introduced the project to the Union. On October 30th, 1922, the first concept of the Declaration already appeared in the bulletin of the *Save the Children International Union*. When on February 23rd, 1923, the General Assembly of the Union convened, two drafts (one a variant of the other) were presented, one with five, the other with seven principles.

A resolution was adopted wherein the *Conseil général* of the Union undertook to formulate a Declaration. The National Committees were consulted and an Editorial Committee was formed (Secretary-General Clouzot, George Werner and Mr. MacKenzie).[8] Eglantyne Jebb proposed the title: 'Declaration of Geneva'. On May 17th, 1923, the Union accepted the concept proposed by the Editorial Committee.

On the evening of February 28th, 1924, at 9 o'clock, an impressive ceremony took place[9] in the Geneva *Museum of Art and History*. In the presence of diplomats, representatives of various International Organisations and Churches, a copy of the *Declaration of Geneva*, signed by all members of the *Save the Children International Union*,[10] was presented to a representative of the Government of the Canton of Geneva. Since then the document has been kept in the State Archives of the District of Geneva. It has been translated into many languages. In June 1923 the Swedish text was already signed by, among others, Ellen Key and the Swedish Minister of Social Affairs, Mr. G. Mallen. Albania, Finland, France, the United Kingdom, Lithuania, the Kingdom of the Serbs, Croats and Slovaks[11] all organised ceremonies to sign the Declaration. Queen Elizabeth signed it in Belgium and Prince Waldemar in Denmark. According to Werner[12] and André Durand,[13] Gustave Ador, former President of the Swiss Confederation and Chairman of the International Committee of the Red Cross, read the *Declaration of Geneva* on November 21st, 1923, in a radio broadcast from the Eiffel Tower.[14]

The most important boost to the status of the *Declaration of Geneva* came from the *League of Nations*.[15] On September 26th, 1924, the League's Assembly discussed the Declaration and the protection of children. The *Fifth Committee* put two resolutions up for vote. Both were adopted. The first resolution stated that the work of the *International Association for the Protection of Children* must be continued under the auspices of the League of Nations; the second resolution urged the Member States of the League of Nations to be guided, when dealing with Child Welfare in their home countries, by the principles mentioned in the *Declaration of Geneva* and endorsed by the Assembly of the *League of Nations*. The Chairman, former President of Switzerland, Giuseppe Motta,[16] mentioned the importance of the *Declaration of Geneva* and called it the *Children's Charter* of the *League of Nations*.[17] With the adoption of the Declaration this 'World Parliament' had gone a step further than the *Treaty of Versailles* which had already mentioned the protection of the young in its Preamble. Although every State was left free to take its own measures, the *Declaration of Geneva* contained the basic principles for Child Welfare.[18] F.P. Walters wrote in his 'History of the League of Nations': "To have brought fifty countries to accept the Geneva Declaration of the Rights of the Child – such acts may continue to produce their effects long after many a frontier dispute has been forgotten."[19]

In its *Preamble*, the *Declaration of Geneva*[20] states that men and women of all nations recognise that "mankind owes to the Child the best it has to give." If the Principles of the *Declaration of Geneva* are not implemented, writes Eglantyne Jebb,[21] and children grow up physically, mentally and morally degenerate, they are not only miserable themselves, they will spread misery around them, and it is impossible to say where the influence of this misery will end." 'The best humanity can give' was understood to include what had already been mentioned in one of the first (British[22]) drafts of such a declaration: "This 'Charter' seeks to summarise those needs of the children that should at all costs be met, even at a time of severe economic pressure."

Principles I and II of the *Declaration* indicate, according to Jebb, the duty of the community towards the individual child. Principle I states that "each child must be provided with the requisite means for his or her normal development, both materially and spiritually". Edward Fuller[23] writes: "It has long since become axiomatic in the child welfare movement that care for the child's well-being must begin months before birth, and this Principle must be applied in the fullest degree if the first paragraph of the Declaration is to be honestly carried out. The child must 'choose its parents wisely'. They must be fully alive to the responsibilities of parenthood, suitably mated both physically and mentally, whole in mind and body and they must consciously derive the advent of the child, believing that they can offer it a place in life which it can worthily fill." It is Fuller's opinion[24] that "in the United Kingdom, this Principle is often violated and that nothing shows that we realise our responsibilities when we allow ill or psychologically and morally deviant people to become parents, and that 'to give the child the best we have' means nothing if children are born in slums or if they are 'products' of psychologically and physically unfit parents." This is a typical Social-Darwinistic point of view and one wonders if Fuller realised that such a statement could have very negative implications.

Since Principle I of the *Declaration of Geneva* deals with external resources that must be provided for physical and mental development, it can be classified in the *adaptive modes* of the *physical* and the *personality subsystem*.

Principle II begins: "The child that is hungry must be fed; the child that is sick must be nursed." Eglantyne Jebb pointed out that in the past priority had often been given to those who were useful to the community,[25] and that public funds had gone to the education of boys who would, in time, defend their country.[26] This attitude reminded her of animals who kill their weak offspring.

The opening of Principle II is concerned with material resources and health. It fits in the *adaptive* and the *integrative modes* of the *physical subsystem*. The same holds true for the other groups mentioned in this Principle: the child that is backward must be helped; the delinquent child must be reclaimed; the orphan and the waif (the homeless child) must be sheltered and succoured. The indication 'backward' probably refers to the 'mentally retarded'. This adjective fits a very heterogeneous group, ranging from children with slight intellectual limitations to profound mental retardation. This Principle is, therefore, also classifiable in the *adaptive mode* of the *social subsystem*. The same holds true for the paragraph relating to the delinquent child, the orphan and the waif.

Editor of *The World's Children*, Edward Fuller explains that it is a lack of funding that prevents the complete execution of Principle II of the Declaration. "We have become quite familiar, for instance, with the closing of departments in hospitals. Less apparent but equally disastrous is the shortage of attendants in children's homes."[27]

Principle III claims "that the child must be the first to receive relief in times of distress." Fuller finds this shortest Principle of the *Declaration of Geneva* of utmost importance. "For it is the only one which, in so many words, insists that the child shall be *first*.[28] This Principle can be classified in the *conservative mode* of the *physical subsystem* (to conserve the child's very being).

Jebb and Fuller[29] insist that this Principle does not only pertain to acts of war, but that children must always have priority.[30]

Principle IV states that "the child must be enabled to earn a livelihood and must be protected from every form of exploitation". Fuller explains that the first part of this Principle concerns vocational training for young people (an investment in the future) and the second part concerns human nature which is weak and makes us take advantage of our fellow-men. In Fuller's comments (1925) on the Declaration he wrote that attempts to make children under the age of fourteen earn money have become rare in Britain, but it is still quite common, even for the very gifted, to stop going to school and start helping their parents earn a living as soon as they are past the age of compulsory education.[31]

The child is viewed as an independent individual whose purpose in life is not to serve others. This view fits in the *adaptive mode* of the *social subsystem* (the concern for employment is an instance of entering a 'give and take' situation). However, the Principle is also concerned with child slavery and the worst of all exploitations: child prostitution. This belongs in the *conservative mode* of the *physical subsystem* (concern for the child's safety).

Principle V states "that the child must be raised in the consciousness that its talents must be devoted to the service of its fellow-men." Jebb[32] comments that if Principles I and IV are not adhered to, Principle V remains an unattainable ideal. Fuller observes that Principle V, like the Preamble, stands out by its *universal quality*. He compares it[33] with the tendency in Great Britain to emphasise nationalist and imperialist ideals in education – particularly in the teaching of history – to the detriment of the ideal of world service which is implied in the *Declaration of Geneva*. According to him "the fifth Principle is, from the point of view of the world future no less than of

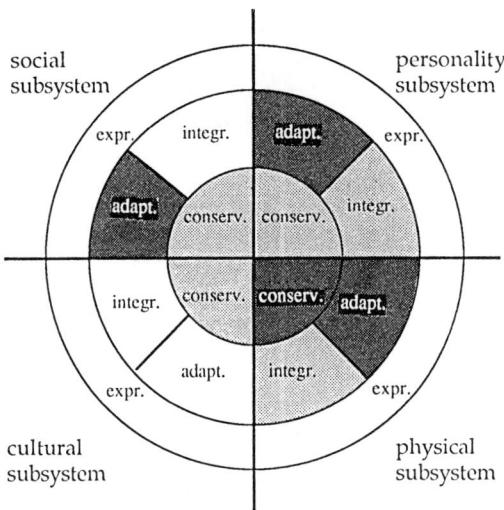

Fig. 10.1. The Declaration of Geneva (1924). Interpreted by the Systemic Quality of Life Model.

the individual, the most important and far-reaching of all Principles of the *Declaration of Geneva*."[34] Principle V expresses values and norms (contributing to society) and the wish that education should be used to these ends. Education often fits in the conservative mode of the cultural subsystem. Although Principle V voices a laudable concern for social harmony and interpersonal consideration, it is doubtful whether it qualifies as a 'right', since it is not clear what claim the child can make in this context (see Hohfeld's definition of a right in Chapter II). The values are still important.

2. THE UNITED NATIONS DECLARATION ON THE RIGHTS OF THE CHILD (1959)

See Appendix XVIII

As early as 1946 the *International Union for Child Welfare*,[35] partially an offspring of Eglantyne Jebb's *Save the Children International Union*, started to lobby the members of the Economic and Social Council of the United Nations (ECOSOC)[36] and its Temporary Social Commission to have the *Declaration of Geneva*, originally adopted by the *League of Nations*, confirmed – with a few minor amendments – by the United Nations.

"The welfare of children, physically, mentally and spiritually, must be the first concern of every nation, particularly having regard to the ravages of the two world wars,"[37], wrote the Temporary Social Commission, a subcommission of the Economic and Social Council. The Commission was therefore of the opinion "that the terms of the *Declaration of Geneva* should be

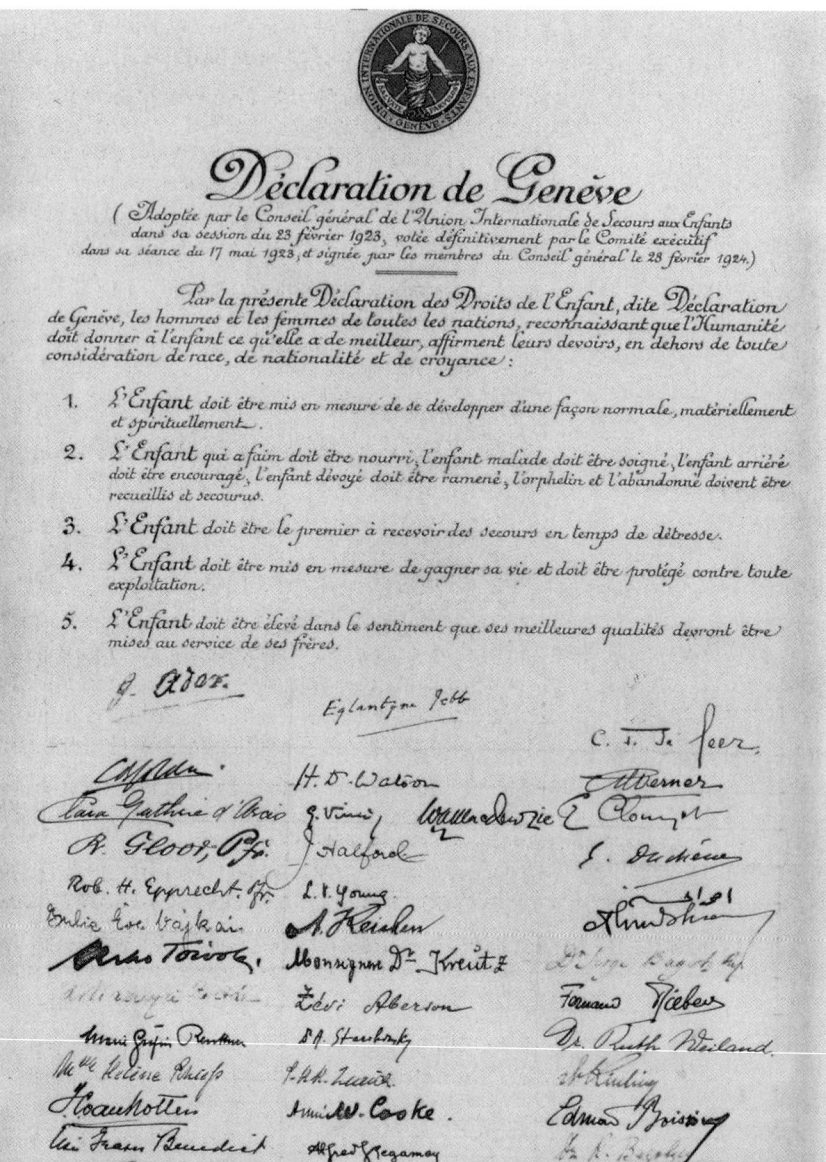

Picture X.1. The Geneva Declaration of February 28, 1924 of the Union Internationale de Secours aux Enfants. (Photographed for this study in the archives by François Martin.)

as binding on the peoples of the world in 1946 as they had been in 1924."[38] ECOSOC agreed to work on an adapted *Declaration of Geneva* which would be proposed in the General Assembly.

In 1948 The General Council of the *International Union for Child Welfare*[39] accepted a revised text of the *Geneva Declaration* and added two clauses to the original text:

1. *The child must be protected beyond and above all considerations of race, nationality or creed.*
   (This principle of non-discrimination, originally mentioned in the Preamble, had received prime importance after the beastly slaughtering of children on racist grounds during the Second World War.)
2. *The child must be cared for with due respect for the family as an entity.*

Process

Before analysing *the contents* of the United Nations Declaration on the Rights of the Child, we shall follow the *process* of deliberations that have led to that Declaration.

In the spring of 1948 a '*Children's Charter*' figured for the first time on the agenda of the *Social Commission*.[40] A long series of discussions which was started on April 19, 1948, would result, eleven years later, in the unanimous adoption by the General Assembly of the *Declaration of the Rights of the Child*.

During the initial meeting, a representative explained that it was the opinion of the Secretary-General of the United Nations that the *Declaration of Geneva* should be the starting-point for future deliberations, and that the Secretary-General had asked the Social Commission to advise him about one of three possibilities:

1. To re-confirm the original text of the *Declaration of Geneva* with a few minor amendments;
2. To use the framework of the *Declaration of Geneva* but amend it in such a way that it would become a *Charter of the Rights of the Child of the United Nations*;
3. To start preparations for a completely new Charter.

The opinion prevailed that the *Declaration of Geneva* which had been proclaimed in 1924, was somewhat outdated, especially in view of the changes that had taken place in the field of health-care and child-welfare. Since then a number of other Declarations had been formulated and proclaimed. These documents had, among other things, drawn the attention to the fact:

– that child-welfare and social security should be integral parts of the social policy, and the duty of the State;

- that growing up in a family had a positive influence on the development of the personality;
- that it was necessary to protect the child against abuse by politicians;
- that juvenile delinquency should be prevented;
- that discrimination, not only based on race, nationality and religious beliefs, but also on gender, the social position of the parents and family circumstances, should be prevented.

Mr. A.J. Altmeyer,[41] the United States representative, proposed in 1948 to formulate a new Charter because the original text of the *Declaration of Geneva* "did not reflect the tremendous development which had taken place in the field of child-welfare since 1924." However, Altmeyer was of the opinion "that the Principles embodied in the *Declaration of Geneva*, as well as additional significant principles that had been generally recognised in more recent statements on children's rights, must be taken into consideration." Lieutenant-Colonel Van Schalkwijk of South-Africa recommended the United Nations "to give great weight to the principles of the *Declaration of Geneva*, and to transform *this document* into a United Nations Charter of the Rights of the Child, embodying the main features of the new conception of child welfare." This view was supported by, among others, the representative of the United Kingdom.

On July 11th, 1950 a *Concept-Declaration of the Rights of the Child*,[42] was proposed by the Social Commission to ECOSOC in Geneva, and discussed by its Social Committee.

Some members of the Social Committee were rather reticent about the idea of a *Declaration of the Rights of the Child* in general. The Chilean Delegate was of the opinion that the *Universal Declaration of Human Rights* had made the *Declaration of the Rights of the Child* superfluous. The Canadian Delegate also did not favour a separate Declaration concerning certain age groups. He pleaded for a thorough review of the course taken by the Social Commission.

On July 13th, 1950, the objections, voiced in the *Social Committee*[43] were rehashed in the plenary meeting of ECOSOC. This time the French Delegate appreciated the opportunity to clarify that a vote for the resolution to *consider* a Declaration and have the Commission on Human Rights look into the matter, as proposed by the Social Commission, was not identical with a vote for such a *Declaration*. That was a modest step foreward.

The representatives of Australia and Pakistan were of the opinion that the question of a *Declaration of the Rights of the Child* yet needed to be studied in depth, and withheld their votes. These and other reservations did not deter ECOSOC. A resolution to deal with a Declaration of the Rights of the Child as soon as possible, originally proposed in the Committee by the representatives of France, India, Mexico and the United States, was again tabled during the eleventh meeting of the General Assembly, and the *Commission on Human Rights* was requested to report to ECOSOC during its

13th meeting. This proposal was adopted with 12 votes against 1, and 2 abstentions.

In the meantime staff members of the Secretary General had done a useful job with the preparation of a memorandum for the *Commission on Human Rights*. They had, for instance, compared the text of the *Social Commission's* Draft Declaration of the Rights of the Child paragraph after paragraph with the text of the *Universal Declaration of Human Rights*.[44]

But the issue was 'forgotten' by the *Commission on Human Rights* for a long time. We may assume that politically it did not have high priority. Meanwhile several Non-Governmental-Organisations had submitted requests to deal with the Declaration as soon as possible. Often such requests had been accompanied by proposals for supplements and/or amendments in the concept-text of the *Social Commission*.[45]

However, when in April 1957 (!) the eighteen members of the *Commission of Human Rights* finally broached the issue,[46] the first subject of their discussion was again whether or not a special *Declaration on the Rights of the Child* was at all desirable.

All the delegates agreed that in view of the vulnerability and physical and mental immaturity of children a special Declaration dealing with their rights was called for in addition to the *Universal Declaration of Human Rights*. Some delegates even would have preferred a *Convention*, since they feared that a *Declaration* would not be binding enough. At long last, the climate was favourable for completing a Declaration.

One of the first problems was the difference between the rights of legitimate and illegitimate children. Some members of the Commission on Human Rights drew the attention to the stigma worn by illegitimate children through no fault of their own, and demanded of the United Nations to protect such children by way of the future Declaration. In 1959 this issue would again be discussed extensively.

A great deal of attention was also given to the duties and responsibilities of the State and the parents. However, the members of the *Human Rights Commission* did not discuss the Concept-Declaration in detail. Some delegates were of the opinion that the Concept-Declaration should be returned to the *Social Commission* for further elaboration, but the representatives of Ceylon, India, Iran and Mexico prevented further delay and proposed in a resolution[47] that the Member-States of the United Nations should deliver their comments to the Secretary General, and that further deliberations would take place in the *Commission on Human Rights*. The Soviet Union proposed that December 1st, 1957, should be the deadline for delivering the comments. All these proposals were accepted.

In July 1957 ECOSOC decided that the Member States needed more time and moved the deadline to December 1st, 1958. It would be the responsibility of the Secretary-General to distribute the comments by the end of December 1958. Twenty-one States reacted. Of these, five declared that they did not have substantial comments. The other sixteen had detailed suggestions. In the spring of 1959 the *Commission on Human Rights* met in New York and again discussed the Concept-Declaration, this time against the background of the comments handed in by the different governments and of new comments made by the *International Union for Child Welfare* and the *International Federation of Women Lawyers*.[48]

As could be expected, the representatives of all the Communist countries wanted a more binding document. This issue would again be discussed during the talks about Paragraph 6 of the Preamble. Poland supported the Declaration because it was a step towards a *Convention*.[49] The delegate of the United States was of the opinion that the Declaration should first be a modern version of the *Declaration of Geneva*. The French delegate, Mr. Juvigny,[50] was of the opinion that "the child was not in a position to exercise his own rights. Adults exercised them for the child and in doing so were subject to certain obligations. Thus it could be said that a child had special legal status resulting from his inability to exercise his rights." The representative of Iraq reminded the Member-States that although the Principles of the Declaration seemed acceptable for all States, they posed practical problems for the Third World countries who did not have the means, for instance, to implement compulsory education. The Italian delegate, Mr. Dominedo, wanted the Declaration first to be short and to the point. He argued that it should be a document from which hope could be drawn and wanted as few references as possible to the role of the State. The Chinese representative agreed with Mr. Dominedo. The Russian representative, Mr. Sapozhnikov, expounded that the *Declaration of the Rights of the Child* should not only include general principles but also the duties of the State and proceedings leading to the realisation of the rights. The philosophies of East and West were diametrically opposed. The Warsaw Pact countries were sticking to the idea of the primary responsibility of the State. Mrs. Lord of the United States represented the view of the Western delegations, that the prime responsibility for the child's welfare lay with the parents and not with the State. Sir Samuel Hoare of the United Kingdom proposed as a compromise that the Declaration should appeal to individuals, local authorities and National Governments. In the initial stages of the deliberations Mr. Sapozhnikov was even opposed to reference to *individuals* working through local authorities and National Governments.[51]

These were not the only value conflicts. Israel and Poland proposed amendments in order to protect illegitimate children. Israel proposed to add that "in particular no child shall be discriminated against by reason of his birth out of wedlock.[52] Mr. Dominedo of Italy expressed respect for the idealistic mentality behind this amendment but "thought it equally necessary to affirm the need to protect the *legitimate* family, which, before the State, constituted the foundation of an organised society."[53] Mr. Cohn of Israel observed that "the amendment proposed by Mr. Dominedo was tantamount to legitimation of discrimination against illegitimate children," and warned the Commission against sanctioning such discrimination. Mr. Dominedo, however, felt himself compelled to defend the rights of the family and feared that the Commission was treading a dangerous path by explicitly declaring that children "whether born in or out of wedlock should enjoy the same rights." If this would be the case his country would vote against the Declaration.

The above was one of the few instances of a serious clash within the Commission. In general the atmosphere between East and West and even between the representatives of Iraq and Israel, was of a constructive nature. The representative of Iraq even declared[54] that the arguments about illegitimate children, brought to the fore by the Israeli representative, seemed quite positive. The final formulation does not mention children born out of wedlock explicitly but states that *all* children will enjoy equal rights.

In the subsequent meetings of the *Commission on Human Rights* Principle after Principle of the Declaration was discussed. In 1953 a particularly delicate Principle had been introduced by the International Catholic Child Bureau, a Non-Governmental Organisation with consultative status at ECOSOC, UNICEF and UNESCO. This N.G.O. wanted the Declaration to mention specifically that "from the moment of conception the child has the right to life and shall be protected from anything liable to impair this right."[55] This offensive, lead by the Catholic lobby, aimed at providing the adversaries of abortion in the various countries with munition. The Italian delegate was the self-appointed leader of this movement that kept popping up, especially during the discussions of Principle 3 of the Preamble. The Italian amendment was rejected in the *Commission on Human Rights*.

The new draft text of the Declaration, as amended and supplemented by the *Commission on Human Rights*, was adopted and sent up to ECOSOC. The Council was now equipped with two Concept-Declarations, one drawn by the *Social Commission* and one by the *Commission on Human Rights*. On July 30th, 1959, ECOSOC recommended presenting the last Concept-Declaration to the General Assembly of the United Nations. The General Assembly decided to delegate the issue to its *Third Committee*, whose task was to deal with issues of social, humanitarian and cultural nature.

This *Third Committee*,[56] chaired by Mrs. Georgette Ciselet, a Senator for the Belgian Liberal Party,[57] needed another twenty-three meetings in order to discuss the issue. Once again some delegates said that their governments would have preferred a Convention to a Declaration. Others would have liked the Declaration to be shorter and contain Principles rather than detailed guidelines. The most important spokesman of this opinion was the representative of the United States. Paul Hofmann, the well-informed reporter of the *New York Times*, wrote that the document would only be acceptable to the government of the United States in "absence of any specific provision for implementation and international enforcement."[58] Anonymous diplomats told Hofmann that "the United States was opposed to any Covenants under United Nations auspices that would call for international supervisory machinery."[59] This, by the way, was also the reason why, for a long time, the United States was one of the few States who had not acceded to the 1948 *Convention on the Prevention and Punishment of the Crime of Genocide* which declared genocide (defined as destruction of a national, ethnic or religious group) punishable by national or international tribunals.

A different approach was taken by the East Bloc countries. They tended to ratify Conventions and Declarations about Human Rights, but made it practically impossible for other countries to supervise their implementation. Hofmann reported in the *New York Times* that "Communist delegates pressed for welfare-state provisions. Most of these amendments were rejected on the ground that interference in the domestic affairs of individual countries must be avoided. The Soviet motions sought, among other things, to provide for free health services and free schooling on all levels, and to outlaw child labour."

The text which was finally proposed by the Third Committee was much weaker than the representatives of the Soviet Union had hoped for. However, the Western States also did not get what they wanted, such as a recognition of the right to religious teachings.

Italy did not give up on the issue of protection of human life from the moment of conception. The Italian delegate, Mrs. Lupinacci, submitted a sub-amendment[60] to a Philippine amendment.[61] In her view the phrasing "from the moment of his conception", should be inserted in the third paragraph of the Preamble. The Philippine amendment employed the broader formula "before as well as after birth," and did not specify when exactly such protection was supposed to begin. The Philippine proposal for the Preambule was adopted[62] with 58 votes to 1 and 10 abstentions.

On Friday afternoon, October 16th, 1959, the discussion about the Concept-Declaration, now consisting of a Preamble and ten Principles, was closed. During the weekend it was translated into the official languages of the United Nations so that all the papers would be ready on Monday morning and the voting could take place after the weekend. The Concept-Declaration was adopted by the Third Committee with 70 votes and two abstentions. Princess Pingpeang Yukanthor of Cambodia explained that she had abstained from voting "to give her country the freedom to adapt the Declaration to the customs and conditions prevailing in Cambodia."[63] Mr. C.J.A. Barratt from South-Africa said that he had "found it necessary to abstain on certain Principles." We may assume that he alluded to Principle 1 and Paragraph 2 of the Preamble, wherein is stated that the rights apply to all children without discrimination because of colour.

The Declaration appeared on November 20th, 1959 on the agenda of the General Assembly. It was unanimously adopted without discussion.

The *New York Times* published an editorial on the Declaration: "The United Nations are making a strong affirmation of our desire to do better in the future than we have done in the past. In that better world no child ought to be allowed to suffer. It is well to have a broad commitment to that end."

Analysis of the Contents of the U.N. Declaration

In the following pages we shall analyse the contents of this very important Declaration in detail. According to Casullo[64] "the most striking feature of the *Declaration of the Rights of the Child* is that there is no definition of 'child' or 'child's rights' and in consequence . . . there is no way to elicit its scope from the wording of its Preamble or its ten Principles."

In *Paragraph 1 of the Preamble* the peoples of the United Nations confirm their faith in fundamental human rights and in the dignity and worth of the human person as represented in the Charter of the United Nations. Moreover they express their determination to promote social progress and better standards of life in larger freedom.

Paragraph 2 of the Preamble refers to the *Universal Declaration of Human Rights*, which proclaimed that everyone is entitled to all the rights and freedoms set forth therein, without distinction of any kind, such as race, colour, sex, language, religion, political or other opinion, national or social origin, property, birth or other status.

In the draft of this Paragraph the Dutch Government[65] made a marginal note to the effect that "in the opinion of the Government of the Netherlands fundamental rights of the child would be adequately protected if the Universal Declaration of Human Rights, which also applies to children, were observed in all countries. In cases where the Universal Declaration of Human Rights is not observed it is doubtful whether anything will be achieved by the adoption of a new instrument dealing especially with the child." This observation must, however, be understood as concerning the Declaration of the Rights of the Child as a whole.

Paragraph 2 laid down the principle of non-discrimination of the Preamble. The clearest interpretation of the intention of this paragraph is given by Sir Samuel Hoare[66] who stressed "that many of the rights in the . . . Declaration – social security, education, etc. – were also rights proclaimed in the Universal Declaration. It was therefore necessary to establish a link, in the Preamble, between the Universal Declaration[67] and the draft Declaration, and that was effected in the second Paragraph."

In the Commission on Human Rights the last few words of this Paragraph: "without distinction of . . . birth or other status," lead to an important debate, on which we already reported earlier in this Chapter. Some delegates wanted explicit mention of children born out of wedlock. The Hungarian delegate proposed in a note dated December 9th, 1958, "that no child shall suffer because of its birth out of wedlock and that all children born in or out of wedlock shall enjoy the same rights," but this phrasing was not adopted.

Paragraph 3 of the Preamble expresses the consensus that the child needs special protection "by reason of his physical and mental immaturity." As we have seen earlier in this Chapter, the argument was about the exact moment this protection should come into effect. Adopted was the phrasing "before as well as after birth."[68]

Paragraph 4 of the Preamble cites as a basis for the subsequent enunciation of Principles of the United Nations Declaration, the original Declaration of Geneva (of 1924), the Universal Declaration of Human Rights, and the statutes of the specialised agencies and international organisations concerned with the welfare of children. Said Mr. Lopez of the Philippines: "It was good for the peoples of the world to be reminded how much already had been done to protect the child."[69] Although not everybody had agreed to refer to the statutes of some U.N. agencies (such as the I.L.O.), no fundamental discussions about this issue took place.

Paragraph 5 of the Preamble reflects that this is a Declaration of good intentions: "whereas mankind owes to the child the best it has to give."

Paragraph 6 of the Preamble originated some very fundamental discussions. According to Mr. Cheng, the Chinese Delegate in the Commission on Human Rights, this happened because "the difference of opinion appeared to derive from two views of the child, one regarding him as the child of an individual, and the other as the child of the State."[70]

Controversial was the statement that men and women as *individuals*, as well as local authorities and Governments were called upon to recognise those rights. In the Commission on Human Rights and in the Third committee of the General Assembly, the U.S.S.R. argued that only *the State* could guarantee many of the rights formulated in the Declaration. Many Western Delegates, on the other hand, maintained that not the State but the family and especially the parents should be primarily responsible for the child's welfare."[71]

Two trends prevail in the final compromise: first, the underlying assumption that *Society* should benefit (the child shall enjoy rights for the good of society), and second, as Sir Samuel Hoare of the United Kingdom expressed it: "The Commission should be wary of adopting any amendment that would give the impression that the text was one that imposed obligations on States, rather than a declaration."[72]

Most of the paragraphs of the Preamble are too general to be classified in the 'Systemic Quality of Life Model'. Only Paragraph 3: ("whereas the child, by reason of his immaturity needs special safeguards and care") belongs in the *conservative mode* of the *physical and of the conservative mode* of the *personality subsystem* (prevention from physical and psychological harm).

The Preamble is followed by ten Principles. That the indication *Principles* is used rather than *Articles* derives from the non-binding character of the *Declaration*. From the very beginning a Principle was looked upon as a further elaboration of the purpose, the nature, and the title of the Declaration.[73]

Principle 1

The major areas of concern of this Principle are "patterns of discrimination (race, colour, sex, language, religion, political opinion, birth, status, property, age and inter-generational justice."[74] These areas of concern are dealt with by stating the general right to enjoy all the rights set forth in the Declaration. Originally[75] this Principle closed the Declaration, but the International Union for Child Welfare[76] attached so much importance to non-discrimination that they proposed that this Principle should be mentioned first and not last. On April 1st, 1959, the Commission on Human Rights decided by eleven votes against none (and six abstentions) on the proposal of France to include Principle 10 of the draft prepared by the Social Commission, as Principle 1 of the new draft.

If we look at an Israeli amendment adopted by the Commission on Human Rights, we see that "without distinction or discrimination of *caste*" did not become part of the final text. Another Israeli proposal, that "all children, whether born in or out of wedlock, shall enjoy these rights," was amended by the United Kingdom. "In Her Majesty's Government's view this reference is quite unnecessary, because the word 'birth' (as has been clearly brought out in the course of discussion of similar provisions in the draft Covenants on Human Rights) includes *inter alia* the consideration both of legitimacy and of illegitimacy... In the view of Her Majesty's Government, it is also undesirable that the enumeration of certain particular grounds of discrimination (which are given only as instances and are to be read with the words 'or other status') should depart from the terms adopted for similar provisions, both in the Universal Declaration and in the draft Covenants on Human Rights. For this reason the word 'caste' as well as the word 'legitimacy' should be deleted."[77]

Bitterly Haim Cohn, the Israeli Delegate to the Commission on Human Rights, observed that "the only point of a Declaration concerning children would be to denounce more vigorously than did the Universal Declaration any form of discrimination which particularly affected children. If the Commission on Human Rights wished to adhere to the terms in the Universal Declaration, as did the representative of the United Kingdom, it would be enough to refer to Article 2 of that document. It was, however, a Declaration on the Rights of the Child that the Commission was considering; it should therefore stress those forms of discrimination which particularly affected children, in particular discrimination based on 'illegitimacy'."

Sir Samuel Hoare of the United Kingdom warned that the Commission should guard against declarations which promised equality in every respect between children whether born in or out of wedlock, when such equality was not possible in practice." And the Delegate of India said that "the word 'caste' appeared to apply to one country only and therefore should not appear in a document which was international in scope."

These two *explicit* broadenings of Principle 1 survived neither in the Commission on Human Rights nor in the Third Committee where the knot was finally cut by the Saudi Arabian Delegate who proposed the general formula: "every child without any exception whatsoever." Says Haim Cohn: "We wanted to do business, not come to a dead stop over semantics." According to him the rights of the group 'children born out of wedlock' are covered by the term: 'or any exception whatsoever'. However, other patterns of discrimination (such as discrimination on grounds of socio-economic status[78]) are explicitly mentioned.

Said P. van Dijk[79] "Equality is strongly emphasised and elaborated upon with an extensive but not comprehensive list of characteristics and reasons that may lead to forbidden discrimination. This Principle of equality is of fundamental importance for the scope of the following Principles. It means that each time the child is mentioned we must read: 'all children without exception whatsoever."

Principle 1 of the Declaration cannot be classified in the 'Systemic Quality of Life Model'. It does not deal with rights, but with universality of the rights formulated in the other Principles.

Principle 2

The major areas of concern in this Principle are international and national protective legislation, age limits for protection in specific areas, and the best interests of the child: articulation, representation and protection.[80]

This Principle says that the child shall enjoy special protection and shall be given opportunities and facilities by law and other means to enable him to develop physically, mentally, morally, spiritually and socially in a healthy and normal manner and in conditions of freedom and dignity.

It is a further elaboration of what had already been formulated in the Universal Declaration of Human Rights,[81] namely that *motherhood and childhood are entitled to special care and assistance*.

Mrs. Wasilkowska of Poland said that Principle 2 "was intended to give effect to the third Paragraph of the Preamble."[82] She proposed that the enactment of laws should be "solely" in the interests of the child, but the United Kingdom and Belgium raised objections.

For the first time protection was not only viewed as something positive. Mr. Jha of India[83] felt that to place such emphasis on the child's need for protection was a negative attitude. This, however, was not approved by the members of the Commission who made efforts to formulate an acceptable text concerning the responsibility of States in the enactment of laws for the purpose of protection.

Principle 2 of the Declaration has several aspects. We read that "the child shall enjoy the benefits from special protection," but we do not get a clear understanding against what the child must be protected. It might be protection from physical harm so that this Principle could be classified in the *conservative mode* of the *physical subsystem*. However, it might also be protection against bad influences on the growing personality. In that case it would fit in the *conservative mode* of the *personality subsystem*.

"The child shall be given opportunities and facilities to enable him to *develop* physically, mentally, morally, spiritually and socially " can be classified in the *expressive mode* (to develop is expressive: to advance the potentials of the child and to promote capabilities) of *all the four subsystems*.. Since the last paragraph of Principle 2 ("the best interests of the child shall be the paramount consideration") compares the rights of children with the rights of other human beings, it is not classifiable in the 'Systemic Quality of Life Model', at least not formally. Yet the context suggests that this paragraph relates to the *conservative mode* of *all the subsystems*.

Principle 3

This Principle refers to the child's right to a name and nationality. "The right to a name" that was proposed for the *Declaration on the Rights of the Child* was an extension of Article 15(1) of the *Universal Declaration on Human Rights* (Everyone has the right to a nationality). Major areas of concern are acquisition of citizenship and problems of statelessness.[84]

According to Mr. Suphamonghon of Thailand "the right to have a name was not really necessary, since it merely recognised a custom that was thousands of years old."[85]

According to Haim Cohn[86] the issue was not whether the principle related to a first or a last name. In some cultures a person has only one name, in others sons are called after the father and one cannot really speak about a family name, etc. That problem has been solved long ago by each culture. But the child's right to a nationality raised complex legal questions. Mr. Suphamonghon of Thailand said in the Third Committee of the General Assembly: "This issue is complex since in the application of national legislations, nationality in some States is based on the principle of *jus sanguinis* and others on the *jus soli*. This led in some cases inevitably to statelessness or multiple nationality."[87]

Dr. Haim Cohn explained the importance of this Principle to me. Since a child is not a qualified petitioner, somebody else must claim the rights for him. However, if the legal guardian does not claim that right there is a serious problem. The function of Principle 3 is to make *someone* responsible for making sure that the child receives what is his due.

In Chapter III we have classified the right to have a name in the *adaptive mode* of the *social subsystem* and the right to a nationality in the *adaptive mode of the social subsystem* and the *conservative mode* of the *physical subsystem*.

Principle 4

Article 22 of the *Universal Declaration* already states that everyone, as a member of society, has the right to social security. Article 25 gives everyone the right "to a standard of living adequate for the health and well-being of himself and of his family, including food, clothing, housing and medical care and necessary social services."

In 1951 the Social Commission proposed: "The child shall enjoy the benefits of social security. He shall be entitled even from before birth to grow and develop in health. He shall have the right to adequate nutrition, housing, recreation and *free* medical services." Major areas of concern were the physical, psychological, emotional and social welfare of the child including health care, nutrition, housing, social assistance, social security, living standards, etc.[88]

Nine years later the discussion in the Commission on Human Rights dealt especially with "free medical services." Mr. Jha of India asked: "Whatever right will be accorded to individuals, must not the corresponding duty of the State also be formulated?"[89] Obviously many countries did not have the financial resources to establish an adequate network of hospitals, clinics, maternity wards and other medical institutions. However, Mr. Sapozhnikov of the U.S.S.R. argued that "if the word 'free' was omitted, the Declaration would be quite ineffectual, since the State could guarantee the right to medical services only if those services were free."

More than others the representative of the United States pleaded for deleting the word 'free'. With him sided the representatives of the United Kingdom, Italy and Belgium. Every country should be free, they argued, to choose the means for attaining the desired goal of ensuring medical services to every child. Mr. Hakim of Lebanon summarised what was probably the decisive factor for the final omitting of the word 'free': "Most countries would not have the financial resources necessary for free medical services for a long time." The same course was followed in relation to 'adequate housing and recreation.'

Principle 4 does mention special care "both to him *and to his mother.*" The Soviet Union pleaded for an even stronger phrasing in favour of the mother, but France tried to weaken it because it referred more to the rights of women than to the rights of children. Mr. Nedbailo of the Ukrainian Soviet Socialist Republic[90] sided with the Soviet Union. It was his opinion that the child, even from before birth, had a right to normal development, and that all protection of the mother was in the best interests of the child."

Principle 4 belongs in the *adaptive mode* (social security, adequate nutrition, housing, medical services, recreation) of the *physical subsystem*. Recreation can also be classified in the *adaptive mode* of the *personality subsystem*. "To grow and develop in health" fits in the *integrative mode* of the *physical subsystem*. Special care and protection belongs in the *conservative mode* of the *physical subsystem*.

Principle 5

This Principle establishes that if the child is handicapped he or she shall be given special treatment, education and care. The text as proposed by the

Social Committee in 1951, is an extension of Article 25(1) of the *Universal Declaration of Human Rights* ("Everyone has the right to security in the event of sickness, disability or other lack of livelihood in circumstances beyond his control"), and Article 25(2) ("Motherhood and childhood are entitled to special care and assistance").

Areas of concern of this Principle are disadvantaged children (socially, racially, economically, etc.). The Principle especially mentions "the child who is physically, mentally or socially handicapped."

The representative of Peru proposed in the Commission on Human Rights to include also delinquent children but later withdrew his proposal. Italy also made an effort in this direction with "the socially maladjusted child, including the delinquent child, may not be separated from his family save by decision of a competent judicial authority." This proposal was rejected.

In the Third Committee of the General Assembly some representatives took a strong stand against the specific mentioning of 'delinquent children' in this context. Most outspoken was Mr. Goris of Belgium who declared that "the Declaration would certainly be read by some delinquent children, and it would be most unfortunate to leave them with the impression that they were a privileged group in the community."

Since Principle 5 does not deal with a specific right but with categories of children to whom rights apply, it can not be classified in the 'Systemic Quality of Life Model'.

Principle 6

Keywords for understanding this principle are "the full and harmonious development of his personality."[91] The rest of the Principle is an elaboration about the kind of environment required for the normal development of the child's personality.

That the child needs "love and understanding" initiated no argument. However, differences in cultures, values and norms were evident. This accounts for the great number of amendments proposed during the discussion of this Principle. The International Catholic Child Bureau in Geneva, for instance, wanted explicit mention of rights of the parents to choose religious education for their children. Representatives of Guatemala and Israel proposed that the child would have the right to be raised in the faith of his or her parents. This was rejected. The major areas of concern of this Principle are protection of children who are deprived of family life, and protection of the family unit against outside intervention, in particular removal of children from their family and intervention in case a family is broken.

Said Mr. Yolga, the representative of Turkey[92] in the Third Committee: "Since every right implied a corresponding obligation, it was reasonable to lay a certain responsibility on the parents."

Principle 6 mentions as a guideline that a child of tender years shall not be separated from his mother, save under exceptional circumstances. The

Iraqi delegate said in the Commission on Human Rights that the expression 'young child' in the English text was inappropriate. "If a particular category of children was to be mentioned, the word 'infant' would be preferable." Mr. Juvigny of France explained that "his delegation had merely wished to insert in the Declaration some guidelines for public authorities of judicial bodies in doubtful cases. By the word 'young' his delegation had wished to indicate, without fixing a specific age limit, that the consequences of separation were particularly serious when the child was very young." The idea was to keep separations to a minimum.

Casullo[93] notes that the importance of Principle 6 is "that it makes public authorities responsible for the provision of particular care to children without families and to those without adequate means of support. This provision illustrates the philosophy based on the notion of 'parens patriae' according to which State interference in the relationship between the child and the family is sometimes justified." The Principle regulates the care for orphans and "those without adequate means of support." Stressed is that the child must grow up "in an atmosphere of affection and of moral and material responsibility."

The French representative in the Commission on Human Rights proposed to supplant 'economic security' by 'moral security'. Dr. Haim Cohn from Israel told his fellow Commission members that "a child had no more right than any other individual to grow up in economic security," and that "it was merely an ideal to be striven for. The child had, however, the right to an opportunity to grow up in the house of his parents, even if they were poor."

"Love and understanding," he said, "were more important than economic security." He preferred the word 'emotional security' to the words 'moral security' proposed by France.

Mr. Sapozhnikov[94] of the Soviet Union had nothing against the words 'economic security', but noted that it was "useless to state that the child was entitled to grow up in economic security without indicating any practical measures enabling him to do so." He thought that children of poor parents required special safeguards. "They were entitled to State assistance to ensure that they received proper care and education. That did not mean that the child should be removed from his family, however poor, without the parents' consent, but that financial assistance should be provided by the State in some form, and that the State should also help to place the child in a boarding school or children's home if the parents so requested."[95]

Sir Samuel Hoare of the United Kingdom could not accept the changes proposed by the U.S.S.R., because he found the expression 'States shall provide' not appropriate in a Declaration and more something for a Convention. Mr. Mitra of India feared that the use of the word 'moral security' was open to various interpretations. It was Sir Samuel Hoare[96] who finally proposed that the text would become: "he shall grow up whenever possible in the care of his parents, and in any case in an atmosphere of affection and moral and material security." (See Appendix XVIII, page 466.)

Finally the Soviet Union proposed an amendment to the effect that the State must assist large families financially and otherwise. Mr. Mitra of India voiced great concern because in his country, where the population was at that time growing by five million annually, such encouragement could not be viewed favourably.

In the Report of the 1959 sessions of the Third Committee, however, the Dutch Ministry of Foreign Affairs wrote acrimoniously: "Although the States had over and again opposed such aims, the Soviet Union succeeded this time to have its amendment accepted by 19 votes against 18 and 31 abstentions." This, according to the Dutch Ministry, accounted for the ending of Principle 6 (which mentions that the State should pay maintenance money to large families.).[97]

If we analyse Principle 6 with the 'Systemic Quality of Life Model' we see that the aim of this Principle (full and harmonious development of the child's personality) stands central and that the other paragraphs are elaborations on means to reach this goal. According to most of the delegates, for instance, the separation of a young child from his or her mother have adverse influence on the child's harmonious development. However, here too cultural differences play a part. Miss Fujita of Japan said in the Third Committee that she could not support the Principle that a child of tender years should not be separated from his mother.

The aim of the Principle and the final consensus about it can best be classified in *all modes* of the *personality subsystem*.

Principle 7

Besides access to education (in particular the denial of access to education for economic or other reasons) areas of concern in Principle 7 are the aims of education and the extra-curricular activities of children (play, recreation and cultural rights).

A very important contribution to the formulation of Principle 7 came from Sir Samuel Hoare of the United Kingdom[98] who submitted an amendment to the Commission on Human Rights to the effect that "education should be free, at least in the elementary stages."

Although free education at all levels was a goal to strive for, at the moment many countries could not achieve it. The wording was taken from the Universal Declaration, but the reference to the fundamental stages of education had been omitted because fundamental education was a term usually referring to adult education."

Mr. Sapozhnikov[99] of the U.S.S.R. pointed out that the expression 'at least in the elementary stages' might be interpreted as meaning only during the first year or so of the child's education. Although this objection was supported by Mexico the wording was adopted.

Mr. Basyn of Belgium[100] interpreted the controversial paragraph as follows: "If the word 'child' was meant to apply to children under ten, the elementary stages would only cover kindergarten and primary education, but if the word 'child' was intended to apply to children up to the age of twelve or fourteen, technical education, ... should also be mentioned. If the child was to become a useful member of society, which was one of the aims of education specified in the original text, he must acquire not only general culture but also a means of earning his living."

Since the final text of Principle 7 includes the words "to become a useful member of society", we may assume that vocational education and training are also a major area of concern of this Principle, even though the text itself and the records of the discussions do not mention much to support this theory. What is mentioned in the records is that free secondary education was for many States still impossible.

What direction must education take? India, Iran and Iraq(!) proposed in an amendment that education should aim at full development of the child's personality, strengthen respect for human rights and fundamental freedoms, offer the child opportunities to develop individual judgement and become a useful member of society, and promote tolerance and understanding.

The first concept of this Principle, drafted by the Social Commission in 1950[101], proposed that "the child shall be given an education which will bestow upon him general culture and enable him to develop his abilities and individual judgement and to become a useful member of society." Mrs. Siegel[102] of the International Confederation of Free Trade Unions (ICFTU) noted that the term 'general culture' was too general." The Australian delegate had already tried to sharpen the issue by proposing "the culture to which he belongs." The Soviet Union went a little further by proposing to include that the aim of this Principle was to make culture accessible to children by way of libraries, reading rooms, music schools, etc. The representative of Argentina proposed that education should ensure "full and harmonious development of his personality."[103] The representative of Uruguay, Mr. Penderes, wanted to see a specific statement of the need to promote the development of the moral and social conscience of the child. In the same committee Miss MacEntee of Ireland[104] noted that the intellectual growth of the child was neglected in the text. The Delegate of Pakistan[105] was of the opinion that the wording "education *will bestow on him* general culture" was too strong in view of the fact that nobody could guarantee that education indeed bestowed a general culture. The text was subsequently changed to "the child shall be given an education *which will promote his culture.*" The delegate of Uruguay contributed a sub-amendment to the effect that the child must be educated towards responsibility. The delegate of Turkey supported this especially "at a time when juvenile delinquency was proving a disturbing problem."[106]

Principle 7 leaves the right to determine the kind of education the child will receive to the parents. As quite a few delegates pointed out, this is more a right of the parents than of the children. However, the obligation that education must be in the best interests of the child is included in the Principle.

The second part of Principle 7 refers to the right of the child to have full opportunity for *play and recreation*. These activities should, like education, be oriented to promote the child's culture and to develop his abilities, judgement, moral and social responsibility. In the Third Committee this paragraph was submitted by Mexico, Peru and Rumania. Mr. Malitza of Rumania[107] explained that "the purpose of recreation was simply to enable the child to develop in health. Play was something quite different. It was an essential activity in which all the child's faculties were called upon. During his free time the child should engage in activities which fostered the full development of his personality and discouraged him from adopting anti-social modes of behaviour."

The International Catholic Child Bureau pleaded for mentioning the right to religious observance and religious education, but in the final text of Principle 7 no space has been devoted to this right. The *Christian Crusade Weekly*[108] pointed bitterly out that "apparently the soul of the child does not matter."

While evaluating the final text of Principle 7, we see that it is rather vague. What for instance is meant with the 'general culture', and with 'in the best interests of the child'?

The general culture, which education (according to the Declaration) must promote, belongs in the *four modes* of the *cultural subsystem*. The effort to make the child, by way of education, into a 'useful member of society' can be classified in the *adaptive mode* of the *social subsystem*. 'Education must contribute to the development of abilities' fits in the *expressive mode* of the *personality subsystem*. 'To develop individual judgement' belongs in the *expressive mode* of the *cultural subsystem* (judgement is a matter of values). 'The sense of moral and social responsibility' which must be developed by education fits in the *adaptive mode* of the *cultural subsystem*.

Play and recreation, being complementary to education, are meant to develop the *personality subsystem*. To the extent that play means *recharging the batteries* it belongs in the *adaptive mode* (see Chapter III).

Principle 8

"The child shall in all circumstances be *among* the first to receive protection and relief."

The word 'among', originally advanced by the Social Commission, had unanimously been rejected by the Commission on Human Rights. However, Mrs. Diemer of the Netherlands had submitted an amendment in the Third Committee to reinstall it. She was guided[109] by the consideration that, no age limit being mentioned in the Declaration, cases might occur where old or physically handicapped persons or pregnant women would have the same or even more right to be helped than big children who could very well help themselves. Mr. Rimmerfors of Sweden said that the Dutch amendment made the Principle too vague. He feared that in situations of natural disasters or armed conflict children would receive less priority than was intended. The Dutch proposal was adopted with 36 votes against 8. Thus the final text does not give absolute priority to the child (as did Principle 3 of the Declaration of Geneva). We can classify this Principle in the *adaptive mode* of the *physical subsystem*.

Principle 9

This Principle states that a child "shall be protected against all forms of neglect, cruelty and exploitation". According to Casullo "this obligation is collective and falls not only on the parents but also on the State and on each member of Society."[110]

One form of child exploitation is child labour. The Declaration states that the child shall not be admitted to employment before an appropriate minimum age. In 1950 the Social Commission had been unable to reach a consensus about linking the minimum age of employment with the school leaving age.[111] This pattern was carried on during the years of discussion. The determination of a minimum age for employment found much resistance. In April 1959 the Commission on Human Rights discussed the issue. A Soviet amendment[112] was adopted, which stated: "To these ends, the States shall enact legislation prohibiting the employment of minors below a certain age limit to be established by law, and also the employment of minors for unhealthy or hazardous work."

Mr. Tarra Murzi of Venezuela pleaded in the Third Committee[113] for a "firm provision prohibiting the employment of children below the age of fourteen years, which was the age established by Conventions of the International Labour Organisation." Since the proposal again met with resistance, Venezuela later proposed as a compromise to change the term 'appropriate age' into 'appropriate minimum age'. The representative of the International Labour Organisation who was invited to voice his opinion supported the proposal which was subsequently adopted with 41 votes against 1 and 27 abstentions.

Another important proposal came from Mr. Malitza of Romania. This proposal aimed at forbidding the trade in children *expressis verbis*.[114] No one raised objections. However, some delegates found that the issue was already covered by the expression 'exploitation'. The Romanian wording: "He shall not be the subject of traffic, nor shall he be bought or sold," (as for purposes of adoption for instance)[115] was sharply attacked by the Mexican Delegate who argued that "buying or selling pre-supposed a contract between two parties competent to conclude a contract. Moreover, a contract of purchase or sale should refer to something that could be bought or sold. To say that a child should not be bought or sold was to admit the possibility of an act which had no legal validity in the legislation of the Member States of the United Nations under which, indeed, human beings could not be sold. Since the second part of the Romanian amendment recognised implicitly that a child could be the subject of a contract of purchase or sale, it contradicted the first part of the same amendment. It was, moreover, inconsistent with the spirit in which the proposal had been made." Most delegates agreed to delete the words "nor shall he be bought or sold"[116], but leaving in it that "he shall not be the subject of traffic in any form". The Soviet proposal to include a paragraph on corporal punishment[117] was very controversial. Particularly the representative of the United Kingdom expressed his opposition to such a Paragraph.

If we analyse Principle 9 with the 'Systemic Quality of Life Model', we find that its main concern is with the protection of children, which can in all cases (abuse, neglect, trafficking, no admission to employment before an appropriate minimum age) be classified in the *conservative mode* of the *physical subsystem*.

Principle 10

This Principle relates to protection as well as to discrimination. It states that the child shall be protected from practices which may foster racial, religious or any other form of discrimination. According to Casullo[118] "this Principle is conceived in bombastic language." She also finds that "difficulties are presented in determining what kind of practices the Principle refers to, but what is more important is that it would be difficult to determine with certainty when a practice fosters discrimination."

The Principle also deals with education in the spirit of peace and friendship among peoples. *Defence for Children International*[119] concludes that the major area of concern of this last paragraph is: education in human rights, tolerance, peace and development.

The first sentence of the Principle states that the child *shall be protected* from practices which may foster discrimination. Mr. Sapozhnikov of the U.S.S.R. explained in the Commission on Human Rights that in his opinion 'shall be protected' indicated that "measures must be taken to that end." "But," said Sir Samuel Hoare of the United Kingdom "the first sentence was open to various interpretations. Did it mean, for example, that the child must be protected against any religion that considered itself the only true religion, on the grounds that such a belief might lead to religious discrimination?" Poland proposed in the Commission on Human Rights[120] that the first sentence should read 'protected by law'. However, Mr. Basyn of Belgium

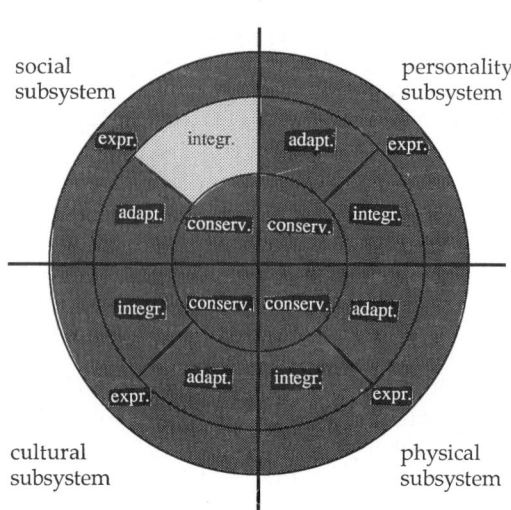

Fig. 10.2. The United Nations Declaration on the Rights of the Child (1959). Interpreted by the Systemic Quality of Life Model.

objected because this was "trying to give the provisions of the Declaration the force of a legal obligation... and it propounded a Principle which was much too absolute and gave the impression that there was no way of protecting the child other than legislation... which was certainly not the case."

India and Mexico submitted in the Third Committee a sub-amendment that read: "the child shall be protected from practices which may foster racial, religious and other forms of discrimination." The words 'racial, religious, and' were maintained after a number of States had tried to eliminate them.[121]

The first sentence of Principle 10 cannot be classified in the 'Systemic Quality of Life Model. It extends beyond the strict domain of rights of the child into an area that can best be described as 'what a better world would look like'. This tendency is pre-eminently present in the second sentence of this Principle. Some delegates had wished to go even further. In the Commission on Human Rights the representative of Poland wanted to add "the right to live in peace." (which proposal was rejected). Although the second sentence ("He shall be brought up in a spirit of understanding, tolerance, etc.") is more a world view than a right, we take into consideration that the drafters intended it to be a right and therefore hesitatingly classify it in the *complete cultural subsystem*.

It is interesting to see that all domains of the 'Systemic Quality of Life Model' are covered by the Declaration.

Picture X.2. Under Chairmanship of Mrs. Georgette Ciselet of Belgium the General Assembly's Third Committee discussed on September 23, 1959 the U.N. Declaration on the Rights of the Child. (Photo: United Nations.)

3. THE UNITED NATIONS CONVENTION ON THE RIGHTS OF THE CHILD (1989)

See Appendix XLI

In 1978 Poland[122] proposed to mark the International Year of the Child (1979) by a United Nations Convention on the Rights of the Child. This proposal met with little enthusiasm. Most of the developing countries felt it was too much a European affair and many European States were not interested in the matter.

Cynthia Price Cohen and Hedwin Naimark[123] believed that the proposed Convention was taken less seriously than previous Human Right Treaties because the first working model presented by Poland to the Commission on Human Rights was virtually identical with the Declaration of the Rights of the Child, with the addition of an implementation mechanism.

Even more serious was the risk the United Nations would be taking if they decided in favour of such a Convention. Sandra Singer[124] explains: "Although a Convention is legally binding and therefore theoretically stronger than a Declaration, experience has shown that a Declaration adopted unanimously has a greater moral impact than a Convention ratified only by a few countries."

Kelly Weisberg[125] expressed her fear that the Convention would, by its very existence, weaken the persuasive moral force of the Declaration of the Rights of the Child. On the other hand, she thought that rejection of the idea of a Convention would boomerang and weaken the moral force of the Declaration.

In the end the opinion prevailed that the *Declaration on the Rights of the*

Child would be the starting point for the discussions on a Convention. The Commission on Human Rights charged an *Open-Ended Working Group on the Question of a Convention on the Rights of the Child*[126] with the task of reviewing and reformulating the text of the proposed Convention.

The Open-Ended Working Group consisted of representatives of the forty-three Member States of the Commission. Moreover observers from other interested Member States of the United Nations and Inter-Governmental Agencies such as ILO, UNHCR and UNICEF, as well as Non-Governmental Organisations (NGOs) in consultative status with ECOSOC, were invited to send delegates who had the right to participate in the discussions. For ten years the Open-Ended Working Group met in Geneva's 'Palais des Nations' during the week before the annual sessions of the Committee on Human Rights.[127] The Open-Ended Working Group was chaired by Adam Lopatka, the former Director of the Institute of State and Law of the Polish Academy of Sciences.

When we study the records of the attendance of Governments,[128] we see that from the 158 Member States of the United Nations, only a small group participated in the discussions. From the developing countries only Argentina, Brazil and the Central African Empire, the Dominican Republic and India sent their delegates to all the sessions of the *Open-Ended Working Group*. Of the Warsaw Pact States Poland and the USSR kept a high profile. Of the Western States Australia, Canada, France, Norway, the United Kingdom and the United States were always present. The East-West ideological differences were obvious.[129] Poland focused, for instance, on material rights (such as the right of the child to the highest attainable standard of health and to medical and rehabilitation facilities). The U.S. focused on non-material rights (such as freedom of thought, conscience and religion).

Many developing countries could not participate in the meetings of the *Open-Ended Working Group* because their Ministries of Foreign Affairs, Justice and Health were over-burdened. One participant of the Working Group, representing a Non-Governmental Organisation,[130] said to me: "Look for instance at the Ministry of Health in Burkino Faso. There are likely only some twenty-five staff members and they have probably no Xerox-machine."

Misunderstandings created by the translating and interpreting of proposals also slowed down the drafting-process. Moreover religious and cultural differences had to be handled with care. For instance a proposal on birth out of wedlock, tabled by the delegation of China[131] faced strong opposition by Algeria, Iraq and Morocco.

Secretary-General Javier Perez de Cuellar praised the drafting process as a model of how the Member States of the United Nations can and should strive to achieve common goals: "Unproductive political confrontations were set aside while delegates from countries with different social and economic systems representing the various cultural, ethical and religious approaches to life, worked together with NGOs in a spirit of harmony and mutual respect and with the best interests of the child as their paramount objective."[132]

Sanford Fox[133] wrote about these sessions: "Perhaps we expect too much from a group that is not wholly expert, does not speak the same language, and views the problem of creating a treaty through a myriad of jurisprudential lenses. But it is the formal approval process that is most directly related to the lowest-common-denominator thesis. This has to do with how the group adopts the text of individual articles for inclusion in the Draft Convention. Articles are accepted by 'consensus'. There is no vote taken and nothing is considered as approved if any of the legations present has some objection to it. This means that each country has a veto. It is not, of course, exercised in those terms; rather a delegate will announce: 'Mr. Chairman, my delegation cannot join consensus on that language.' That kills the provision in question, although sometimes the chairman will follow-up the exercise of a veto by appointing a small group to try to work out compromise language that will hopefully attract a consensus. But failing that, nothing gets into the treaty that is not acceptable to all."

Nigel Cantwell[134] (of Defence for Children International, DCI) wrote that "the Convention was meant to reflect the minimum present-day standards of what things children have rights to; nevertheless, one cannot say that there is a universal approval for the provisions therein. A whole series of Articles will violate some or other countries' national laws." The Convention thus reflects a negotiated consensus rather than a real consensus.

Several NGOs reacted either jointly or individually to the original Polish proposals for the Draft-Convention. However, their involvement in the drafting process at the start of the 1980s was sporadic and badly co-ordinated. Some NGO-representatives who attended the 1983 meeting of the Working Group were convinced that their organisations had special knowledge and experience to contribute to the drafting work, but that the opportunity for doing so was being lost. They decided to organise a mid-year NGO-consultation for interested organisations, aimed at ensuring that NGO-input be well prepared and coherent. From this first consultation a *NGO Ad-Hoc Group on the drafting of the Convention* emerged, which thereafter met twice a year in order to pool ideas and present clear, unified proposals to the United Nations Working Group. *Defence for Children International* served as secretariat for this fifty organisations Ad Hoc Group. On average more than half of these organisations participated in the twice-yearly consultations.[135]

From the moment the Ad Hoc Group was functioning, the idea of a Convention gained momentum. In 1985 UNICEF[136] with its prestige and high-level lobbying possibilities joined the champions on the Convention. From now on the sceptics[137] were fighting a lost battle.

On February 5, 1988, the *Open-Ended Working Group* finished the first reading of the Draft-Convention. After an in-depth *technical review* within the United Nations Secretariat (to ensure that the text contained no contradictions and that it was worded in accordance with the terminology of international legislation) the text came up for second reading (formal review and revision of the draft) in the *Open-Ended Working Group*.

After the text was found to be technically sound it was sent to the *Committee on Human Rights* which accepted it in March 1989. From there it was sent to the Economic and Social Council (ECOSOC), who forwarded it to the General Assembly. In the fall of 1989 the Third Committee of the General Assembly adopted it with only some minor changes.

Finally, on November 20, 1989, the 54–Article Convention, which had been negotiated for ten years, was on the agenda of the General Assembly. After only two minutes of procedural discussion the 158–member Assembly approved it by consensus.

The text was now officially available for ratification by individual Governments. It would enter into force thirty days after ratification by the twentieth State. This happened on September 2, 1990 (a record in the United Nations!).

Although no Government, no organisation and no individual is likely to call the *U.N. Convention on the Rights of the Child* a perfect instrument, it seems that content and spirit make it ratifiable by almost every State.

The *Convention* provides an opportunity and impetus to define and harmonise human rights standards for children, to fill in the many gaps identified in the current provisions, and to set the results of this in-depth reassessment within the context of a single, binding international instrument. It codifies under one title those provisions of international law pertaining to children. It is therefore an important and easily understood advocacy tool – one that promotes children's welfare as an issue of justice rather than one of charity. It provides a framework for UNICEF and other United Nations Agencies and NGOs to define and promote more effectively existing and future programme priorities and will create the impetus for an alliance for action for the world's children. It is an innovative Convention[138] because:

1. It says that State agencies will be responsible for the physical, psychological and social re-integration of a child whose rights are violated.
2. It no longer mentions primarily *only* duties of adults and the State (as formulated in most Declarations), but spells out, for the first time, child participation (for instance the child's right to express an opinion and to have that opinion taken into account). Participation is normally understood as an active and conscious endeavour. The idea that every child has now such rights may make some people nervous and certainly introduces a new element to be reckoned with. States are now being asked to look beyond some of their traditional concepts of childhood. The Convention is the first international instrument that explicitly states that children have a right to 'have a say' in processes affecting their lives.
3. Placements in residential care and foster care will now be subject to constant review ("the right to have all aspects of placement evaluated regularly") and the right to foster care and adoption is recognised (with certain limitations – see later in this chapter, pages 197 and 198).

4. The right to identity has never before been formulated in an international Convention.[139]
5. It will be the first international binding instrument that specifically states that 'traditional practices' such as female circumcision (as still practised on a wide scale in Africa) are harmful.

Another aspect makes the Convention an important instrument. While the 1959 *Declaration on the Rights of the Child* concentrated on the particular needs and rights of children as distinguished from adults, the Convention exceeds these limits and re-iterates most of the general human rights which the Covenant on Civil and Political Rights and the Covenant on Economic, Social and Cultural Rights applied to all persons, including children.

An advantage of the *United Nations Convention on the Rights of the Child* is "that the States which have not ratified the *Covenant on Civil and Political Rights* and the *Covenant on Economic, Social and Cultural Rights* and would not accord the rights set out therein or in other instruments (like the Geneva Conventions on International Humanitarian Law), might still be ready or persuaded to accord those rights at least to children."[140]

Analysis of the Articles of the United Nations Convention on the Rights of the Child

The Preamble of the Convention recalls the basic Principles of the United Nations and reaffirms that children, because of their vulnerability, need special protection. It emphasises the responsibility of the family, the importance of respect for the cultural values of the child's community, and the vital role of international co-operation in achieving the realisation of children's rights.

In regard to the definition of 'the child' the Holy See suggested to incorporate reference to the unborn child by the phrasing "*before* as well as after birth" (taken from the United Nations *Declaration of the Rights of the Child*). This issue was hotly debated.

According to some delegates the definition of 'child' should be contained in Article 1, and nothing in the Preamble should prejudge or slant this definition.[141]

The debate on the amendment proposed by the Holy See in the Working Group was resumed at the fourth meeting, after adoption of Article 1.[142] Again several delegations argued that the proposed text should be deleted in order to ensure the neutrality of the Preamble. It was also stated that, since national legislation on the question of abortion deferred greatly, the Convention could only be widely ratified if it did not take sides on the issue.

Other delegations were of the opinion that the amendment was sufficiently neutral, since it did not specify the length of the period before birth.

At the fifth meeting of the Open-Ended Working Group, the Chairman announced that a compromise text had been elaborated. The new text would amend the beginning of the paragraph to read: "Recognising that, as stated in the *Declaration on the Rights of the Child*, the child, due to the needs of his physical and mental development, needs special safeguards and care, including appropriate legal protection, before as well as after birth".[143]

The danger of such compromises is (as among others Philip Alskon explained) that it is subject to a range of different interpretations. Most people[144] now interpret the Preamble as a statement against abortion. King Boudewijn of Belgium, for instance, caused an upheaval in his country when he quoted the Preamble of the Convention in his 1989 Christmas message on radio and TV,[145] and concluded "This is an important Convention which cannot be bypassed. It means, among other things, that our society must make real efforts to help pregnant women in difficulties." To our taste this pro-life interpretation goes too far.

In fact the issue of the unborn child was approached[146] "within the framework of the Convention's provisions and the context of the culture, tradition and religion of each State Party." Indeed, the paragraph about the unborn child, copied from the 1959 Declaration, was mentioned on purpose in the *Preamble* and not in the binding part of the Convention which starts with "Have agreed as follows". Even this was only possible after the *Open-Ended Working Group* explicitly declared in its report that the controversial quotation would not influence the interpretation of the Convention.[147] In fact the inclusion of such a statement in the *Report of the Open-Ended Working Group* (the so-called Travaux Préparatoires)[148] was so unusual that the Legal Council of the United Nations had to ask special advice for it. According to De Bruijn[149] the legal advisor of the United Nations had been asked for advice and was of the opinion that it was strange that a Declaration must be included in the *Travaux Préparatoires*.

Article 1 deals with the definition of a child. Some delegates pointed out that the age of 18 appeared to be quite late in the light of some national legislations, and that a lower age limit should be recommended. They suggested that, since the General Assembly had set the age limit at 15 in connection with the International Year of the Child, the same position should be adopted in the Convention. They also pointed out that in many parts of the world fourteen is the age of the end of compulsory education and the age girls can legally marry.

Many national legislations used the terminology 'minor', instead of 'child'. Setting the age limit at fourteen would therefore also establish a clear distinction between the concepts *child* (age 0–14) and the *minor* (age 14–18).

Other delegates,[150] however, opposed the lowering of the age limit to 14 or 15 because their domestic legislation embodied protective measures for 'children' beyond that age and they believed that the Convention should apply to as large an age group as possible.

A number of delegates opposed the idea of making the definition of 'child' dependent on the concept of majority age, since this varied widely between countries and also within national legislations, according to whether the civil, penal, political or other aspects of majority were at issue.

Finally it was decided that Article 1 of the Convention would define *all persons under* 18 as children, unless "under the law applicable to the child majority is attained earlier."

Lea Shamgar-Handelman[151] remarked that the legal definition of childhood is a subject for negotiation. "This negotiation takes place between all the parties involved, except the children. As children themselves are restricted from entering this negotiation process, it is those whom are considered to be responsible for their well-being who will do the negotiation of children's rights ... The attempt to standardise children's rights world-wide should be understood as an expression of utopian belief in world democracy, as an ideology of equal sharing of resources among people, and as a deep awareness of world-wide interdependence."

What we observe is that the age limit for different rights has been shifting in different directions. Thus in most countries the age limit for employment and for marriage has gone up, while the age for reaching majority has gone down. In Switzerland at 20, in Austria at 19. In most other States children reach majority on their 18th birthday.

Since Article 1 only states to whom the Convention applies, it can *not* be classified within the 'Systemic Quality of Life Model'.

Article 2 deals with non-discrimination. The United States introduced a proposal which read: "Each State Party to the present Convention shall respect and extend all the rights set forth in this Convention to all children lawfully in its territory." Some delegations, however, could not agree with the limitation to children who were lawfully in the territory of a State Party.[152] It was agreed that the term *jurisdiction* would be included instead of *territory*. The Article now states that the Convention applies to "each child within the *jurisdiction* of the State Party".

Article 3 (the best interests of the child) is fundamental to the Convention in that it stipulates that the child's best interests must be the 'primary consideration' in all actions concerning children.

The DCI/UNICEF briefing kit states that whilst the term 'best interests' leaves room for interpretation, its inclusion as the guiding principle marks an important step forward in terms of the approach to be taken – to children as a group as well as in individual cases – when determining the most appropriate solutions to situations in which they find themselves.

The State is to provide adequate care when parents or others responsible fail to do so. In the Working Group a discussion[153] ensued as to whether, on general humanitarian grounds, the best interests of the child should be the *pre-eminent consideration* in actions undertaken by his parents, guardians, social or State institutions. The imposition of obligations on parents and guardians by an international Convention was questioned. Moreover, the word *paramount* used in the revised Polish draft to qualify the consideration to be given to the interests of the child was considered too broad by some delegates who felt that the best interests of the child should be a *primary* consideration.

The danger lies in the fact that anybody can make a case 'in the best interests' of the child. Ludwig Salgo[154] points out that personal preferences will be mingled with professional standards.

Goldstein, Freud and Solnit[155] maintain that the courts are often all too ready to take children away from their social environment because of the doctrine known as 'in the best interests of the child'. The conviction that every child needs continuity of care led to the position of Goldstein et al.

> "that the child's interests should be paramount consideration *once, but not before* a child's placement becomes the subject of official controversy" and that "so long as a child is a member of a functioning family, his paramount interests lies in the preservation of his family"....

"The person who provides the continuity of care for the child and with whom the child has (or develops) an ongoing relationship, the 'psychological parent', has the right to be protected against intrusion by the State on behalf of other adults," Goldstein, Freud and Solnit claim.

Richards,[156] however, criticises the approach of Goldstein, Freud and Solnit. He writes: "Like many psychoanalytic writers, the *Best Interests* authors greatly emphasise the child's need for a continuous presence of an autonomous and omniscient parent." They point to the intermittent nature of the non-custodial parent's relationship as being a barrier to the custodial parent for being an effective psychological parent. Goldstein, Freud and Solnit, however, acknowledge in *In the Best Interests of the Child* that not only their professional knowledge but also their personal values and norms have led to the statement that "*when* an intervention is necessary, the well-being of the child must be put in the first place and not that of the parents of the family or interests of the youth well-being organisation who handles the affair." Also the point of departure of a minimum of intervention by the State in the family itself ("parents must be able to raise the children as they see fit") is not only based, according to Goldstein et al., on professional knowledge but also on personal values.[157]

Diplomats and other representatives of States (such as the NGOs) were also mainly lead by their own values.

Thus Article 3, however important, stays open for many interpretations based on personal ideas, values and norms. Since it is not clear which interpretation was intended by the drafters, we cannot classify it in the 'Systemic Quality of Life Model'.

Article 4 (implementation of rights) is probably the most important Article of the Convention. Here the States pledge to translate all the rights set forth in the Convention into reality. (Practical details of implementation are dealt with in part II of the Convention Articles 42, 43, 44, and 45.)

In 1981 the Open-Ended Working Group discussed[158] how the obligation of States Parties under the Convention should be laid down to ensure the implementation of the rights recognised in the Convention. Some delegates proposed to include in the text that "States Parties undertake to protect the family." This initiated of course a debate on the relationship between parental authority and the rights of the child. The delegates of Canada[159] and the Netherlands[160] indicated that they would only support a principle dealing with the importance of the family, the parental rights and parental responsibilities in the exercise of their rights over the child, if this would be linked with *the evolving capacities of the child* and the child's need to mature into an independent adulthood.

After intensive consultations and several compromise proposals it was decided to dedicate a separate Article (Article 5) to the proposal of Canada and the Netherlands. For the text of Article 4 a Brazilian proposal was accepted "The States Parties to the present Convention shall undertake all appropriate administrative and legislative measures, in accordance with their available resources, and, where needed, within the framework of international co-operation, for the implementation of the rights recognised in this Convention."

Since this Article deals with a procedural aspect of the Convention, it is not classifiable in the 'Systemic Quality of Life Model'.

Article 5 (parental guidance and the child's evolving capacities) is also an axis around which all the other Articles revolve: Article 12 (the child's opinion), for instance, and Article 13 (freedom of expression) should be seen in this light. The drafters of the United Nations Convention recognised that growth is a gradual process and that as the child's personality grows, the child or adolescent can carry more responsibility. Since, however, no specific developmental psychological theories seemed to have influenced the delegates, this Article can be classified in the *expressive modes* of all four subsystems.[161]

Article 6 has to be interpreted in the context of paragraph 9 of the Preamble (legal protection, before as well as after birth) and of Article 1 of this Convention (definition of a child). The intention was[162] to include a special Article on the child's right to survival (UNICEF can be seen behind this proposal). First the discussion focused on the importance of healthy development after survival. The Italian delegate re-tabled an old discussion. It was his opinion that *life* and survival were complementary and did not exclude each other, and that survival could even mean the decrease in infant mortality. He observed that the rights of the child began at the time of conception and convinced the other delegates to include a paragraph on the inherent right to life.

In relation to the second paragraph of Article 6, the view was expressed that conditions should be defined in order to permit the exercise of the right to *life*, not the right to mere *survival*. The following text for paragraph 2 was accepted: "The States Parties to the present Convention undertake to promote conditions which protect to the maximum extent possible, the life of the child."

The issue of child survival is one of the most tragic issues of our modern era. "Two things are evident," says Dr. Voorhoeve. "Child mortality has been going down in the development countries during the last ten years, and the pattern of disease changes. Children's diseases that were important some twenty years ago, are less so today. Other diseases have clearly 'taken over'. When I started my career, malaria was by far the greatest evil. Second came diarrhoea which in most cases ended by death through dehydration. Third were measles. The fourth cause for mortality was malnutrition.

Malaria seemed in the beginning to be susceptible to quinine-related medicines. The disease was going down and the number of fatal cases was reduced. Recently, however, malaria has returned with double strength. For this we know two reasons. First, more and more parasites have become resistant against quinine. Second, and this sounds paradoxical, the susceptibility increases because nutrition has improved. Animal research in laboratories have shown that there is a clear relation between susceptibility to malaria and good nutrition. A well-fed European is susceptible to malaria, not only by the absence of immunity but possibly also by his better fed condition.

In the sixties and early seventies diarrhoea claimed a very high infant mortality. It used to lead to death by dehydration. This has been changed in a nearly revolutionary way. In earlier times European doctors prescribed a salt solution, generally by infusion. This was only possible in the proximity of a hospital or clinic, until it was discovered in the world-diarrhoea-centre in Bangladesh that the salt solution was much more effective if mixed with a little sugar. This could easily be given orally. Since that time UNICEF hands out the famous bags of sugar and salt."[163]

Today more than sixty percent of the children in the developing countries receive several doses of vaccines before their first birthday, namely for diphtheria, whooping cough, tetanus and polio. Coverage against measles jumped from thirty-six per cent in 1986 to fifty-three per cent in 1987. Improved delivery of polio vaccine alone is sparing about 240,000 children each year from the crippling effects of this disease. Ninety-six countries have programmes to control diarrhoeal diseases (still the main cause of infant and child mortality in the developing world). Knowledge of oral rehydration therapy is spreading so rapidly that fifty per cent of all diarrhoea cases in the developing world can today be treated at home with simple oral rehydration solutions.

UNICEF, together with the World Health Organisation (WHO) and other U.N. Agencies and Non-Governmental Organisations, have been promoting child survival for many years. The technologies are not new. New is the relative ease with which all developing nations, in spite of poverty, have access to the technologies, communicate the opportunities they represent to

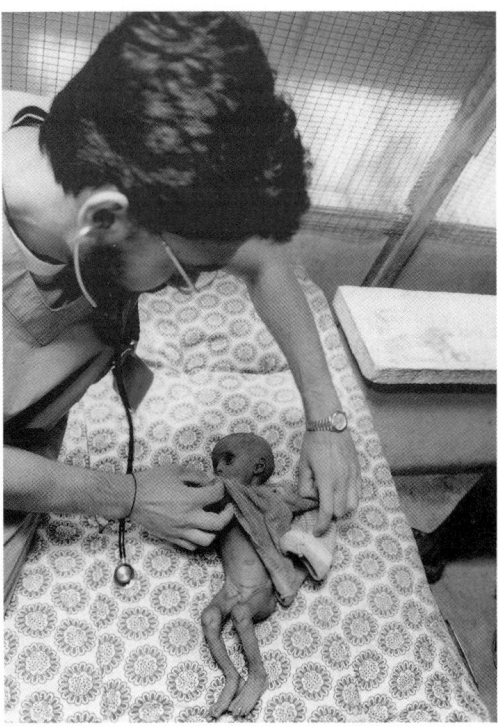

Picture X.3. A dying, malnourished child, brought by his father to the Paediatric Hospital, Mekelle, is examined by a member of the Italian medical team, working in Ethiopia. (Photo: UNICEF Stephenie Hollyman.)

their people, and deliver the goods. As a result, attention has now been focusing on the other half of the equation: "Survival for what?"[164] In a UNICEF Executive Board report[165] from 1986 we read: "While UNICEF has accorded top priority to reducing mortality among infants and young children, it also has recognised that to save the lives of children who do not have the opportunity to grow and develop is a hollow and insufficient victory indeed." Against this background the right *to survival and development* was formulated. Since this right deals with the child's very life, we classify it in the *conservative mode* of *the physical subsystem*.

The 'right to life' (of paragraph 1) belongs in the middle of the 'Systemic Quality of Life Model', in the heart of all the *conservative modes*.

Article 7 recognises the child's right to have a name and be registered immediately after birth.

The representative of the United States said in the Open-Ended Working Group[166] that he wanted to prevent difficulties under the immigration and nationality laws of various States. But his true intentions were revealed when he told he specially wanted to prevent "that stateless children would automatically get the nationality of the State they entered".

Poland and Australia were better inspired, because their proposals for this Article were aimed at *providing every child with a nationality* so as to prevent statelessness among children.[167] Many States will no doubt make a reservation on this point when ratifying the Convention. Morocco already indicated in 1987 that "in accordance with the Moroccan code the nationality of the child follows that of his father (*jus sanguinis*). If born of a Moroccan mother and an unidentified father, the child is also entitled to Moroccan nationality. Moroccan nationality, however, may not be granted to a child born of stateless parents."[168]

Sometimes the right to a name and nationality coincide. In May 1989 many Bulgarian children were expelled from their country because their parents, who were of Turkish origin, refused to adopt Bulgarian names.

In Thailand a child must have a 'blood tie' with a Thai-National in order to obtain the Thai Nationality. Refugee children, therefore, can not obtain a Thai passport.

Article 7 belongs in the *adaptive mode* of the *social subsystem* and the *conservative mode* of the *physical subsystem* (see page 49).

Article 8 (preservation of identity) was introduced in 1985 by the representative of the new democratic government of Argentina,[169] against the background of the 'disappeared children'. After the 1976 military coup hundreds of children and their parents had disappeared. Pregnant women were kidnapped and killed after giving birth! Even today the brave 'Grandmothers of the Plaza de Mayo' still demonstrate every week in Buenos Aires for the return of the disappeared children to their lawful families.

The Argentinean representative insisted on the need for a specific Article to safeguard the personal, legal and family identity of children throughout the world.[170]

We classify this Article in the *conservative mode* of the *social subsystem* (belonging to a family). Since the genetic code was considered important by the delegates, it also belongs in the *conservative mode* of the *social subsystem*. This Article belongs so highly to the conservative mode that we can even classify it in the *conservative mode* of the *conservative-social and conservative-physical sub-subsystems*.

Article 9 deals with separation from parents. Some delegations had repeatedly emphasised that the separation of a child from his parents should preferably be of a temporary or provisional nature, that the separation period should be made as short as possible under national legislation, and that a child should be returned to his parents as soon as circumstances changed favourably making the separation no longer necessary.

This Article concerns the *integrative mode* of the *social subsystem* (intimate relations). However, the right to maintain contact with both parents if separated from one is also formulated. This belongs in the *conservative mode* of the *social subsystem* (belonging).

Already in 1981 the Working Group[171] indicated that the Convention should state "that in cases where both parents lawfully resided in one State-

Party and their child lawfully resided in another State-Party, the States-Parties concerned should deal with applications for family reunification in a positive, humane and expeditious manner. States Parties should charge only moderate fees in connection with such applications and should not modify in any way the rights and obligations of the applicant(s) or of other members of the family concerned. States parties should ensure that applications for the purpose of family reunification of parents with their children which were not granted for any reason might be renewed at the appropriate level and would be considered at reasonably intervals by the authorities of the country of residence or destination, and that fees would be charged only when applications were granted." A separate Article was drafted about Family Reunification.

This became Article 10 which states the right of children and their parents to leave any country and to enter their own in order to be reunited or to maintain the child-parent relationship.

The realisation of this right is often linked with changes in the political situation.[172] In 1986 the Soviet representative objected to the inclusion in the Convention of the specific right of a child's parents to leave any country and to return to it, but in 1989 the USSR had more or less dropped this objection.

On the one hand there is the positive wording that "family reunification shall be dealt with by States Parties *in a positive, humane and expeditious manner.*" On the other hand this paragraph was not followed by a real boost for other international standards.

We classify this Article in the *integrative mode* of the *social subsystem* and, to a lesser extent, in the *conservative mode* of the *social subsystem*.

Article 11 deals with *illicit transfer of children* often also called *child-abduction*. This is a situation in which a child is taken away from one or both parents or guardians although neither the law nor a decision of a competent body allows this. This used to be a rare phenomenon. However, the increased number of divorces, separations, and marriages between nationals of different States, as well as cheaper flights have boosted the number of child-abductions. If the child is abducted from one country to another the situation becomes even more complicated because the parent from whom the child was abducted has to convince the court of the other State that the child should be returned. There is already efficient international law available for this purpose.[173] It was decided therefore that the new Convention would only stimulate States who did not join earlier instruments to promote the conclusion of bilateral or multilateral agreements or access to existing agreements." (See also Article 41.) Article 11 belongs in the *conservative mode* of the *social subsystem* (stability of the social structure of the child).

Article 12 obliges States to give due weight to the views of the child in accordance with his or her age and maturity. This applies especially in any judicial or administrative proceedings affecting the child.[174]

The United States submitted in 1988 a proposals[175] on freedom of expression, freedom of association and peaceful assembly and the right to privacy. These paragraphs were later split in different Articles. Thus the (second) Polish draft of the Convention, which only mentioned the child's right to express his own opinion, was expanded.

Article 12 belongs in the *expressive mode* of the *social subsystem* (give the child a voice, influence, more status). To a lesser extent (when political ideas are voiced) it can also be classified in the *expressive mode* of the *cultural valuative subsystem*.

The Finnish delegation[176] proposed that there should not only be an Article on the right to have opinions, but also an Article on the right of expression. This was to become Article 13. Interesting is that the Chinese delegation supported the view that the child should have the right to fully express his or her views on questions concerning the child.

In a publication (not related to the U.N. Convention) David Moshman[177] writes: "Freedom of expression implies not only freedom to form and express one's own ideas but also freedom not to adopt or express ideas of which one has not been convinced. Requiring a child to make a pledge or sing a song that expresses views contrary to his or her own, would clearly be an abridgment of freedom not to speak."

It is important to mention that the Convention does not mention anything about the freedom of non-expression.

Since ideas and opinions are to be classified in the cultural-valuative subsystem, Article 13 belongs in the *expressive mode* of the *cultural subsystem*.

In Article 14 States-Parties to the Convention are required to respect the right of the child to freedom of thought, conscience and religion.

This is one of the most controversial Articles of the Convention. Quite a number of States are sure to express reservations on this point. In the Working Group this became clear when the representative from Bangladesh[178] expressed his point of view: "This Article appears to run counter to the traditions of the major religious systems of the world and in particular to Islam. It appears to infringe upon the sanctioned practice of a child being reared in the religion of his parents. We believe that the Article will give rise to considerable difficulties in application."

Also the point of view of the representative of Morocco[179] was very clear: "On the question of religion, the rule adopted in Moroccan legislation is that the child shall follow the religion of his father. In this case the child does not have to choose his religion, as the religion of the State is Islam. Islam guarantees freedom of worship to members of other faiths."

In 1989 the Jordanian Ambassador to the Third Committee of the General Assembly also declared to have reservations on this point. Not the religious differences but the ancient east-west points of view were at that time still discussed in connection with Article 14.

When I visited the Israeli Ministry of Justice, as part of a Defence for Children International (Israel Section) delegation, an official from the Ministry told me that in her opinion paragraph 2 of Article 14 did not go far enough and put too much emphasis on the *freedom* of religion. "It is not only a right of the parents to educate the child to their belief, it is also their duty", she told us.

A different view was expressed by some representatives of Non-Governmental Organisations. They felt that the right to choose one's religion was more restricted in the Convention on the Rights of the Child than in the International Covenant on Civil and Political Rights, which states:

(2) "States Parties shall respect the rights and duties of the parents and, when applicable, legal guardians, to provide direction to the child in the exercise of his or her right in a manner consistent with the evolving capacities of the child.
(3) "Freedom to manifest one's religion or beliefs may be subject only to such limitations as are prescribed by law and are necessary to protect public safety, order, health, or morals or the fundamental rights and freedoms of others."

We shall classify Article 14 in the *expressive mode* of the *cultural subsystem*.

Article 15 deals with freedom of association. While the delegations of Australia and Canada expressed their support for the United States' proposal, the representative of the USSR stated in 1986 that he was totally opposed to it and the representatives of Algeria, China, Iraq and Poland said that it would be difficult for them to accept this Article.[180]

The Chinese delegate was of the opinion that the freedoms of association and peaceful assembly could not be enjoyed by children in the same way as they are enjoyed by adults "because the intellect of a child was not as developed as that of an adult."[181]

We shall classify Article 15 in the *expressive mode* of the *social subsystem*.[182]

The drafters of Article 16 (on the right to protection from interference) faced opposition because some delegates[183] feared that such a right might endanger the relationship between the parents and the child. Nevertheless the delegates agreed that the Convention would state that no child shall be subjected to arbitrary or unlawful interference with his or her privacy, family, home, or correspondence, nor to unlawful attacks on his or her honour and reputation.

This Article seems to be designed to avoid damage to the expressive functioning rather than to enhance it. We classify it in the *expressive mode* of the *personality, social and physical subsystems*.

Article 17 deals with access to appropriate information. The (revised) Polish draft read: "Parents, guardians, State organs and social organisations shall protect the child against any harmful influence that mass media, and in particular the radio, film, television, printed materials and exhibitions, on account of their contents, may exert on his mental and moral development." Some delegates had a 'protective approach' (the child's moral, social and spiritual development needed to be protected against harmful influences of the media). Others had a more positive approach and stressed that mass media do more good than harm and that children should take advantage of a diversity of opinion concerning all matters; they expressed sometimes concern for censorship of media. Much of the final phrasing of Article 17 stems from the proposal of the Baha'i International Community.[184] The first paragraph reads as a preamble to the five points of the Article itself. These five points stress, among other things, that States-Parties "encourage the mass media to disseminate information and material of social and cultural benefit to the child encourage the production and dissemination of children's books", etc. The Article also refers to a special category of children (those who belong to a minority group or who are indigenous).

We classify it in the *adaptive mode* of the *cultural subsystem*.

Article 18 (parental responsibilities) formulates the principle that both parents have joint primary responsibility for raising their children, and that the State should support them in this task. According to the records of the debate, this Article was drafted in order to regulate the relationship between parents and State. The first (amended) sentence reads: "Parents or, as the case may be, guardians, have the primary responsibility for the upbringing and development of the child. The best interests of the child will be their basic concern."

When supporting this text, one representative explained that he thought the aim of the first sentence should be to protect parents against excessive intervention of the State. Walter Bennett wrote in 1987 that "there is a confusion over whether this Article in fact assigns a duty to the parents vis-a-vis the child, or attempts to protect the prerogative of the parents from State interference."[185]

In the opinion of the author both elements are to be found in the adopted texts. They are not contradictory. To recognise that parents have the primary responsibility implies that the State should stay in the background.

Since this Article does not deal with the individual life quality of the child, we shall not classify it in the 'Systemic Quality of Life Model'.

Article 19 obliges the State to take all appropriate legislative, administrative, social and educational measures to protect the child from all forms of maltreatment and to investigate and follow up on reported cases of child maltreatment. In general the terms *child abuse and neglect* refer to harm or predictable harm caused through assault, wilful inattention, or failure to provide the necessities of life, to a child under the age of 18, by a parent, guardian or other person responsible for his or her welfare.[186]

Thanks to pressure by NGOs a paragraph has been added about the importance of preventive programmes and treatment programmes. But the aim of the Article remains to prevent maltreatment. This Article therefore belongs in the *conservative mode* of the *physical subsystem*.

Article 20 formulates the State's obligation to provide special protection for children deprived of their families. Clearly, delegates tried to find alternatives for the 'natural family environment' (or 'biological family' as it was sometimes called in the debates.[187])

The problems to which Article 20 tries to find an answer are more urgent than ever. If today's trend persists, we shall have, towards the year 2000, 430 cities with a population of more than one million inhabitants while 45 of the 60 cities with more than 5 million inhabitants will be in the Third World."[188] Nobody knows how many *street children*[189] there are in the world. Some estimates put their number as high as 100 million! According to Judith Ennew[190] some ten million children are completely outside all family control. The other children have some contact with their families which they provide with a vital income.

Unmarried women or widows take care of children for instance in the *SOS Children's Villages* in substitute 'families'.[191] Such projects, however, are largely dependent on charity and cannot provide a large-scale solution. They show that States are still far from taking their obligations as seriously as they should. In principle, however, States pledge by ratifying the Convention to give special protection. This special protection by the State can be classified in the *conservative mode* of the *physical subsystem*.

The Working Group was not only concerned with the State's obligations but also with stimulating the creation of other opportunities for intimacy. It belongs in the *integrative mode* of the *social subsystem*.

Article 21 deals more explicitly with adoption. Originally the representatives of Poland, Australia and Denmark pushed for the following text: "The States Parties to the present Convention shall undertake measures, where appropriate, *to facilitate the process of adoption* of the child who is parentless or who cannot be cared for in his family environment, in order that such a child is provided with a stable family environment."[192] However, since adoption is not a recognised institution under Islamic law, problems arose during the 1986 debates. The representative of Bangladesh[193] said that "in cases of adoption the question of inheritance rights will give rise to complex problems in Islamic jurisdictions since adopted children cannot inherit from adopting fathers. Perhaps a phrasing may be found to protect Islamic conceptions on the subject." With the reference to Kafalah of Islamic[194] law in the previous Article the problem was solved. Article 21 became also applicable to Islamic Law.

Article 21 deals also with *intercountry adoption*, about which several delegates had expressed their concern in 1982. Bilateral agreements and other Conventions on inter-country adoption were discussed. This was necessary in order to prevent the sale of young children for purposes of adoption. The purchase of human beings, whatever the motives of those concerned, is a serious violation of national and international law. It denies the child's right to an identity, erodes the integrity of families in the countries of origin and introduces legal and psychological insecurity in the newly constituted family. In consequence, the international community had begun to take a new interest in more efficient instruments for the prevention and control of this practice. The U.N. Working Group on Contemporary Forms of Slavery had, for instance, added the traffic and sale of children to its agenda. The Hague Conference on Private International Law is preparing a Convention on International Adoption. While many such arrangements are legally managed in the best interests of the child, the concern was that many crude transactions, effected under the guise of adoption, resulted in servitude and other abuses.[195]

The large profits of the intermediaries were another point of concern. We agree with an official of the Israeli Ministry of Justice who expressed her regret that lawyers were not forbidden to play the role of 'go-between' and make a fortune for their services.

Moreover, if the biological parents disagree with adoption this creates a confusion for the child about his or her identity. This concern of the drafters belongs in the *conservative mode* of the *social subsystem*. But allowing adoption and Kafalah must be classified in the *adaptive mode* of the *integrative-social subsystem* (intimate relations).

Article 22 deals with refugee children. Since the United Nations *Declaration on the Rights of the Child*[196] does not mention this sub-population, Denmark proposed in 1982 to introduce an Article in the Convention concerning their rights.[197]

There are today some six million refugee children. Most of them have crossed the border with their mothers, sometimes also with their fathers because of armed conflicts in the country of their origin. If they were sent back their lives would be endangered.

Article 22 says that the States have an obligation to co-operate with the United Nations, Inter-Governmental and Non-Governmental Organisations and to grant refugee children protection. A specialised U.N. Agency, the United Nations High Commissioner for Refugees (UNHCR), takes care of this problem. Moreover the State shall assist the child to trace his or her parents or other relatives and to facilitate re-unification. When relatives cannot be found, the child shall receive the same protection as other children who are temporarily or permanently deprived of a family.

Important are the concerns about 'basic needs' (such as food and housing) which belong in the *adaptive and conservative modes* of the *physical subsystem*. The assistance to reunite the child with his or her parents (paragraph 2) is classifiable in the *integrative mode* of the *social subsystem* (intimacy).

Article 23 deals with another sub-population, namely *handicapped children*.[198] During the 1982 discussion in the Working Group, the Australian representative[199] suggested that the fundamental right of the handicapped child "to enjoy a decent life, as normal and full as possible, and to become as self-reliant as possible", should be placed in the first paragraph. The *United Nations Declaration on the Rights of mentally retarded Persons*[200] states for instance: "The mentally retarded person has, to the maximum degree of feasibility, the same rights as other human beings."[201] Likewise Article 2 of the *Declaration of Rights of Deaf Blind Persons*[202] states: "Deaf-

Picture X.4. A Guatemalan refugee-boy in the settlement of Moya Tecun in South-East Mexico. (Photograph by Finn Stepputat.)

blind persons have the right to expect that their capabilities and their aspirations to lead a normal life within the community and their ability to do so shall be recognised and respected by all governments, administrators, educational and rehabilitation personnel and the general public."

In 1983 the Working Group underlined that disabled children should be considered as a specific category of children who needed special treatment. Attention was focused on the means to ensure the realisation of this right and more specifically on the means of financing services for disabled children. Some Third World representatives voiced the fear that their countries would not be able to finance such projects. Therefore a special paragraph (23.4) was added to this Article 23. However, instead of dealing with concrete help of the rich States to the developing States, there is an 'easy way out'. The paragraph deals with the exchange of appropriate information.

In our opinion the formulation 'to enjoy a full and decent life', is rather vague. What one person sees as a 'full life' the other shall not consider to be full enough.

Article 24 deals with health and health services. In 1988 India proposed that States Parties should "pursue to diminish infant and child mortality."[203] The aim of this proposal was to cover situations in developing countries where almost all the 14 million cases of premature death were due to disease.

It must be noted, however, that the lack of health care is not typical for the Third World. With the exception of Massachusetts, there is no system in the United States that guarantees medical examination and care. In 1984 children made up one-fourth of all Americans younger than sixty-five, but one-third of America's 35 million uninsured persons. In 1988 about 35 million people in the United States were not insured. Un-insured Americans lack adequate access to health care. This is reflected in health outcome data for children. For nearly nine million American children there are no arrangements for financial coverage of health care. "Infant mortality is an ongoing scourge."[204]

Some delegates pleaded for the adding of a paragraph about the importance of information on breast-feeding, hygiene and environmental sanitation. Paragraphs 2(c) and 2(e) cover this concern.

Since paragraph 2(f) ("to develop preventive health care, guidance for parents, and family planning education and services") has proved to be open for different interpretations, it deserves special mention. When I visited the Israeli Ministry of Justice as part of a *Defence for Children International* delegation, an official expressed concern that paragraph 2(f) intended to promote 'family planning'. We, the members of the DCI delegation, gave as our interpretation that focus was on (*sex*) *education*.

Paragraph 3 needs a separate discussion. In 1987 the Working Group decided to consider a proposal by the representative of Rädda Barnen (Swedish Save the Children) which read[205] "The States Parties to the present Convention shall seek to eradicate traditional practices harmful to the health of children and shall take all appropriate action including necessary legislative, administrative, social and educational measures to ensure that children are not subjected to such practices." Everybody knew that Rädda Barnen was aiming at female circumcision, but the delegation of Senegal counselled prudence when dealing with issues that entailed differences in cultural values, and emphasised the dangers of forcing practices into clandestinity by prohibiting them legally.

However, the representative of Italy, referring to the recommendations of the 1985 *Nairobi World Conference of the United Nations Decade for Women*, noted that female circumcision was practised on children without their consent, often in unsanitary circumstances, and caused great suffering. She recognised the importance of plurality of cultures but nevertheless appealed for measures that would eliminate this problem.

Everybody knows that 'traditional practices' as mentioned in Paragraph 3 refers in the first place to female circumcision, and that this vague language was used to avoid problems.[206]

Because of the many dangers connected to female circumcision, we shall classify Paragraph 3 in the *conservative mode* of the *physical subsystem*.

The rest of Article 24 belongs in the *integrative mode* of the *physical subsystem* (ongoing health, preventive care) and the *conservative mode* of the *physical subsystem* (treatment of diseases).

Article 25 deals with a very important and new procedure: periodic review of placement. This Article was proposed in the Working Group by Canada in 1985. A year later it was accepted.[207] The right of children placed by the

State (for reasons of care, protection or treatment) to have all aspects of that placement evaluated regularly has been included in the Convention.

According to Teram and Erickson,[208] however, the "concept of periodic review is 'threatening' since it negates the public display of good faith, and questions whether participants in the organisation are performing their roles properly." They also warn that "although mechanisms to review the institutional placements of children can be a protection of the rights of children, these same mechanisms can create the impression that children's rights are being protected through the provision of a forum for the myth of appropriate service provision." They conclude that "the review procedures can work to benefit the professionals and their organisations rather than protect the child. Unless there is a commitment by professionals to client involvement in decision-making, including exposure to inter-professional conflicts, the periodic review procedure will not be genuine." Here Article 12 (the child's opinion) provides an opening.

We cannot classify this Article in the 'Systemic Quality of Life Model' because it deals with a strictly procedural aspect.

Article 26 deals with the right of children to benefit from social security.[209] Although it is not always clear what this means, we understand from the debates in the Working Group that focus is on *benefits*, which means payment.

Contrary to the International Covenant on Economic, Social and Cultural Rights, the Convention carries a restricting clause of this right. The United States proposed that in granting social security to a child, account must be taken of the financial resources of the child and his or her family.[210] We classify this Article in the *adaptive mode* of the *physical subsystem*.

Article 27 recognises the right of children "to a standard of living adequate for the child's physical, mental, spiritual, moral and social development." The primary responsibility rests, according to the Convention, with the parents. The State's duty is to ensure that this responsibility is fulfilable, if necessary through the recovery of maintenance. If the father of the child lives in another country and does not want to pay maintenance, international agreements should help to enforce this.

Although the standard of living should be adequate to fulfil needs in all domains of the 'Systemic Quality of Life Model', the issue is money. Therefore this Article belongs in the *adaptive mode* of the *physical subsystem*. In 1987 the representative of the USSR said[211] that "the concept of guardianship greatly differed from country to country and, accordingly, the matter of securing child maintenance of parents who are financially responsible for the child, should be sorted out in the context of national legislation." The representative of the United Kingdom greatly sympathised with this point of view.

Article 28 formulates the child's right to education. The representative of Algeria[212] had proposed to include a general clause on the right of the child to education. Such a right is especially relevant for the 115 million children (namely 30% of the children between 6 and 11 and 60% of the children between 12 and 17) who do not go to school.

In Paragraph 1(a) States-Parties pledge to make primary education *free and compulsory*. Paragraph 1(b), about secondary schooling, is less outspoken, probably because many States cannot afford to offer it free in any case. Paragraph 1(e) deals with "measures to encourage regular attendance at schools and the reduction of drop-out rates." Nevertheless, it was predicted at the World Conference on Education for All, in Jomtien, Thailand on March 9, 1990, that of the 100 million children who started schooling in 1990, at least 40 million will drop out before completing primary school.

Education (often classified by us in the adaptive mode of the cultural subsystem) belongs in this case in the *adaptive mode* of the *social subsystem*. (The drafters wanted to make the child play the role of pupil).

In 1985 the representative of the Ukrainian Soviet Socialist Republic (supported by the representative of the Union of Soviet Socialist Republics) pointed out that in many countries degrading and cruel methods of discipline were still inflicted upon children.

The representative of Sweden pointed out that physical punishment was not restricted to schools. He therefore argued that the prohibition of degrading and cruel treatment of children should be dealt with in a separate Paragraph or Article.[213] Article 28 Paragraph 2 urges States-Parties to take "all appropriate measures to ensure that school discipline is administered in a manner consistent with the child's human dignity."

We shall classify this paragraph in the *expressive mode* of the *personality subsystem* (but in the 'negative' sense, as if this paragraph was saying: Do not stop children from expressing themselves).

Article 29 deals with the *aims* of education. Part of this proposal came from the Baha'i International Community (a participant in the NGO-Group).[214]

Paragraph 1(a) mentions that education should be directed to the development of the child's personality and the realisation of his or her full potential. This belongs in the *expressive mode* of the *personality subsystem*.

Paragraph 1(b) gives as one of the aims of education the development of respect for human rights. It is concerned with creating equality.

This we classify in the *integrative and adaptive modes* of the *integrative-social sub-subsystem*.

Paragraph 1(c) is concerned with the development of respect for the child's parents, his or her own cultural identity, language and values, and for the national values of the country in which the child is living, the country from which he or she may originate, and for civilizations different from his or her own." In 1987 the paragraph was proposed by Algeria as: "Children should be educated in a social climate imbued with the national values and the cultural identity of the children, with respect for civilizations different from their own and for the rights of peoples. In no case may children of countries still under colonial domination and foreign occupation or racist regimes be deprived of their cultural and national identity."[215]

The observer for Canada found the term "the child's cultural identity and national values" ambiguous as to whether it was the child's, the State's or the parents' identity and national values that were to be considered. She said that in a multicultural State such a question was not easily answered. She also sought clarification of what 'rights of peoples' were referred to, other than the 'right to self-determination'. Her arguments were accepted and the paragraph got a less nationalistic character ('rights of peoples' was deleted). It belongs in the *adaptive mode* of the *cultural-valuative subsystem*:

The first part of paragraph 1(d) ("the preparation of the child for a responsible life in a free society") is to be classified in the *adaptive mode* of the *social subsystem*. The second part ("the spirit of understanding, peace, tolerance, equality of sexes, and friendship among all peoples, ethnic, national and religious groups and persons of indigenous origin") belongs in the *adaptive mode* of the *integrative-social subsystem*.

Article 30 deals with children of minorities and indigenous populations[216] (such as the Kanaks[217] of New Caledonia, the Indians in the U.S. and Canada, and the Maoris in New Zealand or Aotearoa).

When in 1986 this Article was proposed by the Washington D.C. based Four Directions Council[218], it dealt only with the children of indigenous populations. Later the concern was extended to children of minorities in general.[219] It can be classified in the *expressive mode* of the *cultural subsystem*.

In Article 31 the States Parties recognise the right of children to leisure, play and participation in cultural and artistic activities. The representative of the Federal Republic of Germany stressed the importance of leisure and recreation for the child's development, but expressed doubts with regard to the advisability of proclaiming a universal right in this respect. He indicated his preference for dealing with the issue in the context of the provision against economic and social exploitation. The representative of Japan also expressed doubts concerning the advisability of proclaiming a universal right in this respect. The observer for the Holy See voiced a reservation on the grounds that the Article did not reflect a relationship between the right of the child to rest and leisure and the right of parents to control the rest and leisure activities of their children.[220]

Leisure and recreational activities are classifiable in the *adaptive mode* of the *personality subsystem*.

Play belongs in the *expressive mode* of the *personality subsystem*. The participation in cultural and artistic life are classifiable in the *expressive mode* of the *cultural subsystem*.

Article 32 deals with child labour. The aim of several representatives to include such an Article was specially to protect children from work which is likely to be harmful.[221]

In Article 32 the obligation of the States-Parties is formulated to protect children from engaging in work that is likely to be hazardous (*conservative mode* of the *physical subsystem*) or to interfere with the child's education (*expressive mode* of the *personality subsystem*; *adaptive mode* of the *social subsystem* and the *adaptive mode* of the *cultural subsystem*) or is harmful to the child's health (*integrative mode* of the *physical subsystem*).

Article 33 deals with the child's right to protection from the use of narcotic and psychotropic drugs and from being involved in their production or distribution. In 1986 China tabled this proposal.[222] The Dutch observer said that he welcomed the proposal by China but that he would like clarification concerning the term 'narcotic drugs'. He asked whether it included all kinds of drugs, and suggested the phrasing "to protect children from the abuse of narcotic and psychotropic substances." Eventually the text read: "to protect children from the illicit use of narcotic drugs and psychotropic substances as defined in the relevant international treaties." We classify this Article in the *conservative mode* of the *physical subsystem*.

Article 34 deals with sexual exploitation. In 1986 the delegations of France and the Netherlands[223] proposed a separate Article, which would protect children from prostitution. (Sexual abuse[224] in the family was already dealt with in Article 19). Since venereal diseases and aids endanger the child's life, the main concern of this Article is with the *conservative mode* of the *physical subsystem*. However, the original intention was to protect the child against all abuses of the child's moral, spiritual, mental and physical integrity. Sexual exploitation in its most overt form is tolerated internationally. Sex tourism to Thailand and the Philippines is 'big business'. However, the phenomenon is not limited to these two Asiatic States. Renée Bridel[225] wrote me that "the question of exploitation of the physical person of children 'for immoral purposes' cannot be solved because of a *political* question and a very clandestine matter that many governments try to hush up!

The last paragraph of this Article deals with child pornography. It was proposed by the Norwegian representative in 1987.[226]

The intention can be classified in the *integrative mode* of the *cultural subsystem* (forced conflict with own values) and the *conservative mode* of the *personality subsystem* (the degree of stability needed before the identity is endangered).

Article 35 deals with child-abduction. The concern is here with abduction for prostitution and sale of children for those or any other purpose. Cases are known of children who were abducted for the sale of organs for transplantation![227] Since such practices endanger the child's very existence, Article 35 belongs in the *conservative mode* of the *physical subsystem*.

It is noteworthy that, according to the International Association of Democratic Lawyers[228] and the International Organisation of Police Forces (INTERPOL), no member State has requested speedy co-operation and priority acting to combat trade in human beings!

Article 36 deals with protection from all forms of exploitation not covered by other Articles. The Article was proposed by the Canadian observer,[229] who noted that *Article* 10 of the *International Covenant on Economic, Social and Cultural Rights* dealt with economic and social exploitation. If the Convention contained Articles dealing with economic and sexual exploitation but not with social exploitation, this would be a step backwards with regard to the Covenant. She suggested one Article dealing with all forms of social exploitation.

This started a debate about terminology. The representative of the USSR observed that terms such as moral, spiritual, mental or physical exploitation did not cover all aspects of the interests of the child which needed to be protected. He indicated his preference for a general, overall, approach and a broad wording that would allow for protection from any kind of exploitation. This was accepted. We can, therefore, classify this Article in the *conservative modes* of all *subsystems*.

Article 37 deals with various aspects of physical integrity of the child. It prohibits torture and inhuman or degrading treatment or punishment.

This belongs in the *conservative mode* of the *physical subsystem*.

Capital punishment[230] and life imprisonment without the possibility of release are prohibited for persons below the age of 18. When detained the child has the right to maintain contact with his or her family (*integrative mode* of the *social subsystem*).

Every child deprived of his liberty has the right to legal assistance (*adaptive mode* of the *social subsystem*).

Article 38 (on armed conflicts) was hotly debated. In 1985 the delegations of Belgium, Finland, the Netherlands, Peru, Senegal and Sweden[231] proposed the following:

1. States Parties to the present Convention undertake to respect and to ensure respect for rules of international humanitarian law applicable in armed conflicts which are relevant to children.
2. In order to implement these obligations States Parties to the present Convention shall, in conformity with the relevant rules of international humanitarian law, refrain in particular from recruiting children into the armed forces and shall take all feasible measures to ensure that children do not take part in hostilities.

Noteworthy is that the final text of Paragraph 1 of Article 38 indeed mentions "respect for rules of *international humanitarian law*." Since no other human rights instrument incorporates a humanitarian law provision, this is also a unique aspect of the Convention.

In 1986 NGOs submitted a text which read "The Principle of humanitarian law should also be applicable for the protection of children in situations of internal strife." According to Françoise Krill of the International Committee of the Red Cross',[232] this provision should doubtless have increased the protection afforded to children. However, several governments were against, because it would bring in the Geneva Convention through the 'back door'.

Picture X.5. A 9-year old Ugandan marksman caught up in an armed conflict. (Courtesy: Yann Gamblin/UNICEF.)

"It should be noted," writes Krill, "that the provisions contained in Article 38 must not convey the impression of addressing the entire question, and it must not be forgotten that there are some 25 Articles covering this area which are in force in international humanitarian law."[233]

Paragraph 2 formulates that no child under 15 should take a direct part in hostilities. This paragraph is controversial in three ways.

First the text obliges States Parties to take all *feasible* measures. The International Committee of the Red Cross, several governments (notably Sweden) and most of the NGOs were in favour of obliging States to take all *necessary* rather than all *feasible* measures to prevent children from taking part in hostilities. "In other words," says Françoise Krill "the text which was finally approved means that voluntary participation by children is not totally prohibited."

Secondly, Paragraph 2 forbids that children take a *direct* part in hostilities. From this we can conclude that indirect participation, such as the gathering and transmitting of military information, transporting weapons, munitions and other supplies, is allowed.

The most controversial issue is the age limit stated for involvement in hostilities. As we have seen Article 38 deviates from its own Article 1 ("a child means every human being below the age of 18 years"). Paragraph 2 talks about persons who *have not attained the age of* 15 *years*, and Paragraph 3 states: "States Parties shall refrain from recruiting *any person who has not attained the age of* 15 *years* into their armed forces. In recruiting among those persons *who have attained the age of* 15 *years but who have not attained the age of* 18 *years, States Parties shall endeavour to give priority to those who are oldest.*"

During the debates[234] the representative of Algeria expressed her disagreement with the proposed age limit, and indicated her wish that the age of 18 years, which appeared in Article 1 of the draft Convention, be maintained in the text under discussion. Many organisations agreed. Rädda Barnen (Swedish Save the Children)[235] wrote for instance: "Unfortunately, the formulations agreed so far do not provide further protection for the minors. On the contrary they represent steps backwards. There is no recognition in the text of the absolute ban against targeting civilians, there is no indication that the drafting age ought to be higher than 15. The discussion on the draft United Nations Convention should therefore be reopened on these aspects. The only decent position is that *no child* be drafted for military combat service. Those who, because of their age, are not otherwise recognised as fully responsible citizens should not be sent to the battlefields and be exposed to the risk of being killed."

One of the reasons for defining 15 years as the age limit[236] for taking part in hostilities, was, no doubt, to remain realistic. Unfortunately the interests of some States[237] supporting guerilla movements and counter-revolutionary movements must also have been instrumental. W.G.Rabus[238] calls it a disappointment that "the progressive development which related to the age limits for participating in hostilities, namely that children under 18 may not be forced to become soldiers, was annulled by the Working Group in December 1988."

The Article does not differentiate between international and internal armed conflicts. However, the Fourth Geneva Convention of 1949 and the two Additional Protocols of 1977 offer precisely that.[239] According to Rabus[240] "the gap between the protection in international conflict and the protection in a civil war is being bridged by the contents of Article 38(1)".

Article 38 is classifiable in the *conservative mode* of the *physical subsystem* (protection of the child's life).

Article 39 (rehabilitative care) obliges the States Parties to give appropriate treatment for recovery and re-integration to children who are victims of armed conflicts, torture, but also of neglect, maltreatment and exploitation. "Such recovery and re-integration shall take place in an environment which fosters the health, self-respect and dignity of the child."

We classify this Article in the *integrative mode* of the *physical and personality subsystems*, and also in the *conservative mode* (prevention of further deterioration).

Article 40 (administration of juvenile justice) aims at securing for the child who is in conflict with criminal law, treatment which is consistent with the child's human rights and with his or her age and maturity, and which focuses on the child's re-integration into society.

States oblige themselves to give children who allegedly have committed an offence, legal or other assistance (such as an interpreter) in preparing and presenting their defence. This belongs in the *adaptive mode* of the *social subsystem*.

Already in 1985 the United Nations accepted more detailed guidelines on this issue, although they are not binding as is a Convention (see the so-called 'Beijing-Rules').[241]

Article 41 deals with respect for existing standards. Since the United Nations Convention is a product of compromise, and the existing standards in the various States are not always identical to those mentioned in the Convention, this Article states that in cases of difference, the higher standard applies.[242]

Article 42 – 45 deal more in detail with the implementation process. Thomas Hammarberg, director-general of Rädda Barnen explained[243] how the implementation process is arranged by the drafters of the United Nations Convention: "The Convention itself rules that a monitoring Committee of ten people should be set up. These Committee members should be appointed in their individual capacity and be experts of 'high moral standing and recognised competence in the field.' States Parties undertake to report to this Committee within two years after ratification and thereafter every five years. The Committee, in turn, shall report to the General Assembly every two years."

Governments should make their reports to the Committee widely available to the public in their own countries, so as to encourage public discussion.

Since concrete obligations are not specified, it will be hard to evaluate the implementation of some of the provisions in the Convention, for instance the one on 'child survival'.

In particular the monitoring of the economic and social rights of a more collective nature will require a creative approach by the Committee. The main point is, of course, whether governments demonstrate a genuine ambition to meet such rights.

It has been left to the Committee to work out its own rules of procedure. However, it is spelled out that UNICEF and the United Nations specialised agencies will be entitled to take part in its work. 'Other competent bodies' which might be invited to provide expert advice are mentioned. The phrase alludes to NGOs, who are thereby recognised as contributors to the process. This procedure is different from the usual model in the field of human rights. The thrust is constructive and aid oriented.

The fact that the implementation of the reporting system is not left to the "quiet diplomacy of infrequent, little-known meetings"[244] will not mean "that States loudly proclaim their adherence to human rights treaties and then ignore their implementation", says Dana Fisher. She argues that the attention of NGOs to these procedures "at least raises the possibility of strengthening them, and it will certainly raise the cost of non-compliance to those governments who now hope that the procedures will be largely forgotten." Governments open themselves up for public scrutiny.

In 1987 the representative of the United States[245] announced that his country "would only support the funding of the Committee and its activities *by States Parties* and not *from the general funds of the United Nations*." (A high percentage of the United Nations budget comes from the United States.) However, in the General Assembly 171 States voted for the funding of the committee out of the United Nations budget (The United States was against, Japan abstained). The reasoning behind this decision was that a financial obligation might have deterred some States from ratifying the Convention.

According to the international secretariat of Defence for Children International (DCI) "considerable effort has been made to ensure that concerns of economically disadvantaged countries, as well as the religious and cultural specificities of given societies, are reflected in the text. Finally, alongside the necessary mechanism for overseeing compliance with the Conventions provisions, strong emphasis is placed on the need for international solidarity, co-operation, dialogue and technical assistance in fostering implementation."[246]

According to the Executive Director of UNICEF James P.Grant,[247] the principle that the lives and the normal development of children "should have *first call* on society's concerns, (embodied by the *United Nations Convention on the Rights of the Child*) will hopefully affect the course of political, social and economic progress in all nations over the next decade and beyond." Grant: "If the trench of such a principle could be dug across the battlegrounds of political and economic change in the decade ahead, then civilisation itself would have made a significant advance. Failure to protect the physical, mental and emotional development of children is the principal means by which humanity's difficulties are compounded and its problems perpetuated. And *special measures* to protect children from the inadequacies and mistakes of the adult world is a principle means by which many of mankind's most fundamental problems might ultimately be confronted."[248]

4. THE WORLD DECLARATION ON THE SURVIVAL, PROTECTION AND DEVELOPMENT OF CHILDREN (1990)

See Appendix XLIV

To promote this idea of 'first call' a *World Summit for Children* was held at the United Nations Headquarters in New York on September 30, 1990. It was remarkable that, at a time when World Leaders were occupied with the Gulf crisis and the threat of war,[249] seventy-one Heads of State and Prime Ministers gathered in New York for the sole purpose of giving children a better chance for the future.

In November 1989, almost a year before the Gulf-crisis, with the decline of superpower confrontation, Prime Minister Brian Mulroney of Canada, Presidents Hosni Mubarak of Egypt, Moussa Traoré of Mali, Carlos Salinas de Gortario of Mexico, then Prime Minister Benazir Bhutto of Pakistan and Prime Minister Ingvar Carlsson of Sweden, had called for this World Summit

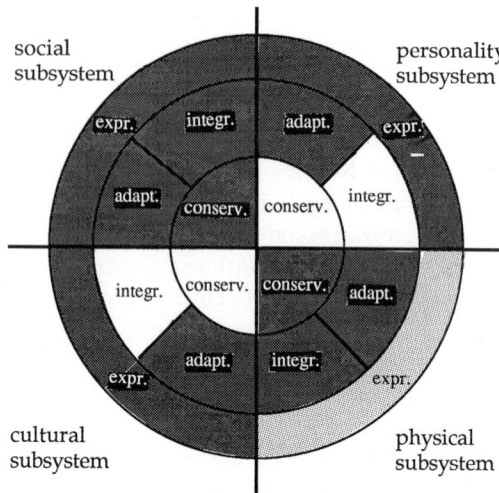

Fig. 10.3. The United Nations Convention on the Rights of the Child (1989), interpreted by the Systemic Quality of Life Model.

for Children. The initiating governments asked UNICEF to provide the secretariat to organise the meeting.

The World Summit for Children marks the first time that leaders around the globe have met for a single purpose, joining hands to try to resolve some of the universal problems that children encounter in developing and surviving to adulthood.

The overall aim of the World Summit was to put children high on the agenda of the 1990s, giving them priority or 'first call' on the world's resources

Picture X.6. The U.N. Convention on the Rights of the Child, adopted on November 20, 1989 by the General Assembly, was opened for signature on January 26, 1990 at the United Nations. During the official signing ceremony sixty-one governments signed the Convention. (Photo: UNICEF/Ruby Mera.)

in good times or bad, war or peace. This implied, according to the organisers, that "the growing minds and bodies of children should have first call on society's capacities, and that children should be able to depend upon these commitments."[250]

"Whether a child is to survive, go to school and be protected from exploitation or abuse should not depend on whether interest rates rise or fall, commodity prices go up or down, a particular political party is in power, a country is at war, nor on any other trough or crest in the endless undulations of political and economic life," UNICEF argued.

According to the organisers of the World Summit, nothing could illustrate the need for this principle more clearly than the damage which the debt crisis has inflicted on children in recent years. In many parts of the world cuts in government spending and a fall in family incomes have meant that infant mortality has risen, malnutrition has increased, and schools and health clinics have been closed. The result is that the poorest and most vulnerable children have been the most exposed to the lash of debt and recession. This is exactly the opposite of the principle of first call.

The principle of *first call* is universally relevant. No matter what the nation and what the cause, the World Summit organisers said, "the time has come to protect children, as far as is humanly possible, from the mistakes, excesses and vicissitudes of the adult world." The real challenge of the First World Summit for Children was to translate that principle into specific aims to be achieved in the decade ahead. As the executive director of UNICEF, James Grant, said: the Heads of State and Prime Ministers should try to "do the do-able."

The World Summit for Children adopted a *Declaration* and gave its blessing to a Plan of Action (drafted by UNICEF-staff members) to save the world's young from hunger, disease and other woes. Moreover, the World Summit gave the *United Nations Convention on the Rights of the Child* additional political weight by mentioning the Convention in the World Summits Declaration as well as in its Plan of Action.

"We have gathered at the World Summit for Children to undertake a joint commitment and to make an urgent universal appeal – to give every child a better future," is the opening paragraph of the Declaration. It takes as its starting point the daily deaths of an estimated 40,000 children around the globe from malnutrition, disease, lack of clean water, inadequate sanitation and drugs. Many could be saved with existing cures and remedies costing pennies, such as vaccination and anti-dehydration formulas.

Among ambitious targets set out in the Plan of Action are the reduction by one-third of mortality rates among children under five years old and the halving of maternity death rates by the year 2000.

Universal access to safe drinking water and to sanitary means of waste disposal is another aim. So is universal access to basic education and completion of elementary education by at least 80 percent of primary school-age youngsters.

By the late 1990s a program to prevent the majority of child deaths and child malnutrition in the decade ahead might need a budget of approximately 2.5 billion dollars per year. This is as much as companies in the United States have been spending yearly for the advertising of cigarettes, and as much as the Soviet Union has monthly been spending on vodka.[251] "If the politicians will give the fight against child deaths and malnutrition a high priority (also in the state budgets), this will be their gift to the people of the twenty-first Century", the organisers of the Summit concluded.

What is the importance of the World Summit Declaration? "There's not that much new in the Declaration," noted Patrick Hennessy (Ireland's representative on the Summit Planning Committee), to a journalist of *Time*[252] Magazine. However, "it is the commitment that is important. And the fact that so many Heads of State have come together is symbolic."

Many people stayed sceptical about this Summit. Child psychiatrist Robert Coles, for instance, told *Time* that he was afraid the Summit would provide politicians with another opportunity to talk about the plight of children without doing anything about it.

Although President Bush came to New York, he greatly disappointed his audience by *not* announcing that the United States would sign or start procedures for ratification of the United Nations Convention on the Rights of the Child.[253] The reason that the United States Government has not signed the Convention is that it forbids execution of minors who have committed capital crimes, and, according to some sources, that the Convention does not take a more explicit stand against abortion.

According to *Time* the Planning Committee struggled for weeks to find a language acceptable to all the participating nations. The United States and Britain, for instance, objected to the original wording on economic policies, resulting from the debt crisis (amounting to enforced poverty of millions of children in the Third World). This wording was subsequently altered. Cuba wanted to add colonialism to the list of dangers to children, but when Britain countered with totalitarian dictatorships the matter was dropped. At the last minute, just after Iraq's invasion of Kuwait, Saudi Arabia added "annexation and aggression," which stayed in.

In Paragraph 20 the World Leaders tell the world that they have agreed to act together. In Paragraph 20(1) they state: "We will work to promote earliest possible ratification and implementation of the Convention on the Rights of the Child. Programmes to encourage information about children's rights should be launched world-wide, taking into account the distinct cultural and social values in different countries." The wording "taking into account the distinct cultural and social values in different countries" gives the politicians an 'escape', not to implement certain rights of the child.

When we analyse this Declaration and compare it with the United Nations Convention on the Rights of the Child, we see that the Declaration is less comprehensive than the Convention. There is a real 'retreat' to the *physical subsystem*. Of course when seventy-one Heads of State and Prime Ministers are brought together, it is to be expected that they do not want to commit themselves on issues liable to confront them with criticism at home. They therefore refrained from formulating rights in the cultural, social and personality domain. The concern in the physical field provided them with the lowest common denominator on which they could agree. Who can be against fighting dehydration, pneumonia, measles, tetanus and the whooping cough?

In Paragraph 20(2) the Heads of State pledge "to work for a solid effort of national and international action to enhance *children's health*" The concern with child health is classifiable in the *integrative mode* of the *physical subsystem*. The concern with *child mortality* belongs in the *conservative mode* of the *physical subsystem*. To promote the provision of *clean water* and *access to sanitation* belongs in the *adaptive mode* of the *physical subsystem*.

In Paragraph 20(3) the politicians state that they "will work for *optimal growth and development in childhood*. This belongs in the *expressive mode* of the *physical subsystem*. The rest of this sub-paragraph shows that 'growth and development' must be understood in the physical sense: "through measures to eradicate hunger, malnutrition and famine". This can be classified in the *adaptive mode* of the *physical subsystem*.

Paragraph 20(4) deals with the status of women in general rather than with the rights of children. It pleads for giving women a higher status in those cultures where this is not yet the case. This concern belongs in the *expressive mode* of the *social subsystem*.

It is interesting to note that *girls* are only mentioned in this respect in the (less important) *Plan of Action for Implementing the World Declaration.*[254] "Women in their various roles play a critical part in the well-being of children. The enhancement of the status of women and their equal access to education, training, credit and other extension services constitute a valuable contribution to a nation's social and economic development. Efforts for the enhancement of women's status and their role in development must begin with the girl child. Equal opportunity should be provided for the girl child to benefit from the health, nutrition, education and other basic services to enable her to grow to her full potential."

The *equal opportunity* element brings also a (weak) *adaptive-physical* (money/salary) and *adaptive-social* concern in the picture.

The promotion of breast-feeding, paragraph 20(4), belongs in the *adaptive mode* of the *physical subsystem*.

Paragraph 20(5) states: "We will work for respect for the role of the family in providing for children and will support the efforts of parents, other caregivers and communities to nurture and care for children from the earliest stages of childhood through adolescence. We also recognise the special needs of children who are separated from their families." The text of this sub-paragraph is not very clear. The nurturing by the family in the physical sense (food, etc.) belongs in the *adaptive mode* of the *physical subsystem*. However, there is another way to understand this sub-paragraph: Introduction of chil-

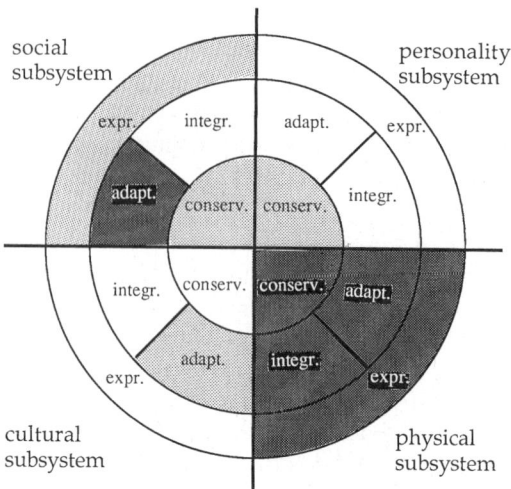

Fig. 10.4. The World Declaration on the Survival, Protection and Development of Children (of the World Summit for Children in New York on September 30, 1990). Interpreted by the Systemic Quality of Life Model.

dren to the culture, values and norms of their society begins in the family. Paragraph 20(5) ends with the statement that the World Leaders "recognise the special needs of children who are separated from their families." What are these *special needs*? One would say: to have a continuous relationship!

The *Plan of Action* states that "Whenever children are separated from their families, arrangements should be made for appropriate alternative family care or institutional placement, due regard being paid to the desirability of continuity in a child's upbringing in his or her own cultural milieu." These arrangements can be classified in the *adaptive mode* of the *physical subsystem*.

Paragraph 20(6) states: "We will work for programmes that reduce illiteracy and provide educational opportunities for all children, irrespective of their background and gender; that prepare children for productive employment and lifelong learning opportunities, i.e. through vocational training; and that enable children to grow to adulthood within a supportive and nurturing cultural and social context." Since such issues as preparation for employment, are well represented in this sub-paragraph, we classify it in the *adaptive mode* of the *social subsystem*. The programmes to reduce illiteracy are mainly concerned with improving the social fit of youngsters.

Paragraph 20(7) is a promise to children in especially difficult circumstances – such as "victims of apartheid and foreign occupation; orphans and street children; children of migrant workers; displaced children and victims of natural and man-made disasters; the disabled and the abused; the socially disadvantaged and the exploited." This can be classified in the *expressive mode* of the *social subsystem*, but in the *negative sense*: politicians promise

Survival, Protection and Development of Children (1990) 215

Picture X.7. "We have gathered at the World Summit for Children to undertake a joint Commitment and to make an urgent appeal – to give every child a better future . . . we ourselves hearby make a solemn commitment to give high priority to the rights of children, to their survival and to their protection and development".

(Photo, Courtesy: UNICEF/Eastman Kodak Company).

216   *Chapter X*

to try and *avoid* dissatisfaction in the expressive mode of the social subsystem. However, the second part of Paragraph 20(7) (dealing with orphans, street children, displaced children, etc.) belongs in the *adaptive mode* of the *physical subsystem*, since we assume that the World Leaders wanted to provide those children with homes. The sentence dealing with refugee children is not very clear. Possibly it is a concern with the (*conservative mode* of the *personality subsystem*) (belonging), since the importance of "new roots in life" is mentioned. The last part of 20(7) ("we do our best to ensure that children are not drawn into becoming victims of the scourge of drugs") is again classifiable in the *conservative mode* of the *physical subsystem*.

In Paragraph 20(8) most of the text, (except the sentence about values of peace, understanding and dialogue in the education of children),[255] deals with physical safety (*conservative mode* of the *physical subsystem*) and the conditions to ensure such safety (*adaptive mode* of the *conservative-physical sub-subsystem*). One such condition is special relief corridors for the benefit of children in times of war. UNICEF's idea of declaring children "a neutral conflict free zone in human relations"[256] is again brought to the fore in this paragraph.

Paragraph 20(9) ("common measures for the protection of the environment") is concerned with the *adaptive mode* of the *physical subsystem*. It can also be seen as a concern for the *conservative mode* of the physical subsystem ("so that children enjoy a safer future"), and for the *integrative mode* of the *physical subsystem* ("so that children enjoy a healthier future").

Paragraph 20(10) ("... work for a global attack on poverty, which would have immediate benefits for children's welfare.") belongs in the *adaptive mode* of the *physical subsystem*

In Paragraph 24 the World Leaders state that they "have decided to adopt and implement a Plan of Action as a framework for more specific national and international undertakings. We appeal to all our colleagues to endorse that Plan. We are prepared to make available the resources to meet these commitments, as part of the priorities of our national plans."

The future will show if the politicians will keep the promises they have pledged at the *World Summit for Children*, and how the *UN Convention on the Rights of the Child* will be implemented in different States.[257]

NOTES

1. Another *Declaration of Geneva* exists, namely of the *World Medical Association*. Adopted during the Association's meeting in September 1948, and subsequently adapted several times, it contains a sort of *promise* to be made by every doctor upon joining the profession. ("I solemnly pledge myself to consecrate my life to the service of humanity ... I shall practice my profession with conscience and dignity ... ", etc.) See for this *Declaration of Geneva*: The World Medical Association Handbook of Declarations, Ferney-Voltaire, France, 1985, p. 3.
2. When I was in Geneva in May 1986, I discovered to my dismay that the International

Union for Child Welfare had gone bankrupt and that much material from their archives could not be found. Only the library of the Union had been sold and sent, packed in crates, to the Asilo Mariuccia Organisation (in Milan!). The President of that organisation wrote me that he had not been able to obtain the necessary space for all the material which, therefore, was still with the shipper. Consequently the greater part of this Chapter is based on what I could find in the Archives of the League of Nations in Geneva and in the library of the 'Save the Children Fund' in London.
3. Lejeune, René, 'Eglantyne Jebb, A Life Devoted to the Service of Children in Distress', in *International Child Welfare Review*, No. 58, September 1983, p. 58.
4. According to George Werner, vice-president of the World Union for Child Welfare, professor of law at the University of Geneva and member of the board of the *Comité International de la Croix-Rouge*. Werner's speech at the occasion of the proclamation of the *Declaration of Geneva*, has been published in the *Revue Internationale de la Croix-Rouge* ('Remise de la Declaration de Genève au Conseil d'Etat de Genève pour ses archives') Sixième année, No. 63, March 1924, pp. 155–156.
5. *International Child Welfare Review*, 'How the Declaration was Born', 1950, No. 7, June, p. 40.
6. In the journal *The World's Children*, Vol.III, 1922–1923, of the Save the Children Fund in London, a concept with four general principles and twenty-eight 'clauses of the charter' appeared (on p. 146). Those twenty-eight elaborations are somewhat similar to the Declaration of the International Council of Women. In Edward Fuller's book *The Right of the Child, A Chapter in Social History*, London, 1951, Victor Gollancz Ltd, we read on page 71 "In 1922 – the Fund's third year – Eglantyne Jebb began to put her ideas on paper, first in the form of a children's Charter for Great Britain, in which she endeavoured to express the basic needs of the day. Simultaneously, the Marchioness of Aberdeen and Temair (1847–1939) a member of the Association of the Save the Children Fund, and the Scottish National Council of Women, over which she presided, were thinking along the same lines and had produced their own draft of the Children's charter. Then a joint committee of the two organisations worked out a composite charter ( ) The intention was that every nation should draft its own charter, reflecting its own needs. Experience showed that this was impracticable." See also: *the World's Children* of April 1923, Vol.III, No. 3, p. 111 in which the English efforts to come to a Declaration are discussed. Mentioned is a 'Charter Committee' under the chairmanship of a Mrs. de Bunsen, that had also been engaged in drafting such a Children's Charter.
7. *International Child Welfare Review*, 1970, No. 7, 'How the Declaration was Born', p. 40.
8. Werner, George, in the *Revue Internationale de la Croix-Rouge*, Op. cit., p. 157, quotes a letter from Eglantyne Jebb.
9. See: *International Child Welfare Review*, No. 7, June 1970, p. 40.
10. Mr. Claude Capaire of the Musée d'Art et d'Histoire in Geneva wrote me in July 1986 that there are no photographs of this meeting in his archives.
11. Werner, George, Op. cit., p. 160.
12. Idem. Also published in the *International Child Welfare Review* in 1970 in the article 'How the Declaration was Born,' Op. cit.
13. Durand, André, *From Serajevo to Hiroshima, History of the International Committee of the Red Cross*, Geneva, 1984, Henry Dunant Institute, p. 165.
14. Unfortunately Roger Herbaut, *Conseiller Technique of the Musée de Radio France* in Paris wrote me in September 1986 that he could find nothing about this special transmission in his archives. Neither was there any report about it in the *Journal de Geneva* of 1923.
15. Although Edward Fuller called this acknowledgement "the most spectacular triumph of Eglantyne Jebb's career" I hardly ever came upon her name or, for that matter on the name of the *Save the Children International Union*, in the archives of the League of Nations.
16. My impression is that the adoption of the *Declaration of Geneva* was more or less automatic and was overshadowed by 'strife for power' and pulling the ropes by the various organis-

ations. More important was the question: What shall we do after the *League of Nations* will have adopted the Declaration of Geneva? Who is going to document the International Child Welfare work and who is going to co-ordinate it?

17. Pfeil, Alfred, *Der Völkebund, Literaturbericht und kritische Darstellung seiner Geschichte*, Darmstadt, 1976, Wissenschaftliche Buchgesellschaft, p. 81. The year 1924 was relatively hey-day for the League of Nations.
18. Chanlett, Eliska and Morier, G.M., 'Declaration of the Rights of the Child' in: *International Child Welfare Review*, 1986, No. 1, p. 4.
19. Walters, F.P., *A History of the League of Nations*, Vol.I, London/New York, 1952, Oxford University Press, p. 187.
20. See Appendix IX.
21. Jebb, Eglantyne, *International Responsibilities for Child Welfare*, Geneva, 1927, Save the Children International Union, p. 6.
22. *The World's Children*, April, 1923, Vol.III, No. 3, p. 111. This quote refers to a draft of a *Children's Charter*, by the British committee under the presidency of a Mrs. de Bunsen.
23. Fuller, Edward, 'Great Britain and the Declaration of Geneva', in: *The World's Children*, Vol.V, October 1924, pp. 27–29. The journal *The World's Children* was and still is published by (Eglantyne Jebb's) *Save the Children Fund*.
24. Idem.
25. Jebb, Eglantyne, *International Responsibilities for Child Welfare*, Geneva, 1927, Save the Children International Union, p. 7.
26. Idem.
27. Fuller, Edward, 'Great Britain and the Declaration of Geneva', in: *The World's Children*, Vol.V, No. 2, Nov. 1924, p. 57.
28. Fuller, Edward, 'Great Britain and the Declaration of Geneva III' in: *The World's Children*, Vol.V, No. 5, p. 75.
29. Jebb, Eglantyne, *Save the Child!*, p. 41. and Fuller, Edward, Article No.III, 1925, Op. cit., pp. 75–76.
30. In May 1988 I flew from New York to Milwaukee and heard a stewardess of the Midwest Express declare while demonstrating the oxygen masks that mothers with children must administer oxygen to themselves before administering it to their children. When I asked the Midwest Express the reason for this, the official in charge of safety explained to me that if the mothers do not take care of themselves first they will soon not be able to take care of their fainting children. A necessary exception of the rules in the Declaration of Geneva.
31. Fuller, Edward, 'Great Britain and the Declaration of Geneva IV', in *The World's Children*, Vol.V, No. 6, March 1985, pp. 88–90.
32. Jebb, Eglantyne, *International Responsibilities for Child Welfare*, 1927, Op. cit., p. 14. Fuller, Edward, 'Great Britain and the Declaration of Geneva V', in: *The World's Children*, Vol.VI, No. 7, April 1925, p. 116.
33. Idem.
34. Idem.
35. The International Union for Child Welfare (IUCW) was a merger between the Brussels-based International Association for Child Welfare, and the Save the Children International Union in Geneva. The IUCW was founded in 1946 but had, regrettably, to be liquidated in the spring of 1986, because the organisation had made debts. See an article of Pascal Auchlin in the *Tribune de Geneva* of December 20th 1985. In 1989 the International Forum for Child Welfare (IFCW) was created. It can be considered as the successor of the IUCW.
36. ECOSOC (Economic and Social Council) works under the responsibility of the General Assembly. It co-ordinates and guides the work done by various United Nations committees in the economic and social field. It gives recommendations to the General Assembly. The Council consists of fifty-four members of whom eighteen are chosen every year for three years. Originally (in the time of the discussions about the *Declaration of the Rights of the Child*) the Council consisted of only eighteen members (read: Member-States). The scope

of ECOSOC now comprises economic, social, cultural, educational, health and human rights issues.
37. United Nations *Report of the Temporary Social Commission*, Session held in New York from April 29 till May 14, 1946, *document E*/41. On September 1959 the Polish Delegate to the 907th Assembly of the Third Commission of the General Assembly said that "in 1946 the temporary Social Commission had already been discussing the possibility of the adoption of a Declaration; it was regrettable that thirteen years had elapsed before the draft had been laid before the General Assembly." See Archive material A/C.3./Sr.907 29 September 1959.
38. See: Document E/41. Temporary Social Commission (1946).
39. *International Child Welfare Review*, 1970, No. 7, p. 40.
40. *Social Commission, Third Session, Summary Record of the Sixteenth Meeting*, Lake Success, New York, Monday, 19 April 1948, E/CN.S/SR.60.
41. Social Commission, E/CN.5/SR.60, p. 15.
42. The concept of the 'draft Declaration on the Rights of the Child' is contained in the report of the Social Commission (Sixth Session), official Records of *The Economic and Social Council*, Fifth Year, Eleventh Session, *Supplement*, No. 3, (E/1678, Annex II). See also: the report of the Social Commission: E/AC.7./L.24,1950.
43. Social Committee of ECOSOC see: E/AC.7/SR.125–128 and E/1755.
44. Memorandum of the Secretary General, see: E/CN.4/512, February 19, 1951. The Secretary General was referring to resolution 309, C(XI) of July 13, 1950 of the Economic and Social Council, Document E/1849, p. 39.
45. For instance:
   a) Suggestions Concerning the Declaration of the Rights of the Child, *Statement submitted by the International Union for Child Welfare, a Non-Governmental Organisation in category B status*, E/CN.4/NGO/44, 20 March 1953.
   b) *Statement submitted by the International Catholic Child Bureau – a NGO in category B status*, E/CN.4/NGO.58, February 18, 1954.
   c) *Statement submitted by the Joint Committee of International Teachers' Federations, a NGO on the Register of the Secretary-General*, E/CN.4/NGO.59, March 1, 1954.
46. *Commission on Human Rights, Report on the Thirteenth Session* (1–26 April 1956), E/2970/Rev.1 and E/CN.4./253/Rev.1.
47. E/CN.4/L.450.
48. a) Statement submitted by the Liaison Committee of Women's International Organisations, a NGO in Category B, consultative status, E/CN.4/NGO/73, April 2, 1957.
   b) *Statement submitted by the International Federation of Women Lawyers, a NGO in Category B consultative status*, E/CN.4/NGO/71, April 1, 1957.
   c) *Communication from the International Union for Child Welfare, a NGO having consultative status in Category B*, E/CN.4/NGO/84, December 31, 1958.
49. Mrs. Wasilkowska (Poland) in: Commission on Human Rights, Monday, 30 March 1959, 19 August 1959, E/CN.4/SR.626.
50. Juvigny (France) in: E/CN.4/SR.629, p. 9 and E/CN.4/SR.626, p. 10.
51. E/CN.4/SR.629,p.12.
52. See: E/CN.4/SN.630, pp. 6–14.
53. Idem, p. 6.
54. Mr. Kittani of Iraq (see: E/CN.4/SR.630, p. 8). "The expression 'child born out of wedlock' was certainly preferable to 'illegitimate child'. Both the Israel and the Polish amendments contained interesting points. The Polish amendment expressed the idea in a positive form but it considered the question only from the limited point of view of legal protection. It would be better, as was done in the Israel amendment, to denounce discrimination against children born out of wedlock in Paragraph 1 of the Principles, which was more general. Some changes should perhaps be made in the Israel amendment, and in particular the idea should be expressed in a positive form. He agreed with the United Kingdom representative that an enumeration could only be indicative and not exhaustive.

In the first Paragraph of the Principle proposed by Israel, the words 'or status – of himself or of either of his parents' should be replaced by the words 'or any other status'.
55. See note 45. See also the Israel amendment E/CN.4/L 525 and that of the United Kingdom, E/CN.4/L.529.
56. *Official Records of the General Assembly Fourteenth Session, Third Committee, Social, Humanitarian and Cultural Questions, Summary Records*, 15 September-7 December 1959, New York, A/C.3/SR.907–929.
57. Clerck, De, Jacques, *Georgette Ciselet ou le Triomphe de l'Obstination*, Bruxelles, 1984, Centre Paul Huimans.
58. Hofmann, Paul, 'U.N. Body Backs Child's Charter' in: *The New York Times*, Tuesday, October 20, 1959, p. 8 (part L).
59. Idem.
60. Italy, sub-amendment, A/C.3/L.735.
61. Philippine amendment, A/C.3/L.734.
62. Third Committee, 913th Meeting, Friday, October 2, 1959.
63. *United Nations General Assembly, Third Committee*, 929th Meeting, Monday 19 October 1959, p. 106, A/C.3/SR.929, Idem, p. 105.
64. Casullo, Caterina, 'The Declaration of the Rights of the Child,' in: *U.N. Secretariat News*, April 15, 1955, Vol.XL, No. 1, p. 11.
65. Government of the Netherlands, Comment, Commission on Human Rights, March 19th, 1959, E/CN.4/7a80/Add.2.
66. Sir Samuel Hoare of the United Kingdom in the Commission on Human Rights, see: E/CN.4/SR.629.
67. See: Peace and Justice Committee of the U.N. International Year of Peace, 1986, *United Nations Declaration of Human Rights*.
68. A similar discussion had occurred around the White House Conference on Child Health and Protection in 1930 where the *Children's Charter* was drafted. However, the outcome in 1930 was different: "Several organisations wanting to get into the Conference were refused, because participating organisations were limited to those dealing specifically with child problems. Those interested in birth control were the most vociferous in complaining about this." Secretary Wilbur of the Conference who was accused of blocking the discussion said: "Our work is with the child. Consequently it starts with conception and not before. We are interested in children – not in *no* children.
69. United Nations General Assembly, Fourteenth Session, Third Committee, 911th meeting, Wednesday September 30th, 1959, *Official Records*, p. 25.
70. Cheng, (China), Human Rights Commission, E/CN.4/SR.69.
71. U.N. Year Book 1959, p. 191.
72. Human Rights Commission, E/CN.4/SR.629.
73. The Economic and Social Council, E/CN.4./512.
74. Defence for Children International, *A DCI Programme for Monitoring Respect for and Violations of Children's Rights*, IEC/10/6(b)1, Geneva, September 1986.
75. The Economic and Social Council, E/1744, p. 4.
76. Commission on Human Rights, *Communication from the International Union for Child Welfare*, E/CN.4/NGO/84, December 31, 1958.
77. Commission on Human Rights, E/CN.4/SR.630.
78. See Note 63. In 1948 an Interim Commission of the WHO and the ILO had already expressed a general interest in the project of a *Declaration on the Rights of the Child* because it could be an "extension of the non-discrimination clause to 'sex' and 'social position' (Children's Charter for the Post-War World) on 'family circumstances' (ILO Resolution) and not only to 'race, nationality or creed'" in: Report of the Social Commission, United Nations.
79. Dijk, Van, P., 'De Internationale Bescherming van de Rechten van het Kind', in: *Familie- en Jeugdrecht*, Vol. 1 (6) 1979, pp. 165–180.
80. Defence for Children International, *A DCI Programme for Monitoring Respect for and Violations of Children's Rights* Op. cit.

81. See Article 25-5 and Article 22.
82. E/CN.4/SR.630.
83. E/CN.4/SR.631.
84. Defence for Children International *A Programme for Monitoring Respect for and Violations of Children's Rights*, Op. cit.
85. United Nations General Assembly, Third Committee, 917th meeting, October 6, 1959.
86. Personal communication of Dr. Haim H. Cohn to the author.
87. Third Committee, October 6, 1959.
88. Defense for Children International, *A programme for Monitoring Respect for and Violations of Children's Rights*, Op. cit.
89. E/CN.4/SR.631.
90. E/CN.4/SR.632.
91. DCI Programme (see Note 51).
92. United Nations General Assembly, Fourteenth Session, *Third Committee*, 920th meeting, October 8, 1959.
93. Casullo, Catherina, 1985, Op. cit.
94. E/CN.4/SR.633.
95. Idem.
96. Idem.
97. Ministerie van Buitenlandse Zaken (Ministry of Foreign Affairs of the Netherlands), 63 *Verslag over de Veertiende Algemene Vergadering van de Verenigde Naties*, New York, September 15 – December 12, 1959, The Hague, 1960, Staatsuitgeverij.
98. United Kingdom amendment, E/CN.4/L.529.
99. E/CN.4/SR.637.
100. E/CN.4/SR.636.
101. Draft Declaration: See E/CN.4/512.
102. E/CN.4/SR.637.
103. Mr. Quijano (Argentina) E/CN.4/SR.636.
104. United Nations General Assembly, Fourteenth Session, *Third Committee*, 921st meeting, October 9, 1959.
105. Idem.
106. Mr. Yolga (Turkey) on October 12, 1959, in the Third Committee, 922nd meeting.
107. Mr. Malitza (Rumania), on October 12, 1959.
108. Williams, Julian, 'Intelligence Digest': The Truth About UNICEF, in *Christian Crusade Weekly*, August 15, 1971, pp. 7-8.
109. Ministry of Foreign Affairs of the Netherlands, 1960, Op. cit., pp. 146-147.
110. Casullo, Caterina, 1985, Op. cit.
111. The Social Commission had agreed on the following text: "The child shall be protected against all forms of neglect, cruelty and exploitation. He shall in no case be caused to engage in any occupation or employment which would prejudice his health or education or interfere with his development.
112. Soviet amendment E/CN.4/L.526. Not accepted was the following sentence: "Criminal liability shall be established for the employment of minors who have not attained the minimum age established by law, and also for the employment of minors for unhealthy or hazardous work.
113. General Assembly, Fourteenth Session, *Third Committee*, 925th meeting, October 14, 1959.
114. Ministry of Foreign Affairs of the Netherlands, 1960, Op. cit., p. 147.
115. In September 1959 'The grave aspect of buying and selling of children for adoption purposes to couples from the United States' was described in the *New York Law Journal*. The Romanian delegate referred to this publication.
116. General Assembly, Fourteenth Session, *Third Committee*, 926th meeting, October 15, 1959.
117. "In particular, the child shall not be subjected to corporal punishment in schools."
118. Casullo, Caterina, 1985, Op. cit.

119. Defence for Children International, A DCI Programme for Monitoring Respect for and Violations of Children's Rights, Op. cit.
120. The Commission on Human Rights discussed this Principle on April 7, 1959. Amendments were submitted by Israel (E/CN.4/L.525), the Soviet Union (E/CN.4/L.526), Poland (E/CN.4/SR.527), the United States of America (E/CN.4/SR.530), the Philippines (E/CN.4/SR.531) and India, Lebanon and Mexico (E/CN.4/SR.543) and a sub-amendment to the United States amendment by India, Lebanon and Mexico (E/CN.4/SR.542). The Israel and Philippine amendments were subsequently withdrawn.
121. Ministry of Foreign Affairs of the Netherlands, *Verslag over de Veertiende Algemene Vergadering*, Op. cit.,p.148.
122. It is interesting to note the observation by Cynthia Price Cohen that the "Polish government had been pressing for a children's rights treaty since the initial discussions of the United Nations Declaration and, in fact, supported the Declaration only in the absence of a treaty, which it thought preferable. Yet, when Poland was called upon to draft a model Convention on the Rights of the Child for the benefit of the Commission on Human Rights, the first draft was virtually a verbatim replication of the United Nations Declaration with the addition of an implementation mechanism.

    Cohen, Cynthia Price, 'Relationships Between the Child, the Family and the State: The United Nations Convention on the Rights of the Child', in: Bayles, Michael, R., and Moffat, Robert, C.L., Eds., *Perspectives on the Family*, Lewiston, N.Y., 1990, Edwin Meller Press. See: proposed text to the Commission on Human Rights for a United Nations Convention on the Rights of the Child; E/CN.4/SR.1349, submitted by Poland.
123. Cohen, Cynthia Price and Naimark, Hedwin, 'The United Nations Convention on the Rights of the Child: Individual Rights Concepts and their Significance for Social Scientists', in: The *American Psychologist*, Vol. 46, No. 2, 1990. See also: DCI/UNICEF, *the Future United Nations Convention on the Rights of the Child*, Document No. 2 (The Future Convention, How it came about), Third Edition, May 1989, p. 2.
124. Singer, Sandra, 'The protection of children during armed conflict situations', in: *International Review of the Red Cross*, May-June 1986), Vol. 36, No. 252, p. 165.
125. Weisberg, Kelly, D., 'The Rights of the Child in the Western World', in: *Review of the International Commission of Jurists*, (1978), No. 21, pp. 43–51.
126. 'Open-ended' because no deadline was set for halting the drafting process.
127. Except in 1988 when the Committee met for an additional fortnight in November and December for a 'second reading'.
128. No records of the years 1979 and 1980 are available.
129. Based on interview with Mr. Jacques Jansen (department 'wetgeving privaatrecht', Ministry of Justice, the Netherlands) on June 4, 1986, and with Michael Longford (of the Department of Health and Social Services) in the fall of 1987 in London.
130. Mr. Nigel Cantwell of Defence for Children International.
131. Proposal by China, E/CN.4/1986/WG.1/CRP.5, reads: "The States Parties to the present Convention shall take all effective measures to ensure that a child born out of wedlock shall enjoy the same legal rights as those enjoyed by a child born in wedlock, in particular the rights enumerated in the present Convention.
132. The Secretary-General was speaking in the General Assembly Meeting of November 20, 1989, after adopting the United Nations Convention.
133. Fox, Sanford, J., 'The Convention on the Rights of the Child: Rights and Potential', in: Verhellen, E. and Spiesschaert, F. (eds.) , *Ombudswork for Children, A way of improving the position of children in Society*, Louvain, 1989, Acco, pp. 409–410.
134. Cantwell, Nigel, 'The International Consensus' on the Rights of the Child' in: *Action for children – unfinished business*, Report of a Symposium in Amsterdam on June 2, 1986, at the Free University, A publication of the Stichting Educatief Centrum Kind en Derde Wereld, The Hague, 1987, p. 47.
135. DCI/UNICEF Briefing kit, Geneva/New York Document No. 2, Third Edition, May 1989, p. 3.

136. UNICEF operates always very carefully. This explains why this U.N. Agency with special experience in the children's matters stood so long in the sidelines.
  On April 18, 1988 James Grant said at the Executive Board of UNICEF "I was a sceptic five years ago, but now I am a believer!"
  When UNICEF finally entered the lobbying game for the Convention, it could lobby influential people. For instance, when the President of Bangladesh, the King of Bhutan, the Prime Minister of India, the President of Maldives, the King of Nepal, the Prime Minister of Pakistan and the President of Sri Lanka met for the second Summit of the *South Asian Association for Regional Cooperation – SAARC* in Bangalore on November 16 and 17, 1986, UNICEF not only lobbied for subscription to the goals of Universal Immunisation by 1990 and for Maternal and Child Nutrition, the provision of safe drinking water and adequate shelter before the year 2000, but also for *an early conclusion and adoption of the Convention on the Rights of the Child.*
  The Summit of the SAARC Heads of State, held in Katmandu in 1987, issued the following statement: "The Heads of State or Government welcomed the first annual review of the Situation of Children in the SAARC Member Countries. They reiterated their commitment made in the 1986 Bangalore Declaration to accord highest priority to the needs of children in national development planning and emphasised that more intensified action should be taken for the welfare and well-being of children. They further reiterated their call for an early conclusion and adoption of a United Nations Convention on the Rights of the Child.
  See: UNICEF, *Towards a United Nations Convention on the Rights of the Child*, New Delhi, UNICEF Regional Office for South Central Asia, February 1988, p. 8.
137. Graaf, J.H., de, 'De betekenis van de Ontwerp-Conventie inzake de Rechten van het Kind', in: Langen, M., de, Graaf, J.H., de, en Kunneman, F.B.M., *Kinderen en Recht*, Deventer/Arnhem, 1989, pp. 14–24. Strong criticism came from Bennett, Walter, H., 'A Critique of the Emerging Convention on the Rights of the Child', in: *Cornell International Law Journal*, Winter 1987, Vol.20, No. 1, pp. 3–49: "It is a precarious undertaking in an international arena where standards and resources vary widely and enforcement machinery is either tentative or non-existent. In the area of international law the importance of the content of the legal norm increases because recognition, observance, and compliance, to a much greater degree than in the domestic area, depend upon the integrity of the norm itself. The norm becomes the focus and bears most of the weight. Where a right is part of a broad instrument containing other rights, and is part of a larger scheme of instruments seeking the same general end, the need for integrity includes not only the necessity for integrity of individual rights, but also mutual support and harmony among rights and the instruments in which they are contained. Promulgation of written children's rights in this context, then, should begin with a comprehensive understanding of the broader scheme of international human rights, careful planning upon how the new norms will fit the scheme, and testing of the proposed norms for both content and form to ensure that they can carry the weight they are expected to bear. The drafting of the Convention on the Rights of the Child has to date omitted much of this process. Instead, it has emphasised coverage of substantive areas rather than planning and scrutiny of content. While this methodology has brought to light long neglected areas of concern, there is a serious question, both as a matter of tactics and international law, whether this should be the primary function of a multilateral convention.
  See also: Detrick, S., ed., *The guide to the Travaux Préparatoires of the U.N. Convention on the Rights of the Child*, Martinus Nijhoff Publishers, Dordrecht, 1992.
  Shabtai Rosenne, an expert in international law (living in Jerusalem) tried to cool down my own enthusiasm for the Convention when he told me that the *Multilateral Treaties Index* (Bowman, M.J., and Harris, P.J., London, 1984, Butterworths) already mentions 833 treaties (up till 1983) and that every self-respecting Agency of the United Nations works on an individual Convention for their field. The practical result is, so he thinks, that such a quantity of Conventions cannot be handled.

138. I thank Mr. Nigel Cantwell of *DCI* for giving me his opinion on the innovative aspects of the Convention, which I followed here.
139. Cerda, Jaime Sergio, 'The Draft Convention on the Rights of the Child: New Rights' in: *Human Rights Quarterly*, 12 (1990), pp. 97–105.
140. Cohn, Haim H., 'The State of Israel and the International Draft Convention on the Rights of the Child', in: Veerman, Philip, E., *Israel and the Future United Nations Convention on the Rights of the Child*, Jerusalem, 1988, Defence for Children, International Israel Section, p. 15 (Library of Congress No.TX 2 834 793). Cohn argues that the State of Israel would qualify as one of the addressees of the Convention.
141. Debates Open-Ended Working Group, Commission on Human Rights, Thirty-sixth session, Agenda item 13, E/CN.4/L.1542, March 10, 1980.
142. Idem; a good guide for the study of the debates is *The Compilation of the On-Going of the Drafting of the United Nations Convention on the Rights of the Child 1978–1987*, Geneva, May 1987, Rädda Barnen International. (edited by Simone EK)
143. See: Lopatka, Adam, 'Convention on the Rights of the Child', in: *Polish Contemporary Law*, no. 1., 1990, pp. 21–34. Lopatka states it was impossible to reach consensus about the issue who is a child.
144. A representative of the National Council of Jewish Women in New York wrote to me: "We have serious difficulty with some of the language in the Preamble and two Articles". They found the statement in the Preamble ambiguous, particularly in light of Article 6. "Our leadership finds that this language has clear implications to which we are opposed, based on our Pro-Choice position.
145. *De Standaard*, Koning Boudewijn in Kerst-boodschap, Centrale rol van gezin bevestigen, December 26, 1989.
146. *Questions and Answers in The Convention on the Rights of the Child*, New York/1989, Geneva, Centre for Human Rights, United Nations and United Nations Children's Fund (UNICEF) brochure.
147. Alston, Philip, 'The status of the unborn child and of abortion under the Draft Convention on the Rights of the Child', in: *Human Rights Quarterly*, 1990, pp. 156–178, Vol. 12.
148. "In adopting this Preamble paragraph, the Working Group does *not* intend to prejudice the interpretation of Article 1 or any other provision of the Convention by States Parties.
149. Bruijn – Lückers, M.L.C.C., de, 'Verdrag inzake de Rechten van het Kind', in: *Familie- en Jeugdrecht*, Vol. 10, (7) 1989, pp. 171–175.
150. Debates Open-Ended Working Group, Commission on Human Rights, Thirty-sixth session, Agenda item 13, E/CN.4/L.1542, March 10, 1980.
151. Shamgar-Handelman, Lea, 'Childhood as a Social Phenomenon', Comment on Article 1 of the U.N. Convention on the Rights of the Child, in: Veerman, Philip E., ed., *Israel and the Future United Nations Convention on the Rights of the Child*, Jerusalem, 1989, DCI-Israel Section (publication registered at the U.S. Library of Congress under Number IX 2 834 793).
152. Dr. Eyal Benvenisti has argued at a DCI–Israel meeting in November 1991 that the Convention applies to the occupied territories (West Bank and Gaza) interpreting *within their jurisdiction* as *under the State Party's effective control*.
153. *Debates U.N. Working Group*, Commission on Human Rights, Thirty-sixth session, Agenda item 13, E/CN.4/L.1542, March 10, 1980.
154. Salgo, Ludwig, 'Das Kindeswohl in der neueren Rechtsprechung der Bundesverfassungsgerichts', in: Bois, du, Reiman, ed., *Praxis und Umfeld der Kinder- und Jugendpsychiatrie*, Bern/Stuttgart/Toronto, 1989, Verlag Hans Huber, p. 168.
155. Goldstein, Joseph, Freud, Anna and Solnit, Albert, J., *Beyond the Best Interests of the Child*, New York, 1973, The Free Press.
156. Richards, M.P.M., 'Behind the Best Interests of the Child: An Examination of the Arguments of Goldstein, Freud and Solnit Concerning Custody and Access at Divorce', in: *Journal of Social Welfare Law*, England, 1986, March, p. 83.
157. Goldstein, Joseph, Freud, Anna and Solnit, Albert, J. *In the Best Interests of the Child*, New York, 1985, The Free Press, p. 10.

158. *Debates U.N. Working Group*1981, E/1981/25.
159. *Debates U.N. Working Group*1981, E/1981/25. The implementation mechanism of the Convention and the monitoring system written into the Convention is dealt with in Articles 42–54.
160. Information from Ms. Jacques Jansen of the Ministry of Justice of the Netherlands.
161. Child psychiatrist D.J. de Levita (Levita, de, D.J., *De Ontwikkeling van het Normale Kind*, Rotterdam, 1975, Academic Hospital Rotterdam, Sophia's Children's Hospital, Department of child-psychiatry (stencil, not published) compares the development of the child with a horse-rider who has to jump a number of obstacles; each phase in life comprises its own task which the child must fulfil. If he succeeds, he can use all his energy for the next task. If something goes wrong, the child will, so to speak, sit lopsidedly in his saddle while tackling the next obstacle and be in danger of stumbling. When in a development phase things go wrong, part of the psychic energy of the child stays there and the child has not enough energy left for the next phase.
162. The proposal came from India (after it was initiated by UNICEF).
163. Interview with Prof.H.W.A. Voorhoeve 'Beeld Kindersterfte in de Tropen Verandert' in: *Foster Parent Post*, December 1987, Vol. 4 (publication of Foster Parent Plan in the Netherlands) p. 8.
164. United Nations Centre for Human Rights and UNICEF, 'Survival and Development', *Background Note No. 4 on the U.N. Convention on the Rights of the Child*, New York/Geneva, s.a. In 1987 14 million children died: about 5 million from diarrhoea related diseases, 1,9 million from the measles, 0,8 million from tetanus, 2,9 million from infections of the bronchial tubes, 1 million from malaria and 2,4 million from other causes. "Dehydration caused by diarrhoea kills 3 million children a year. However, according to UNICEF in *The State of the World's Children*, 1988, almost all these children could be saved if their parents were informed about how to use the low-cost breakthrough known as Oral Rehydration Therapy or ORT".
165. UNICEF, *Children in Especially Difficult Circumstances*, New York, 1986, (UNICEF Executive Board Paper), p. 19, E/ICEF/1986/L.6.
166. Report of the U.N. Working Group, Commission on Human Rights, Thirty-sixth session, Agenda item 13, E/CN.4/L.1542, March 10, 1980.
167. Report of the U.N. Working Group, Commission on Human Rights, E/1981/25 (former Article 2).
168. E/CN.4/1987/WG.1/WP.35, February 25, 1987.
169. *Debates U.N. Working Group*, E/CN.4/1985/64.
170. In the Netherlands a conflict about identity arose in 1944. The foster families who were rescuing Jewish children from the Nazi's, had received a pamphlet from the resistance movement proposing that those children should not be returned to the Jewish Community after the war. After the war the Jewish Community protested. A Commission decided that the Jewish children could live with their relatives.
171. *Debates U.N. Working Group*, E/1981/25.
172. Veerman, Philip, E., 'Ethiopian Children in Israel: Stomachs full of Sorrow', in: *International Children's Rights Monitor*, 1989, Vol. 6, p. 27. See also: Tomasevski, Katarina, 'Family Reunification: Right, Privilege or Utopia?', in: *International Children's Rights Monitor*, 1987, Vol. 4, No. 1, pp. 12–13.
173. *The Hague Convention on the Civil Aspects of International Child Abduction*, originally signed on 25 October 1980 has in slightly more than 10 years been joined by 19 countries as Parties. There is also a *European Convention on Recognition and Enforcement of Decision Concerning Custody of Children and an Restoration of Custody of Children* (Council of Europe, 1980).
174. Bruijn – Lückers, M.L.C.C., de, 'Verdrag inzake de Rechten van het Kind', in: *Familie- en Jeugdrecht*, Vol. 10, No. 7, 1989, pp. 171–151.
175. E/CN.4/1988/W.G.1/WP.18.
176. W/XN.4/1988/W.G.1/CRP.1.p.10.
177. Moshman, David, 'Children's Intellectual Rights: A First Amendment Analysis', in: Moshman, David, editor, *Children's Intellectual Rights*, San Francisco,1986, p. 28.

178. *Paper submitted by the Permanent Representative of Bangladesh*, E/CN.4/1986/39, Annex IV, p. 2.
179. *Debates U.N. Working Group*, E/CN.4/1987/WG.1/WP.35, p. 2.
180. *Debates U.N. Working Group*, E/CN.r/1986/39.
181. *Debates U.N. Working Group*, 1987.
182. In November 1987 the Ministry of the Interior in Israel rejected the registration of 'The Israel Section of Defence for Children International' as a new Association ('Amuthah') because a 16 years old (the chairman of the Youth for Youth Organisation) was one of the founders and signed all documents together with the other (adult) founders. After his signature was withdrawn the Ministry agreed to register the DCI.
183. *Debates U.N. Working Group*, 1988, E/CN.4/1988/WG.1/CRP.l,p.14.
184. Proposal submitted by the Baha'i International Community, E/CN.4/1983/WG.1/WP.2.
185. Bennett, Walter, J., 'A Critique of the Emerging Convention on the Rights of the Child', in: *Cornell International Law Journal*, Vol.20, Winter 1987, No. 1,p.7.
186. Clearinghouse on Child Abuse and Neglect, *Child Abuse and Neglect: an informed approach to a shared concern*, Washington D.C., 1986, U.S. Department of Health and Human Services, Office of Human Development Services.
187. *Debates U.N. Working Group*, 1982, E/CN.4/1982/L.41.
188. Independent Commission on International Humanitarian Issues, presented by Susanna Agnelli, *Street Children, A Growing Urban Tragedy*, London, 1986, Weidenfeld and Nicolson.
189. Here two organisations can be helpful: *Childhope*, an international movement on behalf of street children, and *Streetwise International*, an organisation that organises fact-finding, volunteer expeditions to a number of developing countries.
190. Ennew, Judith, 'Children without Families' in: *The World's Children*, June 18, 1988.
191. Gmeiner, Hermann, *The SOS Children's Village*, Innsbruck, 1980, SOS-Kinderdorf Publications.
192. *Debates U.N. Working Group*, 1982, E/CN.4/1982/L.41.
193. *Debates U.N. Working Group*, 1986, E/CN.4/1986/39, Annex IV, p. 2.
194. Under Islamic Law a father can take a child into his family. This is viewed as a form of *charity*. The child cannot inherit from the father. And he or she is allowed to marry an adoptive sister or brother.
    I thank attorney Dr. Awni Habash in East Jerusalem for explaining this paragraph to me.
195. United Nations Centre for Human Rights and UNICEF, Background Note No. 5, 'Adoption', *The Future United Nations Convention on the Rights of the Child*, p. 1.
196. Underhill, E., 'The Situation of migrant and refugee children in relation to the United Nations Declaration of the Rights of the Child', in: *International Migration*, 17(1–2), 1979, pp. 122–138.
197. *Debates U.N. Working Group*, 1982, E/CN.4/1982/L.41.
198. In the literature about this subject the need for *special* treatment and special schools is sometimes emphasised. Since 1969, however, pleas are sometimes made to apply the *normalisation principle* which endeavours to make the lives of the handicapped as rich and normal as possible. An important author is Wolf Wolfensberger, *Normalization; The Principle of Normalization in Human Services*, Toronto, 1972, National Institute on Mental Retardation.
199. *Debates U.N. Working Group*, 1982, E/CN.4/1982/L.41.
200. United Nations General Assembly, 26th session, agenda item 12, A/RES/2856 (XXVI), 21 Jan. 1972. Resolution adopted by the General Assembly (on the report of the Third Committee, A/8588), 2856 (XXVI). *Declaration on the Rights of Mentally Retarded Persons*. This Declaration is based on the Declaration of General and Special Rights of the Mentally Retarded, promulgated at the closing session of the 4th Congress of the International League of Societies for Persons with Mental Handicaps, held in Jerusalem, October 1986. See: International League of Societies for the Mentally Handicapped, *From Charity to Rights*, 4th International Congress, Published by the League in Bruxelles.

201. The Principles of *Normalization* have lead to such developments as the United Nations Declaration of the Rights of Mentally Retarded Persons.
202. A Declaration of Rights of Deaf-Blind Persons, adopted by the Helen Keller World Conference on Services to Deaf-Blind Youths and Adults, New York, 1977. See: *International Child Welfare Review*, March, 1978, pp. 49–50.
203. *Debates U.N. Working Group*, 1988, E/CN.4/1988/WG.1/WP.14.
204. Weill, James, D., 'The Children's Defense Fund: Aims, Procedures, and Results', lecture delivered at the International Congress on Ombudswork for Children, Gent, Belgium, 1987, p. 6, Children's Defense Fund, Washington D.C.. See also: *Children Without Health*, a brochure from 1981 of the CDF.
205. *Debates U.N. Working Group*, 1987, E/CN.4/1987/25.
206. The Inter-African Committee on Traditional Practices affecting the health of women and children in Geneva, guided by Berhane Ras Work, Ethiopia, does a good job lobbying governments to abolish 'traditional practices'.
207. E/CN.4/1986/W.G.1/W.P.1.
208. Teram, E. and Erickson, G., 'The Protection of Children's Rights as Ceremony and Myth: A Critique of the Review of Institutional Placements in Quebec and Ontario', in *Children and Youth Services Review*, 1988, Vol. 10, pp. 1–17.
209. For a general background article on the Child's Right to Social Security, see: Ozawa, Martha, W., 'Children's Rights to Social Security', in: *Child Welfare*, 53 (10), December 1974, pp. 619–631.
210. *Debates U.N. Working Group*, 1984, E/CN.4/1984/71.
211. *Debates U.N. Working Group*, 1987, E/CN.4/1987/25.
212. *Debates U.N. Working Group*, 1985, E/CN.4/1985/64.
213. *Debates U.N. Working Group*, 1985, E/CN.4/1985/64.
214. *Debates U.N. Working Group*, 1985, E/CN.4/1985/64.
215. *Debates U.N. Working Group*, 1987, E/CN.4/1987/25.
216. Defence for Children International, International Executive Council, 10th Meeting, 27 to 29 March, 1987, London, Item 5(b) on the Agenda, Draft Policy Guidelines on Rights of Children of Indigenous Peoples, IEC/10/5(b)1.
217. Minority Rights Group. *The Kanaks of New Caledonia*, London, 1986, MRG Report No. 71.
218. Proposal Tabled by the Four Directions Council, E/CN.4/1986/39.
219. *Debates U.N. Working Group*, 1987, E/CN.4/1987/25. Prof. Vitit Muntarbhorn from Bangkok (Thailand) explained in his article 'Realizing Indigenous Social Rights', in: *Without Prejudice*, Vol.II, No. 2, 1990, p. 9, that "there are other dangers in defining 'indigenous'. In one country one is not considered to be indigenous if one is an 'integrated Indian', thereby forfeiting those rights ordinarily accruing to indigenous Indians. Demarcating by means of definition may, therefore, lead to the anomalous situation whereby a group or person who was originally indigenous loses certain rights originally attached to such status. The debate becomes more heated over the terms 'indigenous populations' and 'indigenous peoples'. Both terms appear frequently although maybe with different connotations.
220. *Debates U.N. Working Group*, 1985, E/CN.4/1985/64. In a conversation with an official of the Ministry of Justice in Israel I was told that for certain sections of the Jewish population (the very orthodox) it was more important that the child should study. Leisure and play were in this group a problem and the official wondered if Israel should make a reservation here because Article 31 started with "States Parties recognize
221. *Debates U.N. Working Group*, 1986, E/CN.4/1986/39.
222. Proposal Tabled on Drugs, E/Cn.4/1986/W.G.1/W.P.1.
223. Proosal Tabled E/CN.4/1986/39, para.9 and annex II.
224. Armstrong, Louise, *Kiss Daddy Goodnight*, New York, N.Y., 1987, Pocket Books. Also: Finkelnohr, David, *Child Sexual Abuse, New Theory*, New York, 1984, The Free Press.
225. Letter (dated 31.10.1986) from Renée Bridel, Delegate to the United Nations of the International Association of Democratic Lawyers (living in Pully/Lausanne).

226. *Debates U.N. Working Group*, 1987, E/CN.4/1987/25. About pornography see: Pierce, Robert, Lee, 'Child pornography, a hidden dimension of child abuse', in *Child Abuse and Neglect*, 8, 1984, pp. 483–493.
227. *International Children's Rights Monitor* Vol. 4, No. 1, p. 16, 'Adoption for Organs Transplants; in search of the truth'.
228. Sub-Commission on Prevention of Discrimination and Protection of Minorities. Working Group on Slavery, Written statement submitted by the International Association of Democratic Lawyers, a NGO in Consultative Status (Category II), Notes on trade in children, Addendum, E/CN.4/Sub.2/AC.2/1984, NGO, 4/Add.1, 24 August 1984.
229. *Debates U.N. Working Group*, 1987, E/CN.4/1987/25.
230. Countries known to have executed juvenile offendors in the last decade are Barbados, Iran, Iraq, Nigeria, Pakistan, Bangladesh and the USA.
231. *Debates U.N. Working Group*, 1986, E/CN.4/1986/39.
232. Krill, Françoise, 'The U.N. Convention on the Rights of the Child and his Protection in Armed Conflicts', published in the Norwegian periodical 'Human and Rights' *Mennester og Rettigheter* Oslo, Vol. 4, No. 3, 1986. See also: Krill, Françoise, 'United Nations Convention on the rights of the child: a controversial article on children in armed conflicts', in: *Dissemination*, No. 12, August 1989.
233. The four *Geneva Conventions* of August 12, 1949 and the 1977 Additional Protocols give children such protection. Examples of these provisions are: Protection against the effects of the hostilities; Entitlement to care and assistance; Preferential treatment; Measures to preserve their cultural environment and the unity of their families and to provide for their education; The obligation to keep arrested, detained or interned children in premises separate from those for adults. See: *The Geneva Conventions of August* 12, 1949, published in Geneva by the International Committee of the Red Cross, which cover 'the wounded and sick in armed forces in the field'; 'wounded, sick and shipwrecked members of armed forces at sea'; 'the treatment of prisoners of war'; and 'the protection of civilian persons in time of war'), and additionally the 1977 Protocols: (Protocol I, dealing with the protection of victims of international armed conflicts; and Protocol II, dealing with the protection of victims of non-international armed conflicts). The Geneva Conventions have been ratified by 166 parties; Protocol I has been ratified by 86 parties and Protocol II by 76 parties. Examples of Articles dealing with children are: in the fourth Geneva Convention of 1949, Article 17, (concerning evacuation of civilians, which states that combatants "shall endeavour to conclude local agreements for the removal from besieged or encircled areas, of wounded, sick, infirm, and aged persons, children..."), and Article 24 (relating to child welfare, to the effect that combatants "shall take the necessary measures to ensure that children under 15, who are orphaned or are separated from their families as a result of the war, are not left to their own resources, and that their maintenance, the exercise of their religion and their education are facilitated in all circumstances"). Articles in the Protocols specifically concerning children include: Protocol I, Article 77 (on the protection of children, including: "Children shall be the object of special respect and shall be protected against any form of indecent assault. The Parties to the conflict shall provide them with the care and aid they require, whether because of their age or for any other reason; The Parties to the conflict shall take all feasible measures in order that children who have not attained the age of fifteen years do not take a direct part in hostilities and, in particular, they shall refrain from recruiting them into their armed forces (Krill, Françoise, Op. cit., 1986).
234. *Debates U.N. Working Group*, 1986, E/CN.4/1986/39.
235. Commission on Human Rights, 43rd session, Pre-sessional Open-Ended Working Group on the Question of a Convention on the Rights of the Child, 26–30 Jan.1987, E/CN.4/1987/WG.1/WP.3, 5 Jan.1987, Written statement submitted by Rädda Barnen, on behalf of itself and four national organisations of Sweden, Statement on the Draft Convention on the Rights of the Child. A Conference organised in 1991 by the Swedish Red Cross, Rädda Barnen and the Raoul Wallenberg Institute mapped a long term strategy to raise the age limit (Protection in Armed Conflicts article).

236. The International Union for Child Welfare (IUCW) declared during the Diplomatic Conference on the Reaffirmation and Development of International Humanitarian Law (1974–1977), "In a number of developing countries, especially in Africa, children of 14 are already adults."
237. In June 1988 Mike Jupp, the Director of the U.S.A. Section of Defence for Children International, told me that he thought that the U.S.A.'s stand in these matters (against raising the age limit) was made because of its support for groups in America. See also: *Children of War, Report from the Conference on Children of War*, Raoul Wallenberg Institute, Lurd, report no. 10. Officially the USA found the Working Group the wrong forum to amend International Humanitarian Law.
238. Rabus, W.G., 'De bescherming van kinderen in oorlogstijd, mede in het licht van de Ontwerp-Conventie inzake de Rechten van het Kind' in: Langen, M., de, Graaf, J.H., de, en Kunneman, F.B.M., *Kinderen en Recht*, 1989, Deventer en Arnhem, pp. 85–97. Interesting is also the statement by the Dutch representative, Drs. Van Wulfften Palthe, on November 15, 1989, in the U.N.: "My delegation did not wish to break the prevailing consensus on the draft just adopted... We accepted in a spirit of compromise... a number of provisions which could have been formulated differently. One article of the Convention is a case of particular unfortunate standard setting. I refer of course to Article 38... The New Convention... should at least have incorporated the maximum protection of children in armed conflicts provided by already existing standards. States should not be allowed to engage children directly or indirectly in hostilities. Unfortunately, this prohibition which we do find in the Second Additional Protocol to the Geneva Conventions, turned out not to be acceptable to the drafters of our new Convention. Neither was it possible to raise the minimum age for recruiting children into the armed forces My Government would have wished that the child's best interest would also have been at the basis of treating law aimed at securing the protection of children in regard to armed conflicts." See: Dutch Ministry of Foreign Affairs, *Verslag over de Hervatte Drieenveertigste zitting, New York, 23 December 1988 – 18 September 1989, en de Vierenveertigste zitting, New York, 19 September – 29 December 1989, van de Algemene Vergadering van de Verenigde Naties*, The Hague, 1990.
239. Singer, Sandra, 'The protection of children during armed conflict situations', in: *International Review of the Red Cross*, May-June 1986, Vol.26, No. 252, p. 138. See also: Ditli, Maria Teresa, 'Captured child combatants, in: *International Review of the Red Cross*, Sept./Oct. 1990, pp. 421–434.
240. Rabus, Op. cit., p. 97. For different point of view see: Heintze, Hans-Joachim, 'Die Volkerrechtliche Stellung der Kindes im benaffneten Konflikt – Verfestigung einer unbefriedigenden Standards durch die neue UN-Kinderkonvention-in: *Humanitäres Völkerrecht* no. 3, July 1990, pp. 92–98.
241. See also: *U.N. Standard Minimum Rules for the Administration of Juvenile Justice, 'The Beijing-Rules'*, New York, 1986, U.N. Department of Public Information, A/RES/40/33. The General Assembly accepted these rules on November 29, 1985.
242. Prof. Philip Alston (in his article 'Abortion under the Children's Convention', Op. cit.) reports: "During the Working Group's final session, the representative of the Holy See suggested that an alternative way out of the emerging impasse would be to include the words 'before as well as after birth' in the savings clause which subsequently became Article 41. That provision, which has a counterpart in the vast majority of international human rights treaties, states that 'nothing in this Convention shall affect any provisions that are more conducive to the realization of the rights of the child ' In the event, neither he nor any other participant pursued the proposal.
243. Hammarberg, Thomas, 'The U.N. Convention on the Rights of the Child – and How to Make it Work', in: *Human Rights Quarterly*, Feb. 1990, Vol. 12, No. 1, p. 102.
244. Fisher, Dana, D., 'International Reporting Procedures', in: Hannum, Hurst, ed., *Guide to International Human Rights Practice*, Philadelphia, 1984, University of Pennsylvania Press, p. 183.
245. *Debates U.N. Working Group*, 1987, E/CN.4/1987/25.

246. Defence for Children International (DCI) *The Ratification of the Convention on the Rights of the Child*, Geneva, 1990. See also: Salgo, Ludwig, 'Menschenrechte kennen kein Alter', in: *Kindeswohl*, No. 3, 1990, pp. 9–11.
247. Grant, James, P., *The State of the World's Children*, 1990, New York 1990, UNICEF, p. 4.
248. Idem.
249. Brodie-Olles, Marion and Veerman, Philip, E., 'A World Summit for Children', in: *The Jerusalem Post*, September 23, 1990.
250. UNICEF/World Summit Mobilisation, *Giving Children a Future*; *The World Summit for Children*, New York, 1990.
251. Idem. See also: Stanley, Allesandra, 'For Each Leader there was a Child, and a Chance to Savor', in: *The New York Times*, October 1, 1990, p.A.12.
252. Angelo, Bonnie and North, Jeanne-Marie, 'Suffer the Little, Summit addresses the plight of the World's poorest youngsters', in: *Time*, October 1, 1990, No. 40, pp. 52–58.
253. In an unpublished paper ('United States Policy on Children', October 5, 1990) George Kent of the University of Hawaii quotes the *Honolulu Advertiser* of October 1, 1990 ('World Leaders Sign Accord to Aid Children') in which it was cynically noted that President Bush "returned to Washington to announce agreement of a federal budget pack that will sharply limit his administration's spending on child welfare programmes at home and aid abroad".
254. Paragraph 15 of the *Plan of Action for implementing the World Declaration on the Survival, Protection and Development of Children in the 1990s*.
255. These aims are explicitly described in the 1965 *Declaration on the Promotion among Young of the Ideals of Peace, Mutual Respect and Understanding between Peoples*.
256. Thedin, Nils, (Head of the Swedish Delegation to the UNICEF Executive Board) *Statement* at UNICEF Executive Board, 1984.

    In May 1988 Mr. Jack Charnow of UNICEF's History Project explained me the difficulties in providing aid to both sides during active hostilities. According to Charnow, the obstacle is the sovereignty issue which forbids UNICEF to act in any country except with the consent of, and in consultation with the Government concerned.
257. In *some* States a law of implementation by the Parliament is necessary in addition to the ratification by the Government. Treaty law in these States (Israel for example) says that Conventions are not binding unless a law of implementation is passed. To base a claim in court on the convention will only have meaning in court if a law was adopted or if it is part of the international custom. NGO's have to lobby their Parliament members in these States!

CHAPTER XI

National and Regional Declarations

1. THE CHILDREN'S CHARTER OF PRESIDENT HOOVER'S WHITE HOUSE CONFERENCE ON CHILD HEALTH AND PROTECTION (1930)

See Appendix X

In 1922 Herbert Hoover addressed the *American Child Health Association*.[1] Since 1920 he had been United States' President Harding's Minister of Trade, and the invitation by the Health Association was probably due to the fact that from April to September 1919 he had played an important part in initiating the emergency relief operation for Europe (see Chapter VI).

In his speech Hoover said among other things: "The ideal to which we should strive is that there should be no child in America that has not been born under proper conditions, that does not live in hygienic surroundings, that ever suffers from under-nutrition, that does not have prompt and efficient medical attention and inspection, that does not receive primary instruction in the element of hygiene and good health. It should be the purpose of associations like yours to replace ten policemen with a single community nurse."

In 1923 these words were quoted in the Association's periodical[2] under the title: 'The Child's Bill of Rights'. In 1925 Hoover wrote in *McClures Magazine*[3] that a Bill of Rights should be written for children, and he repeated more or less what he had stated in 1922. In 1925 efforts were made to broaden this so-called 'Children's Bill of Rights'. Some points referring to the mental and spiritual well-being of the child were added.[4] President Hoover followed the examples of former Presidents Roosevelt and Wilson. In May 1919 President Wilson had, for instance, called a Conference[5] where "irreducible minimum standards" were adopted (such as the minimum age for labour, which was to be sixteen). President Hoover, however, formulated the results of 'his' Conference in a 'Children's Charter'. Hoover's White House Conference on Child Health and Protection was held in 1930. No less than three thousand experts, amongst them many psychologists, psychiatrists and paediatricians, were invited. Statements were made on education, labour, vocational training, the family, recreation, health, growth and development, the handicapped child and more.[6] A concise summary of the work done by the different committees covered some five hundred pages. The supporting evidence filled many volumes.

In his *Memoirs* Hoover points to some bright spots in these dark times of unemployment.[7] Stressing his own part in the events he writes, for instance, that the 1930 Conference was so successful that it yielded an avalanche of technical reports with recommendations. "However, ... I felt that the reports would not develop popular understanding or make that impression on the country at large which I sought as a support to official action. Therefore, jointly with Mr. Wilbur, I revised what I had some years before stated as the 'Children's Charter' and secured its adoption by the Conference. This document which has been reprinted in several millions of copies has had a wide influence."[8]

Wilbur,[9] since March 1929 Hoover's Minister of Interior, wrote his own *Memoirs* wherein we read that the closing session of the Conference was used to summarise the wealth of excellent recommendations into nineteen paragraphs which were intended to be a 'Declaration of the Rights of the American Child'. According to Wilbur it was John Finley of the New York Times who suggested the title *Children's Charter*.[10] Robinson and Edwards who edited Wilbur's memoirs, write that the *Children's Charter* received the subtitle: 'President Hoover's White House Conference on Child Health and Protection, recognizing the Rights of the Child as the First Rights of Citizenship, pledges itself to these aims for the Children of America'.

According to the then Deputy-Director of the *Children's Bureau* in Washington D.C., Katharine Lenroot,[11] the advantage of the White House Conference was the complexity of problems submitted for discussion, and the necessity for serious thought.

Katharine Lenroot[12] and Grace Abbott[13] pointed out that the problem of providing all American children with shelter, food, clothing, education, recreation and other necessities could not be solved without social change. However, these ladies were no revolutionaries. Their intention was not to condemn capitalism.

Miss Lenroot was of the opinion that the *Children's Charter* was in fact a "statement of general aspirations" concerning the care for children.[14] Various ideals were discussed in the *Charter*. A number of paragraphs, (such as paragraphs 2, 9, 16 and 18) emphasise "the sacredness of the child's personality."[15]

During the *White House Conference* a certain tension arose between the parents and the new professional dispensers of help. President Hoover pointed at the growing role of the experts but underlined that their only function was to provide a service to parents. In 1930 the general feeling about the family was somewhat more casual than it had been during earlier White House Conferences (1909 and 1919). The limitations of the family were recognised. Organisations to help the family supplement parental responsibility were called for. "Our function should be to help parents, not replace them," Hoover told the Conference. Parent education was seen as a possible means to introduce the necessary changes, especially in rural families.

"An interesting feature of all research on the family is the resistance of the rural family to change," we read in the report on the Conference.[16] This is probably what lead to the formulation of Principle XVII: "For every rural child a satisfactory schooling and health services as for the city child." On the one hand the American experts had come together in a mammoth conference in order to stimulate change, on the other hand Americans were not at all ready to let go of their holy cows (autonomy, sanctity and inviolability of the family, aversion against State interference). Although Principle XIX of the Charter mentions a nation-wide service of statistics and scientific research which is supposed to support local activities, Minister of Interior and Chairman of the Conference Wilbur declared during the closing session that there could be no greater danger than to try and enforce the results of this Conference by means of either a too fragmented or a too centralised programme, and that he wanted as few Federal laws concerning these issues as possible.[17]

Public opinion was varied. The New York Times wrote positively about the *Children's Charter*, but in *The Nation*[18] we read: "The White House Conference on Child Health and Protection has come and gone with the blare of publicity that always attends these gatherings summoned by the President, but with little tangible achievement as yet evident to the naked eye.... It is unfair to judge a conference of this character by the resolutions to which it finally agrees, but it is a pity that a gathering of leading experts on Child Welfare could not have been allowed to give the public a more inspiring platform than this string of platitudes."

Be the opinions about the *Charter* as they may, the implementation of its Principles became less and less feasible as the economic depression advanced. In the book 'A Nation in Torment'[19] we read how much bad blood was raised by a picture of President Hoover feeding his dog. Hoover himself denied at various occasions that under-nourishment was widespread but his sources of information were unreliable. We also read in 'A Nation in Torment' that the showman Groucho Marx claimed he knew just how bad things were when he had seen the pigeons in Central Park feed the people!

In 1933 the *Children's Bureau* reported that one out of every five children in the country were undernourished. A teacher in a coal-mining district asked a little girl if she was sick. "No," she said. "I am only hungry." "Then go home and eat something." "Impossible," replied the little girl. "Today is my sister's turn to eat."

If we analyse the Children's Charter, we see that it is in the first place a statement regarding the care of adults for children.

Principle I of the Charter: "For every child spiritual and moral training to help him stand firm under the pressure of life" is typical for the years of the depression. It actually states that *the cultural subsystem provides the infrastructure or basis of operating in all other subsystems* of the human condition. This corresponds with Shye's idea that the cultural-valuative subsystem is the basis for selecting preferred actions in all subsystems. The White House Conference Charter acknowledges the special value of culture in the human condition and the fact that it contributes power and gives strength to children. The issue here is *the use* of the *cultural subsystem* to help the child stand firm against the pressures of life. (Escape into alcoholism was a major problem during the Hoover era.) For a sensible classification of this Principle we must consider the intention of the drafters. Hoover's intention was to strengthen the cultural subsystem's capacity to cope with the pressures of life. He wanted a good set of values to strengthen the character of the child and to affect his or her adaptability. The first Principle must therefore be classified in the *adaptive mode* of the *cultural subsystem* (moral training).

Principle II concerns the 'safety of the child': "For every child understanding and the guarding of his personality as his most precious right" belongs in *all four modes* of the *personality subsystem*.

Principle III: "For every child a home and that love and security which a home provides" is meant to produce a feeling of belonging and must, therefore, be classified in the *conservative mode* of the *social subsystem*. To a lesser extent it also belongs in the *integrative mode* of the *social subsystem* (love means a chance for intimate relationships). The second part of this Principle deals with 'foster care' and belongs in the *adaptive mode* of the *social subsystem*. No mention is made of what children's homes are supposed to offer children. The general impression is that such homes were not considered a very good solution. According to Homer Folks,[20] in 1918 250,000 children in the United States were boarded out, one third of them with foster families. This was considered a bad situation.

Concerning Principle IV ("For each child full preparation for his birth, his mother receiving pre-natal and post-natal care"[21]). Grace Abbott wrote that "certainly no right can be considered more important than the child's right to be well born and to receive the care and protection of a mother who safely survives the ordeal of childbirth. The saving of the lives of mothers and babies is the kind of a national economy which commends itself to everyone."

According to Dr.F.L. Adair,[22] who presided over one of the Committees of the Conference, many cases of mother and/or baby mortality during or immediately after birth could be prevented. The Conference stated that counselling of pregnant women and new mothers by midwives and doctors, and a better curriculum for medical students, were the cures for this problem.

"For every child full preparation for his or her birth, . . . and the establishment of such protective measures to make childbirth safer," can be classified in the *conservative mode* of the *physical subsystem* (safety).

Principle V: ("For every child health protection from birth through adolescence") deals with ongoing health. It belongs in the *integrative mode* of the *physical subsystem*.

Principle VI: ("For every child from birth, through adolescence, promotion of health") belongs in the *integrative mode* of the *physical subsystem*. However, since "wholesome physical and mental recreation" are mentioned, and the aim is that children may acquire the ability to draw psychological nourishment from the environment, Principle VI can also be classified in the *adaptive mode* of the *personality subsystem*.

Principle VII: a) ("For every child a dwelling place, safe, sanitary and wholesome") belongs in the *conservative mode* of the *physical subsystem*. b) ("with reasonable conditions for privacy") deals with controlling one's own physical space, such as a room of one's own. It belongs in the *expressive mode* of the *physical subsystem*. c) ("a home environment harmonious and enriching") belongs in the *adaptive mode* of the *personality subsystem*.

Principle VIII: ("For every child a school which is safe from hazards, sanitary, properly equipped, lighted and ventilated") expresses a concern with the *conservative mode* and the *adaptive mode* of the *physical subsystem*.

The second part of this Principle: ("For young children nursery schools and kindergartens to supplement home care") assumes that mothers can take care of their children and only need supplement home care. What does that mean from the point of view of the child? Here the text is not very clear. To keep the children out of trouble? To help the child to develop himself? We believe it concerns mainly physical care and must therefore be classified in the *adaptive mode* of the *physical subsystem* (maintenance: ongoing supplementing of the needs, especially physical needs) but also in the *conservative mode* and the *integrative mode* of the *physical subsystem* (safety and health). Perhaps it can also be classified in the *integrative mode* of the *social subsystem* (to provide the child with opportunities for intimate relations with peers or with significant adults).

Principle IX: ("For every child a community that recognises and plans for his needs, protects him against physical dangers, moral hazards and disease; provides him with safe and wholesome places for play and recreation; and makes provisions for his cultural and social needs") expresses a concern about the basic things in life. It belongs in the *conservative mode* of *all four subsystems*, although mostly of the *physical subsystem* (protection against physical dangers). There is also a weak reference to moral hazards (cultural subsystem) but, considering the context of physical dangers and disease of the year 1930, we interpret this paragraph as mainly referring to the physical dangers of prostitution and venereal disease.

Principle X: ("For every child an education which, through the discovery and development of his individual abilities, prepares him for life; and through training and vocational guidance prepares him for a living which will yield him the maximum of satisfaction") belongs in the *expressive mode* of the *personality subsystem*.

Principle XI aims at better education. It deals with preparing the child to become a successful member of society. It refers in particular to two social institutions 'parenthood' and 'citizenry'. ("For every child such teaching and training as will prepare him for successful parenthood, home-making and the rights of citizenship; and, for parents, supplementary training to fit them to deal wisely with the problems of parenthood".) Clearly this Principle is classifiable in the *adaptive mode* of the *social subsystem*.

About Principle XII: ("For every child education for safety and protection against accidents to which modern conditions subject him") we read in the reports of the White House Conference that it deals with accidents in industry and on the road. Although in some industries the number of accidents had decreased, the overall number of fatal accidents was higher than the number of soldiers killed in action during the First World War. This Principle belongs in the *conservative mode* of the *physical subsystem*.

Principle XIII: ("For every . . . handicapped child such measures as will . . . train him that he may become an asset to society rather than a liability") belongs in the *adaptive mode* of the *social subsystem*. However, strictly speaking, part of this Principle lies outside the domain of children's rights, since it expresses a viewpoint on society, namely, that handicapped children must be an asset to society.

Typical for the mentality of the Americans who always prefer private initiative to State interference is the sentence: 'Expenses of these services should be borne publicly where they cannot be privately met.'

The Committee on physically and mentally handicapped children of the *White House Conference*, published a supplement to the *Charter*, formulated in a *Bill of Rights for the Handicapped Child*,[23] comprising five Principles (Appendix XI).

Principle XIV has two major concerns. The first part ("For every child who is in conflict with society the right to be dealt with intelligently as society's charge, not society's outcast') is concerned with the *conservative mode* of the *social subsystem*, since it expresses the viewpoint that maladapted children should be retrained or brought back to the fold of society. It shifts the attention from 'the problem child' to the 'problems of the child'.[24] While the intentions of this lucidly proposed Principle are clear, analytically the first part emphasises the general notion 'belonging to society' and hence is classifiable in the *conservative mode* of the *social subsystem*. The second part, calling for the creation of institutions to suit that purpose, fits by definition in the *adaptive mode* of the *social subsystem*.

The purpose of Principle XV is clearly the "safeguarding against social handicaps" and therefore classifiable in *the four modes* of the *social subsystem*. However, it is interesting to note that the thrust of this Principle is directed towards the family as the surest means to attain the stated purpose.

Principle XVI ("For every child protection against labour that stunts growth either physical or mental, that limits education, that deprives children of the right to comradeship, of play and of joy") is (although formulated in the negative) concerned with growth. 'Growth', must in the first place be understood as physical growth, which makes it classifiable in the *expressive mode* of the *physical subsystem*. However, it is also mental growth (play and joy), which makes it classifiable in the *expressive mode* of the *personality subsystem*. The right to comradeship (intimate relationship among equals) clearly belongs in the *integrative mode* of the *social subsystem*.

Principle XVII focuses on a particular sub-population of children: the rural children. There is no concern in this Principle about basic physical needs, perhaps because it is assumed that rural families manage to provide food, housing etc. for themselves. However, the Principle is concerned with means and facilities. "For every rural child a satisfactory surrounding and health services . . . and . . . social . . . facilities" belongs in the *adaptive mode* of the *social subsystem*. Cultural facilities belong in the *adaptive mode* of the *cultural subsystem*. Health services belong in the *adaptive mode* of the *integrative-physical sub-subsystem*. Recreational facilities are to be classified in the *adaptive mode* of the *adaptive-personality sub-subsystem*.

Principle XVIII: ("To supplement the home and the school in the training of youth and to return to them those interests of which modern life tends to cheat children") and ("every stimulation and encouragement should be given to the extension and development of the voluntary youth organisations"), is a recommendation rather than the formulation of a right.

Principle XIX does not formulate rights. It is a policy statement, namely about decentralisation of services. The creation of more possibilities for Federal intervention was feared. Therefore only country-wide services through research are mentioned.

The closing paragraph of the *White House Charter* declares that "all nineteen paragraphs are applicable to *every* child, regardless of race, colour, situation, wherever he may live under the protection of the American flag." The Rights formulated in the Children's Charter were, therefore, relevant for children in Puerto Rico, the Philippines, Hawaii and Alaska.

2. A Children's Charter in Wartime of the United States Department of Labor, Children's Bureau (1942)

See Appendix XII

After France had fallen to the Nazis it became clear in the United States that "everything had now to be tested by its relation to the war effort."[25] At the one hand an invincible fighting force must be built, but on the other hand the welfare and the morale of the civilian population must be maintained. A vulnerable group of this civilian population were the children.

In 1942, between March 16th and 18th, a representative of the Civilian Mobilisation Branch of the Office of Civilian Defence, a representative of the Public Health Service of the Federal Security Agency, a representative

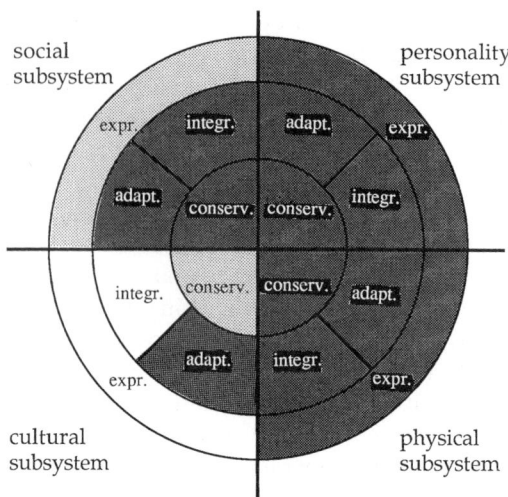

Fig. 11.1. The Children's Charter of the White House. Conference on Health and Protection (1930). Interpreted by the Systemic Quality of Life Model.

of the Surgeon-General, and other experts met in order to discuss the needs of children in wartime. They decided to issue a Declaration.

The Committee who drafted this Declaration, the *Children's Charter in Wartime*, divided its contents under four headings: *danger zones, defence areas, homes in wartime, and the general charge for American children everywhere.*

Picture XI.1. President Herbert Hoover (1930). (Courtesy: Herbert Hoover Presidential Library, West Branch, Iowa, U.S.A.)

Although the Charter was formulated for the United States, the drafters hoped that "it might have some significance up and down the hemisphere, and perhaps elsewhere."[26] The experts discussed the draft and proposed amendments or more adequate formulation where necessary. The meeting took place in the Children's Bureau functioning under the responsibility of the U.S. Labor Department.

The first paragraph of the introduction emphasised that the United States, involved in a total war, fought for the future of their children in a free America and for all children everywhere. As Dr. Casparis stated: "We can't be free unless the whole world is free."[27]

In the second paragraph we read that in the midst of this total war children must be safeguarded, and that we must strive for a "just and lasting peace" which hopefully will be carried forward by the children.

Next follows a discussion *about zones* containing military targets, industrial plants, oil tankers or the like. If necessary, we read in the discussion, children must be evacuated from such danger zones, but "the evacuation should not proceed beyond local jurisdictions unless we are sure the reception area is there and adequate."[28] The Charter itself, however, only mentions that the transfer of children from these danger zones to summer vacation camps can be seen as an exercise for the real evacuation and as an "investment in the children's health."

Dr. Adair stated during the discussion that most lay people thought that to 'guard children from injury' meant guarding them from *physical injury*. He proposed a broader conception. The Charter therefore states that "childhood anxiety can be as devastating as disease, and that adults must help children to meet the anticipations and realities of wartime." This opinion is intended to enlarge the scope of concern from the purely physical to the psychological domain.

The second part of the Charter deals with protection of children from neglect and undue strain in *defence areas*. A thousand communities in the United States were involved in the production of guns, tanks, war-planes and other war material. In a bulletin issued by the Children's Bureau we read that "approximately four hundred 'Defence Areas', embracing about a thousand communities, are scattered throughout the United States." What exactly is meant by 'Defence Areas' is not explained. Mrs. Fowler[29] said during the experts' discussion: "I am a bit worried about the differentiation between defense areas and *homes in wartime*. I think there is considerable overlapping there". The three concepts: 'danger zones', 'defense areas' (where production is directed towards the war effort, fathers work on night shifts, women live in trailer camps and many mothers are employed outside the home[30]) and 'homes in wartime' can, however, be seen as a continuum.

In these thousand defence-area communities, we read in the Charter, there must be adequate health services, education and welfare services. Pediatricians and obstetricians must be appointed and child guidance clinics must be available "to help parents and children overcome insecurity associated with dislocations in family life." School opportunities must be geared to the new demands. Many new recreation leaders, group workers and child welfare workers were needed to staff the recreation centres and help fight mounting juvenile delinquency.

Several experts pleaded for a reference to 'exploitation'. In the text of the Charter, however, no trace of this can be found.

The third part of the Charter deals with *homes in war time*, affected by enlistment or employment. We read: "The home is vital as a centre of security and hope and love. Migration to new and crowded communities, the absence of the father ... and the employment of mothers are creating problems that affect every member of the family. ... Full provision must be made for the economic needs of children whose fathers are in the military service," and "a government insurance program for civilians, injured or killed as a result of war activities, must be set up." Pleas are made for adequate housing. As plans developed for the participation of women in war industry, the responsibility of the community to assist parents plan the best possible care for their children is mentioned. Day care is specifically mentioned. The experts concluded that all parents who are economically unable to maintain a home for their children should be assisted.

The fourth part of the Charter refers to *homes everywhere in the country*. "One would think we were introducing a novelty," said Dr. Adair during the meeting of experts. "But I wondered if we could not better emphasize the idea that we are trying to better things that already exist."[31] The text of the Charter refers to the Children's Charter of the 1930 White House Conference and mentions some points that "take on a new significance in the present war crisis."

In the elaboration of this part a plea is made for certain medical provisions and health supervision from the prenatal period throughout adolescence. "If our country is to be strong, all children must have the food they need for buoyant health and normal growth." School meals were seen as an effective way to supplement nutrition.

The charter states specifically that "in war time more than ever, recreation must be assured for children and youth." Every State, county and city must also see to it that the child welfare and child guidance facilities give appropriate attention to children with special needs. Health services must also be extended to school children, and nursery schools must be made increasingly available to all children. All boys and girls should participate in civilian mobilisation programs, states the Charter. However, special attention must be given to children in rural areas who are more likely to be handicapped by harmful employment, inadequate schools and lack of other community facilities. The war effort must not increase these handicaps.

In our opinion the most important part of the Charter in Wartime is the following statement in the middle of part IV: "Their right to schooling should not be scrapped for the duration. Demands for the employment of children as a necessary war measure should be analyzed to determine whether full use has been made of available adult man power and to distinguish between actual labor shortage and the desire to obtain cheap labor. The education and wholesome development of boys and girls should be the first consideration when decisions are made with regard to their employment or other contribution to our war effort."[32] Indeed, the Ministry of Labor files in the National Archives show that only few boys and girls under fourteen were at all employed, that no children under sixteen worked in manufacturing and mining occupations, and that no children under eighteen were employed in hazardous occupations. There were no drummer boys like there had been in the Civil War and no eleven and twelve year-old boys involved in the war industry.

This *Children's Charter* can be seen as a collection of *guidelines for policy makers*. We shall now classify its different parts in the 'Systemic Quality of Life Model'.

In the Preamble we read that "children must be safeguarded," and "sheltered." In war time this can be understood as protection of the children's very lives. This belongs in the *conservative mode* of the *physical subsystem*. "Children must be nourished," belongs in the *adaptive mode* of the *physical subsystem*, since it seems from the context that physical nourishment was the main concern.

The first guideline ("guard children from injury in danger zones") is concerned with protection from physical injuries and loss of life. This belongs in the *conservative mode* of the *physical subsystem*.

The paragraphs that clarify this guideline are all operational paragraphs suggesting *means* to guard children and can therefore not be classified. The last paragraph stands somewhat apart because it mentions that anxiety is devastating for children. It belongs in the *integrative mode* of the *personality subsystem*.

The second guideline states that the effects of "undue (psychological) strain" on children living in the areas where tanks, planes and other war material are built, can be as devastating as physical injuries. This strain on the child's mind belongs in the *integrative mode* of the *personality subsystem*.

The explanatory paragraphs mention the need for health care and mental health care centres. They also emphasise the need to protect children from neglect. Since it is not clarified what kind of neglect is meant, we assume that the concern is with all the child's individual needs in *all* functioning modes.

In the paragraphs clarifying the third guideline (*strengthening the home life of children whose parents are mobilized for war or war production*), the *physical aspect* of home life is stressed like, for instance, adequate housing which belongs in the *adaptive mode* of the *physical subsystem*. We can classify other facilities mentioned in this paragraph in the *integrative mode* of the *physical subsystem* (medical and hospital care for children). "Full provision for the economic needs of children whose fathers are in the service" belongs in the *adaptive mode* of the *physical subsystem*. Day-care for children belongs in the *adaptive mode* of the *physical subsystem*.

Economic security which is due to the children "of all parents economically unable to maintain a home for their children" belongs in the *adaptive mode* of the *physical subsystem*, and in the *conservative mode* of the *physical subsystem* (compensation for temporary and permanent disability, continuity to the physical conditions of the child).

Although most of the aspects of the third guideline as well as the clarifying paragraphs belong in the *physical subsystem*, we must take into consideration that physical care is often linked to affection (*integrative mode* of the *social subsystem*), safety and security (*conservative mode* of the *social subsystem*). However, the physical aspects are dominant in this guideline.

The fourth guideline states that the values of the American society must be provided for children. "*Equip* . . . children . . . to take part in democracy" belongs in the *adaptive mode* of the *cultural (valuative) subsystem*. This guideline also re-affirms the values of democracy. These values belong in the *conservative mode* of the *cultural subsystem*. The main concern of guideline IV lays in the *cultural subsystem*. However, the following paragraphs of guideline IV can be classified in the *integrative mode* of the *physical subsystem* (health services such as public-health-nursing services) and the *adaptive mode* of the *physical subsystem* (food for children). This paragraph also deals with the social means to give children care, training and nourishment. This can be classified in the *adaptive mode* of the *physical subsystem* and *personality subsystem*. Measures to be taken in the field of health care (such as "complete medical examinations") belong in the *integrative mode* of the *physical subsystems*.

The last paragraph belongs in the *adaptive mode* of the *social subsystem*. Even if there is war, it states, the child should interact with society ("participate in home and community efforts"). The right to play belongs in the *expressive mode* of the *personality subsystem*, and the *expressive mode* of the *physical subsystem*. "Recreation must be assured for children and youth." This belongs in the *adaptive mode* of the *personality subsystem* (mental nourishment).

"School and work to prepare children for the tasks of tomorrow" and "to match the characteristics of each child" are classifiable in the *adaptive mode* of the *social subsystem*.

Two paragraphs (one about young children and one about children in rural areas) are concerned with specific sub-categories of children and can therefore not be classified in the 'Systemic Quality of Life Model'.

Most of the aspects of this Charter lie, as was to be expected in wartime, in the *physical subsystem*. However, it is interesting to note that the *personality subsystem* and the *cultural subsystem* are also emphasised. Thought has not only been given to short-term protection, but also to long-term effects.

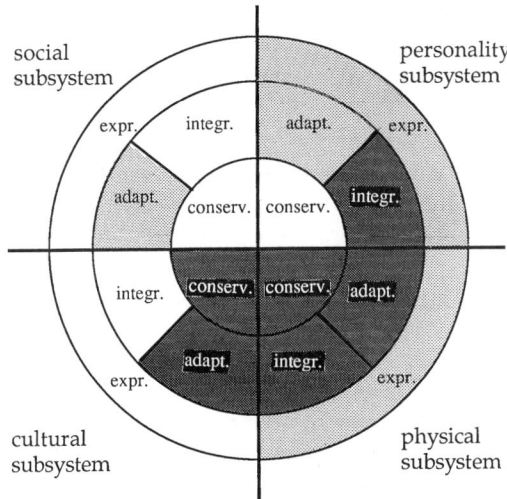

Fig. 11.2. The Children's Charter in Wartime of the U.S. Department of Labor (1942). Interpreted by the Systemic Quality of Life Model.

3. THE DECLARATION OF OPPORTUNITIES FOR CHILDREN (ADOPTED BY THE EIGHTH PAN AMERICAN CHILD CONGRESS, MAY 1942)

See Appendix XIV

By the end of April 1942 diplomats, pediatricians, teachers, social workers, representatives from different governments and representatives of child-welfare organisations travelled from all over North and South America to Washington to attend a Conference about child-welfare in and after the war. The Conference was organised by the *Pan American Union* (today the *Organization of American States*, the OAS). After Pearl Harbour the organisers and their advisors were of the opinion that in the midst of world-wide conflict it was more important than ever for the Governments to consult each other in order to consider the ways in which childhood could be safeguarded.[33]

Twenty-one North- and South-American countries (henceforth called States) had sent representatives. It was the first Conference of this kind in Washington. The first Conference about children by the Pan-American Union had been organised in 1926 in Argentina, the others had taken place in Uruguay, Brazil, Chili, Peru and Mexico. These earlier Conferences, however, had not produced Children's Charters.

On May 2nd, 1942, Bidu Sayao, the Brazilian Prima Donna of the Metropolitan Opera in New York, performed at the opening session in the *Hall of the Americas* in the Pan-American Union building in Washington. Except for a lunch where Mrs. Roosevelt spoke, an evening party in the White House and a few excursions, this Congress worked very hard.[34]

Three issues were central:

* How to guarantee that the needs of children would be satisfied, even in war time;
* Guidelines for planning child-welfare after the war;
* How Inter-American co-operation could contribute to the above mentioned issues.

The *New York Times*[35] was well informed when it announced that the Pan American Union would not only develop plans for collaboration in child-health and welfare but also draft a Declaration of goals of collaboration. It quoted Katharine Lenroot of the Children's Bureau in Washington who stated that the Conference "would give attention to those rights which must be at heart of a just and lasting peace."

All the representatives spoke about the consequences of the Second World War. In some countries food was scarce anyway, in others shipping problems lead to food problems. In others still, health-care facilities originally founded for mothers and children were now exclusively used by the military. Everywhere systems and services, carefully developed for children, were not working specifically for children any more.

The Committee working on plans for child- and youth-care *after* the war decided to re-formulate the goals of the American States concerning education.[36]

The closing session of the Conference was a great happening in the presence of Dr. Manuel Prado Y. Ugarteche, President of Peru. The *Declaration of Opportunities for Children*, written in Spanish, Portuguese, English and French, was signed by the leaders of the twenty-one delegations as well as by the director of the *American International Institute for the Protection of Childhood*, Dr. Robert Berro from Montevideo.[37]

Strikingly, the term *rights* does not appear in the Declaration. To state that children must have certain *opportunities* is weaker than to state that they have a *right* to something. Opportunities can only be realised if the economic circumstances allow it. Rights can be claimed under all circumstances. However, the tone of the Declaration is optimistic.

If we analyse the above Declaration,[38] we observe that the Pan-American Congress values *family life* greatly. It was the Congress' opinion that a family environment must be created for homeless children. Although the answer is found in foster-family care, no mention is made of the fact that foster-parents must receive adequate compensation. The absence of clear regulations in this field is, by the way, probably one of the reasons why foster-care in South America has never become popular. Guidance by social workers and a commitment by the governments to make funds available for home-finding are also not mentioned. Apparently private initiative is taken for granted in child-welfare. This becomes even more evident when we read in the first paragraph of the Declaration how the American States throw the care for needy mothers on the lap of the social workers who are expected to provide assistance until the mothers can improve their economic circumstances through their own efforts. No consideration is given to the fact that the *governments'* policies might themselves be responsible for a great deal of economic misery. Neither is there any suggestion about where the social workers must find the funds to assist the needy mothers. We may assume that the institution 'social work' was identified with 'relief' or 'charity'.

This part of the Declaration (to provide *opportunities* for children) deals mostly with the *framework* which makes family life possible. It belongs in the *adaptive mode* of the *integrative-social sub-subsystem*.

We see the similar attitude of charity in clause (a) of the paragraph about health. Said Dr. Pedro Escudero, the Director-General of the Buenos Aires *National Institute of Nutrition*: "The Latin American continent is living a veritable tragedy of hunger which goes back to the time of its discovery."[39] However, not a word was said about restructuring the economy in such a way as to make it possible for *all* parents to buy adequate food for their children.

The paragraph about *health* states that the child needs "an adequate diet". This belongs in the *adaptive mode* of the *physical subsystem*.

"Periodic medical and psychological supervision" shows concern for the *integrative mode* of the *physical subsystem* (physical health) and the *integrative mode* of the personality subsystem (mental health). But since the *means to achieve this* such as *supervision* are discussed, we classify this paragraph in the *adaptive mode* of the *integrative-physical sub-subsystem* and the *adaptive mode* of the *integrative-personality sub-subsystem*.

"Expert guidance in recreation" deals with the means to achieve (what the drafters consider as 'good') recreation. It belongs in the *adaptive mode* of the *adaptive-personality sub-subsystem*.

We assume that "adequate rest" is meant to be physical rest, such as sleep. We, therefore, classify it in the *integrative mode* of the *physical subsystem*.

"*Guidance* in the proper formation of the personality in all its aspects" belongs in the *adaptive mode* of the *expressive-personality sub-subsystem*.

"Preparation for life in the community" is difficult to classify. If *life in the community* means *conditions for feelings of togetherness* it belongs in the *adaptive mode* of the *integrative-social sub-subsystem*. However, if the *conditions for social institutions* are meant, this concern belongs in the *adaptive mode* of the *adaptive-social sub-subsystem*. If *conditions for feeling of belonging to a community* are meant it belongs in the *adaptive mode* of the *conservative-social sub-subsystem*.

"*Opportunity* for every child to discover his or her special abilities, and to secure *education and training* to develop these powers – mental, physical, and spiritual – during the years necessary to achieve full development" belong in the *adaptive mode of the expressive-personality sub-subsystem*. To achieve these goals the American States plead for "vocational guidance". This belongs in the *adaptive mode* of the *social subsystem*.

246   Chapter XI

"Appropriate and adequate organisation of intellectual, physical, spiritual and cultural education . . . and the full realisation of his capacities and natural talents" are classifiable in the *adaptive mode* of the *expressive-personality, expressive-physical, expressive-cultural* and *expressive social sub-subsystems*.

The next paragraph deals with *responsibility and work*. We interpret responsibility here as enhancing the status of the person who takes such responsibility upon himself. It hints, therefore, at the *expressive mode* of the *social subsystem* (exertion of social influence). It also refers to appropriate interaction with institutions (*adaptive mode* of the *social subsystem*).

The deeper concern of the child-labour legislation is with health (*integrative mode* of the *physical subsystem*) and prevention of accidents that may cost the child his life. It belongs in the *conservative mode* of the *physical subsystem*. The regulations themselves are to be classified in the *adaptive mode* of the *social subsystem*.

The recommendations for the use of *leisure time* cannot be realised without financial help from the governments. The formulation looks more like a statement of good intentions than as a Plan of Action. The concern for recreation belongs in the *adaptive mode* of the *personality subsystem*.

"Opportunity for every child as a citizen to take his place in the life of the community" belongs in the *adaptive mode* of the *integrative-social subsys-

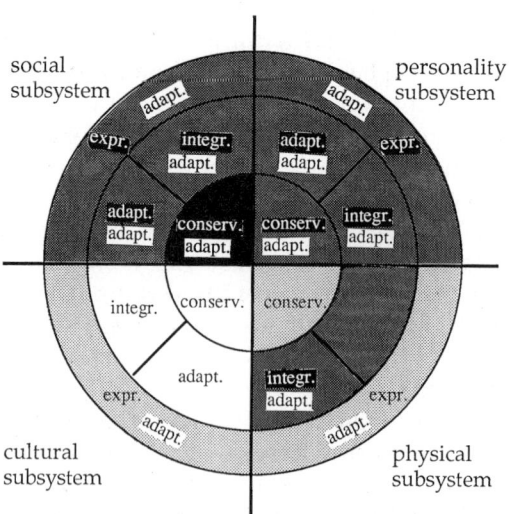

Fig. 11.3. The Declaration of Opportunities for Children (1942) of the Pan American Congress. Interpreted by the Systemic Quality of Life Model.

tem. "To develop the conscience of the child" hints at a preoccupation with educating the conscience, rather than with the conscience itself. This concern belongs in the *adaptive mode* of the *expressive-social sub-subsystem*.

At first sight it seemed as if the drafters of this Declaration were less concerned with rights of children than with *stability of the family*. However, having studied the Declaration closely, we now realise that the ultimate goal was *stability of society* and that stability of the family was seen as the way to achieve law and order. This concern belongs in the (*conservative mode* of the *social subsystem*).

The drafters believed that stability could also be achieved through enhanced interactions between the individual and his or her community. They assumed an *inter-relatedness* between different domains of the quality of life. (In 1979 this assumption has been validated by Shye[40]).

Interesting is the focus of the Declaration on *means* to achieve things (the *adaptive mode* of *all sub-subsystems*). Indeed, the title *Declaration of Opportunities for Children* already indicates that means are the central issue, and that the drafters wished to create a favourable combination of circumstances.

4. THE CHILDREN'S BILL OF RIGHTS OF THE NEW YORK STATE YOUTH COMMISSION (1949)

See Appendix XV

This Declaration has long been forgotten. Having spotted the title in *Selected References on Rights of Children* 1970–1986,[41] we had to organise a real search to unearth the text.[42] This was strange, since in 1949 this *Children's Bill of Rights* had been displayed as a poster in thousands of offices throughout the United States.

The document was the brainchild of the New York State Youth Commission, (founded in 1945 on the recommendation of the then Governor of New York State, Thomas E. Dewey), and of an inter-departmental Committee.[43] The philosophy was that juvenile delinquency could be reduced by better meeting the needs of children, and that "those needs are obvious and understandable when given the consideration they merit. But in a confused and restless world, perhaps some of them have been more talked about than satisfied."

The Youth Commission "recognized that a better public understanding of the problems of youth and public support for programs directed at meeting them, must precede the mustering and effective use of our abundant human and material resources." This important educational undertaking was carried out by publicity, public addresses, public displays, documentary films and by a *Children's Bill of Rights* which set forth, in concise, poster-like form, the needs of children.[44] Besides putting major emphasis upon the needs of chil-

Picture XI.2. Closing session of the 8th Pan American Child Congress, Washington D.C., 1942. (Courtesy: Records of the Children's Bureau, National Archives, Washington DC.)

dren, how and where they should be met, and the importance of the home, the school, the church and the community in the wholesome development of children[45], this *Children's Bill of Rights* drew the attention to two very special rights, principles 5 and 9, not mentioned so explicitly in any other Charter or Declaration.

We shall now analyse this *Children's Bill of Rights* with the 'Systemic Quality of Life Model'.

Principle 1, "the right to the affection and intellectual guidance of understanding parents," belongs in the *adaptive mode* of the *personality subsystem* (external nourishment to personality growth). This principle is part of the 'theory' of the New York State Youth Commission that is the cornerstone of this Charter, that if a child does not receive enough attention, love and discipline, he or she will become delinquent (see especially Principle 5 and 9).

Principle 2 is classifiable in the *adaptive mode* of the *cultural-valuative subsystem* (conforming to standards of society by means of raising a child "in a decent home"), and in the *adaptive mode* of the *physical subsystem* (to be "adequately fed, clothed and sheltered").

Principle 3 belongs in the *adaptive mode* of the *cultural subsystem*, since it mentions provisions for a cultural practice and even recommends a specific kind of cultural framework, ("the rights to benefits of religious guidance and training").

Principle 4 ("sound academic training" and "opportunity for individual development and preparation for living") recommends that practical steps for optimal development of the personality be incorporated in the school programme. Since the concern is for the child's personality, we classify this Principle in the *expressive mode* of the *personality subsystem*.

Principle 5 shows the 'theory' that lies behind this 'Bill', that if a child

Picture XI.3. The Children's Bill of Rights of the New York State Youth Commission.

does not receive constructive discipline, this may lead to delinquency. What exactly must be understood under "constructive discipline" is not explained. For all we know it may be physical punishment. Whatever the case may be, the concern of this Principle is undoubtedly the development and environmental compatibility of the child's *personality*. We classify it in the *adaptive mode* of the *personality subsystem*.

Principle 6 is concerned with safety ("the right to be secure") which belongs in the *conservative mode*. But "secure" in what? This is not specified in the text. Although it is easy to determine in which mode or modes this Principle belongs, the classification in a subsystem raises a problem. At first sight we tend to interpret "wholesome development" as personality development. But when we look at the formulation: "against all influences detrimental to *proper* development", we think that a valuative element also plays an important part. We have therefore classified this Principle in the *conservative mode* of the *cultural subsystem*. However, "*wholesome* development" belongs also in the *conservative mode* of the *personality subsystem*. "Secure in his or her community" suggests that this Principle also belongs in the *conservative mode* of the *social subsystem*.

Principle 7 ("wholesome recreation") belongs in the *adaptive mode* of the *personality subsystem*. However, the specification *individual selection* (with additional stress on the fact that recreation must be *free*), points clearly in the direction of the *expressive mode* of the *personality subsystem*.

Principle 8 is a blanket statement. It formulates the right "to live in a community in which adults practice the belief that the *welfare* of their children is of primary importance." The word 'welfare' covers the complete 'Systemic Quality of Life Model'. This Principle is not so much a *right* as the formulation of the *means* to improve the children's quality of life.

Principle 9 represents again the underlying 'theory' of the New York State Youth Commission. It deals with ways to prevent juvenile delinquency. Years before Bandura and Walters[46] demonstrated the use of observational learning in children, the Youth Commission formulated this idea as "the right to receive good adult example." Although the phrasing of this right does not reveal the focus of concern (a "good example" for what?), it may nevertheless be understood from the context that the major concern is the *social-adaptivity* of the child.

Principle 10 is heavily loaded. The first part of it deals with "the right to a job commensurate with his or her ability, training and experience." This belongs in the *adaptive mode* of the *social subsystem*. The second part of this Principle ("protection against physical or moral employment hazards") belongs in the *conservative mode* of the *physical and cultural subsystems*. However, physical and cultural conservative measures are, in this case, intended to facilitate "wholesome development." Therefore the real concern is to be classified in the *expressive mode* of the *personality subsystem*.

Principle 11 is concerned with special groups of children, namely those who have physical and/or mental handicaps or are socially maladjusted. It is the Youth Commission's opinion that "they have the right to early diagnosis and treatment." The Youth Commission specifies that such diagnosis and treatment must "whenever necessary" be "at public expense." This recommendation about financing cannot be classified in the 'Systemic Quality of Life Model'.

5. The Pledge to Children: Mid-Century White House Conference on Children and Youth (1950)

See Appendix XVI

In June 1950 North-Korean (Communist) forces invaded South Korea. This was the immediate cause of the war. In September and October there was a counter-offensive by a United Nations force (90% American and South-Korean). In December, the White House Conference on Children and Youth took place.

Contrary to President Hoover's Children's Charter, President Truman's *Pledge to Children* deals mainly with issues belonging to the *cultural-valuative subsystem*. President Truman (President since the death of President Roosevelt on April 12, 1945, and re-elected on November 2, 1948) linked the concern for the development of children and youth to the future well-being,

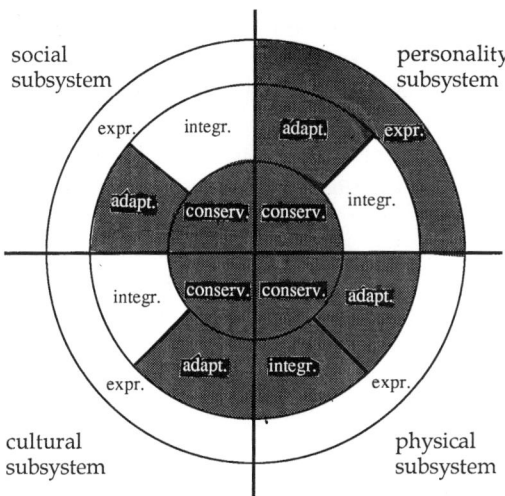

Fig. 11.4. The Children's Bill of Rights of the New York State Youth Commission (1949). Interpreted by the Systemic Quality of Life Model.

not only of these children and youth, but of the nation.[47] He also linked it with educating children in a system of values. "This year," said Truman "you (the participants to the Conference) are mainly concerned with the mental and moral health of our children. And this is exactly what you should be concerned with at this time.[48] . . . As we engage in that struggle, we must preserve the elements of our American way of life that are the basic source of our strength. That is the purpose of this Mid-Century White House Conference on Children and Youth. If you are to give our children the training that will enable them to hold fast to the right course in these dangerous times, we must clearly understand the nature of the crisis. We must understand the nature of the threat created by international communism. . . . Communism attacks our basic values, our belief in God, our belief in the dignity of man and the value of human life, our belief in justice and freedom."[49]

We shall now analyse this *Pledge for Children* with the 'Systemic Quality of Life Model'.

In the first paragraph ("From your earliest infancy we give you love") *love* is the keyword. We classify this paragraph in the *integrative mode* of the *social subsystem*, and to a lesser extent, since it is only indicated by a few words, ("so that you may grow with trust in yourself") in the *integrative mode* of the *personality subsystem*. We can also classify this paragraph in the *conservative mode* of the *personality subsystem* (trust in yourself gives a feeling of security), and in the *conservative mode* of the *social subsystem* (trust in yourself *and others*, stressing growth of social relations, enabled by love).

The second paragraph: "We will recognize your worth as a person," belongs in the *conservative mode* of the *personality subsystem*, since it is concerned with *the feeling* of worth regardless of the deeds in the social context. It can also be classified in the *conservative mode* of the *social subsystem* (we will help you to strengthen your sense of belonging), since it is designed to give the feeling that the individual is part of the fibre of society.

The third paragraph: "We will respect your right to be yourself and at the same time help you to understand the rights of others," belongs in the *adaptive mode* of the *social subsystem*. This paragraph stresses the importance of training for co-operative behaviour in the social sphere (understand the rights of others, so that you may experience co-operative living). We have also interpreted "the right to be yourself," as part of the social-adaptive sphere, since the assumed philosophy behind it is: you have to understand yourself and the social environment, after which an exchange of interests can take place.

The fourth paragraph ("you have the right to develop initiative and imagination so that you may have the opportunity freely to create") clearly belongs in the *expressive mode* of the *personality subsystem*. Key-words in this paragraph are *develop initiative* and *freely*.

The fifth paragraph ("we will encourage your curiosity and your pride in workmanship") belongs partially in the *expressive mode* of the *personality subsystem* (recognised achievements manifested in workmanship) and partially in the *integrative mode* of the *personality subsystem* (balance your potential well with achievements). The paragraph states: "so that you may have the satisfaction that comes from achievement."

In order to classify the sixth paragraph we must use a deeper level of the 'Systemic Quality of Life Model'. This paragraph ("we will provide the conditions for wholesome play that will add to your learning, to your social experience, and to your happiness"), belongs in the *adaptive mode* of the *expressive-personality sub-subsystem*. The paragraph deals with the conditions (adaptive mode) of play.

The seventh paragraph states: "We will illustrate by precept and example the value of integrity and the importance of moral courage." *We will illustrate by precept* belongs in the *adaptive mode* of the *cultural subsystem*. *Integrity* belongs in the *integrative mode* of the *cultural subsystem*. *Moral courage* belongs in the *expressive mode* of the *cultural-valuative subsystem*, since we understand it as courage for expression of morality of individual principles of conscience. However, this is our personal interpretation for which there is no support from the text.

The eighth (very American) paragraph: "We will encourage you always to seek the truth," is highly individualistic. It suggests not only that one should seek the truth but also that one should act upon it, which makes it

The Pledge to Children

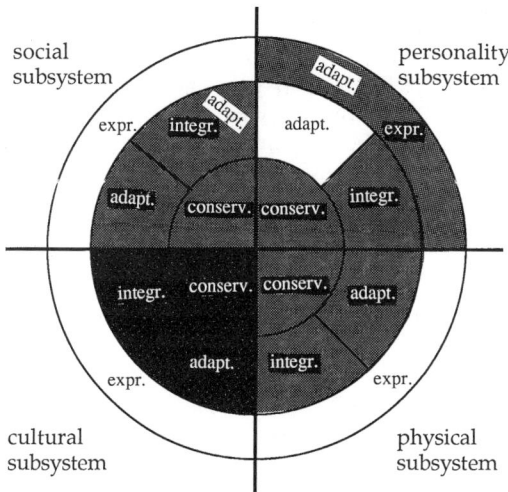

Fig. 11.5. The Pledge to Children (Mid Century White House Conference on Children and Youth, 1950). Interpreted by the Systemic Quality of Life Model.

classifiable in the *expressive mode* of the *personality subsystem*. This paragraph can also be classified in the *conservative mode* of the *cultural-valuative subsystem* (stability of value structure).

This interpretation is supported by the ninth paragraph: "We will *provide* you with all opportunities possible to develop your own faith in God." Truman does not promise the children God, but *opportunities*. The first part of this paragraph belongs, therefore, in the *adaptive mode* of the *cultural subsystem*. The second part ("to develop their own faith in God") belongs in the *expressive mode* of the *cultural subsystem*.

The tenth paragraph ("We will *open the way* for you to enjoy the arts and to use them for deepening your understanding of life") strongly emphasises the *adaptive mode* of the *cultural subsystem*. In this paragraph the idea is also expressed that culture helps the child to understand the interaction between the cultural subsystem and other aspects of life ("deepening your understanding in life").

In the eleventh paragraph the adults express a good intention: "to work towards more equality in a democratic society, to rid ourselves of prejudice and discrimination." To classify these good intentions we must resort to a deeper level of analysis: *the adaptive mode* of the *integrative-social subsystem*.

In the twelfth paragraph the adults express another good intention: "to work to lift the standard of living and to improve economic practices." This work for "a material basis" is classifiable in the *adaptive mode* of the *physical subsystem*.

The thirteenth paragraph expresses the good intention to "provide rewarding educational opportunities." This paragraph lies very much in the personality-sphere. We classify it in the *adaptive mode* of the *personality subsystem*, and also in the *expressive mode* of the *personality subsystem*, since the paragraph continues: "so that you may *develop* your talents." The addition "and contribute to a better world," in which we interpret this better world as a social phenomenon, belongs in the *adaptive mode* of the *social subsystem*.

The fourteenth paragraph promises protection "against exploitation and undue hazards." This belongs in the *conservative mode* of the *physical subsystem*. To help to grow "in health and strength" (ongoing health) belongs in the *integrative mode* of the *physical subsystem*).

We interpret the efforts of adults "to conserve and improve family life", as formulated in the fifteenth paragraph, as emphasising the importance of attachments. We therefore classify it in the *integrative mode* of the *social subsystem*.

The sixteenth paragraph is hard to classify. It lies probably in the *expressive mode* of the *personality subsystem*, since it expresses the intention to develop the child's potentialities.

The seventeenth and last paragraph is a statement about *mobilizing support* to improve conditions of all children and youth in general. It cannot be classified in the 'Systemic Quality of Life Model'.

6. The Children's Charter, Japan (1951)

See Appendix XVII

The Japanese Charter of Children's Rights covers most of the quality of life modes. Missing are, however, the *expressive mode of the social subsystem* (striving for social status) and the *expressive mode of the physical subsystem* (the individual control over the physical environment). Both reflect existing circumstances in Japanese society. Since 1951 more and more emphasis has been laid in Japan on the necessity for individual decision making (less and less emphasis is on an acquired status).

It is interesting to note that the *personality subsystem* is well covered in the Charter, including the *expressive mode*. Striking because in Japanese upbringing *shitsuke* (something like discipline) and etiquette play such an important role. See for instance point 4: "All children shall be educated in accordance with their individuality...". But even here it is placed in the context of responsibilities as members of society.

7. THE CHILDREN'S BILL OF RIGHTS OF THE WHITE HOUSE CONFERENCE ON CHILDREN (1970)

See Appendix XXII

The Chairman of the White House Conference, Stephen Hess, wrote to the author of this study: "I split the Conference in two parts because I felt both children and youth deserved the same attention and I was fearful that otherwise the concerns for adolescents would absorb all the attention and not much energy would be left for the specific concerns for children."[50]

In the 1970s the image of childhood in the United States had changed so much that young people between the ages 14 and 24 were sometimes allowed to enter the world of adults, while children were not. Stephen Hess wrote in his final report: "The differences have become even more pronounced, with youth becoming more and more concerned with what was once considered adult domain of public affairs, while children still live in their own special world."[51]

As many as 3.700 delegates came for a short week to Washington D.C. to talk about at least twenty-six different aspects of child welfare.[52] The twenty-six Committees called themselves *Forums*. Forum 22, consisting of fifteen specialists, and chaired by the Director of the National Commission on Resources for Youth, Mary Conway Kohler, discussed the Rights of the Child. According to Rochelle Beck[53] "the 1970 Children's Bill of Rights was drafted by Mary Kohler."

The Children's Bill of Rights was very much inspired by the recommendations of the Joint Commission on Mental Health of Children, submitted in June 1969 to members of the United States Senate and House of Representatives (see Appendix XXI). Several members of Forum 22 had previously been members of the Joint Commission.

Forum 22 of the White House Conference[54] was concerned with "both pre-court and beyond the ken of the court-rights, as well as with the problems of who protects the child from his protectors, who guards against the guardians, and what mechanisms and which persons provide the best means to gain and protect the rights of children."[55] The Forum on Children's Rights stated: "We conceive of 'rights' as the intrinsic entitlements of every human born (or residing) in the United States. Although adult rights have been specifically delineated in the law and Bills of Rights, children are still considered objects to be protected – indeed, almost possessions. We must recognize their *inherent* rights which, although not exclusively those established by law and enforced by courts, are nonetheless closely related to the law.... Although children are one of our largest and most vulnerable minority groups, they have no voice in political processes and do not directly participate in lobbies on their own behalf. Their rights can be, and frequently are, infringed upon – often by those who claim they are acting in the child's interests.[56] ... The time has come to re-examine such fundamental issues as the extent to which a child is entitled to seek medical and psychiatric assistance, birth control information, and even abortion." As a subject for consideration it was suggested to make such decisions possible without parental consent or even overriding parental opposition. The entire concept of emancipation and its consequences should also be looked into as "the concept that the child is economically subservient to the parent, now embraced in common law and statutory directives."[57]

Among other things, the Forum drew a list of rights which children have in school. It mentioned as the *child's basic right in school, access to a satisfactory education*.[58] It also pleaded for child-advocate services to assert children's rights. It even proposed a National Centre for Child Advocacy. These recommendations, however, were not followed up by President Nixon.

In the analysis of the activities of the Forum, we shall only deal with the six *Specific Rights of Children*[59] which the Forum declared to be "central to a child's well-being."

I. The Right to Grow in a Society Which Respects the Dignity of Life and is Free of Poverty, Discrimination, and Other Forms of Degradation

With this formulation Mary Kohler was clearly trying to encompass all fields of life. It therefore belongs in all subsystems, but it is not easy to decide in which modes to classify it. *Respect for the dignity of the child* belongs in the *conservative mode* of the *physical subsystem*, since the commentary refers to the "tension of war and near-war and . . . the insanity of nuclear holocaust." We can also classify it in the *personality subsystem* (because of the tension).

In the commentaries is also written that "children need the assurance of dignity and a decent standard of living to be able to adopt healthy values, to make free choices concerning their future, and later to love and provide security for their own children." Dignity has to do with *effective expressive functioning*. Without it the child will probably have a low social status. Racism and sexism can hamper such effective expressive functioning.

Professor Irving N. Berlin (Professor in Psychiatry and Pediatrics at the University of New Mexico) who participated in *Forum* 22, explained in a letter to me that the term *degradation* related to "degrading circumstances like no pre-natal or post-natal care, no attention to early neglect and abuse of infants and small children, inadequate early education and poor education for minorities in school, etc." Since the formulating of this first group of rights invites a very broad interpretation, we classify it in *all conservative and expressive modes of all subsystems*.

II. The Right to Be Born Healthy and Wanted Through Childhood

As was the case with the rights formulated by Ellen Key, the first thing we see is that the question of 'to be or not to be' plays a part in "the right to be born healthy." In the commentary we read: "If the parents are degraded by the Society, or if the absence of birth control or abortion facilities produce an unwanted child, the likelihood of their being affectionate and nurturing toward their child is sharply diminished. Several measures can help ensure that our children are wanted and nurtured. All who wish to prevent a pregnancy should have easy access to contraceptive and family planning information; abortions should be available, although never mandatory."[60] As we have done with Ellen Key's rights, we classify this statement *in the centre of the 'Systemic Quality of Life Model' in all four conservative modes*.

III. The Right to Grow up Nurtured by Affectionate Parents. What Exactly Is Meant With "The Right to Grow up Nurtured?"

Mary Kohler comments that for children to be born healthy "pregnant women ... must have adequate nutrition, excellent pre-natal care and skilled delivery." This concern belongs in the *integrative mode* of the *physical subsystem*.

Intimate relationships in the family should be encouraged, says Mary Kohler.[61] "We take children 'too soon' away from their families. ... By 'too soon' I mean that we take children away from their families without having mobilized the kind of help that might enable the family to maintain or reconstitute itself, and the parents, through such help, to function adequately as parents." Strengthening of the intimate bonds belongs in the *integrative mode* of the *social subsystem*. To grow up nurtured belongs, according to our interpretation, in the *adaptive mode* of *all the subsystems*.

IV. The Right to Be a Child During Childhood and to Have Meaningful Choices in the Process of Maturation and Development and a Meaningful Voice in the Community

The significance of *to be a child during childhood* is not obvious. Indeed it probably differs according to cultures. Forum 22 reported: "We force children to make choices much too early; we are too quick to label and categorize them; we maintain all-encompassing and permanent records which stigmatize children. Such practices rob the child of the opportunity to be a child – of the right to play, investigate, explore, relate, test, try out, experiment and rebel, as well as to develop according to sexual and genetic differences.[62] ... Children also have the right to participate in making decisions which affect their lives". This means more power and social status for children. All these statements seem to belong in the *expressive mode* of the *personality subsystem* and, to a lesser extent, in the *expressive mode* of the *physical subsystem*. To make meaningful choices belongs in the *expressive mode* of the *personality subsystem*. To have a meaningful voice in the community belongs in the *expressive mode* of the *social subsystem*.

V. The Right to Be Educated to the Limits of Individual Capacity and Through Processes Designed to Elicit Their Full Potential

The keywords for our classification here are *full potential*. This points at the *expressive mode* of the *personality subsystem*. Whether or not a child will be able to develop to the limits of his or her individual capacity depends on the conditions.

VI. The Right to Have Societal Mechanisms Developed to Make the Foregoing Rights Effective

The aim of this points is to guarantee that the rights granted are indeed realised. 'Rights put social mechanisms in motion' belongs in the *adaptive mode* of the *social subsystem*. The formulation of this paragraph emphasises the institutions in relationship to the implementation of certain value systems. We can therefore, at least to some extent, classify this right in the *adaptive mode* of the *cultural subsystem*.

Professor Berlin wrote me: "The White House Conference on Children in 1970 was essentially a farce without any dissemination of its findings.... None of the large White House Conferences except the first one has had any impact on changing how the Nation treats children. The first White House Conference called by President Theodore Roosevelt came out against child labour and (like the Second Conference in 1919) received the President's support for legislation. The 1970 Conference, however, was not very influential."

8. RIGHTS OF YOUTH, FORMULATED BY THE WHITE HOUSE CONFERENCE ON YOUTH (1971)

See Appendix XXIII

In April 1971 some 1,500 experts on adolescence gathered in Washington D.C. in order to discuss the problems of young people (aged 14–24). "It is time," the experts stated, "now finally to affirm and implement the rights articulated in the Declaration of Independence and the Constitution. Each individual must be given the full rights of life, liberty, and the pursuit of

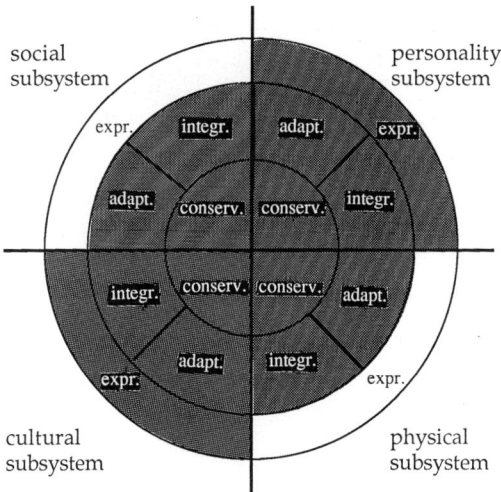

Fig. 11.6. The Children's Charter (Japan, 1951). Interpreted by the Systemic Quality of Life Model.

happiness. The Bill of Rights must be re-interpreted so as to be meaningful to all persons in our society." In addition to this, the Conference formulated four rights of which they declared that they were crucial.

I. The Right to Adequate Food, Clothing, and a Decent Home

We interpret this right as belonging in the *adaptive mode* of the *physical subsystem*. Food and clothing can give us no doubt, but even "a decent (good enough, reasonable) home", since it is mentioned in the same context as food and clothing, obviously refers to the physical subsystem.

II. The Right of the Individual to Do His/Her Thing, So Long as It Does Not Interfere With the Rights of Another

This is a typical American 'right', since the emphasis is on the individual, "who can do his/her thing." What that 'thing' is, is not explained and is of no importance as long as it does not interfere with the rights of another individual. It belongs clearly in the *expressive mode* of the *personality subsystem*.

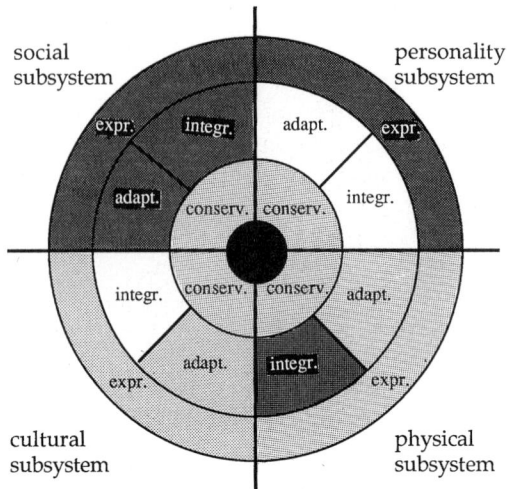

Fig. 11.7. The Children's Bill of Rights, White House Conference on Children (1970). Interpreted by the Systemic Quality of Life Model.

III. The Right to Preserve and Cultivate Ethnic and Cultural Heritages

To *preserve* belongs in the *conservative mode* of the *cultural subsystem*. To *cultivate* belongs in the *expressive mode* of the *conservative-cultural subsystem*, (since the preservation of the heritage is effected through active aspects in society, so that society contributes to the ongoing evolution of the culture).

IV. The Right to Do Whatever Is Necessary to Preserve These Rights

The issue in this paragraph is interaction with Society, namely 'how to obtain something'. This belongs in the *adaptive mode* of the *social subsystem*. It is, however, our opinion, that this paragraph deals in the first place with the interaction with Society about the *values* which were allowed to be expressed as rights. We therefore classify it also in the *adaptive mode* of the *cultural subsystem*.

9. THE CHARTER OF THE RIGHTS OF THE ARAB CHILD[63] OF THE LEAGUE OF ARAB STATES

See Appendix XXXVI

The League of Arab States[64] proclaimed the rights of the *Arab* Child. Noteworthy is that the League and its Council of Ministers of Social Affairs (perhaps unintentionally) did not proclaim the rights of *Children in Arab States*. If we may judge from the title of the Charter, the rights do not apply to the children of non-Arab minorities who live in Arab States.

In May 1984 the Charter received some attention when it was adopted by the Jordanian Cabinet.[65] This step was praised by the Secretary-General of Rädda Barnen ('Swedish Save the Children').[66] In his opening speech of the Amman Symposium on *Protection of Children* Crown Prince Hassan bin Talal said[67]: "Within the regional context, I would like to propose further efforts relating to the Charter of the Arab Child."

In its Preamble the Charter declares that it is a product of religious values (although Islam is not specifically mentioned here). The Arab States claim authorship for humanitarian principles ("the fact that our homeland is the cradle of religions and the homeland of the civilisations and culture expounding the sublime humanitarian principles which has given respect to man"). A large part of the Preamble is a statement on the importance of Arab unity. A statement is made about *Imperialistic* interventions that have interrupted the unity ("understanding the fatal challenge comprising the partitions consecrated by Imperialism whose burdensomeness can only be unravelled through unity"). 'Zionism', which the Arab States consider to be the worst form of imperialism is blamed, together with imperialism itself, for social backwardness of some of the countries. Children's rights stem, according to this Charter, from ancient cultures in which the Arab nations have played a unique role. The last paragraph of the Preamble proclaims to whom this Charter relates: " for the Arab child *from date of birth until the age of fifteen*."

In Part A(a) the view is expressed that children's rights are part of a more general concept of development.

A(b) ("All efforts are made to develop the child's 'personality' by making him love his family and country.") is to be classified in the *conservative mode* of the *cultural subsystem* (to belong to a social network in the large sense of the word). The rest of this paragraph ("and show pride of his country's civilisation and work on pan-Arab unity") belongs in the *expressive mode* of the *cultural subsystem*. It can also be classified in the *conservative mode* of the *social subsystem* (belonging to a culture).

A(c) states that "the family is considered the nucleus of the society," and that its aim is to strengthen the social fibres of society. Traditional institutions will support each other. The family has to provide warmth, security and a high commitment to social structures. We classify this paragraph in the *conservative mode* of the *social subsystem*.

The basic thought in paragraph (d) of Part A is: if the country gives the families support, they, in turn, will be loyal to the social structure. This paragraph belongs in the conservative mode of the social subsystem. However, since it is not concerned with children, it is not directly related to our subject.

B(1) describes the right "to grow up in the family where there is family stability." It belongs in the *conservative mode* of the *social subsystem*. However, since the family is supposed to give affection and warmth (inter-personal relationships) it also belongs in the *integrative mode* of the *social subsystem*. The second part of this paragraph ("whereby his *biological, psychological, spiritual and social needs* are met") belongs in *all four subsystems* of the 'Systemic Quality of Life Model'. The last part of this paragraph (independent personality, participation in a democratic manner, etc.) is to be classified in the *expressive mode* of the *personality and social subsystems*.

B(2) ("the right to social security") refers probably to financial support. It therefore belongs in the *adaptive mode* of the *physical subsystem*. The second part ("the right to health-care and . . . preventive health-care") deals with ongoing health. It belongs in the *integrative mode* of the *physical subsystem*. The end of this paragraph ("to live in a clean house and a clean environment and be given the right to food") belongs in the *adaptive mode* of the *physical subsystem*.

B(3) deals with the right to education. Although education has many purposes, the explanatory words ("education is a cornerstone in the existing change and acquiring trends") hints at a concern in the *adaptive mode* of the *cultural (valuative) subsystem*. This concern belongs also in the *adaptive mode* of the *social subsystem* ("to contribute positively in the daily life of his society"), in the *adaptive mode* of the *physical subsystem* ("guaranteeing himself a good standard of living"), and in the *adaptive mode* of the *personality subsystem* ("the benefit of free time, playing, sports and reading").

In Paragraph 4 of Part B the right to receive comprehensive and integrative social services is stated and the right to contribute to society's construction and development. This interchange can be classified in the *adaptive mode* of the *social subsystem*.

B(5) deals with protection from abuse and exploitation (in the physical and psychological sense). This concern belongs in the *conservative mode* of the *physical and personality subsystems*. The statement "that the youngster should be given the right job at an appropriate time" belongs in the *adaptive mode* of the *social subsystem*. The stipulation that the job should "not subject him to danger" belongs in the *conservative mode* of the *physical and personality subsystems*. "The job he undertakes should not subject him to danger or impede his course of study or limit his bodily, mental or psychological growth," belongs (in the negative sense) in the *expressive mode* of the *personality and physical subsystems*.

In B(6) we read that the child has the right to free movement. This belongs in the (*expressive mode* of the *physical subsystem*). In the same paragraph a plea is made for "the importance of peace, cordiality among nations and love for his brethren in humanity." This is a social issue in the widest sense. It belongs in the *integrative mode* of the *social subsystem*).

After having dealt with good intentions (to conform to the provisions of this Charter, to apply to criteria relating to safety and to work for a just division of wealth) the drafters of this Charter formulate their *aims*. Since no rights are mentioned in this part of the Charter, we shall only discuss some interesting highlights. In paragraph 12 of *Means and Requirements*, we read that "financial support, training and technical support should be given in order to enable them to help the families with more vigour." The text suggests that the family has not been weakened in the Arab countries as is the case in, for instance, the United States. Active co-operation of all concerned has to bring about an *esprit de corps* which will inspire towards cohesion.

Paragraph 13 calls attention to childhood as a developmental stage. It attempts to change current attitudes and make citizens more aware of childhood problems.

Paragraph 14 discusses the role of the mass media ("they are the only source of information to the illiterate"). Media should be used to educate the people, to make people more aware of childhood problems.

Paragraph 15(c) deals with family law. It relates to problems of marriage and home maintenance that may arise in Arab societies. The Charter speaks out for children within the context of a given traditional family structure. It proposes a minimum age for marriage; to control polygamy in accordance with the provisions of Islam; to allow divorce and to organise certain procedures in order to ascertain child-allowances and a home for the child, and to limit the authority of the landlord (be it father or mother). All these issues can be classified in the *adaptive mode* of the *social subsystem*.

The Charter closes with the proposals to bolster Arab co-operation through co-operation on child-welfare issues. The aim is to create "Arab generations full of the spirit of co-operation and restoring the historic initiative of our nation." The Arabs, we read in the Charter, have made an important contribution to civilisation. However, many States fell back to the level of developing countries. This Charter on Children's Rights was seen as an opportunity to restore what was lost ("the historic initiative of our nation").

Some other interesting points conclude the lengthy document. An Arab Fund for the support of child-care and development (an Arab 'UNICEF'!) is proposed; care for children should be supported, preferably through Arab owned industries (for instance an own industry for nutrition (such as baby food) or an Arab toy industry); the protection of the Palestinian child is especially mentioned as a point of concern and as an issue for the political agenda. Finally it is felt that the level of attention for children's issues should not only be increased at a societal level, but that Arab presence "in all institutions, meetings and conferences" should be increased.

10. DECLARATION OF THE RIGHTS OF THE CHILD IN ISRAEL (1989)

See Appendix XLI

In October 1988 the Equal Opportunity Fund, the EOF (a non-profit organisation dedicated to enhancing the quality of care and education of infants and

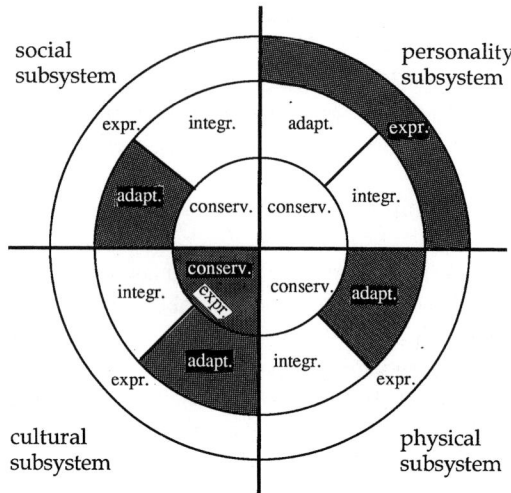

Fig. 11.8. Rights formulated by the White House Conference on Youth (1971). Interpreted by the Systemic Quality of Life Model.

pre-school children in Israel), held a lunch meeting for sponsors. During this meeting Mrs. Jehan Sadat, widow of Egyptian President Anwar Sadat, and EOF-Chairperson, Mrs. Rachel Dayan, widow of the former Israeli Minister of Defence, Moshé Dayan, signed a *Children's Bill of Rights* in Hebrew, Arabic and English, drafted by Amalia Biederman, Director of the EOF, and Yitzhak Kadman, Director of the National Council for the Child.[68]

Amalia Biederman, told me that "to raise money for early childhood

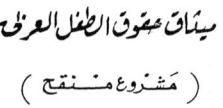

Picture XI.4. First page of the Arab Charter.

education is not easy and we needed a gimmick to bring some donors together."[69] Since this Bill aimed at raising funds rather than at declaring rights, it has been included in the present study as a note[70] rather than as an appendix. Although the EOF's 'Children's Bill of Rights' was itself of little importance, it initiated the idea of a more serious Declaration, which we will now discuss.

The year 1989 marked the 10th anniversary of the International Year of the Child, as well as the 30th anniversary of the United Nations Declaration on the Rights of the Child. UNICEF asked the nations of the world to commemorate these events and to centre activities around the subject of Children's Rights. The Israel National Council for the Child, the EOF, the Organisation 'Variety', the International Cultural Centre for Youth and other organisations working on behalf of child welfare in Israel, decided to publish a *Declaration on the Rights of the Child in Israel.*[71]

On April 3, 1989, the 'Rights of the Child Year' was formally launched in the residence of President Herzog. Here the *Declaration of the Rights of the Child in Israel* was read by two primary school children, in Hebrew by Asaf Brezis and in Arabic by Anan Hyadra. After this moving scene the Declaration was signed by Mrs. Aura Herzog and Supreme Court Justice Gavriel Bach.

November 28, 1989, was 'Children's Rights Day' in the Israeli Parliament (the Knesset). Many Members of Parliament added their signatures to the Declaration.

One critic[72] wrote: "The Declaration has some relevance because important people signed it, but it has no legal validity."

While drafting the Declaration, Dr. Kadman had consulted some experts and several child-welfare organisations. The result was a lengthy document, as well as a shorter version[73] published as a poster and displayed in many child-welfare institutions in Israel. The National Council for the Child uses the abbreviated version and we shall do the same. If necessary we shall refer to the original text and to an explanatory letter Dr. Kadman wrote us.

It strikes the eye that the rights mentioned in this Declaration were proclaimed for "every boy and girl in Israel."

Principle 1 is concerned with the development in *all four subsystems*. In the Hebrew text, which is somewhat more elaborate than the English translation, we read that every child has "the right to receive the opportunity and possibility to grow and develop physically, morally, spiritually, socially in a healthy and proper form in conditions of freedom and honour." *To grow and develop* belongs in the *expressive mode* of *all four subsystems*.

Principle 2 ("the right to a family life") is based on the assumption that living in a family is best. (The pioneers who founded the first kibbutzim would not have agreed.) The Principle also states what the child should receive from the family: "nourishment, suitable housing, protection, love and understanding." The original text subsequently declares that "the child will not be separated from his or her parents except under exceptional circumstances. In such cases the child will have the right to an appropriate substitute home, as similar as possible to the child's own milieu, while keeping contact with his or her natural family." *Family life* is seen as the means to provide nourishment, belonging in the *adaptive mode* of the *physical subsystem*, suitable housing, belonging in the *adaptive mode* of the *physical subsystem*, protection belonging in the *conservative mode* of the *physical subsystem*, love belonging in the *integrative mode* of the *social subsystem*, and understanding belonging in the *integrative mode* of the *social subsystem* and in the *adaptive mode of the personality subsystem*. We have added this last category of the 'Systemic Quality of Life Model' to our list because *understanding* makes it easier for the child to interact with the environment. In this case the environment allows the child to be an individual.

Principle 3 ("the right to an identity – to be given a name and nationality") is in the Hebrew text "to be a subject".[74] Dr. Kadman wrote me that the difference between the English and the Hebrew text was not intentional. However, the right to be a *subject* or a *citizen* is weaker than the right to a *nationality*. When we analysed the Declaration on the Rights of the Child of the United Nations, we already saw that the right to a nationality belongs in the *adaptive mode* of the *social subsystem*, and also in the *adaptive mode* of the *physical subsystem* (physical security, the right to live in a State). The right to a name belongs in the *adaptive mode* of the *social subsystem*.

Principle 4 mentions education[75] as a *means* to "self-realisation, equal opportunity, fulfilling his or her ability and talents."[76] Kindergartens and schools are, in our opinion, 'social institutions' which enable self-realisation etc. We classify this paragraph in the *adaptive mode* of the *expressive-personality sub-subsystem* and the *adaptive mode* of the *expressive-social sub-subsystem*. The reference to self-realisation[77] stems, in our opinion, from a concern for the *adaptive mode* of the *personality subsystem*.

Principle 5 deals with the right to privacy. "Confidentiality and protection of his or her property" are explicitly mentioned. Our interpretation is that absence of *confidentiality* threatens to damage a child's personality. We therefore classify this principle in the *conservative mode* of the *personality subsystem*. However, it belongs also in the *expressive mode* of the *social subsystem* (it can damage his or her social status), and in the *adaptive mode* of the *social subsystem* (inter-action between child and environment). "Protection of his or her property" mainly relates to the *physical belongings of the child. It belongs in the adaptive mode* of the *physical subsystem*.

Principle 6 ("not to be exploited by neglect or cruelty")[78] belongs in the *conservative mode* of the *physical subsystem* and in the *conservative mode* of the *personality subsystem* ("not to be exploited ... by humiliation").

Principle 7 ("the right to ... sensitive treatment within the legal system.")[79] warns that legal proceedings may hurt the child's personality. It belongs in the *conservative mode* of the *personality subsystem*).

Principle 8 states "the right to integration in society and ... to non-discriminatory treatment". Although it is, no doubt, by adaptive-social proce-

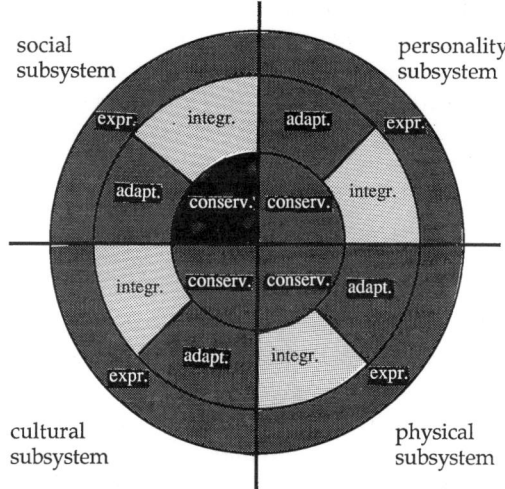

Fig. 11.9. The Charter on the Rights of the Arab Child of the League of Arab States (1984). Interpreted by the Systemic Quality of Life Model.

dures that a person becomes integrated into society, the concern is here with the *expressive mode* of the *personality subsystem* (to express him- or herself without being discriminated against).

Principle 9 ("the right to self-expression") also belongs in the *expressive mode* of the *personality subsystem*.

Principle 10 (priority treatment in cases of emergency) is to be classified in the *conservative mode* of the *physical subsystem*[80], since it is concerned with the child's physical safety.

11. Declaration of the Rights of Mozambican Children (1979)

See Appendix XXXII

An interesting national Declaration has been issued by the socialist African State Mozambique (which became independent on June 25, 1975). In 1979 the Declaration of the Rights of the Mozambican Children was adopted by Mozambique's Legislative Assembly,[81] the 'People's Assembly'. The Declaration is rather unknown, but since it has been published in English as an appendix in the book *The Next Generation*,[82] it will hopefully draw the attention it deserves.[83] In style the Declaration of the one-party State, run by the Front for Liberation of Mozambique (FRELIMO), reminds us of Harry Truman's 1950 *Pledge to the Children*. "You, the children," it starts "are the ones who will carry on the revolution."

The first paragraph of the Mozambican Declaration ("Socialism means justice, means every citizen having the same rights and duties") is classifiable in the *adaptive mode* of the *integrative-social sub-subsystem* (equality is seen as a framework for love).

The second paragraph stresses the right to grow up in security (*conservative mode* of the *social subsystem*) and surrounded by love (*integrative mode* of the *social subsystem*).

The third paragraph stresses the importance of the family. ("You have the right to live in a family.") This belongs in the *integrative mode* of the *social subsystem*. The right to a name is also mentioned in this paragraph. ("You have the right to a name, so that your parents, brothers and sisters can call you and so that you can be known where-ever you are.") This clearly belongs in the *conservative mode* of the *personality subsystem*.

The fourth paragraph ("You have the right to play and practice sports, so that your body develops full of health and energy") belongs in the *expressive mode* of the *physical subsystem*, and in the *integrative mode* of the *physical subsystem*. The child's right to be educated by his or her family is repeated. This concern belongs in the *integrative mode* of the *social subsystem* (intimacy).

Paragraph five ("the right to receive education so that you will become a citizen of tomorrow") stresses the right to education as a means to become socially integrated. It is classifiable in *the adaptive mode* of the *social subsystem*.

"You have the right to know about the world in which you are living and how to transform it," belongs in the *expressive mode* of the *physical subsystem* and in the *expressive mode* of the *social subsystem*.

"The right to know the history and culture of your people," belongs in the *conservative mode* of the *cultural subsystem* (identity).

"The right to learn to master science and technology" belongs in the *expressive mode* of the *physical subsystem*.

The last sentence of paragraph five is an elaboration of children's rights. It states that rights should be an instrument "to understand the world in a scientific and revolutionary way, and to know and love your country and all peoples of the world." It is the task of the schools to teach this.

Ennew and Milne report that "schools are a major component of Mozambican reform, and education takes up about a quarter of public spending. In the years of independence, adults and children have been able to take up educational opportunities which had been denied to black Mozambicans by the Portuguese colonists. Despite scarce resources, teachers who are barely trained themselves, and a curriculum and school system still based largely on the Portuguese model, there have been innovations in both content and method."

Paragraph six repeats the child's right to education and adds that this right is given "so that when you are grown up you can fulfil your duty of serving the people." The last sentence ("You have the right to be educated to respect work, to respect the people's property, and to participate in production") explains that this paragraph is concerned with social adaptation. It belongs in the *adaptive mode* of the *social subsystem*.

Paragraph seven belongs in the *adaptive mode* of the *social subsystem*. Kindergartens are given to the Mozambican toddlers. The Legislative Assembly even promises to "increase their number so that they can have room for every child in the country."

Paragraph eight deals with ongoing health ("You have the right to protection of your health, to live in a healthy environment, to have a good diet, to be taught how to defend yourself against illness. When you are ill you have the right to be treated with the best medical care"). This belongs in the *integrative mode* of the *physical subsystem*.

Since the rate of infant mortality in Mozambique is one of the highest in Africa, this paragraph is certainly also written out of concern for the very life of the children. This belongs in the *conservative mode* of the *physical subsystem*.

The concern expressed in the ninth paragraph is typically African: "You have the right *not* to be submitted to initiation rites, premature marriage or bride-price." No infringement on the *expressive mode* of the *physical subsystem* and of the *personality subsystem* is allowed. The last part of paragraph nine expresses a concern for the physical safety of children and youth. The text is not clear, but we imagine it deals with a concern for the damaging results of child labour. We classify it in the *conservative mode* of the *physical subsystem*.

Paragraph ten ("You have the right not to be subjected to violence and ill treatment") expresses a concern for the *adaptive* and *conservative modes* of the *physical subsystem*.

Unfortunately this paragraph and paragraph eleven, which is concerned with the *conservative mode* of the *physical subsystem* ("In dangerous situations, you have the right to be among the first to receive help and protection") became relevant when in 1980 the Mozambican FRELIMO government had to face an armed insurgency identifying itself as the Mozambican National Resistance (RENAMO).

Since 1980 RENAMO has abducted children in order to train them in military camps to become combatants. Boothby reports[84] that RENAMO has forced many children to kill other human beings, sometimes even members of their own families.

The last paragraph ("the right to take part in the organisation of Mozambican Pioneers") belongs in the *adaptive mode* of the *social subsystem*. It aims at mobilising the children to take part in the revolution and could also be explained as a way to enforce FRELIMO government policies, norms and values. In that case (but the text is not very clear), we can also classify this paragraph in the *adaptive mode* of the *cultural subsystem*.

270   *Chapter XI*

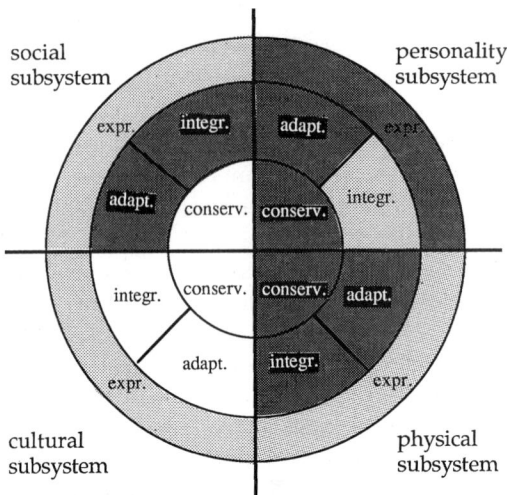

Fig. 11.10. The Declaration of the Rights of the Child in Israel (1989). Interpreted by the Systemic Quality of Life Model.

12. TOWARDS NEW REGIONAL CHARTERS

The drafting of National and Regional Declarations and Conventions on the Rights of the Child is an ongoing process. In January 1984 the International Union for Child Welfare (IUCW) issued a 'first draft' of a *European Convention for the Protection of the Rights of the Child*.[85] In 1979 the Assembly of the *Council of Europe*[86] had already proposed the creation of such a European Convention on the Rights of the Child, but the Committee of Ministers did not follow up this idea.[87] The International Union for Child Welfare presented a memorandum[88] to the Council of Europe in which they claimed that the provisions for protecting children in Europe were seriously inadequate and that such a Convention was therefore necessary.

The IUCW asked: "Is the situation of European children such as to render superfluous any specific implementation of the provisions of the Declaration of the Rights of the Child? Are there no longer any children who are denied their rights, or who do not enjoy the full exercise of the rights mentioned in the Declaration? This is far from being the case. Thousands of children, everywhere in Europe, are undergoing serious physical and psychological mistreatment. Every year hundreds are beaten or tortured to death. Thousands of children are put to work as prostitutes: an official document mentions a horrifying number in the city of Paris alone. The huge numbers exposed to drug addiction are constantly on the increase, and ever younger children are at risk. What about the children in institutions who are denied the right to a family, the right to love, because of the tremendous obstacles set in the way of adoption by regulations inspired by the bourgeois preoccupation with the protection of inherited wealth? In addition, it is in Europe that tens of thousands of immigrants' children are employed in what can justly be called 'forced labour', in 'unacceptable and sometimes dangerous conditions'. To quote only one example, children aged nine to fourteen can be seen in Berlin slaving from the dawn, handling, sorting and washing early fruit and vegetables. The youngest are fed but not paid. See: (*Le Monde*, 18.8.1983)."

With many other examples the IUCW tried to convince the Council of Europe to call a Convention for the Member-States of the Council. However, the Ministers were not yet convinced of the need of such a Convention.

In 1989 it was more and more felt that even after the acceptance of the Universal Standard of the United Nations Convention on the Rights of the Child, a European Convention[88] might push for revisions of some laws of the Member-States (and especially future Easter-European Member-States). When the Council of Europe would consider membership, it would at the same time consider the rights of children in each applying State. Some provisions in former Communist States were good and should be preserved, others should be changed. It became clear that the *United Nations Convention on the Rights of the Child* was not the last word and *regional* Conventions could be used to push for specific issues or, as in the case of Europe, for higher standards.

These new considerations led to recommendations of the Parliamentary Assembly of the Council of Europe to establish new European standards of children's Rights.[89] The new thought was that to establish a Convention would be an easy way out for some governments. However, to add a *protocol* to the European Convention on Human Rights would make the position of children's rights in Europe even stronger.

13. THE CHARTER ON THE RIGHTS AND WELFARE OF THE AFRICAN CHILD (1990)

See Appendix XLV

In other regions, such as Africa, where a monitoring-machinery and a strong secretariat on human rights do not yet exist, a special Convention might strengthen the position of children and their rights.

In 1988 a Convention, the African Charter on the Rights of the Child, was prepared by the Organisation of African Unity (OAU). A strong input came from ANPPCAN, the African Network for the Prevention and Protection Against Child Abuse and Neglect, an African N.G.O. In July 1990 it was approved by the OAU-Assembly and later also by the Committee of Ministers.

A draft Charter on the Rights and Welfare of the African Child was circulated among all OAU Member States. It contained a Preamble, Articles on Rights and Responsibilities, Articles that establish a Committee on the

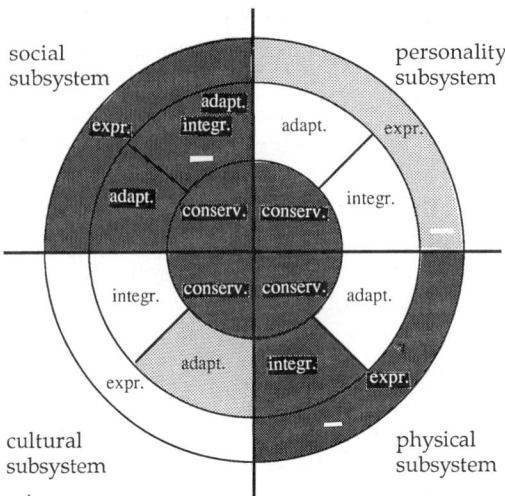

Fig. 11.11. The Declaration of the Rights of Mozambican Children (1979). Interpreted by the Systemic Quality of Life Model.

Rights of the Child and Articles dealing with Administrative dispositions. In April 1990 preparatory meetings for the issuing of this *African Charter* were held in Addis Abbeba.[90] The Sudanese delegate opened by commenting that he was struck by the lack of specificity in the document and wanted guidance as to how it differed from the United Nations Convention. The representatives of Senegal stated that the Preamble was unsatisfactory and that it

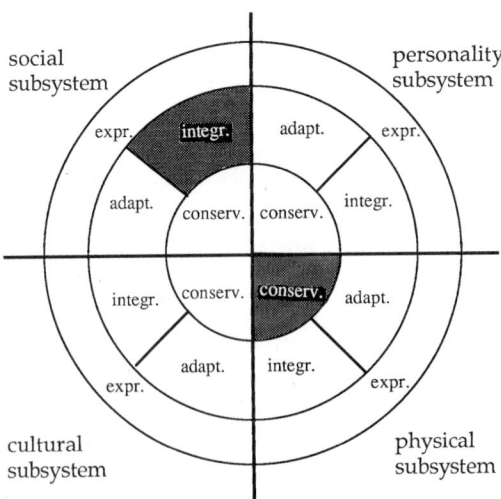

Fig. 11.12. The special emphasis of the African Charter of the Rights of the Child (1990). Interpreted by the Systemic Quality of Life Model.

should reflect the economic and social conditions in Africa more adequately. They insisted on mentioning that more than 50% of the overall population of Africa were young people, and that in some countries 55% of the population were younger than eighteen. The representative of Nigeria mentioned that illegitimate children had specific rights that were not covered by the Draft Charter. The representative of Swaziland wanted Parents' Rights to be mentioned. The representative of Botswana wanted the draft re-written so as to be comprehensible to children. He also raised the question of Sharia (Islamic) law. Representatives of Uganda, Lesotho, Tunisia and Ethiopia also had comments. The representatives of all these States mentioned the importance of drawing up strategies for the implementation of the Charter after it would have been approved. The Summit of the Heads of State of the OAU endorsed the Charter on July 11, 1990. The Convention is now open for ratification by the OAU Member-States.[91] Promises were also made at the OAU Summit in June 1991 in Abuja, Nigeria.

Most of the provisions are similar to the United Nations Convention but several additional Articles relate specifically to Africa. This African Charter is based on the exceptional economic and social conditions in Africa today. According to Amos Wako[92] the inclusion that 'State Parties shall ensure to the maximum extent possible the survival and development of the child' is a positive development in Africa[93] where more than four million children under five years of age die each year because of malnutrition and ill-health. Wako also says that access to health care is a priority in Africa. There is a specific Article condemning Apartheid, and another Article condemning traditional practices such as female circumcision. Special reference is made to the extended family and the responsibility of parents for their children. These issues are to be classified in the *integrative mode* of the *social subsystem* and the *conservative mode* of the *physical subsystem*.

The process of drafting National and Regional Declarations and Conventions will continue.[94] They clearly fulfil a need. While international standards are made and/or approved by international bodies, national and regional Charters are often tuned in with specific cultural settings. If, therefore, certain international standards are elaborated upon and translated into national and regional standards, the international standards (often described in very vague terms) will be strengthened. We should not forget, however, that such national and regional Conventions can also be used as an excuse for not adhering to international standards. It should always be the higher standard that applies.

NOTES

1. A letter, dated April 27th, 1932, by Mrs. Aida de Acosta Breckinridge, director of the department publications and promotion of the *American Child Health Organisation* to Mr.

French Strother in the White House in Washington D.C., and kept in the *Herbert Hoover Presidential Library* in West Branch, Iowa, ack 4/29/32.
2. *Mother and Child*, February 1923, Magazine of the American Child Hygiene Association.
3. Hoover, Herbert. 'May Day, Child Health Day' in *McClures Magazine*, May 1925.
4. Letter by Mrs. A. de Acosta Breckinridge, see Note 1.
5. In the publication *School Life*, of the Department of the Interior, Bureau of Education, Washington D.C., May 16th, 1919, No. 10, Vol.II, p. 1, we read that the White House Conference of 1919 had also adopted what President Wilson called "irreducible minimum standards of child welfare". School Life summarizes as follows: "The standards drawn up, set 16 as the lowest age at which children can go to work in any occupation during the months when school is in session. Nine months' schooling, either full- or part-time, for children between 7 and 8 years of age is proposed as the minimum educational standard. A child of 16 cannot go to work unless he has completed the eighth grade. Education beyond the eighth grade is to be provided for employed children between 16 and 18 years old by attendance at day continuation schools. Tentative standards for public protection of the health of the school child were adapted." National Archives File 10–8–7–2–0.
6. Beck, Rochelle, 'The White House Conferences and Children: An Historical Perspective' in: *Harvard Educational Review*, Vol. 43, No. 4, November 1973, p. 656.
7. After the stock market had collapsed, just before the end of Hoover's term, between 12 and 14 million Americans lost their jobs.
8. Hoover, Herbert, *Memoirs*, Part II, p. 261. According to the *New York Times* of November 27, 1930, p. 20, the President did not close the conference himself. This was done by Ray Wilbur who presented a summary of the conference, also drawn up in nineteen paragraphs (somewhat different from those of the Children's Charter).
9. *The Memoirs of Ray Lyman Wilbur*, 1875–1949, E.E. Robinson and Paul C. Edwards, editors, Stanford, L.A., 1960, Stanford University Press, p. 525. Wilbur presided over the *White House Conference on Child Health and Protection*.
10. Finley's article was mentioned in a note by his editors Robinson and Edwards on page 525 of Wilbur's Memoirs. However, I have not been able to find an article about the conference by John H. Finley in the New York Times. It is highly probable that the editorial of November 24th, 1930, (p.22, section BQ) is his. In this editorial we read: "A law, proposed in the middle of the (First World) War by the British Minister of Education, was sometimes called 'The Children's Charter', but what became a law in the United Kingdom cannot be compared with the concern about the child emanating from what was adopted by the *White House Conference* last Saturday.

The *Children's Charter of* 1898 (whereto this editorial of the New York Times related) in the United Kingdom regulated child labour and made child abuse punishable. The police force and the judicial authorities became authorised to intervene in domestic affairs where child abuse took place or was suspected. They could board children out. See J.S. Heywood *Children in English Society*, Vol.II, Chapter XX, London, 1970–1973, pp. 103–104).
11. Article by Grace Abbott: 'What can we expect of the White House Conference?', found in the records of the *Children's Bureau* (National Archives, Washington D.C., file 0–1–0–4³, Ab.2). Mrs. Abbott was the director of the (Federal) Children's Bureau in Washington D.C.
12. Lenroot, Katharine, F., 'The Challenge of the White House Conference', notes from her lecture at the West Virginia Conference of Social Work (National Archives, Washington, Children's Bureau file 0–1–0–4³ L 542 C).
13. Grace Abbott. See Note 11.
14. Lenroot, Katharine, F., *The Needs of Children in Wartime as seen by the Children's Bureau*, paper presented to the Conference for consideration on March 16,1942.
15. Katharine F. Lenroot, "The Challenge of the White House Conference," Op. cit, saw that this were only Points 1, 2, 3, 7 and 15.
16. *White House Conference on Child Health and Protection*, Washington, D.C., p. 137. The records of the Children's Bureau in the National Archives include about five linear feet of

correspondence relating to the White House Conference on Child Health and Protection which took place on November 19–22, 1930. The Hoover Library recently acquired leaflets published by the Conference and nineteen volumes relating to the Conference published by the Century Company, 1931–36.
17. *New York Times*, 23 November 1930, p. 20.
18. "The Conference Resolutions a 'string of platitudes'" in: *The Nation* (1930), December 3, reprinted in Bremner, Robert, H., editor, *Children and youth in America, A Documentary History*, Vol.II: 1866–1932, Cambridge, Mass., 1971, Harvard University Press, p. 1083.
19. Ellis, Edward Robb, *A Nation in Torment, The Great American Repression* 1929–1939, New York, 1970, Coward-McConn, pp. 239–240.
20. Folks, Chairman, "Socially Handicapped – Dependency and Neglect" in: *White House Conference 1930, addresses and abstracts of Committee Reports*, New York, 1931, The Century Co., pp. 332–333.
21. Abbott, Grace, "analysis of Point IV of the Children's Charter", unpublished, found in the National Archives in Washington, D.C., No. 0–1–0–4³/69, Ab.2.
22. According to Adair about 15,000 mothers and 80,000 babies died every year in the United States.
23. Ellis, William, J. (Chairman of the Section IV – Commission B of the Conference); A Bill of Rights for the Handicapped Child" in: *White House Conference* 1930, pp. 291–292.
24. See the Report of Cabot, Frederick, P. (judge and Chairman of Section IV, Committee C-2) in: White House Conference 1930, Op. cit., 00.341–345.
25. Lenroot, Katharine, F., *The Needs of Children in Wartime as seen by the Children's Bureau*, paper presented to the conference for consideration on March, 16, 1942.
26. Children's Bureau, *Commission on Children in Wartime* (1942) p. 43. in the National Archives in Washington D.C.
27. Apparently the draft dealt only with American children, because Casparis pleaded for the broadening of the first paragraph (in: Children's Bureau 1942 File, National Archives).
28. Mr. Hopkirk in: *Commission on Children in Wartime*, 1942, p. 65, National Archives.
29. Commission on Children in Wartime, p. 57.
30. The text of the Children's Charter sub II (Defense Areas).
31. Commission on Children in Wartime, in National Archives, Washington D.C.
32. Idem.
33. Lenroot, Katharine, F., 'The Significance of the Eighth Pan American Child Congress', in: *Bulletin of the Pan American Union*, Vol.LXXVI, No. 7, July 1942, p. 361.
34. The *New York Times*, May 3, 1942.
35. Idem.
36. Lenroot, Katharine, F., 1942, Op. cit., p. 365.
37. Unfortunately I was not able to locate the signed document. Beverly D. Wharton-Lake, Records Specialist, Records Management Center of the Organization of American States in Washington D.C., wrote me: "I spoke with you recently regarding the Final Act of the 8th Inter-American Conference on Children and had promised to do some further checking for you. Unfortunately, I have been unable to locate here at Headquarters the Final Act with signatures." I therefore assumed that the document was in Montevideo (Uruguay) in the Inter-American Children's Institute. However, upon my request, I received a cable: "Regret to inform you document pertaining to 8th Pan-American Child Congress with signatures not at IACI. Sincerely Rodrigo Crespo, Director IACI.
38. See: *Eighth Pan American Child Congress, Washington, D.C., May 2–9, 1942*, 1942, Washington D.C., U.S. Government Printing Office; Also: *Final Act of the Eighth Pan American Child Congress, Washington, D.C., May 2–9, 1942*, Washington D.C., 1942, Pan American Union, Congress and Conference Series No. 37.
39. Lenroot, Katharina, F., 1942, Op. cit., p. 364. I like to thank Mr. Thomas Walch of the OAS (Columbus Memorial Library) in Washington D.C. for his help.
40. Shye, Samuel, *A Systemic Facet-Theoretical Approach to the Study of Quality of Life*,

Jerusalem, 1979, Israel Institute of Applied Social Research, (study supported by the Ford Foundation).
41. Child Welfare League of America, Inc., *Selected References on Rights of Children* 1970–1986, New York, N.Y.
42. From New York City I phoned the State Archives in Albany, the Assembly Document Room, the General Council Youth Division and ten other State Officials of the State of New York, but in vain; no one had ever heard of this *Children's Bill of Rights*. Finally it was Linda A. Braun, of the State Education Department of the University of the State of New York in Albany, N.Y., and the New York State Library who unearthed the document, which was printed as a poster (No. 590/4 CHYBR).
43. Lee C. Dowling wrote (in his article 'The Program of the New York State Youth Commission' in: *New York State Welfare Conference Proceedings*, 51st Annual Meeting, New York City, 1950): "Early in 1943, Governor Dewey, recognizing the social importance of the problem of juvenile delinquency, as well as the rising tide of crimes committed by youths, took effective action by appointing an inter-departmental committee to study juvenile delinquency and to make recommendations particularly as to a program of prevention.
44. State of New York, *Public Papers of Thomas E. Dewey, Fifty-First Governor of the State of New York*, 1950, p. 105.
45. Idem, p. 113.
46. Bandura, A., Social learning through imitation, in: Jones M.R. (Ed.), *Nebraska symposium on motivation*: 1962, Lincoln, 1962, University of Nebraska Press, pp. 211–269. Bandura, A. and Walters, R.H., *Social learning and personality development*, New York, 1963, Holt, Ninehout and Wilson, LO.
47. Grotberg, Edith, H., editor, 200 *Years of Children*, Washington D.C., 1977, U.S. Department of Health Education and Welfare, p. 411.
48. Bremner, Robert, H., *Children and youth in America, A Documentary History, Vol.III*: 1933–1973, Cambridge, Mass., 1974, Harvard University Press, p. 185.
49. Idem, pp. 183–184.
50. Stephen Hess chaired the 1970 and 1976 Conferences, and works today at the Brookings Institution, Government Studies Program in Washington D.C.
51. Hess, Stephen, letter to President Richard M. Nixon, in: *Report to the President, White House Conference on Children* 1970, Washington D.C., U.S. Government Printing Office.
52. Interesting observations of this White House Conference were made by Thomas J. Cottle. They were published in his book *Private Lives and Public Accounts*, Amherst, 1977, University of Mass. Press, pp. 160–177.
53. Beck, Rochelle, 'The White House Conferences on Children: An Historical Perspective', in: *Harvard Educational Review*, Vol. 43, No. 4, November 1973, p. 664. Prof. Irvin N. Berlin (Professor of Psychiatry and Pediatrics) wrote me on June 27, 1990: "Mary Kohler was Director of The National Council on Children. As a member of that Council and of the White House Conference, several of us got Mary Kohler to present the previous Congressional Commission's concerns about children's rights. Mary Kohler then was an elderly lady with a great concern for children. Her daughter and son-in-law are very well-known sociologists who are child advocates".
54. The following can be found in the Nixon Presidential Materials in the National Archives: Special Files of H.R. Haldeman: Alpha-Subject File, container No. 157, in a folder entitled "White House Conference on Children and Youth Background Material," dated August 14th, 1970. There are other scattered references to the White House Conference on Youth in Haldeman's Files. The White House Central Files: Subject Files relating to Meetings – Conferences (MC), especially MC 4, White House Conference on Children and Youth, contain eight file folders of correspondence, memoranda, reports and addresses by Stephen Hess, the national chairman of the conference; newsletters, newspaper clippings, reports of the conference forums, and the Black Caucus position paper on the conference, as well as other topics. In addition, the first two containers of FG 32, Department of Health, Education and Welfare, should be consulted for supplemental materials.

55. *White House Conference on Children* 1970, Report of Forum 22, p. 345.
56. Idem, p. 347.
57. Idem.
58. The right to an effective assessment of his capability using all new research methodology, especially utilizing that methodology which best evaluates the most effective sensory input modality and therefore gears the learning to the talents and unique potential of the child.
   Freedom to express ideas verbally and in print, as well as by wearing buttons, badges, armbands, or insignia.
   Opportunity to refuse, without penalty or embarrassment to participate in ceremonies and activities expressing loyalty to or agreement with any belief or symbol.
   Due process in any procedure involving loss of the right to attend or fully participate in school activities. Moreover, it should be a child's prerogative to negotiate with school officials on issues involving his rights.
   Freedom from corporal punishment.
   Protection from unauthorized use of school records, the indiscriminate use of tests and similar screening devices, and the release of such data to sources outside the school without the pupil's knowledge and consent. The child and parents should also have the opportunity to review the records periodically and insert clarifying or countervailing material.
   Freedom to follow their own taste in clothing and grooming.
59. These Specific Rights for Children are not only mentioned in *Report of Forum* 22: *The Rights of Children*, White House Conference on Children 1970, pp. 350–361, but also in a Chapter written by Mary Kohler ('To What Are Children Entitled?') in the book: *The Children's Rights Movement*, edited by Beatrice and Ronald Gross, New York, 1977, pp. 217–232. It is strange that only a single footnote refers to the White House Conference of 1970.
60. *Report of Forum* 22, Op. cit.,p.353.
61. Kohler, Mary, 'To what are Children Entitled?' Op. cit., p. 223. This article appeared earlier in the periodical *Social Policy*, March/April 1971, pp. 36–43.
62. *Report of Forum* 22, p. 355.
63. Mr. Nabil Masarweh, Chargé d'Affaires a.i. of the Embassy of Jordan in Brussels, Belgium sent me, to my address in the Netherlands, the Arab text of the *Charter on the Rights of the Arab Child*. It was translated for me into English by Mr. Samir Bayyuk, a translator working for the British Consulate-General in East Jerusalem. A summary of the Charter distributed by the Nour Al-Hussein Foundation in Amman, Jordan, was later used by the author to adapt the translation of Mr. Bayyuk. I like to thank Simone Ek of Rädda Barnen (Swedish Save the Children) for sending me the summary of the Nour Al-Hussein Foundation.
64. Established in March 1945 in Cairo. Aims: to strengthen links between Member States, co-ordinate their political plans in such a way as to permit co-operation between States, safeguard their independence and their sovereignty, and in general consider all matters affecting Arab countries and their interests.
   I could not establish from the available documents in which year, exactly, the Charter of the Rights of the Arab Child was adopted by the Ministers of the League of Arab States.
65. According to the introduction to the Charter of 6 October 1986 (The Nour Al-Hussein Foundation, Amman, Jordan) on the occasion of the publication in Jordan.
66. Mr. Hakan Landelius, Secretary General of Rädda Barnen, in: proceedings of the *International Symposium on the Protection of Children*, Amman, Jordan, November 1984, published by the Independent Commission on International Humanitarian Issues and Rädda Barnen, p. 70.
67. *International Symposium*, Op. cit., pp. 57–58.
68. The E.O.F. tries to push early childhood education in Israel higher up the scale of national priorities.
69. Interview with Amalia Biederman in Tel Aviv in March 1989.
70. The Children's Bill of Rights' of Rahel Dayan and Jehan Sadat signed in New York City

on October 27, 1988. Here is the text of this *Children's Bill of Rights*:
From the moment of his birth the child is a full member of the human race. Children can neither be a property nor can they be used as a means to attain an objective – they are the objective itself.

The child, because of his physical and psychological immaturity, requires exceptional protection and care. His dependence on the adults demands that meticulous attention be paid to guaranteeing his rights so that his present and future well-being and development be ensured. The children of today's world are the citizens of tomorrow and it is they who will determine our future. The Equal Opportunity Fund strives to foster the protection of children's rights in order to achieve and ensure their well-being and optimal development. Therefore, we hereby present our Bill of Children's Rights:

The rights as declared in this Bill pertain to each and every child irrespective of his race, religion, sex, age, background, creed or any other reason for discrimination.

1. It is the right of every child to be given the opportunity to grow and develop physically, mentally, morally, intellectually and socially in normal and healthy circumstances in freedom and respect.
2. Every child has the right to grow up in his parental home, there to be maintained, educated, protected and loved.
3. Every child has the right to be given a name and a nationality on his birth.
4. Every child has the right to social security rooted in state law. It is his right to receive free care and education of optimal scope and standard, in a manner appropriate to his abilities and talents and ensuring the fullest exploitation of his potential.
5. Every child suffering from any disability, illness, impairment or handicap has the right to receive education and treatment best suited to his needs with the aim of his full integration in society.
6. Every child has a right to privacy, confidentiality and protection of property.
7. Every child has the right to proper representation and full legal defence in any litigation which concerns him directly and is entitled to benefit from the principle that the best interest of the child is the prime consideration, over and above any other legal aspects.
8. Every child who has suffered bodily harm or property damage has the right to be interrogated by a suitably trained person and not by a member of the police force and has the right to full protection from harmful public exposure in the course of court proceedings.
9. Every child has the right to be exonerated from criminal responsibility and to receive proper and suitable alternative treatment whenever he has perpetrated a criminal offence while still a minor.
10. Every child has the right to be fully and effectively protected from:
    * Neglect, abuse, cruelty, physical and psychological exploitation in any form whatsoever.
    * Harmful exposure in the communication media.
    * Unfair commercial dealings.
    * Work or employment detrimental to his education, health or development.
    * Harm in times of disasters or emergencies and, at such times, he should be entitled to priority in receiving succour and care.
    To ensure the full implementation of the above rights, society is required to maximize its efforts to:
    * Promote research and study in the field of education, care, protection and advancement of the child.
    * Promote legislation governing children's rights, their lives and welfare.
    * Promote greater investment of funds by government and other public bodies rightly due to projects connected to the advancement of children.
71. National Council for the Child, 1989 *Child Rights Year, Program of Activities and Events*, Jerusalem, 1988.
72. Veerman, Philip, 'On Israel's Declaration on the Rights of the Child', in: *The Jerusalem Post*, April 3, 1989. "The U.N. Declaration on the Rights of the Child, unanimously adopted

by the General Assembly on November 20, 1959, is far more important as far as Israel is concerned, as it has become part of accepted international law. The Israeli Declaration's promulgation today is, nevertheless, a welcome initiative which should raise public consciousness of children's rights. However, the challenge for Israeli child-welfare organisations will come when they begin lobbying for ratification of the planned U.N. Convention on the Rights of the Child by the Israeli Government."

73. There were two abbreviated versions, one comprising ten, the other comprising eleven principles. (Principle 11: 'As a child I have the right to . . .")
74. In Hebrew: rétinut.
75. In the Hebrew text Principle 4 (deleted in the abbreviated English version) "The right of every child to enjoy social security, anchored in law, including children's allowance services (not specified), medical treatment to the child himself and his mother, before birth, during birth and after birth." Social security can be classified in the *adaptive mode* of the *social subsystem*, medical care (ongoing health) and the *integrative mode* of the *physical subsystem*.
76. In the Hebrew text: *Free education*.
77. The Hebrew text mentions "the right to receive free education in maximum scope and quality until the completion of his high school, which should guide his abilities and talents in a way that will suit his or her talents *in the full realisation of his potential*.
78. In the Hebrew text this is Principle 7. It reads: "The right to efficient and full protection from any kind of neglect, exploitation, cruelty, torture or humiliation either physical or mental in his or her parents' home or outside it.

    Principle 8 in the Hebrew text states: "It is the child's right to be protected from unfair exploitation in commerce, advertisements and economic inter-relations. The child should be protected from employment which might hurt his health, education and normal development. The child has the right to be protected against harmful exposure in the mass-media.

    Yitzhak Kadman explained me that his intention of the first paragraph was in the first place to protect children against being cheated by vendors who make them sign for things they do not need. The last paragraph, Kadman explained, aims at avoiding that a child's name would be published in the newspapers if that child had been the victim of sexual abuse. Likewise it aims at protecting the child's name if the father has transgressed the law.
79. In Hebrew this principle states: "The right to enjoy a special attitude from the part of the judicial system and law-makers and full judicial defence in every judicial proceedings that might relate to the child, giving priority to the principle of the best interests of the child in judicial proceedings, and above this the right to receive professional treatment, avoidance of exposure to police investigations and testimony in court in cases of transgressions against his or her body or property.

    Dr. Kadman explained that he meant here: limited arrest periods, separation of minors from adult prisoners, the possibility of erasing a 'criminal record' etc.
80. The Hebrew version comprises as a separate right: "the right to medical treatment, treatment of emotional disturbances and care for the mentally retarded, with the aim of preventing disease and handicap." This is classifiable in the *integrative mode* of the *physical* and *personality subsystems*.
81. I thank Ilene Cohn of 'The children and War Project' of Columbia University in the City of New York. Ilene works often in Mozambique and she wrote me when this Declaration was adopted.
82. Ennew, Judith and Milne, Brian, *The Next Generation*, London, 1989, Red Books p. 217. One of the authors, Brian Milne, wrote to me: "To answer your question about the Mozambican Declaration . . . It was given to us rather casually by someone who had been there and had acquired this translation. We no longer know where that person is and were unable to give direct reference ourselves. It was, we know, drawn up by children (probably youths) but the actual body, organisation or who was involved personally remains unknown. A friend was field officer for Save the Children in Maputo at that time and was unable to find out for us. However, it is, he assured us, quite genuine and had been circulated to N.G.O.s throughout the country".

83. Ennew and Milne, Op. cit., p. 103.
84. Boothby, Neil, *Working in the War Zone, A Look at Psychological Theory and Practice from the Field*, paper presented at the 'Children in War Conference', on June 25, 1990, in Jerusalem. This paper is published in: *Mind and Human Interaction*, Vol.2, No. 2, October 1990, pp. 30–36.
85. International Union for Child Welfare, *First Draft, European Convention for the Protection of the Rights of the Child*.
86. Information given to the author by Trevor Stevens, of the Directorate of Human Rights of the Secretariat General of the Council of Europe in Strasbourg (letter of November 6, 1986).
87. See *Recommendation* 874 for a European Charter. The Committee of Ministers's answer: (reply) doc. 4659 Addendum. See also: Memorandum prepared by the International Union for Child Welfare, *the Rights of the Child, Current Situation and Future Prospects in Europe*, Strasbourg, 10 January, 1984, H/ONG (84)1, Council of Europe.
88. Boucaud, Pascale, *Le Conseil d'Europe et la Protection de l'Enfance; L'opportunité d'une Convention Européenne des Droits de l'Enfant*, Strasbourg, 1989, Direction des droits de l'homme (I also studied the texte provisoire, Strasbourg, September 16, 1987, restricted DH-ED(87)22).
89. Assemblée Parlementaire, Conseil de l'Europe, *Recommandation* 1121 (1990) (1), *relative aux droits des enfants*, FAREC 1121. See also: *Rapport de la Commission des questions juridiques et des droits de l'homme* (Rapporteur: Mme Ekman), Doc.6142.
90. Ebigbo, Peter, O., *Charter on the Rights and Welfare of the African Child*, Uwani-Enugu (Nigeria) 1991, African Network for the Prevention and Protection against Child Abuse and Neglect (ANPPCAN).
91. In March 1991 the organization of African Unity's Chief of the Legal Division reported to the international secretariat of DCI that not one member State of the OAU signed or ratified the new Convention.
92. Wako, S. Amos, Towards an African Charter on the Rights of the Child, in: *The Rights of the Child, Selected Proceedings of a Workshop on the Draft Convention on the Rights of the Child: An African Perspective*, Nairobi May 9–11, 1988, published by ANPPCAN, Nairobi, 1989, pp. 41–47. See also: *The Law Journal* (Kenya), no. 1., vol. 1, 1991.
93. Thanks to Geraldine van Bueren in London, who told me that the version of the *African Charter* published in CHILDWATCH no. 2. April 1991 (ANPPCAN publication) was more recent than in the booklet of Dr. Ebigbu (Note 90), I could correct Appendix XLV. If this is the correct version the African Charter goes further in Article 22 (Armed Conflicts) than the UN Convention on the Rights of the Child (Article 38 on Armed Conflicts). The African Charter states that "*no* child shall take a direct part in hostilities". The UN Convention allows recruiting from fifteen years on. Philista Onyango of ANPPCAN indeed stated at the 'Children of War' Conference (in Stockholm, 1991) that "the African Charter sets the age of majority at 18, and – in contrast to the UN Convention on the Rights of the Child – it does not make exceptions for recruitment into armed forces or entities or participation in armed conflicts".
94. A group of NGO's from eight Latin American countries met in 1988 Buenos Aires. The drafting of a *Latin American Charter on the Rights of the Child* was proposed here. A first draft was adopted there. One of the features of it is that the drafters are against international adaption: It is recommended that "all human being born in Latin America has the right to ensure and preserve his Latin American identity".

CHAPTER XII

Ideological Declarations

1. THE DECLARATION OF THE RIGHTS OF THE CHILD, PROPOSED TO 'PROLET'CULT', (MOSCOW, 1918)

See Appendix VI

The first efforts to arrive at a Declaration of the Rights of the Child were presented four months after the October revolution, at the first national conference of the 'Organisations for Cultural Enlightenment'[1] held in Moscow from February 23rd to 28th, 1918.

The aim of the Prolet'cult movement[2] was to make educational facilities available to the proletariat. Its activities covered art, pedagogy, adult- education and socio-cultural training. The records of the proceedings of the Prolet'cult Congress show that the revolution had not yet produced a blueprint for Soviet society. A great deal of infighting lay in store.

The Communists rejected the educational system of Tsarist Russia.[3] According to Nearing, they combed the world for good suggestions.[4] Already before the October revolution, a number of progressive pedagogues had joined the *New Education Movement* (*Reformpädagogik*) and had even conducted several small-scale educational experiments.[5] According to Oskar Anweiler[6], the influence of the pioneers of the new education movement on the development of educational theories was considerable. The roots of Marxism, says Anweiler, lie in the same conceptual world as those of the most progressive educational ideas in pre-revolutionary Russia.[7] Some Russian schools had already embraced modern educational trends and ideas before the revolution. The various Prolet'cult organisations, too, were interested in raising the intellectual level of the population. Illiteracy was still widespread and this hampered the creation of a modern industrial proletariat. Douglas Holly[8]: "From a nation of peasants with a tiny urban proletarian vanguard decimated by civil war, a modern State had to be forged, capable of defending within its borders the infant-phenomenon of Socialism. This required rapid technicalisation of the work-force, accompanied by what the

Party termed a 'cultural revolution', asserting the cultural hegemony of the proletariat over the remnants of bourgeois and patrician culture."

The pragmatic Lenin distanced himself somewhat from the endeavours to create a new proletarian culture. According to Anweiler, he warned against sky-rocket changes and preferred to view the cultural revolution and its repercussions on schools and training courses in the light of scientific social planning and Karl Marx's theory of class struggle.[9]

At first, the Party accepted the democratic experiments in art, education and science, but soon the icy wind of Stalinism began to prevail and the Party became very suspicious of new ideas.

Anweiler[10]: "The central position of the child, acknowledgement of his or her rights, strong feelings about independence and spontaneity – the liberal elements of Reform Pedagogy – were set against 'pedagogy without children'." Says Nigel Grant: "By the 1930s a halt had been called to what were described, rather unjustly, as 'irresponsible experiments' in the schools, and the Stalin era re-imposed a strict routine of examinations, formal teaching and strict classroom discipline on the traditional continental model. This was geared to the political needs of the Soviet State and the Communist Party."[11]

In 1918 the *Draft-Declaration of the Rights of the Child* was originated by the *Association for Free Education* for the Prolet'cult Congress. This Draft-Declaration comprises seventeen Principles. As far as we know, the English text, translated by us from the German, appears for the first time in print in this study.

Principle 1 states that, as soon as a child is born, he or she has a right to certain vitally important provisions such as health care. It is stressed that this must be the case for all children irrespective of the social status of their parents.

Principle 2 holds the parents, society and the State responsible for the availability of these provisions to all children. Society is rather a vague concept, but we may assume that it refers here to frameworks such as Prolet'cult and the Communist Party. The proposal was submitted by the *Association for Free Education*, and we therefore presume that the drafters intended to involve private initiative. Principles 1 and 2 are classifiable in the *conservative mode* of the *physical subsystem* (worries about life itself).

Principle 3 states that children are not the property of either their parents or Society or the State, and that each child is unique ("the child is a person in his/her own right"), and has the right to be different. This principle is, therefore, classified in the *personality subsystem*.

Principle 4 states that a child has the right to leave his or her parents and to choose and/or dismiss his or her educators. Reasons for leaving the parents are not specified. Whether this is to obtain better food or to avoid being beaten, the child is viewed as a social being with a part to play in relation to other, similar individuals, and competent to choose with whom to interact. This pertains to the *adaptive mode* of the *social subsystem* (the child is seen as a person in his or her own right, with an individual role in society).

Principle 5 advocates the right of the child to individualised education. This relates to *all four modes* of the *personality subsystem*.

Principle 6 states that no child can be forced to attend an educational institution or vocational training centre that is not compatible with his or her individuality. It grants the right to, and acknowledges the capacity of children to form a value judgement vis à vis parents and other educators. It is therefore classifiable in the *adaptive modes* of the *personality* and *social subsystems*.

Principle 7 deals with the pedagogical value of labour. The German Pedagogue Georg Kerschensteiner (1854–1932), the first to mention this idea, was already a widely read author in pre-revolutionary Russia. Russian circles connected with the periodical *Svobodnoe Vospitanie* (Free Education) had also urged that children should learn some productive craft at an early stage. Since this concern implies the right of the child to participate in suitably productive frameworks, if he or she so chooses, it relates to the *adaptive mode* of the *social subsystem* (interaction with social institutions).

Principle 8 affirms that, insofar as rights are concerned, "the child is at all ages equal to the adult person." Since this Principle puts all members of society in a par and claims an *a priori* formal equality, we classify it in the *adaptive mode* of the *social subsystem*. This Principle also contains the possibility of withholding a right on the grounds that the child does not have the required physical and/or mental competence. However, this restriction pertains also to certain categories of adults (the mentally ill, prisoners, senile people etc.).

Principle 9 deals with the freedom to partake in any activity that is not harmful to the physical and spiritual development of the child himself. This belongs in the *expressive modes* of the *physical* and *personality subsystems*.

Principle 10 mentions the fact that children are capable of accepting and abiding by social rules designed for the good of the community as a whole. If this Principle were formulated in terms of a 'right', it would fit in the *conservative mode* of the *social subsystem*.

Principle 11 states that children should have the right to take part in the process of making the rules that govern their lives. To the extent that this Principle is concerned with giving the child a chance to exert his or her influence on the social environment, it is classifiable in the *expressive mode* of the *social subsystem*. The interaction with social organs that regulate society relates to the *adaptive mode* of the *social subsystem*.

Principle 12 states that children should not be forced to partake in religious practice or religious education. This is classifiable in the *expressive mode* of the *cultural subsystem*.

Principle 13 deals with the basic right that "no child may be oppressed because of his or her convictions." This right pertains to the *expressive mode* of the *cultural subsystem*.

Principle 14 states that the child should be allowed to express his or her convictions and thoughts. This relates to the *expressive mode* of the *cultural*

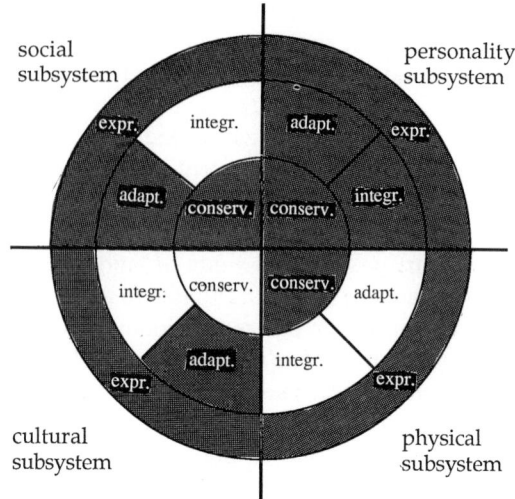

Fig. 12.1. The Draft Declaration of the Rights of the Child presented to the Proletcult-Organisation in 1918. Interpreted with the Systemic Quality of Life Model.

and possibly also the *personality subsystems*. However, the second part of this Principle mentions the need to explain to the child that convictions must be dictated by the well-being of society and its members. It is a matter of continual dialogue with the child. This relates to the *adaptive mode* of the *cultural subsystem*.

Principle 15 deals with freedom of association. A child has the right, just like an adult person, to initiate associations and organisations. This applies not only to sport clubs and the like, but also to political organisations. This Principle relates to the *expressive mode* of the *social subsystem*.

Principle 16 pleads that children and youngsters who have misbehaved or failed be helped rather than punished. The major concern of this Principle is with the *expressive mode* of the *physical subsystem*. The preference for educational means and "clarification" suggests a concern with the *adaptive mode* of the *cultural subsystem*.

Principle 17 stresses that it is the State's duty to guard against infringements of the above mentioned Rights of the Child.

The above Draft-Declaration relates mainly to the *expressive and adaptive modes* of the *social subsystem*. It seems strange that the Draft-Declaration does not deal with the physical subsystem (food, housing etc.)

Although Principle 7, for instance, is in tune with Marxist mainstream ideological thinking, the Draft-Declaration of the Organisation for Free Education was rejected. It was felt that it contained too many elements that could be interpreted as containing anti-collectivism. In Pridik's book *Das Bildungswesen in Sowjetrusland* we read that the Congress summoned Prolet'cult to formulate another Declaration that would be more in agreement with the teachings of Karl Marx. As far as we know[12] Prolet'cult did not respond to this request.

The tragedy of the Soviet Union, says Anweiler[13], is that it started out with ideas based on freedom, equality and fraternity, and ended by repressing all individuality. In the Stalin era, when expressions of free thought were banned, the child became again an object rather than an individual in his or her own right.

Now the Soviet Union itself does not exist anymore, since January 1992, there should be room in Russia to remember the brave educators of 1918 and their first Draft-Declaration on Children's Rights.

2. THE CHILDREN'S CHARTER FOR THE POST-WAR WORLD, PROCLAIMED BY A CONFERENCE OF THE NEW EDUCATION FELLOWSHIP IN LONDON, 1942

See Appendix XIII

During the Second World War, with London the centre of governments in exile, the *New Education Fellowship* under the chairmanship of I. Compton organised a conference of experts in the field of education.[14] On April 11th and 12th, 1942, specialists from nineteen countries met to discuss the situation of children after the war. The outcome was a "statement of the basic and minimum rights of children to be secured and guarded." According to the *New York Times*[15], the organisers sent the text of this *Children's Charter for the Post-War World* to all allied governments and to the BBC with the urgent request that it be broadcasted.

R. A. Butler, chairman of the *English Board of Education*, opened the Conference with the Ambassador of the Soviet Union, a Chinese representative, the American Ambassador, a representative of the government of Free-France and representatives of all the other allied countries seated in the front row. In the *New York Times*[16] we read that a Polish representative to the Conference pleaded for more social contact between English children and refugee children, and that an Indian representative argued that the English children should be educated to be servants rather than rulers of the peoples of the imperium. According to the *Times*, Mr. Butler urged the participants of the Conference not to hesitate, but to stand firm in the belief that a new society can be built through reform in the educational system.

Principle 1 of the Charter states that the educational system should be based on the needs of the children, since their personalities are sacred.

Principle 2 urges that priority should be given by each and every nation to use its resources to feed, clothe and shelter its children.

Principle 3 deals with medical care.

Principle 4 calls for equal opportunity in education.

Principle 5 specifies that this education must take the form of full-time schooling.

Principle 6 states that religious training must be *available*. Although not stated explicitly, the wording suggests that every child should have the right to decide whether or not he or she wished to make use of this opportunity.

The Charter was "not an intellectual *tour de force*" wrote the drafting committee. "We wanted to encourage everybody to take action."[17] It was hoped that in London, Washington or Moscow the Allies would open an *International Office of Education* to plan for the era to come, following the victory over Nazi-Germany. Idealistic themes were advocated (such as the exchange of teachers and students), as well as practical measures relating to matters such as the rebuilding of schools, libraries and laboratories.[18] The primary aim was to ensure that educational reconstruction would become an integral part of allied policy-making.[19]

Although the *Charter* is rather vague, it carries a definite message, one that runs counter to practices in Nazi-Germany where the personality of the child was subordinate to the needs of the State. Hence the first Principle of the *Charter for the Post-War World* declares that "every good educational system must be based on the needs of the child."

Shye points out that different needs sometimes stand in contradiction to one another. It is, therefore, important to balance such needs. In the *Charter* the concept of 'needs' is somewhat too general and over-simplistic and cannot be classified accurately. However, since the individual needs of the child are emphasised, we classify it in *all four modes* of the *personality subsystem*.

The second and third Principles (right to food, clothing, shelter and medical care) belong in the *adaptive mode* of the *physical subsystem*. See page 456.

Equal opportunity in education (Principle 4) must be viewed against the background of the wish to create a socially harmonious society. Equality suggests the social subsystem. Since the aim is harmony, this Principle relates to the *integrative mode* of the *social subsystem*.

Principle 5 ("for every child full-time schooling") deals with compulsory education. The Principle is not only concerned with the 'need of the child' to be educated, but also with preparing him or her for the future by means of education. (In our opinion, these two elements are liable to be contradictory or contrary to the actual needs of a child.) Since attention is drawn here to the need to prepare the child for the task of earning a living, we could classify this Principle in the adaptive mode of the physical subsystem. Since the Principle is concerned with providing children with the tools to become integrated in a working society, we could also classify it in the adaptive mode of the social subsystem. Finally, since education is a means to instill values and norms, the Principle could be classified in the adaptive mode of the cultural subsystem. However, in view of the declared aims of the Charter and the New Education Fellowship Movement, we interpret the central aim behind Principle 5 as being to give children the chance to develop their potential capacities. We have therefore decided to classify this Principle in the *expressive mode* of the *personality subsystem*.

Why religious education must be made available is not explained. It seems,

The Draft Charter of Children's Rights

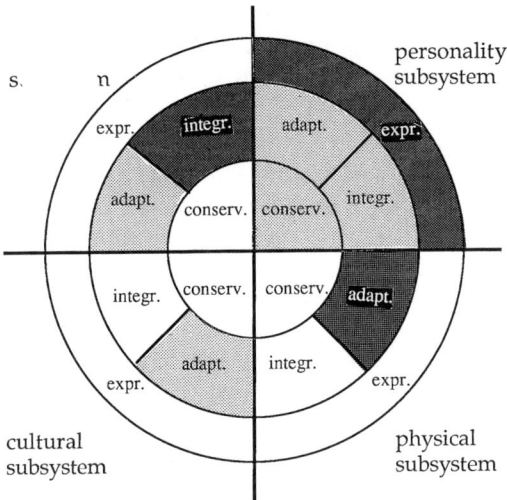

Fig. 12.2. The Children's Charter for the Post-War World of the Inter-allied Conference of Educational Experts (1942). (Organized by the New Education Fellowship.) Interpreted by the Systemic Quality of Life Model.

however, that Principle 6 is concerned with the nurturing of individual values as opposed to the Nazi ideology in which religion is subordinate to the needs of the State and no consideration is given to the religious experience of the individual. In our opinion the intention of this Principle was to highlight the right to self-expression. This pertains to the *expressive mode* of the *personality subsystem*.[20]

3. THE DRAFT CHARTER OF CHILDREN'S RIGHTS OF THE BRITISH MAGAZINE 'WHERE' (1971)

See Appendix XXIV

Referring to the Draft-Charter of the Magazine *Where*, Family lawyer John Eekelaar[21] wrote that "the proclamation of children's rights has hitherto mainly taken the form of a propagandist exercise." In our opinion, however, this *Draft Charter* is a very original and interesting piece of work and well worth looking into.

The editor of *Where*[22], in explaining the purpose of the Draft Charter, states: "It is no more than a draft. It is printed to provoke discussion... It is offered to make us think about the way we treat children and the way we *should* treat children. In places it may be ill-phrased. Some 'rights' may be missing, others may be stated too vaguely, or too narrowly... Before you turn to the charter, we must make it clear that teachers and parents also have rights."[23] The *Draft Charter of Children's Rights* was, according to the editor, "an ideal statement of how the world might be. As such," he wrote, "it perhaps says too little about means and all about ends. But the detailed spelling out of how a better, fairer world can be achieved would fill many volumes. It would also have to bow to the facts of life as they are today. Changing this, whether for child or adult, would be a Herculean task."

Leila Berg, who helped with the preparation of the Charter, wrote me about the social context in which we must place this document:

> "In 1965 a certain school in London was closed although children and parents marched to Government offices begging it be kept open. It was a political matter. There was an enormous amount of publicity about it all in press, television, radio. I wrote a book about it: 'Risinghill, Death of a Comprehensive School', which, after two years of work was published in 1968 by Penguin. It occasioned a further uproar. The book added to other voices to change things. Many things happened as a result, e.g. the beating of children which went on to a very large extent in English schools began to be questioned, and an organisation called S.T.O.P.P. was formed to end this practice; after twenty years campaigning a law has at last been passed banning it, though not in all schools even now. The 1960s had been a time of great tumult, educationally and racially, and many books were published about the situation, both here and in the United States. 'Children's rights' and 'Children's Charters' (which tied in with the United Nations one) began to be talked about. My book had also made very clear that very many children were living in conditions that middle-class people had no knowledge of."

According to the Advisory Centre for Education (ACE)[24] and Hazel Wigmore[25], the idea to draft the Charter came from educationalist Brian Jackson, who founded the magazine *Where* and was actively campaigning for the appointment of a Minister for Children who would co-ordinate all the fragmented services for children. Many officials asked him what exactly such a cabinet minister would be supposed to do. Jackson[26] used the Charter itself in his attempt to answer this question.

The Charter is divided into five parts. Part One deals with *the laying of the foundations for adult life*.

Point 1 states that every child has the right to "love from the family." Since it is specified that this love aims at "normal development", the main concern of this Point is with the growth of the personality. We classify it, therefore, in the *expressive mode* of the *personality subsystem*.

The text of the Draft-Charter does not reveal the actual concern of the right to education (*Point 2*). However, the work of the ACE (Advisory Centre for Education) focused not on the cultural-valuative aspects but on the claim that young people should be provided with good education. As such it is an interactional process between the individual child as a role carrier, and the environment. It pertains to the *adaptive mode* of the *social subsystem*.

Point 3 states the right "to food." This would belong in the adaptive mode of the physical subsystem, but for the addition: "nourishing enough to promote vitality," which brings us to a deeper level of the 'Systemic Quality of Life Model': the *expressive mode* of the *adaptive-physical sub-subsystem*.

Point 4 of Part One is rather unique. It is one of the few places in a Charter for the Rights of the Child that is concerned with *adequate sleep* of children. Sleep has the effect of re-balancing the body and mind. We classify it in the *integrative modes* of the *physical* and *personality subsystems*.

"The right to warmth" (*Point 5*) is too briefly formulated to give a good impression of what the drafters had in mind. We assume that the intention was 'interpersonal close relationships'. This relates to the *integrative mode* of the *social subsystem*.

Point 6 ("the right to tranquillity and privacy") is also too briefly formulated to give an adequate impression of the intention. Did the drafters want to reduce noise (adaptive mode of the personality subsystem), or did they have internal calm in mind (integrative mode of the personality subsystem)? Since tranquillity and privacy are mentioned in the same breath, we interpret it as meaning that the child might gain peace from being on his or her own. As such it belongs in the *adaptive mode* of the *personality subsystem*. This is confirmed in Leila Berg's letter to me: "Tranquillity is to be free from continuous anxieties, fears, distractions – to be able to be calm and quiet."

Point 7 ("free association with other children") emphasises relationships with peers which promotes interpersonal interactions. It pertains to the *expressive* and *integrative modes* of the *social subsystem*.

The concerns of *Points 8 and 9* ("space to play in and space to explore") are classifiable in the *expressive mode* of the *physical subsystem*.

Point 10 ("access to toys and books that will deepen and widen experience") clearly must be viewed in the context of more individual nourishment for personality growth and development. Toys and books are the means to this end. Point 10, therefore, relates to the *adaptive mode* of the *personality sub-subsystem*.

Point 11 ("the right to access to excursions outside the home that will deepen and widen experience") is very difficult to classify. The best we can do is to view 'widening experience' in a positive ethical light, for instance, to give expression to the personal interests of a child. As such it is classifiable in the *expressive mode* of the *personality subsystem*.

Point 12 stands out by its originality. "The right to respect from society for one's parents" must be interpreted before it can be classified. We understand that it is meant to indirectly promote the identity and social status of the proletarian child in the eyes of middle class adults. If we see it in this light, we can classify it in the *expressive mode* of the *social subsystem*.

Part Two (one long paragraph without separate points) deals with "the special right of protection from *psychological* exploitation by adults." This concern belongs in the *conservative mode* of the *personality subsystem*. "The special right of shelter or protection from *social exploitation*" pertains to the *conservative mode* of the *social subsystem*. (Strangely, protection from physical and sexual abuse are not mentioned here.) The "need of children to be protected from the danger of *harming themselves*" belongs in the *conservative mode* of the *physical subsystem*.

Part Three comprises fifteen paragraphs.

Paragraph 1 takes the form of the sweeping statement: "all children have the right to protection from, and compensation for, the consequences of *any* inadequacy in their homes or backgrounds." Protection (*conservative mode*) from and compensation for (*adaptive mode*) refer to *any* inadequacies in *all four subsystems* of the 'Systemic Quality of Life Model'.

The spirit of the uniquely phrased *Paragraph 2* ("children have the right to protection from any excessive claim made on them by their parents or others in authority over them. In particular, no one shall have the power to infringe a child's rights"), conveys the importance of taking the rights of the child seriously. We classify this concern in *all the modes* of the *personality subsystem*.

Paragraph 3 ("the right to freedom from religious or political indoctrination") institutes a negative phrasing of the right to freely express religious and political beliefs. We classify it in the *expressive mode* of the *cultural subsystem*.

Paragraph 4 states that the emphasis of this declaration is on *all* children and interprets the definition of a child as *any child*.

Paragraph 5 ("all children are entitled to freedom of association both within school and outside.") is classifiable in the *expressive mode* of the *personality subsystem*. Since this paragraph tries to broaden the social influence of children, it also relates to the *expressive mode* of the *social subsystem*. Less obvious is the classification in the *integrative mode* of the *social subsystem* (interactions among the child's various social roles). Finally, since a statement is made about children having "the right to publish their *opinions*" this paragraph also pertains to the *expressive mode* of the *cultural subsystem*.

Paragraph 6 relates to the right to *freedom of expression*. This relates to the *expressive mode* of the *personality subsystem*.

Paragraph 7 deals with the child's interaction with the social environment. The concern is with improving and institutionalising the balance between the child (as a budding role carrier) and society. The intention is to map procedures of such institutionalised ways of interacting with society that can tip the balance in the favour of the child. "Suitable trained and appointed people can," states the Charter "take complaints and grievances." We classify this paragraph in the *adaptive mode* of the *social subsystem*.

Paragraph 8 ("the right to exercise choice in the school curriculum") belongs in the *expressive mode* of the *personality subsystems*). The concern is with personality growth. The school is a social institution where values are expressed. We classify this paragraph in the *expressive* mode of the *social* and *cultural subsystems*.

Paragraph 9 which was particularly appealing to youngsters in the Beatles era, deals with personal appearance (such as dress and hair style). It is classifiable in the *expressive mode* of the *physical subsystem* (control over one's body).

Paragraph 10 ("freedom of movement") can by definition be classified in the *expressive mode* of the *physical subsystem*.

Paragraph 11 states that "every child shall have the freedom to play a full part in his choice of school." Contrary to *Paragraph* 8 which stipulates that the influence on important decisions "should grow as the child matures", no such connection is made here. This paragraph can only be analysed on a deeper level: to play a full part must be seen against the background of the part that others (such as the parents) play in these matters. This paragraph is classifiable in the *adaptive mode* of the *social subsystem*. However, the word *freedom* is emphasised. Within the social-adaptive context we find the concern to give the child a voice. This pertains to the *expressive mode* of the *adaptive-social sub-subsystem*.

Paragraph 12 deals with "freedom from physical assault". It therefore relates to the *conservative mode* of the *physical subsystem*. The issue in the second part of this paragraph was, at the time, especially relevant for Britain (with its widespread corporal punishment). The *Where* Charter stated that "no person shall have the right to subject a child to such punishment as is intended to mentally or physically humiliate the child, or to reduce his self-respect."

In *Paragraph 13*, the authors of the Draft-Charter plead for "privacy of person and thought." We interpret this paragraph as the right of the child to his or her own thoughts, and classify it (in the negative sense) in the *expressive mode* of the *cultural subsystem*.

Paragraph 14 is a balanced statement. Contrary to the pleas of the kiddy-libbers who want to give children the right to be employed, and to the pleas of those who focus on safeguarding children from employment, the *Where* Charter recognises 'the right to employment' but states that "no person shall have the right to compel a child to enter employment against his will." This paragraph can be classified in the *adaptive mode* of the *social subsystem*.

Paragraph 15 of *Part Three* pleads for providing children with knowledge so that they will be able to cope with the society in which they live. This belongs in the *adaptive mode* of the *social subsystem*. This paragraph also deals with contraceptives (*adaptive mode* of the *physical subsystem*) and religion (*adaptive mode* of the *cultural subsystem*).

Part Four is an important statement, formulated in terms of children as human beings equal to other human beings. However, it does not express any specific rights of children and we shall therefore not classify it.

Part Five formulates the right of the child to know his rights, and the duty

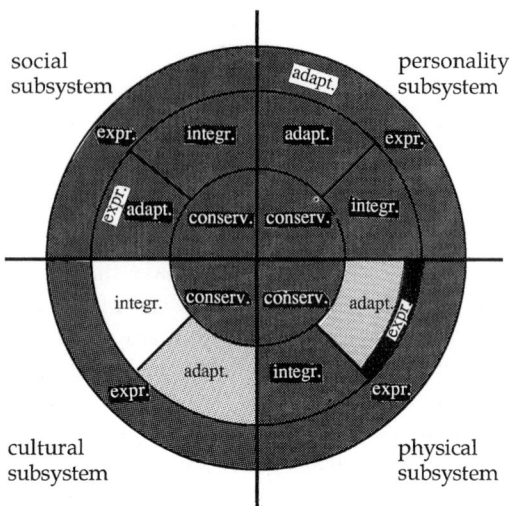

Fig. 12.3. The Draft Charter of Children's Rights of the British Magazine Where (1971), as Interpreted by the System Quality of Life Model.

of adults to inform the children about their rights. We consider *knowing* as *behaviour*, and classify this right in the *adaptive mode* of the *expressive-personality sub-subsystem*.

According to Hazel Wigmore, the Draft-Charter helped to draw the attention of the British public to the fact that children had no vote and, therefore, no influence. The debate initiated by this Draft-Charter focused, according to Wigmore, not so much on its content as on possible means to put at least some paragraphs into practice.

4. THE TEN COMMANDMENTS FOR ADULTS OF PROFESSOR LEONHARD FROESE (MARBURG, GERMANY, 1979)

See Appendix XXX

On the eve of the celebrations marking the start of the International Year of the Child (1979) in the Federal Republic of Germany, Leonhard Froese (Professor of comparative education, history of education and youth policy at the Philipps University in Marburg) published his 'Ten Commandments for Adults'.[27] At a press conference[28] he handed the proposal over to a representative of the State of Hessen, requesting that it be passed on to the Commission for the International Year of the Child. Froese's aim was to effect change in the mentality of politicians, parents, teachers and other educators, and thereby to improve the situation of children.

The First Commandment of Marburg's Mount Sinai is "Thou shalt regard the child as the highest good ever entrusted to you." Froese does not specify ways to provide for the needs of children, but rather proposes general attitudes to be adopted by adults. From Froese's explanation we learn that his intention was to make people see the child as an individual in his or her own right. We therefore classify this 'Commandment' in the complete *personality subsystem*. Froese: "Everywhere in the world and in all layers of population there are prejudices against children. Sometimes because of the colour of their skin: a white family, for instance, won't take a black child in; at other times because of religion: parents from one belief wouldn't like their children to marry someone from a different belief; in a third case because of so called national reasons: young people from one country wage war against their age-peers from another country; in yet another case, because of class differences: people belonging to one class condemn those of another class (this, in the opinion of the author of this study, is not really a children's rights issue); finally because of sex: boys are wished for and claimed, girls are rejected and/or even given away or sold."

The Second Commandment ("Thou shalt not form the child in thine own image") is a warning against excessive attempts to restrict the child or to shape him or her according to the image that the adult has about how children should be. Froese writes that "it is dangerous for the development of the child when philosophical, religious, political or other opinions are forced upon him or her." However, value-free education is not possible since educators always pass values on to children. Our interpretation of this Commandment is that it warns against coercive practices. Since this Commandment deals with the right to self-expression, we classify it in the *expressive mode* of the *personality and cultural subsystems*.

Froese's Third Commandment is the positive counterpart of the Second Commandment. "Children need free space for the unfolding of their physical, intellectual and spiritual powers." We classify it in the *expressive mode* of the *physical, personality and cultural subsystems*.

Froese's Fourth Commandment ("Thou shalt respect the child's personality") demands that the child be allowed to grow and develop according to his or her individuality. This pertains to the *expressive mode* of the *personality subsystem*.

The Fifth Commandment states: "Thou shalt not use force against the child." The meaning of this Commandment is elaborated in Froese's explanation: "The use of force by adults against children sows in them the seeds of force. Children learn to recognise force as a means of asserting themselves over those who are weaker. Hence corporal punishment should be forbidden throughout the world." Since this Commandment is not explained in terms of the good of the child, but rather in terms of the good of the world, we shall not classify it.

The Sixth Commandment reads: "Thou shalt not destroy the confidence of a child." Since the concern is with self-esteem, we classify this Commandment in the *conservative mode* of the *personality subsystem*. This Commandment is presented not only in terms of the rights of the child but also in terms of the good of the world. As Froese puts it: "It is the greatest disappointment – disillusionment for a child when the people around him or her prove unworthy of his or her trust. Trust will then be replaced by mistrust; goodwill by suspicion; hope by resignation. These can lead to aggression, radical behaviour and even terrorism."[29]

The Seventh Commandment ("Thou shalt protect the child against death") relates to the *conservative mode* of the *physical subsystem*. Froese explains: "There is no greater misdeed than the killing of children by adults. Leaving aside the interruption of pregnancy under certain conditions, this includes: the legal killing of the unborn or the newly born, death through inadequate nutrition or physical violence, death at the place of work or on the road."

About his Eighth Commandment ("Thou shalt not tempt a child to lie") Froese states: "Adults transfer their own imperfect social relationships to the children that are entrusted to them when they set them an example of treating the truth lightly. When honesty is no longer the basis of relationships, comradeship and friendship, partnership and love are replaced by enmity and hatred." In answer to the question of whether or not an adult is entitled to tell a dying child that he or she will recover one day, Froese states: "Only in a situation of mutual trust does the difference between the lie and the untruth in life's border situations – such as in a serious illness – eventually become manageable for the child." Froese's explanation of this Commandment deals with adults as *models* for children. This is even more evident in the (original) German text: "Du sollst Kinder nicht zur Lüge *verleiten*", (Thou shalt not *seduce* the child to lie). Since the concern here is with the interaction of values held by children and adults, we classify this Commandment in the *integrative mode* of the *cultural-valuative subsystem*.

The Ninth Commandment ("Thou shalt recognise the needs of the child") cannot be classified, since no specific right is emphasised. Froese's explanation of *the right to sleep* is interesting: "The satisfaction of basic needs such as hunger, thirst and sleep belongs to the natural rights of man. This applies also very much to children. It is only when these needs have been met, that social norms and human values can successfully be conveyed to the child." Froese continues: "To the basic needs of the child belongs not only the love of parents, brothers, sisters and fellow human beings, but also, from a certain degree of maturity onward, sexual love."

The last of the 'Ten Commandments' ("Thou shalt grant the child his or her own rights") pertains to the *adaptive mode* of the *social subsystem*. We base our classification on Froese's explanation: "Efforts to level the differences between races, peoples, classes and sexes have stopped before they reached the most helpless group in society. The emancipation of 'the last minority' remains to be achieved. As children do not reach their full 'voice' until late in their youth, they cannot represent their interests either as individuals or as a group." If the child cannot speak out for him- or herself, adults should represent them, argues Froese. The focus is on social institutionalis-

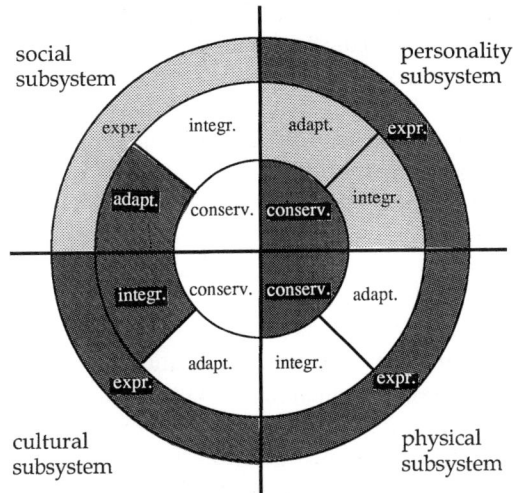

Fig. 12.4. The Ten Commandments for Adults of Prof. Leonhard Froese (1979) as Interpreted by the Systematic Quality of Life Model.

ation. Froese states: "It is therefore necessary that the child be rooted in the legal system as an independent legal subject so that it is possible for him or her to pursue his or her own rights with the help of the judicial system."

Rights of children lead to duties of adults and, therefore, a formulation of duties of adults is more or less a 'Declaration of Children's Rights'. However, it is sometimes difficult to classify a Declaration of *Children's Rights*.

5. THE YOUTH CHARTER-ACT PROPOSED BY JAMES WALLACE, M.P. (1985)

See Appendix XXXVII

Back-bencher James Wallace presented his Bill[30] to promote opportunities for young people on January 9th, 1985, at the first session of the House of Commons that year (International Youth Year). In it he proposed the establishment of a *Youth Charter*, giving rights and representation to young people. After the first reading, a date was set for the second reading: April 19th, 1985. "It was never seriously expected to proceed to legislation," wrote Jim Wallace in a letter to me.[31] ". . . nor indeed to reach a second reading debate. In fact, although I had named a day for debate when the Bill was read out, there was certainly no time to debate it and the Government Whip was able to block its progress by simply shouting 'Object!'[32] Nevertheless, I certainly do not regret having pursued this initiative. Although the Bill was never likely to reach the Statute Book, it did attract a certain amount of publicity when I presented the Bill to Parliament... It was a worthwhile opportunity to promote the cause of young people."

On January 9th, 1985, Wallace told the Commons why he was proposing his Youth Charter[33]: "In proposing a Youth Charter, it would be all too easy for me to fall into the trap of patronising the young or telling them what is best for them. Rather than do that, the Charter would seek to establish rights and to create a framework within which young people could participate more fully in the affairs of the community and the decisions that affect or shape their lives."

The right of youngsters to participate in decision-making is a central feature of Wallace's Charter. ("Within six months of the appointed day every borough council in London, district council in the remainder of England and Wales and district or island council in Scotland shall bring forward a scheme for the establishing of *youth councils* for their area.")

In the House of Commons[34] Wallace stated: "We hope for greater involvement by young people in decision-making... At the local level we believe that there should be a right of youth representation on a number of local committees, including health councils, school and college boards and local education authority committees. We also recommend democratically elected local Youth Councils. They would be a forum in which young people could express their anxieties to statutory bodies in their areas." In analysing Wallace's Charter according to the 'Systemic Quality of Life Model', the right to participate in decision-making (to give youngsters more power) is clearly classifiable in the *expressive mode* of the *social subsystem*.

In the House of Commons Wallace went on to say that to give more power to youngsters meant to give them political power: "We would propose a lower voting age and a lower age for candidature." This concern is voiced in the first paragraph of the proposed Youth Charter in which Wallace argues that "statutory bodies, governmental bodies and local authorities should encourage young people's civic and political participation; to this end young people shall be entitled to the maximum possible involvement in decision-making in all areas which affect themselves and their lives." In this same paragraph, Wallace proposes that the governmental bodies "shall promote young people's self-esteem and personal development." Since this paragraph is designed to promote self-esteem we classify it in the *integrative mode* of the *personality subsystem*, and since it aims at promoting personality development it also pertains to the *expressive mode* of the *personality subsystem*

The second paragraph deals with greater involvement by young people in decision-making ("young people shall be entitled to be represented "). It is classifiable in the *expressive mode* of the *social subsystem*.

Bob Franklin, the radical British campaigner for children's rights,[35] claimed that "to give young people rights is of little use unless they also achieve an understanding of how to exercise these rights. The mere possession of rights without this knowledge can lead to the worst sort of tokenism,

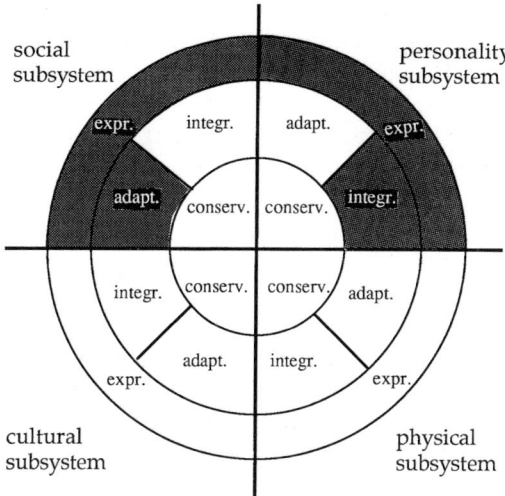

Fig. 12.5. The proposed Youth Charter-Act of James Wallace, M.P. (1985). Interpreted by the Systemic Quality of Life Model.

with young people being manipulated by more experienced participants." Wallace took this statement into account. In his third paragraph he pleads that "the option of an extensive programme of social and political education" be made available to young people. This paragraph is classifiable in the *adaptive mode* of the *social subsystem* (giving children more power).

The fourth paragraph ("Young people shall be entitled to a significant role in the planning and managing of the local youth service.") is also classified in the *expressive mode* of the *social subsystem*.

The fifth paragraph ("young people shall so far as possible be given the economic independence . . .") seems, at first glance, to belong to the adaptive mode of the social subsystem, since resources must be allocated to help the youngsters function well in society. However, if we read the whole paragraph ("young people shall be given the economic independence and the necessary advice to make an informed choice . . ."), we understand that Wallace was aiming at strengthening the cognitive part of the personality of youngsters in order to enable them to make informed choices. Paragraph 5, therefore, relates to the *expressive mode* of the *personality subsystem*.

6. THE LABOUR PARTY CHARTER FOR YOUNG PEOPLE (LONDON, 1985)

See Appendix XXXVII

The International Year of the Child also saw the British Labour Party present its *Labour Charter for Young People*. Labour's Neil Kinnock declared: "Labour backs young people. That's why young people are backing Labour. Together we can build a better future."[36] Although the intention of the Party was obviously to attract future voters, the instrument proposed is interesting enough to warrant analysis in this study. No explicit definition is given of the term 'young people', but, broadly speaking, the text deals with young people aged fourteen to twenty-four.

The short introduction states that "Labour believes young people should have opportunity, choice and independence." The term 'opportunity' is explained by what follows: "We want young people at 16 to have real jobs, good education and training – and a chance to earn as they learn." This belongs in the *adaptive mode* of the *social subsystem*.

Since the main concern of the proposed Youth Charter relates to the *adaptive mode* of the *social subsystem*, this area in the graphic representation of the 'Systemic Quality of Life Model' has been shaded darker than the rest (see Fig. 12.6.). Other important aims of the Charter are choice and independence (the opportunity to express personal preferences, and more social power), both classifiable in the *expressive mode* of the *personality and social subsystems*.

According to a *Newsweek* cover story dealing with this issue in 1985[37], the lack of job-opportunities was a real problem in Britain. ". . . in the past five years, the number of unemployed youths under age 25 in European Community countries has swelled from 2,9 million to more than 4,4 million, and accounts for an estimated 37% of Western Europe's total unemployed." "hat's a pretty major chunk of a generation," said Britain's Ivor Richard, a former social affairs chief of the Brussels-based European Commission. "The task of putting Western Europe's unemployed youth to work is daunting. Joblessness among British youth has reached 1,2 million, or about 23% of the labour force under 25. . . . Studies in Britain have suggested that unemployment is worst among the children of immigrants who came to Western-Europe during the boom-years of the 1960s . . . Now they are subject to widespread job discrimination that has a distinct racial edge." *Newsweek* quotes Prime Minister Margaret Thatcher as saying: "The economy is expanding. Investment is at an all-time record, the standard of living is at an all-time high, and there are great expansions in the Youth Training Scheme from which they will benefit."[38] *Newsweek* notes that "with variations, that is also the policy of most West European governments."[39]

Principle One of the Labour Party Charter elaborates on the meaning of 'opportunity' for young people and can therefore be classified in the *adaptive mode* of the *social subsystem*.

The same is true for *Principle Two* which deals with education, training and work experience that will fit the skills of young people to society's needs so that they can find employment ("the right at 16 to at least two years' education," etc.)

Principle Three deals with the means to achieve gainful employment ("the right at 16 and 17 to a negotiated wage if employed, with paid release to college; at least 36 English Pounds a week training allowance if on a training scheme.") This, too, relates to the *adaptive mode* of the *social subsystem*.

Principle Four ("The right to 27 English Pounds a week if in full-time study") probably aims at promoting the child's independence from his or her parents. This is classifiable in the *expressive mode* of the *social and the personality subsystems*.

Principle Five relates to fulfilment of the potential of all young people (not only the children of rich parents). It pertains, therefore, to the *expressive mode* of the *personality subsystem*.

Principle Six ("the right of unemployed 18 to 24 year old to more jobs and better training opportunities") is classifiable in the *adaptive mode* of the *social subsystem*.

Principle Seven (housing) pertains to the *adaptive mode* of the *physical subsystem*. In the explanation we read: "We need to increase public provision in this area to ease the pressures on young people leaving home – and on the parents and relatives they live with. Labour believes that local authorities should make rented accommodation more accessible."[40] This relates to the earlier mentioned 'independence' and we therefore classify it in the *expressive mode* of the *social subsystem*.

Principle Eight formulates the "right to sport and leisure facilities" and a "youth service which meets young people's needs." It relates to the *adaptive modes* of the *personality subsystem* and of the *physical subsystem*.

Principle Nine states that the rights mentioned above apply to everybody ("regardless of race, gender, class or sexuality"). It cannot be classified according to the 'Systemic Quality of Life Model'.

Principle Ten (physical security of young persons) belongs in the *conservative mode* of the *physical subsystem*. In the commentary the Labour Party[41] clarifies that its policies will reduce the risk of a nuclear holocaust; that money will be spent on creating jobs, not on nuclear arms and on fighting the evils of unemployment, poverty and disease."

Finally, a general remark about this Charter: These rights were discussed in the framework of political measures that (according to the British Labour Party) ought to be taken.

7. THE 'CHILDREN'S LEGAL CENTRE' MANIFESTO FOR CHILDREN
(LONDON, 1987)

See Appendix XLI

On May 5th, 1987, the Children's Legal Centre in London called on politicians "to adopt policies which help people whose votes they do not need – the country's 13.5 million under-18s who are too young to vote."[42]

In a press release the 'Children's Legal Centre' stated that "the Children's Manifesto aims to give children and young people greater rights to participate

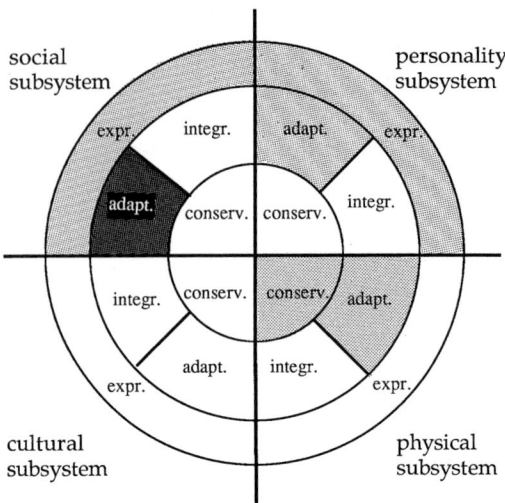

Fig. 12.6. The British Labour Party Charter for Young People (1985). Interpreted by the Systemic Quality of Life Model.

in society and increase independence, and to protect the services they require." "But what were its real aims?" I asked Martin Rosenbaum, a campaigner who had worked three years for the Children's Legal Centre. Rosenbaum[43]: "At the time that we produced it, the elections in the United Kingdom were not far away. In the run-up to the general elections, we wanted the political parties to incorporate some of the proposals in their party programmes. We also sent the Manifesto to hundreds of members of parliament. But actually it was already much too late to influence them. But we got a lot of publicity."[44]

The Manifesto was not a Charter advocating general principles. It was very concrete and practical. Martin Rosenbaum: "We hoped that this Manifesto would remind politicians and voters of the interests and needs of children and young people. Because they cannot vote, they are too easily ignored." The spirit of the Manifesto is therefore classifiable in the *expressive mode* of the *social subsystem* (more influence and more power for children).

The proposals of the Children's Legal Centre are grouped according to themes: I: Participation; II: Protection and Safeguards; III: Provisions and Services; IV: Civil Rights.

Section I deals with a number of principles. The first is that "young people aged 16 and 17 should be allowed to vote in elections." This point drew much publicity.[45] The measure, if implemented in the United Kingdom at the time, would have extended the right to vote to 1,800,000 young people who, according to the Manifesto, were considered old enough to leave school, have full-time jobs and get married, yet were not allowed any say in the choice of government. Since this paragraph aims at improving the social fit of youngsters and the balance between 'give and take', and since elections are a social institution, we classify it weakly in the *adaptive mode* of the *social subsystem*, and more strongly in the *expressive mode* of the *social subsystem*.

The second paragraph of Section I states that education authorities and schools should adapt themselves to the children and not the other way round. This statement pertains to the (*adaptive mode* of the *social subsystem*). From the explanation given by the Children's Legal Centre it becomes evident that the aim is "to give children some say in the running of their schools". This aim relates to the *expressive mode* of the *social subsystem*.

The third paragraph proposes change in the 1986 Education Act. According to the 1986 Act, young people under 18 cannot become school governors. The Manifesto calls for creating the possibility to appoint pupil governors. This obviously would give children more power. Although the paragraph deals with a technical matter, we classify it in the *expressive mode* of the *social subsystem*.

The fourth paragraph proposes that a *legal duty* be imposed on parents and guardians to ensure that "wishes and feelings of children about decisions which affect them should be given due consideration." This pertains to the *expressive mode* of the *social subsystem*.

The fifth paragraph proposes that children in care (especially residential care) should be allowed to participate in their own case conferences and (six-monthly) reviews of placement. 'Case conferences' should not be held behind closed doors in the residential treatment facilities or psychiatric hospitals and the patients or clients should be allowed to have a say in their affairs. This proposal relates to the *expressive mode* of the *social subsystem*.

Section II deals with *protection and safeguards*, and proposes that legislation should establish independent complaints' procedures for all institutions which cater for children and young people (such as schools, hospitals, children's homes etc.). Such a complaint procedure would help children and youngsters improve their social fit. It belongs, therefore, in the *adaptive mode* of the *social subsystem*.

The second paragraph is an extension of the first. It indicates how these complaints proceedings can best be institutionalised and is therefore also classifiable in the *adaptive mode* of the *social subsystem*.

The third paragraph is a 'pure' protection paragraph. It deals with the *legal protection from physical punishment* in all institutions as well as in the family. In 1987, corporal punishment was due to be abolished in State-funded education and child care institutions. The Children's Legal Centre demanded that this law be extended to apply to other institutions and to families. Since the humiliation of corporal punishment can harm the personality development of the child, this paragraph belongs in the *conservative mode* of the *physical subsystem*, and in the *conservative mode* of the *personality subsystem*.

The fourth paragraph deals with handicapped children. It pleads for such children to be included in the regular social networks and that their isolation be avoided. We classify this concern in the *conservative mode* of the *social subsystem*, stated in negative terms, i.e. 'protection' (by way of isolation) should be avoided.

The fifth paragraph deals with immigration rules which pose numerous problems for black children in the United Kingdom. The *British Nationality Act* 1981 discriminates against children whose parents are unmarried. Quite often, the parents of black children are not married, one parent living, for instance, in Jamaica and the other in London. This makes family reunification difficult. Since family reunification and intimate relationships are the concern of this paragraph, we classify it in the *integrative mode* of the *social subsystem*. Since the family is a social institution, we also classify it (weakly) in the *adaptive mode* of the *social subsystem*.

The sixth paragraph calls for the strengthening of an already existing Act, with the aim of "improving relations between police and young people." This pertains to the *adaptive mode* of the *social subsystem*.

The seventh paragraph calls for all child employees to be covered by employment protection legislation. The main concern of this paragraph is with the relationship between the young worker and his employer (although some other matters such as health concerns also play a part). The paragraph pleads for implementation of the *Employment of Children Act* 1973 (introducing "consistency to the regulations governing employment of children under 16 years old). This is classifiable in the *adaptive mode* of the *social subsystem*.

The last paragraph of Section II makes a very important, and in our opinion highly commendable, claim: "An independent body should be established to assess and advise on the environmental implications for children of central and local governmental planning decisions." This would help make the child feel comfortable in the physical environment. This pertains to the *adaptive mode* of the *physical subsystem*. The child should also be allowed to express his or her opinion about environmental decisions[46]. We classify this concern in the *expressive mode* of the *adaptive-physical sub-subsystem*.

Section III (Provisions and Services) begins with an introduction which relates both to the *adaptive mode* of the *physical subsystem* (provisions and services should meet the needs of children who are entitled to adequate transport, health etc.) and the *adaptive mode* of the *social subsystem* (social services, employment and training opportunities).

The first paragraph demands that the social security system provide children and young people with adequate living standards. As the Children's Legal Centre promotes the idea of more power over financial resources, this paragraph is classified in the *expressive* and in the *adaptive modes* of the *physical subsystem*.

The second paragraph deals with the right of homeless youngsters to be "entitled to get help with housing". This relates to the *adaptive mode* of the *physical subsystem*.

The third paragraph calls for the establishment of a *family court system* (a model developed in New Zealand). This proposal must be viewed as a reaction to the malfunctioning of the prevailing system. The New Zealand model is not only a judicial institution; additional (counselling) services under the umbrella of the court are also available. According to one of the campaigners such a system[47] would deal more effectively with the stress of family breakdown. The aspect of 'quality of life' that would be improved (or in which disastrous consequences of family breakdown could be prevented) pertains to in the field of inter-personal relationships and is, therefore, classified in the *integrative mode* of the *social subsystem*.[48]

The fourth paragraph deals with a special population (young people with disabilities). It is not related to 'quality of life' in general.

Section IV deals with civil rights. "Whenever practicable, possession of rights should not depend on arbitrary age limits but on maturity and the ability to understand the implications of those rights." However, the Manifesto does not specify who should decide whether or not a child is mature enough. Seven interesting paragraphs follow:

The first paragraph argues that young people should have the right to participate in legal action on their own behalf (for instance by having the right to initiate legal proceedings). This relates to the *expressive mode* of the *social subsystem*.

The second paragraph states that young people should be able to leave home (if there is a breakdown of relations with parents) and place themselves in voluntary care (which would lead to placement in a children's home or foster family). This paragraph relates mainly to the *adaptive mode* of the *social subsystem* (change of social institution from family to children's home). It also pertains to the *expressive mode* of the *physical subsystem* (environment), and in the *expressive mode* of the *personality and social subsystems*.

The third paragraph is a general plea *against* curtailing the *expressive-physical* functioning mode of youngsters by depriving them of their liberty. The incarceration of juvenile delinquents must be reduced to a minimum.

The fourth paragraph gives children who are placed in a foster family the right to be placed with a family of their own race. It deals primarily with identity and is classified in the *conservative mode* of the *personality and social subsystems* (continuity needed to affirm personality identity).

The fifth paragraph claims that wrong or negative information concerning the rights of children under 16 years old has, in the past, been given by teachers (about the right to confidential advice). This is interpreted by us as meaning that care must be taken to avoid the degradation of the youngster by giving incorrect information. This paragraph (stated in negative terms: do *not* degrade the child) relates to the *expressive mode* of the *social subsystem*.

The sixth paragraph deals with the child's right to receive sex education, which should be included in the school curriculum. This is the right to receive something (adaptive mode) which itself (sex education) lies in the field of cognitive behaviour. It belongs, therefore, in the *adaptive mode* of the *expressive-personality sub-subsystem*.

The seventh paragraph pleads for the right of access to education-, medi-

304   Chapter XII

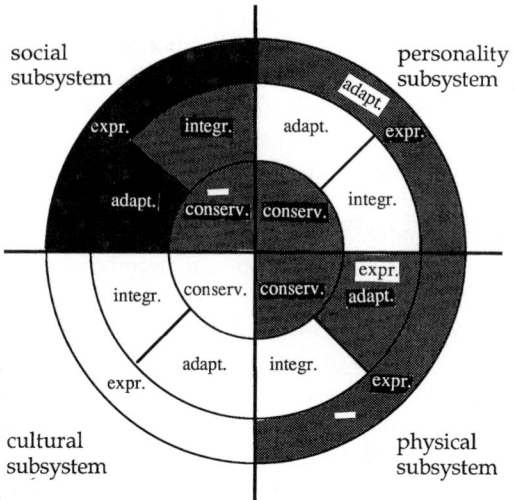

Fig. 12.7. The Manifesto for Children of the Children's Legal Centre (London, 1987). Interpreted by the Systemic Quality of Life Model.

cal-, social service-, probation-, housing- etc. files, since inadequate information can seriously affect the social status of a youngster. This right is classifiable in the *expressive mode* of the *social subsystem*.

In May 1987 Martin Rosenbaum[49] told the Magazine *New Society* that "a substantial part of this Manifesto could quickly be implemented." Indeed, three years later some elements were included in the New Children's Act (such as the right to apply for separate representation in family proceedings) but, says Rosenbaum, "much still applies, such as our plea of 1987 that youngsters of 16 should have the right to vote and a say in the running of their schools."[50]

8. 'Children's and Young People's Charter' (Labour Party, London, 1990)

It is to be expected that new social reformers will stand up and formulate Declarations of Children's Rights. The latest such ideological document is the British Labour Party's *Giving Children a Voice* (published in the summer of 1990), which is an attempt to put "children and the rights of children firmly on the political agenda."[51] On November 19, 1990, Joan Lestor, MP, Labour's Spokesperson for Children launched at a news conference the *Children's and Young People's Charter*. She claimed that in this Charter[52] the rights of the UN Convention on the Rights of the Child are translated in UK terms. "It also makes a statement about our attitude toward children and young people and our aspirations for them". Joan Lestor explained further about why she made a Charter: "I hope it will help bring about much-needed social change, providing children with a basis to enforce their individual rights". With 'the right to a good start in life' she meant: "to enjoy equal opportunities through access to quality education, health care and housing".[53] This declaration focusses mainly on the *conservative mode of the physical subsystem* and the *adaptive mode of the social subsystem*.

NOTES

1. I first saw this Declaration in Dutch translation in: Vos, Jaap, F., 'De 1918–Onderwijswet in de U.S.S.R.: een kort hoofdstuk over de vrijwording van het onderwijs' in: *INFO, Informatiebladen van de Afdeling Onderwijskunde van de Rijksuniversiteit te Groningen*, 1970, Vol.I, No. 4, pp. 146–157.
Originally the Declaration was published in: Pridik, Heinrich, ed. *Das Bildungswesen in Sowjet Russland, Vorträge, Leitsätze und Resolutionen der Ersten Moskauer Allstädtlischen Konferenz der Kulturell-aufklärenden Organisationen (Mosko-Prolet'cult) vom 23-28 Febr. 1918)*, Annaberg i. Erzgib, 1921, Neuropädagogischer Verlag.
2. Prolet'cult (also Prolet'kult) is short for *Proletarskaja Kul'tura*, (proletarian culture). See: *Proletarische Kulturrevolution in Sowjetrussland (1917–1921)*, Munich, June 1969, Taschenbuchverlag GmbH. and Co. KG, p. 11.
3. Widmayer, Ruth, 'The Evolution of Soviet Educational Policy', in: *Harvard Educational Review*, Summer 1954, p. 159, quoted by Hunt, Herold, L., *The Changing Soviet School*, Cambridge, Mass., 1960, The Riverside Press, p. 51.
4. Nearing, Scott, *Education in Soviet Russia*, New York, 1926, International Publishers, p. 8.
5. Anweiler, Oskar, 'Der internationale Zusammenhang der Reformpädagogik zu Beginn des 20. Jahrhunderts' in: *Bildung und Erziehung*, Vol. XIV, 1961.
6. Anweiler, Oskar, *Geschichte der Schule und Pädagogik in Russland, vom Ende des Zarenreiches bis zum Beginn der Stalin-Aera*, Berlin, 1964, Ost-Europa Institut, Berlin, p. 64.
7. Some of the reform pedagogues eventually co-operated with or even joined the Communist movement, like, for instance, S.T. Sackij (1878–1934) whose thinking had initially been more in line with that of Tolstoj and the American John Dewey. Others, like Konstantin Venttsel (1857–1947), author of *The Struggle for the Free School* (1906) and leader of *The House of Free Children* (1906–1909), resisted adaptation somewhat longer. In the *Great Soviet Encyclopedia* we read: "Venttsel did not immediately understand that new social conditions for the creation of a genuinely free school had come into existence after the victory of the Great October Socialist Revolution; for some time he continued to defend his idea of the 'autonomy' of schools with regard to the State, and to advocate non-political education." The difference between Sackij and Venttsel was not only that Sackij joined Marxism. On the ancient educational question of whether to direct the child's learning or to allow the child to develop on his/her own, Sackij opted for the former approach, and Venttsel for the latter approach.
8. Holly, Douglas, 'Learning and the Economy: Education under the Bolsheviks 1917–1929', in: *History of Education*, 1982, Vol. 11, No. 1, p. 42.
9. Nevertheless Lenin did not restrict Lunacarskij and Krupskaya. Anatoly Vasilievic Lunacarskij (1875–1933) was the first people's commissioner for education and vocational training in the Soviet Union. Naderda Konstantinova Krupskaja (1869–1939) was married to Lenin. It was Lenin himself who recommended that Luncarskij work together with Krupskaja. He also allowed the Prolet'cult organisations freedom of action. However, party and government officials did not trust them. Perhaps this was related to the fact that by the middle of 1920, Prolet'cult had half a million members. In 1918, however, this was not yet a problem.

10. Anweiler, Oskar, 1964, Op. cit. p. 64.
11. Grant, Nigel, *Soviet Education*, Harmondsworth, Middlesex, 1964, Penguin Books, p. 22.
12. In the book *Proletarische Kulturrevolution in Sovjetrussland* (1917–1921), we read in a note on page 147: "It was impossible to establish if this was indeed done." It is my opinion that Jaap Vos (see note 1) is mistaken when he writes that "the conference, among other things, *resulted* in the Declaration of the Rights of the Child." In Pridik's book *Das Bildungswesen in Sowjetrussland* we read that the Congress of the Prolet'cult rejected the Declaration in a resolution, but that it called upon Prolet'cult to formulate another Declaration that would be more in agreement with the spirit of Marxist doctrine. The same information is given in the book *Proletarische Kulturrevolution in Sowjetrussland* (1917–1920) *in a note on page 191. See: Pridik, Op. cit. pp. 42–43. Also: correspondence with Prof. O. Anweiler of the Institut für Pädagogik der Ruhr-Universität Bochum* did not unearth a (new) Declaration of the Rights of the Child by Prolet'cult. We, therefore, conclude that the project was probably abandoned due to other priorities. On October 16th, 1918, however, another *Declaration* was drafted by the State Commission for Education and Vocational Training, in a bid to provide a blueprint of the ideal school. This free-of-charge united labour school would be instrumental in the effort to create a renewed Russia. Apart from emphasising the connection of the school with labour, this Declaration also dealt with principles related to autonomy. Students aged twelve and over would have the right to participate in meetings of the school council. It also advocates the rights of the student to his/her individual development. See: Orlova, Nina, V., 'The Protection of Children's Rights and Interests in the USSR' in: *International Child Welfare Review*, October 1969, No. 4, p. 15.
13. Anweiler, O., 1964, Op. cit.
14. The first international meeting of progressive educators took place in Calais in 1921.
15. *New York Times*, April 13th 1942, 'British Group Adopts Children's Charter; Government to be Responsible for Care and Education.'
16. Idem.
 The information is given in the New York Times. I could not find anything on this subject in the London *Times*.
17. Boyd, William and Rawson, Wyatt, *The Story of the New Education*, London, 1965, Heinemann, pp. 121–123.
 As pointed out to me by Dr. Frank A. Stone, Professor of International Education of the Isaac N. Thut World Education Center in Storrs (Connecticut, U.S.A.), the *New Education Fellowship* is now called *The World Education Fellowship*. Its archives are in London at the University of London's Institute of Education.
18. *The Times*, April 13th, 1942, p. 2.
19. Boyd and Rawson, Op. cit., pp. 122–123.
20. Nowadays the Fellowship promotes the same principle. See: Miller, Laurence, 'Enhancing Human Rights Through School Communities' in *The New Era*, Vol. 68, No. 1., 1987, pp. 11–13.
21. Eekelaar, J.M., 'What are parental rights'? in *Law Quarterly Review* (1973), Vol. 89, April, p. 211.
22. *Where* (information on education) 1971, April, p. 105.
 The Consumer Association in Britain has a magazine called *Which*, recommending which products to buy. Brian Jackson founded a sister magazine focusing on where to send your child to school, where to find good colleges for your high school children and so on.
23. *Where*, April 1971, p. 105.
24. Letter to the author from Elizabeth Wallis of the Advisory Centre for Education (ACE), dated March 13th, 1990.
25. Telephone interview with Hazel Wigmore, May 25th, 1990.
26. Jackson was a very creative man who had launched many ideas such as an early concept of an Open University (which Jackson developed with Michael Young, now Lord Young of Dartington), Advisory Centres for Education in shopping centres, the child care switchboard idea, using local radio to give information on services for children, and paying teachers to spend time in holiday resorts to talk with parents and children about education.
 The National Council for Civil Liberties also advised *Where*. See: Lilly, Mark, *The NCCL – The First 50 Years*, London, NCCC.
27. Froese, Leonhard, *Zehn Gebote für Erwachsene, Texte für den Umgang mit Kindern*, Frankfurt am Main, 1979, Suhrkamp Verlag, p. 197.

28. 'Zehn Postulate aus Marburg zum Internationalen Jahr des Kindes', in: *Marburger Universitäts-Zeiting*, 10.1.1979.
29. Terrorism probably means here the Baader-Meinhof group.
30. *A Bill to promote opportunities for young people in the International Youth Year, 1985 by establishing a Youth Charter giving rights and responsibilities to young people*; *and for connected purposes, ordered to be brought in by Mr. James Wallace, Mr. David Alton, Mr. Simon Hughes, Mr. Alex Carlisle, Mr. Malcolm Bruce and Mr. A. Beith, ordered by The House of Commons, to be printed, 9 January 1985, London, HMSO (Bill 55, 49/2)*.
31. Letter to the author from James Wallace, M.P. (Orkney and Shetland), dated August 7th, 1989.
32. Mr. Wallace writes in his letter to me: "I am sure you will find such Parliamentary procedure archaic and curious, to put it mildly". Indeed, I do.
33. *Parliamentary Debates*; *House of Commons*, 1985, p. 787.
34. Idem, p. 788.
35. Franklin, Bob, 'Children's Political Rights', in Franklin, Bob ed., *The Rights of Children*, Oxford/New York, 1986, Basil Blackwell, p. 47. Mr. Franklin is a sociologist.
36. Labour Party, *Labour's Charter for Young People*; *Labour's Jobs and Industry Campaign*, London, 1985, p. 20.
37. Garrison, Lloyd, 'Lost in the Eighties; Many Europeans Face Life Without Work', in *Newsweek*, August 19th, 1985, No. 33, p. 14.
38. Idem, p. 19.
39. Idem.
40. Labour Party, *Labour's Charter for Young People*, Op. cit.
41. Ms. Patricia Hewitt of the Institute for Public Policy Research in London wrote in a letter to the author: "As far as I remember this Labour Party Charter for Young People was drafted by Labour Party Staff together with front-bench Parliamentary spokesmen dealing with children's rights issues".
42. The Children's Legal Centre, 'Children's Manifesto' published (press release), London, May 5th, 1987.
43. Telephone interview with Martin Rosenbaum, May 1990.
44. I saw clippings from *The Star* (May 6), the *Glasgow Herald* (May 5), *Today* (May 5) and *New Society* (May 8).
45. MacDermid, Alan, 'Votes-at-16 Children's Charter', in: *Glasgow Herald*, May 5, 1987.
46. In 1979 an interesting experiment was conducted in Rotterdam (the Netherlands). In the neighbourhood 'Oude Noorden' children were successfully involved in a housing improvement scheme. The intention was to give children more influence in this field. The children, who had prepared themselves thoroughly in advance, were given the opportunity to discuss their ideas with an alderman. See: Dansen, Eva; Zeeuw, Jan Willem de, and Lemmen, Piet, *Kinderen kiezen zelf, Verslag van een kinderinspraakproject*, Rotterdam, 1981, Stichting Ruimte.
47. Sautoy, de Tany, 'A Court for Families', in *Concern* (Magazine of the National Children's Bureau), No. 61, Winter 1986/87, p. 16.
48. De Sautoy mentions yet another aspect of quality of life: "If sensible relationships can be managed despite breakdown in the interests of the next generation, then that can only be for the long term benefit of this country's social stability."
49. *New Society*, May 8, 1987.
50. Telephone interview with Martin Rosenbaum.
51. 'Labour Party Launch New Charter for Children', in: *Childright*, July/August 1990, No. 68, p. 4.
52. *Children's and Young People's Charter* (London, 1990)

    – The right to respect
    – The right to information about yourself
    – The right to be protected from harm
    – The right to have a say in your life
    – The right to a good start in life
    – The right to feel and be secure

    All children – living with their families or living in care – are entitled to the same rights.
53. Joan Lestor, MP, Labour's Spokesperson for Children, News Release, November 19, 1990.

Picture XIII.1. The youngest breaker boys. (Photo: Lewis Hines. Courtesy: George Eastman House, International Museum of Photography, Rochester, N.Y., U.S.A.)

CHAPTER XIII

Specified and Sectarian Declarations and Conventions

1. ILO CONVENTIONS FIXING MINIMUM AGE

See Appendices I and II

In July 1900, the International Congress of Labour Legislation met in Paris. Signor Luzzatti, the Italian Delegate, addressed the Congress as follows: "I come from a country where industry is only just beginning to develop. I would be thankful if international legislation could be worked out to give Italian workmen the protection which is not afforded to them by their national legislation."[1] He said that, when he had pushed for the prohibition of night work in cotton mills, he was told that he should first get such legislation introduced in competing neighbouring states. An international solution was badly needed. On July 28th, 1900, the Statutes of the International Association for Labour Legislation were approved. The Association took upon itself "by preparation of memoranda or otherwise" to promote uniformity among the various systems of labour laws.

According to Ayusawa[2] "progress accelerated when, on April 15, 1904, the French and Italian governments entered into a treaty whereby equal benefits of legal protection and privileges were assured to the workers of both countries residing in either country."

Ayusawa explains that conditions in France and Italy were very different. Apart from the legal provision of weekly rest periods, "Italian labour legislation lagged behind that of France in practically every respect, so this treaty meant a considerable step forward for Italy."

The reason we mention this Convention in our study is that for the first time, an inspectorate was instituted to protect children, especially child emigrants:

Article 2 of the Convention stated[3]:

(a) *In order to avoid error or false declarations, the two governments shall define the character of the documents to be presented to Italian Consulates by young Italians engaged to work in France, as well as the form of the certificates to be furnished by the said Consulates to the Mayoral offices before delivering employment books to children as prescribed by child labour legislation. Labour inspectors shall require the presentation of the certificates upon each visit and shall confiscate employment books wrongfully possessed.*

(b) *The French government shall organise Protection Committees including among their members as many Italians as possible in industrial regions where large numbers of young Italians not living with their families are employed through middlemen.*

(c) *The same measures shall be adopted for the protection of young French workers in Italy.*

Italy promised to improve its network of inspectors. Article 4 stated:

On signing this Agreement, the Italian Government will complete the organisation, throughout the whole Kingdom, and more particularly in those regions where industry is developed, of a factory inspection system operating under the authority of the State, and affording, for the application of the laws, guarantees analogous to those of the factory inspection system of France.

The inspectors shall enforce the observance of the laws in force on the work of women and children, and especially the provisions which relate to:

1. The prohibition of night work;
2. The age of admission to work in industrial shops;
3. The length of the workday;
4. The obligation of weekly rest.

The Italian Government engaged to publish an annual detailed report on the application of the laws and regulations relative to the work of women and children. The French Government assumed the same obligation.

The rest of the Convention dealt with matters not specifically related to children, such as simplified transfer of bank accounts.

Analysing these Articles with the 'Systemic Quality of Life Model', we find that the major concern is with the fear of permanent damage to the health of working children. We classify this concern in the *conservative mode* of the *physical subsystem*.

On January 31st, 1913, the Swiss Federal Council proposed, by means of a circular[4] sent to the governments of nineteen States, that international negotiations be initiated with the aim of prohibiting industrial night work for young workers and of fixing a maximum ten-hour working day for women and young workers employed in industrial concerns. "We take the liberty of asking your Excellency kindly to proceed with the appointment of the representatives of your Government, and to inform us as soon as possible of their names."

In June 1913, the International Conference on Labour Legislation took place in Berne. This led to a draft *International Convention Respecting the Prohibition of Night Work of Young Persons Employed in Industrial Occupations.*

The Convention stated that "the prohibition shall be absolute in all cases up to the age of fourteen years."[5] The Convention applied to "all industrial undertakings employing more than ten persons." It was not intended to apply to "undertakings where only members of the family are employed."

On July 14th, 1914, the Swiss Federal Government sent out another circular[6] proposing "that a Diplomatic Conference should meet on September 3rd, 1914, in order to convert the principles adopted by the Technical Conference of 1913 into International Agreements." However, the First World War broke out before such a Conference could take place.[7]

With the establishment of the International Labour Organisation (I.L.O.) an effective framework was created to promote better Conventions and to monitor the situation in all States.

In 1919, the I.L.O. brought together for the first time, governments, employers and trade unions for united action towards social justice and better living conditions everywhere.[8] Historically the I.L.O. is an outgrowth of the social thought of the Nineteenth Century. Many influential social reformers believed that if a country's industry introduced measures to improve working conditions, this would automatically raise the cost of labour, putting it at an economic disadvantage compared to other countries and industries. They therefore tried to persuade the governments of Europe to make better working conditions and shorter hours the subject of *international* agreements.[9] Child labour, too, "escaped in 1919 from the localising restraint of national boundaries," and was now considered an international problem.[10]

The I.L.O., which dealt with these types of problems, was founded in 1919 after trade unions in several countries requested that the Peace Conference set up a Labour Commission. On April 11th, 1919, this Labour Commission agreed on a document which, as Part XIII of the Treaty of Versailles, became the Charter of the I.L.O. Its first General Assembly (called the International Labour Conference) was held in October 1919 in Washington.[11] On the agenda of the Conference were listed, among other things, employment of children: (a) minimum age of employment; (b) employment during the night in industry; and (c) employment in unhealthy processes.[12] Also on the agenda was the employment of women before, and after childbirth, (including the question of maternity benefits). It was agreed that "work should be prohibited for six weeks after childbirth."[13] In addition, the I.L.O. Conference proposed that women should receive a "benefit sufficient for their maintenance and that of their child in satisfactory hygienic conditions."[14]

Forty-five countries had already established a minimum age of fourteen for work in industries. In France, Germany, the Netherlands, South Australia and (for boys) Sweden, the minimum age for work in factories was thirteen; in Argentina, Brazil, Italy, Japan, Mexico and Portugal it was twelve; in

Rumania eleven, in Austria ten and in India nine. The General Assembly (the International Labour Conference) agreed to a fixed minimum age of fourteen for work in industry in a Convention.

Some insight into the structure of the I.L.O. of those days is required in order to understand the importance of such a *Convention*, Grace Abbott[15] explained the uniqueness of the organisation: The I.L.O. included government-, worker-, and employer-delegates, both in the Conference and in the Governing Body. The Conference consisted of four delegates from each nation – two representing the government, one employer and one worker, each appointed from the most representative organisation of employers and workers. By a two-thirds vote of delegates to the Conference, so-called 'Labour Conventions' were adopted and then transmitted to the member nations for ratification. Each Government was obliged, as a member of the organisation, to submit them to the competent authority for a decision about ratification.

After preliminary discussions with States where the minimum age for work in industry had not yet been declared to be fourteen, the organising committee for the Labour Conference decided to recommend the following: "The Committee submits for the consideration of the Conference a draft Convention prohibiting the employment in industrial work of children below the age of *fourteen*."

For most Western States[16] the age of fourteen was quite acceptable. However, the Commission on Children's Employment, responsible for preparing the Labour Conference, was faced with strong objections from Asiatic countries where child labour under the age of fourteen was widespread and where the financial means for introducing fast changes were lacking.[17] "Should modifications of the Convention be allowed in the case of those countries with special climatic and industrial conditions?"[18] asked Sir Malcolm Delevinge of the United Kingdom. "No," replied Miss Margaret Bondfield with great emotion, while speaking on behalf of the British Workers' Delegation. "This question of child labour has been discussed by the whole world and we do not think the Indian Government should be so detached from world discussions as not to be prepared with recommendations on this subject in 1919."[19] Nevertheless, she proposed an amendment which allowed India to detach itself partially and which was subsequently adopted in section 6 of the Convention: "With regard to one of the main objections, namely the nature of the Indian industries, we have carefully drafted this amendment to exclude all those industries that could be considered purely native industries or that are small industries. It is especially drafted to refer only to those industries which are being modelled on Western ideas, which are to some extent under control of factory legislation and which are mainly supervised by Western people. . . .Our main point is that in textiles, in engineering, in all those great industries where a factory act has already been being applied, it should be quite possible to have the Western safeguards; and it is that point that we particularly wish to impress upon the Indian government. . . .It seems to us that with regard to the question of mines, railways, and docks, the nature of the employment will be sufficient reason for safeguarding the employment of children on those properties."[20]

The Conference indeed decided that exceptions were justified for India when Oriental industrial methods prevailed, but that in industries where Western methods were already applied, implementation of the Convention was expected. Article 6 read: *The provisions of Article 2 (children under the age of fourteen shall not be employed or work in any public or private industrial undertaking) shall not apply to India. However, in India children under twelve years of age shall not be employed*:

(a) *in factories working with power and employing more than ten persons*;
(b) *in mines, quarries, and other works for the extraction of minerals from the earth*;
(c) *in the transport of passengers or goods or mails by rail, or in the handling of goods at docks, quays and wharves, but excluding transport by hand.*

This was not enough for the Indian Government. It now raised reservations relating to the "difficulties which local customs would place in the way of organising adequate primary education."[21]

We cannot deduce from the discussion in the I.L.O. whether the Oriental industrial methods were any better for children than the so-called Western methods. A start had to be made somewhere with the prohibition of child labour, and the industries already working according to Western methods were best equipped to introduce such a change.

The I.L.O. Convention was accepted with 93 votes for and 3 votes against.

In the course of the years more than forty States have ratified this fifth Convention of the I.L.O. However, the Diplomatic Branch of the National Archives of the United States in Washington D.C. notified me that: "It appears that while the United States accepted membership in the International Labour Organisation in 1934, it did not ratify the Convention fixing the minimum age for admission of children in industrial employment of 1919."[22]

The 1919 Conference also adopted *Convention No. 6, concerning the night work of young persons employed in industry*. Of special importance in this Convention is the provision that young persons under eighteen years of age should not be employed during the night in any public or private industrial undertaking or in any branch thereof, unless with only members of the same family. See Appendix II, page 421.

Once again India asked for preferential treatment, and so did Japan. In Japan the age limit was to be fifteen until July 1st, 1925 and sixteen thereafter, while in India such night work was allowed from the age of fourteen and the sphere of application was to be defined by law. Belgium's request to except the glass industry was rejected by the Conference.[23]

314   Chapter XIII

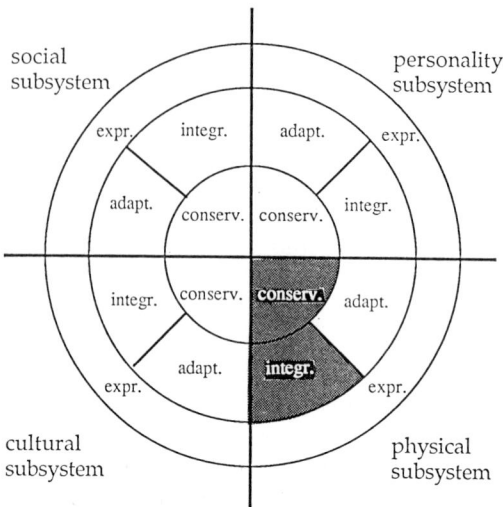

Fig. 13.1. I.L.O. Conventions 5 and 6. Interpreted by the Systemic Qulaity of Life Model.

By 1921 the Convention on nightwork was nevertheless ratified by India! Japan had taken no legislative measures, but had already applied the Convention in spinning works and in certain public departments, such as the central telephone office in Tokyo where more than 4000 girls had been employed.[24]

Conventions 5 and 6 marked the beginning of a series of I.L.O. Conventions with regard to children's labour.[25] Apart from concern about children working in industries, a 1920 Convention required that children under the age of fourteen could only be employed in agriculture after school hours. For employment at sea, the minimum age was fixed at fourteen by the 1920 Convention; the 1921 Convention adopted a proposal that young persons must reach the age of eighteen before being admitted to employment at sea as stokers and trimmers (whose task it is to arrange the cargo in a way that makes the boat assume a desired position in the water).

In Shye's 'Systemic Quality of Life Model' the above Conventions fit in the *integrative mode* (ongoing health) and *conservative mode* (physical security) of the *physical subsystem*.

2. ILO CONVENTION NO. 138 CONCERNING THE MINIMUM AGE FOR ADMISSION TO EMPLOYMENT (1973)

See Appendix XXVIII

In 1973 the International Labour Conference re-examined the problem of employment or work of children and young persons. The Conference decided to lay down new comprehensive standards aimed at the protection of working children and the gradual elimination of child labour. At the Conference a new Convention was adopted. It replaced earlier I.L.O. Conventions relating to minimum age for admission to employment, such as Convention No. 5 (1919) and Convention No. 59 (1937) on Minimum Age. Both concerned labour and industry (with a minimum age, respectively 14 and 15 years). Two others, No. 33 (1932) and No. 60 (1937) concerned non-industrial labour (also with a minimum age of 14 and 15 years) while six others related to special sectors (agriculture, mining, sea-faring and sea-fishing). (See page 373–375.)

In order to replace these ten Conventions by one general instrument, and hoping to inspire national policy and legislation, the new Convention (No.138) stated that every State Party to the Convention should undertake to progressively raise the minimum age for admission to employment or work "to a level consistent with the fullest physical and mental development of young persons" (Article 1). The acceptance of this Convention showed that the *principle* of minimum age for admission to employment or work had been universally recognised. Bequele[26] stresses "that child labour laws are not intended to supplant, or be carried out apart from, socio-economic changes; they are intended to reinforce and complement them wherever possible, to deal with the worst forms of the exploitation of children wherever they exist and to provide minimum levels of protection wherever such labour is unavoidable."

Article 2 defines to whom the Convention applies. This is an important issue. However, it cannot be analysed in the framework of the 'Systemic Quality of Life Model'.

Article 2 (sub 3) specifies that the minimum age must be "not less than the age of completion of compulsory schooling and, in any case, shall not be less than 15 years." However, the same Article (sub 4) mentions the possibility of (temporary) exceptions to this rule: " a Member whose economy and educational facilities are insufficiently developed may . . .initially specify a minimum age of 14 years." Although the proposed minimum age of 15 had drawn a majority in the Commission (consisting of employees and some government representatives), the employers declared in the Plenary that they would submit an amendment to re-state the minimum age at 14 years. But, the Draft-Convention did not succeed in drawing the two-third majority in the Plenary. The solution was found in a compromise that kept the minimum age at 15 but offered the developing countries the alternative age of 14. Such countries would be required to state the specified age in a declaration attached to the ratification document. This age may subsequently be raised by means of a new declaration by the State.

Although the Convention specifies 15 as the basic minimum age, Recommendation No. 146 (Paragraph 7), adopted in the same year the International Labour Conference, states that the objective of Members should be to raise this age to 16, and that if it is still below 15 years, urgent steps should be taken to raise it to that level.

Doek[27] points out that "This Convention gives us the possibility to define the term 'child labour' because it is an internationally accepted set of rules although the number of countries that have ratified the Convention is still disappointingly low." According to Doek, "the Convention makes it possible to describe *child labour* (as an undesired phenomenon) *as work, within or without employment, by a person younger than* 15 *years, on a more than incidental base* (*which, therefore, makes regular schooling impossible*). Especially understood in this context is work with a high probability of danger for health, safety and morality of young people under 18 years of age."

Article 3 of the Convention states that a minimum age of at least 18 years shall be set for work that can damage health. According to Lee Swepston[28] the term *employment*, used in Convention 138, has been a source of misunderstandings "even for those governments who have ratified the instrument". The Conference discussions make clear that the term 'employment' covers all economic activity, regardless of the formal status of young persons. However, after examining reports submitted by countries which have ratified the Convention, the Committee of Experts has pointed out that the coverage of the legislation of several countries is not the same as that of the Convention. In these countries the relevant legislation is applicable only to labour relations in which the young person works has signed a contract. In each case, the Committee has asked the government to indicate what provisions exist to ensure that young persons under the minimum age cannot be admitted to employment or work, even in the absence of an official employment relationship. In carrying out the General Survey, the Committee found that the legislation of only a minority of countries covers both employment and work in the sense of the Convention."[29] The most difficult task for governments is to cover those young persons who are working in the 'informal' sector of the economy (for instance in family undertakings).

Article 4 allows the "competent authorities" to "exclude from application of the Convention limited categories of employment or work". Which categories may be excluded is not specified, but Article 5 (sub 3) states certain provisions of the Convention that shall be applicable as a minimum.

Another exception allowed under this Convention is formulated in Article 5(1) which states that a Member whose economy and administration facilities are insufficiently developed may initially limit the Convention's scope by declaring it applicable only to certain economic sectors. However, regular reports must be made concerning the general position regarding the employment or work of young persons or children in the excluded sectors.

Article 7 of the Convention authorises light work from the age of 13 to 15 years, whereby the interpretation of the term 'light work' is left to the discretion of the governments.

Article 8 allows lowering the age for artistic performances. No minimum age is mentioned.

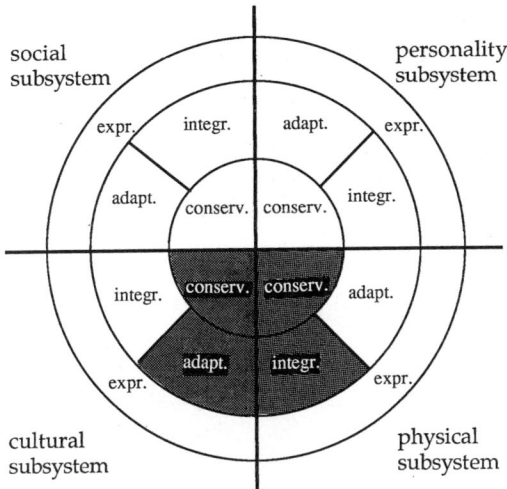

Fig. 13.2. I.L.O. Convention 138 Concerning Minimum Age for Admission to Employment (1973). Interpreted by the Systemic Quality of Life Model.

Article 9 lays down three basic requirements: identification of the persons responsible for compliance; the establishment of enforcement measures, including penalties; and keeping registers of young persons employed or working. (See page 488.)

The Committee of Experts concluded that a great number of countries had given only limited attention to the need to place special restrictions on work by young persons which might jeopardise their health, safety or morals: this despite the fact that the International Labour Conference had adopted the largest number of instruments and provisions on these issues. The Committee recommended that "special attention be paid to industrial and maritime work as a first step, since work in these sectors is inherently hazardous, but that the dangers found in agriculture and other forms of activity should by no means be ignored. Even where it had not been possible to fix a minimum age for employment or work, it should be possible in most countries to prohibit some types of work for children who were too young to perform them." Clearly, even after the 1973 Convention, we still have a long way to go before reaching our goal.[30]

In analysing I.L.O. Convention 138 according to the 'Systemic Quality of Life Model', we classify its concerns in the *conservative mode* of the *physical subsystem* (safety), in the *integrative mode* of the *physical subsystem* (danger to health), in the *conservative mode* of the *cultural subsystem* (morality), and in the *adaptive mode* of the *cultural subsystem* (education).

Picture XIII.2. A child (five years old) selling candy at one o'clock at night in Rio de Janairo. (Photo by Antonio Nery, O Globo newspaper, Rio de Janairo.)

3. THE DECLARATION OF THE RIGHTS OF THE ADOLESCENT (1922)

See Appendix VII

Two International Socialist Youth Organisations, the *Young Workers International*, mainly concerned with education, and the *International Union of Socialist Youth Organisations*, concerned with politics, met in 1922 in Salzburg in order to unite all working-class youth organisations.[31] Kimml: Thus was the first systematic effort "devoted to a joint agitation for the protection of youth." The two organisations jointly drafted a 'minimum programme for the protection of youth'. George Werner[32] refers to this programme as the *Declaration of the Rights of the Adolescent*. By means of this *Declaration* the young workers enthusiastically demanded the recognition of their most urgent demands for shorter working hours, holiday periods, prohibition of night work, reform of the system of industrial training and continuation schools, etc.[33] It is our interpretation that the intention of the drafters was that more education, better working conditions for young workers, etc. (*adaptive mode* of the social subsystem would lead to more power of young workers (*expressive mode* of the *social subsystem*). Although the Young Workers supported the new I.L.O. Conventions, they felt that they fell short of the minimum demands of the working class. Capitalism, they complained, was "directing its systematic offensive in the first place against the apprentices and young workers: their wages were the first to be reduced; their working hours the first to be increased; their rights the first to be disregarded."[34]

The Conference in Salzburg called on the Young Workers "to carry on the old struggle for national and international legal protection with redoubled energy and new weapons mere resolutions and protests on the one hand, and protest demonstrations on the other, are as futile a weapon against the tremendous power of present-day capitalism as cavalry attacks against massed artillery fire. Capitalism can only be effectively opposed by its own methods: by international action."[35]

In 1923, one year after the Declaration of the Rights of the Adolescent,[36] a new organisation, the Socialist Youth International, took up the torch of the earlier groups and pressed the Labour Organisations and Trade Unions to formulate minimum claims. Its representatives demanded: "reform of compulsory continuation schools, organisation and extension of vocational guidance, and compulsory elementary education up to the age of admission to wage earning work." They also demanded, as a first step, ratification of the "Conventions and Recommendations of the International Labour Conference of the I.L.O.[37]

In the 'Systemic Quality of Life Model' the above Declaration can be classified in the *integrative mode* (worries about ongoing health), and the *conservative mode* (physical security) of the *physical subsystem*. The worries for ongoing health and physical safety were, for instance, reflected in the proposed "compulsory medical examination of young persons before admission to employment" and in the "prohibition of night work and underground work as in mines."

Interestingly, a report of the Socialist Youth International, interpreting the Salzburg Meeting, mentions (in relation to the Declaration) a need of young workers for a stable social situation "not to be kicked in the street as rubbish when you are no longer needed." To the extent that this aspect is part of the Declaration, (even if not explicitly mentioned) this concern belongs in the *conservative mode* of the *social subsystem* (continuity and stability in social relations) and the *adaptive mode of the social subsystem*.

4. THE YOUTH CHARTER (ADOPTED IN OSLO AT THE THIRTEENTH WORLD CONGRESS OF THE INTERNATIONAL CONFEDERATION OF FREE TRADE UNIONS, ICFTU IN 1983)

See Appendix XXXIV

The ICFTU has 141 affiliates in 97 States and territories in all five continents. It has a membership of 87 million workers. It promotes the interests of working people everywhere, works for constantly rising living standards, full employment and adequate social security, and defends the fundamental human- and trade-union rights.[38] Within the ICFTU framework, a 'Youth Committee' deals with the creation and up-dating of protective standards for young workers and trainees. The ICFTU's aims are expressed in a Youth Charter.[39]

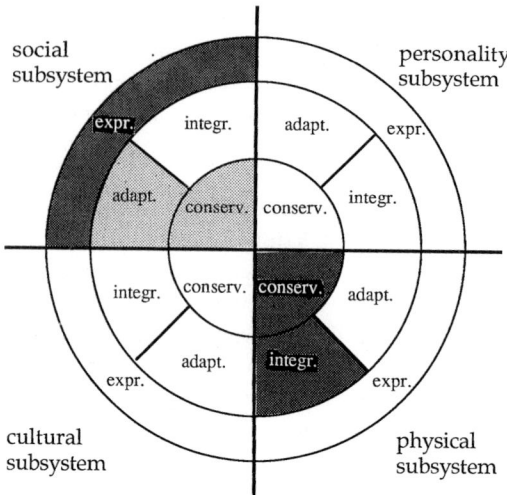

Fig. 13.3. The Delcaration of the Rights of the Adolescent (1922). Interpreted by the Systemic Qality of Life Model.

Tim Noonan, the Youth Secretary, wrote me that the ICFTU Youth Charter was based on the views, expressed in the meetings of the 'Working Group of Young Workers' Questions' which took place between the 12th and 13th ICFTU World Congresses. The Charter was endorsed by the ICFTU Youth Committee at its meeting prior to the Oslo Congress.

The aim of the Charter[40] was to provide overall guidance for the ICFTU's youth programmes, and to function as a policy framework for the deliberations of the ICFTU Youth Committee. As a document adopted by an ICFTU World Congress, it is the key ICFTU Policy Document on Youth Questions.[41]

Mr. Noonan noted that it would be difficult to quantify the impact of the Charter in promoting youth rights in recent years, but "it has certainly contributed to the development of policies on youth affairs by many ICFTU affiliates. The major direct impact has occurred through their activities and programmes in the work place and in national and local political and community affairs. In addition, the Charter serves as the basis for ICFTU input on youth affairs into international fora, particularly the United Nations system."

Interestingly, the concept 'youth' is very broad. Mr. Noonan writes for instance:[42] "Taking into account the various definitions of the age categories constituting 'youth' amongst ICFTU affiliates, the Charter is aimed generally at people between the ages of 15 and 35. It should be borne in mind that the application of the Charter in different countries depends to an extent on national circumstances (some ICFTU affiliates have, for example, set the maximum age limit for 'youth' at 23 or 24 years). While the principal emphasis of the Charter is on rights and opportunities of young workers, the Charter also deals with education, training and broader social questions, affecting young people in general."

The Charter is a lengthy document. Specific sections of it are used from time to time in Trade Union youth-education activities where the subject matter coincides with material included in the Charter.

The interests of the drafters (Trade Unions) are not forgotten in the Charter. Paragraph 14, for instance states that "young people should be introduced into the practical work of the trade union as early as possible, and that they should be adequately prepared for their coming tasks as active trade unionists. Special attention should be given to young workers beginning at their work place, and to those seeking work. To achieve this aim, special membership arrangements should be made." These concerns are classifiable in the *adaptive mode* of the *social subsystem* of the Shye's 'Systemic Quality of Life Model'.

The first paragraph of Section B of the Charter (Programme of Demands) claims "the right of freedom of association." This is classified in the *expressive mode* of the *social subsystem*. However, since explicit mention is made of the right to join a youth movement, it can also be classified in the *adaptive mode* of the *social subsystem* (interaction between the individual youngster as carrier of social roles and the environment.)

The second paragraph deals with education. It is loaded with concerns pertaining to the *adaptive mode* of the *social subsystem* (" which will prepare young persons for employment . . . vocational guidance designed to enable the individual to make a better choice of occupation"). (See page 506.)

The third paragraph demands, among other things, *freely chosen* employment. This concern can only be analysed on a deeper level: *the expressive mode* of the *adaptive-social sub-subsystem*.

The fourth paragraph ("employment of children under the age of 16 must be forbidden") relates to the *conservative mode* of the *social subsystem*. The rest of the paragraph deals with various problems (such as the transition from school to working-life). All these concerns belong in the *adaptive mode* of the *social subsystem*.

The fifth paragraph of Section B highlights vocational and advanced vocational training aspects. These can be classified in the *adaptive mode* of the *social subsystem*.

The sixth paragraph promotes the idea of *paid educational leave*. This pertains to the *expressive mode* of the *personality subsystem* (since its aim is the realisation of the right of youngsters to realise their potential). However, since it increases the young worker's chances to fit into society, we can also classify it in the *adaptive mode* of the *social subsystem*.

The seventh paragraph deals with protective labour legislation (safety). This pertains to the *conservative mode* of the *physical subsystem*. There is also a concern about ongoing health (medical check-ups at regular intervals) which we classify in the *integrative mode* of the *physical subsystem*.

The eighth paragraph pleads for regulation of working hours for youngsters under 18. The aim, we read, is "to develop their personalities in the broadest sense." This relates to the *expressive mode* of the *personality subsystem*. However, this paragraph is also concerned with health and safety. This relates to the *integrative and conservative modes* of the *physical subsystem*.

The ninth paragraph ("the pay of apprentices and trainees should be based on the principle of equal pay for work of equal value and nature") deals with *equality* and *social justice*. These issues are on the border between the *integrative* and the *adaptive modes* of the *social subsystem*.

Paragraph ten states that "in cases of unemployment, sickness, industrial accidents and diseases, young workers should enjoy full social insurance protection." Here the ICFTU tries to assure some (minimal) standard of living. This concern belongs in the *adaptive mode* of the *physical subsystem*.

Paragraph eleven deals with holidays and paid leave. Since the main concern is here with personal growth, it pertains to the *expressive mode* of the *personality subsystem*.

Paragraph twelve (leisure) deals with 'reloading the batteries' of the young workers. This concern is classifiable in the *adaptive mode* of the *personality subsystem*.

The concern expressed in Paragraph 13 (employment and under-employment) relates to the *adaptive mode* of the *social subsystem*

Paragraph fourteen has already been discussed in the beginning of the analysis of this Chapter.

Paragraph fifteen deals with *young migrant workers*. The ICFTU pleads that the interests of young migrants should not be in conflict with the fact that they are workers. The concern is about these migrant workers as human beings and as *workers*. Solidarity with the migrants implies a certain intimacy. This pertains to the *integrative mode* of the *social subsystem*.

The larger part of paragraph sixteen, ("after completing their military service, young workers must have the right to return to their former employment" and "rights acquired by young persons at the place of work must be maintained during their absence") is classifiable in the *adaptive mode* of the *social subsystem*. The right to become a conscientious objector, however, relates to the *integrative mode* of the *cultural subsystem* (interactions among the values held by individuals).

Paragraph seventeen is concerned with preventing juvenile delinquency, and with keeping offenders integrated in society. It relates to the *conservative mode* of the *social subsystem*).

Paragraph eighteen deals with *marriage*. Probably with apartheid in mind, the drafters of the ICFTU Charter proclaim that "women and men have the right to marry and found a family." (*Family* is a social institution. We therefore classify this paragraph in the *adaptive mode* of the *social subsystem*).

Paragraph 19 states that from age 18 onwards, young people should be considered as adults. This belongs in the *adaptive mode* of the *social subsystem*.

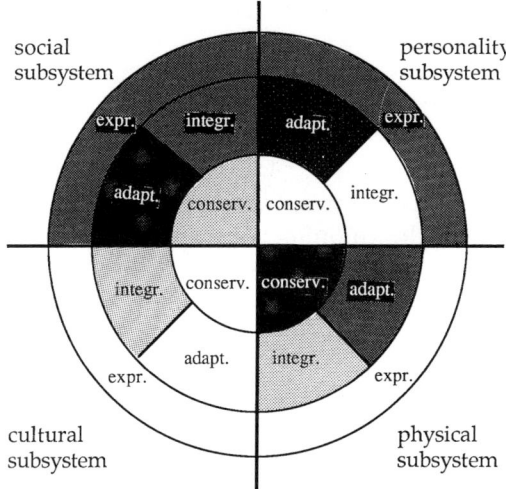

Fig. 13.4. Youth Charter of The International Confederation of Free Trade Unions (ICFTU) (1983). Interpreted by the Systematic Quality of Life Model.

Paragraph 20 is more concerned with women than with children, although there is an indirect concern for the health of the unborn child. This relates to the *conservative mode* of the *physical subsystem*.

Paragraph 21 (more power for young people, also in "the work of their Trade Union – organisation") pertains to the *expressive mode* of *the social subsystem*.

Paragraph 22 (development) relates to the *integrative mode* of the *social subsystem*.

Paragraph 23 is a formulation of the importance of international solidarity ("it is essential that young workers realise and understand the mutual interests between workers in different countries") and class-consciousness. It pleads for social justice and a new economic order. This concern is classifiable in the *integrative and conservative modes* of the *social subsystem*.

5. INTERNATIONAL AGREEMENTS RELATING TO THE TRAFFIC OF WOMEN AND CHILDREN (1904, 1910, 1921)

See Appendices III, IV and V

On September 27, 1901, the International Association of Labour Legislation held its first meeting in Basel. Professor Toniolo, president of the Italian Section, presented a memorandum on the traffic of Italian children. International regulation on this issue was proposed. In 1904 the *International Agree-*

ment for the Suppression of the White Slave Traffic was published. The most important articles for our study are:

Article 1

Each of the Contracting Governments undertakes to establish or name some authority charged with the co-ordination of all information relative to the procuring of women or girls for immoral purposes abroad; this authority shall be empowered to correspond directly with the similar department established in each of the other Contracting States.[43]

Article 2

Each of the Governments undertakes to have a watch kept, especially in railway stations, ports of embarkation, and *en route* for persons in charge of women and girls destined for an immoral life. With this object instructions shall be given to the officials and all other qualified persons to obtain, within legal limits, all information likely to lead to the detection of criminal traffic.

In July 1924, however, the League of Nations issued a statement, regretting the observation that many States had failed to communicate with one another, not only in cases of actual offence but also in cases of suspicion, where co-operation was even more important.[44]

Traffic in Women and Children was widespread at the turn of the Century. Governments tried to fight the phenomenon with the 1904 *International Agreement* and with two Conventions, one in 1910 and the other, in 1921.[45]

The International Convention of 1910 *request that White Slave Traffic should be made punishable*:

Article 1

Whoever, in order to gratify the passions of another person, has procured, enticed, or led away, even with her consent, a woman or girl under age, for immoral purposes, shall be punished, notwithstanding that the various acts constituting the offence may have been committed in different countries.

Article 2

Whoever, in order to gratify the passions of another person, has, by fraud, or by means of violence, threats, abuse of authority, or any other method of compulsion, procured, enticed, or led away a woman or girl over age, for immoral purposes, shall also be punished, notwithstanding that the various acts constituting the offence may have been committed in different countries.

This regulation was not always implemented by the States Parties to the Convention. In 1924, for instance, Italy was criticised by the League of Nations because, although it did have regulations in regard to prostitution ("the object of which was to maintain public order and prevent the spreading of venereal diseases"), their bearing on the traffic in women and children was not clearly stated.[46]

Using Shye's 'Systemic Quality of Life Model', we classify the first three international agreements in the *conservative mode* of the *physical subsystem* since the central issue was public health, especially the fear of venereal disease. Unlike influenza, venereal disease could, in those days, permanently damage physical functioning and even threaten life. There is also a concern for promoting the compatibility between the child's behaviour and society's norms and values. This relates to the *adaptive mode* of the *cultural subsystem*.[47]

In the archives of the League of Nations in Geneva, I found a letter (dated February 1925[48]) wherein a shift in the emphasis from protection to prevention is mentioned:

> *Dear Arthur,... the point is that in combining child welfare with the committee for the suppression of the traffic in women and girls, the whole movement is getting off on the wrong foot. Such a combination represents an idea that was prevalent perhaps twenty-five or more years ago when child welfare was conceived to be exclusively a business of protecting children from external assault. Newer ideas, however, have been introduced and now, when we here in America speak of child welfare, we think of it in more positive and affirmative terms – not only health, but in the general release of those forces of childhood which make for happiness and balanced life. The emphasis has come to be not so much to protect the child from external situations as to develop the child and remove the inhibitions which might cramp or narrow its life.*

6. THE CHILDREN'S CHARTER OF THE INTERNATIONAL COUNCIL OF WOMEN (1922)

See Appendix VIII

The *International Council of Women* (ICW) was founded in 1888 as an umbrella organisation for women's movements.[49] In September 1920, the Council convened for the fifth time[50] in order to talk about the welfare of the Commonwealth, the family and the individual.[51] Photographs show the wealthy ladies wrapped in their fur stoles, grouped around the Scottish Marchioness of Aberdeen and Temair who acted as Chairperson. On the

326   *Chapter XIII*

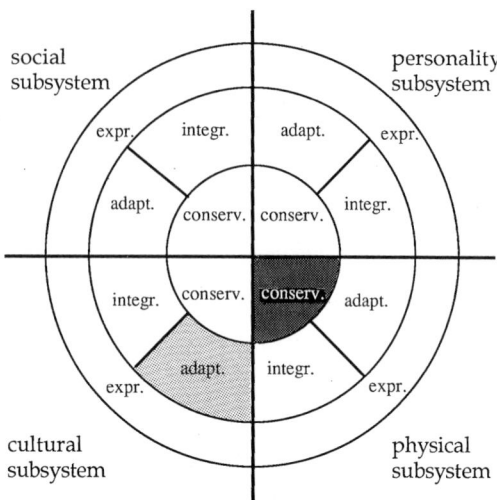

Fig. 13.5. International Agreement relative to the Traffic of women and children (1910 and 1921). Interpreted by the Systemic Quality by the Systemic Quality of Life Model.

agenda of the 1920 Conference, held in Kristiania (Norway) were economic and industrial problems, public health care, the concept of the League of Nations, and their repercussions on women.[52]

The Women's Councils of Italy and the United States submitted resolutions, requesting that the *International Women's Council* formulate a Children's Charter with minimum rights for children of all countries.[53] A Committee was appointed[54] to draft such a Charter. In 1922 this Committee met in the Hague (the Netherlands). The result of their work was presented to the Executive of the ICW, who forwarded it to the National Councils with a recommendation "to adapt it to the needs of their respective countries and then to present it to their Governments." The Charter consisted of seven sections, each divided into a number of paragraphs.

Section I, *Prenatal Care*, demands "instruction in sexual hygiene for boys and girls by specially trained teachers." From the text we understand that the aim is to prevent the spread of venereal diseases leading to degeneration.

Couples about to marry must be shown their responsibility towards the next generation; community nurses and midwives must advise and help pregnant women; work must be forbidden by law during six weeks before and after childbirth; medical care must be available during the period of breast feeding etc. Section I also demands that the causes of mother and child mortality be explained.

In Shye's 'Systemic Quality of Life Model' Section I is classifiable in the *conservative mode* (permanent bodily damage by venereal diseases) and the *integrative mode* (ongoing health) of the *physical subsystem*.

Section II, *Care of mothers and children up to school age*, demands, among other things, treatment of eye diseases in order to prevent infantile blindness; convalescent homes and holiday homes for mothers and young children who need to regain strength; playgrounds and playrooms with trained play teachers.

Prevention of blindness pertains to the *conservative mode* of the *physical subsystem*. Convalescent homes for mothers belongs in the *integrative mode* of the *physical subsystem*. It is interesting that for the first time (in 1922) importance is attached to play and recreation under the guidance of professional teachers. Play is classifiable in the *expressive mode* of the *personality subsystem*. Recreation relates to the *adaptive mode* of the *personality subsystem*.

The main concern of Section III, *Children of School Age* is with physical health (schoolhouses with suitable sanitary arrangements etc.). This is classifiable in the *integrative mode* of the *physical subsystem*. Vaccination against smallpox and other diseases and is classifiable in the *conservative mode* of the *physical subsystem*. Education in moral laws pertains to the *adaptive mode* of the *cultural subsystem*. Adequate playground, recreation centres and libraries belong in the *adaptive mode* of the *cultural subsystem* and the *adaptive mode* of the *personality subsystem*.

Section IV deals with *Children in Employment*. Paragraphs 1 and 2, demanding "prohibition of the employment of boys and girls under eighteen at night and in dangerous trades," correspond to the fifth and sixth Conventions of the International Labour Organisation (I.L.O.). The concern relates to the *integrative and conservative modes* of the *physical subsystem* (prevention of accidents).

Section V, *Delinquent Children*, demands provisions "preventing the delinquent, abnormal, defective and neglected child from drifting into crime." Insofar as this Section is concerned with the containment of children within 'decent society', it pertains to the *conservative mode* of the *social subsystem*. The last paragraph of Section V, demanding that the State should assume guardianship "in cases where parents are found guilty of cruelty, neglect and desertion," belongs in the *conservative mode* of the *physical subsystem*.[55]

Two other subjects discussed by the International Council of Women, concern 'children born out of wedlock'[56] and 'children of aliens to different countries'. These subjects proved to be so controversial that no consensus was reached. No reference to them is therefore made in the Charter.

Although we have not dealt with each and every detail of the Children's Charter, it is clear that the International Council of Women greatly valued financial investment by the authorities in order to raise the quality of life. The majority of the demands are classifiable in the *physical subsystem*. Of course improvement in the physical subsystem positively affects the other three subsystems.

The women's plan to discuss the *Charter* again during their next meeting,[57]

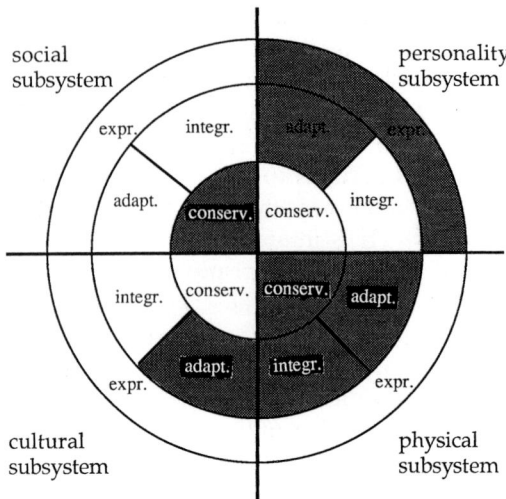

Fig. 13.6. The Children's Charter of 1922 of the I.C.W. (International Council of Women). Interpreted by the Systemic Quality of Life Model.

was abandoned for fear that this would be at cross-purposes with the efforts of the League of Nations to formulate a *Declaration of the Rights of the Child.*

7. A Bill of Rights for Children, Proposed by Henry Foster and Doris Freed (1972)

See Appendix XXV

In 1972 the *New York Law Journal* published in its regular feature column three articles by Professor Henry Foster (Matrimonial Lawyer and Professor at the New York University School of Law) and Doris Freed (then Counsel to the Firm Deisan & Gordon). These articles,[58] which appeared under the title 'A Bill of Rights for Children', were not purely scientific but the result of the practical knowledge of an expert lawyer in private practice and a 'down to earth' academician.

In 1974, Foster published an elaboration of these three articles[59]. Henry Foster[60] died on June 26th, 1988. In the summer of 1988, I talked extensively with Doris Freed in her office in the Chrysler Building in New York.

"To stipulate a 'Bill of Rights for Children'," wrote Foster and Freed, "does not rid them of moral and legal obligations." On the contrary, it was intended "to enhance their sense of responsibility."[61] The authors formulated ten Principles.[62] The premise behind the ... Principles is that children are people," they wrote. "They are entitled to assert individual interests in their own right, to have a fair consideration given to their claims, and to have their best interests judged in terms of pragmatic consequences." Foster and Freed did not consider the child as an adult. They wrote, for instance, "Although marriage is 'a basic civil right of man' we would not argue that a child of three has a constitutional right to marry. The child of three, however, should not be treated as an object, and in custody proceedings between his parents, it is our contention that he should receive legal protection and representation."[63] "Children must be treated fairly if we want them to mature into responsible adulthood," Foster and Freed write. "We therefore best reckon with the child's point of view and his sense of fairness."[64] Foster and Freed represent a lawyer's point of view, but express great knowledge of child-psychology. Foster and Freed's 'Bill of Rights for Children' is often quoted (especially in the field of family law). It is an important piece of work that deserves to be analysed in this study.

The first Principle ("the right to receive parental love and affection") means the right to an affectionate relationship with someone who stands in the position of a parent towards the child. This is not necessarily his or her biological parent but may be someone with whom the child has a psychological relationship."[65] The consequence of this Principle is that the bond "between the *de facto* parents and the child should always be a crucial factor in resolving difficult custody and adoption cases," writes Foster.[66] "The *psychological* well-being should be the focal point."[67] Since, according to Foster and Freed, the psychological relationship between the *de facto* parent(s) and the child offer the child the best chances for optimal personality development, this Principle pertains to the *expressive mode* of the *personality subsystem*.

The second Principle ("the right to be supported, maintained and educated") is formulated as a right of the child but is in fact a duty of the parents. Foster: "the tragedy is that these parental duties or rights of children, were until relatively recently not backed up by effective legal sanctions."[68] However, Foster admits that "today most States have multiple actions and remedies to enforce the child support obligation, ranging from criminal, quasi-criminal to civil actions."[69]

The two expert Attorneys at Law were only too familiar with the gap between legislation and court practice in many cities (where over-burdened courts normally rushed through these support hearings). Foster speaks from experience when he says that, owing to lack of time, sometimes the father does not receive a chance to state his point of view, and that he often leaves the courtroom, determined not to pay the child support money if he can avoid it. Basing himself on his rich experience, Foster offers all sorts of practical suggestions such as informal pre-trial conferences with both parties, during which the father is allowed to air his side of the family difficulty and to suggest the amount of money he is willing to pay. Foster and Freed argue that if the amount is reasonable such a hearing has the function of making the father morally obliged to agree with the support order. Interestingly, they view the child's right to be supported, maintained and educated, as a duty of *parents* rather than of *the State*. This is also typical for the United States, where many people are afraid of State interference. Since they claim that financial support is a right, it is classifiable in the *adaptive mode* of the *physical subsystem* of the 'Systemic Quality of Life Model'.

If the third Principle ("the child's right to be regarded as a person") were accepted, appreciated and implemented, write Foster and Freed, "the other Principles would fall neatly into place." In his book, Foster mentions the original third Principle as number one. Foster: "A great deal of the difficulty with minors derives from the refusal to accept them as individuals, with their own needs, interests and desires To fail to treat a minor as a person, at home, in school or before the law, is to deny him humanity."[70] Foster would even grant minors the right to sue and be sued in their own name. According to him, the minor and his counsel would make relevant decisions "if minors became *sui juris*, and were real parties in interest, there would be greater autonomy for them and an assurance that their point of view would be presented."[71]

To the extent that the third Principle represents an effort to accept minors as individuals and accord them more self-determination and responsibility[72], it relates to the *expressive mode* of the *personality subsystem*. The part concerned with giving children more power is classifiable in the *expressive mode* of the *social subsystem*. The central concern here is the effort to have the child's uniqueness honoured ("right to individuality and autonomy"). This relates to *all modes* of the *personality subsystem*.

The fourth Principle, the right to "fair treatment from all in authority", (for instance, not to be denied the privilege against self-incrimination, the right to counsel, the right to confrontation) seems to deal only with juvenile court proceedings, but according to Foster and Freed "is not limited to the forensic area."[73] Foster: "Children are entitled to reasoned argument in lieu of ultimati; understanding is promoted, if not achieved, when reasons are given for decisions. Many adults fail to appreciate that fair procedure and rules are essential for a just determination of controversies." This Principle deals with the right to be treated individually, but because of the statement *from all authority* we classify it in the *integrative mode* of the *social subsystem* (interactions among the individual's various social roles) and, to a lesser extent, also in the *expressive mode* of the *social subsystem* (not cutting down the child's possibility to influence).

The fifth Principle (the moral and legal right "to be heard and listened to") is mainly concerned with the fact that "children have individual interests *apart* from and sometimes *in conflict with* the interests of parents and Society."[74] According to Foster and Freed "the most significant and practical reform that could be made in the area of children and the law," would be independent representation by counsel (for instance when the parents divorce). In Foster's book,[75] the right "to be heard and listened to," is linked to "the right to receive fair treatment." Foster: "Lawyers usually have not pressed the interests of children *qua* children. There is also a pervasive paternalism derived from the feudal status of children and the concept that children are not people, but objects of paternal rights."[76] Foster and Freed explain that the right to be heard and listened to would facilitate interaction with the authorities. It therefore pertains to the *adaptive mode* of the *social subsystem*. However, the main concern is that the child should be seen as an individual in his or her own right, and not as the object of parental rights. The true intention of this Principle is therefore classifiable in all the *four modes* of the *personality subsystem*.

In the sixth Principle ("the right to earn and keep his own earnings"), Foster and Freed revolt against the denigration of minors and the regulations in many States that make the parents legally entitled to their children's money (earned, for instance, for delivering newspapers or baby-sitting). This Principle belongs to the *adaptive and the expressive modes* of the *physical subsystem* (earnings). However, from the context in which it appears, we understand that the drafters were again concerned with the *expressive mode* of the *personality subsystem* ("at some stage of child development a continued parent-child relationship should be a matter of mutual consent insofar as contact and economic incidents are concerned").[77]

About the seventh Principle ("to seek and obtain medical care and treatment"), Foster and Freed state that "here again autonomy is denied and it follows from the status of minority that minors lack legal capacity to give valid consent."[78] Foster and Freed fear that the "usual rule which requires parental consent for medical treatment deters large numbers of young people from seeking and obtaining medical attention when needed or as early as is desirable." They point out that "pregnancy, contraceptive information, drug abuse, and emotional disturbances are among the sensitive issues where a rule requiring parental consent for treatment may be counter-productive."[79] Since the concern is for physical and mental health, we classify the seventh Principle in the *integrative mode* of the *physical and personality subsystems*. The goal (physical and mental health) pertains to the *expressive mode* of the *personality subsystem*.

In the eighth Principle Foster and Freed plead for "the right to emancipate from the parent-child relationship", which would give the individual greater freedom to shape, if necessary, the social framework (such as the family) of which he is a part. In this context the word 'emancipation' is used in the legal sense, as has been explained in Chapter II. Foster and Freed argue that "the status of a minor could be terminated by emancipation which has the legal consequence of relieving the minor from parental control and from the duty of rendering filial services, and terminating the parental duty of support, maintenance and education".[80] Foster and Freed note that up till the present time, only the parent(s) could decide about emancipation. In their opinion, emancipation should apply in both directions. "Why should emancipation be a parental prerogative, but not a privilege to minors?" In Foster's book the seventh and the eighth Principle are inseparable. From the explanation we understand that the eighth Principle pertains to the *adaptive mode* of the *social subsystem*.

The ninth Principle ("to be free of legal disabilities" etc.) is concerned with the child's interaction with society. Foster: "There is a current need to change the philosophical base so that children will be recognized as legal persons, and hence removed from their common law status as non-persons. There must be a strong justification for any impairment for their legal rights and for the imposition of any disability or incapacities."[81] According to Foster and Freed, compulsory school attendance, child labour laws, limitations on property and on the signing of contracts, are outdated. It is our opinion that Foster and Freed had especially the middle class children in mind, and that they would be opposed to child labour if this meant child exploitation. These concerns are classified in the *adaptive mode* of the *social subsystem*.

The tenth Principle is an elaboration of the social interaction between children as carriers of social roles, and society. In this interaction the child has, among other things, the right "to receive special care, consideration and protection in the administration of law or justice." Foster and Freed advocate, for instance, that school administrations should be forced "to adopt fair procedures and the rudiments of due process for disciplinary hearings at school."[82] Before a student is, for instance, suspended for behavioral or medical reasons, he must, according to Foster and Freed, be accorded a fair hearing by the Principal, and the Principal's decision should be subject to appeal. Foster and Freed claim that the solution to such problems is "to provide for the implementation of the right to counsel."[83] This concern relates to the *adaptive mode* of the *social subsystem*.

8. THE RIGHTS OF CHILDREN IN DIVORCE ACTIONS (WISCONSIN, U.S.A., 1966)

See Appendices XIX and XX

In 1966, Circuit Judge Robert W. Hansen published a *Bill of Rights of Children in Divorce Actions*,[84] based on decisions of the Wisconsin Supreme Court by the Milwaukee Family Court Judges. Hansen tells us that a printed copy of this *Bill of Rights* is presented to divorce-seeking parents.[85]

The Wisconsin statutes do not specifically require the preparation and distribution of a Bill of Rights for Children.[86] However, in a letter to me, Assistant-Attorney General of the State of Wisconsin, Donald P. Johns, wrote that "this practice appears to have been started voluntarily in one or two Wisconsin counties in the early or mid-1970s. When, in 1977, the divorce statutes were amended to require, among other things, the dissemination of

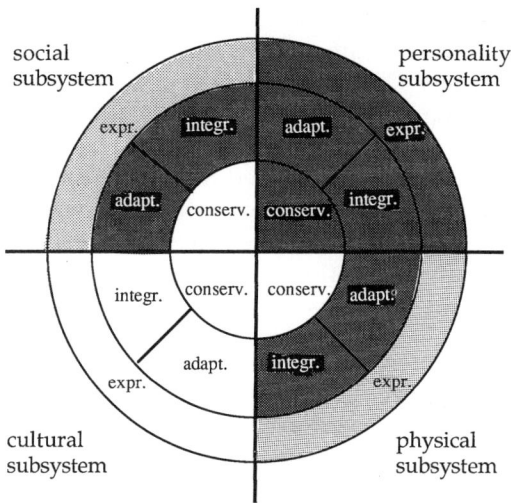

Fig. 13.7. The 'Bill of Rights for Children' of Henry foster and Doris Freed (1972). Interpreted by the Systemic Quality of Life Model.

more information about the divorce procedure to the parties, most counties created or adopted a document similar to the enclosed Bill of Rights."[87]

In another letter Johns added: "It appears that most of the seventy-two counties in Wisconsin distribute some form of a children's Bill of Rights similar to the one we recently forwarded to you. However, the exact format and wording might change from county to county. Nobody seems to know exactly when the document I forwarded was drafted, but it probably was a few years before 1981 as your letter suggests."[88]

Hansen writes[89] that "the Wisconsin story of protecting the rights of children in divorce actions begins with the enactment by the Wisconsin Legislature of a Wisconsin Family Code." The Wisconsin Supreme Court had to spell out what this Family Code implied for children. "The State's Appellate Court soon moved to put muscle power and heart power into the concept that more was involved in a divorce action than the rights or wishes of the two contending parties. Many post-Code decisions have dealt with questions of custody and visitations, but the landmark decision in this field is the 1963 case of *Kritzik v. Kritzik*. Written by Associate Justice Horace Wilkie, this decision dealt with a rather narrow question of whether a custodian ex-wife could send a child to a summer camp and the non-custodian ex-husband be required to pay for such recreational or educational experience. But the issue gave the Supreme Court the opportunity to say the following on the rights of children and the responsibility of the Trial Court in custody matters:

"In making his determinations as to what conditions of a divorce judgment would serve the interests of the children involved, the Trial Court does not function solely as an arbiter between two private parties. Rather, in his role as a Family Court, the Trial Court represents the interests of society in promoting the stability and best interests of the family. It is his task to determine what provisions and terms would best guarantee an opportunity for the children involved to grow to mature and responsible citizens, regardless of the desires of the respective parties. This power reflected a recognition that children involved in a divorce are always disadvantaged parties and that the law must take affirmative steps to protect their welfare".

Such 'affirmative steps', prescribed by the *Kritzik* decision include the right of the Trial Court to direct that a social investigation be made as to the well-being of the children. "Whenever there is a dispute concerning child custody or a reason for concern for the welfare of minors involved in divorce actions, the Milwaukee Family Court now directs that an inquiry, investigation or evaluation of alternatives as to the custody placement be made by the Family Conciliation Department."[90]

We shall first analyse the Bill of Rights assembled by the Family-Court Judges of Milwaukee (A), and thereafter, as an example of similar bills, the one drafted by the staff of the Dane County Family Court Counselling Services in Madison (B).

A.

Principle I of the Milwaukee *Bill of Rights of Children in Divorce Actions* ('the child is a human being and not a pawn, etc.) is a general statement which can be classified in the *complete personality subsystem* of the 'Systemic Quality of Life Model'. (See Appendix XIX for this Declaration.)

Principle II deals with the child's right to grow and develop. To grow to maturity pertains to the *expressive mode* (realising one's potential) of *all the subsystems*.

Principle III states "the right to the day by day love, care, discipline and protection of the parent having custody of the children." From the parent-figure the child must receive love, care, discipline and protection (in that order, according to the Bill of Rights). 'Guardianship' is seen as a means to provide the children with love (*integrative mode* of the *social subsystem*) and belonging (*conservative mode* of the *social subsystem*).

The first part of Principle IV ("the right to know the non-custodian parent") emphasises that the child is part of a social network of relationships. It relates to the *conservative mode* of the *social subsystem*. The second part of this Principle deals with intimate relationships ("the benefit of such parent's love"). This pertains to the *integrative mode* of the *social subsystem*.

The aim of Principle V is to preserve the social and psychological integrity of the child. It urges the divorcing parents not to degrade each other in front of the children. The concern for the social and psychological integrity of the child pertains to the *integrative mode* of the *social and personality subsystems*. Another possible interpretation would classify it in the *conservative mode* of the *personality and social subsystems* (see Principle IV of the next Children's Bill of Rights).

Principle VI ("the right to have moral and ethical values developed") deals with moral and ethical values and thus pleads for the strengthening of the *complete cultural-valuative field* which will influence personal motivation, self-control, identity, etc.

Principle VII ("the right to the most adequate level of economic support") deals with economic support and is classifiable in the *adaptive mode* of the *physical subsystem*.

Principle VIII mentions the right to "the same opportunities for education that the child would have had if the family unit had not been broken." This Principle pleads for continuity in the *adaptive mode* of the *social subsystem*. Perhaps the Principle can also be understood as 'Do not deprive the child of cultural opportunities' (education can be considered as a way to transfer values). In that case, the concern is with the *adaptive mode* of the *cultural subsystem*.

Principle IX pleads for "periodic review of custodial arrangements and child support orders . . . as *the benefit* of the child may require," but does not specify which benefit of the child is meant. We can, therefore, not classify this Principle in the 'Systemic Quality of Life Model'.

Principle X states that if parents divorce, the children are always disadvantaged parties. However, if the parents do not function well or fight too much about the children, a *guardian ad litem* should be appointed to protect the child's interests. Since the nature of these interests is not specified, we assume that they pertain to all modes and subsystems.[91]

B.

Principle I of *The Children's Bill of Rights by the Staff of the Dane County Court Counselling Services* (see Appendix XX) emphasises the importance of a *"continuing relationship with both parents."* This is classifiable in the *integrative mode* of the *social subsystem*. We will explain this further in analysing Principle IX.[92]

Principle II states that the child is a unique individual. Since this Principle deals with the entire 'quality of life' system, it is difficult to classify. We may, however, assume that the emphasis is on the *personality subsystem*.

Principle III is also very general ("the right to continuing care and guidance"). Is *care* here only *physical care*? Since the text is vague, we shall classify this Principle in the *adaptive mode* of *all the subsystems*.

Principle IV is a call for each parent not to degrade the other ("the right to know and appreciate what is good in each parent without one parent degrading the other"). The child often sees him- or herself as an image of both parents. Thus, if one of the parents is degraded, this will affect the child's self-image. It is therefore important that the child learns what is good in each parent. Our interpretation of this Principle is that it belongs in the *conservative mode* of the *personality and the social subsystems*.

Principle V ("The right to express love etc. for each parent without having to stifle that love because of fear of disapproval by the other parent.") deals with one of the most important problems of children of divorced or divorcing parents: the *loyalty conflict*. The child fears that if he or she expresses affection to one parent, the other parent will not love him or her any more. The Principle is a plea for such situations to be avoided. It relates to the *expressive mode* of the *personality subsystem*.

Principle VI ("the right to know that the parents' decision to divorce was not the responsibility of the child") is also extremely important. The intention is to ensure that guilt does not become part of the child's personality. This concern is classifiable in the *conservative mode* of the *personality subsystem*.

Principle VII ("the right not to be a source of argument between the parents") deals with the same consideration, and belongs also in the *conservative mode* of the *personality subsystem*. As a marginal note we point out that children of couples who are not divorced or divorcing are also frequently a source of argument between their parents. However, *the right* not to be a source of argument is very difficult to enforce.

Principle VIII ("the right to honest answers to questions about the changing family relationships") pleads for proper interaction with the child as a human being and a member of society. This concern pertains to the (*adaptive mode* of the *personality and social subsystems*).

Principle IX consists of two parts. They can only be analysed on a deeper level: "The right to be able to experience regular and consistent contact with both parents" deals with the stability of the relationship and relates to the *conservative mode* of the *integrative-social sub-sub-subsystem*. The second part, ("the right to know the reason for cancelation of time or change of plans"), pertains to the *adaptive mode* of the *integrative-social subsystem*.

Since for small children the parents are the microcosmos of social relations, Principle X ("the right to have a relaxed, secure relationship with both parents etc.") expresses the right to the whole network of relationships. In the case of small children, we classify this Principle in the *conservative mode* of the *social subsystem*. In the case of older children Principle X is classifiable in the *integrative mode* of the *social subsystem*. However, the last part of the Principle ("without being placed in a position to manipulate one parent against the other") reveals the true intention. Like Principle IX, stability is the main concern of the drafters. This pertains to the *conservative mode* of the *integrative-social sub-subsystem*.

The Rights of Children in Divorce Actions 337

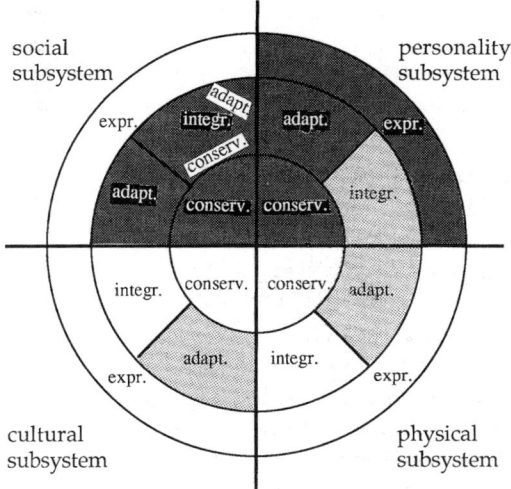

Fig. 13.8.1. The 'Bill of Rights of Children in Divorce Actions' (Milwaukee, Wisconsin, 1966). Interpreted by the Systemic Quality of Life Model.

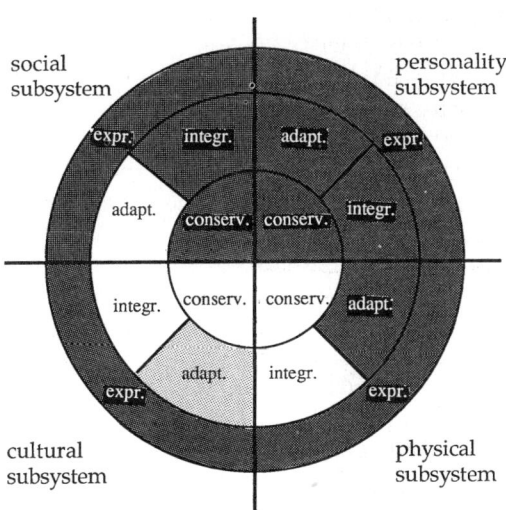

Fig. 13.8.2. The Children's bill of Rights, of the Dane County Family Court Counseling Services (Madison, Wisconsin). Interpreted by the Systemic Quality of Life Model.

338   Chapter XIII

9. A Bill of Rights for Foster Children (1973)

See Appendix XXVI

On April 14th, 1973, President Nixon announced his support for the 'National Action for Foster Children Week'. The President said: "We have to renew our determination to assure foster children that we care about them and their well-being." The National Action for Foster Children Committee organised a meeting in Philadelphia in the historical Hall where the American *Constitution*[93] had been discussed and adopted. Now, like then,[94] the 'delegates' adopted the Bill with an unanimous "Aye."

Several American foster children had been invited to witness the signing of the *Bill of Rights of Foster Children* by Frederick C. Green (Adjunct-Director of the *Children's Bureau*), Bruce Mallott (President of the *National Action for Foster Children Committee*), *and Mrs. Cox (President of the North American Indian Women's Association)*, and to accept the document symbolically.

Apart from reiterating the 'inalienable rights' of *all* children, this Declaration emphasises the *special* rights of foster children. The drafters argued that foster children had often been deprived in early infancy, and that they were, therefore, entitled to assistance with adjustment problems in their emotional, physical, intellectual, social and spiritual growth (see Article VI). The Declaration also mentions the need to help the child accept the fact that the biological parents do not take care of him or her (Article III), and the right to be represented by an attorney, for instance for evaluation of problems that may arise when the Juvenile Judge places a child in a foster family (Article IX). The "right to be cherished by a family" (Article I) and "the right to be nurtured by foster parents who have been selected to meet his individual needs" (Article II)[95] deal with the special characteristics of foster care. The second part of Article II notes that foster parents ("who are provided services and support") should be helped to fulfil their task well. The Bill of Rights calls for the child (and his natural parents) to be involved in major decisions that affect the child's life (Article X).

Jacob Sprauce,[96] one of the foremen of the American Association of Foster Families, noted that the publicity given to the meeting in Philadelphia had helped to counter the negative connotations associated with the term 'foster child' in the United States. Many people think that children who are *in foster care* have been placed away from home because they have trespassed the law. According to Sprauce this prejudice is still prevalent since the National Action for Foster Children Committee[97] was much too weak to brandish a fist to the authorities in order to initiate the necessary changes and influence public opinion. According to Sprauce the idea to proclaim a *Bill of Rights for Foster Children* was good, but what one really needed was an organisation that was strong enough to follow up the proclamations. In 1983 the *National Association of Foster Parents* launched the (revised)

Declaration again during a meeting in Northfolk (West Virginia). At this meeting, it was decided to replace the term 'foster children' by *children in care*.

If we analyse the 1973 Bill of Rights for this special sub-population according to Shye's 'Systemic Quality of Life Model', we see that Article I deals with the now largely accepted opinion that children make affectional bonds with those adults who act as their parents, irrespective of blood relationship. "The child has a right to be cherished by a family..."[98] says Article I. The rationale of this formulation is that if the child cannot, for whatever reason, continue to live with his or her natural parents, he or she must be placed with new parental figures with whom attachment is possible. If the child learns (again) to trust his new 'psychological parents', he will later learn to trust larger societal frameworks beyond the family unit. The right "to be cherished by a family of his own" is, therefore, classifiable in the *conservative mode* of the *social subsystem* (fundamental sense of belonging and trust).

The first part of Article II, ("to be nurtured by foster parents... to meet his individual needs,") deals with adjusting conditions and resources to the child's individuality. This concern relates to the *adaptive mode* of the *personality and physical subsystems* (in that order). The second part of Article II deals with "specialized education for the foster parents, so that the family will be better equipped to enable the child to reach his potential. Although the child will indirectly benefit from this concern, we shall not classify it as a right of the child..."

Article III deals with giving the child sensitive, continuing help in understanding and accepting his 'new social reality' (the foster family). This concern pertains to the *adaptive mode* of the *social and the personality subsystems*. The second part of Article III aims at encouraging a feeling of confidence and self-worth (to evaluate oneself). This pertains to the *conservative and integrative modes* of the *personality subsystem* (interactions among personality characteristics).

In Article IV we read that the child needs "continuing loving care." We classify this concern in the *integrative mode* of the *social subsystem* (intimate relationships). This Article also mentions the child's right to "respect as a unique human being." This relates to *the whole personality subsystem*. The Article specifies that children need "loving care and respect as a human being" in order to "trust in himself" (classifiable in the *conservative mode* of the *personality subsystem*), and "trust in others" (classifiable in the *integrative and conservative modes* of the *social subsystem*) (see Principle V of the Milwaukee Bill of Rights).

Article V formulates the right of the child to 'belong' to a neighbourhood of people. 'To belong' is classifiable in the *conservative mode* of the *social subsystem*. To the extent that the drafters considered the neighbourhood as a social institution, the concern pertains to the *adaptive mode* of the *social subsystem*.

Article VI deals with the right "to receive help." Help "in his

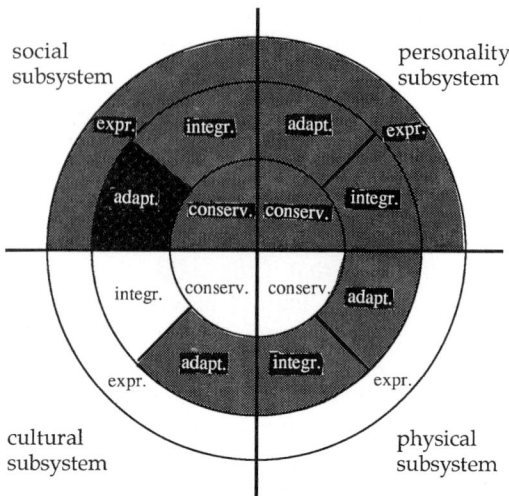

Fig. 13.9. The 'Bill of Rights for Foster Children' (1973). Interpreted by the Systemic Quality of Life Model.

emotional... intellectual growth" pertains to the *adaptive mode* of the *personality subsystem*. Help "in his physical growth" relates to the *physical subsystem*. Help "in his social growth" pertains to the *social subsystem*. Help "in his spiritual growth" pertains to the *cultural and personality subsystems*.

Article VII (the right "to receive education, training and career guidance") belongs in the *adaptive mode* of the *social subsystem*. To the extent that the concern is with preparing the child "for a useful and satisfying life," it can also be classified in the *integrative mode* of the *personality subsystem*.

Article VIII deals with preparing a child for citizenship and parenthood. It is classifiable in the *adaptive mode* of the *social subsystem*.

Since Article IX deals with proceedings, it is not classified in the 'Systemic Quality of Life Model'.

Article X ("to receive high quality of child welfare services") relates to the *adaptive mode* of the *social subsystem*. Since reference is made to social status that might affect the life of the child ("his own involvement in major decisions that affect his life"), this Article is also classifiable in the *expressive mode* of the *social subsystem*.

Summarising the analysis of this 'Bill of Rights for Foster Children' we can say that its main concern lies with the *adaptive mode* of *all subsystems* (with special emphasis on the social and personality subsystems). Only Principle X expresses a concern for the expressive mode. The question is raised whether the failure to deal with the expressive mode is accidental or a tacit manifestation of an attitude that is *protective* rather than focused on self-determination.

10. THE UN DECLARATION RELATING TO FOSTER PLACEMENT AND ADOPTION (1986)

The United Nations Declaration on Social and Legal Principles Relating to the Protection and Welfare of Children, with Special Reference to Foster Placement and Adoption Nationally and Internationally

See Appendix XL

In 1975 the Secretary-General of the United Nations asked a group of experts to draw up a Declaration on the social and legal principles regarding national and international adoption and the placement of children in foster families. In 1979 the experts delivered a draft for such a Declaration at the office of the Secretary-General, but it was not before 1985 that the General Assembly, on the initiative of the Netherlands, called the Member States in order to complete this Draft-Declaration. This Consultation, chaired by the Dutch Legal Counsellor Jaap Walkate, took place in New York from September 16th to 27th, 1985.

Jacques Jansen, an advisor to the Chairman wrote: "While proposing some changes in the original work-document drafted in the 1970s, we took in due consideration the many detailed comments by the Member-States. An important obstacle appeared to be that prominently Islamic countries had raised insurmountable objections against adoption."[99] The strategy that finally led to a consensus about this very sensitive subject was phrased by the Chairman of the Consultation: "The Declaration does not intend in any way to impose on States the obligation to adopt national legislation establishing such legal institutions as foster placement or adoption, but is based on the assumption that, if such institutions exist, States should consider the principles of the Declaration as relevant and . . . when adopted . . . should have the status of a recommendation to Member States of the United Nations."[100]

Marie-Françoise Lücker-Babel: "Since a significant proportion (12 of the 24) of the Articles . . . are phrased in the form of wishes or qualified recommendations, the text carries less impact than other international instruments. Even among comparable, i.e. non-binding, texts, there are many drafted in more specific terms."[101]

On December 3rd, 1986, the Declaration, consisting of a Preamble, Section A (General Family and Child Welfare), Section B (Foster Placement) and Section C (Adoption), was unanimously adopted by the General Assembly of the United Nations.

The first paragraph of the Preamble recalls the Universal Declaration of Human Rights and the different Human Rights Conventions. This explains that the protection of welfare of children is based on respect for human rights and that the drafters base their concern for children on general concerns.

The *second paragraph* of the Preamble comes nearer to the specific concerns by recalling the United Nations Declaration on the Rights of the Child.

The *third paragraph* of the Preamble ("the child shall wherever possible, grow up in the care and under the responsibility of his parents, and in any case, in an atmosphere of affection and of moral and material security") reaffirms *Principle* 6, *Paragraph* 2 of the United Nations Declarations on the Rights of the Child. The drafters of the new Declaration thus emphasise a concern that we classify in the *conservative mode* of the *physical subsystem* (continuity of physical structure), in the *conservative mode* of the *cultural and physical subsystems* (moral and material security), and in the *integrative mode* of the *social subsystem* (in an atmosphere of affection).

Paragraph 4 of the Preamble mentions the motivation for this Declaration (concern about the large number of children who are abandoned or became orphans). It expresses a concern with security and is classified in the *conservative mode* of the *physical subsystem*. The best interests of the child, mentioned in Paragraph 4, relates to the complete 'Systemic Quality of Life Model'.

Paragraph 6 of the Preamble pays respect to 'Kefalah' or the solution under Islamic Law for taking care of abandoned children and orphans. 'Kefalah' also guarantees that the community will fulfil its obligations towards these children. Under Islamic Law, a man can take a child into his family, but he cannot arrange for the child to inherit from him. And different from adoption, a boy taken in by an Islamic man can marry that man's daughter.

Marie-Françoise Lücker-Babel writes: "The restrictive wording in the Preamble to the Declaration is worth noting. Although universality is an essential aspect of human rights – to deny it would automatically lead to segregation between all kinds of human groups. The Declaration provides a sizeable loophole: 'Recognizing that under the principal legal systems of the world, various other alternative valuable institutions exist, such as the 'Kefalah' of Islamic Law,' it affirms that the 'universal principles' it proclaims do not *impose* on States such legal institutions as foster placement or adoption. As a result, even the general recommendations relating to general family and child welfare could be interpreted in so restrictive a sense as to be inapplicable to valuable institutions not covered by the definitions of foster placement or adoption.[102] . . . This means that these institutions would be exempt from every specific international ruling, which would immediately place innumerable children outside the field of application of the most recent text dealing with the issue. Such an interpretation would be regrettable."[103]

Article 1 is a suggestion to States to give high priority to family welfare.

Article 2 widens the perspective from child welfare to family welfare. It states that child welfare depends upon "good family welfare."

As we have seen, *Article* 3 suggests as a good child-welfare policy that "the first priority for a child is to be cared for by his or her own parents."

The original formulation by the experts had been: "every child has the right to a family." Lücker-Babel states that "article 3 of the Declaration should, ideally, enable a far greater number of children to remain with the family, and hence in the national community into which they are born."[104] If the natural parents are incapable of caring for the child, alternative care should be provided by the relatives of the child's parents, another substitute family "or if necessary, by an appropriate institution." The United Nations explicitly prefer care in a family to care in an institution. In this respect, it defers from the 1988 International Federation of Educative Communities (FICE) Congress who, in their 'Malmö-Declaration'[105], "urged all persons in society and government... to consider 'Children's Homes' and comparable provisions not as a last resort for children needing care, but as an important available intervention to be used at an appropriate time in the development of those children for whom it is desirable."

On the other hand *Article* 4 "wants" as Jansen pointed out, "to promote a world policy wherein care, other than in the natural or a foster family, ergo in an institution or children's home, will be reduced to absolute *ultimum remedium*"[106]

Article 5 states that "in all matters relating to the placement of a child outside the care of the child's own parents, the best interests of the child should be the paramount consideration."

The best interests of the child is specified: "His or her need for affection" pertains to the *integrative mode* of the *social subsystem*. "The right to security" pertains to the *conservative mode* of the *physical and personality subsystems*). "Continuing care" belongs in the *adaptive mode* of the *physical subsystem*).[107]

Article 6 recommends that persons responsible for foster placement or adoption should be professionally trained.

Article 7 stipulates that if national child welfare services do not function adequately, appropriate actions should be considered by governments. But what about local and regional child welfare services? The Declaration does not provide an answer to this question.

Article 8 ("the child should at all times have a name, a nationality and a legal representative") is classifiable in the *adaptive mode* of the *social subsystem*. The child's name and nationality can be changed, but at all times he or she must possess both. Most declarations on the rights of the child do not mention the child's right to have a legal representative. Article 8 does not elaborate on the subject, thus leaving it open for different interpretations. Lücker-Babel writes that "the representative should preferably be independent of the persons and agencies directly concerned, until such time as a final decision on the placement is reached in the country of origin and the adoption is finally pronounced in the host country. The presence of a legal representative external to the case being processed should be regarded as a means of curtailing abuses."[108]

Although *Article* 9 recognises the importance of the child's social identity, it is not formulated as a right, but as "*the need* of a foster or adopted child." We classify this Article in the *conservative mode* of the *social subsystem*. Lücker-Babel writes: "An absolute right would, in fact, conflict with the right of other individuals directly related with the adoption (namely the natural parents)"[109]

In some societies, the bearing of a child out of wedlock is looked upon as so negative that the biological mother's very life may be endangered if her secret is revealed by action initiated by the child. Sometimes 'knowing his or her identity' can also be in conflict with the best interests of the child. For instance, should a social worker be obliged to tell an adopted child the truth if the child was after birth thrown in the garbage can? In some cases such information may be too heavy to live with.

Part B of this Declaration deals with foster placement. The most important statement in this connection is that foster placement should be of a temporary nature. The fact that *permanent* placement in a foster family (without subsequent adoption) may sometimes be in the best interests of a child is ignored in the Declaration.

Article 12 recommends that the prospective foster parents, the child and the natural parents should be involved in the decision-making process. According to Jansen,[110] the addition "as appropriate (to the child and his or her parents)" aimed at leaving room for exceptions, for instance if the child is still too young or if the behaviour of the natural parent(s) is not appropriate. The Article also recommends that a competent authority or agency should be responsible for supervision "to ensure the welfare of the child."

Part C deals with adoption.

Article 13 states that the primary aim of adoption is "to provide the child who cannot be cared for by his or her own parents with a permanent family." Continuing care ("a permanent family") is classifiable in the *adaptive mode* of the *physical subsystem*. Bearing in mind that care in a permanent family does not refer only to physical care, we assume that *Article* 13 pertains to the *other subsystems*, too.

Article 14 *and* 15, and the first part of *Article* 16 are concerned with selection and placement. The second part of *Article* 16 recommends that "legislation should ensure that the child is recognized in law as a member of the adoptive family and enjoys all rights pertinent thereto." According to Jansen,[111] a preference is voiced for the *adoptio plena* whereby the child is part of the adoptive family, not only in the social but also in the legal sense, so that he or she will be totally integrated in the adoptive family. Lücker-Babel notes that this paragraph "is phrased as an appeal to the authorities rather than as an acknowledgment of the specific rights."[112] This pertains to the *conservative mode* of the *social subsystem*.

From *Article* 17 onwards the Articles are concerned with *intercountry* adoption. The taking away of a child from his or her own culture may be considered *only* if no appropriate manner of care can be offered to the child in its own State. Jansen: "If there was anything at all about which the Delegations in New York came to a complete consensus, it was about this Article."[113] This is classified in the *conservative mode* of the *cultural subsystem*.

Article 18 is a recommendation to governments to provide protection for children who are involved in intercountry adoption. Adequate policy, legislation and supervision must be procured by the State.

According to Lücker-Babel, *Article* 19 prohibits for the first time abduction and any other form of illegal separation of the child from his or her family.[114]

Article 20 condemns improper financial gain as the result of adoption. Articles 18, 19 and 20 are concerned with the very life and health of the child. They are, therefore, classifiable in the *conservative mode* of the *physical subsystem*, and also in the *conservative mode* of the *social subsystem*.

Article 21 recommends special precautions by the States when the adoption takes place through agents (middlemen).

Article 22 states that before a child is allowed to leave the State in which he or she lives, it must be established that he or she is free for adoption, and also that the child will be able to join his or her prospective adoptive parents and obtain their nationality. This concern pertains to the *adaptive mode* of the *social subsystem*.

Article 23 states that 'as a rule' the legal validity of the adoption should be assured in each of the States involved.

Article 24 "due weight shall be given to the child's cultural and religious background and interests" seems to run contrary to the reality of intercountry adoption, since 'acquisition' of a new cultural and religious background is virtually inevitable. In our opinion, this article is an empty slogan, included to satisfy the States of origin.

Lücker-Babel concludes that "neither the lengthy, complicated title nor its 24 articles are actually focused on children... The Declaration fails to grant a central place to the rights of the child... Any prospect of improvement is contingent on acceptance of the Declaration as a minimal requirement and on the institution of appropriate measures."[115]

Unfortunately, the 1965 *Hague Convention on jurisdiction, applicable law and recognition of decrees relating to Adoption* did not become the important instrument hoped for, since only a few States ratified it. The 1986 United Nations Declaration was thus 'reculer pour mieux sauter'(a few steps back to make a jump to a new Convention about adoption). Since then talks have indeed started about a new Convention in the framework of the Hague Conference on Private International Law. The chances for a new, more effective and more widely supported Convention, have increased.[116]

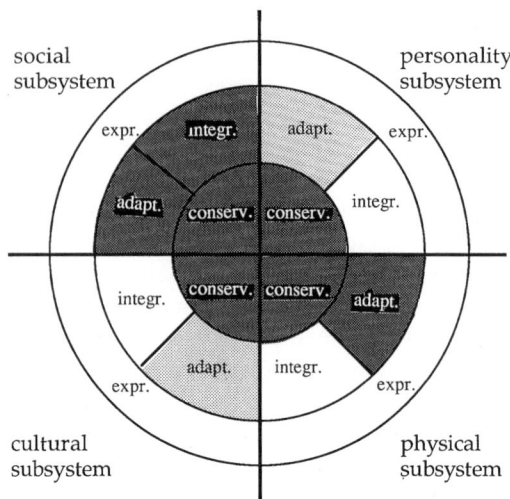

Fig. 13.10. De U.N. Declaration Relating to Foster Placement and Adoption (1986). Interpreted by the Systemic Quality of Life Model.

11. THE CHARTER OF RIGHTS FOR CHILDREN IN CARE OF THE LONDON BOROUGHS CHILDREN'S REGIONAL PLANNING COMMITTEE (AUGUST 1986)

See Appendix XXXIX

In June 1975, the National Children's Bureau in London organised a one-day Conference of young people in care.[117] During the Conference, a working group of youngsters was set up which produced, among other things, a *Charter of Rights for Young People in Care*.[118] A *National Association of Young People in Care* was formed. Other organisations[119], such as the *Residential Care Association*[120] also tried to speak and voices were even heard demanding a special *Charter of Rights for Residents*. Ron Walton, for instance, wrote that "much bitterness and frustration could be avoided if the management of social services and the staff of Homes were to take the initiative in opening up the question of rights with residents. Not all conflicts would be resolved by this approach, but they would be set in a climate of greater trust and constructive effort."[121] The social workers now pleaded for "an appeals sub-committee with professional advice in each local authority" and "involving clients and their relatives in the decision to admit and discharge them."[122]

The National Children's Bureau produced a list of essential elements for an effective complaints procedure for children in care.[123]

The pleas of the National Association of Young People in Care were heard by the London Boroughs Children's Regional Planning Committee (a voluntary Joint Committee of the London Boroughs under the powers of the

Local Government Act 1972), consisting of one elected member from each of London's thirty-two Boroughs and the City of London and co-opted members representing voluntary child care organisations, magistrates, education and probation services.

The Committee[124] insisted on consulting young people in care about the documents drafted by a regional working party of members and officers. This working party included one representative of the National Association of Young People in Care. In August 1986, the Committee published a *Charter of Rights for Children in Care*. The aim was to offer London Boroughs a model policy which would assist them in drawing up their own policies and guidelines.[125] In a letter to me, John Ogden wrote that the "'Charter of Rights' was published alongside a child care policy paper, both of which were approved by the Children's Regional Planning Committee, which in such matters has only an advisory function. Therefore the status of the document is that of guidance, particularly to the London Boroughs."

The Charter, a rather 'wordy' document, was the forerunner of similar documents produced by all Local Authorities in the United Kingdom.

We have analysed this Charter as an example of several such Charters[126] that were published in England and Scotland.

Under Paragraph 1 we find:

i) "the right to expect first consideration to promoting his or her welfare etc." pertains to the complete 'Systemic Quality of Life Model'.
ii) deals with "the child's right to have his or her interests legally represented in care proceedings, wardship proceedings and criminal proceedings; the right to appeal against a care order and the right to apply for the discharge of a care order." These rights belong in the *adaptive mode* of the *social subsystem*.
iii) formulates the right of young people to express their opinions and to have these taken into account. Attempts to give children in care more power are classifiable in the *expressive mode* of the *social subsystem*.
iv) "a right to be the subject of a six monthly review": This is not classified, since it deals with a procedural matter.
v) Part one: "The right to vote if they are over 18," pertains to the *expressive mode* of the *social subsystem*. Part two: "The right not to be subject to detention etc." relates to the *adaptive mode* of the *social subsystem*).
vi) states that the child (when accused of criminal offenses while in care) has the right to "a legally independent solicitor, not from the care authority's or residential home's solicitor." This right is classifiable in the *adaptive mode* of the *social subsystem*.
vii) the right "to an independent visitor" also relates to the *adaptive mode* of the *social subsystem*.

348   *Chapter XIII*

viii) contact with the child's own family pertains to the *integrative mode* of the *social subsystem*.
ix) is an interesting statement. It requires the local authorities to enable children to practise their religion, including "spiritual guidance, the observation of dietary rules, clothing rules and the right to attend places of worship and festivals, consistent with their beliefs." This concern belongs in the *adaptive mode* of the *cultural subsystem*.
x) deals with inspection of foster homes and residential care. This is a procedural matter and is therefore not classified in the 'Systemic Quality of Life Model'.
xi) "good access to independent legal advice" proposes facilitating contact between the child and Society. This relates to the *adaptive mode* of the *social subsystem*.
xii) demands that children in care receive a "mainstream education alongside other children of their age group." Since the wording of this paragraph is not quite clear, we interpret the intention to be that children in care should be enabled to mingle with their peers who are not in care in order to maintain a sense of belonging to society. This concern is classifiable in the *conservative mode* of the *social subsystem*.
xiii) and xiv) mention the protection of children's rights under the education system. This we interpret as a plea for *individualised* attention to each pupil. It pertains to the *expressive mode* of the *personality subsystem*.

Under the heading 2.A. we find Paragraph

i) which is too general to be classified.
ii) "the right to be informed of the decision making-processes ... and to be encouraged to take part in them" relates to the *expressive mode* of the *social subsystem*.
iii) the right to "attend and *contribute* to their case reviews" etc. also pertains to the *expressive mode* of the *social subsystem*.
iv) deals with files and records of the child. The Charter states that the children should be able to see reports written about them. It is interesting to note that this "may include access to information about parents or other family members when the content is important for decisions on the children's future." The idea seems to be that whatever is recorded in the file must be relevant to the child, and he or she should, therefore, have the right of access to such information even if this infringes upon the privacy of others. We classify this right in the *adaptive mode* of the *social subsystem*.
v) states that "children in care should be able to expect security of placement; to know that they will not be moved at whim or without their needs being the first consideration in decisions to move them."

This obviously refers to the fact that several Children's Homes in the United Kingdom were closed under protest of the children. It pertains to the *conservative mode* of the *physical subsystem*. Since this right pleads for stability, we can also classify it in the *conservative mode* of the *social subsystem*.

vi) "the right to see relatives as frequently as parties concerned wish to do so" belongs in the *integrative mode* of the *social subsystem*. However, since the idea of a so-called care plan creates a *framework* for intimacy, we classify it (on a deeper level) in the *adaptive mode* of the *integrative social sub-subsystem*.

vii) regular visits from social workers is classifiable in the *adaptive mode* of the *social subsystem*.

viii) gives credit to the child's expressive abilities. It states that the children in care "should be able to make representations to a senior person in the care authority if they are experiencing difficulties of communication with their social workers". By increasing the expressive power of the child, it is hoped that he or she will function better in the *expressive mode* of the *social-adaptive sub-subsystem*.

ix) deals with privacy. The right "to receive private telephone calls and see visitors privately" relates to intimacy in social relations. It pertains to the *integrative mode* of the *social subsystem*. Another element of this important paragraph, ("a place to lock private papers or valuables; a safe place to keep treasured personal possessions; freedom to send and receive private letters") is classifiable in the *expressive mode* of the *physical subsystem*.

x) "the right not to have intimate details of the child's life and family passed to other people," is designed to protect the child's social status. This relates to the negative (don't damage!) of the *expressive mode* of the *social subsystem*.

xi) emphasises the importance of personal clothing. This relates to the *expressive mode* of the *personality and physical subsystem*.

xii) states that children may not be subject to cruel or degrading punishments. Moreover, children in care have the right to know what punishments may or may not be used. To the extent that the concern is with the health of the youngster (which could be impaired by physical punishment), we classify this right in the *conservative mode* of the *physical subsystem*. However, insofar as this right is intended to protect the child's self-image, we classify it in the *conservative mode* of the *personality subsystem*. The right to know which punishments are or are not allowed (to adapt to what is allowed and reject what is not allowed) relates to the *adaptive mode* of the *social subsystem*.

xiii) is not very clear: "Children should be able to expect consistency from their care authorities." It would seem that the intention of the London Boroughs Children's Regional Planning Committee was that the values instilled in children in care should be the same at home, in school, and in care. We classify this concern in the *adaptive mode* of the *cultural subsystem*. As a marginal note, it should be noted that there is a dark side to this policy. Once a child has been raised within a rigidly kept value system, he or she must have a real motivation to change and/or make known his or her wish to change.

xiv) and xiv refer to procedures.

Part B of this wordy Charter has ten paragraphs relating to the right to normal development.

i) deals with preservation of identity and self esteem. This points strongly to the *personality subsystem* and especially to the *conservative mode* (identity).

ii) refers to the sense of belonging to a family network. This is classifiable in the *conservative mode* of the *social subsystem* and in the *integrative mode* of the *social subsystem* (intimacy).

iii) deserves a closer look. "Children learn (as we all learn) by taking risks, experiencing and being taught to cope with, the normal hazards of life in our society. Over-protective, bureaucratic regulations which prevent children in care from taking part in the normal activities of their age group are a denial of their needs and impede the learning which they should expect a 'good parent' to provide." Since the word *risk* seems to be the keyword of this paragraph, we classify it in the *expressive mode* of *all subsystem*.

iv) states that the activities of children in care should be as 'normal' as possible (visiting friends, staying there overnight, taking part in school visits etc.). This we classify in the *integrative mode* of the *social subsystem* (balance among the child's social roles).

v) "continuity of health care, medical and dental treatment" has *continuity* as its catchword. This would seem to point to a concern for effective functioning in the conservative mode. However, we should not be misled into classifying this paragraph in the conservative mode of the physical subsystem. The concern of this paragraph is a *framework* for health care. This pertains to the *adaptive mode* of the *integrative-physical sub-subsystem*.

vi) "Children should be able to expect continuity of education" belongs in the *conservative mode* of the *social subsystem* (don't change everything because the child is in residential or foster care!) However, the paragraph has also a *social-adaptive* concern (the child should attend an adequate school).

vii) emphasises that children from ethnic minorities should be able to keep contact with their community. This concern is classifiable in the *conservative mode* of the *social subsystem*.

viii) expresses concern about the sexual development of the child in care.

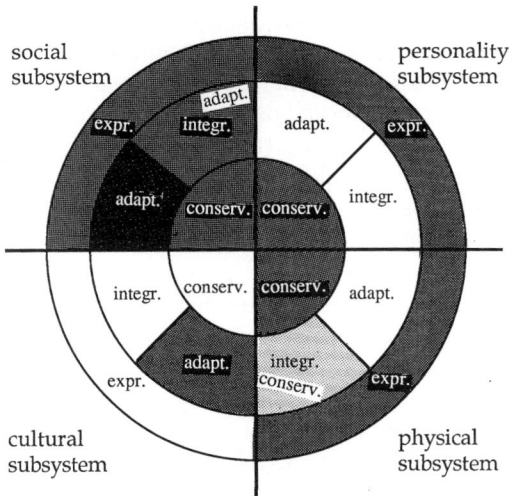

Fig. 13.11. The Charter of Rights for Children in Care of the London Boroughs Children's Regional Planning Committee (August 1986). Interpreted by the Systemic Quality of Life Model.

This is classifiable in the *integrative mode* of the *physical subsystem*, in the *integrative mode* of the *social subsystem*: (intimacy, intimate relationships), and in the *integrative mode* of the *personality subsystem*.

ix) states that children in care should be prepared for the life *after* the residential (treatment) home or foster home. This relates to the *adaptive mode* of the *social subsystem*. Special mention is made of teaching children in care how to deal with money. This pertains to the *expressive mode* of the *physical subsystem*.

x) states that, after leaving care, children should be able to take continued support for granted. Since former pupils of good residential facilities describe the transition as "stepping from a warm bath into a cold shower," this is an important theme. It pertains to the *adaptive mode* of the *social subsystem*.

12. A BILL OF RIGHTS FOR JUVENILES (NEW YORK STATE DIVISION FOR YOUTH, 1973)

See Appendix XXVII

In 1973 about 50,000 children in the United States were confined in so-called *training schools*.[127] James D. Silbert and Alan Sussman, both legal

Ombudsmen[128] acquainted with these places of residential treatment in New York State from the inside, wrote: "In the name of treatment, thousands of orphans, truants, runaways, and delinquents are deprived of their liberty. Given neither the full constitutional protections of an adult nor the treatment, training, and rehabilitation promised to children, they suffer a double irony: often they are confined in penal-like institutions for non-criminal behaviour punishable *only* because they are children, and frequently the period of confinement for illegal acts is longer than it would be for adults convicted of similar crimes "

"Unlike convicted adults," Silbert and Sussman continue, "convicted juveniles are not meant to suffer any civil disabilities. Thus, they take with them to the training school not only all the rights that have been and are being granted adult prisoners, but all those possessed by free children as well, except the right to leave the institution at will, and others, absolutely necessary for, and rationally related to, the purpose of confinement – that is, treatment."

In 1972 the New York State Division for Youth tried to introduce some improvements. The fact that James Silbert, Alan Sussman and two other attorneys were appointed as Ombudsmen in Training Schools was itself a laudable effort to improve the legal position of youngsters in training schools. Notwithstanding the conflicting loyalties in which these Ombudsmen became involved[129], it should be recognised that the authorities in New York State did try to improve the difficult situation. However, Silbert and Sussman became very sceptical about the efficacy of such efforts. In a footnote to an article about their experiences they wrote: "At the time this article was being written, the Division for Youth promulgated State-wide regulations prohibiting, among other practices, mandatory religious service attendance, mail censorship, and required hairstyles in the training schools. It remains to be seen whether such regulations will be duly enforced and whether the residents will be informed of their new rights."[130] This is the background against which we shall analyse the *Bill of rights for Juveniles*.

Section I of the Bill of the New York State Division for Youth states that when an individual is placed in a (closed) institution, it does not follow that he or she has lost "certain basic rights."

Section II deals with *dress code*.

II(a) states that "students have the right to wear personal clothing or combinations of their own clothing and clothing issued by the Youth Division." This right, which we can view as a negotiating process between inmate and training school, relates to the *adaptive mode* of the *physical subsystem* (clothing as a means to keep warm). To the extent that clothing implies personal preferences, we can classify it in the *expressive mode* of the *personality subsystem*.

Point (IIb) ("clothing issued by the Division shall be available to those children lacking personal clothing...") is classifiable in the *adaptive mode* of the *physical subsystem*.

The right (mentioned under c) of inmates "to discriminate themselves from others with a particular item of jewellery," belongs in the *expressive mode* of the *personality subsystem*.

Point (d) "students may be prohibited from possessing items of clothing or jewellery which could be utilised in such a way as to endanger themselves or others" is a restriction rather than a right.

Point (e) "to follow the same criteria of cleanliness of their own clothing" is not a right but an obligation.

Point (f) (dealing with cleaning materials) can be classified in the *adaptive mode* of the *physical subsystem*.

Point (g) "development of self-esteem and individuality," pertains to the *expressive mode* of the *personality subsystem*.

Section III deals with personal appearance.

Point (a) of this Section gives students the right to determine the length and style of their hair. Ever since the Beatles this has been an important issue. We can classify it in the *expressive mode* of the *personality subsystem*.

The same applies for point (b) concerning facial hair.

Point (c) concerns health and safety and would fit in the integrative and conservative mode of the physical subsystem if it were phrased in the terms of a right, which it is not.

Point (d) is not a right but describes a procedure. (See page 483.)

Section IV deals with religious freedom.

Point (a) which deals with the right to participate in religious observances, refers not to *the faith of their own choice*, but to *the faith of their parents*. We classify this right in the *adaptive mode* of the *cultural subsystem* and, to a lesser extent, in the *expressive mode* of the *cultural subsystem*.

Under (b) we find the right to "counselling to members of their faith by authorised representatives of religious denominations " This also pertains to the *adaptive mode* of the *cultural subsystem*.

Point (c) "The use of physical force, punishment or coercion to compel attendance or participation in religious observances is prohibited" is stated in the negative (Do not!). It pertains to the *expressive mode* of the *cultural subsystem*.

Section V deals with mail censorship.

Without censorship the inmate can express himself more accurately. We therefore classify Point (a) of this Section in the *expressive mode* of the *personality subsystem*.

Point (b) gives inmates the right to receive mail without censorship, except if the institution suspects contraband or cash. This right relates to the *expressive mode* of the *social subsystem* (control your own information), of the *physical subsystem* (guard your own belongings), and of the *personality subsystem* (self-expression of personality). We can also classify this right in the *adaptive mode* of the *social subsystem*.

Point (c) ("the right to mail minimum one letter per week at State expense") relates to the *adaptive mode* of the *social subsystem* (the training

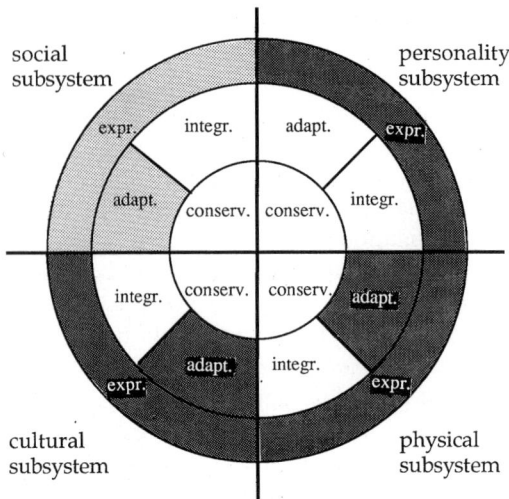

Fig. 13.12. The 'Bill of Rights of Juveniles' (New York State Division for Youth 1973). Interpreted by the Systemic Quality of Life Model.

school – institution), and in the *expressive mode* of the *personality subsystem* (to write letters).

Point (d) deals with money sent to the inmates. This money shall either be given to them or be kept for them "in order to prevent stealing". In any case, its concern is with privacy. This pertains to the *expressive mode* of the *physical subsystem*.

Point (e) ("packages are subject to inspection") is again a restriction, not a right.

After serving a number of years as Ombudsmen in these facilities, Silbert and Sussman expressed the opinion that "rights alone will not make training schools suitable places to train or rehabilitate a child, and unless these institutions can offer the treatment they are required by law to provide, without destroying the lives of the children they pretend to help, their doors should be closed forever."[131]

13. Charters for Children in Hospital

See Appendix XXXV and Notes 139, 140 *and* 145

In the fifties and sixties, the phenomenon of *separation anxiety* became known[132] and the public at large came to recognise that the hospitalisation of a child induced such separation anxiety. When children are hospitalised, they are often separated from their parents. On top of the fear of treatment, perhaps even an operation, in an unfamiliar environment, comes the child's inability to grasp the temporary nature of the separation from his or her parents.

Psychoanalysts[133] have given us insight into children's fantasies, their perception of hospitalisation constituting punishment, the phenomenon of regression and anger as a result of the separation, and the importance of allowing the child to keep a teddy bear or small blanket representing his or her parents (called by Donald Winnicott a 'transitional object').

In 1959, the Ministry of Health of the United Kingdom issued the *Welfare of Children in Hospital Report* (better known as the *Platt Report*) which stated that possibilities must be created for parents to stay with their children in hospital.[134]

In 1961, the pressure group *Mother Care for Children in Hospital* (later called the *National Association for the Welfare of Children in Hospital, NAWCH) was founded.*

In 1984, the NAWCH formulated a *Charter for Children in Hospital* in order to raise the quality of services for children in hospital. This Charter was the first of its kind. In a letter to me, Jenny Davison of the NAWCH wrote that it "was formulated by procedures which have become a model for later standard setting: (a) wide ranging discussions with a mixed group of consumers and providers to determine the clauses; (b) presentation of results to all interested agencies for comments; (c) return to the Association for further discussion and comments; (d) collection of endorsements from all professional organisations involved in children's health care."

The NAWCH Charter was approved by the Royal College of Nursing and the British Pediatric Association.[135] Thus, approval was not legally binding but simply meant that these two organisations supported the rights of children in hospital as formulated by the NAWCH.

The first Principle confronts us with the dangers of dislocation from the physical environment. It warns us against separating the child from his or her social relations. This concern belongs in the *conservative mode* of the *social subsystem*. Intimacy between the child and the parents relates to the *integrative mode* of the *social subsystem*. To the extent that separation anxiety can cause psychological discomfort it pertains to the *integrative mode* of the *personality subsystem*.

The second Principle ("children in hospital shall have the right to have their parents with them at all times") emphasises that even when the child is not physically in his or her familiar environment, the social network should, at all times, be maintained. The social structure of the individual is classified in the *conservative mode* of the *social subsystem*. The concern for the interpersonal relations is classifiable in the *integrative mode* of the *social subsystem*. To the extent that the dislodging may have adverse effects on the child's personality structure, we classify this Principle in the *conservative mode* of the *personality subsystem*.

The third Principle deals with the very important "right to information appropriate to age and understanding." Although in cases of emergency there may be no time for adequate preparation, we should, if possible, tell children what to expect. The Dutch child-psychiatrist Wim Strubbe who worked for many years in a children's hospital, points out that "it is of fundamental importance for the person who gives the information to be in touch with the fantasies of the child, and to explain that 'you can suddenly get ill' and 'the operation is necessary to make you healthy again'". Strubbe: "Giving information without dealing with anxiety and talking about fantasies has little or no psychological effect."[136] The idea behind information is that the child's *expressive-personality functioning* becomes better *adapted* to the foreign (hospital) environment. Information has to be presented on the level of the child, with maximum consideration for his or her personality. The emergence of specific perceptions and emotions peculiar to the individual pertains to the expressive mode of the personality subsystem. However, we interpret this principle on a deeper level and classify it in the *adaptive mode* of the *expressive-personality sub-subsystem*.

The fourth Principle consists of two parts: (a) "the right to informed participation in all decisions etc."[137] This relates to the *expressive mode* of the *social and physical subsystems*; (b) "protection from unnecessary medical treatment." This belongs in the *conservative mode* of the *physical subsystem*. However, we can also classify this concern in the *adaptive mode* of the *physical subsystem*.

Principle five ("children shall be treated with tact and understanding") is concerned with respect for the child's individuality. This pertains to the *expressive mode* of the *personality subsystem*. Principle five also deals with respect for privacy. Privacy is often classified in the physical subsystem (an own room for instance). In the present case ("the child's privacy shall be respected"), however, we interpret it as the favourable interaction between the child's personality and the human environment. This relates to the *adaptive mode* of the *personality subsystem*.

Principle six ("children shall enjoy the care of appropriately trained staff") relates rather vaguely to quality of life in general. Nurses and others who work with children in hospital should be trained to understand the special physical and emotional needs of children, so that they can help the child and the parents to deal with the child's anger, fears and behaviour, typical in certain developmental phases. We interpret this as meaning that children have the right to express all their fears, and that the response of the environment should be appropriate. This right pertains to the *expressive modes* of the *physical and the personality subsystems*.

Principle seven ("children shall be able to wear their own clothes and have their own personal possessions") deals with the *expressive mode* of the *physical subsystem*.[138]

Principle eight demands that children of same developmental stages have the opportunity to play together. The aim here is to facilitate the expression of feelings. This pertains to the *expressive mode* of the *personality subsystem*.

Principle nine calls for the environment to be adapted ("furnished and equipped") to the children. We classify this Principle in the *adaptive mode* of the *physical subsystem*. It also contains a concern with safety. This is classifiable in the *conservative mode* of the *physical subsystem*.

The last Principle demands that children in hospital have "full opportunity to play, recreation and education." Play relates to the *expressive mode* of the *personality subsystem*. Recreation ('reloading the batteries') belongs in the *adaptive mode* of the *personality subsystem*. The Principle does not specify what is meant by education in this context. However, the intention is probably that education should not be discontinued because the child is unable to go to school. Tutors can visit the child in the hospital. Since we lack detailed information about the intention, we shall classify education in the *adaptive mode* of the *cultural subsystem*.

In 1988 NAWCH developed the Quality Checklist for Caring for Children in Hospital. This Checklist translated the Principles of the Charter into standards to be used to assess the quality of services for children in each district of the health authority. NAWCH received funding to conduct follow up on how the Checklist was being used. The NAWCH Quality Review reports about the findings of this study.

The Review has three main purposes: (a) to draw up a profile of existing services for children; (b) to widen understanding of what 'quality' means in children's services; (c) to enhance communication between staff and children. The Quality Review provides basic achievable standards to monitor services and plan developments.

The NAWCH Charter stimulated organisations in other European countries to formulate their own *Charters*. The Belgian Organisation *Land en Ziekenhuis* ('Child and Hospital') presented such a Charter on December 20th, 1984, and the Dutch 'Landelijke Vereniging Kind en Ziekenhuis' ('National Association Child and Hospital') presented their Charter on March 23rd, 1985.[139]

A European Charter

On January 19, 1984, the European Parliament adopted a resolution on a *European Charter on the Rights of Patients*. Article 5 of this resolution stated that the rights of sick children should be dealt with in a special Charter.

On December 18, 1984, European Parliament Member Kenneth D. Collins called for a European Charter for children in hospitals and outlined[140] the principles on which it should be based. The matter was referred to the Committee for the Environment, Public Health and Consumer Protection of the European Parliament. The Committee proposed that the following points be added to the proposal: "(a) Opposition to any form of pharmacological or therapeutic experimentation should be stressed; only parents well aware of the risks and benefits of such treatment should be allowed to give their consent, and should reserve the right to withdraw such consent; (b) recrea-

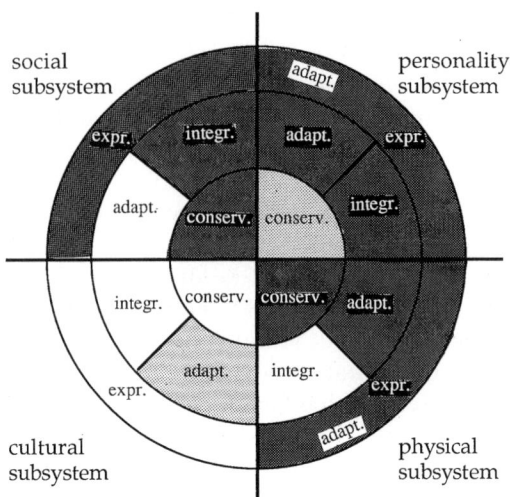

Fig. 13.13. The Charter for Children in Hospital of the NAWCH (1984). Interpreted by the Systemic Quality of Life Model.

tional activities and education must have an important role. Hence in hospitals yet to be built, space must be set aside for this purpose, and rebuilding or conversion work must be carried out in existing ones; (c) in order to ensure that recreational and educational activities are effectively and efficiently carried out, specialised staff, such as recreation teachers, play workers and specialised nurses must be trained; (d) the appropriate authority must provide schooling, especially for older children, by seconding teachers to hospitals. Teaching must continue at home when children are admitted to day-hospital."[141]

The Committee on Legal Affairs and Citizens Rights of the European Parliament was rather sceptical about the enterprise: "It should be observed," they wrote, "that a number of so called 'children's rights' should in fact be conceived as pertaining to the parents, for example the one on the provision of information on the child's condition and treatment. It may also be that certain of the guidelines suggested by Mr. Collins could be, if properly drafted, turned into enforceable rights, though the necessity to do this remains to be demonstrated. A proposal by delegate Mrs. Squarcialupi that any form of pharmacological or therapeutic experimentation should only be carried out on children with the informed consent of the parents is clearly a good one, but is more appropriate for treatment within the sphere of classical human rights, to physical integrity, than in the type of Charter under discussion, which deals with hospital conditions for child patients. It may be taken for granted that the European Parliament would be unanimously in favour of action to alleviate any distress sick children would endure through being in hospital. Nonetheless, it remains to be demonstrated that an instrument such as a European Charter, as distinct from an agreed set of guidelines distributed to all hospitals with child patients, would contribute to the achievement of this aim: equally, it remains to be shown that the European Community is the most appropriate forum for such action. Finally, the so-called 'rights' proposed are not, for the most part, suitable for being put into legal form."[142]

Nevertheless on May 13, 1986, the European Parliament[143] adopted the idea of such an European Charter. In May 1988, a meeting of all the European Associations[144] for Children in Hospital, hosted by 'Kind in Ziekenhuis' in Leyden (the Netherlands) agreed on a *European Charter for children in hospital*.[145] This Charter (the so-called banner) was forwarded to the European Commission.

In July 1990 Ken Collins wrote to me that the European Parliament had agreed to draft a Charter, "but so far we haven't been able to move things forward in the Member States of European Community, so sadly we don't actually have such a thing in force."

14. RIGHTS OF THE CHILD FORMULATED BY THE JOINT COMMISSION ON MENTAL HEALTH OF CHILDREN (U.S.A., 1969)

See Appendix XXI

In 1966 the National Institute of Mental Health in the United States estimated that 1,400,000 children under the age of eighteen needed psychiatric care.[146] But surveys in 1969 showed that nearly 1,000,000 of those children were not receiving any treatment. From these and other studies, the Joint Commission on Mental Health of Children concluded that "it is an undeniable fact that there is not a single community in the United States which provides an acceptable standard of services for its mentally ill children, running a spectrum from early therapeutic intervention to social restoration in the home, in the school, and in the community."[147] What happened to all these children who were not receiving help for emotional problems? According to the Joint Commission they were "bounced around from training schools to reformatories to jails and whipped through all kinds of understaffed welfare agencies."[148]

The Commission wrote: "It is not unusual in this year 1969 to tour one of these massive warehouses for the mentally ill and come upon a child, aged nine or ten, confined on a ward with eighty or ninety sick adults."[149] The Clinical Sub-Committee of the Joint Commission noted that the admission of teenagers to the State hospitals had risen by about 150 % between 1959 and 1969. There were only few private residential treatment centres, and only parents from the higher income group could afford such therapeutic services. Moreover, for every child admitted, ten or more were turned away due to lack of space.

A member of the Commission[150] noted that the United States was aware of the problem, but did not support funds to treat and care for these children "because it had given up on them."[151] The Commission also noted that "the child-rearing program of our communities, if properly carried out, will be one of the largest 'industries' in the country, one of the largest in manpower utilization and therefore costs. It is our opinion that this is as it should be. If vast expenditures, both human and monetary, are not made, it will in the long run be costly in terms of mental illness, human malfunctioning, and therefore under-productivity."[152] The Commission therefore concluded that if "we are true to our heritage, we must recognize that we are confronted not merely with the needs of children but with their *inalienable* rights."[153]

The recommendations of the Joint Commission were aimed at two major goals: "to ensure proper diagnosis, treatment, and care for mentally ill children and youth who presently receive the lowest priority for service, and to strengthen and improve the quality of all youngsters' lives."[154]

"We know a great deal about *why* abnormal development occurs," wrote the Commission. "At least enough to allow us to say in these recommendations what *can be done* to prevent or treat much of what goes wrong." The Commission believed that certain rights must be granted to children in order "to optimize the mental health of the young."[155] The rights formulated by the Joint Commission are centred around perceived social problems. Most of the areas in the 'Systemic Quality of Life Model' pertaining to these rights are indicated with dots, and only the *adaptive mode* of the *social subsystem* are shaded black.

The first right advanced by the Commission is "the right to be wanted." The mental health experts knew only too well how 'to be born unwanted' can influence the psychological development of the child. The Commission's explanation states that often "parents unfortunately had no access to or knowledge of the benefits of birth control information and devices." This shows that we are dealing with Ellen Key's central question of 'to be or not to be' or 'to choose one's parents wisely', which makes this 'right' classifiable in the centre of the 'Systemic Quality of Life Model'.

The second right ("to be born healthy") is very much connected with the first right, since it implies that if one is not born healthy, it is better not to be born at all. This is also classifiable in the *centre of the 'Systemic Quality of Life Model'*. It is our opinion that the Joint Commission did not mean that if a child was born handicapped it should be killed.

The third right deals with a healthy environment. The explanation describes how bad the situation was in 1969 ("yet, thousands of children and youth become physically handicapped or acquire chronic damage to their health from preventable accidents and diseases, largely because of impoverished environments. . ."). The concern is that children who grow up in unhealthy environments will become dependent on Society. Prevention of handicaps can be classified in the *conservative mode* of the *physical and personality subsystems*.

The formulation of the fourth right, ("satisfaction of basic needs") does not specify what is meant by 'basic needs'. The explanation, however, emphasises concerns that belong in the *adaptive mode* of the *physical subsystem* (nutrition, housing), the *integrative mode* of the *physical subsystem* (ongoing health) and the *integrative mode* of the *personality subsystem* (mental health). No explanation is given of the term *further educational handicaps*, but we understand from the context that the source of these handicaps is poverty of the parents. We therefore classify this right in the *adaptive mode* of the *social subsystem*.

The next right deals with "continuous loving care," the lack of which leads, according to the Joint Commission, to emotional disturbances and "lack of necessary motivation . . . to cope in our society." Love and intimacy belong in the *integrative mode* of *the social subsystem*. The hypothesis here is that if a child does not get continuous loving care early in life, this will lead to disturbances later in life. In this connection Professor Michael Rutter (child psychiatrist in London) who I interviewed in 1985, told me that, according to psychoanalytic theory, the personality of the individual is established during the first three years and that any changes that occur later in life take always place within the already established structure.[156] He himself, however, adheres nowadays to a different theory, based on his research with girls who grew up in residential treatment centres and whose behaviour he followed up until adulthood. Most of the girls who were 'coping well' had a stable marriage with a non-deviant man. These girls scored as well as the control-group of girls who had not been in care. Having established this fact, Professor Rutter searched for other factors, such as: Are the chances to conclude a good marriage higher if one has had no problems as a child? According to his research this was not the case. According to Professor Rutter's findings, a good relationship in early adulthood was very important. From this he concluded that after years of problems in childhood, positive experiences during early adulthood were decisive. More research is needed to prove who is right, Professor Rutter or the Joint Commission.

Another important right formulated by the Joint Commission is "the right to acquire the intellectual and emotional skills necessary to achieve individual aspirations and to cope effectively in our society." The explanation indicates that this right which is linked to avoiding non-adaptability, relates to the *adaptive mode* of the *social subsystem*. The meaning of "the right to acquire" is unclear. The explanation talks about enabling the child to develop his potential. In our opinion this is, indeed, the goal of education. We classify this goal in the *expressive mode* of the *personality subsystem*.

The Joint Commission states that "countless others are denied the opportunities to develop to their fullest potential through effective vocational training, meaningful work experiences or higher education". As exposed elsewhere, however,[157] for some youngsters "the 'capacity to learn' is disturbed and has to be restored to enable them to develop to their fullest potential" Many youngsters must first learn how to learn. The Joint Commission also states that "we fail to provide avenues for learning adult roles and for

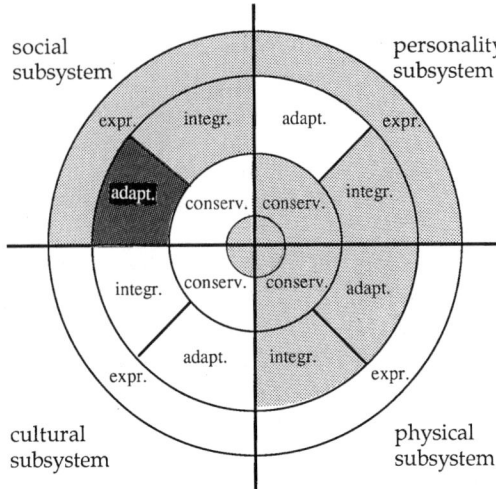

Fig. 13.14. The Right of the Child as formulated by the Joint Commission on Mental Health of Children (1969).

acquiring leadership skills," etc. The right to cope effectively in society is classifiable in the *expressive mode* of the social subsystem.

The last right formulated by the Joint Commission on Mental Health of Children ("the right to receive care and treatment through facilities which are appropriate to their needs and which keep them as closely as possible within their normal social setting") points to the task of the Commission itself. Facilities to which the child is entitled are in the preventive sphere and if this does not have the desired effect, further treatment is demanded. The explanation mentions care for "the emotionally disturbed, the mentally ill, the mentally retarded, the handicapped and the delinquent". The right to such care can be classified in the *adaptive mode* of *all the subsystems*.

As a marginal note, we stress again that it is easier to formulate rights than to enforce them. Clearly the 'right to loving care' should primarily be understood as a 'need'.

From the report of the Joint Commission we understand that the implementation of Rights is the task of the Society. In 1987, however, this was far from being the case. Twelve years after the report of the Joint Commission, President Ronald Reagan approved "cuts in programs, family planning services, child immunizations, aid to families with dependent children, food stamps, school lunches and breakfasts, public housing for poor people, compensatory education to enable disadvantaged children to keep up in school, and day-care services to enable poor and single and teen mothers to work."[158] One would think that the Joint Commission had never existed.

15. THE CHILDREN AND YOUTH BILL OF RIGHTS OF THE NATIONAL ASSOCIATION OF SOCIAL WORKERS, NASW, (U.S.A., 1975)

See Appendix XXIX

In 1975, the Delegate Assembly of the United States National Association of Social Workers (NASW) approved for the first time a *policy statement* about children's rights. This Assembly meets every two years to approve general social policy statements and set broad programme goals for the Association.[159] Policies are submitted by units or Chapters of the Association and are then revised and approved by the 300 member Delegate Assembly.

The 1975 statement on Rights of Children was formally introduced[160] to the NASW by Mrs. Carol Perry of the New York City Chapter of the NASW. It was subsequently replaced by a substitute motion which was unanimously adopted by the Assembly.

Natalie Young, representing a group of social workers from South-East Louisiana, told the Delegates that her support for the Children and Youth Bill of Rights reflected "a change in attitude from viewing children as property to viewing children as developing persons."[161] This, indeed, is how the Policy Statement starts:[162] "Historically, children have been considered as property... In the past, basic rights given to adults have not been applied to children. This has resulted in circumstances of gross injustice and isolation".

The introductory paragraphs ('background') of this *Children and Youth Bill of Rights* focuses on 'children' vis à vis social institutions such as the family, the school or the courts, and belongs, therefore, in the *adaptive mode* of the *social subsystem*.[163]

The first right formulated by the NASW is "the right to sound preparation for Life." Like Ellen Key's 'right of the child to choose its own parents wisely' (see Chapter V), this right is concerned with the very existence of the child. The 'to be or not to be' nature of this right is confirmed by the sentence: "Potential parents should have access to genetic information to evaluate the probabilities of transmitting hereditary diseases. Sound preparation also includes the right to adequate prenatal care and protection from trauma during the birth process." We also read that "children are entitled to a good beginning. Such preparation is based on being wanted and cared for, to assist potential parents to decide when it is best for them to have a child."

The second right, formulated by the NASW, is the "right to individuality." This concern belongs mainly in the *personality subsystem*. "Children have the right to be children," is classifiable in the *conservative mode* of the *personality subsystem*. "The right to play as a foundation for the development of mastery and competence,"[164] pertains to the *expressive mode* of the *personality subsystem*.

The section about "the Right to Positive Social Identity," deals with various issues. As already explained in Chapter III, the identity of the child refers to the *conservative mode* of the *personality subsystem*. Although the spirit of this section focuses on identity, the concern should be classified in the *expressive mode* of the *cultural subsystem*. The following will clarify this: the NASW states that identity "should include pride in racial and ethnic characteristics, family and national culture, and unique individual differences," that children should be allowed to express their individuality by exercising the right to speak languages other than English and by expressing social and ethnic characteristics in dress, and that (when age-appropriate) children and youngsters should have "freedom to choose their religion."

Next the "Right to a Good Parenting Experience," is mentioned. In our opinion this right is very difficult to enforce. We can only strive for external conditions to be as favourable as possible. The rest depends on the personality of the father and of the mother. Under the same heading we find "the right to continuous nurturing care" and "the right to consistent parental controls and expectations." The right to *care* belongs in the *adaptive mode* of the *physical subsystem*, and the *adaptive mode* of the *personality subsystem*. Consistent parental controls and expectations can also express care for the child and help shape the child's identity. We therefore classify them in the *conservative mode* of the *personality subsystem*. This paragraph is also concerned about fitting foster children in the best possible family-environment. This fitting process relates to the *adaptive mode* of the *social subsystem*. As a guideline, the NASW recommends that the child's intimate relations with the psychological parents to whom he or she is most attached should not be ignored, and that the child's own opinion should be taken into consideration: "When that decision is to be made about who the child's parents may be, the child is entitled to participate in the decision . . . ." This concern relates to the *expressive mode* of the *social subsystem*.

The "Right to a Healthy Environment" is classifiable in different modes and subsystems. "The child should have access to adequate housing," and "Children should have freedom from pollution of air, water and food" pertains to the *adaptive mode* of the *physical subsystem*. "The child has the right to safety and security," pertains to the *conservative mode* of the *physical subsystem*. The section continues: "Children should receive environmental support conducive to health and development." Health relates to the *integrative mode* of the *physical subsystem*; development belongs in the *expressive mode* of the *physical subsystem*. The *adaptive mode* of the *personality subsystem* is represented by "provisions of recreational space," (recreation means to reload the child's batteries). "Beautification of the environment" pertains to the *adaptive mode* of the *cultural subsystem*.

The next section states that children have the right to "health care to prevent and treat potentially handicapping diseases and disabilities." The first part of this section relates to the *integrative mode* of the *physical subsystem*. "To prevent disabilities" is classifiable in the *conservative mode* of the *physical subsystem*. "Mental health care" relates to the *integrative mode* of the personality subsystem. "Information about their own bodies," which the

NASW also mentions under the heading 'health' is classifiable in the *expressive mode* of the *personality subsystem*, the reasoning being that the child, having received the information, will be able to do something with it. "The right to adequate nutrition" pertains to the *adaptive mode* of the *physical subsystem*.

Next follows the "Right to a Relevant Education." The NASW proposes that "children should be guaranteed access to high-quality education from pre-school to maturity, in order *to develop to their fullest potential*." It would seem impossible to secure the potential of everyone and certain compromises are necessary. The NASW does not suggest how to solve this problem (which would have been indicated for a social policy statement of this kind). We only read that "atypical children must have opportunities geared to there specific needs, including the opportunity to participate with normal children to the maximum of their ability." Since the NASW pays a great deal of attention to 'personal growth', and even observes that "education is a highly individualised process," we classify this section in the *expressive mode* of the *personality subsystem*. The plea to let each child "participate in the design of his or her learning experience," pertains to the *expressive mode* of the *social subsystem*.

The central issue of "the Right to Participatory Citizenship" means "to get acquainted with social roles and career possibilities." This section belongs, therefore, in the *adaptive mode* of the *social subsystem*. The observation that this right can contribute "to the development of self-identity," makes it also classifiable in the *conservative mode* of the *personality subsystem*.

In "the Right to Representation," the NASW pleads for more social power, and for giving the vote to children and youngsters on school boards, city planning councils, health and social service boards, legislative panels, and task forces at every level of government. This Right belongs in the *expressive mode* of the *social subsystem* (giving children more power).

The next section ("the Right to Legal Status, Legal Protection and Legal Redress") is concerned with creating interaction opportunities so that the child's opinion can be heard and considered. This concern pertains to the *adaptive mode* of the *social subsystem*. In order to help children get their opinion across, the NASW pleads for "the right to appropriate representation in judicial and quasi-judicial proceedings, including custody proceedings, in which their interests may be affected directly." The second part of this section expresses concern for the children's safety when deprived of their liberty, and demands, for instance, "freedom from incarceration with adult offenders." This concern pertains to the *conservative mode* of the *physical and personality subsystems*.

The section dealing with "the Right to Services" is difficult to classify. It deals with the question of how to secure quality of life in all its aspects through social services for some sub-populations ("children who are dependent on society for care and protection or who have special needs"). The background of this section is contained in Judit Shild's speech in the Delegate

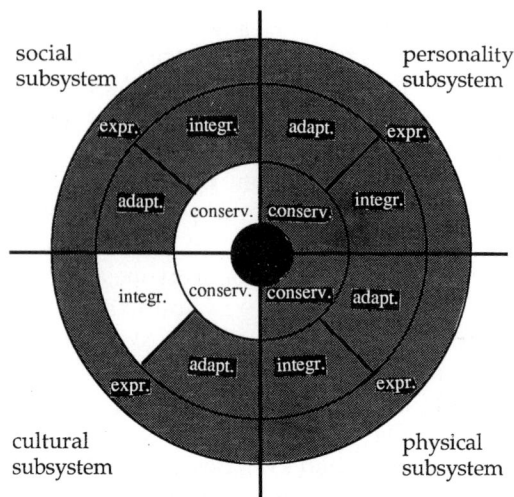

Fig. 13.15. The NASW Children and Youth Bil of rights (1975). Interpreted with the Systemic Quality of Life Model.

Assembly:[165] "The introduction of this Bill of Rights is crucial for this Delegate Assembly. Those of us in Illinois have experienced for the past several years an attempt to dismantle services for children. We have had to develop our own basis and our own kind of position paper from which we could operate. We know that this is beginning to be a nation-wide trend, and therefore we urge support of the proposal." Relying on this background information, we are inclined to classify this section in the *adaptive mode* of the *social subsystem*.

The last section ("The Right to Advocacy") relates to the *adaptive mode* of the *social subsystem*. The NASW sees the "right to advocacy" as a mechanism by which the situation of children can be improved ("to ensure that they will be guaranteed full benefit of the legal rights established by our society").

16. THE DECLARATION OF THE PSYCHOLOGICAL RIGHTS OF THE CHILD OF THE INTERNATIONAL ASSOCIATION OF SCHOOL PSYCHOLOGISTS (1979)

See Appendix XXXI

Milton Shore wrote that "one area in which psychologists have shown a particular interest is defining the rights of children and youth ... Psychologists have been attempting to gain a consensus on children's rights so that legislators and those working with children and youth can thus be held accountable."[166]

In a 1978 newsletter of an International Group of School Psychologists

(I.P.S.)[167] we read: "Because of their important work with children having behaviour and learning difficulties in the schools around the world, School Psychologists are in a unique position to draw the attention of the world to the unmet psychological and educational needs of the child," and that "I.S.P.'s wide international contacts with committed people working in the schools puts it in a position to initiate the process to produce a truly International Declaration of the Psychological Rights of the Child."[168] In the same newsletter this network of School Psychologists, with Calvin D. Catterall as its leading force, issued a tentative Declaration on the Psychological Rights of the Child.

The intention of the I.P.S. was to produce a "most powerful yet practical statement of the Child's Psychological Rights."[169] Calvin Catterall explained that such a Declaration would be most useful "if it

(1) covered the entire psychological domain of development in sufficient detail to enable all countries to evaluate the effectiveness of present programs attempting to provide for these needs and rights;
(2) would be stated with sufficient flexibility, however, so that the need could be provided for with a great deal of adaptability within the context of different cultures and levels of economic development;
(3) should provide practical goals for the future development of improved levels of services for children as well as for all the countries of the world to improve the psychological climate in which their children and youth will grow."[170]

In our opinion the above aims are rather pretentious. Be that as it may, the question is: What are these *Psychological* Rights? According to Stuart N. Hart[171] "they will be considered to focus on cognitive, affective or volitional dimensions of human experience rather than physical dimensions. Under such a broad definitional umbrella, the 'first' right in the United Nations Declaration on the Rights of the Child which deals with affection, love, and understanding, would be basically psychological in nature, while the second right, dealing with nutrition and medical care would not." The word 'first' in the above sentence does not relate to Principle one, but to the importance for psychologists of the issues in the United Nations Declaration on the Rights of the Child.

The tentative Declaration[172] "covered the entire domain of psychological and intellectual development and . . . only those factors which were considered to be essentially psychological in nature were included."[173] The tentative Declaration was sent for comments to all of the Ministers of Education in the world. Psychologists from 'all over the world' were invited to comment. The final *Declaration of the Psychological Rights of the Child* was discussed at the Third International Colloquium of the International Association of School Psychologists, held in York,[174], England, in July 1979, where it underwent further modification by a Committee of Psychologists of the I.S.P. headed by Dr. Stuart Hart. On July 12th, 1979, the Declaration was adopted by the I.S.P. membership. It was hoped that the Declaration would be transformed into a 'yardstick' against which the value of existing services could be measured, and the need for new programmes be determined.[175]

If we analyse this *Declaration of the Psychological Rights of the Child*, we see that internal processes are often emphasised. As it is often difficult to guarantee rights in the domain of feeling, learning, etc., we might expect the formulated Psychological Rights to belong only in the personality subsystem of the 'Systemic Quality of Life Model'. This, however, is not the case.

The Declaration itself comprises three Areas, each subdivided in three Rights. The first Area deals with *Love and Freedom from Fear*. The first Right formulated in this Area is "the right to love, affection, and understanding." This point, which was not included in the tentative Declaration, is classifiable in the *integrative mode* of the *social subsystem*.

The formulation of the second Right in this Area explains that "freedom from fear" means "freedom from fear of psychological and physical harm or abuse." This Right pertains to the *conservative mode* of the *personality and physical subsystems*. It is noteworthy that in the eyes of the drafters of this Declaration *fear* is, by definition, determined to be negative. In our opinion fear is an unpleasant and often strong emotion caused by anticipation or awareness of danger. Fear warns us of impending danger, and has, therefore, a positive function, too. We find it strange that psychologists regard "freedom from fear" to be a right. Although explicitly stated, the intention is probably that the environment should be organised in such a way that the child will not be exposed to *constant* fear ("of psychological and physical harm or abuse"). This concern is classifiable in the *adaptive mode* of the personality subsystem. Since constant fear constitutes a threat to the psychological development of the child, this right is also classified in the *conservative mode* of the *personality subsystem*.

The meaning of the right "to protection and advocacy", is rather vague. Nowhere is it explained *against what* a child must be protected. Stuart Hart[176] says that application of the theories of Piaget, Kohlberg and others may help to determine the appropriate time for a shift in emphasis from 'protection' to 'choice' rights for a given population and a particular time. Since Hart emphasises age-appropriate protection-measures to be taken (or not taken) by adults, we classify this right in the *adaptive mode* of the *social subsystem*. Although protection and advocacy (adults as spokesmen for children) are not the same, here *advocacy* and *protection* are mentioned in one and the same breath. As advocacy facilitates the interaction between the child and society,[177] we conclude that the Right "to protection and advocacy" relates to the *adaptive mode* of the *social subsystem*.

Next follow three Rights in the Area of *Personal, Spiritual, and Social Development*. "The Right to personal identity and independence and the freedom to express these" belongs in the *conservative mode* of the *personality subsystem* (identity, being a separate human being), and in the *expressive mode* of the *personality subsystem* (to be able to express the distinctiveness).

"The Right to opportunities for spiritual and moral development", does not belong in the cultural-valuative subsystem (as might perhaps be expected), but in the *expressive mode* of the *personality subsystem*, since the concern is promotion of an optimal *moral development* (as described by Kohlberg[178]). We assume that spiritual and moral development are meant to be the same (namely moral development as mentioned by Kohlberg).

The last Right in the Second Area ("the right to satisfying inter-personal relationships"[179]) pertains to the *integrative mode* of the *social subsystem*, and the *adaptive mode* of the *social subsystem* ("the right to responsible group membership"). Classification in the *social subsystem* is based on the keyword 'responsible' which suggests formal group membership.

The third Area deals with *education and play*. We interpret "the right to formal and informal education and any necessary special resources" as part of the development of the personality. It belongs, therefore, in the *expressive mode* of the *personality subsystem*.

The Right "to full opportunity to play, recreation and fantasy," is classifiable in the *expressive mode* (play), the *adaptive mode* (recreation), and the *expressive mode* (fantasy) of the *personality subsystem*.

The Right "to optimum physical and psychological development and encouragement toward this" relates to the *expressive mode* of the *physical subsystem*, as well as in the *expressive mode* of the *personality subsystem*. As a marginal note we draw the attention to the fact that *optimum development* is not the same for everybody, and that one person may find that he has given enough *encouragement* for such development, while another may think that it has been too little. These considerations make the enforcement of this right difficult.

The Declaration of the Psychological Rights of the Child is hardly known outside the circle of school-psychologists. Inside this circle, however, it has contributed to the notion that maltreatment and abuse are not necessarily or in the first place a physical matter.[180] However, the issues typical for psychologists (tests, psychotherapy, confidentiality) are not mentioned in this Declaration. Those issues are dealt with in another declaration to which we refer: Gerald Koocher and his 'Bill of Rights for Children in Psychotherapy'.[181]

17. THE MALTA DECLARATION OF THE CHILD'S RIGHT TO PLAY (OF THE INTERNATIONAL PLAYGROUND ASSOCIATION, NOVEMBER 1977)

See Appendix XXXII

"Children's right to play generally is given a low priority if it is considered at all. Play is often looked upon as a useless occupation or even as a luxury,

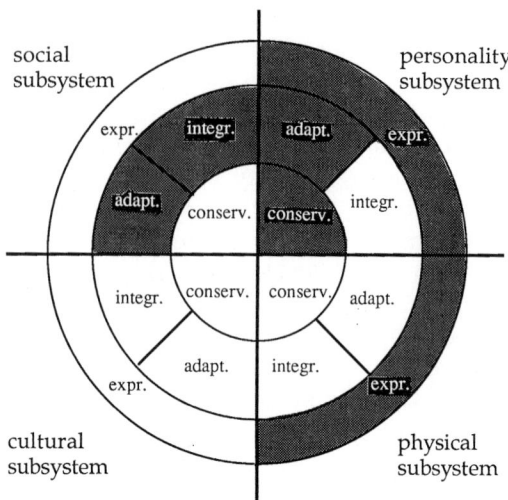

Fig. 13.16. The Declaration of the Psychological rights of the Child, adopted by the International Association of School Psychologists. Interpreted by the Systemic Quality of Life Model.

yet we know how fundamentally important it is. The International Year of the Child, 1979, may be the golden opportunity to focus attention on this."[182] This is how Arvid Bengtsson addressed the International Playground Association (IPA) in 1977.

In order not to lose this golden opportunity, the board of directors of the IPA invited representatives of the Association of interested Non-Governmental Organisations recognised by the Economic and Social Council of the United Nations (ECOSOC) and UNESCO, and representatives of the developing countries, to take part in a week's consultation about various aspects of the 'Child's Right to Play'. The Malta Playing Field Association acted as host. The aim was to produce "Strategies of Action," on a co-operative basis, not only for the International Year of the Child, but on an ongoing long-term basis.

A small group prepared a final document, which resulted in the *Malta Declaration of the Child's Right to Play*." The then Secretary of the IPA, (now called the *International Association for the Child's Right to Play*), who is today President of the Association, wrote to me that the initiative to formulate a Declaration came – if he remembered correctly – from the UNESCO-representative Mr. A. Chiba who noted that such an instrument would be valuable during the International Year of the Child. "We must appeal", said Mr. Chiba[183] "to all parents, on the occasion of the International Year of the Child, to convince them that the child's right to play should be fully recognised and encouraged, for the child to lead a meaningful and enriched life at home, at school and in the community." He emphasised that "the result of this consultation should be to provide the world community with an opportunity to give a fresh look at the child's life, which is being menaced by so many different factors at present, and to re-think how to promote and facilitate children's sound and happy growth in life."[184] On the one hand, Mr. Chiba stated that the Twentieth Century "undoubtedly was the one in which play had been given due recognition and importance in the education of children," on the other hand he voiced great concern about recent developments. Chiba: "Now, quo vadis homo ludens? The nature of children's play is changing as their environment changes... For us, the major issue is how to protect children from the dehumanisation process of modern society, how to retain human and humane nature and how to encourage children's initiative, spontaneity, creativeness and imagination. Schools, parents and society in general not only do not recognise these qualities and the usefulness of play, but also try to discourage it and want to make children conform to certain norms and values established by adults, thus killing children's spontaneity and even creativeness fostered through play."[185] Chiba also feared that children were becoming more passive, would watch only television, read comics and spend most of their time indoors. Chiba: "The most dangerous fact is that they know very little about themselves or how to play."

A number of child psychologists and pediatricians had already pointed out that neglect or enrichment in the senso-motoric field strongly affected the behaviour and development of children. In the Netherlands, the ideas of the child psychologist Wilhelmina J. Bladergroen[186] became popular. She believed that certain learning disabilities could be retraced to deprivation in early childhood. According to her, the lack of senso-motoric experiences resulted in a lower or unharmonious level of functioning. These opinions induced others to point at the effect of living in flats and amidst fast traffic.[187] Thus Ackermans[188] showed that some aspects of urban development threatened to influence the development of children negatively. In 1972, at a Congress in Vienna, the IPA had decided to press for the end of building high-rise apartment buildings.

The IPA (which had at that time National Correspondents in 22 countries)[189] stated in the Malta Declaration that "play is a means of learning to live," and appealed to all countries and organisations "to consider seriously the implementation of measures to reverse the alarming trends... and to place high on its list of priorities the development of long term programmes to ensure for all time *the child's right to play*".

The Malta Declaration includes proposals for action in the field of health, education, welfare, leisure and planning.

With regard to play, the Malta Declaration argues that: A child learns the different roles by play, expresses his or her present personality through play, and develops further through play. Speaking of non-living systems (machines) we can say: "Let's use it to full capacity. It won't make the machine better

372   Chapter XIII

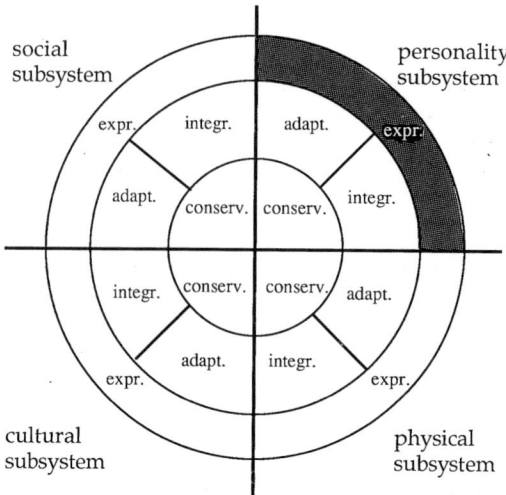

Fig. 13.17. The Malta Declaration of the Child's Rights to Play (1977). Interpreted by the Systemic Quality of Life Model.

or worse." In living systems there is a gradual shift in potential. When children play, they are not only expressing themselves, but they are also strengthening their identity and becoming more mature human beings.

The participants to the Malta Consultation were especially concerned with personality development. They assumed that the child's expressive actions would, in the long run, lead to his or her 'normal' development. The personality of the child is, to a large extent, formed by play. The IPA's point of view (expressed in the Malta Declaration) that the child develops physically, mentally, emotionally and socially through play is classifiable in the *expressive mode* of the *personality subsystem*.

NOTES

1. *Bulletin of the International Labour Office*, Nos.1,2,3, Vol. 1, 1906, p. 150 (in the appendix).
2. Ayusava, Iwao Frederick, *International Labor Legislation*, New York, 1920, Columbia University, Studies in History, Economics and Public Law, Vol.XCI, No. 2, p. 430.
   See also the statement of Mr. Zmirou of the I.L.O. in the Third Committee of the U.N. General Assembly on October 13, 1959, A/C.3/SR.926.
3. *Nouveau Receuil Général de Traités et Autres Actes Relatifs aux Rapports de Droit International*, Continuation du Grand Receuil de G.Fr. de Martens par Felix Stoerk, Leipzig, 1905, Librairie Dietrich, pp. 367–370. The English translation can be found in: Lowe, Boutelle Ellsworth, *The International Protection of Labor*, New York, 1935, The MacMillan Comp. pp. 180–184.
4. *Bulletin of the International Labour Office*, Vol.VIII, 1913, p. 248.
5. International Labour Office, *The International Labour Code* 1951, A systematic arrangement of the Conventions and Recommendations adapted by the International Labour

Conference, 1919–1951, with Appendices embodying other standards of social policy, Vol.II (Appendices), p. 1180.
6. *Bulletin of the International Labour Office*, Vol.IX, 1914, No. 7.
7. *The International Labour Code* 1951, Op. cit., p. 1182. I thank Mrs. Linda Stod of the Central Library and Documentation Branch of the International Labour Office in Geneva for helping me to find the documents mentioned here.
8. The International Labour Organisation, *Backgrounder*, Geneva, 1987, Bureau of Public Information, I.L.O., p. 1.
9. Idem.
10. *The New International Year Book* 1919, New York, 1920, Dodd, Mead and Comp. p. 150.
11. Shotwell, James Thomas (Ed.), *The Origins of the International Labour Organisation*, New York, 1934.
12. League of Nations, *International Labour Conference*, First Annual Meeting, October 29, 1919 – November 29, 1919, Washington, D.C., Government Printing Office, 1920.
13. League of Nations, International Labour Office, 'The International Labour Office and the Protection of Children', in: *International Labour Review*, Vol.III, Nos.1–2, July–August 1921, p. 13.
14. Idem, p. 14.
15. Abbott, Grace, *The Child And The State, Volume I, Legal Status in the Family Apprenticeship and Child Labor*, Chicago, Ill., 1938, The University of Chicago Press, p. 639.
16. Poland and Sweden were willing to accept fourteen as the minimum age. (Sweden only for industrial occupations.) Serbia was prepared to adopt fourteen as the age limit in districts where industrial conditions were favourable, but proposed to adopt *twelve* in less developed districts. In Czechoslovakia and the Netherlands, bills proposing to fix the age limit at fourteen were already pending before the legislature.
17. League of Nations, *Report on the Employment of Women and Children and the Berne Conventions of* 1906, prepared by the Organising Committee for the International Labour Conference, Washington, 1919, London, Harrison & Sons.
18. League of Nations, *International Labour Conference, First Annual Meeting*, o.c., p. 96.
19. Idem.
20. On October 15, 1989, representatives of some seventy voluntary organisations in India adopted the *Bhopal Statement on Child Labour in India*. This recent Statement calls attention to the "incredible hazards" faced by child labourers in a wide range of industries.
21. *International Labour Review*, Vol.III, Nos.1–2, July–August 1921, p. 16.
22. According to a letter, written to me by I. Dane Hartgrave of the Diplomatic Branch of the National Archives in Washington.
23. In many countries, children were employed for night work in the pottery industry. When the chairman of a Dutch Parliamentary Inquiry Committee asked Pierre Regout (one of the owners of the Sphinx factories) in 1887 if he allowed children to work at night, the answer was: "I know also that children sometimes do not go to bed without falling ill. But students sometimes study all night to prepare for an exam." See: Vink, Bart, 'Honderd jaar De Sphinx: Van kinderarbeid tot dat rijke gevoel' in *Intermediair*, Vol.23, Feb.13,1987.
24. *International Labour Review*, Vol.III, Nos.1–2, July–August 1921, p. 17.
25. List of I.L.O. Instruments Containing Standards Regarding Youth. *Minimum age*

  – (Industry) Convention, 1919 (No.5).
  – (Sea) Convention, 1920 (No.7).
  – (Agriculture) Convention, 1921 (No.10).
  – (Trimmers and Stokers) Convention, 1921 (No.15).
  – (Non–Industrial Employment) Convention, 1932 (No.33).
  – (Sea) Convention (Revised), 1936 (No.58).
  – (Industry) Convention (Revised), 1937 (No.59).
  – (Non–Industrial Employment) Convention (Revised), 1937 (No.60).
  – (Fishermen) Convention, 1959 (No.112).

- (Underground Work) Convention, 1965 (No.123).
- Convention, 1973 (No.138). (Minimum Age)
- (Non–Industrial Employment) **Recommendation**, 1932 (No.41).
- (Family Undertakings) Recommendation, 1937 (No.52).
- (Coal Mines) Recommendation, 1953 (No.96).
- (Underground Work) Recommendation, 1965 (No.124).
- Recommendation, 1973 (No.146).

Medical examination

- of Young Persons (Sea) Convention, 1921 (No.16).
- of Young Persons (Industry) Convention, 1946 (No.77).
- of Young Persons (Non–Industrial Occupations) Convention, 1946 (No.78).
- (Fishermen) Convention, 1959 (No.113). Radiation Protection Convention, 1960 (No.115).
- of Young Persons (Underground Work) Convention, 1965 (No.124). Maximum Weight Convention, 1967 (No.127). Benzene Convention, 1971 (No.136). Occupational Safety and Health Convention, 1981 (No.155).
- of Young Persons Recommendation, 1946 (No.79). Radiation Protection Recommendation, 1960 (No.114). Maximum Weight Recommendation, 1967 (No.128). Benzene recommendation, 1971 (No.144).

Night work

- of Young Persons (Industry) Convention 1919 (No.6.).
- of Young Persons (Non-Industrial Occupations) Convention, 1946 (No.79).
- of Young Persons (Industry) Convention (Revised), 1948 (No.90).
- of Children and Young Persons (Agriculture) Recommendation, 1921 (No.14).
- of Young Persons (Non-Industrial Occupations) Recommendation, 1946 (No.0).

Other conditions of work

Night Work (Women) Convention, 1919 (No.4).
White Lead (Painting) Convention, 1921 (No.13).
Holidays With Pay Convention, 1936 (No.52).
Safety Provisions (Building) Convention, 1937 (No.62).
Holidays With Pay (Agriculture) Convention, 1952 (No.101).
Lead Poisoning (Women and Children) Recommendation, 1919 (No.4).
Holidays With Pay Recommendation, 1936 (No.47).
Safety Provisions (Building) Recommendation, 1937 (No.53).
Holidays With Pay (Agriculture) Recommendation, 1952 (No.93).
Conditions of Employment of Young Persons (Underground Work) Recommendation, 1965 (No.125).
Protection of Young Seafarers Recommendation, 1976 (No.153).

Employment and training

Unemployment Provision Convention, 1934 (No.44).
Employment Service Convention, 1948 (No.88).
Human Resources Development Convention, 1975 (No.142).
Unemployment of Young Persons Recommendation, 1935 (No.45).
Employment Service Recommendation, 1948 (No.83).
Special Youth Schemes Recommendation, 1970 (No.136).
Human Resources Development Recommendation, 1975 (No.150).

Employment Policy (Supplementary Provisions) Recommendation, 1984 (No.169).

Migrant workers

Migration for Employment Convention (Revised), 1949 (No.97).
Migration (Protection of Females at Sea) Recommendation, 1926 (No.26).
Migration for Employment Recommendation (Revised), 1949 (No.86).

26. Bequele, Assefa, 'Child Labour: A framework for policies and programmes', in: *Child Labour: A Briefing Manual*, Geneva, 1986, International Labour Office, p. 17.
27. Doek, J.E., *Kinderarbeid en Ontwikkelingssamenwerking*, Amsterdam, 1987, Vrije Universiteit, Report by order of the Ministry of Foreign Affairs, Directorate-General International Co-operation, p. 5.
28. Swepston, Lee, 'Child Labour: Its regulation by I.L.O. standards and National Legislation', in: *Child Labour: A Briefing Manual*, Op. cit.
29. *Minimum Age*, General Survey by the Committee of Experts on the Application of Conventions and Recommendations, International Labour Conference, 67th Session, Geneva, 1981, I.L.O.
30. International Labour Office, Report V. *Youth* Geneva 1986, International Labour Conference, 72nd Session, p. 25.
31. Kimml, Anton, 'The struggle for the Protection and Rights of Youth', in: *The Socialist Youth International*, s.d. Berlin, p. 16.
    See also: Ollenhauer, Erich, 'Historical Survey', in: *The Socialist Youth International*, Op. cit., p. 6.
32. Werner, Georges, 'Remise de la Déclaration de Genève' au Conseil d'Etat de Genève pour ses Archives", in: *Revue Internationale de la Croix-Rouge*, sixième année, No. 63, Mars 1924, pp. 155–156.
33. Kimml, Anton, Op. cit., p. 16.
34. *The Protection of Young Workers throughout the World; A Summary of the protective legislative measures for Young Workers in the various countries*, Amsterdam, 1922, International Federation of Trade Unions, p. 42.
35. Idem, pp. 43–44.
36. The Socialist Youth International's programme for the protection of youth, in: *The Socialist Youth International*, Op. cit., p. 38.
37. I thank Mieke Yzerman of the *International Institute of Social History* in Amsterdam, and Linda Stoddart, Deputy-Librarian of the Central Library and Documentation Branch of the *International Labour Office*, Geneva, for their help in locating this material.
38. *Free Labour World*, Magazine of the ICFTU, No. 16/87, 18 December, 1987.
39. *ICFTU Trade Union Youth Work in Favour of Development: Examples of Activities*, Brussels.
40. Letter to the author, dated April 30, 1990, from Tim Noonan, Youth Secretary of the ICFTU.
41. The other Resolutions on Youth adopted by the ICFTU World Congress are also important. In one such Resolution the World Congress of the ICFTU in Melbourne (1988) insisted, for instance, on the urgency of tackling young persons' problems by providing youth with a broadly based education, appropriate and modern vocational training, while focusing on the need to expand full-time employment opportunities aimed at absorbing youth into the labour market and developing their human resources potential. The World Congress also stressed that governments must adopt positive measures to provide youths with a place in society and that they should respect the rights of youth to equal standards and conditions in employment, apply internationally agreed standards on the minimum age for employment and the abolition of child labour, and provide properly supervised quality training, leading to real employment prospects.
42. Letter from Tim Noonan, Op. cit.

43. *International Agreement for the Suppression of the White Slave Trade* between Austria-Hungary, Belgium, Brazil, Denmark, France, Germany, Great-Britain, Italy, the Netherlands, Portugal, Russia, Spain, Sweden, Norway and Switzerland. Although Their Majesties of Belgium, Germany, Denmark, Spain, France, Italy and The Netherlands declared that the Convention was also applicable to their colonies, the major concern was the trade in *White* rather than in Brown or Black Slaves (see title of the Agreement).
44. Societé des Nations, *Journal Officièl*, July 1924, p. 937.
45. 1904, March 18, International Agreement for the Suppression of White Slave Traffic; 1910, May 4, Convention for the Suppression of the White Slave Traffic; 1921, September 30, International Convention for the Suppression of Traffic in Women and Children.
   When I asked the International Abolitionist Federation in Lausanne about the attitude of the I.A.F. towards these Conventions, I was told that their attitude was positive although insufficient towards the 1904 and 1921 Conventions, and that they had participated in efforts to broaden the 1921 Convention in order to make life difficult for traffickers and pimps. Unfortunately, the Council of the League of Nations did not, at the time, follow up these efforts. In 1937, (thanks to the tenaciousness of the I.A.F.), the project for a new Convention was again taken up. In 1949, the effort was finally realised and accepted by the ECOSOC (Economic and Social Council) of the U.N. (Convention du 2 Décembre 1949 pour la répression de la traité des êtres humains et de l'exploitation de la prostitution d'autrui).
46. *Societé des Nations*, Journal Officièl, July 1924, p. 9340.
47. For a number of States this was not important. Panama, for instance, stated that "from an ethical point of view it could not but condemn prostitution and the traffic in women, but that these considerations of a pure theoretical nature were not sufficiently cogent to prevent the recognition that prostitution was inevitable and its regulation in the interests of public health a necessity." (See: Societé des Nations, *Journal Officièl*, July 1924.)
48. A copy of a letter received by the Registry of the League of Nations on February 18, 1925, and written on February 6, 1925, but not signed on the carbon copy found in the archives.
49. Tuttle, Lisa, *Encyclopedia of Feminism*, New York, 1986, Facts File Publications.
50. The meetings were held successively in London (1899), Berlin (1904), Toronto (1909), Rome (1914), Kristiania (1920) and the Hague (1922).
51. Backer, Fru Anna, Editor, *International Council of Women, Combined First and Second Annual Report of the Seventh Quinquennial Period*, 1922, p. 12.
52. The Marchioness of Aberdeen and Temair, editor, *International Council of Women, Report on the Quinquennial meeting*, *Kristiania* 1920, Aberdeen, Scotland, March 1921, The Rosemount Press.
53. Backer, Op. cit., p. 324.
54. On the authority of Resolution 23 of the International Council of Women in 1920, a separate commission for the well-being of youth was appointed with the Marchioness of Aberdeen and Temair as Chairwoman. Members were among others Mrs. Frederick Schoft (U.S.A.), Mrs. Ogilvie Gordon (United Kingdom), Countess Teresa Spalletti-Ruf (Italy) and Miss Christiton (from Yugoslavia, but residing in London). An *Educational Committee*, convening at the same time, discussed matters such as the supervision of movie screenings in cinemas and the appointment by the governments of censorship committees wherein women, too, would participate. The Educational Committee employed itself also, for a while, with the drafting of the Charter. It advised the Committee for the Well-being of Youth to include in this Charter: "education during eight years, full-time and compulsory, until an age not lower than fourteen, followed by two years of compulsory full- or part-time complementary education.
55. On April 9, 1912, President William H. Taft of the U.S.A. signed a law which created the *Children's Bureau*.
56. When the *International Council of Women* met in Norway, the discussions included the topic of *Children born out of Wedlock*. A resolution was adopted to the effect that "all States should take legislative measures ensuring children born out of wedlock the right to

their father's name, and that rules must exist for the purpose of establishing the identity of the father with a view to adequate maintenance of the child." The concept-resolution, proposed by the American Delegation to Kristiania went even further: The American women demanded the right of a child born out of wedlock "to inherit from both parents and that this must be legalised." This was more than many members of the commission could agree with, and the resolution was adopted after the clause relating to inheritance was erased from the text. The result was Resolution 24: *Rights of Children born out of Wedlock*. It is interesting to note that the *Code Napoleon* on which much of the French, Belgian and Dutch legislature was originally based, forbad investigation into the identity of the father, except in cases of abduction. (See Krause, Harry, D., 'Reflections on Child Support, from Debt Collection to Social Policy' in: Kahn, Alfred, I., and Kamerman, Sheila, B., *Child Support*, Newbury Park, Calif., 1988, p. 272.) Also discussed in Kristiania were the problems of foreign children who encountered many set-backs due to their lack of 'definite status'.

57. A telephone conversation with Mrs. E.E. Monro, the archivist of the International Council of Women, June 26th, 1988. Mrs. Monro lives in South Africa.
58. Foster, Henry, H. and Freed, Doris, Jonas, 'A Bill of Rights for Children', in *New York Law Journal*, Vol. 168, June 28, August 23 and September 29, 1972.
59. Foster, Henry, H., *A 'Bill of Rights' for Children*, Springfield, Ill., 1974, Charles C. Thomas Publishers.
60. On the day I was to meet Professor Foster in New York City, Mrs. Foster phoned me to say that he had died that morning from a heart attack.
61. Foster and Freed, 'A Bill of Rights for Children', Op. cit. The Articles appeared as one article in the *Family Law Quarterly* 6, 1972, pp. 343–375. They were also published in Katz, Sanford, N., ed., *The Youngest Minority, Lawyers in Defense of Children*, 1974, American Bar Association Press.
62. Foster reformulated this in his book in eight Principles. In the present study we have kept to the original 1972 Principles of Foster and Freed.
63. Foster and Freed, 'A Bill of Rights for Children', in *Family Law Quarterly* 1972, 6, p. 345.
64. Foster, Henry, H., 1974, Op. cit., p.xi.
65. Idem, p. 16.
66. Idem.
67. Idem, p. 29.
68. Idem, p. 31.
69. Idem, p. 32.
70. Foster and Freed, Op. cit., pp. 352–353.
71. Foster, Henry, H., Op. cit., p. 10.
72. Idem, p. 9.
73. Idem, p. 41.
74. Foster and Freed, Op. cit., p. 356.
75. Foster, Henry, H., 1974, Op. cit., p. 38. In the book this right is linked to the right to receive fair treatment.
76. Idem, p. 45.
77. Foster, H., Op. cit., p. 53.
78. Foster and Freed, 'Law and the Family', in: *New York Law Journal* August 25, 1972, Vol. 168, No. 39.
79. Idem.
80. Idem.
81. Foster, H., Op. cit., p. 60.
82. Foster, Henry, H. and Freed, Doris Jonas, 'A Bill of Rights for Children', in: *Family Law Quarterly*, 1972, 6, p. 372.
83. Idem, p. 373.
84. Hansen, Robert, W., 'The Role and Rights of Children in Divorce Actions', in: *Journal*

of Family Law, Vol. 6, 1966, No. 1, pp. 1–14.
85. This is presented to them, according to Hansen, at the time of the preliminary hearings in court.
86. 1987–1988, *Wis.Stat.* Actions Affecting the Family (see sections 767.11 and 767.081).
87. Letter from Donald P. Johns, Assistant-Attorney General, of April 5, 1990, written to me after I wrote to Governor Tommy G. Thompson.
88. Dennis Austin, Deputy Law Librarian of the Supreme Court of Wisconsin (State Law Library) in Madison wrote me: "As far as I can determine, the Bill of Rights for Children as discussed in the article by Judge Robert Hansen, published in 1966, was never enacted by the Wisconsin Legislature. It seems that this Bill of Rights was only used for some time as a guideline by some of the Circuit Court Judges in Milwaukee, County Wisconsin. Some of the thoughts contained in the Bill of Rights were perhaps used in 1978, when the Children's Code was adopted. There are also sections in the Wisconsin divorce statutes that relate to the "best interest of the child."
89. Hansen, Op. cit., p. 2.
90. Idem, p. 4.
91. *Protection* can of course be classified in the *conservative mode* of the *physical subsystem*. However, from the context in which it appears, we understand that the social subsystem was meant.
92. It is important to view these rights against the background of the important work by Judith Wallerstein and Joan B. Kelly (*Surviving the Breakup: How Children and their Parents Cope with Divorce*, New York, 1980, Basic Books.)
93. In 1789, the American *Constitution* was adopted in Philadelphia.
94. The election of representatives was more symbolical than real.
95. "Rights of Foster Children", in: *Children Today*, Vol.2, No. 4, July-August 1973, p. 20.
96. Telephone conversation between the author and Jacob Sprauce in King George, Virginia, July 1988.
97. The *National Action for Foster Children Committee* consisted of foster parents and interested citizens. It also co-ordinated regional and local committees.
98. Hegar, Rebecca, L., 'Foster Children's and Parents' Rights to a Family' in *Social Service Review*, 1983, Vol. 57, No. 3.
99. Jansen, Jacques (Legal Counsellor of the Ministry of Justice in The Netherlands), "According to a U.N. Declaration dealing with foster families and intercountry adoption" in *Familie en Jeugdrecht* 7–8, 1985, December, p. 235.
100. Walkate, Jaap, A., *Report by the Chairman of the Consultations on the Draft Declaration on Social and Legal Principles Relating to the Protection and Welfare of Children*, with Special Reference to Foster Placement and Adoption, Nationally and Internationally, held pursuant to General Assembly Resolution 39/89, 16–27 September 1985, New York, p. 2.
101. Lücker-Babel, Marie-Françoise, 'The U.N. Declaration Relating to Adoption and Foster Placement: New Safeguards for Children?' in: the *International Children's Rights Monitor*, Vol. 4, No. 3/4, 1987, p. 28.
102. Idem, p. 25.
103. Idem.
104. Idem.
105. FICE (Fédération Internationale des Communautés Educatives), *Malmö Declaration*, August 28th, 1986, FICE-International, Zurich.
106. Jansen, Jacques, Op. cit., p. 238.
107. It is important to compare this Article with Article 20 (sub 3) of the *U.N. Convention on the Rights of the Child*, which states that "when considering solutions, due regard shall be paid to the desirability of continuity in a child's upbringing
108. Lücker-Babel, Op. cit., p. 26.
109. Idem.
110. Jansen, Jacques, Op. cit., p. 239.
111. Idem, p. 240.

Notes

112. Lücker-Babel, Op. cit., p. 24.
113. Jansen, Op. cit., p. 240.
114. Lücker-Babel, Op. cit., p. 27.
115. Idem, and pp. 24 and 28.
116. See: Loon, J.H.A. van, *Report on Intercountry Adoption*, The Hague, 1990, The Hague Conference on Private International Law, Prel. Doc. No. 1.
117. Page, Raissa and Clark, G.A., *Who Cares? Young People in Care Speak Out*, London, 1977, National Children's Bureau.
118. Charter of rights for young people in care.
    We have drawn up this charter for 'young people' because we feel it is the responsibility of the residential worker and social worker to make sure that younger kids get a good deal.

    1. the right to be accepted and treated as an individual member of society. Also the right to be treated with the same respect given to any other valid member of the human race.
    2. The right to know who we are. To know our parents and brothers and sisters. To have factual information about our family origins and background.
    3. The right to be able to make our own decisions and to have real influence over those decisions we are sometimes considered too thick to participate in.
    4. The right to privacy. We understand that in care it is not always possible to choose who we are going to live and share our lives with. But we are still human beings and are still entitled to the essential amount of privacy needed before cracking up.
    5. The right to be given an insight into the use of money by handling it, using it and paying the consequences if we misuse it, e.g. being given the money in our hand to buy the clothes our clothing allowance will allow.
    6. The right to choose those who will represent us whether it be legally or otherwise, e.g. social workers. Also the right to choose those whom we wish to confide in.
    7. Finally, the right to be as much a part of society as the next person and not to be labelled in any way. In short, to live.

    These rights can be interpreted how you like. But don't misuse them or distort them for your own devices.
    Copyright: *Who cares?* published by the National Children's Bureau, London, 1977.
119. An active group is for instance *A Voice for the Child in Care*, a network of people concerned about children in care. Their aim is to help children in care to have a voice in their lives by trying to ensure that, as far as their age allows, every child can take part when plans are being made or decisions taken about their future.
120. Now called *Social Care Association*.
121. Walton, Ron, 'Charter of Rights: The End or the Beginning?', in: Walton, R.G. and Elliott, T., editors, *Residential Care*, 1980, Pergamon Press, pp. 239–241.
122. British Association of Social Workers (BASW), *Clients are fellow citizens*, Report of the Working Party on Client Participation in Social Work, Birmingham, 1980. See also the draft regulations for children's homes published in *Childright*, March 1984, No. 5 ('regulating care').
123. National Children's Bureau, *Essential Elements in Establishing an Effective Complaints Procedure for Children in Care*, London, s.a. See also: James, Gwen and Wadcock, Dave, Signpost, *A Guide for a Person given the Responsibility of Setting up a Complaints Procedure for Young People in Care*, London, 1985, National Children's Bureau.
124. Ogden, John, Principal Advisor, London Boroughs Children's Regional Planning Committee, *Giving Young People a Say*, London, unpublished paper.
125. 'New Charter sets out rights for young people in care', in: *Childright*, March 1986, No. 25, pp. 6–7.
126. *Charter of Rights for Children in Care* adopted in Kingston-upon-Thames in September 1986.

1. Children in care have the right to full and accurate information on the legislation under which they have come into care and how they can be discharged from care.
2. Children accused of criminal offenses while in care should receive equal protection from the law as if they were in the care of their own parents. This applies particularly in cases where a child is charged with offenses on residential premises or in foster homes; in these circumstances the person attending the police station 'in loco parentis' should be a practitioner other than the foster parents, and not a member of staff from the home in which the offence is alleged to have taken place. The child should have legal advice from an *independent* solicitor.
3. Children in care have a legal right to attend and contribute to their case reviews. They have the right to expect a key worker to write out an individual 'care plan' and discuss the content of the Case Plan with them.
4. Children in care have a right to security of placement, to know that they will not be moved at whim or without their needs first being considered, and should be involved in this process where possible.

    Children in care have a right to expect regular and frequent visits from their field social workers.
5. Children have a right to ask for help from the Director of Social Services or other independent sources of help. See Children in Care Booklet for details.
6. Children have a right to see parents, brothers and sisters and other relatives. Equally they have the right to refuse to see parents or other relatives following discussion with their social worker.
7. Children have a right to privacy. This should include a place to lock private papers or valuables; a safe place for treasured personal possessions; the right to send and receive private letters; make and receive private telephone calls.

    7(b) The right to privacy includes the right not to have staff or residents gossip about a child's personal or family life.

    It is a right that only essential information should be given to school, youth clubs, community health services etc.
8. Young People (after age 14) have the right to access to their files (from 1st January 1987) as laid down by the Borough's Procedure Manual to include Statutory Review Papers and in particular their care plans.
9. Children have the right not to be made subject to cruel or degrading or humiliating punishments by social workers, teachers or foster parents. They should know what punishments can or cannot be used by their carers.

    The following are contrary to good practice:

    Any form of physical punishment;
    Stopping a child from visiting his/her family or from receiving visits;
    Refusal of basic food and drink;
    Being made to wear night clothes or remain unclothed during the day;
    Use of sedation when this is not required by the child's medical condition or prescribed by a medical practitioner;
    Locking children and young people in any room;

If children don't behave, Residential Social Workers and foster parents can:

Stop you hurting other children or yourself;
Defend themselves by use of reasonable restraint, if they are attacked;
After discussion with a young person and their social workers, change plans for visits home, for a while;
Stop children going on outings or playing out; stop children watching TV etc.;

Give out extra tasks such as clearing up;
Hold pocket money back for a while;
Make children pay out of their pocket money for damage e.g. breaking a window;
Take any dangerous things away (such as knives and matches etc.);
Try to stop damage to property;
Insist on short periods of 'time out' from the rest of the group;

10. Children placed in a residential or foster home or homes managed by other authorities have a right to know who makes the decision regarding their schooling, changes in where they live as well as details of their daily life, clothes, pocket money, leisure activities.
11. Children have a right to be brought up by adults who will value them as people and will not subject them to racism, sexism, discrimination against physical or mental disability or any other form of discrimination which will affect their self-confidence or self-esteem.
12. Children have a right to enjoy normal experiences of living without undue rules and regulations.
13. Children have a right to keep contact with families and friends. Arrangements should be made with the person who is in charge of their day to day care. Any overnight stay or holiday should be planned in order to make sure children/young people will be safe.
14. Children in care have the right, where possible, to keep their own doctors and dentists.
15. Whenever possible and desirable children in care have a right to remain in their own schools.
    People looking after them should keep a careful record of their work and progress at school to make sure that all their skills and abilities can be developed.
16. Young people have the right to further education beyond school leaving age if they so wish. Handicapped and distressed children may need additional help beyond 19 years.
17. Children have the right to follow their own religion including eating special food, wearing clothes and hairstyles that their religion specifies and going to festivals and practices. Their religion should be treated with respect. They should be told of their nearest religious centre or religious leaders. Children have the right not to be forced into religious practices against their will.
    Other agencies such as Education, Health Services etc. should be reminded of the above recognition.
18. Children and young people have the right to grow up in a home which encourages normal sexual development and enables good relationships with children and adults of all sexes. This requires that Carers should make sure children have the opportunity to meet members of the opposite sex.
19. Children have the right to information on health, and counselling on sex should be made available.
20. Young people in care have the right to be prepared for adult living and eventual independence. This should prepare them to handle money, enjoy their spare time, to be familiar with personal documents and to know the whereabouts of birth certificates, passports, medical cards.

Young people in care have the right to support in establishing themselves as independent adults beyond their 18th birthday. They have a right to financial help and support on leaving care (including accommodation) as would be provided by any 'good and caring family' (as provided under Section 27 of 1980 Act).
Draft Charter of Rights for Young People in Care, National Association of Young People in Care (1978).

All young people in care should have:
Files:

1. The Right to know that files exist and to have their purpose explained to them. All previous decisions should be explained.
2. The Right to read information kept on them.
3. The Right to help and support if such information is painful.
4. The Right to control who has access to their file.
5. The Right to add their own comments and opinions.
6. The Right to check, challenge and change any wrong information.
7. The Right to have files stored in a safe and secure place.
8. The Right to have the file kept brief and to the point.
9. The Right to have only one file kept on a young person.
10. The Right to be involved in the setting-up and updating of the file.
11. The Right to have files written in simple, clear language and not used in any way to label people.
12. The Right to have the file when that young person has left Care.

Rules, Punishment and Discipline:

13. The Right not to be beaten or have other degrading punishments given.
14. The Right not to be given drugs.
15. The Right not to have violence used against them.
16. The Right not to be locked up.
17. The Right to be given full information about the places where they will live and details of the rules and regulations.
18. The Right to information about life in Care by having booklets giving full explanations.
19. The Right to have a say in how the home is run.
20. The Right not to have home visits, pocket money and bedtimes used as a punishment.
21. The Right to decide punishments at House Meetings.
22. The Right to have punishments recorded in a punishment book and to have full access to the book.
23. The Right to complain, to be listened to and to be taken seriously.
24. The Right to be able to complain and appeal through a complaints procedure.
25. The Right to proper legal advice and help.

Dignity, Privacy and Personal Freedom:

26. The Right to Privacy.
27. The Right to have enough space of our own, not to be overcrowded.
28. The Right to buy our own clothes, food and toiletries.
29. The Right not to be embarrassed (for example, not to have to travel in a Social Services Minibus).
30. The Right to choose their sexual partner.
31. The Right to choose their own sexual lives, including being gay, lesbian or bisexual.
32. The Right to choose their own friends, of their own age, or from the staff etc.
33. The Right to belong to groups in the community, like Youth Clubs or other organisations, the same as any young person.
34. The Right to belong to the culture of choice, i.e. Rasta, or Punk or Mod, or anything else.
35. The Right to belong to the religion of choice and to practice it freely.
36. The Right to have no religion, not to be forced to go to church, watch TV religious programmes or have to say grace before meals.

37. The Right to choose the kind of food to eat, e.g. vegetarian or Asian etc.
38. The Right to choose and cook their own meals.
39. The Right to write letters or use the telephone in private whenever needed. Plus the Right to receive mail and calls without these being intercepted.
40. The Right to smoke or not to smoke, or have to breathe other peoples' smoke polluted air.
41. The Right not to be talked about needlessly to other people.
42. The Right to be told if advertisements are being used for fostering or adoption. Plus the Right to object. Also to take a part in drawing them up.
43. The Right to use whatever name, and surname, they want to use.
44. The Right to belong to N.A.Y.P.I.C.
45. The Right for girls and boys to have equal treatment. No sexism.
46. The Right to change the social worker.
47. The Right not to be discriminated against for any reason.
48. The Right not to have racist treatment.
49. The Right of black young people to choose which foster parents they have.
50. The Right to have a black person involved in fostering procedure.
51. The Right to have a foster home in a black community.
52. The Right to be black in a white society.
53. The Right of young black people to be provided with references to their cultural history and background.
54. The Right to change things in Care that young people do not agree with plus the Right to be consulted when new policies are made.
55. The Right not to be in Care for longer than is needed.

Proper Care:

56. The Right to a warm safe life.
57. The Right to have nourishing, tasty and adequate food.
58. The Right to get enough pocket money each week or whenever it is needed.
59. The Right to Birthday, Christmas and holiday allowances.
60. The Right to a good holiday each year.
61. The Right, if handicapped, to equal opportunities in housing, leisure, education and employment.
62. The Right to special help if handicapped and to be able to live as normal a life as possible, including integration into ordinary homes within communities.
63. The Right to give and expect to be given love.
64. the right to full education and training, including the right to go to college or have full opportunities for work.
65. The Right to proper medical care.
66. The Right to full advice on contraception, pregnancy or abortion and other alternatives. This should be made available regardless of the viewpoints of staff to all those of age.
67. The Right to decent and non-segregated facilities should be available to girls in Care with their babies.

Home and Family:

68. The Right to live at home if at all possible.
69. The Right to be placed as near to home as possible.
70. The Right to see parents and family when wanted or the Right to refuse.
71. The Right to have enough time at home if living away in Care including weekends and holidays.
72. The Right to be placed with brothers and sisters (siblings) if they are also in Care.

73. The Right to stay at the same schools that they went to from home if this is possible. Not to be moved round from school to school.

Reviews and Case Conferences:

74. The Right to attend reviews and case conferences for the whole time.
75. The Right to be consulted about who attends their review (especially parent(s), employers).
76. The Right to bring along a friend of their choice.
77. The Right to have disagreements recorded along with everyone else's.
78. The Right to have a say as to where the reviews should be held and the time they are held.
79. The Right to appeal against any decisions taken at reviews.
80. The Right to know what the Department/Organisation's policy on reviews is.
81. The Right to see written reports/letters prepared for reviews.
82. The Right to chair their own review.
83. The Right to have a say in all assessments whether for court, for social services, or for special education etc.

Leaving Care and After Care:

84. The Right not to be over-protected, and to be prepared properly for leaving Care, from as soon as the young person comes into Care.
85. The Right to proper help when leaving Care.
86. The Right to financial help when no longer in Care, including the Right to a realistic grant to meet all needs on leaving Care.
87. The Right to other help and support once left Care.
88. The Right to expect proper accommodation to be provided if having to move out of a children's home or foster home.
89. The Right to financial assistance and support for further education.
90. The Right to have experience of cooking, ironing, washing, budgeting etc.
91. The Right to have Birth Certificates, Medical Cards, and School Reports etc.
92. The Right to know who young people can get help from when they leave Care.
93. The Right to know how to register with a doctor, dentist etc.
94. The Right to continued support up to any age once left Care.
95. The Right to full help from social services and other agencies in tracing their origins.
96. The Right to full access to all past care-givers.
97. The Right not to have their age (e.g. 18 years) used as a reason for making them leave Care.
98. The Right to be resettled in their place of origin regardless of expense.
99. The Right to help in establishing a social life to prevent loneliness when living out of care (e.g. after care groups).
100. The Right to choose when to leave Care.

Charter of Rights for Young People in Care, approved by the 'Who Cares' Scotland Conference at Largs in November 1986.

General

1. The right to have a Booklet of Rights when coming into care.

Reviews

2. The right to attend all reviews and case conferences for the whole time. (Children 12

and over *always*, children under 12 if mature enough – this rule to apply to all the Rights.)
3. The right to have a say on who attends.
4. The right to have all reports discussed with you before the review (including your own).
5. The right to appeal about review decisions.

Files

6. The right to read your own files and to have help and support to understand the contents.
7. The right to have your own file kept up to date in simple language and to have your disagreements added.
8. The right to have a say in who reads your file.

Rules

9. The right to have a written set of rules agreed by staff and young people.
10. The right to be consulted about major changes.
11. The Right not to be abused or locked up or denied home leave as punishment.
12. The right to have complaints taken seriously and to have an appeals procedure.
13. The right to take part in "Who Cares".

Privacy and Freedom

14. (The right to have a room of your own which you should be able to lock, or to share a room with a locker for your private property.
15. The right to choose your own friends and to send and receive mail without interference and to make private phone calls.
16. The right to practise your own religion or not, and have your ethnic background respected.
17. The right to smoke (or not) within agreed rules.

Home and Family

18. The Right for brothers and sisters to stay together in care.
19. The right to choose when to see your own family (or not).

Allowances

20. The right to nationally agreed pocket money, birthday, Christmas presents and holiday allowances.
21. The right to a proper clothing allowance and involvement in how it's spent.
22. The right to help with Education, Training, and Development, Employment and Housing.

Staff

23. The right to see your own social worker and residential worker when you need them.
24. The right to request a change of social worker or key worker.

Personal Care

25. The Right for girls in care who become pregnant to have and keep their babies in their own home.
26. The right to have a choice about fostering.

Leaving Care

27. The right to staff support after leaving care.
28. The right to help in getting accommodation and the right to financial support in setting up a new home.
29. The right to proper preparation before leaving care. For example, learning about cooking, buying food, ironing, washing, living on your own, reading meters, changing plugs, budgeting.
30. The right to leave care by agreement, and not to have age used as a reason.
31. The right to keep in touch after leaving care.

127. According to the U.S. National Center for Social Statistics quoted by Silbert, James, D., and Sussman, Alan 'Rights of Juveniles Confined in Training Schools' in: *Crime and Delinquency*, October 1974, p. 347.
128. Idem.
129. In July 1988, in a telephone conversation with the author, former Ombudsman James D. Silbert (Attorney at Law in New York) said: "It was a very frustrating job. The Ombudsman was really treated with suspicion. The kids wanted me to do more than I really could, and when I could not answer their expectations this created mistrust. Also the staff members were all the time 'looking over their shoulders' and in the end, I got the feeling nobody really wanted me there."

Silbert and Sussman wrote two interesting articles 'The Rights of Juveniles confined in Training Schools' as mentioned in note 127, and 'The Experience of a Training School Ombudsman' in the *Brooklyn Law Review*, Vol. 40, 1974, pp. 605–633. Silbert and Sussman worked with the most difficult youngsters, who had been referred by other training schools due to their problematic behaviour. In these articles Silbert and Sussman formulated:

'Rights of Juveniles Confined in Training Schools' by James D. Silbert and Alan Sussman, 1974.

I. Post-Adjudication, Legal Rights Pertaining to Commitment

A. Rights to challenge legality of confinement.
B. Right to an attorney.
C. Right to release upon expiration of commitment order or determination that further treatment is not needed, whichever sooner.
D. Right to a parole revocation-hearing with counsel.
E. Right to extension of placement hearing.
F. Right to maintain a civil suit.

II. Procedural Due Process Guarantees

A. Right to Notice and knowledge of written rules and regulations.
B. Right to be free from arbitrary institutional punishment.
C. Right to be free from arbitrary transfers.

III. Right to Treatment

A. Right to treatment.
B. Right not to receive treatment.

IV. Individual Rights

A. Right to be free from cruel and unusual punishment.
B. Right to expression and choice of personal appearance.

- C. Right to co-educational activities.
- D. Right to worship or not worship as one pleases.
- E. Right to receive and send uncensored mail.
- F. Right to vote.
- G. Right to adequate compensation for work.
- H. Right to Confidentiality of Training School Records.

130. *Brooklyn Law Review*, 1974, Op. cit., p. 633. The authors' scepticism about information given to inmates are based on their experiences: "For example one of the institutions, on its own accord, proudly announced that its male residents had been granted the *right* to wear their own clothing if they so chose. Only the staff, however, was informed of the change. The Ombudsman suggested to the superintendent of the training school that such an announcement ought to be posted in each cottage so that every child would be aware of it and, hopefully, would conclude that law and institutional rules could work for him. The superintendent replied that such a plan, though meritorious, was unworkable, since posting might cause disruptions and ultimately work against the best interests of the children. In other words, the residents were not even allowed to be informed of the few rights they did possess."
131. *Brooklyn Law Review* Op. cit., p. 633.
132. Films made by the English couple James and Joyce Robertson greatly contributed to this. Also James Robertson's book: *Young Children in Hospital*, London, 1970, Tavistock Publications. John Bowlby's report: (*Maternal Care and Mental Health*, Geneva, 1951, World Health Organisation) is also an important contribution, especially the popular version of this report published by Pelican Books in 1953: *Child Care and the Growth of Love*)
133. For instance: Nagera, H., 'Children's Reactions to Hospitalisation and Illness', in: *Child Psychiatry and Human Development*, 9 (1978), pp. 3–19 and: Provence, S., Lipton, R.C., *Infants in Institutions*, New York, 1962, International University Press.
134. The Platt Report also stated that separate children's wards must be set up, and that trained staff should care for children.
135. Letter (dated August 4, 1989) from Jenny Davison (Acting Director of the NAWCH), to the author.
136. Strubbe, W., *Anders dan gewoon. Inleiding in de kinderpsychiatrie*, Nijkerk, 1989, Published by Intro, p. 104.
137. The formulation issued by the 'Raad voor het Jeugdbeleid' (Council on Youth Policy) in the Netherlands is interesting: "Within the rights for minor patients, hides the dilemma of parental power and medical power. If only the parents decide about medical treatment, no justice is done to the personal stand of the minor: the right to integrity of his or her body. However, if we give the young person a great measure of responsibility, this creates a new dependency, namely on the medical powers, especially if we take into account the insecurity everybody experiences when dealing with medical treatment. If we try to establish rules in this respect, we stumble over the character of legal age limits: these are clear but general and arbitrary. The question is whether age limits do enough justice to the growing phase of each young person the position of a child changes all the time: a child grows, becomes bigger and also more mature. And along with the changed position of the child, the positions of all concerned also change.
138. The concern, in this case, is not that the child can choose his clothes, a concern which pertains to the expressive mode of the personality subsystem.
139. Charter Dutch National Association "Kind en Ziekenhuis" (Child and Hospital), March 1985.

   1. *Children* will not be admitted to a hospital if the care they require can be administered at home, in day care or in an outpatient department.
   2. *Children* have a right to medical treatment by doctors specialized in treating children.

3. *Children* and/or their parents have a right to information appropriate to their age and limits of comprehension.
4. *Children* and/or their parents have a right to all necessary information to give consent to methods of treatment and/or operations to be performed.
5. *Children* will be protected from unnecessary medical treatment.
6. *Children* will be cared for and will be treated in hospital departments with patients of their own age and in surroundings which are suited in every way to children with highest possible safety standards.
7. *Children* have a right to have their parents with them at all times. Parents are encouraged and supported to help their child in hospital. Parents are kept informed about rules of the department and will be encouraged to care for their child.
8. *Children* are to be cared for and treated by specially instructed personnel with expert knowledge of the physical and psychological needs of children of various age groups.
9. *Children* will be given the opportunity in hospital to play, to be creative and to receive schooling adjusted to their age and condition; they may have visitors of every age group.
10. *Children* may wear their own clothes in hospital and may have their personal belongings around them. Their privacy will be respected.

140. *Proposition de résolution* présentée par M. Collins, conformément à l'article 47 du Règlement sur une Charte européenne des enfants hospitalisés. Auteur, intervenants: Collins, Kenneth D. – Note that the document has been superseded by Doc. A2-25/86.
Also: Resolution on a European charter for children in hospital. Texts adopted by the European Parliament.
The European Parliament

– having regard to the motion for a resolution tabled by Mr. Collins (Doc. 2–1256/84);
– having regard to paragraph 5 of its resolution of 19 January 1984 on a European charter on the rights of patients, which states that the rights of sick children should be dealt with in a special charter;
– having regard to the report of the Committee of the Environment, Public Health and Consumer Protection and the opinions of the Committee on Legal Affairs and Citizens' Rights and the Committee on Youth, Culture, Education, Information and Sport (Doc. A2–25/86);
– stressing the soundness of the recitals contained in the charter, especially recitals A and E, which mention the Community dimension of the problem;

1. stresses that the right to the best possible medical treatment is a fundamental right, especially for children, who have their whole life in front of them;
2. is concerned that the budgetary cuts in many Member States hit the public health sector in particular and that this has inevitable repercussions on the health of the population and thus of children;
3. calls on the Commission to submit as soon as possible a proposal for a European charter on the rights of patients and for a European charter on the rights of children in hospital, in order to give real meaning to Youth Year;
4. requests that the charter for children in hospital should incorporate the following rights;

   a) the right to be admitted to hospital only if the treatment they require cannot be provided at home or on a day basis, and has been so planned as to ensure that they are hospitalized as soon as possible and for the shortest possible time;
   b) the right of children to day care without incurring additional costs for the parents;
   c) the right to have with them as much as possible during their stay their parents or the person acting in *loco parentis*, not as passive bystanders, but as active participants in hospital life, with no additional costs being incurred thereby; however, the exercise of

this right must not prejudice or stand in the way of the best possible administration of the treatment which the child has to receive;
d) the right to be fully informed – as far as their age, degree of mental development and emotional and psychological state allow – about the medical treatment they are undergoing and the positive prospects it offers;
e) the right of the child to individual supervision and care, with, as far as possible, the same nurses and assistants being detailed to look after them;
f) the right to refuse (through their parents or the person acting in *loco parentis*) to serve as research subjects and to refuse any care or examination when the primary purpose is educational or informational rather than therapeutic;
g) the right of the parents or the person acting in *loco parentis* to be given all available information concerning the child's illness and welfare, insofar as this does not conflict with the child's fundamental right to privacy;
h) the right of the parents or the person acting in *loco parentis* to authorize the treatment which the child is to undergo;
i) the right of the parents or the person acting in *loco parentis* to appropriate support and psychosocial counselling by specially trained staff;
j) the right not to be subjected to pharmacological or therapeutic experimentation. Only the parents or the person acting in *loco parentis* having been duly informed of the risks and benefits of such treatment, may give their consent and must retain the right to withdraw this consent.
k) the right of children in hospital, where they are involved in therapeutic experimentation, to protection by the Helsinki Declaration of the World Medical Assembly and its subsequent updates;
l) the right to be protected from unnecessary medical treatment and physical or emotional distress;
m) the right (and the means) to contact their parents or the person acting in *loco parentis* in times of stress;
n) the right to be treated with tact, civility and understanding and to have their privacy respected;
o) the right to be cared for throughout their hospital stay by appropriately trained staff, fully aware of the physical and emotional needs of each age group;
p) the right to be cared for in hospital with other children, avoiding as far as possible admission to adult wards;
q) the right to an environment furnished and equipped to meet hospital requirements and the educational and recreational needs of children, and in conformity with current safety standards;
r) the right to continue their schooling during their stay in hospital, teachers and teaching materials being supplied by the educational authorities, particularly in the case of prolonged stays in hospital providing that this activity does not have an adverse effect on the child's well-being or hinder its treatment;
s) the right to use books, audiovisual aids and toys appropriate for their age group during their stay in hospital;
t) the right to be taught even when they are admitted to day-hospital or are convalescing in their own homes;
u) the right to be guaranteed the treatment they need – if necessary with the intervention of the legal authorities – in the event of their parents or the person acting in *loco parentis* refusing such treatment on religious grounds, or because of cultural backwardness, prejudice or in the event of their being unable to cope adequately in an emergency;
v) the right to the necessary financial, moral and psychological support when undergoing examinations and/or treatment which have to be carried out abroad;
w) the right of parents or the person acting in *loco parentis* to invoke the charter where children require hospital treatment or check-ups in non-Community countries;

5. also calls upon the Commission to submit proposals to ensure that national statistics on health and hospital admission include standardized data for each age range so that such data may be comparable;
6. appreciates the contribution which voluntary associations can make as regards giving effect to many of the above-mentioned rights and carrying out additional tasks involved in helping young patients;
7. instructs its President to forward this resolution to the Commission, the Council, the Council of Europe, UNICEF and the World Health Organization.

141. European Parliament, Workers Documents, 1986–1987, April 14, 1986, Series A, Document A-2-25/86, *Report drawn up on behalf of the Committee on the Environment, Public Health and Consumer Protection on a European Charter for Children in Hospital*, Rapporteur: Mrs. U. Squarcialupi.
142. European Parliament, the Committee on Legal Affairs and Citizen's Rights. On 27 June 1985, the Committee on Legal Affairs and Citizens' Rights appointed Mrs. Boot as draftsman. The Committee considered the draft opinion at its meeting of 22 and 23 January 1986, and adopted the conclusion unanimously.

    I thank the Direction Générale de l'Information et des Relations Publiques of the European Parliament in Strasbourg (and especially Mr. S. Frindel) and Joëlle Marty of the Directorate-General for Research in Brussels) for their help.
143. *Official Journal of the European Communities*, *Vol.*29, 16 *June*, 1986, *No.*C.148/30–31.
144. Landelijke Vereniging Kind en Ziekenhuis, *Report on the First European Conference 'Children and Hospital'*, May 11, 12 and 13, 1988 at Oud Poelgeest, Oegstgeest, The Netherlands.
145. Charter for Children in Hospital, agreed on at the First European Conference 'Children in Hospital' May 13, 1988.

The right to the best possible medical treatment is a fundamental right, especially for children.
1. Children shall be admitted to hospital only if the care they require cannot be equally well provided at home or on a day basis.
2. Children in hospital shall have the right to have their parents or parent substitute with them at all times.
3. Accommodation should be offered to all parents, and they should be helped and encouraged to stay. Parents should not need to incur additional costs or suffer loss of income. In order to share in the care of their child, parents should be kept informed about ward routine and their active participation encouraged.
4. Children and parents shall have the right to be informed in a manner appropriate to age and understanding. Steps should be taken to mitigate physical or emotional stress.
5. Children and parents have the right to informed participation in all decisions involving their health care. Every child shall be protected from unnecessary medical treatment and investigation.
6. Children shall be cared for together with children who have the same developmental needs and shall not be admitted to adult wards. There should be no age restriction for visitors to children in hospital.
7. Children shall have full opportunity for play, recreation and education suited to their age and condition and shall be in an environment designed, furnished, staffed and equipped to meet their needs.
8. Children shall be cared for by staff whose training and skills enable them to respond to the physical, emotional and developmental needs of children and families.
9. Continuity of care should be ensured by the team caring for the children.

10. Children shall be treated with tact and understanding and their privacy shall be respected at all times.

146. Quoted in *Crisis in Child Mental Health: Challenge for the 1970s; Report of the Joint Commission on Mental Health of Children*, New York, 1969, Harper and Row, p. 5.
147. Idem, p. 7.
148. Idem.
149. Idem, p. 5.
150. Judge David Bazelon, Chief Judge of the U.S. Court of Appeals in Washington D.C.
151. *Crisis in Child Mental Health*, Op. cit., p. 7.
152. Idem, Preface, p.XIX.
153. Idem, p. 8.
154. Idem, p. 14.
155. Idem.
156. Drapers, Jan and Veerman, Philip, 'Schooluitvallers – een visie van Prof. H.C. Michael Rutter', in: Fijtel, Anton and Veerman, Philip, *Onderwijs en Jeugdhulpverlening*, Amsterdam, 1985, Stichting voor het Kind, pp. 42–43.
157. Veerman, Philip, E., 'Therapeutic Tutoring as a Method of Preventing School-Dropout', in: Chigier, E. (ed.), *Special Education and Social Handicap*, London, 1985, Freund Publishing House, p. 143.
158. Wright Edelman, Marian, *Families in Peril, An Agenda for Social Change* Cambridge, Mass., 1987, Harvard University Press, pp. 40–41.
159. This information was provided to me by Joan Levy Zlotnik, ACSW, Staff Director of the Commission on Family and Primary Associations of the National Association of Social Workers (NASW) in Silver Spring near Washington D.C. in a letter dated January 4th, 1990.
160. According to Charles Wright. Information found in the *minutes of the 1975–NASW Delegate Assembly, pertaining to the Bill of Rights for Children and Youth*.
161. Minutes of the NASW Delegate Assembly, p. 22.
162. National Association of Social Workers, *Social Work Speaks: NASW Policy Statements*, Washington D.C., 1987. *This book is a compilation of policies adopted and revised by NASW's key policy making body (the Delegate Assembly)*.
163. This is confirmed by what Ms. Carbino of the NASW Wisconsin Chapter said about the Bill of Rights: "It is important for you to note that rights are approached in relation to all societal institutions, not just families; for example we are also talking about court and detention systems, school systems, substitute care institutions and so on." (In: p. 21 of the *Minutes of the Assembly*).
164. We interpret *mastery* according to Otto Fenichel's definition in *The Psychoanalytic Theory of Neurosis*, London, 1946, Routledge & Kegan Paul, p. 45. Fenichel described how during infancy the child already tries to grip what is going on in the world around him or her. In this period the issue of goal-orientedness versus inferiority is an important part of life. Fenichel also described the feeling of playing an active part in the world, which he called *active mastery*. To conquer one's fear contributes much to 'active mastery of the world' and produces a feeling of triumph.
Robert W. White ('Adler and the future of ego-psychology', in: *The Journal of Individual Psychology*, Vol.XIII, No. 2, November 1957, pp. 437–454) wrote about the same subject from a different theoretical orientation. He presumes an inborn need to be effective which, if the conditions are right, leads to a 'sense of *competence*'.
The Minutes of the Delegate Assembly of the NASW do not identify the background of their reference to 'mastery'. We shall assume that it originated from a certain familiarity with the work of the above-mentioned authors.
165. NASW Delegate Assembly, 1975, *Minutes*,, p. 23.

166. Shore, Milton, F., 'Legislation, Advocacy, and the Rights of Children and Youth', in *American Psychologist*, Vol. 34, No. 10, October 1970, p. 1018.
167. *International School Psychology World Go Round*, Vol. 6, No. 2, 1978, June, p. 1.
168. Idem.
169. Catterall, Calvin, D., 'The Psychological Rights of the Child', 1979, unpublished paper found in a file in the library of UNICEF, at UNICEF House in New York.
170. Idem. See also: Catterall, C.D., 'Defining and promoting children's psychological rights', in: *School Psychology International*, 1979, 1(1), pp. 2–3.
171. Hart, Stuart, N., 'The History of Children's Psychological Rights', in: *Viewpoints in Teaching and Learning*, Vol. 58, No. 1, Winter 1982, p. 9.
172. *The Tentative Declaration of the Psychological Rights of the Child.*
    Right I: Personal Identity. The right to have a name, a feeling of identity, to be wanted, and to have a feeling of personal worth regardless of sex or identification with any religious, political, or ethnic group.
    Right II: Emotional Support from Adults. The right to both physical and psychological care and support from his or her parents and/or other adults in the culture, especially during the dependent stages of infancy and childhood.
    Right III: Participate in and Learn from Play and Fantasy. The right to the time and opportunity to participate in and learn from play and from other structured and non-structured activities.
    Right IV: Freedom from Fear of Physical Harm of Abuse. The right to be protected from all forms of neglect, cruelty, physical hurt, or exploitation and/or the dangers of man-made events such as riots or war.
    Right V: Encouragement. The right to encouragement from adults and peers to use his or her abilities, to explore new activities, to risk, and to accept, when necessary, the effects of adversity, defeat, and disappointment.
    Right VI: Satisfying Relationships with Others. The right to the opportunity to develop and foster positive, satisfying relationships with other children and adults.
    Right VII: Growing Awareness of Strengths. The right to be aware of individual differences, to overcome one's weaknesses, and, at the same time, to become aware of, to be proud of, and to make use of one's strengths in facing the responsibilities of life.
    Right VIII: Make Age-Appropriate Decisions. The right to an opportunity to make appropriate decisions about what he or she can and cannot do, including the right to be thought of as wrong or different by others, in order to assist him or her to become a mature adult.
    Right IX: Appropriate Education. The right to obtain the facts necessary to function within their culture and to develop their cognitive potential in an appropriate educational program that helps them to move towards taking a productive place in the culture and, when desirable or necessary, to move freely from one culture to another.
    Right X: Specialized Services. The right to specialized physical, educational, and psychological services to meet the child's unique needs in as normal and non stigmatizing a setting as possible.
173. Catterall, Calvin, D., 'Formulation of the Declaration of the Psychological Rights of the Child', in: *Viewpoints in Teaching and Learning*, Vol. 58, No. 1, Winter 1982, p. 18. See also: Nixon, M., 'The Psychological Rights of the Child and Schooling' in: *Viewpoints in Teaching and Learning* 1982, 58, 1, pp. 99–112.
174. The Declaration has not become very well-known; when I wrote to the Department of Psychology of the University of York in the U.K. (where the I.P.S. meeting took place and the Declaration was adopted), in order to receive more information, the answer was: "Sorry, we cannot help you." Dr. Catterall had died in an accident in France four years earlier. It was Zoran Pavlovic of the Institute of Criminology of the Edvard Kardelj University of Ljubljana in Yugoslavia who put me on the track of Stuart Hall and his *Office for the Study of the Psychological Rights of the Child* at Indiana University – Purdue University at Indianapolis in the U.S.A.

175. Catterall, Calvin, D., 'Formulation of the Declaration of Psychological Rights of the Child', Op. cit., p. 21.
176. Hart, Stuart, N., 1982, Op. cit., p. 12.
177. The Joint Commission on Mental Health of Children defined child advocacy as follows: "The child deserves an advocate to represent him and his needs in the society in which he lives – an advocate who will insist that programs and services based on sound child development knowledge be available to every child as a public utility. Advocacy will further insist on the promotion of National State and community responsibility and initiative in developing comprehensive and systematic programs of prevention and treatment, increasing the accountability of those who minister relevant programs. Advocacy will also further co-ordinating and organizing resources for supportive effective and co-ordinated programs for our children and youth".
178. Kohlberg, L., 'A Moral Development and Identification' in: Stevenson, H.W. (ed.) *Child Psychology, Part I*, Chicago, 1963, University of Chicago Press.
179. This was much stronger in the Tentative Declaration. Right VI in the original text dealt more extensively with "satisfying relationships with others." A satisfying relationship for one person, however, does not necessarily constitute a satisfying relationship for another. One wonders how this can possibly be guaranteed as a right.
180. Brassard, M.R., Germain, R. and Hart, S.N. (Eds.) *Psychological Maltreatment of Children and Youth*, Elmsford, N.Y., 1987, Pergamon. See also: Garbarino, J., Guttman, E., Seeley, J., *The Psychologically Battered Child: Strategies for Identification, Assessment and Intervention*, San Francisco, 1986, Jossey-Bass. Also: Hart, S.N., *Psychological Maltreatment: Emphasis on Prevention*: in: *School Psychology International*, 1988, 9, pp. 243–255. Also: Hart, S.N., 'Psychological Maltreatments in Schooling', in: *Psychological Review*, 1987, 16, pp. 169–180.
181. Bengtsson, Arvid, 'Play – an overall view' in: The Report of the Consultation on the Child's Right to Play held in Malta, 8th -12th November, 1977, *IPA Newsletter*, Vol.VI, No. 7, Jan.1978, p. 3. Arvid Bengtsson was the IPA-President in that year.
182. Koocher, Gerald, P., 'A Bill of Right, for Children in Psychotherapy' in: Koocher, Gerald, P., ed. *Children's Rights and the Mental Health Professions*, New York/London/Sydney/Toronto, 1977, A Wiley-Interscience Publication, pp. 25–32.
183. Chiba, A., 'The Educational Aspects', in: *IPA Newsletter*, Op. cit., p. 14.
184. Idem, p. 10.
185. Idem, p. 11.
186. Bladergroen, Wilhelmina, I., 'Het belang van spelen', in: *De Koepel*, 7, No. 11, November 1952, pp. 284–289. Idem, 'Kinderspel, Ontwikkelingsnoodzaak' in *Kleuterwereld* 9, 1964, 01, No. 5, pp. 105–111.
187. Fiedeldy Dop, Ph. H. 'Psychohygiënische Aspecten', in: Vink, A.P.A., Red., *Criteria voor Milieubeheer, Verslag van een Studie Conferentie*, Utrecht, 1971, Oostbroek.
188. Ackermans, E., *De Woonomgeving als Speelgelegenheid*, Groningen, 1970, Wolters-Noordhoff.
189. Letter to me from Nic Nilsson, President of the IPA. Today the IPA has national representatives/correspondents in 38 countries.

CHAPTER XIV

Summary and Conclusions

In this study about Children's Rights and the Changing Image of Childhood, we have tried to answer the following questions:

1. Did the Image of Childhood change during our century and how?
2. Is it possible to study Children's Rights systematically in different parts of the world and in different periods of this century?

To answer these questions we investigated:

- Primary sources, such as writings by pioneers in the field of Children's Rights;
- Declarations and Conventions in the field of Children's Rights;
- Secondary sources, such as scientific monographs and articles about the child's position in society, and how this position and its perception is reflected in laws and rights;
- Oral history material concerning our subject, collected by the author.

The period we investigated ranges from the publication of Ellen Key's book 'The Century of the Child' in 1900 until the first session of the U.N. Committee on the Rights of the Child (September–October 1991).

To *describe* the development of society's perception of childhood and of society's willingness to secure children rights is one thing, to *evaluate* this development is another. What is a positive development, what a negative one? When can we speak about 'progress', when about 'backtracking', when about a 'negative development'?

Like all judgements in the field of social sciences these are value judgements, and although we think that value judgements and subjectivity are positive characteristics rather than something to be ashamed of, we intend to achieve as broad a consensus as possible in our conclusions about the rights and the social position of children without engaging in an ideologically based contest.

We therefore happily welcomed Samuel Shye's *Systemic Quality of Life*

Model as a most objective tool (Chapter III). This Model provides us with a conceptual framework for observing effectiveness of functioning in sixteen content areas. We classified the children's rights material studied in these sixteen content areas. When this efficient tool is internalised it is extremely helpful in analysing the work of pioneers and the contents of Declarations and Conventions. Moreover the Model claims to be exclusive and exhaustive. The observational items it produces cover the entire quality of life field and do not overlap. The more positive the quality of life proposed by a Declaration or Convention, the more content areas of Shye's model will be covered. An optimal 'quality of life' situation will show us a completely covered model.

This means that every concept of (derived) rights for children, originally formulated with many words filling numerous pages, can now be shown as one small graphic representation. These pictures are comparable because they show the same sixteen sectors of human well-being and use an uniform terminology. This enables us to measure developments as objectively as possible. Surely, where some favour rights in the material field and others give priority to immaterial rights, subjectivity is still not excluded. However, a picture wherein more sectors are covered means the achievement of more rights than one in which less sectors are covered. This can generally be accepted as an objective measurement for progress or decline.

We rejected basing children's rights on the *needs* of children (Chapter IV), since we found the concept of *effectiveness* of the 'Systemic Quality of Life Model' more value-free and therefore more acceptable as a basis for children's rights.

Comparing the products of our efforts enables us to draw the following conclusions:

The perception of the child changed from the *object* of rights in need of protection to the *subject* of rights whose opinion is voiced and asked for.

Whereas in the beginning of this century children's rights were advocated by individuals (Chapters V, VI and VII), their cause became more and more the concern of social and political institutions and was at the same time brought to an international (or supranational) level.

Simultaneously there was a shift from a *charitable* towards a *political* concept. The expanding of range and the shift from one activity to the other are illustrated by the story of Eglantyne Jebb. She started her public activities by founding the London based *Save the Children's Fund*, a voluntary organisation solely concerned with the well-being of children which viewed charity as help between world-neighbours rather than as a patronising gift, and ended it by drafting the *Declaration of Geneva*, which was adopted by the League of Nations in 1924. (Chapters V and X).

There are also some negative aspects to this shift. First, such a wide range is beyond a child's perception. As long as children were only objects of rights this was no problem. However, now that children are allowed to voice their wishes and complaints, the global range has an alienating effect. (A child will not easily pick up the phone to call the Chairman of the Committee on the Rights of the Child of the United Nations.)[1] Therefore the need was felt for narrowing the scope to an individual level. New spokesmen for children were appointed whose task was to accommodate the child's interests (Chapter VIII).

The issue of *universality* of Children's Rights is important but complicated because it is difficult to reach consensus with many representatives of different ethnic backgrounds, nationalities and religions. The 'need to have enemies' is the foe of the universality of Children's Rights.

Although Children's Rights documents often reflect temporary political and economic circumstances – which explains the need for periodical evaluations – some issues in the field of Children's Rights are of an *enduring* nature. Ellen Key's assumption that sometimes a child would be better off if he or she had never been born, for instance, still bears relevance with regard to new phenomena, such as AIDS instead of the (nowadays curable) syphilis of her days.

Another ongoing discussion centres on the definition of the concept 'child'. Is a child a micro-adult or a *species sui generis*? This question must be answered before we can ask: "Can we simply apply human rights to adults and children alike, or are children's rights a category apart?" Janusz Korczak emphasised the child's 'right to respect'. All his writings, however, prove that he wanted to respect the child *as a child* and did not want to burden him or her with adult worries. He demanded that we respect a child's tears for a lost toy *like* we respect an adult's tears about a lost love, not *as the same*.

In the Sixties a group called *The Children's Liberation Movement* formulated Children's Rights in an extreme way (Chapter IX). Important representatives of this movement are John Holt, Richard Farson and Howard Cohen. These 'Kiddie Libbers' are only giving children more power. They do not recognise that the human being called 'child' is a creature still in development and that, therefore, there are still limits to his or her abilities. It is our opinion that the unlimited rights the Kiddie Libbers want to give to children withhold from them the most essential right: *to be a child*!

It is absolutely not justified to put Korczak in the category of strictly anti-authoritarian and 'laisser faire' pedagogues and he definitely does not belong to the 'Kiddie Libbers'.

The concept of 'the child' which prevails in pedagogic literature is a Western concept (Chapter I). As a result of the specific historical development of the Western World, pedagogics itself originated in the West and remained for centuries a Western monopoly, due to the more prosperous conditions which existed there. However, since in our century the whole world has become a 'global village', the people of the Western world were daily confronted with the dramatic difference between children living in their own environment and those from the so-called 'Third World'. Therefore, we should henceforth abstain from talking about 'the' child.

The development of the 'Children's Rights Movement' shows that in regions and times of poverty the Movement focuses mainly on the physical aspects of life, whereas more wealth results in demands for non-material rights for children. Concepts like 'child', 'right' and 'society' are tied to place and time. Therefore the concepts 'children' and 'children's rights' allude in fact to one specific interpretation of these concepts.

The way children are conceptualised in society creates what we call the *Image of Childhood* of that particular society. It has been an assumption of this study that ideas concerning the rights of children are strictly dependent on the prevailing 'Image of Childhood'.

In areas where the 'Image of Childhood' is reflected in ideas about 'Children's Rights' we have definitely found a change. From the Declarations and Conventions we studied we found that in the beginning of the Century concerns concentrated mainly on *physical safety and security*, whereas nowadays *inter-actional processes* between the individual child as carrier of a social role, and adult institutions are in focus.

Thus our major finding is that *there has been a change in the image of childhood as reflected in ideas of children's rights*.

In order to find lines of development, we divided all the Declarations and Conventions into the following categories:

(a) Declarations and Conventions representing an international consensus;
(b) National Declarations;
(c) Regional Declarations;
(d) Ideological Declarations;
(e) Specified and Sectarian Declarations and Conventions.

Each category was mapped with the help of Shye's 'Systemic Quality of Life Model'.

(a) *International (or Supranational) Declarations and Conventions* (Chapter X). When studying the international documents (Chapter X), we learn that, whereas the 'Declaration of Geneva' (1924) was concerned with nursing the sick, feeding the hungry, providing the physical resources necessary for physical and mental development and securing conditions for individual growth, the 'U.N. Convention on the Rights of the Child' of 1989 covered *all* the functioning modes of the 'Systemic Quality of Life Model'. This is a development from a specific to a comprehensive reference of human life quality, or *an ascending line between 1924 to 1959 and on to 1989*.

Between 1978 and 1989 the Nations of the World showed a remarkable political will to achieve a better standard of living for children, by adopting the 'U.N. Convention on the Rights of the Child'. In 1924 and 1959 the international consensus also focussed on special protection and assistance. New in 1989 is that the child is entitled to participate in decisionmaking of matters affecting him or her. The *expressive mode of the cultural subsystem* and the *expressive mode of the personality subsystem* receive now attention in the UN Convention.

We see backtracking in the recent Declaration on the Survival, Protection and Development issued by the World Summit for Children. This can be explained by the fact that this Declaration was predetermined by UNICEF who is afraid of becoming 'too political' and tries to stay away from issues concerning rights of children other than child's right to survival and related issues. This Declaration is only in a limited way also a 'Declaration on the Rights of the Child'.

(b) *National and Regional Declarations* (Chapter XI). When analysing and mapping National and Regional Declarations we took the different geographic contexts into consideration as well as the fact that some Declarations came into existence under extra-ordinary circumstances, such as the Second World War (the 'Children's Charter in Wartime' of 1942). Hence we cannot distinguish a clear trend in this material as was the case with the International Documents. However, we do see an effort to strengthen the cohesion of Society. The more monistic the region or the ethnicity of the drafters, the more concrete are the cultural value aspects they express. (See the Charter of the Rights of the Arab Child). The rights to food and shelter and the means to facilitate personality growth and mental stimulation are favoured by all National and Regional Declarations.

(c) *Ideological Declarations* (Chapter XII). The demands of the drafters of these Declarations are based on a political, social or philosophical ideology. The common denominator of Ideological Declarations is the emphasis on the interaction with social institutions. This represents the point of view of social reformers who obviously have a high awareness of how changes in social organisms should and could be brought about. The first Ideological Declaration (the Draft-Declaration of the Prolet'cult Organisation in the former Soviet Union) formulated in 1918, consistently emphasised the importance of self-expression of children and adolescents in the various domains of human existence. Notwithstanding the bad economic situation of that period, physical concerns (such as health, food and shelter) were ignored! Contrary to what the drafters of the Prolet'cult Declaration did, reformers of our own days tend to stress specific concerns. The 'Ten Commandments for Adults' by Professor Leonhard Froese (1979), for instance, emphasises personal identity and personal safety. The (proposed) Youth Charter Act of a member of the Labour Party in Britain (1985) focuses on self-actualization and on giving youngsters a higher social status. However, no physical or cultural concerns were formulated by this social reformer of the Labour Party.

(d) *Specified and Sectarian Declarations and Conventions* (Chapter XIII). In this category we find documents of groups of professionals (such as psychologists and social workers) or Declarations on a single issue (such as the right to play), and demands of interest groups (such as the International Council of Women and the Socialist Youth). Understandably each group focused on its specific interest area, except for the International Council of Women who covered a wide range of physical and educational aspects.

Never in history has so much attention been paid to Children's Rights as in our own times. This can, for instance, be illustrated by the World Summit for Children which brought together seventy-one Heads of States and Prime Ministers in order to put Children's Rights higher on the Agenda for the next decades. This growing recognition and popularity of Children's Rights, however, is not free from the danger of becoming *a fashion*. It may well be in the spotlight for a certain period but be left in the dark again when the spotlight switches to another subject. It is therefore the task of the Children's Rights Movement to provide a secure foundation for its work.

It is characteristic for the state of the Children's Rights Movement that there is no academic journal on the subject, (only several newsletters). This is probably due to the fact that 'Children's Rights' is an inter-disciplinary subject. With the present study we hope to pave the way for an inter-disciplinary journal focusing on the Rights of the Child.

Since we see it as a pedagogic task not only to *describe* but also to *prescribe*, we formulated, together with Samuel Shye, on the basis of his 'Systemic Quality of Life Model' what we consider to be the ideal Declaration of the Rights of the Child (See Appendix XLIV).

NOTES

1. The task of the Committee is not to look into individual complaints but to monitor compliance of the States parties, mostly through the study of their reports.

CHAPTER XV

Suggestions for Further Research

We have investigated and analysed the works of the pioneers in the struggle for Children's Rights, the resulting Declarations and Conventions, and the vast secondary literature dealing with the subject.

The 'realm' of children's rights, however, consists of many additional provinces which also deserve investigation, but cannot possibly be covered within one single book. For such research, too, the Systemic Quality of Life Model will, no doubt, prove to be a useful instrument.

This afterword points to directions in which research could be continued. We would like to propose that systematic analysis will be undertaken of:

1. Relevant decisions by Parliaments;
2. Relevant rulings by Supreme Courts and comparable international bodies;
3. The conceptualisation of children's rights by children themselves;
4. Children's Rights in the Third World.

We also propose to develop indicators for the level of implementation of children's rights.

1. Decisions by Parliaments

Example: *Corporal punishment in schools in the United Kingdom*. According to Ian Gibson[1] "beating has always been common in British schools, the schoolmaster's legal right to administer corporal punishment deriving from the fact that society has considered him to stand *in loco parentis* to the children under his care ... The English vice began at home, spread to the home's most obvious extension, the school (particularly the boarding school), and hence the courts, the prisons, the Army and the Navy, the Colonies – and the brothels ... The British Empire," argues Gibson, "was founded on the lash."

In 1976, considerable pressure was put upon the British Government when Mrs. Grace Campbell and Mrs. Jane Cosans[2] applied to the European Commission of Human Rights in Strasbourg, alleging that the United Kingdom was in breach of the European Convention on Human Rights because

Picture XV.1. In the summer of 1987 Amalia Lewis (then 84 years of age) received the Levingston Hall Juvenile Justice Award of the American Bar Association (ABA). From left to right: Eugene Thomas (of the ABA), Mrs. Amalia Lewis, Sergeant First Class Gerald Gault and Roberrt McGrate (ABA).

of the use of corporal punishment in schools and the lack of respect for their objections (as parents) against it.

In 1986, after a debate in the House of Commons, corporal punishment in schools was abandoned[3] by 231 against 230 votes. In that year, the leading cane manufacturer in England retired![4]

In 1972, the Riksdag (Swedish Parliament) decided against abolishment legislation.[6] And in 1977, the Swedish Government appointed the Commission for the Rights of the Child. A few months later, this Commission proposed that spanking, *including spanking within the family*, be forbidden in Sweden. In 1979, the Code relating to Parenthood and Guardianship[7] was amended. It now forbids spanking as well as other humiliating treatment such as "locking children in closets, subjecting them to threats, intimidation, ostracism or direct ridicule."

With regard to the image of childhood, it is interesting that the arguments[5] of both supporters and opponents of caning were not concerned with the quality of life of the child, but with the quality of functioning of the *school*.

2. SUPREME COURT AND INTERNATIONAL BODIES

Example: *Depriving a youngster of his liberty*. On June 14, 1964, fifteen-year old Gerald Gault was confined to the Arizona Industrial Training School, a

Picture XV.2. The proud winner, Robert E. Reynolds, Director of Hazelwood East High School, St. Louis (Missouri) with an issue of the school newspaper *Spectrum*. His decision, in 1983, to censure an issue of *Spectrum* was contested to the level of the Supreme Court of the United States and resulted in the postponement of the right to freedom of speech until the age of majority. (Photo: Larry Williams, St. Louis Post Dispatch.)

closed institution, for having used 'dirty language' in an anonymous phone call to a female neighbour. When he appeared before the Juvenile Court, neither he nor his parents had been informed of Gerald's right to be assisted by a lawyer, and of his right to remain silent.[8] Since the Juvenile Court was supposed to have an informal atmosphere, no minutes of the session were made. Nor was the offended neighbour called to give evidence about the phone call. Only later did an attorney (Mrs. Amalia Lewis[9]) appeal, on Gerald's behalf, to the Supreme Court of Arizona and the United States Supreme Court. Here it was ruled that Gerald's constitutional rights had been violated and that the fourteenth amendment[10] should not be applied exclusively to adults, but also to minors. Commenting on this landslide decision, Janet Friedman Stansby[11] concluded that "children brought before the juvenile court could now no longer be treated as second class citizens."

Example: *Parent-child relationships*. The 'Parham versus J.R.' case[12] and the 'Jon Nielsen versus Denmark' case[13] deserve to be studied in this connection. In the first case, the issue was whether parents and guardians can force their children to be hospitalised in a psychiatric hospital.

"On a policy level," says Barbara Landau, "the confusion is related to the ongoing difficulty of sorting out the balance of power, or perhaps the balance of responsibilities among parents, the State and minors."[14] On June 20, 1979, the ruling of the Supreme Court of the United States about the 'Parham versus J.R.' case tipped the balance in favour of parents and guardians.

In the 'Jon Nielsen versus Denmark' case, the European Commission of Human Rights in Strasbourg decided in favour of the minor. This ruling was welcomed as a "European boost to children's rights." However, on November 20, 1988, the European Court on Human Rights decided that Jon's placement in a psychiatric department of a hospital was *not* depriving him of his liberty and that the European Convention on Human Rights was not relevant in his case. The fact, however, that nine judges voted against and seven in favour of the minor's rights, can, in our opinion, be seen as proof that ideas on children's rights were changing.

Referring to the overestimating of parental power, Miek de Langen,[15] for instance, suggested that "the position of children in the eighties deteriorated." However, in other areas, the balance tipped in favour of minors, as in the case concerning abortion where the court recognised minors' competence in decision making (United States Supreme Court ruling in the case of 'Bellotti versus Baird';[16] and the House of Lords which hears appeals from the Court of Appeal in England and Wales and Northern Ireland in the Gillick case.[17])

Example: *Postponed rights*. Zimring[18] wrote that certain children's rights should "properly be viewed as *postponing* rather than *denying* the exercise of liberty." There is, for instance, a fundamental difference between refusing a person a drink in a bar because he or she is black, and refusing a person a drink because he or she is under age. The same can be said with regard to the selling of reading material (the 'Ginsberg versus the State of New York' case). Mr. Ginsberg, the owner of *Sam Stationery and Luncheonette* in Bellmore, Long Island, New York State, sold, among other things, newspapers and magazines, including so-called 'girlie magazines'. The Supreme Court of the State of New York judged that Mr. Ginsberg was breaking the New York State Penal Law by selling these magazines (which did contain some nudity but were not really pornographic) to a 16 year old boy on two occasions in 1965. The United States Supreme Court supported the ruling of the New York State Supreme Court. The argumentation was one of protecting children.

'The Hazelwood School District versus Cathy Kuhlmeier' case[19] deals with the censuring of two school paper articles (one about teen-age pregnancy, the other about divorce) by the principal of the school. Three members of the newspaper staff, Cathy Kuhlmeier, Leanne Tippett and Leslie Smart, sued, claiming that their First Amendment rights (dealing with the freedom of speech) had been violated.

On January 13, 1988, the United States Supreme Court "held that the school officials did not violate the students' free speech rights by removing objectionable material from the school newspaper." With this ruling, the Court severely limited its earlier ruling in the case *Tinker versus Des Moins* (discussed in Chapter II). The argumentation was that in the case of school papers, the school was responsible for the opinions expressed in the articles.

Example: *Inequality-Equality*. The world-famous case 'Brown versus Board of Education'[20] is the most remarkable example in this category. Antoine Foster calls this case "one of the first specific children's rights precedents."[21] A television documentary[22] described the case as follows: "Seven-year-old Linda Brown, who lived in Topeka (Kansas), had to cross the railroad tracks in a nearby switching yard and wait for a rickety bus to take her to a black school. It wasn't the worst that black children had to endure, but soft-spoken Oliver Brown was fed up with his child having to go to the other side of town when there was a good school much closer to home – a white school." The Supreme Court decision led to the dismantling of the system according to which schools for whites and schools for blacks were limited to certain districts. A timetable was set for integration. This decision by the United States Supreme Court overturned the 1896 decision ('Plessy versus Ferguson') holding that segregation was constitutional as long as the segregated schools were "separate but equal."

The lawyers of the National Association for the Advancement of Colored People (NAACP) who had brought the Brown case to Washington D.C., used as an argument that segregation could harm the self-image of black children and that this would lead to a negative identity.[23]

3. THE CONCEPTUALISATION OF CHILDREN'S RIGHTS BY CHILDREN THEMSELVES

In the beginning of this Century[24] there was a promising start, but only recently has there been any important research on this topic. This research, conducted by Gary B. Melton,[25] involved twelve vignettes dealing with inter-personal conflict in which a child might assert a right, such as school punishment without due process, access to school records, parent's reading a girl's diary, a child seeking treatment independently.

Melton and his assistants told ninety third-, fifth-, and seventh-grade children in the Boston area that they were interested in "what kids think about things that happen to kids." Replies to questions raised by the vignettes were scored both according to the level of conceptualisation indicated, and according to whether the child advocated the expression of a right by the child in the story.

When asked: "What is a right?" the average third-grader had some understanding of the concept. Most first-graders, however, were unable to give a correct definition or example. According to Melton, older children tended to express less egocentric views than younger children. Older children perceived rights as being based on criteria of fairness and competence to exercise self-determination, rather than of what authorities allow children to do.[26] Cognitive development,[27] moral development,[28] emotional maturity,[29] par-

Picture XIV.3. Just like other black children, the daughter of Reverend Brown, Linda (7) was not allowed to attend her neighbourhood primary school in her place of residence, Topeka (Kansas). This was the privilege of white children. The case was brought before the Supreme Court of the United States (*Brown* v. *The Board of Education of Topeka*) and resulted in the recognition that the law maintained that all children should be treated equally. It also made clear that children can appeal to the courts (through their parents or guardians) if they feel that the State is not treating them correctly. (Photo: Carl Iwasaki, Life Magazine.)

ental attitudes,[30] social class,[31] school climate and people's attitudes relating to children's rights, all influence children's concepts of their rights.

Only recently have authors begun to perceive *the child's experience with rights* as a variable of major importance with regard to the conceptualisation of these rights. It is therefore important that children are confronted at an early age with concepts related to rights.[32]

4. CHILDREN'S RIGHTS IN THE THIRD WORLD

Third World children are still so busy demanding their basic rights, that matters relating to school councils and school statutes are of little concern to them.

In May 1986, large numbers of *street-children* from all over Brazil came to Brazilia[33] in order to draw attention to their situation. However, not a single Member of the Brazilian Congress appeared to listen to their plight. For research to be helpful here, it would have to be *action research* pointing out why the injustices still exist and in which areas.

Picture XV.4. May 1986: Brasil's streetchildren ask the Congress in Brasilia to help them. (Photo: Agencia JB.)

Warning

I would like to conclude this study by drawing the attention to a warning,[34] voiced by Professor M.J. Cohen who points out that excessive juridification may produce an inflexible generation going only by the book of Statutes.[35]

To illustrate this point, I shall give an example taken from my work at the Psychological Special Education Institute in Amsterdam, the Netherlands (PPI-Amsterdam): In 1981, the mother of a fourteen-year old client decided to have her daughter's surname changed. The father had died long ago and the mother did not wish to be reminded of "that terrible alcoholic." My client, however, was of a different opinion. Without consulting her daughter, the mother had submitted a request to the Queen for a change of her daughter's surname. In 1981, the procedure in the Netherlands demanded that the police deal with the person submitting the request. If there were no discernable problems, the child (provided he or she was over twelve years of age) was also heard. In this case the police officer only talked with my client over the phone. "My mother was standing behind me," the girl told me. "What could I do but say that I agreed?"

As our conversation proceeded, the child decided not to pursue the matter. Nor did she want the social worker who worked with the mother to discuss the issue. My client often talked about leaving home, but realised that she would have to wait several years before she could rent a room and become independent. In the meantime she had to live with her mother and it would not serve her interests to set her mother against her.

Further research would be helpful in distinguishing when a youngster should be encouraged to take the 'rights-approach', and when not.

5. Creating Indicators for the Level of Implementation of Children's Rights

Now the UN Convention on the Rights of the Child has been ratified by more than one hundred States, we have a checklist.[36] On the basis of the Systemic Quality of Life Model indicators, based on well thought out scaling procedures can be developed for evaluating periodically the quality of life in the different states. Such an instrument would be a more objective base to evaluate children's rights on than periodic reports[37] provided by State Parties. Such research would be welcome in addition to reports of States Parties.

Notes

1. Gibson, Ian, *The English Vice; Beating, Sex and Shame in Victorian England and After*, 1978, London, Duckworth, p. 64.
2. See: Zellick, Graham, et al., editors, *European Human Rights Reports*, Vol. 4, 1982, 'Campbell and Cosans v. United Kingdom', pp. 293–312. See also: 'Case of Campbell and Cosans', in: *Publications of the European Court of Human Rights, Series A: Judgments and Decisions*, Vol. 48, Strasbourg/Cologne/Berlin/Bonn/Munich, Council of Europe and Carl Heymanns Verlag.
3. *Parliamentarian Debates* (Hansard), Vol. 102, No. 155, London, 1986, HMSO (debate on 22 July 1986 – Education Bill), p. 231.
4. Wilby, Peter, 'How abolitionists have dealt caning in class a fatal blow', in: *Independent*, 1986, 6 November 1986.
5. See: Parliamentary Debates.
6. Swedish Ministry of Justice, *Can you bring up children successfully without smacking and spanking?*, Stockholm, sine anno.
7. The actual text of the new legislation, which form Chap. 6, par. 3, 2nd section of *the Code relating to Parenthood and Guardianship*, reads: "A child may not be subjected to physical punishment or other injurious or humiliating treatment".
   For a discussion on the Swedish Bill, See: Olson, Dennis Alan, "The Swedish Ban of Corporal Punishment", in *Brigham Young University Law Review*, 1984, No. 3, p. 448.
   Also: Bainsby, Wendy, 'Children's Rights in Sweden: Where to Draw the Line?' in: *Australian Child and Family Welfare*, 1979, Summer, Vol. 4, pp. 33–35.
   Also: Adamo, Amelia, 'New Rights for Children and Parents in Sweden', in: *Children Today*, 1981, November–December, pp. 15–17.
   Also: Ekdahl, Bertil, 'The Swedish Law on Physical Punishment', in: Rädda Barnen (Swedish Save the Children), *The Ombudsman and Child Maltreatment*, Stockholm and Geneva, 1980. In Norway similar legislation was adopted.
8. In Re Gault, 389, U.S.1(1967). See: Friedman Stansby, Janet, "In Re Gault: Children Are People", in: Wilkerson, Albert, E., *The Rights of Children, Emergent Concepts in Law and*

Society, Philadelphia, 1973, Temple University Press, p. 301.
Also: Neigher, A., "The Gault Decisions: due process and the Juvenile Courts", in: *Federal Probation*, 1967, 31, No. 4, p. 8.
Also: Noyes, A.D., 'Has Gault changed the Juvenile Court Concept?' in: *Crime and Delinquency*, 1970, 16, No. 2.
9. I thank Mrs. Lewis for our interesting telephone conversation in May 1988.
10. "All persons born or naturalised in the United States, and subject to the jurisdiction thereof, are citizens of the United States and of the State wherein they reside. No State shall make or enforce any law which shall abridge the privileges or immunities of citizens of the United States; nor shall any State deprive any person of life, liberty, or property, without due process of law; nor deny to any person within its jurisdiction the equal protection of the laws."
11. See Chapter of Janet Friedman Stansby in the study *The Rights of Children* Op. cit., p. 286.
12. Parham v. J.R. et al, 442 U.S., 1979, pp. 584–620. See also: Rubin, Eva, R., *The Supreme Court and the American Family*, Westport, Conn., 1986, Greenwood Press, p. 173, Frank, Carol C., "Children's Rights after the Supreme Court's Decision on 'Parham v. J.L. and J.R.'" in: *Child Welfare*, Vol. LIX, No. 6, June 1980, p. 376.
13. Council of Europe, European Commission on Human Rights, *Decision of the Commission, Jon Nielsen* (10929/84) *against Denmark*, Strasbourg, 1984. See also: 28 November 1988, *European Court of Human Rights*, Series A, 144, Children's Legal Centre, 'European boost to Children's Rights', in: *Childright*, July/August 1987, No. 39, p. 3.
Also: Bruin – Lückers, M.L.C.C., de, 'De Zaak Nielsen, Europees Hof voor de rechten van de mens, 28 November 1988', in: *Tijdschrift Familie- en Jeugdrecht*, 1990, 5, pp. 112–114.
14. Landau, Barbara, "The rights of Minors to consent to treatment and to residential care", in: Landau, Barbara, editor, *Children's Rights in the Practice of Family Law*, Toronto, 1986, Carswell.
15. Langen, M., de, 'De betekenis van Artikel 8 EVRM voor het familierecht' in: Boer, J., de; Langen, M. de; Swart, A.H.J., Prae-adviezen, in: *Handelingen Nederlandse Juristen Vereniging*, 120e, vol. 1990–I, Zwolle, 1990, W.E.J. Tjeenk Willink.
16. 'Bellotti v. Baird II', 1979, p. 634. See also: Lewis, Catherine C., 'Minors' Competence to Consent to Abortion' in: the *American Psychologist*, January, 1987, Vol. 42, pp. 84–88.
17. *The Weekly Law Reports*, London, 1985, Vol. 3, The Incorporated Council of Law Reporting for England and Wales, pp. 831/875. See also: *The All England Law Reports*, London, 1985, Vol. 1, pp. 533–559.
Judgement, Die Jovis 17 Octobris 1985, in: *Record, in the House of Lords, on Appeal*, Op. Cit. See: Parkinson, P.N., 'The Gillick Case: Just What Has it Decided?', in: *Family Law*, Vol. 16, 1986, January, pp. 11–14.
Children's Legal Centre, 'Wider implications of Gillick', in: *Childright*, April 1986, No. 26, p. 17.
Eekelaar, John, 'Gillick: further limits on parents' rights to punish', in: *Childright*, June 1986, No. 28, pp. 9–10.
Also: De Cruz, S.P., 'Parents, doctors and children: The Gillick Case and beyond', in: *Journal of Social Welfare Law*, 1987, pp. 93–108.
Also: Freemann, M.D.A., 'Taking Children's Rights Seriously', in: *Children and Society*, 1987–1988, 4, pp. 299–319.
Also: Bainham, Andrew, 'The Balance of Power in Family Decisions', in: *Cambridge Law Journal*, 45(2), July 1986, pp. 262–284.
18. Zimring, Franklin E., *The Changing Legal World of Adolescence*, New York, 1982, The Free Press, p. 27.
19. The United States Law Week, 1988, 56, 4079–4087.
20. 'Brown v. Board of Education', 347 US 483, 1954.
21. Foster, Antoinette, M., *An Examination and Analysis of the Changes and Concept of*

Children's Rights as Reflected in Court Decisions on Child Welfare, Education and Juvenile Court Procedures Between 1859 *and the Present*, The University of Connecticut, 1978, UMI-Dissertation, Information Service, Ann Arbor, Michigan.
22. Williams, Juan, *Eyes on the Prize; America's Civil Rights Years*, 1954–1965, New York/Harmondsworth, Middlesex, 1987/1988, p. 21.
23. Kluger, Richard, *Simple Justice*, New York, 1975, Alfred A. Knopf Publ. House. See also: Clark, K.B. and Clark, M.P., 'Racial Identification in Negro Children, in: Newcamb, T.M. and Hartley, E.L., eds., *Readings in Social Psychology*, New York, 1947, Holt, Rinehart and Winston, pp. 169–178.
24. Barnes, Earl, 'Study of Children's Rights as seen by themselves', in: *The Paedologist*, Vol.2, No. 3, November 1900, pp. 142–144.
25. Melton, Gary, B., 'Children's Concepts and Their Rights', in: *Journal of Clinical Child Psychology*, Fall 1980, pp. 186–190.
26. Idem, p. 187.
27. Piaget, Jean and Inhelder, B., *The Growth of Logical Thinking from Childhood to Adolescence*, New York, 1958, Basic Books.
   Also: Piaget, Jean, *The Moral Judgement of the Child*, New York, 1932, Harcourt, Brace and World Publishers.
28. Kohlberg, Lawrence and Gilligan, C., 'The Adolescent as a Philosopher: The discovery of the self in a post-conventional world', in: *Daedalus*, 1971, 100: pp. 1051–1086.
29. Guyer, Melvin, J.; Harrison, Saul, I.; and Rieveschl Jan L., 'Child Psychiatry and the Law', Development Rights to Privacy and Independent Decision-Making', in: *Journal of the American Academy of Child Psychiatry*: Vol.21, 1982, No. 3, pp. 298–302.
30. "Through interaction with their parents, children do not only learn social values, what to expect of role patterns and what is 'proper behaviour', but also about decision-making " is the opinion of Sconzoni, John and Szinovacr, Maximiliane, *Family Decision-Making*, Beverly Hills and London, 1980, Sage Publications Inc., p. 187. The authors continue: "If their parents use coercion, so will the children. Parents who discuss and bargain for mutual profit directly or indirectly, teach children to respect the other's viewpoint, to strive for mutually satisfactory outcomes, and to view decision-making as a reciprocal process." Of course, it is also important in the process of decision-making whether or not a child understands the subject about which a decision has to be taken. As children advance in age and their cognitive and emotional possibilities grow, they can, according to the authors, be a party to the decision-making process. "The success of a family group in reaching decisions is not merely a function of its members' individual decision-making abilities. People who make individual decisions easily and without crippling second thoughts are often unable to make decisions together," states Ralph H. Turner in his book *Family Interaction*, New York, 1970, John Wiley and Sons, p. 101. According to Turner the decision-making process in the family can take different directions. The first possibility is that all members of the family believe that the best decision has been taken. The second possibility is that some members of the family have the feeling that the decision has been imposed upon them or that the conversation about the subject has been ineffective. Also a single member of the family can keep a foul taste about the decision in question. The third possibility is that one or more members of a family feel that they have been compelled to subscribe to a decision that does not suit them, in which case they may refuse to conform and will perhaps retable the discussion.

    That children must have an active part in the decision-making process has been more and more emphasised during the last decennia. "It is likely that this norm is further reinforced by the current emphasis on democratic or egalitarian interactions, a trend sometimes expressed in the Children's Right Movement". In a *Commission for the Rights of the Child* of the Swedish Government, Professor Ulla Jacobson of the University of Stockholm has, for instance, emphasised that, ideally, every family should function as a mini-democracy. See: Bainsby, Wendy: 'Children's Rights in Sweden: Where to Draw the Line' in: *Australian Child and Family Welfare*, Vol. 4, Summer 1979, p. 34. Statements like the above seem to be based upon ideal relationships in the Western nuclear family of the higher middle class.

Grolnick and Ryan studied the effect of three different parent styles on the development of autonomy and competence in children. They found that autonomy support from the parents positively predicted children's self-regulation. "By fostering autonomy in their children, parents prepare them better for an educational environment that requires independent mastery and self-regulation." An alternative interpretation, also by Grolnick and Ryan, is that children who exhibit little autonomous self-regulation 'pull' for external control and punitiveness from their parents while those who are more independent make provisions of autonomy support more rewarding and effective." (Grolnick, Wendy S., and Ryan, Richard M., *Parent Styles Associated with Children's Self-Regulating and Competence in Schools*, Rochester, Department of Psychology, University of Rochester, 1988). See also: Frommonn, A., 'Die Rechte von Kindern innerhalb ihrer Familien', in: Neue Praxis 4/1979, p. 352–362.

31. Melton found that social class was an important variable to influence children's concepts of their rights. Melton's findings confirm Koocher's thesis that "children reared in the less entitled groups may grow up to see themselves as having fewer rights, less access to self-actualization, and less opportunity for self-determination." Poor children, says Melton, are relatively slow to acquire a view of rights as having any relevance to themselves.
32. A good example of teaching rights at school can be found in *Ealing, every child is given space to grow: Towards a charter for all children in school*, London Borough of Ealing 1989.
33. *O Globo*, May 5, 1986, 'Menores carentes reunem – se para debater problemas de 36 milhoes'.
    I thank Sergio Zalis for helping me find my way in the archives and photo-archives of the newspapers *O Globo* and *Jornal do Brasil*.
34. Cohen, M.I., 'Leerlingenstatuut en onderwijsrecht' in: *Onderwijsrecht*, 4, 1985, pp. 13–18.
35. Phil Donahue (Multimedia Entertainment Inc., Cincinnati, Ohio, U.S.A., 1988, Transcript No. 031588) had a television programme on this topic. It was called: *Can children sue their parents*? and dealt, for instance, with the case of a daughter (over 18 years of age) who had stored her TV set with her mother before going on a vacation. When the daughter came back, the mother refused to return the TV. The daughter sued her mother in court.
36. The new Committee on the Rights of the Child groups the different items of the convention under six sections:

    – general principles
    – civil rights and freedoms
    – family environment and alternative care
    – basic health and welfare
    – education, leisure and cultural activities
    – special protection measures

    This grouping serves as a guideline for the initial reports to be submitted by the State Parties.
37. I want to warn that some government officials are of the opinion that those who are monitoring the protection of children's rights should play a role in drafting or writing the report for the state party. This will be a conflict of interest, since ombudsmen or members of monitoring committees have to be *independent* from the government.

Appendices

Appendix I
ILO Convention Fixing the Minimum Age for Admission of Children to Industrial
  Employment (1919) 416

Appendix II
ILO Convention Concerning the Night Work of Young Persons Employed in Industry
  (1919) 420

Appendix III
International Agreement for the Suppression of the White Slave Traffic (1904) 424

Appendix IV
International *Convention* for the Suppression of the White Slave Traffic (1910) 427

Appendix V
International Convention for the Suppression of the Traffic in Women and Children
  (1922) 432

Appendix VI
The Declaration of the Rights of the Child Proposed to Prolet'cult' (Moscow 1918) 435

Appendix VII
Programme of Immediate Demands/Declaration of the Rights of the Adolescent (1922) 438

Appendix VIII
The Children's Charter of the International Council of Women's Children's Charter
  (1922) 439

Appendix IX
Declaration of Geneva (1924) 444

Appendix X
The Children's Charter of President Hoover's White House Conference on Child Health and
  Protection (1930) 445

Appendix XI
Bill of Rights for the Handicapped Child (1930) 449

Appendix XII
A Children's Charter in Wartime (1942) 450

Appendix XIII
The Children's Charter for the Post-War World (1942) 456

Appendix XIV
Declaration of Opportunities for Children (1942)   457

Appendix XV
Children's Bill of Rights of the New York State Youth Commission (1949)   460

Appendix XVI
The Pledge to Children (1950)   461

Appendix XVII
The Children's Charter, Japan (1951)   463

Appendix XVIII
The United Nations Declaration on the Rights of the Child (1959)   465

Appendix XIX
The Bill of Rights of Children in Divorce Actions (1966)   468

Appendix XX
Children's Bill of Rights of the Dane County Family Court Counselling Services (Sine anno)   469

Appendix XXI
Rights of Children, Formulated by the Joint Commission on Mental Health of Children (1969)   470

Appendix XXII
Children's Bill of Rights, Formulated by the White House Conference on Children and Youth (1970)   473

Appendix XXIII
Rights of Youth, Formulated by the White House Conference on Youth (1971)   474

Appendix XXIV
The Draft Charter of Children's Rights of the British Magazine 'Where' (1971)   476

Appendix XXV
A Bill of Rights for Children, Proposed by Henry Foster and Doris Freed (1972)   479

Appendix XXVI
A Bill of Rights for Foster Children (1973)   480

Appendix XXVII
Bill of Rights for Juveniles (1973)   482

Appendix XXVIII
ILO Convention Concerning Minimum Age for Admission to Employment (1973)   484

Appendix XXIX
The Children and Youth Bill of Rights of the NASW (1975)   493

Appendices

Appendix XXX
Ten Commandments for Adults (1979) — 497

Appendix XXXI
Declaration of the Psychological Rights of the Child (1979) — 498

Appendix XXXII
Declaration of the Rights of Mozambican Children (1979) — 499

Appendix XXXIII
The Malta Declaration of the Child's Right to Play (1977) — 501

Appendix XXXIV
ICFTU Youth Charter (1983) — 504

Appendix XXXV
Charter for Children in Hospital of the National Association for the Welfare of Children in Hospital, NAWCH, (1984) — 516

Appendix XXXVI
The Charter on the Rights of the Arab Child of the League of Arab States — 517

Appendix XXXVII
The Youth Charter Act, Proposed by James Wallace, M.P. (1985) — 527

Appendix XXXVIII
The Labour Party Charter for Young People, (London, 1985) — 530

Appendix XXXIX
London Boroughs Children's Regional Planning Committee, Charter of Rights for Children in Care (1986) — 531

Appendix XL
The United Nations Declaration Relating to Foster Placement and Adoption (1986) — 540

Appendix XLI
A Manifesto for Children of the Children's Legal Centre (London, May 1987) — 545

Appendix XLII
Declaration of the Rights of the Child in Israel (1989) — 552

Appendix XLIII
The UN Convention on the Rights of the Child (1989) — 553

Appendix XLIV
World Declaration on the Survival, Protection and Development of Children (1990) — 574

Appendix XLV
Charter on the Rights and Welfare of the African Child (1990) — 579

Appendix XLVI
Declaration on the Rights of the Child, based on the 'Systemic Quality of Life Model', by Philip E. Veerman and Samuel Shye (1992) — 598

APPENDIX I

ILO Convention Fixing the Minimum Age for Admission of Children to Industrial Employment (1919)

CONVENTION 5

The General Conference of the International Labour Organisation,

Having been convened by the Government of the United States of America at Washington on the 29th day of October 1919, and

Having decided upon the adoption of certain proposals with regard to the 'employment of children: minimum age of employment', which is part of the fourth item in the agenda for the Washington meeting of the Conference, and

Having determined that these proposals shall take the form of an International Convention,

adopts the following Convention, which may be cited as the Minimum age (Industry) Convention, 1919, for ratification by the Members of the International Labour Organisation in accordance with the provisions of the Constitution of the International Labour Organisation:

Article 1.

1. For the purpose of this Convention, the term 'industrial undertaking' includes particularly –

    (a) mines, quarries and other works for the extraction of minerals from the earth:
    (b) industries in which articles are manufactured, altered, cleaned, repaired, ornamented, finished, adapted for sale, broken up or demolished, or in which materials are transformed; including ship-building, and the generation, transformation, and transmission of electricity and motive power of any kind;

(c) construction, reconstruction, maintenance, repair, alteration, or demolition of any building, railway, tramway, harbour, dock, pier, canal, inland waterway, road, tunnel, bridge, viaduct, sewer, drain, well, telegraphic or telephonic installation, electrical undertaking, gas work, water work, or other work of construction, as well as the preparation for or laying the foundations of any such work or structure;

(d) transport of passengers or goods by road or rail or inland waterway, including the handling of goods at docks, quays, wharves, and warehouses, but excluding transport by hand.

2. The competent authority in each country shall define the line of division which separates industry from commerce and agriculture.

Article 2.
Children under the age of fourteen years shall not be employed or work in any public or private industrial undertaking, or in any branch thereof, other than an undertaking in which only members of the same family are employed.

Article 3.
The provisions of Article 2 shall not apply to work done by children in technical schools, provided that such work is approved and supervised by public authority.

Article 4.
In order to facilitate the enforcement of the provisions of this Convention, every employer in an industrial undertaking shall be required to keep a register of all persons under the age of sixteen years employed by him, and of the dates of their births.

Article 5.
1. In connection with the application of this Convention to Japan, the following modifications of Article 2 may be made:

    (a) children over twelve years of age may be admitted into employment if they have finished the course in the elementary school;
    (b) as regards children between the ages of twelve and fourteen already employed, transitional regulations may be made.

2. The provisions in the present Japanese law admitting children under the age of twelve years to certain light and easy employments shall be repealed.

Article 6.

The provisions of Article 2 shall not apply to India, but in India children under twelve years of age shall not be employed–

>   (a) in manufactories working with power and employing more than ten persons;
>   (b) in mines, quarries, and other works for the extraction of minerals from the earth;
>   (c) in the transport of passengers of goods, or mails, by rail, or in the handling of goods at docks, quays, and wharves, but excluding transport by hand.

Article 7.

The formal ratifications of this Convention, under the conditions set forth in the Constitution of the International Labour Organisation, shall be communicated to the Director-General of the International Labour Office for registration.

Article 8.
>   1. Each Member of the International Labour Organisation which ratifies this Convention engages to apply it to its colonies, protectorates, and possessions which are not fully self-governing -
>   (a) except where owing to the local conditions its provisions are inapplicable; or
>   (b) subject to such modifications as may be necessary to adapt its provisions to local conditions.
>
>   2. Each Member shall notify to the International Labour Office the action taken in respect to each of its colonies, protectorates, and possessions which are not fully self-governing.

Article 9.

As soon as the ratifications of two Members of the International Labour Organisation have been registered with the International Labour Office, the Director-General of the International Labour Office shall so notify all the Members of the International Labour Organisation.

Article 10.

This Convention shall come into force at the date on which such notification is issued by the Director-General of the International Labour Office, but it shall then be binding only upon those Members which have registered their ratifications with the International Labour Office.

Article 11.
Each Member which ratifies this Convention agrees to bring its provisions into operation not later than 1 July 1922, and to take such action as may be necessary to make these provisions effective.

Article 12.
A Member which has ratified this Convention may denounce it after the expiration of ten years from the date on which the Convention first comes into force, by an act communicated to the Director-General of the International Labour Office for registration. Such denunciation shall not take effect until one year after the date on which it is registered with the International Labour Office.

Article 13.
At least once in ten years, the Governing Body of the International Labour Office shall present to the General Conference a report on the working of this Convention, and shall consider the desirability of placing on the agenda of the Conference the question of its revision or modification.

Article 14.
The French and English texts of this Convention shall both be authentic.

APPENDIX II

ILO Convention Concerning the Night Work of Young Persons Employed in Industry (1919)

CONVENTION 6

The General Conference of the International Labour Organisation,

Having been convened by the Government of the United States of America at Washington, on the 29th day of October 1919, and

Having decided upon the adoption of certain proposals with regard to the 'employment of children: during the night', which is part of the fourth item in the agenda for the Washington meeting of the Conference, and

Having determined that these proposals shall take the form of an international Convention,

Adopts the following Convention, which may be cited as the *Night Work of Young Persons* (*Industry*) *Convention*, 1919, for ratification by the Members of the International Labour Organisation in accordance with the Provisions of the Constitution of the International Labour Organisation:

Article 1.

1. For the purpose of this Convention, the term 'industrial undertaking' includes particularly –

    (a) mines, quarries, and other works for the extraction of minerals from the earth;
    (b) industries in which articles are manufactured, altered, cleaned, repaired, ornamented, finished, adapted for sale, broken up, or demolished, or in which materials are transformed; including ship building, and the generation, transformation, and transmission of electricity or motive power of any kind;
    (c) construction, reconstruction, maintenance, repair, alteration, or demolition of any building, railway, tramway, harbour, dock, pier, canal, inland waterway, road, tunnel, bridge, viaduct, sewer, drain, well, telegraphic or telephonic installation, electrical undertaking,

gas work, water work, or other work of construction as well as the preparation for or laying the foundations of any such work or structure;

(d) transport of passengers or goods by road or rail, including the handling of goods at docks, quays, wharves, and warehouses, but excluding transport by hand.

2. The competent authority in each country shall define the line of division which separates industry from commerce and agriculture.

Article 2.

1. Young persons under eighteen years of age shall not be employed during the night in any public or private industrial undertaking, or in any branch thereof, other than an undertaking in which only members of the same family are employed, except as hereinafter provided for.
2. Young persons over the age of sixteen may be employed during the night in the following industrial undertakings on work which, by reason of the nature of the process, is required to be carried on continuously day and night:

   (a) manufacture of iron and steel; processes in which reverberatory or regenerative furnaces are used, and galvanising of sheet metal or wire (except the pickling process);
   (b) glass work;
   (c) manufacture of paper;
   (d) manufacture of raw sugar;
   (e) gold mining reduction work.

Article 3.

1. For the purpose of this Convention, the term 'night' signifies a period of at least eleven consecutive hours, including the interval between ten o'clock in the evening and five o'clock in the morning.
2. In coal and lignite mines work may be carried on in the interval between ten o'clock in the evening and five o'clock in the morning, if an interval of ordinarily fifteen hours, and in no case of less than thirteen hours, separates two periods of work.
3. Where night work in the baking industry is prohibited for all workers, the interval between nine o'clock in the evening and four o'clock in the morning may be substituted in the baking industry for the interval between ten o'clock in the evening and five o'clock in the morning.
4. In those tropical countries in which work is suspended during the middle

of the day, the night period may be shorter than eleven hours if compensatory rest is accorded during the day.

Article 4.
The provisions of Articles 2 and 3 shall not apply to the night work of young persons between the ages of sixteen and eighteen years in case of emergencies which could not have been controlled or foreseen, which are not of a periodical character, and which interfere with the normal working of the industrial undertaking.

Article 5.
In the application of this convention to Japan, until 1 July 1925, Article 2 shall apply only to young persons under fifteen years of age and thereafter it shall apply only to young persons under sixteen years of age.

Article 6.
In the application of this Convention to India, the term 'industrial undertaking' shall include only 'factories' as defined in the Indian Factory Act, and Article 2 shall not apply to male young persons over fourteen years of age.

Article 7.
The prohibition of night work may be suspended by the Government, for young persons between the ages of sixteen and eighteen years, when in case of serious emergency the public interest demands it.

Article 8.

1. The formal ratifications of this Convention, under the conditions set forth in the Constitution of the International Labour Organisation, shall be communicated to the Director-General of the International Labour Office for registration.

Article 9.

1. Each Member of the International Labour Organisation which ratifies this Convention engages to apply it to its colonies, protectorates and possessions which are not fully self-governing –
   (a) except where owing to the local conditions its provisions are inapplicable; or
   (b) subject to such modifications as may be necessary to adapt its provisions to local conditions.
2. Each Member shall notify to the International Labour Office the action

taken in respect to each of its colonies, protectorates and possessions which are not fully self-governing.

Article 10.
As soon as the ratifications of two Members of the International Labour Organisation have been registered with the International Labour Office, the Director-General of the International Labour Office shall so notify all the Members of the International Labour Organisation.

Article 11.
This Convention shall come into force at the date on which such notification is issued by the Director-General of the International Labour Office, and it shall then be binding only upon those Members which have registered their ratifications with the International Labour Office. Thereafter this Convention will come into force for any other Member at the date on which its ratification is registered with the International Labour Office.

Article 12.
Each Member which ratifies this Convention agrees to bring its provisions into operation not later than 1 July 1922, and to take such action as may be necessary to make these provisions effective.

Article 13.
A Member which has ratified this Convention may denounce it after the expiration of ten years from the date on which the Convention first comes into force, by an act communicated to the Director-General of the International Labour Office for registration. Such denunciation shall not take effect until one year after the date on which it is registered with the International Labour Office.

Article 14.
At least once in ten years the Governing Body of the International Labour Office shall present to the General Conference a report on the working of this Convention, and shall consider the desirability of placing on the agenda of the Conference the question of its revision or modification.

Article 15.
The French and English texts of this Convention shall both be authentic.

APPENDIX III

International Agreement for the Suppression of the White Slave Traffic (1904)

Signed at Paris, May 18, 1904, ratification deposited at Paris, January 18, 1905.

Article 1.
Each of the Contracting Governments undertakes to establish or name some authority charged with the co-ordination of all information relative to the procuring of women or girls for immoral purposes abroad; this authority shall be empowered to correspond direct with the similar department established in each of the other Contracting States.

Article 2.
Each of the Governments undertakes to have a watch kept, especially in railway stations, ports of embarkation, and *en route* for persons in charge of women and girls destined for an immoral life. With this object instructions shall be given to the officials and all other qualified persons to obtain, within legal limits, all information likely to lead to the detection of criminal traffic.

The arrival of persons who clearly appear to be the principals, accomplices in, or victims of, such traffic shall be notified, when it occurs, either to the authorities of the place of destination, or to the Diplomatic or Consular Agents interested, or to any other competent authorities.

Article 3.
The Governments undertake, when the case arises, and within legal limits, to have the declarations taken of women or girls of foreign nationality who are prostitutes, in order to establish their identity and civil status, and to discover who has caused them to leave their country. The information obtained shall be communicated to the authorities of the country of origin of the said women or girls, with a view to their eventual repatriation.

The Governments undertake, within legal limits, and as far as can be done, to entrust temporarily, and with a view to their eventual repatriation, the victims of a criminal traffic when destitute to public or private charitable institutions, or to private individuals offering the necessary security.

The Governments also undertake, within legal limits, and as far as possible, to send back to their country of origin those women and girls who desire it, or who may be claimed by persons exercising authority over them. Repatriation shall only take place after agreement as to identity and nationality, as well as place and date of arrival at the frontiers. Each of the Contracting Countries shall facilitate transit through its territory.

Correspondence relative to repatriation shall be direct as far as possible.

Article 4.
Where the woman or girl to be repatriated cannot herself repay the cost of transfer, and has neither husband, relations, nor guardian to pay for her, the cost of repatriation shall be borne by the country where she is in residence as far as the nearest frontier or port of embarkation in the direction of the country of origin, and by the country of origin as regards the rest.

Article 5.
The provisions of the foregoing Articles 3 and 4 shall not affect any private Conventions existing between the Contracting Governments.

Article 6.
The Contracting Governments undertake, within legal limits, to exercise supervision, as far as possible, over the offices or agencies engaged in finding employment for women or girls abroad.

Article 7.
Non-Signatory States can adhere to the present Agreement. For this purpose they shall notify their intention, through the diplomatic channel, to the French Government, who shall acquaint all the Contracting States.

Article 8.
The present Agreement shall come into force six months after the exchange of ratifications. If one of the Contracting Parties denounces it, this denunciation shall only have effect as regards that party, and that only twelve months after the date of denunciation.

Article 9.
The present Agreement shall be ratified, and the ratifications shall be exchanged, at Paris with the least possible delay.

In faith whereof the respective Plenipotentiaries have signed the present Agreement, and thereunto affixed their seals.

Done at Paris, the 18th May, 1904, in single copy, which shall be deposited in the archives of the Ministry of Foreign Affairs of the French Republic, and of which one copy, certified correct, shall be sent to each Contracting Party.

APPENDIX IV

International *Convention* for the Suppression of the White Slave Traffic (1910)

Signed at Paris, May 4, 1910. British Ratification deposited at Paris, August 8, 1912.

The Sovereigns, Heads of States, and Governments of the Powers hereinafter designated,

Being equally desirous of taking the most effective steps for the suppression of the traffic known as the "White Slave Traffic," have resolved to conclude a Convention with this object, and a draft thereof having been drawn up at a first Conference which met at Paris from the 15th to the 25th July, 1902, they have appointed their Plenipotentiaries, who met at a second Conference at Paris from the 18th April to the 4th May, 1910, and agreed upon the following provisions:

Article 1.
Whoever, in order to gratify the passions of another person, has procured, enticed, or led away, even with her consent, a woman or girl under age, for immoral purposes, shall be punished, notwithstanding that the various acts constituting the offence may have been committed in different countries.

Article 2.
Whoever, in order to gratify the passions of another person, has, by fraud, or by means of violence, threats, abuse of authority, or any other method of compulsion, procured, enticed, or led away a woman or girl over age, for immoral purposes, shall also be punished, notwithstanding that the various acts constituting the offence may have been committed in different countries.

Article 3.
The Contracting Parties whose legislation may not at present be sufficient to deal with the offenses contemplated by the two preceding Articles engage to take or to propose to their respective legislatures the necessary steps to punish these offenses according to their gravity.

Article 4.
The Contracting Parties shall communicate to each other, through the intermediary of the Government of the French Republic, the laws which have already been or may in future be passed in their States relating to the object of the present Convention.

Article 5.
The offenses contemplated in Articles 1 and 2 shall, from the day on which the present Convention comes into force, be deemed to be lawfully included in the list of offenses for which extradition may be granted in accordance with Conventions already existing between the Contracting Parties.

In cases in which the above provision cannot be made effective without amending existing legislation, the Contracting Parties engage to take or to propose to their respective legislatures the necessary measures.

Article 6.
The transmission of Letters of Request relating to offenses covered by the present Convention shall be effected:

1. Either by direct communication between the judicial authorities;
2. Or through the intermediary of the diplomatic or consular agent of the demanding State in the country to which the demand is addressed. This agent shall forward the Letter of Request direct to the competent judicial authority, and will receive direct from that authority the documents establishing the execution of the Letter of Request; (in these two cases a copy of the Letter of Request shall always be addressed at the same time to the superior authority of the State to which the demand is addressed);
3. Or through the diplomatic channel.

Each Contracting Party shall make known, by a communication addressed to each of the other Contracting Parties, the method or methods of transmission which it recognises for Letters of Request emanating from that State.

All difficulties which may arise in connection with transmissions effected in cases 1 ad 2 of the present Article shall be settled through the diplomatic channel.

In the absence of any different understanding, the Letter of Request must be drawn up either in the language of the State on whom the demand is made or in the language agreed upon between the two States concerned, or else it must be accompanied by a translation made in one of these two languages and duly certified by a diplomatic or consular agent of the demanding State, or by a sworn translator of the State on whom the demand is made.

The execution of the Letters of Request shall not entail repayment of expenses of any kind whatever.

Article 7.
The Contracting Parties undertake to communicate to each other the records of convictions in respect of offenses covered by the present Convention where the various acts constituting such offenses have been committed in different countries.

These documents shall be forwarded direct by the authorities designated in conformity with Article 1 of the Agreement concluded at Paris on 18th May, 1904, to the corresponding authorities of the other Contracting States.

Article 8.
Non-Signatory States may accede to the present Convention. For this purpose they shall notify their intention by a declaration which shall be deposited in the archives of the Government of the French Republic. The latter shall communicate a certified copy thereof through the diplomatic channel to each of the Contracting States, and shall inform them at the same time of the date of such deposit. The laws of the acceding State relative to the object of the present Convention shall also be communicated with the said declaration.

Six months after the date of the deposit of the said declaration the Convention shall come into force throughout the extent of the territory of the acceding State, which will thus become a Contracting State.

Accession to the Convention shall necessarily entail, without special notification, a concomitant accession to the Agreement of the 18th May, 1904, in its entirety, which shall take effect, on the same date as the Convention itself, throughout the territory of the acceding State.

The preceding stipulation does not, however, derogate from Article 7 of the aforementioned Agreement of the 18th May, 1904, which remains applicable in cases where a State prefers to accede solely to that Agreement.

Article 9.
The present Convention completed by a *Final Protocol* which forms an integral part thereof, shall be ratified, and the ratifications shall be deposited at Paris as soon as six of the Contracting States are in a position to do so.

A protocol recording all deposits of ratifications shall be drawn up, of which a certified copy shall be transmitted through the diplomatic channel to each of the Contracting States.

The present Convention shall come into force six months after the date of the deposit of the ratifications.

Article 10.
In case one of the Contracting States shall denounce the Convention, such denunciation shall only have effect as regards that State.

The denunciation shall be notified by a declaration which shall be deposited in the archives of the Government of the French Republic. The latter shall communicate a certified copy, through the diplomatic channel, to each of the Contracting States, and shall inform them at the same time of the date of deposit.

Twelve months after that date the Convention shall cease to take effect throughout the territory of the State which has denounced it.

The denunciation of the Convention shall not entail as of right a concomitant denunciation of the Agreement of the 18th May, 1904, unless it should be so expressly mentioned in the declaration; if not, the Contracting State must, in order to denounce the said Agreement, proceed in conformity with Article 8 of that Agreement.

Article 11.
If a Contracting State desires the present Convention to come into force in one or more of its colonies, possessions or consular judicial districts, it shall notify its intention to that effect by a declaration which shall be deposited in the archives of the Government of the French Republic. The latter shall communicate a certified copy thereof, through the diplomatic channel, to each of the Contracting States, and shall inform them at the same time of the date of deposit.

The said declaration as regards colonies, possessions, or consular judicial districts, shall also communicate the laws which have been therein enacted relative to the object of the present Convention. Laws which may in future be enacted therein shall be equally communicated to the Contracting States in conformity with Article 4.

Six months after the date of deposit of the said declaration, the Convention shall come into force in the colonies, possessions, and consular judicial districts mentioned in such declaration.

The demanding State shall make known, by a communication addressed to each of the other Contracting States, which method or methods of transmission it recognises for Letters of Request destined for those colonies, possessions, or consular judicial districts in respect of which the declaration mentioned in the first paragraph of the present Article shall have been made.

The denunciation of the Convention by one of the Contracting States on behalf of one or more of its colonies, possessions, and consular judicial districts, shall be made under the forms and conditions laid down by the first paragraph of the present Article. Such denunciation shall take effect twelve months after the date of the deposit of the declaration thereof in the archives of the Government of the French Republic.

Accession to the Convention by a Contracting State on behalf of one or more of its colonies, possessions, or consular judicial districts shall entail, as of right and without special notification, a concomitant accession to the Agreement of the 18th May, 1904, in its entirety. The said Agreement shall come into force therein on the same date as the Convention itself. Nevertheless, the denunciation of the convention by a Contracting State on behalf of one or more of its colonies, possessions, or consular judicial districts shall not necessarily entail a concomitant denunciation of the Agreement of the 18th May, 1904, unless it should be so expressly mentioned in the declaration; moreover, the declarations which the Powers signatories of the Agreement of the 18th May, 1904, have been enabled to make respecting the accession of their colonies to the said Agreement are maintained.

Nevertheless, from and after the date of the coming into force of the present Convention, accessions to and denunciations of that Agreement as regards the colonies, possessions, or consular judicial districts of the Contracting States, shall be made in conformity with the stipulations of the present Article.

Article 12.
The present Convention, which shall be dated the 4th May, 1910, may be signed in Paris up to the 31st July following, by the Plenipotentiaries of the Powers represented at the second Conference for the Suppression of the 'White Slave Traffic'.

Done at Paris, the 4th May, 1910, in a single copy, of which a certified copy shall be communicated to each of the Signatory Powers.

Appendix V

International Convention for the Suppression of the Traffic in Women and Children (1922)

Opened for Signature at Geneva from September *30, 1921*, to March *31, 1922*

Article 1.
The High Contracting Parties agree that, in the event of their not being already Parties to the Agreement of the 18th May, 1904, and the Convention of the 4th May, 1910, mentioned above, they will transmit, with the least possible delay, their ratifications of, or adhesions to, those instruments in the manner laid down therein.

Article 2.
The High Contracting Parties agree to take all measures to discover and prosecute persons who are engaged in the traffic in children of both sexes and who commit offenses within the meaning of Article 1 of the Convention of the 4th May, 1910.

Article 3.
The High Contracting Parties agree to take the necessary steps to secure the punishment of attempts to commit, and, within legal limits, of acts preparatory to the commission of, the offenses specified in Articles 1 and 2 of the Convention of the 4th May, 1910.

Article 4.
The High Contracting Parties agree that, in cases where there are no extradition Conventions in force between them, they will take all measures within their power to extradite or provide for the extradition of persons accused or convicted of the offenses specified in Articles 1 and 2 of the Convention of the 4th May, 1910.

Article 5.
In paragraph B of the final Protocol of the Convention of 1910, the words 'twenty completed years of age' shall be replaced by the words 'twenty-one completed years of age'.

Article 6.
The High Contracting Parties agree, in case they have not already taken legislative or administrative measures regarding licensing and supervision of employment agencies and offices, to prescribe such regulations as are required to ensure the protection of women and children seeking employment in another country.

Article 7.
The High Contracting Parties undertake in connection with immigration and emigration to adopt such administrative and legislative measures as are required to check the traffic in women and children. In particular, they undertake to make such regulations as are required for the protection of women and children travelling on emigrant ships, not only at the points of departure and arrival, but also during the journey, and to arrange for the exhibition, in railway stations and in ports, of notices warning women and children of the danger of the traffic and indicating the places where they can obtain accommodation and assistance.

Article 8.
The present Convention, of which the French and the English texts are both authentic, shall bear this day's date, and shall be open for signature until the 31st March, 1922.

Article 9.
The present Convention is subject to ratification. The instruments of ratification shall be transmitted to the Secretary-General of the League of Nations, who will notify the recept of them to the other Members of the League and to States admitted to sign the Convention. The instruments of ratification shall be deposited in the archives of the Secretariat.

In order to comply with the provisions of Article 18 of the Covenant of the League of Nations, the Secretary-General will register the present Convention upon the deposit of the first ratification.

Article 10.
Members of the League of Nations which have not signed the present Convention before the 1st April, 1922, may accede to it.

The same applies to States not Members of the League to which the Council of the League may decide officially to communicate the present Convention.

Accession will be notified to the Secretary-General of the League, who will notify all Powers concerned of the accession and of the date on which it was notified.

Article 11.
The present Convention shall come into force in respect of each Party on the date of the deposit of its ratification or act of accession.

Article 12.
The present Convention may be denounced by any Member of the League or by any State which is a party thereto, on giving twelve months' notice of its intention to denounce. Denunciation shall be effected by notification in writing addressed to the Secretary-General of the League of Nations. Copies of such notification shall be transmitted forthwith by him to all other Parties, notifying them of the date it was received.

The denunciation shall take effect one year after the date on which it was notified to the Secretary-General, and shall operate only in respect of the notifying Power.

Article 13.
A special record shall be kept by the Secretary-General of the League of Nations, showing which of the Parties have signed, ratified, acceded to or denounced the present Convention. This record shall be open to the Members of the League at all times; it shall be published as often as possible, in accordance with the directions of the Council.

Article 14.
Any Member of State signing the present Convention may declare that the signature does not include any or all of its colonies, overseas possessions, protectorates or territories under its sovereignty or authority, and may subsequently adhere separately on behalf of any such colony, overseas possession, protectorate or territory so excluded in its declaration.

Denunciation may also be made separately in respect of any such colony, overseas possession, protectorate or territory under its sovereignty or authority, and the provisions of Article 12 shall apply to any such denunciation.

Done at Geneva, the 30th day of September, 1921, in a single copy, which shall remain deposited in the archives of the League of Nations.

APPENDIX VI

The Declaration of the Rights of the Child Proposed to Prolet'cult' (Moscow 1918)

1. Each child born into the world has the right to live: for instance, sanitary conditions suited to his/her tender age shall be assured; the child's maintenance and development shall never be neglected; the child shall be provided with the means to cope with the trials of life. These conditions must be fulfilled irrespective of the social status of the child's parents.
2. The responsibility for providing suitable sanitary conditions to children resides with the parents, Society, and the State. The role and extent of the responsibility of each of these components shall be determined by law.
3. Every child, whatever his/her age, is a person in his/her own right. No child may, under any circumstances, be considered as the property of his/her parents, Society or the State.
4. Every child has the right to choose his/her nearest educators and to dissociate him/herself from his/her parents and leave them if they prove to be bad educators. The child has this right at every age; if such a move does take place, the State and Society must ensure that this does not result in a worsening of the child's material position.
5. Every child has the right to freely develop all of his/her inherent strengths, capabilities and talents: the right to an education suited to his/her individuality. To this end, the child must unconditionally and at all ages be entrusted to educational institutions or training courses that guarantee optimal conditions for the harmonious development of all aspects of the child's nature and personality.
6. No child, at any age, shall be forced to attend an educational institution or training centre. Education and development programmes in all the stages are the free concern of the child. Every child has the right to leave education and development programmes incompatible with his/her individuality.
7. Insofar as his/her abilities and talents permit, each child, from his/her earliest childhood, shall participate in social (public) educational labour necessary for the good of the people as a whole. This labour, however,

must not only not endanger the child's psychological health or hamper his/her spiritual growth, but it must be in full agreement with the complete system of his/her education and development. Participation in socially necessary educational work gives the child the opportunity to realise one of the most important rights of children: the right to feel that they are not parasites but active members and builders of life and that their lives can have social worth, not only in the future, but also in the present.

8. With regard to freedom and rights, the child is, at all ages, viewed as equal to the adult person. If a right is not granted to a child, this may only be because the child does not have the necessary physical and spiritual capacity to use it. If, however, the child has the capacity, age may not stand in the way of realisation of the right.

9. The freedom consists of being allowed to do everything on the condition that it will not harm the physical and spiritual development of the child or other people. Thus, no boundaries shall stand in the way of the child exercising his/her natural rights, other than those dictated by the laws of the child's own normal physical and spiritual development, as well as the guarantee that other members of Society, too, are in a position to act on the same right.

10. Within their own peer groups, or in their relationships with the adults in their surroundings, children shall be expected to adhere to certain rules that forbid acts that are harmful to Society as a whole. No obstacle shall be put in the way of interest and activity that does not fall under such rules. No child shall be forced to act contrary to this ruling.

11. Children must be granted the right to participate in the compilation of rules that will control their lives and their talents.

12. No one, neither parents nor Society nor the State, shall force a child to be instructed in any particular religion or to practice its rites. Religious education must always be left to the free choice of the child.

13. No child may be oppressed because of his/her convictions. However, the implementation of convictions shall not encroach upon the equal rights of other members of Society – adults or children.

14. Each child shall be allowed to express his/her opinions and thoughts whether in writing or verbally, just like adults. This right may only be restricted by dictates relating to the well-being of Society, in accordance with teachings of the child's educators and the limits of the child's understanding. All restrictions on this right shall be clearly determined by law.

15. Each child has the right to found, together with other children or adults, organisations, associations and the like, just like adults. Possible restrictions, dictated by the well-being of the child and his normal physical and spiritual development, must be clearly determined by law.

16. No child may be deprived of his/her liberty or submitted to punishment. If a child has misbehaved or failed, he/she shall be rehabilitated with the help of appropriate educational institutions rather than by punishment and other repressive actions.
17. The State and Society shall employ every means possible to ensure that all the above mentioned rights of the child shall, in no way, be infringed upon; they shall protect these rights against all attempts to violate them, and force those who fail in their duty to the younger generation, to mend their ways.

APPENDIX VII

Programme of Immediate Demands/Declaration of the Rights of the Adolescent (1922)

Adopted by the Joint Conference of the Young Workers' International and the International Union of Socialist Youth Organisations at Salzburg, August 21st, 1922, often called 'the Declaration of the Rights of the Adolescent'

1. Absolute prohibition of remunerated employment during pre-school and compulsory school age.
2. Prohibition of any extension of the 8 hours day with inclusion of the compulsory school hours. Actual working time may not exceed 6 hours. Continuation school instruction during daytime only.
3. Compulsory medical examination of young persons before admission to employment.
4. Absolute prohibition of piece work, night work, underground work and work in unhealthy industries or occupations.
5. Thirty-six hours rest on Sundays; Saturday half holiday.
6. Holidays with full pay up to the age of 18.
7. Observance of these rules to be supervised by Juvenile Boards with the co-operation of workers' representative.
8. Reform of the apprenticeship system.
9. Reform of compulsory continuation school instruction.

APPENDIX VIII

The Children's Charter of the International Council of Women (1922)

This Charter is based on the principle that every child is born with the inalienable right to have the opportunity of full physical, mental and spiritual development.

It is the privilege, no less than the duty of parents, to provide such opportunities for their children. In the event of parents not being able, for whatsoever reason, to discharge this duty, the community is bound to secure the fulfilment thereof.

The provisions enumerated under the following headings are based on the recognition of this principle.

I. Pre-Natal Care

1. Schemes to be devised, in co-operation between parents and teachers, whereby carefully prepared instruction in sex hygiene for both boys and girls, adapted to their age and understanding, will be given by specially trained teachers.
2. Education of general public regarding the causes of maternal and infant mortality, and how they can be prevented by means of Maternity and Child Welfare Exhibitions, Lectures, etc.
3. Education of the general public regarding the responsibilities of persons about to marry, with the view of raising the standard of health and morals.
4. Public Health Nurses and District Nurses who are trained to act as advisers to expectant mothers in co-operation with doctors, and fully trained midwives. Such nurses to give advice only and not to give treatment.
5. Clinics – including Dental Clinics and Venereal Diseases Clinics, under special medical direction, where expectant mothers can be treated when necessary.
6. Instruction of expectant mothers through Maternity and Infant Welfare Centres, etc.

7. An adequate medical, midwifery and nursing service for childbirth.
8. Midwives to be registered, and required by law to show adequate training and to be licensed and supervised.
9. Legal prohibition of work for women for six weeks before, and six weeks after child-birth, together with Maternity benefits for all working women, and all needy mothers, with free Hospital and Nursing care during the same period as above and whilst they are nursing their children.
10. Voluntary Care Committees to be appointed in regard to all these matters under the Local Health Authorities, in which a fair protection of women should be included.

II. CARE OF MOTHERS AND CHILDREN UP TO SCHOOL AGE

1. Compulsory notification of births and still-births to Public Health Authorities, within three days after birth.
2. Compulsory registration of births within six months.
3. Prevention of infantile blindness by enforcing adequate laws for treatment of eyes of every infant at birth.
4. Provision of maternity and infant centres, through which medical consultations, home visiting by Public Health Nurses, and advice and instruction of mothers in the upbringing, feeding and clothing of their children should be organised.
5. Dental Clinics for mothers and children – ear, eye, nose and throat clinics – venereal, and tuberculosis and other clinics to be available where medical treatment should be provided.
6. Hospitals and Homes for children requiring special treatment and for defective children.
7. Preventoria, Convalescent and Holiday Homes for mothers and young children needing change of air, rest, and nourishing food.
8. Laws requiring Local Authorities to make adequate provision for a sufficient and pure milk supply, with special arrangements whereby it shall be made available for the use of mothers and young children and invalids.
9. Playgrounds and Play-rooms with specially trained Play Teachers, paid or voluntary, for young children.
10. Licensing and strict supervision of all institutions undertaking the care and education of young children.
11. Scheme for boarding out orphan and deserted children in suitable families under State supervision.

III. CHILDREN OF SCHOOL AGE

1. Adequate provision by the State for a system of education for all citizens including the Kindergarten Schools, Continuation Schools, Technical and Vocational Schools and Universities, and including provision for children living in isolated districts. Such system to be free in elementary schools, and to provide ample facilities by maintenance grants and scholarships for children who show promise of being able to take advantage of higher education.
2. Special Schools for backward children and for those suffering from mental or physical defects.
3. Properly constructed School-houses with suitable sanitary arrangements, bath and cloak-rooms, and heating facilities when required. Overcrowding to be avoided.
4. Adequate salaries and pensions for teachers so that the teaching profession may attract the best type of young men and women and that they, being free from financial anxieties, shall be able to give their best to the children under their care.
5. Schemes for Parents and Teachers Conferences, and joint Committees, so that full co-operation may be obtained between the home and the school in the education of the child.
6. Adequate Playground, Recreation Centres and Libraries under specially trained teachers and leaders, paid or voluntary.
7. Open-air Schools and Classes with opportunities for rest during school hours for children disposed to tuberculosis and others recommended by the School Doctor for open-air treatment.
8. Provision of School Meals for children recommended by School Doctor.
9. Periodical physical examinations by Physicians, together with opportunities to obtain necessary treatment as recommended by such physician.
10. Adequate Staff of School Physicians and School Nurses, who shall assist Physician at examination of children and visit the homes of the children to ensure the carrying out of physician's orders, and to assist and instruct the mothers in the care and feeding of their children.
11. Available Clinics for dentistry, nose, throat, eye, ear, skin and orthopaedic work – also for free vaccination against smallpox and such other diseases, as may be ordered by the State.
12. Sufficient Hospital accommodation for the treatment of children's diseases.
13. Preventoria and Convalescent Homes under adequate supervision.
14. Education of children in laws of health.
15. Compulsory education regarding the care of infants in all schools and Continuation schools.
16. Education in moral laws, thrift and citizenship, with opportunities for

religious instruction by the different religious bodies to which the children's parents belong.
17. Care and After-care Committees in connection with every School or Institution for the care of children.
18. Full-time education up to age of 14, and part-time attendance at Continuation Classes up to 18.
19. Some State provision for the endowment and maintenance of needy mothers and children until the latter reach wage-earning age.

IV. Children in Employment

1. Prohibition of the employment of children in industry under the age of 14.
2. Prohibition of the employment of boys and girls under 18 at night and in dangerous trades.
3. The hours spent by young persons under 18 at Continuation Schools to be counted as part of working day.
4. Advisory Committees and Bureaux appointed for the advice and guidance of parents and children, when the latter are of an age to prepare themselves for entering a trade of profession, and to help them to get suitably placed when they take up work.

V. Delinquent children

1. Juvenile Courts to be established, entirely apart from Criminal Courts, and presided over by specially appointed Judges to deal with all cases of delinquent children from a parental standpoint, and with the object of preventing the delinquent, abnormal defective or neglected child from drifting into crime. A sufficient supply of suitable Remand-Homes to be provided for purposes of observation.
2. No person considered a child in the eyes of the law, to be sentenced to imprisonment.
3. Juvenile probation systems to be established under which delinquent and neglected children are to be placed under the supervision of paid or voluntary probation officers, who shall regularly report to the Court.
4. Special Probation and Training Schools to be established where persistent delinquents and neglected children can be detained by decision of the Juvenile court.
5. In cases where parents are found unfit for the guardianship of their children, or are found guilty of cruelty, neglect and desertion, the State to assume guardianship and to make such arrangements for the children's upbringing as may seem best, charging the parents for maintenance wherever possible.

VI. CHILDREN'S STATE DEPARTMENTS

It is strongly advised that a State Department to watch over the interests of children from every point of view be established in every country.

Note: The Children's Bureau at Washington has accomplished much valuable work and has issued a series of books and pamphlets as the result of much careful field work and investigation which are of the utmost interest for all Child Welfare workers.

State Departments for Children have also been established in Canada, New Zealand and Yugoslavia.

VII. INTERNATIONAL CONFERENCES

Periodical International Conferences between the official representatives of State Departments established to watch over the interests of children and the representatives of voluntary organisations connected with children are strongly recommended and could not fail to yield valuable results. Such Conferences might also enable schemes to be devised for carrying out the policy of the Children's Charter in countries which, in consequence of the War, cannot themselves provide adequately for their children.

The Reports published by the International Conferences for the protection of Childhood held at Brussels in 1918 and 1921 contain reports and papers on various subjects relating to children which are of great value.

APPENDIX IX

Declaration of Geneva (1924)

By the present Declaration of the Rights of the Child, commonly known as the 'Declaration of Geneva', men and women of all nations, recognising that mankind owes to the Child the best that it has to give, declare and accept it as their duty that, beyond and above all considerations of race, nationality or creed:

1. The child must be given the means requisite for its normal development, both materially and spiritually.
2. The child that is hungry must be fed; the child that is sick must be nursed; the child that is backward must be helped; the delinquent child must be reclaimed; and the orphan and the waif must be sheltered and succoured.
3. The child must be the first to receive relief in times of distress.
4. The child must be put in a position to earn a livelihood, and must be protected against every form of exploitation.
5. The child must be brought up in the consciousness that its talents must be devoted to the service of its fellow-men.

APPENDIX X

The Children's Charter of President Hoover's White House Conference on Child Health and Protection (1930)

I

For every child spiritual and moral training to help him to stand firm under the pressure of life.

II

For every child understanding and the guarding of his personality as his most precious right.

III

For every child a home and that love and security which a home provides, and for that child who must receive foster care, the nearest substitute for his own home.

IV

For every child full preparation for his birth, his mother receiving pre-natal and post-natal care; and the establishment of such protective measures as will make child bearing safer.

V

For every child health protection from birth through adolescence including: periodical health examinations and, where needed, care of specialists and hospital treatment; regular dental examinations and care of the teeth; protective and preventive measures against communicable diseases; the insuring of pure food, pure milk, and pure water.

VI

For every child from birth, through adolescence, promotion of health including health instruction and a health program, wholesome physical and mental recreation, with teachers and leaders adequately trained.

VII

For every child a dwelling place safe, sanitary, and wholesome, with reasonable provisions for privacy, free from conditions which tend to thwart his development; and a home environment harmonious and enriching.

VIII

For every child a school which is safe from hazards, sanitary, properly equipped, lighted, and ventilated. For younger children nursery schools and kindergartens to supplement home care.

IX

For every child a community which recognises and plans for his needs, protects him against physical dangers, moral hazards, and disease; provides him with safe and wholesome places for play and recreation; and makes provision for his cultural and social needs.

X

For every child an education which, through the discovery and development of his individual abilities, prepares him for life; and through training and vocational guidance prepares him for a living which will yield him the maximum of satisfaction.

XI

For every child such teaching and training as will prepare him for successful parenthood, home-making, and the rights of citizenship; and, for parents, supplementary training to fit them to deal wisely with the problems of parenthood.

XII

For every child education for safety and protection against accidents to which modern conditions subject him – those to which he is directly exposed and those which, through loss or maiming of his parents, affect him indirectly.

XIII

For every child who is blind, deaf, crippled, or otherwise physically handicapped, and for the child who is mentally handicapped, such measures as will early discover and diagnose his handicap, provide care and treatment, and so train him that he may become an asset to society rather than a liability. Expenses of these services should be borne publicly where they cannot be privately met.

XIV

For every child who is in conflict with society the right to be dealt with intelligently as society's charge, not society's outcast; with the home, the school, the church, the court, and the institution when needed, shaped to return him whenever possible to the normal stream of life.

XV

For every child the right to grow up in a family with an adequate standard of living and the security of a stable income as the surest safeguard against social handicaps.

XVI

For every child protection against labour that stunts growth either physical or mental, that limits education, that deprives children of the right to comradeship, of play, and of joy.

XVII

For every rural child a satisfactory schooling and health services as for the city child, and an extension to rural families of social, recreational, and cultural facilities.

XVIII

To supplement the home and the school in the training of youth, and to return to them those interests of which modern life tends to cheat children, every stimulation and encouragement should be given to the extension and development of the voluntary youth organisations.

XIX

To make everywhere available these minimum protections of the health and welfare of children, there should be a district, county, or community organisation for health, education, and welfare, with full-time officials, co-ordinating with a state-wide program which will be responsive to a nation-wide service of general information, statistics, and scientific research. This should include:

(a) trained full-time public health officials, with public health nurses, sanitary inspection and laboratory workers;
(b) available hospital beds;
(c) full-time public welfare service for the relief, aid, and guidance of children in special need due to poverty, misfortune, or behaviour difficulties, and for the protection of children from abuse, neglect, exploitation, or moral hazard.

For every child these rights, regardless of race, or color, or situation, wherever he may live under the protection of the American flag.

APPENDIX XI

Bill of Rights for the Handicapped Child (1930)

Presented by a Committee on handicapped children at the White House Conference on Child Health and Protection, 1930

The handicapped child has a right:

1. To as vigorous a body as human skill can give him.
2. To an education so adapted to his handicap that he can be economically independent and have the chance for the fullest life of which he is capable.
3. To be brought up and educated by those who understand the nature of the burden he has to bear and who consider it a privilege to help him bear it.
4. To grow up in a world which does not set him apart, which looks at him, not with scorn or pity or ridicule – but which welcomes him, exactly as it welcomes every child, which offer him identical privileges and identical responsibilities.
5. To a life on which his handicap casts no shadow, but which is full day by day with those things which make it worth while, with comradeship, love, work, play, laughter, and tears – a life in which these things bring continually increasing growth, richness, release of energies, joy in achievement.

APPENDIX XII

A Children's Charter in Wartime of the U.S. Department of Labor Children's Bureau (1942)

1. We are in total war against the aggressor nations. We are fighting again for human freedom and especially for the future of our children in a free world.
2. Children must be safeguarded – and they can be safeguarded – in the midst of this total war so that they can live and share in that future. They must be nourished, sheltered, and protected even in the stress of war production so that they will be strong to carry forward a just and lasting peace.
3. Our American Republics sprang from a sturdy yearning for tolerance, independence, and self-government. The American home has emerged from the search for freedom. Within it the child lives and learns through his own efforts the meaning and responsibilities of freedom.
4. We have faith in the children of the New World – faith that if our generation does its part now, they will renew the living principles in our common life, and make the most of them.
5. Both as a wartime responsibility and as stepping-stones to our future – and to theirs – we call upon citizens, young and old, to join together to –

    I. Guard children from injury in danger zones.
    II. Protect children from neglect, exploitation, and undue strain in defense areas.
    III. Strengthen the home life of children whose parents are mobilized for war or war production.
    IV. Conserve, equip, and free children of every race and creed to take their part in democracy.

This charter put in terms of the children of the United States

I. DANGER ZONES

Guard children from injury in danger zones

These danger zones line our coasts along the Atlantic, the Pacific, and the Gulf – especially where there are military targets, industrial plants, business centres, oil tanks or the like; also, closely built home areas which might be bombed in an effort to break the morale of defense production workers.

These zones are a first charge on our Civilian Defense program but there is no certainty that inland districts and communities will not be subject to air raids or other forms of attack.

Children first in all plans for protection. The first step is their registration and identification.

Evacuation of children from such zones, if needed, as a sound precaution; advance plans for adequate reception and care in their places of refuge. Mothers to go with their children whenever possible.

'War vacations' for city children. By the expansion of summer vacation camps conducted under proper supervision, staffed in part by volunteers, and utilizing surplus commodities, and other aids, great numbers of children can be removed from exposed districts at relatively little expense. These camp demonstrations would be an admirable test of evacuation methods and an investment for health.

Appropriate immunization of all children against communicable disease.

Helping children to meet the anticipations and realities of wartime. Childhood anxiety can be as devastating as disease. Not only parents, but doctors, nurses, teachers, recreation leaders, settlement workers, child-welfare and child-guidance workers can help to preserve the child's sense of security, which is his greatest need.

II. DEFENSE AREAS

Protect children from neglect and undue strain in defense areas.

Vital to the cause of the United Nations is an ever-increasing stream of guns, tanks, and planes and other war equipment and materials from the United States. A thousand communities are involved in their production. Broken working time due to sickness of the worker, or his wife or child, or to disturbed family life handicaps production at countless points.

Therefore, the following are essential:

Adequate health, education, and welfare services must be maintained for children and their parents in each of the thousand communities where war production or military camps are established. To accomplish this will require proper staffing with doctors, health officers, nurses, social workers, teachers, recreation leaders and librarians. It will call for adequate hospitals, clinics, schools, playgrounds, recreational facilities, and day-care centres. Each of these communities will need to mobilize all of its resources within a co-ordinated plan. Many will need assistance to supplement existing staff and equipment.

The assignment of obstetricians and paediatricians to defense areas should be given special consideration.

Child-guidance clinics should be provided wherever possible to help parents and children overcome insecurity associated with dislocations in family life. Such dislocations exaggerate the normal anxieties of children and create situations that require special service.

School opportunities must be expanded to meet the new demands of expanding populations. This should include nursery schools for young children.

Recreation leaders, group workers, and child-welfare workers are urgently needed in defense communities, where crowded conditions mean overtaxing of facilities for play of little children and of recreation centres for older boys and girls; increase in harmful employment of children; and mounting juvenile delinquency.

III. HOMES IN WARTIME.

Strengthen the home life of children whose parents are mobilized for war or war production.

To children in wartime the home is vital as a centre of security and hope and love. To our fighting men the safety and protection of their families is the centre of what they fight for. To men on the production front the welfare of their families and homes is basic to morale.

Migration to new and crowded communities, the absence of the father in military service, priorities unemployment on the one hand, and the employment of mothers on the other, are creating problems in homes that affect every member of the family.

Children of our fighting men. Full provision must be made for the economic needs of children whose fathers are in the service and for medical and hospital care for wives and children.

A Government insurance program for civilians injured or killed as a result of war activities should supplement our social security program.

Adequate housing is essential to the protection of home life. In housing projects facilities should be provided for health services and group activities for children.

Employment of mothers and day care of children. As plans develop for the participation of women in war industry, it must be recognized that the care of young children is the first responsibility of mothers. For children whose mothers are employed or planning to enter employment, it is the responsibility of the community, through adequate planning and support, to see that parents have assistance in planning for their needs and that the children have the best possible care – not forgetting health supervision, opportunity for nursery education and play for the youngest, recreation outside of school hours for those who attend school.

Day care for children in crowded areas where home facilities are limited. Such children should have opportunities similar to those provided for children of working mothers.

Economic security. To all parents economically unable to maintain a home for their children, Government help should be extended through such measures as aid to dependent children, general assistance, and benefits for temporary and permanent disability.

IV. CHILDREN THE COUNTRY OVER

Conserve, equip, and free children of every race and creed to take their part in democracy.

The Children's Charter drawn up at the White House Conference in 1930 and the recommendations of the 1940 Conference are still a challenge to the people. Here it is only in point to single out certain factors that take on new significance in the present war crisis.

Health and children. Good health in childhood lays the foundation for good health in later life. Children should have health supervision from the prenatal period through adolescence. Special planning is needed to overcome present and future shortages of doctors and nurses. As soon as possible every county in the United States should have public-health-nursing service, prenatal clinics, delivery care, child-health conferences, and clinic and hospital service for sick children.

Food for children. The needs of children must be considered first in the event of national or local shortages of foods, especially of milk and the other protective foods. If our country is to be strong, all children must have the food they need for buoyant health and normal growth, and information must be available to parents concerning the family food requirements. Family incomes should be sufficient to assure to each member of the family the right amounts and the right kinds of food. School meals are an effective means of supplementing home nutrition and educating children and their families in good food habits. The extension of penny milk to all children is an important aid in assuring to them their full share of this essential food.

Social services for children. Communities should be equipped to supplement the care and training given by home and school when the welfare of the child demands it. Child-welfare and child-guidance resources of the State, county, and city governments should be expanded to provide appropriate service and care for all children with special needs.

The right to play. More than ever in wartime recreation must be assured for children and youth through the full use and expansion as needed of all public and private leisure-time activities.

School and work. It is essential that children and youth be sound and well-prepared in body and mind for the tasks of today and tomorrow. Their right to schooling should not be scrapped for the duration. Demands for the employment of children as a necessary war measure should be analyzed to determine whether full use has been made of available adult man power and to distinguish between actual labor shortage and the desire to obtain cheap labor. The education and wholesome development of boys and girls should be the first consideration in making decisions with regard to their employment or other contribution to our war effort. This means that no boy or girl shall be employed at wages that undermine the wages for adult labor; none under 14 years of age shall be part of the labor force; none under 16 shall be employed in manufacturing and mining occupations; none under 18 in hazardous occupations.

Health and education. A measure urgently needed at this time is complete medical examinations of all boys and girls of high-school age at regular intervals, with provision for correction of remediable defects. Provision should be made for a Nation-wide extension of health services for school children including medical care as needed and health instruction, developed through the co-operation of health and education authorities. The need for health supervision and medical care for youth has been demonstrated until there is no longer any possibility of disregarding it.

Young children. In the war period special consideration should be given to the needs of all young children for security in the home and for opportunity to grow through association with other children in play and through the reassurance given by adults who have learned to understand their needs. Opportunity for nursery education should be made increasingly available to help meet situations created by the war.

Children in rural areas. More than half of the children of the Nation live in country districts. Far more than city children they are likely to be handicapped by early and harmful employment, inadequate schools, and lack of other community facilities. The war effort must not increase these handicaps.

Participation in civilian-mobilization programs. Boys and girls should participate in home and community efforts of the war through activities appropriate to their age and ability.

Every city, county, and State should review the needs of its children and youth in the light of these principles through a children's wartime commission or council or an existing organization designated to serve in this capacity, and should devise means to meet evident needs through the co-operative action of Federal, State, and local governments and private agencies.

Every effort should be made to keep the public informed of activities and needs in all phases of service for children and to provide for participation of professional associations, organized labor, farm groups, and other organizations of citizens concerned with children, in the planning and development of these programs.

Provision should be made as rapidly as possible for training the professional workers needed to provide for extension of community programmes to increasing numbers of children.

There should be no State lines nor barriers of race or creed impeding what we do for children in our war effort. They may not live in danger zones or defense areas; they will still be subject to the strains of these times. They should not be forgotten Americans. Their future is our future.

APPENDIX XIII

The Children's Charter for the Post-War World (1942)

Adopted on April 12th, 1942, in London at the Conference of educational experts.

The Inter-Allied Conference convened by the New Education Fellowship and meeting in London on April 11th and 12th, 1942, humbly request the Governments of the Allied Nations to approve and adopt the following Charter for Children as a statement of the basic and minimum rights of children to be secured and guarded, above and beyond all considerations of sex, race, nationality, creed or social position.

1. The personality of the child is sacred; and the needs of the child must be the foundation of any good educational system.
2. The right of every child to proper food, clothing and shelter shall be accepted as a first charge on the resources of the nation.
3. For every child there shall always be available medical attention and treatment.
4. All children shall have equal opportunity of access to the nation's stores of knowledge and wisdom.
5. There shall be full-time schooling for every child.
6. Religious training should be available for all children.

APPENDIX XIV

Declaration of Opportunities for Children (1942)

Adopted by the Eighth Pan American Child Congress (1942)

Family Life

Opportunity for every child to grow up within the loving care and affectionate discipline of family life.

To this end the creation of a family atmosphere suitable for the child's development is necessary and the following measures are essential:

(a) Every child should live in a family having an adequate standard of living and a stable economic foundation.
(b) The State should take measures to assure the economic stability of the family.
(c) It should be the concern of the State that homeless children be cared for in a suitable family environment.
(d) Only when the needs of homeless children cannot be met adequately in foster families should such children be placed in an institution.
(e) Poverty of the mother should not be a cause for complete separation from her child; welfare organizations should provide assistance to needy mothers until they can improve their economic circumstances through their own efforts.

Health

Opportunity for every child to obtain the essential elements of wholesome, healthful living – good nutrition, healthful recreation, and sufficient rest – and to learn to give due value to physical, emotional, and intellectual development; not only from the point of view of his personal welfare, but of the welfare of those who surround him.

To this end it is necessary to safeguard the physical and mental health of the child from birth until the age at which he becomes a contributing member of the community, for which the following are required:

(a) Adequate diet.
(b) Periodic medical and psychological supervision, and adequate medical care during illness.
(c) Expert guidance in recreation.
(d) Adequate rest.
(e) Guidance in the proper formation of the personality, in all its aspects.
(f) Preparation for life in the community.

EDUCATION

Opportunity for every child to discover his special abilities, and to secure education and training to develop these powers – mental, physical, and spiritual – during the years necessary to achieve full development.

To this end it is necessary to provide appropriate education for each child in accordance with his age and mental capacity, such provision to include especially the following:

(a) Vocational guidance.
(b) Appropriate and adequate organization of intellectual, physical, spiritual, and cultural education during the time required for the attainment of maturity, and the full realization of his capacities and natural talents.

RESPONSIBILITY AND WORK

Opportunity for every child to develop responsibility and to learn to participate in the life of the community.

To this end it is necessary to provide opportunities for work, and to create a sense of personal responsibility under conditions appropriate to his age and capacity, employing such measures as:

(a) Teaching the child to control himself and to conduct his life in a manner that will enable him to assume appropriate responsibility at each stage of his development.
(b) Promoting child-labour legislation, fixing a minimum age for entrance into gainful employment, limiting the hours of work for children to a maximum of 6 hours a day, and establishing compulsory registration of employed minors under 16.

Leisure Time

Opportunity for every child to use creatively part of his free time in developing skills and practising activities of his choice, individual as well as social.

To this end it is necessary to foster provisions for suitable recreation and leisure-time activities.

Citizenship

Opportunity for every child as a citizen to take his place in the life of the community.

To this end it is necessary to develop the conscience of the child concerning his obligation to contribute to the progress of the community and to prepare himself for the responsibilities of citizenship, so that he may realize from his early years that the rights he enjoys in a democracy are accompanied by inescapable obligations which require the unselfish and socially desirable use of those privileges.

And, Finally,

Opportunity for every Child to take part, creatively, in transforming the raw materials of human life into usefulness or beauty – as artist or craftsman; as worker on the soil or in mine, mill, or factory; as a member of organizations for community betterment; or as scholar, scientist, or spiritual leader.

APPENDIX XV

Children's Bill of Rights of the New York State Youth Commission (1949)

New York State Youth Commission, Albany, New York (1949)
For each child regardless of race, colour or creed –

1. The right to the affection and intelligent guidance of understanding parents.
2. The right to be raised in a decent home in which he or she is adequately fed, clothed and sheltered.
3. The right to the benefits of religious guidance and training.
4. The right to a school program, which, in addition to sound academic training, offers maximum opportunity for individual development and preparation for living.
5. The right to receive constructive discipline for the proper development of good character, conduct and habits.
6. The right to be secure in his or her community against all influences detrimental to proper and wholesome development.
7. The right to the individual selection of free and wholesome recreation.
8. The right to live in a community in which adults practice the belief that the welfare of their children is of primary importance.
9. The right to receive good adult example.
10. The right to a job commensurate with his or her ability, training and experience, and protection against physical or moral employment hazards which adversely affect wholesome development.
11. The right to early diagnosis and treatment of physical handicaps and mental and social maladjustments, at public expense whenever necessary.

APPENDIX XVI

The Pledge to Children (1950)

Mid-Century White House Conference on Children and Youth (1950)

To you, our children, who hold within you our most cherished hopes, we, the members of the Mid-Century White House Conference on Children and Youth, relying on your full response, make this pledge:

From your earliest infancy we give you our love, so that you may grow with trust in yourself and in others.

We will recognize your worth as a person and we will help you to strengthen your sense of belonging.

We will respect your right to be yourself and at the same time help you to understand the rights of others, so that you may experience co-operative living.

We will help you to develop initiative and imagination, so that you may have the opportunity freely to create.

We will encourage your curiosity and your pride in workmanship, so that you may have the satisfaction that comes from achievement.

We will provide the conditions for wholesome play that will add to your social experience, and to your happiness.

We will illustrate by precept and example the value of integrity and the importance of moral courage.

We will encourage you always to seek the truth.

We will provide you with all opportunities possible to develop your own faith in God.

We will open the way for you to enjoy the arts and to use them for deepening your understanding of life.

We will work to rid ourselves of prejudice and discrimination, so that together we may achieve a truly democratic society.

We will work to lift the standard of living and to improve our economic practices, so that you may have the material basis for a full life.

We will provide you with rewarding educational opportunities, so that you may develop your talents and contribute to a better world.

We will protect you against exploitation and undue hazards and help you grow in health and strength.

We will work to conserve and improve family life and, as needed, to provide foster care according to your inherent rights.

We will intensify our search for new knowledge in order to guide you more effectively as you develop your potentialities.

As you grow from child to youth to adult, establishing a family life of your own and accepting larger social responsibilities, we will work with you to improve conditions for all children and youth.

Aware that these promises to you cannot be fully met in a world at war, we ask you to join us in a firm dedication to the building of a world society based on freedom, justice and mutual respect.

So may you grow in joy, in faith in God and in man, and in those qualities of vision and of the spirit that will sustain us all and give us new hope for the future.

APPENDIX XVII

The Children's Charter, Japan (1951)

Proclaimed on May 5, 1951

Preamble

We, the people of Japan, in accordance with the spirit of the Constitution, do adopt this Charter to establish correct ideas toward children and thus bring about the well-being of all children.

General Principles

The child shall be respected as a human being.
The child shall be given due regard as a member of society.
The child shall be brought up in a good environment.

Text

1. All children shall be assured healthy minds and bodies and shall be guaranteed freedom from want.
2. All children shall be entitled to be brought up in their own homes with proper love, knowledge and skill. Those children not having homes shall be brought up in an environment having similar advantages.
3. All children shall be provided with adequate nourishment, housing and clothing and shall be protected against disease and injury.
4. All children shall be educated in accordance with their individuality and capacity and so guided that they will honestly and independently discharge their responsibilities as members of society.
5. All children shall be so guided that they may love nature, respect science and art, and accept the virtues of morality.

6. All children shall be assured access to schooling and be provided with complete educational facilities.
7. All children shall be provided with opportunity to receive vocational guidance and training.
8. All children shall be fully protected against exploitation in labour that their mental and physical development shall not be retarded, their opportunities to receive education not be lost and that their lives as children not be hampered.
9. All children shall be assured access to wholesome recreational and cultural resources and be protected against evil environments.
10. All children shall be protected against abuse, exploitation, neglect and other harmful treatment. Children who have committed wrongful acts shall be provided with adequate protection and guidance.
11. All children who are mentally or physically handicapped shall be provided with appropriate medical care, education and protection.
12. All children shall be so guided that they may be united with one another in the spirit of love and sincerity and as good citizens devote themselves to the peace and culture of mankind.

APPENDIX XVIII

The United Nations Declaration on the Rights of the Child (1959)

Preamble
Whereas the peoples of the United Nations have, in the Charter, reaffirmed their faith in fundamental human rights, and in the dignity and worth of the human person, and have determined to promote social progress and better standards of life in larger freedom,

Whereas the United Nations has, in the Universal Declaration of Human Rights, proclaimed that everyone is entitled to all the rights and freedoms set forth therein, without distinction of any kind, such as race, colour, sex, language, religion, political or other opinion, national or social origin, property, birth or other status,

Whereas the child, by reason of his physical and mental immaturity, needs special safeguards and care, including appropriate legal protection, before as well as after birth,

Whereas the need for such special safeguards has been stated in the Geneva Declaration of the Rights of the Child of 1924, and recognized in the Universal Declaration of Human Rights and in the statutes of specialized agencies and international organizations concerned with the welfare of children,

Whereas mankind owes to the child the best it has to give,

Now therefore, the General Assembly proclaims this Declaration of the Rights of the Child to the end that he may have a happy childhood and enjoy for his own good and for the good of society the rights and freedoms herein set forth, and calls upon parents, upon men and women as individuals and upon voluntary organizations, local authorities and national governments to recognize these rights and strive for their observance by legislative and other measures progressively taken in accordance with the following principles:

Principle 1:
The child shall enjoy all the rights set forth in this Declaration. All children, without any exception whatsoever, shall be entitled to these rights, without

distinction or discrimination on account of race, colour, sex, language, religion, political or other opinion, national or social origin, property, birth or other status, whether of himself or of his family.

Principle 2:
The child shall enjoy special protection, and shall be given opportunities and facilities, by law and by other means, to enable him to develop physically, mentally, morally, spiritually and socially in a healthy and normal manner and in conditions of freedom and dignity. In the enactment of laws for this purpose the best interests of the child shall be the paramount consideration.

Principle 3:
The child shall be entitled from his birth to a name and a nationality.

Principle 4:
The child shall enjoy the benefits of social security. He shall be entitled to grow and develop in health; to this end special care and protection shall be provided both to him and to his mother, including adequate pre-natal and post-natal care. The child shall have the right to adequate nutrition, housing, recreation and medical services.

Principle 5:
The child who is physically, mentally or socially handicapped shall be given the special treatment, education and care required by his particular condition.

Principle 6:
The child, for the full and harmonious development of his personality, needs love and understanding. He shall, wherever possible, grow up in the care and under the responsibility of his parents, and in any case in an atmosphere of affection and of moral and material security; a child of tender years shall not, save in exceptional circumstances, be separated from his mother. Society and the public authorities shall have the duty to extend particular care to children without a family and to those without adequate means of support. Payment of state and other assistance toward the maintenance of children of large families is desirable.

Principle 7:
The child is entitled to receive education, which shall be free and compulsory, at least in the elementary stages. He shall be given an education which will promote his general culture, and enable him on a basis of equal opportunity to develop his abilities, his individual judgment, and his sense of moral and social responsibility, and to become a useful member of society.

The best interests of the child shall be the guiding principle of those responsible for his education and guidance; that responsibility lies in the first place with his parents.

The child shall have full opportunity for play and recreation, which should be directed towards the same purposes as education; society and the public authorities shall endeavour to promote the enjoyment of this right.

Principle 8:
The child shall in all circumstances be among the first to receive protection and relief.

Principle 9:
The child shall be protected against all forms of neglect, cruelty and exploitation. He shall not be the subject of traffic, in any form.

The child shall not be admitted to employment before an appropriate minimum age; he shall in no case be caused or permitted to engage in any occupation or employment which would prejudice his health or education, or interfere with his physical, mental or moral development.

Principle 10:
The child shall be protected from practices which may foster racial, religious and any other form of discrimination. He shall be brought up in a spirit of understanding, tolerance, friendship among peoples, peace and universal brotherhood and in full consciousness that his energy and talents should be devoted to the service of his fellow men.

APPENDIX XIX

The Bill of Rights of Children in Divorce Actions (1966)

Assembled by the Family Court Judges of Milwaukee, Wisconsin, USA, in 1966

I. The right to be treated as an interested and affected person and not as a pawn, possession or chattel of either or both parents.
II. The right to grow to maturity in that home environment which will best guarantee an opportunity for the child to grow to mature and responsible citizenship.
III. The right to the day by day love, care, discipline and protection of the parent having custody of the children.
IV. The right to know the non-custodian parent and to have the benefit of such parent's love and guidance through adequate visitations.
V. The right to a positive and constructive relationship with both parents, with neither parent to be permitted to degrade or downgrade the other in the mind of the child.
VI. The right to have moral and ethical values developed by precept and practices and to have limits set for behaviour so that the child early in life may develop self-discipline and self-control.
VII. The right to the most adequate level of economic support that can be provided by the best efforts of both parents.
VIII. The right to the same opportunities for education that the child would have had if the family unit had not been broken.
IX. The right to periodic review of custodial arrangements and child support orders as the circumstances of the parents and the benefit of the child may require.
X. The right to recognition that children involved in a divorce are always disadvantaged parties and that the law must take affirmative steps to protect their welfare, including, where indicated, a social investigation to determine, and the appointment of a guardian *ad litem* to protect their interests.

APPENDIX XX

Children's Bill of Rights of the Dane County Family Court Counselling Services (Sine anno)

As they proceed with the process of dissolving their adult relationship, both parents recognize and acknowledge the following minimum rights of their children:

1. Right to a continuing relationship with both parents.
2. Right to be treated as an important human being with unique feelings, ideas and desires.
3. Right to continuing care and guidance from both parents.
4. Right to know and appreciate what is good in each parent without one parent degrading the other.
5. Right to express love, affection and respect for each parent without having to stifle that love because of fear of disapproval by the other parent.
6. Right to know that the parents' decision to divorce was not the responsibility of the child.
7. Right not to be a source of argument between the parents.
8. Right to honest answers to questions about the changing family relationships.
9. Right to be able to experience regular and consistent contact with both parents and to know the reason for cancelation of time or change of plans.
10. Right to have a relaxed, secure relationship with both parents without being placed in a position to manipulate one parent against the other.

APPENDIX XXI

Rights of Children, Formulated by The Joint Commission on Mental Health of Children (1969)

Challenge for the 1970s
We believe that lives which are uprooted, thwarted, and denied the growth of their inherent capacities are mentally unhealthy, as are those determined by rigidity, conformity, deprivation, impulsivity, and hostility. Unfulfilled lives cost us twice – once in the loss of human resources, in the apathetic, unhappy, frustrated, and violent souls in our midst, and again in the loss of productivity to our society, and the economic costs of dependency. We believe that, if we are to optimize the mental health of our young and if we are to develop our human resources, every infant must be granted:

The right to be wanted,
yet millions of unwanted children continue to be born – often with tragic consequences – largely because their parents have not had access to or knowledge of the benefits of birth control information and devices.

The right to be born healthy,
yet approximately 1,000,000 children will be born this year to women who get no medical aid during their pregnancy or no adequate obstetrical care for delivery; thus many will be born with brain damage from disorders of pregnancy. For some, protein and vitamin supplements might have prevented such tragedy.

The right to live in a healthy environment,
yet thousands of children and youth become physically handicapped or acquire chronic damage to their health from preventable accidents and diseases, largely because of impoverished environments. Even greater numbers living in poverty will become psychologically handicapped and damaged, unable to compete in school or on a job or to fulfil their inherent capabilities – they will become dependents of, rather than contributors to, our society.

The right to satisfaction of basic needs,
yet approximately one-fourth of our children face the probability of malnutrition, inadequate housing, untreated physical and mental disorders, educational handicaps, and indoctrination into a life of marginal work and opportunity.

The right to continuous loving care,
yet millions of our young never acquire the necessary motivation or intellectual and emotional skills required to cope effectively in our society because they do not receive consistent emotionally satisfying care. Society does little to help parents. There are few programs which provide good day care, which aid in developing more adequate child-rearing techniques, or which assist in times of temporary family crisis or where children are neglected or abused.

The right to acquire the intellectual and emotional skills necessary to achieve individual aspirations and to cope effectively in our society,
yet each year almost 1,000,000 of our youth drop out of school and enter the adult world with inadequate skills and with diminished chances of becoming productive citizens; countless others are denied the opportunities to develop to their fullest potential through effective vocational training, meaningful work experiences, or higher education. For all of our children and youth the transition to adulthood is made difficult. We fail to provide avenues for learning adult roles and for acquiring leadership skills or some approved means by which youths' voice can influence a world in which they too must live.

We know that when these rights are granted, development will proceed favourably for most infants. Few children, however, encounter continuously those ideal circumstances that maximize their hereditary potential for health, competence, and humanity. At conception, at birth, and throughout development there are vast variations and inequalities in the life chances of our young. Undoubtedly many will continue to be psychologically damaged. If our more unfortunate are to become functioning and productive citizens, we believe they must be granted:

The right to receive care and treatment through facilities which are appropriate to their needs and which keep them as closely as possible within their normal social setting,
yet several millions of our children and youth – the emotionally disturbed, the mentally ill, the mentally retarded, the handicapped, and the delinquent – are not receiving such care. The reasons are innumerable. Many go untreated because the services are fragmented, or non-existent, or because they discriminate by cost, class, or colour. Other young people are diagnosed and

labelled without regard to their level of functioning. They are removed from their homes, schools, and communities and confined to hospital wards with psychotic adults or to depersonalized institutions which deliver little more than custodial care.

APPENDIX XXII

Children's Bill of Rights, Formulated by the White House Conference on Children and Youth (1970)

I. The right to grow in a society which respects the dignity of life and is free of poverty, discrimination, and other forms of degradation.
II. The right to be born and be healthy and wanted through childhood.
III. The right to grow up nurtured by affectionate parents.
IV. The right to be a child during childhood, to have meaningful choices in the process of maturation and development, and to have a meaningful voice in the community.
V. The right to be educated to the limits of one's capability and through processes designed to elicit one's full potential.
VI. The right to have societal mechanisms to enforce the foregoing rights.

APPENDIX XXIII

Rights of Youth, Formulated by the White House Conference on Youth (1971)

To the people:
 We are in the midst of a political, social and cultural revolution. Uncontrolled technology and the exploitation of people by people threaten to dehumanize our society. We must reaffirm the recognition of Life as the Supreme Value which will not bear manipulation for other ends.

The approach of the two hundredth anniversary of the Revolution which gave birth to the United States of America leads us to re-examine the foundations of this country. We find that the high ideals upon which this country was ostensibly founded have never been a reality for all peoples from the beginning to the present day. The Constitution itself was both racist and sexist in its conception. The greatest blemish on the history of the United States of America is slavery and its evil legacy. The annihilation of Indians, genocide, exploitation of labour, and militaristic expansion have been among the important short-comings which have undermined the ideals to which the people of this country have aspired.

It is time now finally to affirm and implement the rights articulated in the Declaration of Independence and the Constitution. Each individual must be given the full rights of life, liberty, and the pursuit of happiness, the Bill of Rights must be reinterpreted so as to be meaningful to all persons in our society. In addition the following rights are crucial:

- The Right to adequate food, clothing, and a decent home.
- The Right of the individual to do her/his thing, so long as it does not interfere with the rights of another.
- The Right to preserve and cultivate ethnic and cultural heritages.
- The Right to do whatever is necessary to preserve these Rights.

Governments and nation-states are created to secure and protect these rights. Through the acquiescence of its citizenry the government and other power structures of this nation have not fulfilled their responsibilities to the people, seeming instead to be concerned primarily with their self-perpetuation through serving the interests of the powerful at the expense of the people. In so far as any branch, agency, or member of the government or other power structure neglects its responsibility, it forfeits its legitimacy. We proclaim the following grievances:

- Denial of equal opportunity has led to privation in the midst of plenty.
- Repression has denied the free exercise of political rights in a "free society".
- The system of justice lacks legitimacy for vast segments of the people, particularly minority groups and the poor.
- Free cultural expression is discouraged in a supposedly pluralistic society.
- Appeals to chauvinism, nationalism and militarism smother the individual's right to conscientious free choice of action and belief.
- A war which is abhorrent to the majority of Americans and which inflicts inestimable anguish on a foreign people continues.
- The government and the people have allowed economic and political power to be concentrated in institutions which are not responsive or answerable to the people, resulting in the waste and destruction of human and natural resources, and the failure to meet the people's needs.
- The fear of youth identifying with adults and vice-versa, the fear of people identifying with themselves, the fear of people identifying with their race, the fear of people identifying with a country – all create a climate of fear which permeates this nation.
- Internal divisiveness has contributed to a loss of national purpose.

APPENDIX XXIV

The Draft Charter of Children's Rights of the British Magazine 'Where' (1971)

PART ONE: LAYING THE FOUNDATIONS FOR ADULT LIFE

Every child, girl or boy, has the right from birth, irrespective of income, social class, domicile, race, religion, physical or mental endowment, to:

1. love from the family, to secure normal development and the natural growth of independence,
2. education,
3. food nourishing enough to promote vitality,
4. adequate sleep,
5. warmth,
6. tranquillity and privacy,
7. free association with other children,
8. space to play in,
9. space to explore,
10. access to toys and books that will deepen and widen experience,
11. access to excursions outside the home that will deepen and widen experience,
12. respect from society for one's parents,

PART TWO: CHILDREN'S SPECIAL NEED FOR PROTECTION

All children have the special right of shelter or protection from psychological or social exploitation by adults, or those in authority, during the vulnerable years of transition from infancy to maturity. They also need to be protected from the danger of harming themselves through ignorance or lack of experience and foresight.

All succeeding paragraphs must be read in the light of this section.

PART THREE: THE SPECTRUM OF RIGHTS

1. All children have the right to protection from, and compensation for, the consequences of any inadequacies in their homes and backgrounds.
2. Children have the right to protection from any excessive claims made on them by their parents or others in authority over them. In particular, no one shall have the power to infringe a child's rights.
3. Children have the right to freedom from religious or political indoctrination.
4. No child shall be discriminated against by any person on any grounds whatsoever, including race, sex, religion, ability or any other physical or mental characteristic over which the child has no control.
5. All children are entitled to freedom of association both within school and outside.
6. Children have a right to freedom of expression, both written and verbal. They have the right to publish their opinions on any matter whatsoever.
7. Children shall have freedom of access to suitably trained and appointed people to whom they can take complaints and grievances. They shall have the freedom to make complaints about teachers, parents and others, without fear of reprisal.
8. Children have a right to exercise choice in the school curriculum. Such choice should grow as the child matures.
9. A child's personal appearance is his own and his family's concern. No child shall be deprived of any right or benefit as a consequence of his mode of dress, style of hair, make-up or any other aspect of dress or appearance.
10. Children shall have freedom of movement.
11. Every child shall have the freedom to play a full part in his choice of school.
12. Children shall have freedom from physical assault, whether under the guise of punishment or in any other form. No person shall have the right to subject a child to such punishment as is intended to mentally or physically humiliate the child, or to reduce his self-respect.
14. Children have the right to engage in paid employment appropriate to their years. But no person shall have the right to compel a child to enter employment against his will.
15. Children have the right, at the appropriate age, to such knowledge as is necessary to understand the society in which they live. This shall include knowledge of sex, contraception, religion, drugs including

alcohol and tobacco, and other problems which openly confront every growing child.

Part Four: Others Have Rights Also

The exercise of these rights by children is to be on the terms of their equality with others, whether peers or adults. Other than children's additional right to special protection during their vulnerable years, their rights are no greater than the rights of others, and no less. At no stage shall any individual child's rights infringe or restrict the rights of any other individual. Children's rights are no different in nature, nor do they demand any different kind of interpretation than is applied to the rights of adults.

Part Five: The Duty to Inform

Every child has the right to know his rights.

APPENDIX XXV

A Bill of Rights for Children, Proposed by Henry Foster and Doris Freed (1972)

A child has a moral right and should have a legal right:

1. to receive parental love and affection, discipline and guidance, and to grow to maturity in a home environment which enables him to develop into a mature and responsible adult;
2. to be supported, maintained, and educated to the best of parental ability, in return for which he has the moral duty to honour his father and mother;
3. to be regarded as a person, within the family, at school, and before the law;
4. to receive fair treatment from all in authority;
5. to be heard and listened to;
6. to earn and keep his own earnings;
7. to seek and obtain medical care and treatment and counselling;
8. to emancipation from the parent-child relationship when that relationship has broken down and the child has left home due to abuse, neglect, serious family conflict, or other sufficient cause, and his best interests would be served by the termination of parental authority;
9. to be free of legal disabilities or incapacities save where such are convincingly shown to be necessary and protective of the actual best interests of the child; and
10. to receive special care, consideration, and protection in the administration of law or justice so that his best interests always are a paramount factor.

APPENDIX XXVI

A Bill of Rights for Foster Children (1973)

Even more than for other children, society has a responsibility along with parents for the well-being of foster children. Citizens are responsible for acting to insure their welfare.

Every foster child is endowed with the rights inherently belonging to all children. In addition, because of the temporary or permanent separation from and loss of parents and other family members, the foster child requires special safeguards, resources, and care.

Every Foster Child has the Inherent Rights:

Article I

To be cherished by a family of his own, either his family helped by readily available services and supports to reassume his care, or an adoptive family or by plan, a continuing foster family.

Article II

To be nurtured by foster parents who have been selected to meet his individual needs and who are provided services and supports, including specialized education, so that they can grow in their ability to enable the child to reach his potential.

Article III

To receive sensitive, continuing help in understanding and accepting the reasons for his own family's inability to take care of him, and in developing confidence in his own self-worth.

Article IV

To receive continuing loving care and respect as a unique human being – a child growing in trust in himself and others.

Article V

To grow up in freedom and dignity in a neighbourhood of people who accept him with understanding, respect and friendship.

Article VI

To receive help in overcoming deprivation or whatever distortion in his emotional, physical, intellectual, social and spiritual growth may have resulted from his early experiences.

Article VII

To receive education, training, and career guidance to prepare him for a useful and satisfying life.

Article VIII

To receive preparation for citizenship and parenthood through interaction with foster parents and other adults who are consistent role models.

Article IX

To be represented by an attorney at law in administrative or judicial proceedings with access to fair hearings and court review of decisions, so that his best interests are safeguarded.

Article X

To receive a high quality of child welfare services, including involvement of the natural parents and his own involvement in major decisions that affect his life.

APPENDIX XXVII

Bill of Rights for Juveniles (1973)

New York State Division for Youth, December 7th, 1973

Section I: Introduction

In recognition of the fact that juveniles residing in Division for Youth facilities have certain basic rights which are not lost or made negotiable by the fact of their institutionalization, the division herein commences listing specific inalienable rights applicable to all children in our care.

Section II: Dress Code

(a) Students have the right to wear their personal clothing if they so choose, or wear combinations of their own clothing and clothing issued by the Division in cases where their own clothing does not meet all of their clothing needs.
(b) Clothing issued by the Division shall be available to those children lacking personal clothing or who choose to wear issued clothing.
(c) Students have the right to wear items of jewellery.
(d) Students may be prohibited from possessing items of clothing or jewellery which could be utilized in such a way as to endanger themselves or others; however, such restrictions are to be reasonable.
(e) Students have the obligation to follow the same criteria of cleanliness for their own clothing as is required for issued clothing, and any student who violates his obligation, may lose his right to wear the item or items of personal clothing not kept in a clean condition.
(f) The Division has the obligation to provide students with reasonable means of cleaning their personal clothing.
(g) Development of self-esteem and individuality through interest in appearance and grooming is to be encouraged.

Section III: Personal Appearance

(a) *Hair Style*: Restrictions on the right of students to determine the length and style of their hair is prohibited, except in individual cases where such restrictions are necessary for reasons of health.
(b) *Facial Hair*: Restrictions on the right of students to grow facial hair are prohibited, except in individual cases where such restrictions are necessary for reasons of health.
(c) *Health and Safety*: Students may be required to observe reasonable precautions where the length and style of their hair could possibly pose a health or safety problem unless said precautions are taken.
(d) *Prior Approval*: Where the involuntary removal of a student's hair is determined advisable for reasons of health, the superintendent or director of the facility involved shall make a written request to the facility's middle manager, with a copy to the facility's ombudsman, stating the reasons necessitating such removal and shall not proceed until approval for such action is received.

Section IV: Religious Freedom

(a) The Division has the obligation to afford its students the right to participate in the religious observances of their parents's faith.
(b) Counselling to members of their faith by authorized representatives of religious denominations is permissible at all Division facilities.
(c) The use of physical force, punishment or coercion to compel attendance or participation in religious observances is prohibited.

Section V: Mail Censorship

(a) A student has the unrestricted right to send mail without prior censorship or prior reading.
(b) A student has the right to receive mail without prior reading or prior censorship; however, if the institution suspects the delivery of contraband or cash, it may require the student to open the mail in the presence of a staff member.
(c) A student has the right to mail a minimum of one letter per week at State expense and any number of additional letters at his own expense.
(d) All cash sent to students shall be given to the student or held for his benefit in accordance with the procedures of the institution; however, such procedures shall be in writing and approved by the director of his designee.
(e) Packages are exempt from these provisions and are subject to inspection.

APPENDIX XXVIII

ILO Convention Concerning Minimum Age for Admission to Employment (1973)

International Labour Conference, Convention 138 (1973)
  The General Conference of the International Labour Organisation,
  Having been convened at Geneva by the Governing Body of the International Labour Office, and having met in its Fifty-eighth Session on 6 June 1973, and
  Having decided upon the adoption of certain proposals with regard to minimum age for admission to employment, which is the fourth item on the agenda of the session, and
  Noting the terms of the Minimum Age (Industry) Convention, 1919, the Minimum Age (Sea) Convention, 1920, the Minimum Age (Agriculture) Convention, 1921, the Minimum Age (Trimmers and Stokers) Convention, 1921, the Minimum Age (Non-Industrial Employment) Convention, 1932, the Minimum Age (Sea) Convention (Revised), 1936, the Minimum Age (Industry) Convention (Revised), 1937, the Minimum Age (Non-Industrial Employment) Convention (Revised), 1937, the Minimum Age (Fishermen) Convention, 1959, and the Minimum Age (Underground Work) Convention, 1965, and
  Considering that the time has come to establish a general instrument on the subject, which would gradually replace the existing ones applicable to limited economic sectors, with a view to achieving the total abolition of child labour, and
  Having determined that this instrument shall take the form of an international Convention,
  adopts this twenty-sixth day of June of the year one thousand nine hundred and seventy-three the following Convention, which may be cited as the Minimum Age Convention, 1973:

ARTICLE 1.

Each Member for which this Convention is in force undertakes to pursue a national policy designed to ensure the effective abolition of child labour and

APPENDIX XXIX

The Children and Youth Bill of Rights of the NASW (1975)

Policy Statement, approved by the 1975 Delegate Assembly of the National Association of Social Workers (NASW) of the United States.

BACKGROUND

Historically, children have been considered as property. Early laws governing the relationship between parents and children relegated children to little more than chattel. Nineteenth-century reformers challenged this philosophy and initiated legislation to protect children from undue hardship and to provide for their more basic developmental needs. Despite legal advances made on their behalf, however, children too often have remained second-class citizens.

Ironically, legislation intended to protect the rights of children often has had the opposite effect. Lacking legal parity with adults, children frequently have, in the words of former Supreme Court Justice Abe Fortas, received "the worst of both worlds: . . . neither the protection accorded to adults nor the solicitous care and regenerative treatment postulated for children."

It is essential that public social policy recognize children as individuals with rights, including the right to be part of a family. The well-being of children is advanced most frequently by public social policy that supports the well-being of the family. Children's needs as dependent persons requiring nurture must be reconciled with the protection of children's basic human rights and civil liberties. The guarantee of such protection should not deny children greater participation in society. In the past, basic rights extended for adults have not applied to children. This has resulted in circumstances of gross injustice and isolation. Children should not be kept infants until sudden adulthood. Rather, emancipation from dependence should be a gradual process from greater protection to greater participation and responsibility at key stages of maturity.

Policy Statement

The Right to Sound Preparation for Life. Children are entitled to a good beginning. Such preparation is based on being wanted and cared for and should include adequate family planning to assist potential parents to decide when it is best for them to have a child. Potential parents should have access to genetic information to evaluate the probabilities of transmitting hereditary diseases. Sound preparation also should include the right to adequate prenatal care and protection from trauma during the birth process.

The Right to Individuality. Children have the right to be children. They should be given the opportunity to be spontaneous and curious and should have the right to play, as a foundation for the development of mastery and competence.

The Right to a Positive Social Identity. Law should consider children as persons, not as property. Children have the right to develop a positive social identity. Identity as a person should include pride in racial and ethnic characteristics, family and national culture, and unique and individual differences. Such identity can be achieved only when the child is free from discrimination because of racial or ethnic origins, language, political or social origins, sexual orientation, or origin of birth. Children should be permitted to express such individuality by exercising the right to speak other than English freely and without derision; to express social and ethnic characteristics in dress; and, when age-appropriate, should have freedom to choose their religion, including the option to choose none.

The Right to a Good Parenting Experience. Every child has a right to continuous nurturing care and consistent parental controls and expectations. This right is based on the expectations that parents receive sufficient preparation and support in family living so that the family experience can be conducive to healthy development. When that decision is to be made about who the child's parents may be, the child is entitled to participate in the decision, appropriate to his or her age and the capacity to understand the situation. The child's family should be determined by the child's psychological parents, who may or may not be the biological or legal parents and who may not necessarily have current physical or legal custody. Family status should not be determined by arbitrary community definitions of adequate parents. This does not deny the rights of natural parents.

The Right to a Healthy Environment. The child should have access to the following rights of all persons: freedom from want, adequate housing, safety, and security. Children should receive environmental supports conducive to health and development. Children should have freedom from pollution of air, water, and food. Provisions of recreational space and beautification of the environment are vital to aesthetic development and to a sense of respect for self, other persons, and the environment.

The Right to Health. Children have a right to total health care at all critical stages of development from conception to maturity. They have the right to adequate nutrition and to health care to prevent and treat potentially handicapping diseases and disabilities. Comprehensive care includes care appropriate to various age categories, physical and mental health care, and information about their own bodies.

The Right to a Relevant Education. Children should be guaranteed access to high-quality education from pre-school to maturity to develop to their fullest potential. They should have access to education regardless of residence, race, physical or mental health handicap, or social class. Such education shall meet the standards of sufficient preparation for maturity, employment, parenthood, and citizenship in a changing and complex society. Education is a highly individualized process within which each child has the right to participate in the design of his or her learning experience. Atypical children must have opportunities geared to their specific needs, including the opportunity to participate with normal children to the maximum of their ability.

The Right to Participatory Citizenship. Children have the right to a socially recognized and sanctioned role in society. Responsible participation by children in society includes opportunities for interaction between generations that contribute to the development of self-identity, acquisition of roles, and career possibilities. Gradual age-appropriate participation in social institutions that affect their lives provides developing individuals with preparatory experiences in citizenship.

The Right to Representation. Children have the right to have their interests represented by children and youths on decision-making bodies that directly affect their lives. Although adult advocates or representatives appropriately may continue efforts on behalf of children, they are not a substitute for representatives who are, themselves, minors. Children and youths, within reasonable limits of age and personal competence, as is true of the adult population, are entitled and able to be representatives of other minors. The process of selection and representational procedures to encourage competence building should be observed. Whenever possible, such representation should include voting power on school boards, city planning councils, health and social service boards, legislative panels, and task forces at every level of government.

The Right to Legal Status, Legal Protection, and Legal Redress. Children shall have all the safeguards and protections of due process guaranteed to adults by the Fourteenth Amendment to the Constitution, the Bill of Rights, and statutory law. These safeguards include the right to protection from physical and psychological grievances against parents and social institutions that are damaging or interfering with their welfare or rights. Children have the right to appropriate representation in judicial and quasi-judicial proceedings, including custody proceedings, in which their interests may be affected directly.

Children should have freedom from incarceration for offenses that, if committed by an adult, would not be considered criminal acts; freedom from incarceration with adult offenders; and freedom from incarceration beyond minimum length and conditions necessary for their safety and the safety of others. Children should have the same right to privacy and confidentiality afforded to adults, in addition to special provisions to protect minors.

The Right to Services. Children who are dependent on society for care and protection or who have special needs must be given the opportunity to achieve the highest level of social functioning of which they are capable. Services must be mandated legislatively, with input from knowledgeable citizens and professionals. A comprehensive, integrated system of services must be established for families with children and for children separated from their families.

The Right to Advocacy. Children must have effective advocacy services to ensure that they will be guaranteed full benefit of the legal rights established by our society for the protection and well-being of all citizens, adult or children.

Reprinted with permission from *Social Work Speaks*: *NASW Policy Statements*, June 1988, pp. 20–21. Copyright 1988, National Association of Social Workers, Inc.

APPENDIX XXX

Ten Commandments for Adults by Professor Leonhard Froese (Marburg, West Germany, 1979)

I. Thou shalt regard the child as the highest good ever entrusted to you.
II. Thou shalt not form the child in thine own image.
III. Thou shalt give the child more freedom.
IV. Thou shalt respect the child's personality.
V. Thou shalt not use force against the child.
VI. Thou shalt not destroy the confidence of a child.
VII. Thou shalt protect the child against death.
VIII. Thou shalt not tempt a child to lie.
IX. Thou shalt recognize what a child needs.
X. Thou shalt grant the child its own right.

APPENDIX XXXI

Declaration of the Psychological Rights of the Child (1979)

Adopted by the International Association of School Psychologists on July 12, 1979.

AREA I: LOVE AND FREEDOM FROM FEAR

Right I: The right to love, affection, and understanding.
Right II: The right to freedom from fear of psychological and physical harm or abuse.
Right III: The right to protection and advocacy.

AREA II: PERSONAL, SPIRITUAL, AND SOCIAL DEVELOPMENT

Right IV: The right to personal identity and independence and the freedom to express these.
Right V: The right to opportunities for spiritual and moral development.
Right VI: The right to satisfying interpersonal relationships and responsible group membership.

AREA III: THE RIGHT TO EDUCATION AND PLAY.

Right VII: The right to formal and informal education and necessary special resources.
Right VIII: The right to full opportunity for play, recreation, and fantasy.
Right IX: The right to optimum physical and psychological development and the encouragement toward this.

APPENDIX XXXII

Declaration of the Rights of Mozambican Children (1979)

First – You, the children, are the ones who will carry on the Revolution. You are the hope of the future that shines in your smiles when you are happy. You are the guarantees of our socialist nation. Socialism means justice, means every citizen having the same rights and duties. What is written here is that every child has the same rights.

Second – You have the right to grow up in a climate of peace and security, surrounded by love and understanding.

Third – You have the right to live in a family. You have the right to a name, so that your parents, brothers and sisters and friends can call you and so that you can be known wherever you are. If you do not have your own family, you have the right to live in a family that loves you like their own child.

Fourth – In order to grow up strong and healthy, you have the right to be fed, sheltered, clothed and educated by your family. You have the right to play and to practise sports, so that your body develops full of health and energy.

Fifth – You have the right to receive an education so that you will become a citizen of tomorrow. You have the right to know about the world in which you are living and how to transform it, to know the history and culture of your people, to learn to master science and technology. Your school should teach you to understand the world in a scientific and revolutionary way, and to know and love your country and all the peoples of the world.

Sixth – You have the right to an education so that when you are grown up you can fulfil your duty of serving the people. You have the right to be educated to respect work, to respect the people's property, and to participate in production.

Seventh – The kindergartens, where you learn and play with children of your age, and the schools, are mainly for you. We will steadily increase their number so that they can have room for every child in the country.

Eighth – You have the right to protection of your health, to live in a healthy environment, to have a good diet, to be taught how to defend yourself against illness. When you are ill you have the right to be treated with the best of medical care, and with tenderness and affection.

Ninth – You have the right not to be submitted to initiation rites, premature marriage or brideprice. They are against the principles of our Revolution. You have the right not to be employed or engaged in activities that harm your health, your education, your physical development or your brain.

Tenth – You have the right to have the mistakes you make explained so that you understand and do not repeat them. You have the right not to be subjected to violence and ill treatment.

Eleventh – In dangerous situations, you have the right to be among the first to receive help and protection.

Twelfth – So that you can begin to take part in the Revolution, and so that you can learn to live in an organized way and get to know other children like yourselves, you have the right to take part in the Organization of Mozambican Pioneers.

APPENDIX XXXIII

The Malta Declaration of the Child's Right to Play (1977)

(Of the International Playground Association, November 1977)

The Malta Consultation declares that play, along with the basic needs of nutrition, health, shelter and education, is vital for the development of the potential of all children.

The child is the foundation for the world's future

Play is not the mere passing of time. Play is life. It is instinctive. It is voluntary. It is spontaneous. It is natural. It is exploratory. It is communication. It is expression. It combines action and thought. It gives satisfaction and a feeling of achievement. Play has occurred at all times throughout history and in all cultures. Play touches all aspects of life. Through play the child develops physically, mentally, emotionally and socially. Play is a means of learning to live.

The Consultation is extremely concerned by a number of alarming trends, such as:

* Society's indifference to the importance of play.
* The over-emphasis on academic studies in schools.
* The de-humanising of settlements, inappropriate housing forms, such as high-rise, inadequate environmental planning and bad traffic management.
* The increasing commercial exploitation of children through mass communication, mass production, leading to the deterioration of individual values and cultural traditions.
* The inadequate preparation of children to live in a rapidly changing society.

Proposals for Action

Health: Play is essential for the physical and mental health of the child
* Establish programmes for professionals and parents about the benefits of play from birth onwards.

* Incorporate play into community programmes designed to maintain the child's health.
* Promote play as an integral part of the treatment plan for children in hospitals and other settings.

Education: *Play is part of education for life*
* Provide opportunities for initiative, interaction, creativity and socialisation in the formal education system.
* Include the study of the importance of play in the training of all professionals working with or for children.
* Involve schools, colleges and public buildings in the life of the community and permit fuller use of these buildings and facilities.

Welfare: *Play is an essential part of family and community welfare*
* Promote measures that strengthen the close relationship between parent and child.
* Ensure that play is accepted as an integral part of social development and social care.
* Provide community based services of which play is a part in order to foster the acceptance of children with handicaps as full members of the community so that no child, whether for physical, mental or emotional reasons shall be detained in an institution.

Leisure: *The child needs time to play*
* Provide the space and adequate free time for children to choose and develop individual and group interests.
* Encourage more people from different backgrounds and ages to be involved with children.
* Stop the commercial exploitation of children's play e.g. manipulative advertising, war toys and violence in entertainment.

Planning: *The child must have priority in the planning of human settlements*
* Give priority to the child in existing and projected human settlements in view of the child's great vulnerability, small size and limited range of activity.
* Ban immediately the building of all high-rise housing and take urgent steps to mitigate the effect of existing developments on children.
* Take steps to enable the child to move about the community in safety by providing traffic segregation, improved public transportation and better traffic management.

The Malta Consultation

- Believing firmly that the International Year of the Child will provide opportunities to arouse world opinion for the improvement of the life of the child,
- Affirming its belief in the United Nations' Declaration of the Rights of the Child,
- Acknowledging that each country is responsible for preparing its own sources of action in the light of its culture, climate and social, political and economic structure,
- Recognizing that the full participation of people is essential in planning and developing programmes and services for children to meet their needs, wishes and aspirations,
- Assuring its co-operation with other international organisations involved with children,

Appeals to all countries and organisations to consider seriously the implementation of measures to reverse the alarming trends, some of which are identified in this statement, and to place high on its list of priorities the development of long term programmes to ensure for all time *The Child's Right to Play*.

APPENDIX XXXIV

ICFTU Youth Charter (1983)

Adopted in 1983 in Oslo at the Thirteenth World Congress of the International Confederation of Free Trade Unions

A. Preamble

Among the workers represented by the ICFTU throughout the world, the proportion of young workers is steadily increasing. This is why the ICFTU has set itself – among its important tasks in the framework of its constant and general struggle for the emancipation of the working class – the tasks of solving the economic, social and cultural problems which young workers have to face, and of fighting for the rights and improvement of conditions of young workers whether they are already at work or in the training process.

By establishing its Youth Section, the ICFTU has shown its determination to support this work on behalf of the world's young workers. Moreover, by intensifying its action in favour of young workers, the ICFTU also aims at contributing to the achievement of another permanent objective of the international free trade union movement; the strengthening of our movement through the active involvement of young trade unionists in this work. The following programme is intended to form a basis for future activities. It is based on the very principles of the defence of human dignity and the rights and living standards of workers, as laid down in the Universal Declaration of Human Rights and in the Constitution of the ICFTU.

The ICFTU, assisted by its Youth Committee, will pursue the following general objectives in its programme of work in favour of young workers:

* to promote the organisation of young workers in developing countries;
* to organise trade union education and training programmes for young workers;
* to promote the implementation of field projects of a social-economic nature aimed at alleviating the problems of young workers in developing countries;

* to encourage the participation of trade union youth in population education activities;
* to contribute to the action-oriented examination of specific problems of young workers;
* to propagate the contents of the ICFTU Youth Charter;
* to encourage in a general way, activities which may contribute to the strengthening of international solidarity amongst the trade union youth at world level;
* to represent the views and interests of the international trade union movement at youth events organised by the UN, its specialised agencies and other international bodies;
* to encourage the full participation of young trade unionists in the work of the ICFTU towards the establishment of peace, security and disarmament;
* to promote equal rights and opportunities for male and female youngsters by setting up a positive programme for young women.

For the implementation of the demands put forward in this Charter, the different degrees of industrial development in the individual countries must be taken into consideration. The programme establishes long-term aims common to all free trade unions, and starts from the premise that the internationally recognised human rights must be safeguarded in all countries – without distinction on the grounds of race, sex, religion or ideology – as the basis of free and democratic development.

On behalf of young workers organised in the free trade unions, the ICFTU calls on all of its affiliated organisations and on other friendly trade union bodies and their associated political forces to do everything in their power to implement this programme to further the interests of young workers, trainees and students. The ICFTU affiliates are requested to promote active youth work as an integral part of their organisations, and to guarantee that the necessary support be made available. We also appeal to all governments and international organisations to undertake action within their respective spheres of competence to meet, in a true spirit of social justice, the just demands of young people in employment or undergoing training.

The ICFTU recognises that the fulfilment of this programme must be based upon the establishment and support of free and democratic trade unions for the protection of workers' rights, and for the achievement of an international society of peace, liberty and progress, free from all forms of colonialism and exploitation, and accordingly we support all efforts to achieve these goals. Along these lines, the international free trade union movement calls upon all youth organisations to fight side by side with it for the realisation of this Charter for young workers.

B. Programme of Demands

1. *The right of freedom of association*

Every person must be guaranteed the right to freedom of association and a free choice to join a youth movement. Freedom of opinion, as laid down in the Universal Declaration of Human Rights, must also be guaranteed. No disadvantage must arise for young people as a result of joining trade unions.

2. *Education*

Education at all levels should be provided for all young people, according to their own free choice and irrespective of their social origin or material possibilities. It must aim at promoting the development of each individual's abilities and his interest in social and political affairs from youth onwards so as to foster a democratic attitude towards life, and in order to act responsibly and democratically in the work-place and society.

Basic literacy (reading, writing and arithmetic) courses must be guaranteed to all young people. Furthermore, the process of educational reforms should take place assuring the inclusion and integration of practical skills into schooling systems, which will prepare young persons for employment. Appropriate skills and practical training should be oriented to the level of national development and aspirations of youth.

The introduction of a system of continuous education should be the main objective of all forces involved in the process of educational reform. Such a system must guarantee, as educational aims, the development of the individual's capabilities, knowledge and insight into society.

Compulsory and free education up to the age of 16 should be considered as an immediate measure in this context.

Vocational guidance designed to enable the individual to make a better choice of occupation should be an integral part of educational programmes.

Free facilities for education and vocational training must be guaranteed by the provision of education grants from public funds, and from industry for industrial training.

3. *The right to training and employment*

In accordance with Article 23 of the Universal Declaration of Human Rights, the ICFTU, representing free and democratic trade unions, claims the right to training and full productive and freely chosen employment for all.

4. *The transition to active employment*

The employment of children under the age of 16 must be forbidden.

Trade unions themselves should have the right and fully utilise possibilities to contact young people in schools and training institutions, in order to assist and inform them on employment conditions and the importance of joining trade unions.

Particular emphasis during the last few years at school should be given to the full preparation of students for employment and for the vocation they have chosen. This should include instruction on the significance, functions and aims of the trade unions.

Vocational guidance must be compulsory, free of charge, free of discrimination, and independent, and should give every possible consideration to the inclinations and capabilities of young people. Schools and vocational guidance bodies must work in close consultation. The transition from school to working life entails re-adjustment for young people and, in this difficult phase of adaptation to the entirely new atmosphere of working life, it is particularly important for trade unions and work councils to assist young workers in facing their problems and represent their interests.

In particular, specific job training schemes for youth should be oriented to ensure continuous and full opportunities for young people in and leaving schools. Schemes should be sufficiently expanded to the extent needed in respective nations in order to eliminate youth unemployment. Schemes should be based on the principle that trainees' and apprentices' time is working time, not only school time, and adequate remuneration as outlined in paragraph 8 should be enforced.

5. *Vocational and advanced vocational training*

The relevant instruments of the International Labour Organisation must be ratified, observed and fully implemented by all governments.

Vocational training systems and programmes must be conceived in the framework of continuous education, which is a right for everyone and which must be based on the needs and possibilities of the workers and not on those of industry and capital. Opportunities for training and retraining must be guaranteed to workers whenever they wish, without any conditions attached, and must involve no financial disadvantages for them.

Vocational training should be carried out in suitable training establishments with adequate facilities. The basic training must be sufficiently comprehensive to facilitate future adaptations to technological change. Where vocational training is given in the undertakings, there should be inspection by independent institutions which include trade union participation, in order to check whether all necessary facilities are provided. For the purpose, uniform guidelines should be established.

Trade unions must have the right to participate fully in the elaboration, formulation and implementation of vocational training programmes. After having received basic vocational training, the workers must be afforded adequate facilities for advanced vocational training to perfect the vocational skills which have been acquired.

Special protective measures must be adopted for apprentices in order to provide them with genuine training possibilities, and to prevent the exploitation of these young people as a cheap and ill-considered labour force. The continuous training of teachers is of crucial importance for the quality of education. Due attention must be given to this factor, in vocational as well as in general education.

6. *Paid educational leave*

Paid educational leave should be recognised, as set out in ILO Convention 140, through legislation or collective agreements as a social right everywhere and for everyone. As an instrument of continuous education, it should be as broad as possible and open to all kinds of education and training required by the individual, so as to accommodate the principle of study and working life in alternation.

7. *Protective labour legislation*

On entry into employment, young workers should undergo a thorough medical examination – free-of-charge – by an independent body with the co-operation of the trade unions, and their general state of health should thereafter be checked at regular intervals. Workers under the age of 18 must not be engaged in work which is dangerous, conducted underground or at night. No worker should be required to perform unsafe or unhealthy work.

Young workers and trainees must be ensured the right to instruction on work safety within vocational training programmes. In addition, there must be comprehensive schemes for health
protection, with adequate occupational health services at plant and local levels.

Suitable controls are to be provided in order to enforce regulations protecting young workers and trainees. Instructions on hygiene requirements and on the prevention of industrial accidents are indispensable.

The relevant ILO Conventions 77 and 78, and Recommendation 79, must be ratified and applied.

8. *Working hours*

Working hours for young people under the age of 18 should not be longer than those of adults, so that young workers under this age are given the best chance to reach physical maturity and develop their personalities in the broadest sense. After an uninterrupted working period of four hours, these should be assured a work break of at least 30 minutes, calculated as working hours.

Young workers should not be subjected to longer working hours than the normal standard, or to overtime work.

Suitable premises for relaxation must be provided for young workers during work-breaks.

Young workers should be guaranteed a continuous weekly leisure period of at least two days.

9. *Remuneration*

The remuneration of young workers must be based on the principle of equal pay for work of equal value, as laid down in ILO Convention 100. Minimum wages for young workers should, in principle, be determined by free collective bargaining with employers. In countries where this system is not sufficient, a social minimum wage should be provided and guaranteed to all workers by law, regardless of age or any other basis of discrimination.

The pay of apprentices and trainees should be based on the principle of equal pay for work of equal value and nature. Pay should be determined in a proper ratio to a skilled worker's wage.

10. *Social insurance*

In cases of unemployment, sickness, industrial accidents and diseases, or other incapacity, young workers should enjoy full social insurance protection. Social insurance protection should also be extended to any dependants of the young insured person.

11. *Holidays*

The annual paid leave entitlement of young workers under 18 should be longer than that of adults, and should amount to at least 36 working days per year.

12. *Leisure*

Adequate leisure time is particularly important to the young workers. It is necessary to provide the young person with the time and necessary facilities needed for relaxation. Suitable facilities must be put at his/her disposal.

The young should have access to all cultural values. They must be provided with more scope for meaningful use of their leisure time, and should have the right to decide for themselves as to its use.

Here an important task falls to the trade unions, which should see to it that the community provides the necessary facilities. Yet the trade unions themselves should:

* promote the formation of youth groups with the unions;
* develop their own cultural work;
* organise events corresponding to the inclination and to the needs of youth;
* ensure that young workers have access to cultural institutions land events, and that every support be granted;
* make young workers aware about the risks related to the use of alcohol, drugs and other products dangerous to their mental and physical health;
* provide facilities offering young people sufficient leisure opportunities;
* promote the study of foreign languages, exchange schemes and meetings, so that the young learn to know and respect each other in a spirit of international friendship; and
* promote social tourism.

13. *Unemployment and underemployment*

The fight against unemployment and underemployment, particularly among young workers, is one of the chief concerns of the free trade unions. The introduction and maintenance of full employment in a free and peaceful world is one of the most important aims of the ICFTU and its affiliated organisations.

The ICFTU fully supports the right of all workers to full, productive and freely chosen employment. The ICFTU continues to pressure governments to adopt employment policies which will provide employment for all who are available for and seeking work, that such employment be as productive as possible, remunerated by a social wage collectively agreed to. Employment should be freely chosen with the fullest possible opportunity for each worker to qualify for and to use his skills and endowments in a job for which he is well suited, irrespective of race, colour, sex, religion, political opinion, national extraction or social origin.

Government policies should ensure full employment and national growth without the exportation of unemployed to other nations.

Youth unemployment, as a particularly distinctive phenomenon, should be combatted at all costs without displacement of employment in other groups, in order to ensure that all school leavers and trainees completing training can obtain employment.

Whenever the labour market situation or other compelling reasons make a change in their occupations unavoidable, young workers must be afforded the opportunity of retraining free of charge.

14. *Young workers in trade unions*

Young people would be introduced into the practical work of the trade union as early as possible and be adequately prepared for their coming tasks as active trade unionists. Special attention should be given to young workers beginning at their work-place, and to those seeking work. To achieve this aim, special membership arrangements should be made. Those young workers who secure employment but subsequently become unemployed, should continue in membership of the union appropriate for that area of employment. Young workers who qualify for employment in a trade or profession should be allowed (associate or student) membership of the appropriate union. Consequently, youth work should be a constituent part of the programme of every union, and find corresponding support.

It is recommended that consideration be given to the creation of possibilities for the expression of youth opinion at all levels of trade union work, on matters affecting the interests of youth.

Furthermore, the formation of youth groups in trade unions should be encouraged, including development of cultural work and the organisation of events corresponding to the aspirations and needs of youth.

It should be recognised that youth work can make a positive contribution to the entrance of new members while making a dynamic contribution to the trade union as a whole.

Young workers organised in the ICFTU call on all young people to assume their part of responsibility and join the trade unions. In the trade union organisation they will find the moral support and the concrete help to achieve the demands contained in this programme and will be able – true to trade union tradition – to contribute in the best way in building up a world of progress, peace and justice.

Young workers in the ICFTU underline the necessity of co-operation and work in the spirit of international solidarity, peace, security and disarmament.

They are profoundly anxious about the threat of arms and armament industry, and call on the ICFTU and all member unions to appeal to the governments concerned and the United Nations to do all that is possible to settle peacefully disputes between countries, avoid wars by implementing the ICFTU policy on peace, security and disarmament.

ICFTU achievements for working youth throughout the world will depend also in future on all affiliated unions working in solidarity. In this respect it will rest with the ICFTU Youth Committee to purposefully represent and to promote the interests of all young workers in keeping within the principles of this Youth Charter in the ICFTU, according to its Rules and its Resolutions.

15. *Young migrant workers*

Measures should be adopted by governments to encourage the integration of young migrant workers into the social life of the nation – young migrant workers, legally residing in a nation, should enjoy effective equality of opportunity and treatment with nationals of the nation concerned. The problem of illegal migration is of great concern. Illegal migration should be brought to a halt. The human rights of the workers should be respected and their situation regularised. Along with all other rights enjoyed by nationals, the ICFTU underlines the right of exercise of the trade union rights and eligibility for office in trade unions and in labour management relations bodies, including bodies representing workers in undertakings.

In any case, the trade union should be in a position to encourage the participation of young migrant workers in trade union life by the following means:

* concentration should be given to organising young migrant workers;
* convincing them that their rights as workers and their working conditions can only be defended in an effective way by the trade unions;
* encouraging and motivating them to participate in trade union training courses;
* leading them to participate in vocational training or guidance courses;
* enabling and motivating them to participate more in the different activities which trade unions organise for these young members and which can range from educational, cultural and sports activities to access to trade union youth centres;
* inviting them to participate more in trade union meetings and seminars;
* extending the migrant workers' service within their organisations in order to be able to intensify their work of help and guidance to these workers on the social and vocational level;
* host countries should provide language training to migrant workers;
* employers using illegal migrant labour should be brought to sanction.

In all these duties, the information element plays an important role.

16. *Military or alternative service*

Compulsory military service wherever it exists should be regarded as a temporary interruption of employment.

Young people must have the right to refuse to do military service on grounds of conscience. In the event of an alternative service being provided, the young people concerned should be called upon to undertake other work of social value.

After completing their military service, young workers must have the right to return to their former employment.

Rights acquired by young persons at the place of work must be maintained during their absence on military service, and their entitlements to social insurance benefits must not be affected by such absence.

All dependants of persons undergoing military or alternative service must continue to enjoy undiminished social insurance protection.

During military or alternative service, a means of ensuring trade union membership, without payment of union dues, should be provided for.

The right of the trade unions to maintain contact with members undergoing military or alternative service should be guaranteed everywhere. The trade unions, for their part, should inform young persons before their period of service about all their rights and obligations in this connection.

17. *Juvenile delinquency*

It can be expected that suitable protection for young people, as well as advice and assistance, will contribute greatly to preventing juvenile delinquency. Juvenile courts and social workers should take a personal interest in juvenile delinquents with a view to guiding and encouraging them, and giving them a chance to become integrated in society. Penal legislation should take into account the degree of maturity of the young criminal offenders and make special provision for their punishment, paying due regard to the need for humane treatment.

For young offenders up to 18, the main emphasis should be on rehabilitation. Even after completion of the punishment, the young person should continue to be cared for.

18. *Marriage*

In conformity with Article 16 of the Universal Declaration of Human Rights, women and men have the right to marry and found a family, regardless of race, nationality or religion. Marriage shall be entered into only with the free and full consent of the future partners.

19. *Age of reaching adulthood*

From the age of 18 onwards, young people should be considered as adults and thus benefit from all the legal and social provisions of that status.

20. *Maternity protection*

The ICFTU programme for maternity protection has been outlined in the ICFTU's Charter on the Rights of Working Women, and is supported by the ICFTU Youth Committee.

21. *Trade union representation*

The trade unions should be represented on all bodies concerned with youth questions, above all on those which deal with vocational problems and social protection for young people.

In view of the particular problems of young workers and trainees, and with the aim of establishing closer relations between young trade union members and their organisations, young people should be given the proper means to take part fully in the work of their trade union organisation at all levels.

National circumstances and union practices should determine the possibility that at plant level, youth elect its own representatives to co-operate with adult representatives in looking after the interests of young workers.

22. *Development and the role of trade union youth*

Hundreds of millions of people continue to live in hunger, poverty, ignorance and disease; similarly, low growth and unemployment threatens the successful implementation of the demands, as set out in the Youth Charter. Trade union youth have a special contribution to make in the question of development.

The role of the trade union youth has been outlined in the ICFTU Development Charter.

23. *Education on development*

The establishment of social justice is a necessary pre-requisite to the creation of any new international economic order. It is essential that young workers – as up-coming generations of leaders – realise and understand the mutual interests between workers in different countries. Work in this field will reinforce the understanding of the role that trade unions can play in society, integrating young workers and assisting youth to obtain training and jobs relevant to national situations; particular stress must be laid upon adequately equipping young workers by educational and technical training. International solidarity action must appropriately assist trade union youth in the developing countries in their development process.

24. *Action for development*

The trade unions must resist the worldwide threat of economic decline, and press governments to adopt co-ordinated action for full employment, economic expansion and a new international economic and social order.

Young workers should orient activities in order to strengthen the growth and principles of free and democratic trade unions around the world. Young workers in the ICFTU should be more involved in training and assistance programmes in developing countries, particularly in helping youth to acquire basic skills and training for employment, while actively propagating the demands of the ICFTU Youth Charter.

APPENDIX XXXV

Charter for Children in Hospital of the National Association for the Welfare of Children in Hospital, NAWCH (1984)

November 19, 1984

1. Children shall be admitted to hospital only if the care they require cannot be equally well provided at home or on a day basis.
2. Children in hospital shall have the right to have their parents with them at all times provided this is in the best interest of the child. Accommodation should therefore be offered to all parents, and they should be helped and encouraged to stay. In order to share in the care of their child, parents should be fully informed about ward routine and their active participation encouraged.
3. Children and/or their parents shall have the right to information appropriate to age and understanding.
4. Children and/or their parents shall have the right to informed participation in all decisions involving their health care. Every child shall be protected from unnecessary medical treatment and steps taken to mitigate physical or emotional distress.
5. Children shall be treated with tact and understanding and at all times their privacy shall be respected.
6. Children shall enjoy the care of appropriately trained staff, fully aware of the physical and emotional needs of each age group.
7. Children shall be able to wear their own clothes and have their own personal possessions.
8. Children shall be cared for with other children of the same age group.
9. Children shall be in an environment furnished and equipped to meet their requirements, and which conforms to recognised standards of safety and supervision.
10. Children shall have full opportunity for play, recreation and education suited to their age and condition.

APPENDIX XXXVI

The Charter on the Rights of the Arab Child of the League of Arab States

In the name of God, most Gracious, most Merciful,

We issue this Charter holding ourselves responsible towards its principles and provisions and taking it as a basis for our policies and efforts in the field of Child Growth and Care.

This Charter has been drafted in pursuit of our religious belief and from the fact that our homeland is the cradle of religions and the homeland of the civilisations and culture expounding the sublime humanitarian principles which have given respect to man, ascertained and insisted on his right to progressive human existence and to decent life inundated with freedom, justice and equality and asserting man's role in society and his existence on earth in general.

Further, it is in pursuit of the practical facts of our factual existence, aspirations for a progressive future and equality for the Arab nations, understanding the fatal challenge comprising the partitions consecrated by Imperialism whose burdensomeness can only be unravelled through unity, economical and social backwardness which can be remedied through comprehensive social and economical development, imperialism in all shapes and kinds the worst of which is the Zionist imperialistic settlement and which cannot be counteracted except with total liberation and cultural and intellectual campaign thus asserting Arab heritage and knowledge. The Charter also takes into account the recognition that our Arab nation did embrace all along its long history certain social characteristics which helped in the advancement of man's civilisation; in addition, we are in the belief that the child of today is the man of tomorrow and the more we give him attention the more we are on the path of glory.

The Charter also speaks about our concern with regard to the future of the Arab nation, continuity of its heritage and walk to unity with the perseverance of its civilisation and historic role. Further, we want to insure the implementation of this Charter is because of our admittance that the efforts exercised for child growth and care in the Arab World are still insufficient and inefficient with regard to the hopes pinned on our children for the future of their nation, taking into account the U.N. Charter, the Universal Declaration of Human Rights, the U.N. Declaration on the Rights of the Child and other international instruments.

Finally, in pursuit of the rules, principles and objectives contained in the Charter of the League of Arab States and its specialised agencies, Arab States Joint Social Work Charter, Arab States Social Work Strategy, Strategy of Arab Education Development, issues by the Arab Summits on joint Arab efforts containing the Arab Economic Work Strategy relating to providing comprehensive protection and care for the Arab child from date of birth until the age of fifteen, this Charter is based on the above-mentioned observations.

THE BASIC PRINCIPLES

The Charter contains the foregoing principles:

A. Basic rules

a. Child care and preservation of children's rights are basic elements of the social development structure and indeed they constitute the essence of the comprehensive development. No doubt, development is the intended civilised change aimed at a happy and prosperous future. Therefore, childhood is the future and its voice and image are vital for its formulation and a priority for providing everything useful. Further, providing the necessary attention and protection to our children is a national and a humanitarian demand emanating from our spiritual and social beliefs and from our heritage.

b. The right upbringing of our children is a national responsibility for both the State and the people. All efforts are made to develop the child's personality by making him love his family and country and show pride of his country's civilisation and work on pan-Arab unity.

c. The family is considered the nucleus of the society based on integration guided by religion, good conduct and national love. The government, however, carries the responsibility for protecting it against feebleness and disintegration. Members of the family must be given complete security and basic services which would enhance its social calibre and productivity so that in return the members will be endowed with warmth, passion, satisfaction, clear minds, social security and cultural advancement.

d. We have to support the families to enable them to fulfil their responsibilities towards their children. In fact, this is the basis of our efforts for child growth and development; the State is responsible to ensure the family with social and economical stability.

e. We are committed to securing the rights mentioned in the U.N. Declaration on the Rights of the Child for Arab children with no discrimination.

B. Basic rights for the Arab child

1. We confirm and guarantee the right of the child to grow up in the family where there is family stability coupled with affection and warmth. Also, he should be given the right place in the family and receive the necessary attention whereby his biological, psychological, spiritual and social needs are met. He should be given the facilities to enable him to build up an independent personality, to have freedom of speech and participation in a democratic manner with no discrimination for age or sex.
2. We confirm and guarantee the right of the child for social security and health care and will provide him with preventive health care such as medical treatment for him and his mother from the date of his birth. Further, he should live in a clean house and clean environment and be given the right food.
3. We confirm and guarantee the child's right for free education both in the pre-schooling, the basic and compulsory education periods. This is in consideration that education is the corner stone in the existing change and in acquiring trends, expertise and the capabilities with which he can encounter all new situations through renovated knowledge. This will enable him to assume discipline and discard all obsolete customs, thus developing practical and scientific notion, cogent appreciation, love for work and good performance. He will also be able to contribute positively in the daily life of his society and nation, while guaranteeing for himself a good standard of living, the right for continued education and benefit of free time, playing, sports and reading.
4. We confirm and guarantee his right to comprehensive and integrative social services in all stages of childhood in both the rural and urban areas and particularly among the poor, disabled and needy children so as to enable them to live happily and become members of society. They will then contribute to its construction and development.
5. We confirm and guarantee the right of the child to have State protection from abuse and exploitation both physically and psychologically even if it were from members of his family. He should also be given the right job and at a appropriate age. The nature of the job he undertakes should not subject him to danger or impede his course of study or limit his bodily, mental or psychological growth. In the event of a disaster, the child and in particular the disabled child should receive priority attention in protection and aid.
6. We confirm and guarantee the right of the child to have a free movement and to grow up with philanthropic feelings and while realising

the importance of peace, cordiality among nations and love for his brethren in humanity.

PROTECTION OF RIGHTS AND CONTROL OF PROGRAMMES

1. We undertake to protect these rights and legalise and adapt them in each Arab country and conform to the provisions of this Charter, regionally and on the national level. The child's best interests should always be paramount.
2. We undertake to apply the curricula relating to safety, to adapt the preventive and development methods, as the comprehensive and integrated social development is the only solution of the child's cause. No doubt child protection against any sort of disability is much better than providing the remedy after the accident.
3. We undertake to create regional and national conformity in providing the basic needs and delivering our services, taking into consideration its fair and equal distribution. We also undertake through the common Arab effort to bridge the existing gap of growth and child care which is prevalent at present among the various Arab countries.

THE OBJECTIVES

This Charter aims at the accomplishment of the following:
The supreme objective of this Charter is to bring about generations of Arab children having the portrait of the future that we want. Children that can make future generations possessing sound mind and sound body and having conscience and a pleasant personality. Further, they will possess the unfailing calibre to offer and rejuvenate Arab generations that believe in God, adhere to the principles of their religion, understand their national mission, bear allegiance to their country, have confidence in their country, abide by the principles of justice and peace and look for lofty examples in the humanitarian human conduct on individual as well as on group level.

Under these supreme objectives the following is emphasised:

1. We give security to family life by providing the basic necessities and social security so that the children grow up in an atmosphere of stability under the guardianship of the state where job opportunities are made available for all citizens who are sincere workers and who aim at increasing production. Further, we guarantee that the mother will be given the facilities to provide ample attention to her children.
2. We guarantee to provide full medical attention which is a democratic right made accessible to every Arab child and to his mother both in the fields of protection and treatment.

3. We guarantee the establishment of a sound educational system in every part of the Arab World being democratic in its presentation and nationalistic in its obligation. From a nationalistic point of view, this system of education must be compulsory and free at all stages for all those who can continue their studies from the kindergarten to higher education with no discrimination for financial abilities, social origin or political stance. A special strategic guidance must also be adopted for the development of Arab education.
4. We ask for the establishment of an advanced social service of a progressive nature of which all children can make use of and especially those of the poor families. However, special attention must be given to the more needy and those who live at far away places. On the other hand, the social defence methods should protect against digression and provide the remedy for those who have deviated the path of righteousness.
5. We intend to establish certain methods in guardianship and education that will suit the disabled children and the gifted children; allowing the former to integrate in normal productive life and offering the latter the opportunity to enrich their talents for their own good and for the good of their country.

Means and Requirements

Application of the principles of the Charter, the realisation of the objectives and adoption of the methods stated, all of these require the mobilisation of all the national resources and application of the tested methods which have proved their efficiency particularly in the Arab World.

* To make child care and development a priority in the political decision.
* To accelerate the national comprehensive development and adapt to scientific planning of child development, taking into account using the right programmes, administering and making a follow-up on the results.
* To establish national child welfare committee in each Arab country comprising of official, non-official and public representatives are included. This national committee will co-ordinate matters and among her urgent duties are:

1. To carry out research studies and a comprehensive survey in order to evaluate the present situation of children in terms of economic, social, medical, cultural and educational aspects to serve as a basis for scientific planning for child protection and efforts.
2. To set up a comprehensive plan in the light of the contents of this Charter and the strategic social work in the Arab World. The plan must include priorities and steps for execution of work together with

the time consumed and the required resources needed within the framework of the national plan for the social and economical development.
3. To adopt the method of integration in delivering basic services.
4. To put more emphasis on training which includes specialised professional leadership courses in the fields of mother- and child-care. Training must also apply to the local leadership. This trend requires a review of several of the systems and specialised programmes and training programmes dedicated to those employed in the fields of child care and development, with special emphasis on environmental problems and the simplified methods used in offering efficient services.
5. To establish a spectrum of institutions and public facilities to be able to deliver basic services to the children in different environments with a special attention to the rural areas and poor quarters in the city. The services should be given at places which people frequent such as schools, social centres and mosques.
6. To be committed to the strategy of the development of education and culture in the Arab world and to provide all necessities for its implementation.
7. To duplicate efforts of *pre-school child care* and encourage the establishment of day-care centres, kindergarten classes, playgrounds, gardens and children's clubs. The reason is that this developmental stage is quite vital for his present and future in moulding his personality and in bringing him up in the right way.
8. To support institutions serving children in the remote, rural and poor urban areas and make accessible general health services.
9. To pay special attention to statistics and research and support the institutions that carry this work out, and work on the establishment of additional institutions at both the regional and national levels.
10. To make available the necessary financial and man-power resources for the implementation of the child care programmes, and to draw a firm policy for financing these plans and programmes which would lead to its efficiency and continuity.
11. To develop the administrational and organisational institutions able to meet any future requirements and demands.
12. To encourage community participation in child care and development and strengthen its social and national institutions and unions. Financial support, training and technical support should be given in order to enable them to help the families with more vigour and present the suitable local programmes for the children. The social and national institutions must be given the authority to participate in decision making, planning, programming, execution, follow-up and evaluation. Roles should be distributed between the national and local committees. Active participation in this vital field of all concerned will provide the possibilities and huge resources and will bring about a

school in co-operation and in the training of citizens to do general work and develop in the society *an esprit de corps*.
13. This requires a high level of awareness among all community members in the Arab World which in turn calls for concentrated efforts to educate Arab communities in child's cause and necessary child care and development. Further, social alertness must be used as an instrument for paving the way and informing the citizens of childhood problems and their consequences. Consultation and mobilisation of efforts have to be directed towards positive move and constructive work. In the field of knowledge the importance of efforts is justified because of the suffering of the majority in the Arab social sectors where there is a lack of knowledge in the developmental stages. The rich, the poor, the educated, the illiterate, men and women are all alike in this respect as a field study and the replies received from the respective governments have revealed. Further, this subject is being ignored by schools and the information circles have not given it due importance, despite the fact that a few books and articles have dealt with it in a non-simplified manner.
14. For these purposes we have to make use of mass-media as much as possible since this is required because illiteracy is so wide-spread in our society. The mass-media have an important role to play since they are spread all over the Arab World. They have their own influence on public opinion and are the only source of information to the illiterate. Therefore the mass-media are requested to devote a major part of their efforts and programmes to childhood problems through their specialised programmes and their important role in educating children and adults.

    Our imported programmes must be carefully selected in order to avoid the importing of damaging ones and those that have a negative influence on our children.
15. Sound laws and legislations are the main way of guaranteeing rights among which are children's rights. They are also a means of confirming our adherence to this Charter and the realisation of its objectives. This action, however, requires the presence of the legal and the legislative frameworks to give the security for the children's rights as stated in the Charter. The legislative framework must adopt the following:

    1) Constitutional protection for safeguarding the rights of the child and giving details of such rights.
    2) Legislation and laws:

        a. To adjust public laws for the benefit of child and family in accordance with the provision of the Charter.
        b. Enactment of special legislation relating to child-care and pro-

tection. This legislation must be separate from public laws and must endorse the legal status of the child and must provide him and his family with the necessary protection and care.
  c. Family laws based on the principles of the best interests of the child and the family and the enforcement of the following legal rights:

     a) To define the minimum age for marriage and requesting those proposing to marry to undergo the necessary medical tests in order to ascertain their medical fitness.
     b) To control polygamy in accordance with the provisions of Islam.
     c) To allow divorce.
     d) To organise procedures for making payments concerning the child (in case of divorce) in accordance with the father or supporter's income.
     e) To ensure the child's rights to a convenient home and limit the authority of the landlord (whether father or mother) in the free disposal of the house, especially if the State has offered a house or a plot of land as a protection to the family, and ensure its continuity and coherence.
  d. Amendments to present laws and regulations with details of this Charter to ensure proper guardianship and protection to the child, or issuing separate laws in connection with the following:

     a) A child protection law to organise family and institutionalised protection.
     b) A juvenile protection law to ensure the child's rights to receive social care and special treatment.
     c) A law relating to special groups by which they can be ensured of social and economical care to involve them in normal productive life.
     d) A law relating to illegitimate children to ensure their rights, guardianship, financial and psychological care.

JOINT ARAB ACTION IN THE FIELD OF CHILD CARE AND DEVELOPMENT

The approval with regard to child development and guardianship and treating it as a national priority allows for dedicating the present Arab co-operation, bolstering it and giving it continuous development. In this respect, we would like to highlight the following:

  a. We would like to establish an Arab Child Welfare Organisation having the responsibility of co-ordinating Arab efforts in the field of child care and child development and suggesting the policies and national programmes and plans. Further, the organisation will be required to help the Arab states determine their policies, programmes and projects and provide the material and technical expertise to those who need it. It will be also empowered to carry out research work, exchange of expertise, provide pioneer projects, make known successful experiments and assume full responsibility with regard to giving a better standard of living for the child in the Arab world which will eventually lead to creating Arab generations full of the spirit of co-operation and restoring the historic initiative to our nation.

b. We would like to found an Arab Fund for the support of child care and development the resources of which will be used in the Arab countries' programmes and in the programmes of the above mentioned new Arab Organisation for Childhood. The fund will be mainly used for national projects, joint programmes and meeting the basic needs of the children in the poor Arab countries.

c. Strengthening Arab co-operation in the field of standardisation of terminology and all technical terms and basic statistical terms as a means to carrying out comparative studies in research and be helpful for the training and exchange of information. Undoubtedly, this will also mean that total support should be given to the responsible bodies in charge of these various activities.

d. Giving priority to local industries that are related to the child's development specially emphasising the products the absence of which creates a huge gap and a hindrance to the efforts of the Arab countries in the field of child care such as the founding of an Arab industry for syringes and inoculation. This is in addition to an Arab industry for the nutrition of children and teaching, cultural and entertaining instruments. We also recommend the establishment of an Arab toy industry.

e. Establishing an Arab centre for children's literature and magazines since this is a vital part in their lives.

f. This charter emphasises the importance of protection of the Palestinian child in all stages of development whether in the occupied territories or abroad. The Charter also declares that the institutions and Palestinian societies that take care of the child must be given full support. Further, we support the Palestinian people in their struggle to restore their legitimate rights in order to establish their State.

g. Ensuring the Arab presence in all institutions, meetings and conferences which deal with child development and we request that the Arab nation will double its efforts in this humanitarian subject.

General Provisions

1. Each Arab State will take the necessary measures within its financial and economical resources for the implementation of the provisions of the Charter by all suitable means.

2. The Arab states will have to submit periodic reports to the Arab League of Nations in connection with the procedures undertaken and achievements performed in the spirit of the provisions of the Charter. The reports must include the difficulties the parties concerned meet in the implementation of the provisions of the Charter.
3. This Charter becomes effective once it is ratified by the Council of Arab Ministers of Social Affairs.

The Youth Charter Act, Proposed by James Wallace, M.P. (1985)

Bill to promote opportunities for young people in International Youth Year 1985 by establishing a Youth Charter giving rights and representation to young people; and for connected purposes.

Be it enacted by the Queen's most Excellent Majesty, by and with the advice and consent of the Lords Spiritual and Temporal, and Commons, in this present Parliament assembled, and by the authority of the same, as follows:

A.

 (1) References in this Act to the Youth Charter are to the Charter set out in the Schedule to this Act.
 (2) Every local authority, education authority, police authority and health authority in England, Scotland and Wales shall have regard to the Youth Charter, as shall local and national boards of the Manpower Services Commission.
 (3) The bodies set out in subsection (2) above shall within six months of the appointed day bring forward proposals for implementing those parts of the Charter which apply to their work.

B.

 (1) The Representation of the People Act 1983 shall be amended as follows.
 (2) In sections 1(1)(c) and 2(1)(c) for the figures '18' there shall be substituted '16'.

C.

 (1) Within six months of the appointed day every–

(a) borough council in London;
(b) district council in the remainder of England and Wales; and
(c) district or island council in Scotland shall bring forward a scheme for the establishment of youth councils for their area.

(2) In addition to any other purposes which a youth council may pursue, the general purposes of a youth council shall be to ascertain, co-ordinate and express to the local authorities for its area, and to public authorities, the views of the young people it represents, and to take such action in the interests of those young people as appears to it to be expedient and practicable.
(3) Youth councils shall have regard to the Youth Charter.

D.

In this Act–

- 'appointed day' means the day on which this Act shall come into force.
- 'local authority' means in London the Greater London Council, London borough councils and the Common Council, in the remainder of England and Wales county and district councils, and in Scotland, regional, island and district councils.
- 'health authority' shall have the meaning assigned to it by the National Health Service Act 1977, as amended.
- 'police authority' shall have the meaning assigned to it by the Education Act 1944 and the Education (Scotland) Act 1980.
- 'school governing body' shall have the meaning assigned to it by the Education Act 1980.

E.

(1) This Act may be cited as the Youth Charter Act 1985.
(2) This Act shall come into force one month after the day on which it receives Royal Assent.
(3) This Act extends to Northern Ireland.

1. A prominent role of statutory bodies, governmental bodies and local authorities shall be to promote young people's self-esteem and personal development, and to encourage their civic and political participation; to this end, young people shall be entitled to the maximum possible involvement in decision-making in all areas which affect themselves and their lives as is consistent with efficient and responsible government and public administration.
2. Young people shall be entitled to be represented on health authorities,

police authorities and educational governing bodies, and to be co-opted onto the committees of local authorities and education authorities.
3. To enable them to use such representation to best effect, all young people shall have made available to them the option of an extensive programme of social and political education.
4. Young people shall be entitled to a significant role in the planning and managing of the local youth service.
5. Young people shall so far as possible be given the economic independence and the necessary advice to make an informed choice on reaching the school leaving age between employment, training and further full time education.

APPENDIX XXXVIII

The Labour Party Charter for Young People, (London, 1985)

Labour believes young people should have opportunity, choice and independence. We want young people at 16 to have real jobs, good education and training – and a chance to earn as they learn.

* *the right at 14 and 15 to good quality comprehensive education* providing them with the skills, knowledge and confidence to have more control over their lives.
* *the right at 16 to at least two years' education, training and work experience.*
* *the right at 16 and 17 to a negotiated wage* if employed, with paid release to college; at least 36 a week training allowance if on a training scheme with trade unions negotiating a topping up;
* *the right to 27 a week if in full-time study*; with the right to supplementary benefit if unemployed.
* *the right of all qualified young people 18 and above to a place in higher education* and to be paid a living grant.
* *the right of unemployed 18 to 24 year olds to more jobs and better training opportunities.*
* *the right to better housing opportunities*: more rented accommodation and improved access to council housing.
* *the right to sport and leisure facilities and a youth service* which meets young people's needs and gives them a say in the running of their services.
* *the right to equal opportunities* regardless of race, gender, class or sexuality.
* *the right to live in a safe, secure Britain – free of nuclear weapons.*

APPENDIX XXXIX

London Boroughs Children's Regional Planning Committee, Charter of Rights for Children in Care, (August 1986)

PREAMBLE

This Charter has been prepared in conjunction with the Child Care Policy Statement by the LBCRPC Working Party. It draws on existing material produced by local authorities and voluntary organisations, predominantly found in Guides for Children in Care but also in some existing general directories of rights for children and young people, and from writings of 'Who Cares' groups and the National Association of Young People in Care.

The working party began by asking the question "Do children in care need special consideration for their rights over and above that given to other children?" The answer to this is "yes" on two grounds:

1. Children in care are particularly vulnerable because corporate parenting by a large agency can lead to confusions over areas of responsibility. Unless care is taken there may be no individuals to whom the child's welfare is a primary, overriding concern of their lives, as would be the case with good natural parents. Even to the most conscientious social worker, the child is only one of a large number of clients for whom he or she is responsible, and other means are necessary to ensure adequate protection of the child's interest.
2. Children in care are affected by decisions and policies which influence the major events and the minor details of their lives, and which are made at points far removed from them. Unlike children in their own homes, they may have no regular contact with the members or officers who make these decisions and hence have limited negotiating powers over their own lives.

The working party accept that the concept of 'rights' is a difficult one, on which there are many different viewpoints. It is a term which is commonly used in two senses: the legal right, which is expressed in legislation or the common law and enforceable in the courts; and the moral right, which we assume when we talk about 'human rights' or 'justice' as distinct from law. It is our view that any discussion of children's rights in care must include the moral, as well as the legal dimensions. Legal rights sometimes mean very little in practical terms unless the spirit of the law is followed as well as the letter; and there are many areas in which children's rights are at present ill-protected by law, but it is still very clear what standards of care should be offered. The charter makes a distinction throughout between the rights which children can claim in law, and those which they should be able to expect adults *in loco parentis* to regard as obligations.

1. *Legal Rights*: Legal rights may be framed in Acts of Parliament, in regulations or other documents which are prepared in accordance with Acts of Parliament, in the common law, or in agreements to which the British Government are party by reasons of its signature to the European Convention on Human Rights. For children in care, rights are more often expressed in terms of the local authority's duty, than the child's rights, but the failure of a local authority to carry out its duty may be challenged in the courts on behalf of the child.

    i) The child in care has a legal right to expect that the local authority will give first consideration to promoting the child's welfare throughout his or her childhood.
    ii) Children in care have rights under the legislation by which they came into care. This includes the child's right to have his or her interests legally represented in care proceedings, wardship proceedings and criminal proceedings; the right to appeal against a care order and the right to apply for the discharge of a care order; the right to a Guardian ad Litem should there be a conflict of interests between the child and his or her parents in legal proceedings. Good practice requires that particular care is taken to protect the rights of children in care under temporary orders (remands, Place of Safety, interim care orders) in order to enable them to present their own case to court. Individual information of the child's legal rights should be given either when a child comes into care, or (in the case of very young children) when they become old enough to understand their situation.
    iii) Children in care have a legal right to be consulted about decisions which affect their future, and to have their wishes and feelings taken into account. This has been held in court to apply when decisions are taken on the closure of residential homes and changes of placement.
    iv) Children in care have a legal right to be the subject of a six monthly

review, at which discharge from care should be considered, and if the child is to remain in care, his or her long term needs taken into account.

v) Children in care are entitled to normal civil rights to which anyone in our society is entitled: the right to vote if they are over 18, the right not to be subject to detention or other exceptional restrictions on liberty unless this has been authorised by a court.

vi) Children accused of criminal offenses while in care should receive equal protection from the law and the 'Judges Rules' as if they were in the care of their parents. This is particularly important in cases where the child is charged with offenses on residential premises or in foster homes; in these circumstances good practice requires that the person attending the police station *in loco parentis* should if possible be the child's parents; if not, a practitioner other than the foster parents or a member of staff from the home in which the offence is alleged to have taken place. The child should have legal advice from an independent solicitor. Where the alleged offence is unconnected with the child's dwelling place, the child's parents, foster parents or residential workers should act *in loco parentis* while the child is interviewed by police.

vii) Children who live and attend school on the same premises and who have no contact with parents are entitled to the appointment of an independent visitor, who must not be an employee of the care authority, and who will represent the child's interests. This right belongs to some children in care placed in community homes with education, (including those in the private sector), observation and assessment centres, youth treatment centres, secure units, special boarding schools and some hospitals. Good practice would extend this to others in long term residential care and to children in care who are in penal establishments, and give children a voice in the selection of the visitor. This would ensure that there is one person to whom the child's needs are an overriding concern.

viii) The Code of Practice on Access by Parents of Children in Care requires the local authority to promote and sustain the child's contact with his or her family, and to take into account the child's wishes about contact with his or her family. Prevention of contact with parents or relatives must not be used as a punishment or means of control of the child.

ix) The Community Homes Regulations and the Boarding Out Regulations lay a duty on the local authority to enable the child to practise his or her religion. This should include the right to spiritual guidance, the observation of dietary rules, clothing rules and the right to attend places of worship and festivals, consistent with their beliefs. Good practice requires that children's religion should be treated with respect by carers. This right should be taken into account when placements are chosen, particularly for children of religions where opportunities for religious pursuits may be restricted to some localities. Children should always be advised of the nearest religious centres, and put in touch with the local religious leaders if they wish. Equally children have the moral right not to be forced into religious observation against their will. It should be recognised that there are children in care for whom practising their religion provides continuity with their past experience, and children who might find strength in the development of a religious faith, if given encouragement.

x) The Boarding Out Regulations lay down minimum levels of visits which social workers must make to children in foster homes. Good practice requires that fieldworkers' visits to children in residential care, long stay hospitals or other settings will be at least as frequent and regular.

xi) Children in care have the same legal rights as any other citizen with respect to legal advice to enable them to put their case in any legal proceedings to which they are party, and to ensure that their legal rights are enforceable. This requires that the local authority will ensure that children in their care have good access to independent legal advice. This is particularly so in the case of children detained in secure provision, who are unable to mobilise such advice for themselves.

xii) Children in care have a right to mainstream education alongside other children of their age group. When children have special educational needs, attempts should be made wherever possible to have these met within the normal education system in accordance with the 1981 Education Act.

xiii) Children's rights under the education system should be protected. This includes the right to further education beyond school leaving age for those who wish to undertake it, and the right to a statement of special educational needs for all handicapped or disturbed children needing special educational help up to and beyond the age of 19.

xiv) Children placed in community homes with education, unlike other children, have the legal right to leave school on their 16th birthday. They should be allowed to exercise this right if they wish, but good practice requires that they should also be able to complete their education if they wish. They should not be forced to leave the home solely because they have finished attendance at school.

2. *Moral obligations which should be acknowledged by local authorities*: Many of these 'moral rights' which local authorities should concede, follow from a commitment to carry out in full the legal rights detailed above. Foremost among these moral rights are the child's right to expect

good social work practice from those employed in care for him or her, and the child's right to have his or her normal development encouraged. The former stems from the social consensus that people who are employed and paid to do a job should do it competently, a reasonable expectation which all citizens have when using services provided from public funds. The latter stems from the local authority's duty to promote the child's welfare throughout his or her childhood, and rights considered under this heading are those which generally come in the category of 'good parenting'. These issues are not so much those of professional social work practice, but of organising services to avoid creating disadvantages for the child in care.

A. The Right to Good Social Work Practice

i) A child should be able to expect his or her social workers to make an individual care plan and that the care plan will give forethought to the objectives of care and the child's future needs until the expected time of discharge from care. For older children it would be appropriate to put this plan into writing for and with the child.

ii) Children in care should be able to expect to be informed of the decision-making processes which affect their lives and encouraged to take part in them. This is particularly important when the decisions concern changes in placement, changes in legal status, or changes in arrangements for access by parents.

iii) Following from this, children should be able to attend and contribute to their case reviews and to attend case conferences which affect their future. Where case conferences are organised by bodies other than the care authority, the care authority should press the child's claim to attend. Reviews should provide an opportunity for children to express grievances, if necessary, through a nominated person in whom the child feels able to confide, with safeguards to reassure the child that reprisals will not follow.

iv) Children should have access to files and other reports which concern them, and be able to see reports written about them. This may include access to information about parents or other family members when the content is important for decisions on the children's future.

v) Children in care should be able to expect security of placement; to know that they will not be moved at whim or without their needs being the first consideration in decisions to move them. They should be able to expect that the continuity of their family and community networks will be preserved and that its importance to their chances of returning home is recognised.

vi) Children should be able to expect to see parents, siblings and other relatives as frequently as they and the relatives concerned wish to do so. Equally they have the right to refuse to see parents or other relatives. The frequency and extent of visits should be agreed by all parties concerned and included in the care plan.

vii) Children in care should be able to expect regular and frequent visits from their field social workers, which will be incorporated into their care plan.

viii) They should be able to make representations to a senior person in the care authority if they are experiencing difficulties of communication with their social workers.

ix) Resources for privacy for children in care should be available. As a minimum they should include a place to lock private papers or valuables; a safe place to keep treasured personal possessions; freedom to send and receive private letters; make and receive private telephone calls and see visitors privately. These rights need particular safeguarding for children in residential care, where privacy may be vulnerable to other children as well as to staff, and for children in secure units where demands for security may conflict with the right to privacy. Children should not be made subject to procedures such as searches of their person or property except in circumstances in which the person carrying out such actions is authorised to do so, and the need to protect the child or other children justifies the invasion of privacy.

x) The right to privacy includes the right not to have intimate details of the child's life and family passed to other people who have no direct concern with these matters and who would not be given such information about children living at home. Details of the child's background should not normally be given to schools, youth services, community health services or other community services, although these services will need to know that the child is in care. When it is essential to give personal details to protect the child's interests, the child should be told this, and the reasons explained.

xi) The child should be able to expect to have his or her own personal clothing, and not to be forced to wear communal clothing.

xii) Children have the basic human right not to be made subject to cruel or degrading punishments by social workers, teachers or foster parents. They should know what punishments can or cannot be used for their carers within the policy of their care authority.

We consider the following punishments are contrary to good practice; beating; stopping the child from visiting his or her family or from receiving visits; refusal of basic food; being made to wear night clothes or remain unclothed during the day; the use of sedation when this is not required by the child's medical condition. These punishments should not be used in residential homes or foster homes. Residential staff and foster parents should also be given clear guidance by care authorities as to the limits of acceptable punishment.

xiii) Children should be able to expect consistency from their care authorities; when they are placed in homes or boarding schools run by another agency, whether local authority, voluntary, or private, the care plan should ensure that their care authorities' policies on punishment, privacy, visiting, access to records, etc., will be followed by that home or school.

xiv) Children placed in a residential placement or foster home not managed directly by their care authority should be able to know where the decision-making power rests in relation both to major issues affecting their future such as schooling and changes of placement, and to the details of their daily life such as clothes, pocket money, and leisure activities.

xv) Children have the right to know to whom they can turn for help if they are unhappy about any aspect of their care. In the first resort they should have access to an informal, internal procedure which enables them to make direct contact with a senior officer of the care authority by post and telephone. In the last resort they should have direct access to other sources of help, which could include elected members with special interests or responsibilities for children in care, or a local independent 'ombudsman' for children in care. Special provision should be made for children in secure accommodation to have access to senior staff and independent adults.

B. THE RIGHT TO NORMAL DEVELOPMENT

i) The child should be able to take for granted the preservation of his or her identity and self-esteem. Children should be brought up by adults who will value them as people and who will not subject them to racism, sexism, discrimination against physical or mental disability, or any other form of discrimination which could affect their self-confidence and ability to value themselves.

ii) Children in care should be able to take for granted the preservation of their family and friendship and other social networks into adult life. Thoughtlessness in choice or changes of placement, or in access and visiting arrangements for friends and relatives, including siblings, contributes to the loneliness which is often experienced in later life by children who have grown up in care.

iii) Children learn (as we all learn) by taking risks, experiencing and being taught to cope with, the normal hazards of life in our society. Over-protective, bureaucratic regulations which prevent children in care from taking part in the normal activities of their age group are a denial of their needs and impede the learning which they should expect a 'good parent' to provide.

iv) Following from these, it is evident that children in care should be able, with the permission of their immediate responsible carers (heads of residential homes or foster parents) to visit friends, or relatives, stay overnight with friends or relatives, spend holidays with friends or relatives, take part in school visits, and similar activities, without having to surmount complex procedures to obtain approval for such normal behaviour.

v) Children in care should be able to expect continuity of health care, medical and dental treatment. Wherever possible, they should continue to be attended by medical and dental practitioners who treated them before admission to care, and placement choice should take this into account. Children should have their own medical record which stays with the child, rather than in a central filing system, and older children should have a copy of the record under their own control. Children should know which adults are responsible for giving permission for treatment.

vi) Children should be able to expect continuity of education. They are often educationally disadvantaged at the point of admission to care; being in care should not add to this disadvantage and care authorities should practice positive discrimination to overcome it. Placements should be chosen, wherever possible, to enable children to continue at the school which they have attended, and appropriate transport made available if needed. An educational record giving details of the child's work and progress should be maintained by the care authority and go with the child to new placements; older children should have their own copy of the record.

vii) Children from ethnic minorities should be able to take for granted that they will have regular contact with their ethnic communities, and placements in which their needs for such contact will be met.

viii) Children in care should be able to grow up in an environment which encourages normal sexual development and enables good relationships to develop with children and adults of both sexes. Children should receive appropriate help and guidance to understand and cope with their own physical and sexual development, and the significance of sexual relationships. This requires carers to ensure opportunities for friendship and contact with the opposite sex, particularly for children placed in single sex residential homes and schools; this also requires good sexual counselling to be available for children, many of whom may have seen only damaging or hostile relationships prior to coming into care.

ix) Children in care should be able to take for granted that they will have the chance to learn the skills needed for independent adult life. Care should prepare them to handle money, to plan their own use of time, to be familiar with routine personal documentation and take charge of personal documents such as birth certificates and passports, to be able to cope with employment, with the understanding and use of public services, with the domestic skills for running their own household, and with the capacity to care for their own children if and when the time comes. In the past public care has de-skilled children in all these areas, and positive planning is needed to ensure that we do better in the future.

x) Finally, children in care should be able to take for granted that they will be supported in establishing themselves as independent adults, and will not be abandoned by their care authority on their 18th birthday. They should receive the financial and other help on and after leaving care which a 'good family' would provide for its young.

APPENDIX XL

The United Nations Declaration Relating to Foster Placement and Adoption (1986)

(*Declaration on Social and Legal Principles relating to the Protection and Welfare of children, with Special Reference to Foster Placement and Adoption Nationally and Internationally*)

United Nations, Resolution 41/85, 3 December 1986
The General Assembly, recalling its resolution 36/167 of 16 December 1981, 37/115 of 16 December 1982, 38/142 of 19 December 1983 and 39/89 of 13 December 1984 and decision 40/422 of 11 December 1985,

taking note of the draft Declaration on Social and Legal Principles relating to the Protection and Welfare of Children, with Special Reference to Foster Placement and Adoption Nationally and Internationally, as submitted to it by the Economic and Social Council by its resolution 1979/28 of 9 May 1979,

taking note with appreciation of the work done on this question in its Third and Sixth Committees, as well as the efforts made by Member States representing different legal systems, during the consultations held at Headquarters from 16 to 27 September 1985 and early in the forty-first session, to join in the common endeavour of completing the work on the draft Declaration,

adopts the Declaration on Social and Legal Principles relating to the Protection and Welfare of Children, with Special Reference to Foster Placement and Adoption Nationally and Internationally, the text of which is annexed to the present resolution.

ANNEX

The General Assembly,recalling the Universal Declaration of Human Rights, the International Covenant on Economic, Social and Cultural Rights, the International Covenant on Civil and Political Rights, the International Convention on the Elimination of All Forms of Racial Discrimination and the Convention on the Elimination of All Forms of Discrimination against Women,

recalling also the Declaration on the Rights of the Child, which it proclaimed by its resolution 1386 (XIV) of 20 November 1959,

reaffirming principle 6 of that Declaration, which states that the child shall, wherever possible, grow up in the care and under the responsibility of his parents and, in any case, in an atmosphere of affection and of moral and material security,

concerned at the large number of children who are abandoned or become orphans owing to violence, internal disturbance, armed conflicts, natural disasters, economic crises or social problems,

bearing in mind that in all foster placement and adoption procedures the best interests of the child should be the paramount consideration,

recognizing that under the principal legal systems of the world, various other alternative valuable institutions exist, such as the Kafala of Islamic Law, which provide substitute care to children who cannot be cared for by their own parents,

recognizing further that only where a particular institution is recognized and regulated by the domestic law of a State would the provisions of this Declaration relating to that institution be relevant and that such provisions would in no way affect the existing alternative institutions in other legal systems,

conscious of the need to proclaim universal principles to be taken into account in cases where procedures are instituted relating to foster placement or adoption of a child, either nationally or internationally,

bearing in mind, however, that the principles set forth hereunder do not impose on States such legal institutions as foster placement or adoption,

proclaims the following principles:

A. GENERAL FAMILY AND CHILD WELFARE

Article 1
Every state depends upon good family welfare.

Article 2
Child welfare depends upon good family welfare.

Article 3
The first priority for a child is to be cared for by his or her own parents.

Article 4
When care by the child's own parents is unavailable or inappropriate, care by relatives of the child's parents, by another substitute – foster or adoptive – family or, if necessary, by an appropriate institution should be considered.

Article 5
In all matters relating to the placement of a child outside the care of the child's own parents, the best interests of the child, particularly his or her need for affection and right to security and continuing care, should be the paramount consideration.

Article 6
Persons responsible for foster placement or adoption procedures should have professional or other appropriate training.

Article 7
Governments should determine the adequacy of their national child welfare services and consider appropriate actions.

Article 8
The child should at all times have a name, a nationality and a legal representative. The child should not, as a result of foster placement, adoption or any alternative regime, be deprived of his or her name, nationality or legal representative unless the child thereby acquires a new name, nationality or legal representative.

Article 9
The need of a foster or an adopted child to know about his or her background should be recognized by persons responsible for the child's care, unless this is contrary to the child's best interests.

B. Foster Placement

Article 10
Foster placement of children should be regulated by law.

Article 11
Foster family care, though temporary in nature, may continue, if necessary, until adulthood but should not preclude either prior return to the child's own parents or adoption.

Article 12
In all matters of foster family care the prospective foster parents and, as appropriate, the child and his or her own parents should be properly involved. A competent authority or agency should be responsible for supervision to ensure the welfare of the child.

C. ADOPTION

Article 13
The primary aim of adoption is to provide the child who cannot be cared for by his or her own parents with a permanent family.

Article 14
In considering possible adoption placements, persons responsible for them should select the most appropriate environment for the child.

Article 15
Sufficient time and adequate counselling should be given to the child's own parents, the prospective adoptive parents and, as appropriate, the child in order to reach a decision on the child's future as early as possible.

Article 16
The relationship between the child to be adopted and the prospective adoptive parents should be observed by child welfare agencies or services prior to the adoption. Legislation should ensure that the child is recognized in law as a member of the adoptive family and enjoys all the rights pertinent thereto.

Article 17
If a child cannot be placed in a foster or an adoptive family or cannot in any suitable manner be cared for in the country of origin, intercountry adoption may be considered as an alternative means of providing the child with a family.

Article 18
Governments should establish policy, legislation and effective supervision for the protection of children involved in intercountry adoption. Intercountry adoption should, wherever possible, only be undertaken when such measures have been established in the States concerned.

Article 19
Policies should be established and laws enacted, where necessary, for the prohibition of abduction and of any other act for illicit placement of children.

Article 20
In intercountry adoption, placements should, as a rule, be made through competent authorities or agencies with application of safeguards and standards equivalent to those existing in respect of national adoption. In no case should the placement result in improper financial gain for those involved in it.

Article 21
In intercountry adoption through persons acting as agents for prospective adoptive parents special precautions should be taken in order to protect the child's legal and social interests.

Article 22
No intercountry adoption should be considered before it has been established that the child is legally free for adoption and that any pertinent documents necessary to complete the adoption, such as the consent of competent authorities, will become available. It must also be established that the child will be able to migrate and to join the prospective adoptive parents and may obtain their nationality.

Article 23
In intercountry adoption, as a rule, the legal validity of the adoption should be assured in each of the countries involved.

Article 24
Where the nationality of the child differs from that of the prospective adoptive parents, all due weight shall be given to both the law of the State of which the child is the national and the law of the prospective adoptive parents. In this connection due regard shall be given to the child's cultural and religious background and interests.

APPENDIX XLI

A Manifesto for Children of the Children's Legal Centre (London, May 1987)

This is a 'manifesto' for the largest category of disenfranchised: children and young people. It is not a comprehensive programme but it consists of some important measures to be taken by the central government which the *Children's Legal Centre* believes will benefit children and young people and which the Centre would like to see adopted by the parties fighting the general election.

Because under-18s are excluded from the electorate not enough attention is paid to how party programmes can affect them. The Centre hopes this manifesto will help focus the attention of politicians and the wider public on the interests of this group whose votes politicians do not yet have to seek.

Our proposals are grouped according to themes: participation; protection and safeguards; provision and services; and civil rights. Children are often placed in vulnerable situations and they need adequate protection and safeguards. They must be properly provided for by society so they can develop their potential. But children and young people deserve more than this – they also deserve more basic rights, greater independence and a bigger say in decisions which affect their lives.

Of course it requires much more than government action to tackle many of the problems facing this country's children and young people. The immense problem of child abuse, both physical and sexual, stems in the Centre's view from deeply rooted negative attitudes towards children. Until children are generally recognised as individual human beings in their own right – with growing rights to self-determination rather than expected to obey adults automatically – then all too frequently they will continue to be dominated, degraded and abused by some adults, and often they will feel powerless to complain or take any other action to help themselves. This will not change overnight, but the Centre believes that as well as promoting the interests of children directly the proposals listed here would also help foster the necessary wider changes in attitudes.

I. PARTICIPATION

At all levels of society – from national and local government policy down to the various institutions they are part of and their own family – children and young people often have little or no say in important decisions which affect their lives. The Centre proposes the following legislative framework on which greater participation in decision-making could be founded.

Young people aged 16 and 17 should be able to vote in elections.

These young people are considered old enough to leave school, have full-time jobs and get married, yet they are not allowed to have a say in the choice of government. Those who are working pay tax and so are subject to 'taxation without representation'. This measure would give about 1,800,000 young people the right to vote.

There should be a legal duty on education authorities and schools that as far as practicable they should ascertain the wishes and feelings of children regarding the decisions which affect their schooling and give them due consideration, taking into account their maturity and understanding.

The Child Care Act 1980 imposes a similar requirement on local authorities for decisions concerning the lives of children in care. This would bring educational legislation into line and help to give children some say in the running of their schools.

Secondary schools should have pupil governors directly elected by the pupils.

The Education (No.2) Act 1986 forbids the appointment of anyone under 18 as a school governor. As it comes into force over the next two years it will mean the sacking of hundreds of pupil governors and prevent formal involvements by pupils in the way schools are currently run.

There should be a legal duty on parents and guardians that as far as practical they should ascertain the wishes and feelings of children about decisions which affect them and give them due consideration, taking into account their maturity and understanding.

Naturally many parents do this anyway and of course such a provision would sometimes be difficult to enforce. However the Centre believes that a legal statement of principle would strongly encourage parents and guardians in this direction.

Children should be able to participate in their own case conferences and (for those in care) their six-monthly reviews.

Professionals in all sectors – health, education, care, crime etc. – make crucial decisions about children behind closed doors in meetings or 'case conferences'. Children in care have their 'case' reviewed every six months by law. Natural justice demands that children should have the opportunity to attend these conferences or reviews to hear what is said about them and to contribute to the decision-making; practice has also shown that everyone profits from a more open approach.

II. PROTECTION AND SAFEGUARDS

In situations where they are vulnerable children and young people need protection. They also have the right to be safe from discrimination on grounds such as race, sex, disability and sexual orientation. Furthermore, it is essential that when things go wrong there are mechanisms which children and young people can use to get them put right.

Legislation should establish independent complaints procedures for all institutions which cater for children and young people such as schools, hospitals, children's homes and youth custody and detention centres.

For people in an institution where they may have little or no power a vital safeguard is an adequate complaints procedure – one which will ensure their complaints are investigated properly and to which they can turn without fear of victimisation. The Centre's work on detention centres for example demonstrates how it is frequently this fear which allows highly disturbing situations to continue. To be effective procedures must be independent and children should be able to use them directly rather than having to use adults as intermediaries.

The Commissioners for Administration (the Parliamentary local government and health services 'ombudsmen') should cover all services for children with the power to initiate their own inquiries and children's complaints should be expedited.

Certain areas such as matters within the clinical discretion of doctors and internal school decisions are excluded from the scope of the Commissioners' work. They also cannot launch an investigation into any matter unless they receive a complaint about it. Extending their powers and speeding up children's complaints (since lapse of time is more significant for them) would provide a necessary back-up safeguard to the separate complaints procedures outlined above.

Children and young people should have legal protection from physical punishment in all institutions and the family.

Despite their physical vulnerability children are the only section of society who can legally be assaulted, and this fosters attitudes which lead to some adults going much 'too far'. Corporal punishment will soon be abolished in state-funded education and child care institutions and this protection should be extended universally.

Children and young people with disabilities should be legally protected from discrimination and have the right to integrated services and provision.

Anti-discrimination legislation is needed to outlaw discrimination on the grounds of disability, as well as preventing placement in long-stay hospitals, segregation in special schools and in specialist children's homes.

All children whose parents are British citizens or settled in the UK should have equal rights to family life in this country, and nationality and immigration legislation should be amended so that the welfare of children is a paramount consideration.

The way the Home Office implements the immigration rules, particularly by contriving delays in handling applications from the Indian sub-continent, discriminates against black children and young people. The rules themselves make immigration harder for adopted children and children of single parents. The British Nationality Act 1981 discriminates against children whose parents are unmarried by denying them the chance to inherit British nationality through their father if their mother is not British. (This is the one omission from the current and long-overdue Family Law Reform Bill which otherwise removes legal discrimination against 'illegitimate' children). These forms of discrimination should be eliminated. In all other areas of family law the welfare of children is a paramount consideration for courts, and nationality and immigration law should be brought into line.

The rights of young people under arrest should be protected by giving the Codes of Practice under the Police and Criminal Evidence Act 1984 the force of law.

The Codes of Practice set down police procedures when interviewing arrested young people at police stations (e.g. that a parent or guardian should be present). They do not have the force of law and a breach of the Codes can only give rise to disciplinary proceedings against an officer. Giving the Codes of Practice the force of law would allow better protection for young people, help eliminate bad police practice and go towards improving relations between the police and young people.

Young workers – including Youth Training Scheme (YTS) trainees – should be covered by all employment protection legislation.

The employment rights of young people are extremely limited. They often cannot take employers to industrial tribunals because they have not fulfilled the necessary employment qualification periods. Under-16s cannot receive sick pay because they do not pay national insurance and are not classified as 'employee's under health and safety legislation. Under-18s are excluded from redundancy payments. The Wages Act 1986 abolished the minimum wage rates guaranteed in some jobs for under-21s. YTS trainees do not have rights to appeal against unfair dismissal, and because of their status as 'trainees' rather than 'employees' they do not receive state compensation and benefits for injuries. Young workers should be protected from low pay, instant dismissal, unsafe working conditions etc.

The Employment of Children Act 1973 should be implemented.

This Act, passed by Parliament, but not yet brought into force, would introduce consistency to the regulations governing employment of under-16s which vary dramatically across the country. But it is also important that children should still have opportunities for part-time work without being exploited.

An independent body should be established to assess and advise on the environmental implications for children of central and local government planning decisions.

One of the tasks of the children's ombudsman in Norway is to examine proposed transport, housing, commercial, industrial etc. developments from the perspective of children. Children's perspectives are generally not considered in making environmental decisions in this country.

III. PROVISION AND SERVICES

Provision and services should meet the needs of children and young people, who (in addition to the proposals below) are entitled to adequately resourced education, transport, health and social services, and employment and training opportunities. The Children's Legal Centre is particularly concerned that government policy should assist rather than obstruct the natural process of young people's growing independence, and that the legal system should cater appropriately for children.

The social security system should provide children and young people with adequate living standards and promote growing independence rather than perpetuating financial dependence on parents.

This would include increasing child benefit to reflect the actual cost of raising a child, providing mandatory educational maintenance allowances for over-16s at school or in further education, increasing YTS allowances, removing the current time limits on board and lodging allowances for young people on supplementary benefit and abandoning the introduction of lower benefit levels for people under 25.

16–18 year olds who are homeless should be treated as being in priority need and therefore entitled to help with housing.

This involves amending the Housing Act 1985 which does not categorise young people as a priority. Young people are particularly badly affected by the scarcity of rented accommodation and by the absence of a requirement on councils to house those who are 'intentionally' homeless, since this is taken to include young people leaving the parental home. This measure would at least go some way towards improving the desperate housing situation faced by young people.

A Family Court should be established to deal with all matters and cases involving children, including divorce, custody, access, care proceedings and juvenile crime.

The current system of justice for families which involves three different tiers of courts is complex and confusing, leading to inconsistent judicial decisions and increasing the distress of children involved in court proceedings. A Family Court would simplify the procedures and ensure that all court personnel dealing with such cases have relevant training and expertise.

Young people with disabilities should have access to the services they need.

The Disabled Persons (Services, Consultation and Representation) Act 1986 should be brought into force in full so that local authorities must assess the special needs for services of young people with disabilities. In particular the Government should bring in the sections providing for the right to have an advocate and extend it to health services. Further resources should be provided to help local authorities provide services under the Chronically Sick and Disabled Persons Act 1970 such as home helps, aids and adaptations, and assistance with transport: where local authorities are failing to provide adequate services there should be a right to challenge this in court.

IV. CIVIL RIGHTS

Whenever practicable possession of rights should not depend on arbitrary age limits but on maturity and ability to understand the implications of exercising those rights. This principle is in line with the Gillick ruling by the House of Lords. The European Convention on Human Rights contains no lower age limit and children and young people are just as entitled to the fundamental freedoms of thought, expression, assembly etc. within it as adults. But there are many other civil rights which children need.

Young people of sufficient understanding should have full rights to participate in civil legal action on their own behalf and to apply for legal aid.

In particular they should be able to initiate proceedings and be present and independently represented at hearings in all matters relating to parental relationships such as custody or access.

Young people should be able to place themselves in voluntary care in cases of irretrievable breakdown of relationship with parents.

At present young people cannot initiate care proceedings, nor can they put themselves into 'voluntary' care: they are totally dependent on either professionals or parents. The Government has recognised that 16 and 17 year-olds should be able to negotiate informal admissions to care on their own behalf. This right should be extended to all children, and where parents or social workers object the matter should be settled by a court hearing.

Children and young people should not be deprived of their liberty except in circumstances where their behaviour is a danger to themselves or others.

Over the last decade numbers of young people locked up in both the penal and welfare systems have risen dramatically. Yet restriction of liberty has been shown to be ineffective as a deterrent to juvenile crime, or as a cure for 'difficult' behaviour such as running away, self-mutilation or violent aggression towards staff. Custody for young people should be limited to those for whom containment is proved (before a court at regular intervals) to be the only possible option – because either they or others would otherwise be in danger. Resources should be redistributed towards alternatives to custody.

Children placed for fostering should have a right to be placed with a family of their own race.

Many black children have experienced difficulties when placed with white families. As well as recruiting more black foster and adoptive parents, it is important the wishes of children to be placed with families of their own race are respected.

Government circulars should be issued to remind professionals of the rights of children and young people to confidential advice and counselling.

Some recent advice to teachers and others has suggested that under-16s do not have rights to confidential advice. Appropriate government departments should issue circulars to teachers, advice and youth counselling agencies to state that the wishes of a young person for confidentiality should be respected unless there is an immediate risk of serious physical injury.

Children and young people should have the right to receive sex education.

Under the Education (No.2) Act 1986 school governing bodies will be able to prohibit sex education entirely or allow parents to withdraw their children from it, so some children will miss this important part of the curriculum. This provision should be repealed.

Children and young people should have a right of access to the educational, medical, social services, probation, housing etc. files held on them.

Personal files which are kept secret from the subject of those files frequently contain inaccurate or misleading information which can be seriously damaging. Secrecy also builds a barrier between professionals and clients which young people particularly find disconcerting. Opening up files would improve practice and mean a better relationship between professional and client.

APPENDIX XLII

Declaration of the Rights of the Child in Israel (1989)

Abbreviated version

Every girl and boy in Israel is entitled to enjoy the rights listed in this charter – irrespective of his or her age, sex, race, beliefs, religion, origin, physical or mental state, or any other personal characteristic.

1. Every child has the right *to physical and mental development* – in security, in peace, in health, in equality, in honour and in freedom.
2. Every child has the right *to a family life* – to nourishment, suitable housing, protection, love and understanding.
3. Every child has the right *to an identity* – to be given a name and nationality.
4. Every child has the right *to an education* – to self-realisation, equal opportunity, to fulfilling his or her ability and talents.
5. Every child has the right *to privacy* – to confidentiality and protection of his or her property.
6. Every child has the right *not to be exploited* – by neglect, humiliation or cruelty.
7. Every child has the right *to legal consideration* – to special and sensitive treatment within the legal system.
8. Every child has the right *to integration into society* – to equality, and to non-discriminatory treatment.
9. Every child has the right *to self-expression* – in opinion, in feelings, in experience, and in actions.
10. Every child has the right *to relief* – to priority in treatment for illness, in time of accident or emergency.

APPENDIX XLIII

The UN Convention on the Rights of the Child

Adopted by the General Assembly of the United Nations on 20 November 1989, and in force since September 2, 1990

PREAMBLE

The States Parties to the present Convention,
Considering that in accordance with the principles proclaimed in the Charter of the United Nations, recognition of the inherent dignity and of the equal and inalienable rights of all members of the human family is the foundation of freedom, justice and peace in the world,
Bearing in mind that the peoples of the United Nations have, in the Charter, reaffirmed their faith in fundamental human rights and in the dignity and worth of the human person, and have determined to promote social progress and better standards of life in larger freedom,
Recognizing that the United Nations has, in the Universal Declaration of Human Rights and in the international Covenants on Human Rights, proclaimed and agreed that everyone is entitled to all the rights and freedoms set forth therein, without distinction of any kind, such as race, colour, sex, language, religion, political or other opinion, national or social origin, property, birth or other status,
Recalling that, in the Universal Declaration of Human Rights, the United Nations has proclaimed that childhood is entitled to special care and assistance,
Convinced that the family, as the fundamental group of society and the natural environment for the growth and well-being of all its members and particularly children, should be afforded the necessary protection and assistance so that it can fully assume its responsibilities within the community.
Recognizing that the child, for the full and harmonious development of his or her personality, should grow up in a family environment, in an atmosphere of happiness, love and understanding,
Considering that the child should be fully prepared to live an individual

life in society, and brought up in the spirit of the ideals proclaimed in the Charter of the United Nations, and in particular in the spirit of peace, dignity, tolerance, freedom, equality and solidarity,

Bearing in mind that the need for extending particular care to the child has been stated in the Geneva Declaration on the Rights of the Child of 1924 and in the Declaration of the Rights of the Child adopted by the United Nations in 1959 and recognized in the Universal Declaration of Human Rights, in the International Covenant on Civil and Political Rights (in particular in articles 23 and 24), in the international Covenant on Economic, Social and Cultural Rights (in particular in its article 10) and in the statutes and relevant instruments of specialized agencies and international organizations concerned with the welfare of children,

Bearing in mind that, as indicated in the Declaration of the Rights of the Child adopted by the General Assembly of the United Nations on 20 November 1959, 'the child, by reason of his physical and mental immaturity, needs special safeguards and care, including appropriate legal protection, before as well as after birth,'

Recalling the provisions of the Declaration on Social and Legal Principles relating to the Protection and Welfare of Children, with Special Reference to Foster Placement and Adoption Nationally and Internationally (General Assembly Resolution 41/85 of 3 December 1986); the United Nations Standard Minimum Rules for the Administration of Juvenile Justice ('The Beijing Rules') (General Assembly Resolution 40/33 of 29 November 1985); and the Declaration on the Protection of Women and Children in Emergency and Armed Conflict (General Assembly Resolution 3318 (XXIX) of 14 December 1974),

Recognizing that in all countries in the world there are children living in exceptionally difficult conditions, and that such children need special consideration,

Taking due account of the importance of the traditions and cultural values of each people for the protection and harmonious development of the child,

Recognizing the importance of internal co-operation for improving the living conditions of children in every country, in particular in the developing countries,

Have agreed as follows:

Part I

Article 1: Definition of a child
For the purposes of the present Convention a child means every human being below the age of 18 years unless, under the law applicable to the child, majority is attained earlier.

Article 2: Non-discrimination
1. The States Parties to the present Convention shall respect and ensure the rights set forth in this Convention to each child within their jurisdiction without discrimination of any kind, irrespective of the child's or his or her parents's or legal guardians's race, colour, sex, language, religion, political or other opinion, national, ethnic or social origin, property, disability, birth or other status.
2. States Parties shall take all appropriate measures to ensure that the child is protected against all forms of discrimination or punishment on the basis of the status, activities, expressed opinions, or beliefs of the child's parents, legal guardians, or family members.

Article 3: Best interests of the child
1. In all actions concerning children, whether undertaken by public or private social welfare institutions, courts of law, administrative authorities or legislative bodies, the best interests of the child shall be a primary consideration.
2. States Parties undertake to ensure the child such protection and care as is necessary for his or her well-being, taking into account the rights and duties of his or her parents, legal guardians, or other individuals legally responsible for him or her, and, to this end, shall take all appropriate legislative and administrative measures.
3. States Parties shall ensure that the institutions, services and facilities responsible for the care or protection of children shall conform with the standards established by competent authorities, particularly in the areas of safety, health, in the number and suitability of their staff as well as competent supervision.

Article 4: Implementation of rights
States Parties shall undertake all appropriate legislative, administrative, and other measures, for the implementation of the rights recognized in this Convention. In regard to economic, social and cultural rights, States Parties shall undertake such measures to the maximum extent of their available resources and, where needed, within the framework of international co-operation.

Article 5: Parental guidance and the child's evolving capacities
States Parties shall respect the responsibilities, rights, and duties of parents or, where applicable, the members of the extended family or community as provided for by the local custom, legal guardians or other persons legally responsible for the child, to provide, in a manner consistent with the evolving capacities of the child, appropriate direction and guidance in the exercise by the child of the rights recognized in the present Convention.

Article 6: Survival and development
1. States Parties recognize that every child has the inherent right to life.
2. States Parties shall ensure to the maximum extent possible the survival and development of the child.

Article 7: Name and nationality
1. The child shall be registered immediately after birth and shall have the right from birth to a name, the right to acquire a nationality, and, as far as possible, the right to know and be cared for by his or her parents.
2. States Parties shall ensure the implementation of these rights in accordance with their national law and their obligations under the relevant international instruments in this field, in particular where the child would otherwise be stateless.

Article 8: Preservation of identity
1. States Parties undertake to respect the right of the child to preserve his or her identity, including nationality, name and family relations as recognized by law without unlawful interference.
2. Where a child is illegally deprived of some or all of the elements of his or her identity, States Parties shall provide appropriate assistance and protection, with a view to speedily re-establishing his or her identity.

Article 9: Separation from parents
1. States Parties shall ensure that a child shall not be separated from his or her parents against their will, except when competent authorities subject to judicial review determine, in accordance with applicable law and procedures, that such separation is necessary for the best interests of the child. Such determination may be necessary in a particular case such as one involving abuse or neglect of the child by the parents, or one where the parents are living separately and a decision must be made as to the child's place of residence.
2. In any proceedings pursuant to paragraph 1, all interested parties shall be given an opportunity to participate in the proceedings and make their views known.
3. States Parties shall respect the right of the child who is separated from one or both parents to maintain personal relations and direct contact with both parents on a regular basis, except if it is contrary to the child's best interests.
4. Where such separation result from any action initiated by a State Party, such as the detention, imprisonment, exile, deportation or death (including death arising from any cause while the person is in the custody of the State) of one or both parents or of the child, that State Party shall, upon request, provide the parents, the child or, if appropriate,

another member of the family with the essential information concerning the whereabouts of the absent member(s) of the family unless the provision of the information would be detrimental to the well-being of the child. States Parties shall further ensure that the submission of such a request shall of itself entail no adverse consequences for the person(s) concerned.

Article 10: Family reunification
1. In accordance with the obligations of States Parties under article 9, paragraph 1, applications by a child or his or her parents to enter or leave a State Party for the purpose of family reunification shall be dealt with by States Parties in a positive, humane and expeditious manner. States Parties shall further ensure that the submission of such a request shall entail no adverse consequences for the applicants and for the members of their family.
2. A child whose parents reside in different States shall have the right to maintain on regular basis save in exceptional circumstances personal relations and direct contacts with both parents. Towards that end and in accordance with the obligation of States Parties under article 9, paragraph 2, States Parties shall respect the right of the child and his or her parents to leave any country, including their own, and to enter their own country. The right to leave any country shall be subject only to such restrictions as are prescribed by law and which are necessary to protect the national security, public order (*ordre public*), public health or morals or the rights and freedoms of others and are consistent with the other rights recognized in the present Convention.

Article 11: Illicit transfer and non-return
1. State Party shall take measures to combat the illicit transfer and non-return of children abroad.
2. To this end States Parties shall promote the conclusion of bilateral or multilateral agreements or accession to existing agreements.

Article 12: The child's opinion
1. States Parties shall assure to the child who is capable of forming his or her own views the right to express those views freely in all matters affecting the child, the views of the child being given due weight in accordance with the age and maturity of the child.
2. For this purpose, the child shall in particular be provided the opportunity to be heard in any judicial and administrative proceedings affecting the child, either directly, or through a representative or an appropriate body, in a manner consistent with the procedural rules of national law.

Article 13: Freedom of expression
1. The child shall have the right to freedom of expression; this right shall include freedom to seek, receive and impart information and ideas of all kinds, regardless of frontiers, either orally, in writing or in print, in the form of art, or through any other media of the child's choice.
2. The exercise of this right may be subject to certain restrictions, but these shall only be such as are provided by law and are necessary:
   (a) for respect of the rights or reputations of others; or
   (b) for the protection of national security or of public order (*ordre public*), or of public health or morals.

Article 14: Freedom of thought, conscience and religion
1. States Parties shall respect the right of the child to freedom of thought, conscience and religion.
2. States Parties shall respect the rights and duties of the parents and, when applicable, legal guardians, to provide direction to the child in the exercise of his or her right in a manner consistent with the evolving capacities of the child.
3. Freedom to manifest one's religion or beliefs may be subject only to such limitations as are prescribed by law and are necessary to protect public safety, order, health, or morals or the fundamental rights and freedoms of others.

Article 15: Freedom of association
1. States Parties recognize the rights of the child to freedom of association and to freedom of peaceful assembly.
2. No restrictions may be placed on the exercise of these rights other than those imposed in conformity with the law and which are necessary in a democratic society in the interests of national security or public safety, public order (*ordre public*), the protection of public health or morals or the protection of the rights and freedoms of others.

Article 16: Protection of privacy
1. No child shall be subjected to arbitrary or unlawful interference with his or her privacy, family, home or correspondence, nor to unlawful attacks on his or her honour and reputation.
2. The child has the right to the protection of the law against such interference or attacks.

Article 17: Access to appropriate information
States Parties recognize the important function performed by the mass media and shall ensure that the child has access to information and material from a diversity of national and international sources, especially those aimed at

the promotion of his or her social, spiritual and moral well-being and physical and mental health. To this end, States Parties shall:

(a) Encourage the mass media to disseminate information and material of social and cultural benefit to the child and in accordance with the spirit of article 29;
(b) Encourage international co-operation in the production, exchange and dissemination of such information and material from a diversity of cultural, national and international sources;
(c) Encourage the production and dissemination of children's books;
(d) Encourage the mass media to have particular regard to the linguistic needs of the child who belongs to a minority group or who is indigenous;
(e) Encourage the development of appropriate guidelines for the protection of the child from information and material injurious to his or her well-being bearing in mind the provisions of articles 13 and 18.

Article 18: Parental responsibilities
1. States Parties shall use their best efforts to ensure recognition of the principle that both parents have common responsibilities for the upbringing and development of the child. Parents or, as the case may be, legal guardians, have the primary responsibility for the upbringing and development of the child. The best interest of the child will be their basic concern.
2. For the purpose of guaranteeing and promoting the rights set forth in this Convention, States Parties shall render appropriate assistance to parents and legal guardians in the performance of their child-rearing responsibilities and shall ensure the development of institutions, facilities and services for the care of children.
3. States Parties shall take all appropriate measures to ensure that children of working parents have the right to benefit from child care services and facilities for which they are eligible.

Article 19: Protection from abuse and neglect
1. States Parties shall take all appropriate legislative, administrative, social and educational measures to protect the child from all forms of physical or mental violence, injury or abuse, neglect or negligent treatment, maltreatment or exploitation including sexual abuse, while in the care of parent(s), legal guardian(s) or any other person who has the care of the child.
2. Such protective measures should, as appropriate, include effective procedures for the establishment of social programmes to provide necessary support for the child and for those who have the care of the child, as well as for other forms of prevention and for identification, reporting,

referral, investigation, treatment, and follow-up of instances of child maltreatment described heretofore, and, as appropriate, for judicial involvement.

Article 20: Protection of children without families
1. A child temporarily or permanently deprived of his or her family environment, or in whose own best interests cannot be allowed to remain in that environment, shall be entitled to special protection and assistance provided by the State.
2. States Parties shall in accordance with their national laws ensure alternative care for such a child.
3. Such care could include, *inter alia*, foster placement, Kafala of Islamic law, adoption, or if necessary placement in suitable institutions for the care of children. When considering solutions, due regard shall be paid to the desirability of continuity in a child's upbringing and to the child's ethnic, religious, cultural and linguistic background.

Article 21: Adoption
States Parties which recognize and/or permit the system of adoption shall ensure that the best interests of the child shall be the paramount consideration and they shall:
 (a) ensure that the adoption of a child is authorized only by competent authorities who determine, in accordance with applicable law and procedures and on the basis of all pertinent and reliable information, that the adoption is permissible in view of the child's status concerning parents, relatives and legal guardians and that, if required, the persons concerned have given their informed consent to the adoption on the basis of such counselling as may be necessary;
 (b) recognize that intercountry adoption may be considered as an alternative means of child's care, if the child cannot be placed in a foster or an adoptive family or cannot in any suitable manner be cared for in the child's country of origin;
 (c) ensure that the child concerned by intercountry adoption enjoys safeguards and standards equivalent to those existing in the case of national adoption;
 (d) take all appropriate measures to ensure that, in intercountry adoption, the placement does not result in improper financial gain for those involved in it;
 (e) promote, where appropriate, the objectives of this article by concluding bilateral or multilateral arrangements or agreements, and endeavour, within this framework, to ensure that the placement of the child in another country is carried out by competent authorities or organs.

Article 22: *Refugee children*
 1. States Parties shall take appropriate measures to ensure that a child who is seeking refugee status or who is considered a refugee in accordance with applicable international or domestic law and procedures shall, whether unaccompanied or accompanied by his or her parents or by any other person, receive appropriate protection and humanitarian assistance in the enjoyment of applicable rights set forth in this Convention and in other international human rights or humanitarian instruments to which the said States are Parties.
 2. For this purpose, States Parties shall provide, as they consider appropriate, co-operation in any efforts by the United Nations and other competent inter-governmental organizations or non-governmental organizations co-operating with the United Nations to protect and assist such a child and to trace the parents or other members of the family of any refugee child in order to obtain information necessary for reunification with his or her family. In cases where no parents or other members of the family can be found, the child shall be accorded the same protection as any other child permanently or temporarily deprived of his or her family environment for any reason, as set forth in the present Convention.

Article 23: *Handicapped children*
 1. States Parties recognize that a mentally or physically disabled child should enjoy a full and decent life, in conditions which ensure dignity, promote self-reliance, and facilitate the child's active participation in the community.
 2. States Parties recognize the right of the disabled child to special care and shall encourage and ensure the extension, subject to available resources, to the eligible child and those responsible for his or her care, of assistance for which application is made and which is appropriate to the child's condition and to the circumstances of the parents or others caring for the child.
 3. Recognizing the special needs of a disabled child, assistance extended in accordance with paragraph 2 shall be provided free of charge, whenever possible, taking into account the financial resources of the parents or others caring for the child, and shall be designed to ensure that the disabled child has effective access to and receives education, training, health care services, rehabilitation services, preparation for employment and recreation opportunities in a manner conducive to the child's achieving the fullest possible social integration and individual development, including his or her cultural and spiritual development.
 4. States Parties shall promote in the spirit of international co-operation the exchange of appropriate information in the field of preventive health care and of medical, psychological and functional treatment of disabled

children, including dissemination of and access to information concerning methods of rehabilitation education and vocational services, with the aim of enabling States Parties to improve their capabilities and skills and to widen their experience in these areas. In this regard, particular account shall be taken of the needs of developing countries.

Article 24: Health and health services
1. States Parties recognize the right of the child to the enjoyment of the highest attainable standard of health and to facilities for the treatment of illness and rehabilitation of health. States Parties shall strive to ensure that no child is deprived of his or her right of access to such health care services.
2. States Parties shall pursue full implementation of this right and, in particular, shall take appropriate measures:

   (a) to diminish infant and child mortality,
   (b) to ensure the provision of necessary medical assistance and health care to all children with emphasis on the development of primary health care.
   (c) to combat disease and malnutrition including within the framework of primary health care, through *inter alia* the application of readily available technology and through the provision of adequate nutritious foods and clean drinking water, taking into consideration the dangers and risks of environmental pollution,
   (d) to ensure appropriate pre- and post-natal health care for mothers,
   (e) to ensure that all segments of society, in particular parents and children, are informed, have access to education and are supported in the use of, basic knowledge of child health and nutrition, the advantages of breast-feeding, hygiene and environmental sanitation and the prevention of accidents.
   (f) to develop preventive health care, guidance for parents, and family planning education and services.

3. States Parties shall take all effective and appropriate measures with a view to abolishing traditional practices prejudicial to the health of children.
4. States Parties undertake to promote and encourage international co-operation with a view to achieving progressively the full realization of the right recognized in this article. In this regard, particular account shall be taken of the needs of developing countries.

Article 25: Periodic review of placement
States Parties recognize the right of a child who has been placed by the competent authorities for the purposes of care, protection, or treatment of

his or her physical or mental health, to a periodic review of the treatment provided to the child and all other circumstances relevant to his or her placement.

Article 26: Social security
1. States Parties shall recognize for every child the right to benefit from social security, including social insurance, and shall take the necessary measures to achieve the full realization of this right in accordance with their national law.
2. The benefits should, where appropriate, be granted taking into account the resources and the circumstances of the child and persons having responsibility for the maintenance of the child as well as any other consideration relevant to an application for benefits made by or on behalf of the child.

Article 27: Standard of living
1. States Parties recognize the right of every child to a standard of living adequate for the child's physical, mental, spiritual, moral and social development.
2. The parent(s) or other responsible for the child have the primary responsibility to secure, within their abilities and financial capacities, the conditions of living necessary for the child's development.
3. States Parties in accordance with national conditions and within their means shall take appropriate measures to assist parents and other responsible for the child to implement this right and shall in case of need provide material assistance and support programmes, particularly with regard to nutrition, clothing and housing.
4. States Parties shall take all appropriate measures to secure the recovery of maintenance for the child from the parents or other persons having financial responsibility for the child, both within the State Party and from abroad. In particular, where the person having financial responsibility for the child lives in a State different from that of the child, States Parties shall promote the accession to international agreements or the conclusion of such agreements as well as the making of other appropriate arrangements.

Article 28: Education
1. States Parties recognize the right of the child to education, and with a view to achieving this right progressively and on the basis of equal opportunity, they shall, in particular:

   (a) make primary education compulsory and available free to all:
   (b) encourage the development of different forms of secondary education, including general and vocational education, make them

available and accessible to every child, and take appropriate measures such as the introduction of free education and offering financial assistance in case of need;
(c) make higher education accessible to all on the basis of capacity by every appropriate means;
(d) make educational and vocational information and guidance available and accessible to all children;
(e) take measures to encourage regular attendance at schools and the reduction of drop-out rates.

2. States Parties shall take all appropriate measures to ensure that school discipline is administered in a manner consistent with the child's human dignity and in conformity with the present Convention.
3. States Parties shall promote and encourage international co-operation in matters relating to education, in particular with a view to contributing to the elimination of ignorance and illiteracy throughout the world and facilitating access to scientific and technical knowledge and modern teaching methods. In this regard, particular account shall be taken of the needs of developing countries.

Article 29: Aims of education
1. States Parties agree that the education of the child shall be directed to:

(a) the development of the child's personality, talents and mental and physical abilities to their fullest potential;
(b) the development of respect for human rights and fundamental freedoms, and for the principles enshrined in the Charter of the United Nations;
(c) the development of respect for the child's parents, his or her own cultural identity, language and values, for the national values of the country in which the child is living, the country from which he or she may originate, and for civilizations different from his or her own;
(d) the preparation of the child for responsible life in a free society, in the spirit of understanding, peace, tolerance, equality of sexes, and friendship among all peoples, ethnic, national and religious groups and persons of indigenous origin;
(e) the development of respect for the natural environment.

2. No part of this article or article 28 shall be construed so as to interfere with the liberty of individuals and bodies to establish and direct educational institutions, subject always to the observance of the principles set forth in paragraph 1 of this article and to the requirements that the

education given in such institutions shall conform to such minimum standards as may be laid down by the State.

Article 30: Children of minorities or indigenous populations
In those States in which ethnic, religious or linguistic minorities or persons of indigenous origin exist, a child belonging to such a minority or who is indigenous shall not be denied the right, in community with other members of his or her group, to enjoy his or her own culture, to profess and practice his or her own religion, or to use his or her own language.

Article 31: Leisure, recreation and cultural activities
1. States Parties recognize the right of the child to rest and leisure, to engage in play and recreational activities appropriate to the age of the child and to participate freely in cultural life and the arts.
2. States Parties shall take legislative, administrative, social and educational measures to ensure the implementation of this article. To this end, and having regard to the relevant provisions of other international instruments, States Parties shall in particular:

    (a) provide for a minimum age or minimum ages for admission to employment;
    (b) provide for appropriate regulation of the hours and conditions of employment; and
    (c) provide for appropriate penalties or other sanctions to ensure the effective enforcement of this article.

Article 32: Child labour
1. States Parties recognize the right of the child to be protected from economic exploitation and from performing any work that is likely to be hazardous or to interfere with the child's education, or to be harmful to the child's health or physical, mental, spiritual, moral or social development.
2. States Parties shall take legislative, administrative, social and educational measures to ensure the implementation of this article. To this end, and having regard to the relevant provisions of other international instruments, States Parties shall in particular:

    (a) provide for a minimum age or minimum ages for admissions to employment;
    (b) provide for appropriate regulation of the hours and conditions of employment; and
    (c) provide for appropriate penalties or other sanctions to ensure the effective enforcement of this article.

Article 33: Drug abuse
States Parties shall take all appropriate measures, including legislative, administrative, social and educational measures, to protect children from the illicit use of narcotic drugs and psychotropic substances as defined in the relevant international treaties, and to prevent the use of children in the illicit production and trafficking of such substances.

Article 34: Sexual exploitation
States Parties undertake to protect the child from all forms of sexual exploitation and sexual abuse. For these purposes States Parties shall in particular take all appropriate national, bilateral and multilateral measures to prevent:

(a) the inducement or coercion of a child to engage in any unlawful sexual activity;
(b) the exploitative use of children in prostitution or other unlawful sexual practices;
(c) the exploitative use of children in pornographic performances and materials.

Article 35: Sale, trafficking and abduction
States Parties shall take all appropriate national, bilateral and multilateral measures to prevent the abduction, the sale of or traffic in children for any purpose or in any form.

Article 36: Other forms of exploitation
States Parties shall protect the child against all other forms of exploitation prejudicial to any aspects of the child's welfare.

Article 37: Torture and deprivation of liberty
States Parties shall ensure that:

(a) no child shall be subjected to torture or other cruel, inhuman or degrading treatment or punishment. Neither capital punishment nor life imprisonment without possibility of release shall be imposed for offenses committed by persons below 18 years of age;
(b) no child shall be deprived of his or her liberty unlawfully or arbitrarily. The arrest, detention or imprisonment of a child shall be in conformity with the law and shall be used only as a measure of last resort and for the shortest appropriate period of time:
(c) every child deprived of liberty shall be treated with humanity and respect for the inherent dignity of the human person, and in a manner which takes into account the needs of persons of their age. In particular every child deprived of liberty shall be separated from adults unless it is considered in the child's best interest not to do so and shall have

the right to maintain contact with his or her family through correspondence and visits, save in exceptional circumstances;
(d) every child deprived of his or her liberty shall have the right to prompt access to legal and other appropriate assistance as well as the right to challenge the legality of the deprivation of his or her liberty before a court or other competent, independent and impartial authority and to a prompt decision on any such action.

Article 38: Armed conflicts
1. States Parties undertake to respect and to ensure respect for rules of international humanitarian law applicable to them in armed conflicts which are relevant to the child.
2. States Parties shall take all feasible measures to ensure that persons who have not attained the age of 15 years do not take a direct part in hostilities.
3. States Parties shall refrain from recruiting any person who has not attained the age of 15 years into their armed forces. In recruiting among those persons who have attained the age of 15 years but who have not attained the age of 18 years, States Parties shall endeavour to give priority to those who are oldest.
4. In accordance with their obligations under international humanitarian law to protect the civilian population in armed conflicts, States Parties shall take all feasible measures to ensure protection and care of children who are affected by an armed conflict.

Article 39: Rehabilitative care
States Parties shall take all appropriate measures to promote physical and psychological recovery and social re-integration of a child victim of: any form of neglect, exploitation, or abuse; torture or any other form of cruel, inhuman or degrading treatment or punishment; or armed conflicts. Such recovery and re-integration shall take place in an environment which fosters the health, self-respect and dignity of the child.

Article 40: Administration of juvenile justice
1. States Parties recognize the right of every child alleged as, accused of, or recognized as having infringed the penal law, to be treated in a manner consistent with the promotion of the child's sense of dignity and worth, which reinforces the child's respect for the human rights and fundamental freedoms of others and which takes into account the child's age and the desirability of promoting the child's re-integration and the child's assuming a constructive role in society.
2. To this end, and having regard to the relevant provisions of international instruments, States Parties shall, in particular, ensure that:

(a) No child shall be alleged as, be accused of, or recognized as having infringed the penal law by reason of acts or omissions which were not prohibited by national or international law at the time they were committed;

(b) Every child alleged as or accused of having infringed the penal law has at least the following guarantees:

i) to be presumed innocent until proven guilty according to law;

ii) to be informed promptly and directly of the charges against him or her, and if appropriate through his or her parents or legal guardian, and to have legal or other appropriate assistance in the preparation and presentation of his or her defence:

iii) to have the matter determined without delay by a competent, independent and impartial authority or judicial body in a fair hearing according to law, in the presence of legal or other appropriate assistance and, unless it is considered not to be in the best interest of the child, in particular, taking into account his or her age or situation, his or her parents or legal guardians;

iv) not to be compelled to give testimony or to confess guilt; to examine or have examined adverse witnesses and to obtain the participation and examination of witnesses on his or her behalf under conditions of equality;

v) if considered to have infringed the penal law, to have this decision and any measures imposed in consequence thereof reviewed by a higher competent, independent and impartial authority or judicial body according to law;

vi) to have the free assistance of an interpreter if the child cannot understand or speak the language used;

vii) to have his or her privacy fully respected at all stages of the proceedings.

3. States Parties shall seek to promote the establishment of laws, procedures, authorities and institutions specifically applicable to children alleged as, accused of, or recognized as having infringed the penal law, and in particular:

(a) the establishment of a minimum age below which children shall be presumed not to have the capacity to infringe the penal law;

(b) whenever appropriate and desirable, measures for dealing with such children without resorting to judicial proceedings, providing that human rights and legal safeguards are fully respected.

4. A variety of dispositions, such as care, guidance and supervision orders; counselling; probation; foster care; education and vocational training programmes and other alternatives to institutional care shall be avail-

able to ensure that children are dealt with in a manner appropriate to their well-being and proportionate both to their circumstances and the offence.

Article 41: Respect for existing standards
Nothing in this Convention shall affect any provisions that are more conducive to the realization of the rights of the child and that may be contained in:

(a) the law or a State Party; or
(b) international law in force for that State.

PART II: IMPLEMENTATION AND ENTRY INTO FORCE

Article 42
States Parties undertake to make the principles and provisions of the Convention widely known, by appropriate and active means, to adults and children alike.

Article 43
1. For the purpose of examining the progress made by States Parties in achieving the realization of the obligations undertaken in the present Convention, there shall be established a Committee on the Rights of the Child, which shall carry out the functions hereinafter provided.
2. The Committee shall consist of 10 experts of high moral standing and recognized competence in the field covered by this Convention. The members of the Committee shall be elected by States Parties from among their nationals and shall serve in their personal capacity, consideration being given to equitable geographical distribution as well as to the principal legal systems.
3. The members of the Committee shall be elected by secret ballot from a list of persons nominated by States Parties. Each State Party may nominate one person from among its own nationals.
4. The initial election to the Committee shall be held no later than six months after the date of the entry into force of the present Convention and thereafter every second year. At least four months before the date of each election, the Secretary General of the United Nations shall address a letter to States Parties inviting them to submit their nominations within two months. The Secretary-General shall subsequently prepare a list in alphabetical order of all persons thus nominated, indicating States Parties which have nominated them, and shall submit it to the States Parties to the present Convention.

5. The elections shall be held at meetings of States Parties convened by the Secretary-General at United Nations Headquarters. At those meetings, for which two-thirds of States Parties shall constitute a quorum, the persons elected to the Committee shall be those who obtain the largest number of votes and an absolute majority of the votes of the representatives of States Parties present and voting.
6. The members of the Committee shall be elected for a term of four years. They shall be eligible for re-election if renominated. The term of five of the members elected at the first election shall expire at the end of two years; immediately after the first election the names of these five members shall be chosen by lot by the Chairman of the meeting.
7. If a member of the Committee dies or resigns or declares that for any other cause he or she can no longer perform the duties of the Committee, the State Party which nominated the member shall appoint another expert from among its nationals to serve for the remainder of the term, subject to the approval of the Committee.
8. The Committee shall establish its own rules of procedure.
9. The Committee shall elect its officers for a period of two years.
10. The meetings of the Committee shall normally be held at the United Nations Headquarters or at any other convenient place as determined by the Committee. The Committee shall normally meet annually. The duration of the meetings of the Committee shall be determined, as reviewed, if necessary, by a meeting of the States Parties to the present Committee, subject to the approval of the General Assembly. The Secretary-General of the United Nations shall provide the necessary staff and facilities for the effective performance of the functions of the Committee under the present Convention.
12. With the approval of the General Assembly, the members of the Committee established under the present Convention shall receive emoluments from the United Nations resources on such terms and conditions as the Assembly may decide.

Article 44
1. States Parties undertake to submit to the Committee, through the Secretary-General of the United Nations, reports on the measures they have adopted which give effect to the rights recognized herein and on the progress made on the enjoyment of those rights:

    (a) within two years of the entry into force of the Committee for the State Party concerned,
    (b) thereafter every five years.

2. Reports made under this article shall indicate factors and difficulties, if

any, affecting the degree of fulfilment of the obligations under the present Convention. Reports shall also contain sufficient information to provide the Committee with a comprehensive understanding of the implementation of the Committee in the country concerned.
3. A State Party which has submitted a comprehensive initial report to the Committee need not in its subsequent reports submitted in accordance with paragraph 1(b) repeat basic information previously provided.
4. The Committee may request from States Parties further information relevant to the implementation of the Convention.
5. The Committee shall submit to the General Assembly of the United Nations through the Economic and Social Council, every two years, reports on its activities.
6. States Parties shall make their reports widely available to the public in their own countries.

Article 45
In order to foster the effective implementation of the Convention and to encourage international co-operation in the field covered by the Convention:

(a) The specialized agencies, UNICEF and other United Nations organs shall be entitled to be represented at the consideration of the implementation of such provisions of the present Convention as fall within the scope of their mandate. The Committee may invite the specialized agencies, UNICEF and other competent bodies as it may consider appropriate to provide expert advice on the implementation of the Convention in areas falling within the scope of their respective mandates. The Committee may invite the specialized agencies, UNICEF and other United Nations organs to submit reports on the implementation of the Convention in areas falling within the scope of their activities.
(b) The Committee shall transmit, as it may consider appropriate, to the specialized agencies, UNICEF and other competent bodies, any reports from States Parties that contain a request, or indicate a need, for technical advice or assistance along with the Committee's observations and suggestions, if any, on these requests or indications.
(c) The Committee may recommend to the General Assembly to request the Secretary-General to undertake on its behalf studies on specific issues relating to the rights of the child.
(d) The Committee may make suggestions and general recommendations based on information received pursuant to articles 44 and 45 of this Convention. Such suggestions and general recommendations shall be transmitted to any State Party concerned and reported to the General Assembly, together with comments, if any, from States Parties.

Part III

Article 46
The present Convention shall be open for signature by all States.

Article 47
The present Convention is subject to ratification. Instruments of ratification shall be deposited with the Secretary-General of the United Nations.

Article 48
The present Convention shall remain open for accession by any State. The instruments of accession shall be deposited with the Secretary-General of the United Nations.

Article 49
1. The present Convention shall enter into force on the thirtieth day following the date of deposit with the Secretary-General of the United Nations of the twentieth instrument of ratification or accession.
2. For each State ratifying or acceding to the Convention after the deposit of the twentieth instrument of ratification or accession, the Convention shall enter into force on the thirtieth day after the deposit by such State of its instrument of ratification or accession.

Article 50
1. Any State Party may propose an amendment and file it with the Secretary-General of the United Nations. The Secretary-General shall thereupon communicate the proposed amendment to States Parties with a request that they indicate whether they favour a conference of States Parties for the purpose of considering and voting upon the proposals. In the event that within four months from the date of such communication at least one-third of the States Parties favour such a conference, the Secretary-General shall convene the conference under the auspices of the United Nations. Any amendment adopted by a majority of States Parties present and voting at the conference shall be submitted to the General Assembly of the United Nations for approval.
2. An amendment adopted in accordance with paragraph (1) of this article shall enter into force when it has been approved by the General Assembly of the United Nations and accepted by a two-thirds majority of States Parties.
3. When an amendment enters into force, it shall be binding on those States Parties which have accepted it, other States Parties still being bound by the provisions of this Convention and any earlier amendments which they have accepted.

Article 51
1. The Secretary-General of the United Nations shall receive and circulate to all States the text of reservations made by States at the time of ratification or accession.
2. A reservation incompatible with the object and purpose of the present Convention shall not be permitted.
3. Reservations may be withdrawn at any time by notification to this effect addressed to the Secretary-General of the United Nations who shall then inform all States. Such notification shall take effect on the date on which it is received by the Secretary-General.

Article 52
A State Party may denounce this Convention by written notification to the Secretary-General of the United Nations. Denunciation becomes effective one year after the date of receipt of the notification by the Secretary-General.

Article 53
The Secretary-General of the United Nations is designated as the depositary of the present Convention.

Article 54
The original of the present Convention, of which the Arabic, Chinese, English, French, Russian and Spanish texts are equally authentic, shall be deposited with the Secretary-General of the United Nations.

In witness thereof the undersigned plenipotentiaries, being duly authorized thereto by their respective governments, have signed the present Convention.

APPENDIX XLIV

World Declaration on the Survival, Protection and Development of Children (1990)

New York, 30 September 1990

1. We have gathered at the World Summit for Children to undertake a joint commitment and to make an urgent universal appeal – to give every child a better future.
2. The children of the world are innocent, vulnerable and dependent. They are also curious, active and full of hope. Their time should be one of joy and peace, of playing, learning and growing. Their future should be shaped in harmony and co-operation. Their lives should mature, as they broaden their perspectives and gain new experiences.
3. But for many children, the reality of childhood is altogether different.

The Challenge

4. Each day, countless children around the world are exposed to dangers that hamper their growth and development. They suffer immensely as casualties of war and violence; as victims of racial discrimination, apartheid, aggression, foreign occupation and annexation; as refugees and displaced children, forced to abandon their homes and their roots; as disabled; or as victims of neglect, cruelty and exploitation.
5. Each day, millions of children suffer from the scourges of poverty and economic crisis – from hunger and homelessness, from epidemics and illiteracy, from degradation of the environment. They suffer from the grave effects of the problems of external indebtedness and also from the lack of sustained and sustainable growth in many developing countries, particularly the least developed ones.
6. Each day, 40,000 children die from malnutrition and disease, including acquired immunodeficiency syndrome (AIDS), from the lack of clean water and inadequate sanitation and from the effects of the drug problem.
7. These are challenges that we, as political leaders, must meet.

The Opportunity

8. Together, our nations have the means and the knowledge to protect the lives and to diminish enormously the suffering of children, to promote the full development of their human potential and to make them aware of their needs, rights and opportunities. The Convention on the Rights of the Child provides a new opportunity to make respect for children's rights and welfare truly universal.

9. Recent improvements in the international political climate can facilitate this task. Through international co-operation and solidarity it should now be possible to achieve concrete results in many fields – to revitalize economic growth and development, to protect the environment, to prevent the spread of fatal and crippling diseases and to achieve greater social and economic justice. The current moves towards disarmament also mean that significant resources could be released for purposes other than military ones. Improving the well-being of children must be a very high priority when these resources are reallocated.

The Task

10. Enhancement of children's health and nutrition is a first duty, and also a task for which solutions are now within reach. The lives of tens of thousands of boys and girls can be saved every day, because the causes of their death are readily preventable. Child and infant mortality is unacceptably high in many parts of the world, but can be lowered dramatically with means that are already known and easily accessible.

11. Further attention, care and support should be accorded to disabled children, as well as to other children in very difficult circumstances.

12. Strengthening the role of women in general and ensuring their equal rights will be to the advantage of the world's children. Girls must be given equal treatment and opportunities from the very beginning.

13. At present, over 100 million children are without basic schooling, and two thirds of them are girls. The provision of basic education and literacy for all are among the most important contributions that can be made to the development of the world's children.

14. Half a million mothers die each year from causes related to childbirth. Safe motherhood must be promoted in all possible ways. Emphasis must be placed on responsible planning of family size and on child spacing. The family, as a fundamental group and natural environment for the growth and well-being of children, should be given all necessary protection and assistance.

15. All children must be given the chance to find their identity and realize

their worth in a safe and supportive environment, through families and other care-givers committed to their welfare. They must be prepared for responsible life in a free society. They should, from their early years, be encouraged to participate in the cultural life of their societies.

16. Economic conditions will continue to influence greatly the fate of children, especially in developing nations. For the sake of the future of all children, it is urgently necessary to ensure or reactivate sustained and sustainable economic growth and development in all countries and also to continue to give urgent attention to an early, broad and durable solution to the external debt problems facing developing debtor countries.
17. These tasks require a continued and concerted effort by all nations, through national action and international co-operation.

The Commitment

18. The well-being of children requires political action at the highest level. We are determined to take that action.
19. We ourselves hereby make a solemn commitment to give high priority to the rights of children, to their survival and to their protection and development. This will also ensure the well-being of all societies.
20. We have agreed that we will act together, in international co-operation, as well as in our respective countries. We now commit ourselves to the following 10–point programme to protect the rights of children and to improve their lives:

   (1) We will work to promote earliest possible ratification and implementation of the Convention on the Rights of the Child. Programmes to encourage information about children's rights should be launched world-wide, taking into account the distinct cultural and social values in different countries.
   (2) We will work for a solid effort of national and international action to enhance children's health, to promote pre-natal care and to lower infant and child mortality in all countries and among all peoples. We will promote the provision of clean water in all communities for all their children, as well as universal access to sanitation.
   (3) We will work for optimal growth and development in childhood, through measures to eradicate hunger, malnutrition and famine, and thus to relieve millions of children of tragic sufferings in a world that has the means to feed all its citizens.
   (4) We will work to strengthen the role and status of women. We

will promote responsible planning of family size, child spacing, breastfeeding and safe motherhood.

(5) We will work for respect for the role of the family in providing for children and will support the efforts of parents, other caregivers and communities to nurture and care for children, from the earliest stages of childhood through adolescence. We also recognize the special needs of children who are separated from their families.

(6) We will work for programmes that reduce illiteracy and provide educational opportunities for all children, irrespective of their background and gender; that prepare children for productive employment and lifelong learning opportunities, i.e. through vocational training; and that enable children to grow to adulthood within a supportive and nurturing cultural and social context.

(7) We will work to ameliorate the plight of millions of children who live under especially difficult circumstances – as victims of apartheid and foreign occupation; orphans and street children and children of migrant workers; the displaced children and victims of natural and man-made disasters; the disabled and the abused, the socially disadvantaged and the exploited. Refugee children must be helped to find new roots in life. We will work for special protection of the working child and for the abolition of illegal child labour. We will do our best to ensure that children are not drawn into becoming victims of the scourge of illicit drugs.

(8) We will work carefully to protect children from the scourge of war and to take measures to prevent further armed conflicts, in order to give children everywhere a peaceful and secure future. We will promote the values of peace, understanding and dialogue in the education of children. The essential needs of children and families must be protected even in times of war and in violence-ridden areas. We ask that periods of tranquillity and special relief corridors be observed for the benefit of children, where war and violence are still taking place.

(9) We will work for common measures for the protection of the environment, at all levels, so that all children can enjoy a safer and healthier future.

(10) We will work for a global attack on poverty, which would have immediate benefits for children's welfare. The vulnerability and special needs of the children of the developing countries, and in particular the least developed ones, deserve priority. But growth and development need promotion in all States, through national action and international co-operation. That calls for transfers of appropriate additional resources to developing

countries as well as improved terms of trade, further trade liberalization and measures for debt relief. It also implies structural adjustments that promote world economic growth, particularly in developing countries, while ensuring the well-being of the most vulnerable sectors of the populations, in particular the children.

THE NEXT STEPS

21. The World Summit for Children has presented us with a challenge to take action. We have agreed to take up that challenge.
22. Among the partnerships we seek, we turn especially to children themselves. We appeal to them to participate in this effort.
23. We also seek the support of the United Nations system, as well as other international and regional organizations, in the universal effort to promote the well-being of children. We ask for greater involvement on the part of non-governmental organizations, in complementing national efforts and joint international action in this field.
24. We have decided to adopt and implement a Plan of Action, as a framework for more specific national and international undertaking. We appeal to all our colleagues to endorse that Plan. We are prepared to make available the resources to meet these commitments, as part of the priorities of our national plans.
25. We do this not only for the present generation, but for all generations to come. There can be no task nobler than giving every child a better future.

APPENDIX XLV

Charter on the Rights and Welfare of the African Child (1990)

Preamble

The African States Members of the Organization of African Unity, Parties to the present Convention entitled "African Charter on the Rights and Welfare of the Child".

Recalling that the Assembly of Heads of State and Government of the Organization of African Unity, meeting at its Sixteenth Ordinary Session in Monrovia, Liberia from 17 to 20 July, 1979 recognized the need to take all appropriate measures to promote and protect the rights and welfare of the African child;

Considering that the Charter of the Organization of African Unity recognizes the paramountcy of Human Rights and the African Charter on Human and Peoples' Rights proclaimed and agreed that everyone is entitled to all the rights and freedoms recognized and guaranteed therein, without distinction of any kind such as race, ethnic group, colour, sex, language, religion, political or any other opinion, national and social origin, fortune, birth or status;

Noting with concern that the situation of many African children remains critical as a result of inadequate social conditions, natural disasters, armed conflicts, economic deprivation, exploitation, hunger, disability and that the child, by reason of his physical and mental immaturity, needs special safeguard and care;

Recognizing that the child occupies a unique and privileged position in the African society and that for the full and harmonious development of his personality, the child should grow up in a family environment in an atmosphere of happiness, love and understanding;

Recognizing that the child due to the needs of his physical and mental development requires particular care with regard to health, physical, mental, moral and social development, and requires legal protection in conditions of freedom, dignity and security;

Taking into consideration the virtues of their cultural heritage, historical background and the values of the African civilization which should inspire and characterize their reflection on the concept of the rights and welfare of the child;

Considering that the promotion and protection of the rights and welfare of the child also implies the performance of duties on the part of everyone;

Reaffirming adherance to the principles of the rights and welfare of the child contained in the declarations, conventions and other instruments of the Organization of African Unity and in the United Nations and in particular the United Nations Convention on the Rights of the Child;

HAVE AGREED AS FOLLOWS:

PART I: RIGHTS AND DUTIES

CHAPTER ONE

Rights and Welfare of the Child

ARTICLE 1

1. The Member States of the Organization of African Unity Parties to the present Charter shall recognize the rights, freedoms and duties enshrined in this Charter and shall undertake to take the necessary steps, in accordance with their Constitutional process and with the provisions of the present Charter, to adopt such legislative or other measures as may be necessary to give effect to the provisions of this Charter.
2. Nothing in this Charter shall affect any provisions that are more conducive to the realization of the rights and welfare of the child contained in the law of a State Party or in any other international convention or agreement in force in that State.
3. Any custom, tradition, cultural or religious practice that is inconsistent with the rights, duties and obligations contained in the present Charter shall to the extent to such inconsistency be null and void.

ARTICLE 2

According to the present Charter, a child means every human being up to the age of 18 years whether such a child is born out of wedlock or in wedlock.

Article 3

Every child shall be entitled to the enjoyment of the rights and freedoms recognized and guaranteed in this Charter irrespective of the child's or his parents or legal guardian's race, ethnic group, colour, sex, language, religion, political or other opinion, national and social origin, fortune, birth or other status.

Article 4

1. In all actions concerning the child undertaken by any person or authority the best interests of the child shall be the primary consideration.
2. In all judicial or administrative proceedings affecting a child who is capable of forming his own views, an opportunity shall be provided for the views of the child to be heard either directly or through a disinterested representative as a party to the proceedings, and those views shall be taken into consideration by the relevant authority in accordance with the provisions of appropriate laws.

Article 5

1. Every child has an inherent right to life. This right shall be protected by law. No child shall be arbitrarily deprived of his life.
2. States Parties to the present Charter shall ensure, to the maximum extent possible, the survival and development of the child.
3. Sentence of death shall not be imposed for crimes committed by children.

Article 6

1. Every child shall have the right from his birth to a name.
2. Every child shall be registered immediately after birth.
3. Every child has the right to acquire a nationality.
4. States Parties to the present Charter shall undertake to ensure that their Constitutional Processes recognize the principles according to which a child shall acquire the nationality of the state in the territory of which he has been born if, at the time of the child's birth, he is not entitled nationality by any other state in accordance with its laws.

Article 7

Every child who is freely capable of forming his own views shall be assured the right to express his opinions freely in all matters and to disseminate his opinions subject to such restrictions as are prescribed by law.

Article 8

Every child shall have the right to free association and freedom of peaceful assembly in conformity with the law.

Article 9

1. Every child shall have the right to freedom of thought, conscience and religion.
2. Parents and where applicable legal guardians have the right to provide guidance and direction in the exercise of these rights to a degree and in a manner consistent with the evolving capacities of the child and a duty to facilitate the enjoyment of these rights subject to national laws and policies.

Article 10

No child shall be subjected to arbitrary or unlawful interference with his privacy, family, home or correspondence, or to attacks upon his honour or reputation. The child has the right to the protection of the law against such interference or attacks.

Article 11

1. Every child shall have the right to education.
2. The education of the child shall be directed to:
    a) the promotion and development of the child's personality, talents and mental and physical abilities to their fullest potential;
    b) fostering respect for human rights and fundamental freedoms with particular reference to those set out in the provisions of various African instruments on human and peoples' rights and international human rights declarations and conventions;
    c) the preservation and strengthening of positive African morals, traditional values and cultures;

d) the preparation of the child for responsible life in a free society, in the spirit of understanding, tolerance, dialogue, mutual respect and friendship among all peoples, ethnic, tribal and religious groups;
e) the preservation of national independence and territorial integrity;
f) the promotion and achievements of African unity and solidarity;
g) the development of respect for the environment and natural resources.

3. States Parties to the present Charter shall take all appropriate measures with a view to achieving the full realization of this right and shall in particular:
   a) provide free and compulsory basic education;
   b) encourage the development of secondary education in its different forms and to progressively make it free and accessible to all;
   c) make higher education accessible to all on the basis of capacity and ability by every appropriate means;
   d) take measures to encourage regular attendance at schools and the reduction of drop-outs;
   e) take special measures to ensure that children from disadvantaged groups of communities have equal access to education.

4. States Parties to the present Charter shall respect the rights and duties of parents, and where applicable, of legal guardians to choose for their children schools, other than those established by public authorities, which conform to such minimum standards as may be approved by the state, to ensure the religious and moral education of the child in a manner with the evolving capacities of the child.
5. States Parties to the present Charter shall take all appropriate measures to ensure that a child who is subjected to school or parental discipline shall be treated with humanity and with respect for the inherent dignity of the child and in conformity with the present Charter.
6. States Parties to the present Charter shall take all appropriate measures to ensure that children who become mothers before completing their education shall have an opportunity to continue with their education on the basis of their individual ability.
7. No part of this article shall be construed as to interfere with the liberty of individuals and bodies to establish and direct educational institutions subject to the observance of the principles set out in paragraph 1 of this Article and the requirement that the education given in such institutions shall conform to such minimum standards as may be laid down by the State.

Article 12

1. States Parties recognize the right of the child to rest and leisure, to engage in play and recreational activities appropriate to the age of the child and to participate freely in cultural life and the arts.
2. States Parties shall respect and promote the right of the child to fully participate in cultural end artistic life and shall encourage the provision of appropriate and equal opportunities for cultural, artistic, recreational end leisure activity.

Article 13

1. Every child who is mentally or physically disabled shall have the right to special measures of protection in keeping with his physical and moral needs and under conditions which ensure his dignity, promote his self-reliance and active participation in the community.
2. States Parties to the present Charter shall ensure, subject to available resources, to a disabled child and to those responsible for his care, of assistance for which application is made and which is appropriate to the child's condition and in the particular shall ensure that the disabled child has effective access to training, preparation for employment and recreation opportunities in a manner conducive to the child achieving the fullest possible social integration, individual development and his cultural and moral development.
3. The States Parties to the present Charter shall use their available resources with a view to achieving progressively the full convenience of the mentally or physically disabled person to movement and access to public highway buildings and other places to which the disabled may legitimately want to have access to.

Article 14

1. Every child shall have the right to enjoy the best attainable state of physical, mental and spritual health.
2. States Parties to the present Charter shall undertake to pursue the full implementation of this right and in particular shall take measures:

   a) to diminish infant and child mortality;
   b) to ensure the provision of necessary medical assistance and health care to all children with emphasis on the development of primary health care;
   c) to ensure the provision of adequate nutrition and safe drinking water;

d) to combat disease and malnutrition within the framework of primary health care through the application of appropriate technology;
e) to ensure appropriate health care for expectant and nursing mothers;
f) to develop preventive health care and family planning education;
g) to integrate basic health service programmes in national development plans;
h) to ensure that all sectors of the society, in particular, parents, children community leaders and community workers are informed and supported in the use of basic knowledge of child health and nutrition, the advantages of breastfeeding, hygiene and environmental sanitation and the prevention of domestic and other accidents;
i) to ensure the meaningful participation of non- governmental organizations, local communities and the beneficiary population in the planning and management of basic service programmes for children.
j) to support through technical and financial means the mobilization of local community resources in the development of primary health care for children.

Article 15

1. Every child shall be protected from all froms of economic exploitation and from performing any work that is likely to be hazardous or to interfere with the child's physical, mental, spiritual, moral, or social development.
2. States Parties to the present Charter shall take all appropriate legislative and administrative measuers to ensure the full implementation of the Article which covers both the formal sectors of employment and having regard to the relevant provisions of the International Labour Organization instruments relating to children, States Parties shall in particular:

a) provide through legislation, minimum ages for admission to every employment;
b) provide for appropriate regulation of hours and conditions of employment;
c) provide for appropriate penalties or other sanctions to ensure the effective enforcement of this Article;
d) promote the dissemination of information on the hazards of child labour to all sectors of the community.

Article 16

1. States Parties to the present Charter shall take specific legislative, administrative, social and educational measures to protect the child from all forms of physical or mental injury or abuse, neglect or maltreatment including sexual abuse, while in the care of a parent, legal guardian or any other person who has the care of the child.
2. Protective measures under this Article shall include effective procedures for the establishment of special monitoring units to provide necessary support for the child and for those who have the care of the child, as well other forms of prevention and for identification, reporting, referral, investigation, treatment, and follow-up of instances of child abuse and neglect.

Article 17

1. Every child accused or found guilty of having infringed penal law shall have the right to special treatment in a manner consistent with the child's sense of dignity and worth and which reinforces the child's respect for human rights and fundamental freedoms of others.
2. States Parties to the present Charter shall in particular:

   a) ensure that no child who is detained or imprisoned or otherwise deprived of its liberty is subjected to torture, inhuman, degrading treatment or punishment.
   b) ensure that children are separated from adults in their place of detention or imprisonment.
   c) ensure that every child accused or infringing the penal law:

      i) shall be presumed innocent until proven guilty;
      ii) shall be informed promptly in a language that he understands and in detail of the charge against him,
      iii) shall be afforded legal and other appropriate assistance in the preparation and presentation of his defence,
      iv) shall have the matter determined as speedily as possible by an impartial tribunal and if found guilty be entitled to an appeal by a higher tribunal;
      v) shall prohibit the press and the public from trial.
      vi) shall have the assistance of an interpreter if the child cannot understand the language used;
      vii) shall not be compelled to give testimony or confess guilt.

3. The essential aim of treatment of every child during the trial and also

if found guilty of infringing the penal law shall be its reformation, reintegration into its family and social rehabilitation.
4. There shall be a minimum age below which children shall be presumed not to have the capacity to infringe the penal law.

Article 18

1. The family shall be the natural unit and basis of society. It shall be protected by the state which shall take care of its physical health and morals.
2. States Parties to the present Charter shall take appropriate steps to ensure equality of rights and responsibilities of spouses as to marriage and its dissolution. In case of dissolution, provision shall be made for the necessary protection of the children.
3. No child shall be deprived of maintenance by reference to the parents marital status.

Article 19

1. Every child shall be entitled to the enjoyment of parental care and shall, whenever possible, have his place of residence determined by his parents. No child shall be separated from his parents against his will, except when a competent authority subject to judicial review determine in accordance with the appropriate law, that such separation is in the best interest of the child.
2. Every child who is separated from one or both parents shall have the right to maintain personal relations and direct contact with both parents on a regular basis.
3. Where separation results from the action of a State-Party, the State Party shall provide the child, or if appropriate, another member of the family with essential information concerning the whereabouts of the absent member or members of the family. State Parties shall ensure that the submission of such a request shall not entail any adverse consequences for the person or persons in whose respect it is made.
4. Where a child is apprehended by a State Party, his parents or guardians shall as soon as reasonably practical be notified of such apprehension by that State Party.

Article 20

1. Parents or others responsible for the child shall have the primary responsibility for the upbringing and development of the child and shall have the duty:

    a) to ensure that the best interest of the child are their basic concern at all times;
    b) to secure, within their abilities and financial capacities, conditions of living necessary to the child's development; and
    c) to ensure that domestic discipline is administered in moderation and that the child is treated with humanity and with respect for his inherent dignity.

2. States Parties to the present Charter, in accordance with their means and national conditions shall take all appropriate measures:

    a) to assist parents and others responsible for the child and in case of need provide material assistance and support programmes particularly with regard to nutrition, health, education, clothing and housing;
    b) to assist parents and others responsible for the child in the performance of child-rearing and ensure the development of institutions for the care of children; and
    c) to ensure that the children of working parents benefit from child care services and facilities.

Article 21

1. States Parties to the present Charter shall take all appropriate measures to abolish customs and practices harmful to the welfare, normal growth and development of the child and in particular:

    a) those customs and practices prejudicial to the health or life of the child, and
    b) those customs and practices discriminatory to the child on the grounds of sex or other status.

2. Child marriage and the betrothal of young girls shall be prohibited and effective action, including legislation, shall be taken to specify the minimum age of marriage and make registration of marriage in an official registry compulsary.

Article 22

1. States Parties to this Chapter shall undertake to respect and ensure respect for rules of international humanitarian law applicable in armed conflicts which are relevant to the child.
2. States Parties to the present Charter shall take all necessary measures to ensure that no child shall take a direct part in hostilities and refrain in particular, from recruiting any child.
3. States Parties to the present Charter shall, in accordance with their obligations under international humanitarian law, protect the civilian population in armed conflicts and shall take all feasible measures to ensure the protection and care of children who are affected by armed conflict. Such rules shall also apply to children in situations of internal armed conflict, tension or strife.

Article 23

1. States Parties to the present Charter shall take all appropriate measures to ensure that a child who is seeking refugee status or who is considered a refugee in accordance with applicable international or domestic law shall, whether unaccompanied or accompanied by parents, legal guardians or close relatives, recieve appropriate protection and humanitarian assistance in the enjoyment of the rights set out in this Charter and other international human rights and humanitarian instruments to which the States are Parties.
2. States Parties shall undertake to co-operate with existing international organizations which protect and assist refugees in their efforts to protect and assist such a child and to trace the parents or other close relatives of an unaccompanied refugee child in order to obtain information necessary for reunification with the family.
3. Where no parents, legal guardians or close relatives can be found, the child shall be accorded the same protection as any other child permanently to temporarily deprived of his family environment for any reason.
4. The provisions of this Article apply *Mutatis Mutandis* to internally displaced children whether through natural disasters, internal conflicts and strife, breakdown of economic and social order or howsoever caused.

Article 24

States Parties which recognize the system of adoption shall ensure that the best interest of the child shall be the paramount consideration and they shall:

a) establish competent authorities to determine matters of adoption;
b) such competent authorities shall determine in accordance with appplicable law and procedure and on the basis of all relevant and reliable information, that the adoption is permissible in view of the child's status concerning parents, relatives and guardians and that, if required, the appropriate persons concerned have given their informed consent to the adoption on the basis of such counselling as may be necessary;
c) recognize that inter-country adoption may be considered as an alternative means of child's care, if the child cannot be placed in a foster or an adoptive family or cannot in any suitable manner be cared for in the child's country of origin;
d) ensure that the child concerned by inter-country adoption enjoys safeguards and standards equivalent to those existing in the case of national adoption;
e) take all appropriate measures to ensure that, in inter-country adoption, the placement does not result in improper financial gain for those involved in it;
f) promote, where appropriate, the objectives of this Article by concluding bilateral or multilateral arrangements or agreements, and endeavour, within this framework, to ensure that the placement of the child in another country is carried out by competent authorities or organs;
g) establish a machinery to monitor the wellbeing of the adopted child.

Article 25

1. Every child who is permanently or temporarily deprived of his family environment for any reason shall be entitled to special protection and assistance.
2. States Parties to the present Charter shall ensure that a child who is parentless, or who is temporarily or permanently deprived of his family environment, or who in his best interest cannot be brought up or allowed to remain in that environment shall be provided with alternative family care, which include, among others, foster placement, or placement in suitable institutions for the care of children.
3. When considering alternative family care of the child and the best interests of the child, due regard shall be paid to the desirability of

continuity in a child's up-bringing and to the child's ethnic, religious or linguistic background.

Article 26

States Parties to the present Charter shall individually and collectively undertake to accord the highest priority to the special needs of children living under *Apartheid* and in states subject to military destabilization by the *Apartheid* regime. States Parties shall also undertake to provide, whenever possible, material assistance to such children and to direct their efforts towards the elimination of racial discrimination and *Apartheid* on the African continent.

Article 27

1. States Parties to the present Charter shall undertake to protect the Child from all forms of sexual exploitation and sexual abuse and shall in particular take measures to prevent:

    a) the inducement or coercion of a child to engage in any sexual activity;
    b) the use of children in prostitution or other sexual practices;
    c) the use of children in pornographic performances and material.

Article 28

States Parties to the present Charter shall take all appropriate measures to protect the child from illegal use of narcotic and psychotropic substances as defined in the relevant international treaties, and to prevent the use of children in the illegal production and trafficking of such substances.

Article 29

States Parties to the present Charter shall take appropriate measures to prevent the abduction, the sale of, or traffic in children for any purpose or in any form, by any person including parents or legal guardians of the child.

Article 30

States Parties to the present Charter shall undertake to provide special treatment to expectant mothers and to mothers of infants and young children who have been accused or found guilty of infringing the penal law and shall in particular:

    a) establish special alternative institutions for holding such mothers; and
    b) establish and promote measures alternative to institutional confinement for the treatment of such mothers;
    c) a non-custodial sentence will always be first considered when sentencing such mothers;
    d) a child shall not be imprisoned with its mother;
    e) a death sentence shall not be imposed on such mothers;
    f) the essential aim of the penitentiary system will be the reformation, the integration of the mother to the family and social rehabilitation.

Article 31

Every child shall have duties towards his family and society, the State and other legally recognized communities and the international community. The child, subject to his age and ability, and such limitations as may be contained in the present Charter, shall have the duty:

1. To work for the cohesion of the family, to respect his parents at all times and to maintain them in case of needs.
2. To serve his national community by placing his physical and intellectual abilities at its service.
3. To preserve and strengthen social and national solidarity.
4. To preserve and strengthen African Cultural values in his relations with other members of the society, in the spirit of tolerance, dialogue and consultation and to contribute to the moral well-being of society.
5. To preserve and strengthen the independance and the integrity of his country.
6. To contribute to the best of his abilities, at all times and at all levels, to the promotion and achievement of African Unity.

Part II

CHAPTER TWO

Establishment and Organization of the Committee on the Rights and Welfare of the Child

ARTICLE 32

An African Committee of Experts on the rights and welfare of the child hereinafter called "the Committee" shall be established within the Organization of African Unity to promote and protect the rights and welfare of the Child.

ARTICLE 33

1. The Committee shall consist of 11 members of high moral standing, integrity, impartiality and competence in matters of rights and welfare of the child.
2. The members of the Committee shall serve in their personal capacity.
3. The Committee shall not include more than one national of the same State.

ARTICLE 34

The members of the Committee shall be elected by secret ballot by the Assembly of Heads of State and Government from a list of persons nominated by the States Parties to the present Charter.

ARTICLE 35

Each State Party to the present Charter may not nominate more than two candidates. The candidates must have one of the nationalities of the States Parties to the present Charter. When two candidates are nominated by a state one of them may not be a national of that state.

Article 36

1. The Secretary-General of the Organization of African Unity shall invite State Parties to the present Charter at least six months before the elections to nominate candidates.
2. The Secretary-General of the Organization of African Unity shall make a list of persons nominated and communicate it to the Heads of State and Government at least two months before the elections.

Article 37

1. The members of the Committee shall be elected for a term of five years and may be re-elected only once, but the term of four of the members elected at the first election shall expire after two years and the terms of six others, after four years.
2. Immediately after the first election, the Chairman of the Assembly of Heads of State and Government of the Organization of African Unity shall draw lots to determine the names of those members referred to in Paragraph 1 of this Article.
3. The Secretary-General of the Organization of African Unity shall convene the first meeting of the Committee at the Headquarters of the Organization within six months of the Constitution of the Committee, and thereafter the Committee shall be convened by its Chairman whenever necessary but at least once a year.

Article 38

If a member of the Committee vacates his office for any reason other than the normal expiration of a term, the state which nominated that member shall appoint another member from among its nationals to serve for the remainder of the term – subject to the approval of the Committee.

Article 39

1. The Committee shall elect its officers for a period of two years.
2. The Committee shall establish its own Rules of Procedure.
3. Seven Committee members shall forn the quorum.
4. In case of an equality of votes, the Chairman shall have a casting vote.
5. The working languages of the Committee shall be the official languages of the OAU.

Article 41

In discharging their duties, members of the Committee shall enjoy privileges and immunities provided for in the General Convention on the Privileges and Immunities of the Organization of African Unity.

CHAPTER THREE

Mandate and Procedure of the Committee

Article 42

The functions of the Committee shall be:

a) To promote the rights enshrined in this Charter and in particular:

  i) collect document, commission inter-disciplinary assessment of situations on African problems in the fields of the rights and welfare of the child, organize meetings, encourage national and local institutions concerned with the rights and welfare of the child, and where necessary give its views and make recommandations to Governments;
  ii) to formulate and lay down principles and rules aiming at solving problems relating to the rights and welfare of children in Africa;
  iii) co-operate with other African and International Institutions and Organizations concerned with the promotion and protection of the rights and welfare of the child.

b) To monitor the implementation and ensure protection of the rights enshrined in this Charter.
c) Interpret the provisions of the present Charter at the request of a State Party, an Institution of the Organization of African Unity or any other Institution recognized by the Organization of African Unity.
d) Perform such other tasks as may be entrusted to it by the Assembly of Heads of State and Government, Secretary-General of the OAU and any other Organs of the OAU.

Article 43

1. Every State Party to the present Charter shall undertake to submit to the Committee through the Secretary-General of the Organization of

African Unity reports on the measures they have adopted which give effect to the provisions of this Charter and on the progress made in the enjoyment of these rights.

a) within two years of the entry into force of the Charter for the State Party concerned, and
b) thereafter, every four years.

2. Every report made under this Article shall:

a) contain sufficient information on the law and practice of each of the rights, duties and obligation contained in the present Charter to provide the Committee with comprehensive understanding of the implementation of the Charter in the relevant country; and
b) shall indicate factors and difficulties, if any, affecting the fulfilment of the obligations imposed under the Charter.

3. A State Party which has submitted a comprehensive first report to the Committee need not, in its subsequent reports submitted in accordance with paragraph 1(a) of this Article, repeat the basic information previously provided.

Article 44

The Committee may receive communication, from any group or non-government organization recognized by the Organization of African Unity or the United Nations relating to any matter covered by this Charter.

Article 45

1. The Committee may, resort to any appropriate method of investigating any matter falling within the ambit of the present Charter, request from the States Parties any information relevant to the implementation of the Charter and may also resort to any appropriate method of investigating the measures a State Party has adopted to implement the Charter.
2. The Committee shall submit to the Ordinary Session of the Assembly of Heads of State and Government through the Economic and Social Commission of the Organization of African Unity, every two years, reports on its activities and on any communication made under Article 46 of this Charter.

3. The Committee shall publish its Report after it has been considered by the Assembly of Heads of State and Government.

CHAPTER FOUR

Miscellaneous Provisions

ARTICLE 46

The Committee shall draw inspiration from International Law on Human Rights, particularly from the provisions of the African Charter on Human and People's Rights, the Charter of the Organization of African Unity, the Universal Declaration of Human Rights, the United Nations Convention on the Rights of the Child and other instruments adopted by the United Nations and by African Countries in the field of human rights.

ARTICLE 47

1. The present Charter shall be open to signature, ratification or adherence of the Member States of the Organization of African Unity.
2. The instruments of ratification or adherence to the present Charter shall be deposited with the Secretary-General of the Organization of African Unity.
3. The present Charter shall come into force 30 days after the reception by the Secretary-General of the Organization of African Unity of the instruments of ratification of adherence of 15 Member Staes of the Organization of African Unity.

ARTICLE 48

1. The present Charter may be amended or revised if any State Party makes a written request to that effect to the Secretary-General of the Organization of African Unity, provided that the proposed amendment is not submitted to the Assembly of Heads of State and Government for consideration until all the States Parties have been duly notified of it and the Committee has given its opinion on the amendment.
2. An amendment shall be approved by a simple majority of the State Parties.

APPENDIX XLVI

Declaration on the Rights of the Child, Based on the 'Systemic Quality of Life Model', by Philip E. Veerman and Samuel Shye (1992)

The aim of the present Declaration is not to 'proclaim' the rights of the child, as many other Declarations on the Rights of the Child have done. These other Declarations are a description of what, in a certain period, in a given culture, people thought were the rights of the child.

The present Declaration is based on the 'Systemic Quality of Life Model'. It aims at enabling parents and policy-makers to take into account *all* aspects of life without giving more importance to one aspect than to another, and thus to relate to children's rights in a balanced way. It is therefore more of a checklist for future drafters of Declarations and Conventions, and can be used as a basis on which to make a choice at a particular time and place.

Because of the special vulnerability of children, the younger the child, the more protection he or she should have and the more particular his or her rights should be. As the child approaches majority the weight of these special children's rights diminishes, and he or she should gradually be given the rights of adults.

All children, without exception, are entitled to all the rights set forth in this Declaration and no discrimination whatsoever should be put into practice as to the application of all or any one of these rights.

Each paragraph of this Declaration is first phrased in the rather abstract terminology of the 'Systemic Quality of Life Model'. Then some concrete examples are given. Since the 'Systemic Quality of Life Model' claims universality, the reader should not be distracted by the cultural relativity of these examples. Indeed, as the importance of interaction between and adaption to given cultures is built into the 'Systemic Quality of Life Model', the cultural relativism of some of the examples should not be an excuse for the non-application of the consequences of this Declaration.

When a child is small the adult-guardian will supplement those functioning levels that cannot yet be attained by the child. However, every child has the right to practice his or her growing competencies and evolving capacities. When possible, the adult should stop supplementing those functioning levels in which the child can already function effectively.

It is the aim of education that the child will some day (as an adult) function effectively in all sixteen functioning modes. We hereby present a system of interrelated rights, based on the 'Systemic Quality of Life Model'. None of these rights can be over-emphasised at the expense of another right. We focus on the *individual* child or adolescent and his or her individual life quality. We do not preclude any sound theory or claim that the attainment of a certain quality of life is associated with one social structure or another. We also do not claim that a particular social theory is most likely to produce happiness. Our proposal includes criteria for happiness against which various theories and their implementation can be evaluated.

The rights of the child here presented, are based on the components of the 'Systemic Quality of Life Model' which are considered vital for all human beings. However, since we are dealing with children, specific concerns must be taken into consideration. As it is our experience that parents and educators often weigh aspects of the *expressive mode* against aspects of the *conservative mode*, and aspects of the *adaptive mode* against aspects of the *integrative* mode, we want to ensure that in each and every one of the sixteen functioning modes a minimum level of effective functioning is always present. No one mode is more important than another.

Of course the child's temperament and his or her level of physical and emotional maturity must be taken into account by the educator or parent. However, risks must also be taken in order to stimulate self-determined behaviour.

We call upon our readers to unite in lobbies for Children's Rights, and to fight against unjust situations.

Educators and governments must provide as much information about children's rights as possible. This will enable children and youth to draw their own conclusions.

I. Rights in the *Personality* domain

1. *The expressive mode of the personality subsystem: e.g. self actualization.* The child has the right to adequate opportunities for actualising his or her individual aspirations through creative activities (such as play) that express his or her unique personality. The child should be allowed to explore his or her own individual forms of expressions.

   – A child who is deprived of self-actualization through past or present circumstances, should be given *skilled* encouragement and reinforcement so that he or she may restore the self-expressive capabilities.

2. *The adaptive mode of the personality subsystem*: *e.g. recreation*. The child has the right to a congenial psychological environment which enhances recreation and suitable relaxation.

   – If under constant pressure the child is deprived of a minimum level of necessary recreation, special measures should be taken to detach him or her from the pressuring circumstances, and to enable him or herself to recuperate.

3. *The integrative mode of the personality subsystem*: *e.g. promoting a balanced personality*. The right to live in conditions that limit excessive stress on the child and promote a good state of mental health.

   – When a child is too anxious or under undue stress, he or she has the right to adequate treatment.

4. *The conservative mode of the personality subsystem*: *e.g. promoting self-confidence*. The child has the right to maintain his or her individual identity, to be free from attacks on his or her person, and to be respected as a unique human individual. The child has the right to receive protection from abuse that may cause mental damage.

   – Children with severe mental disorders shall be given skilled therapy and care.

II. Rights in the *Physical* domain

1. *The expressive mode of the physical subsystem*: *e.g. physical development*. The child has the right to adequate opportunities for free exploration of his or her physical environment through activities of his or her choice. The child has the right to play with physical objects, to have experiences of his or her choice (handicrafts, excursions, etc.), and to have the level of privacy of his or her choice.

   – If the child is deprived of his or her liberty (i.e. through some handicap or through hospitalisation or incarceration) he or she should be given enough opportunities to participate in sports and games or other physical activities of his or her choice.

2. *The adaptive mode of the physical subsystem*: *e.g. food and housing*. The child has the right to a comfortable physical environment with adequate housing and suitable nutrition.

   – The child that is deprived of minimum standards in the above mentioned field should be compensated for this deficiency. When a child is in need of food or shelter measures should be taken to relieve this condition.

3. *The integrative mode of the physical subsystem: e.g. measures that promote health.* The child has the right to the provision of optimal, preventive and continuous health care.

   – If the child is sick, he or she should receive proper care and treatment.

4. *The conservative mode of the physical subsystem: e.g. a stable environment.* The child has the right to physical security and stability. This includes, but is not restricted to, protection from danger, from neglect and from physical and sexual abuse. It also includes protection from abrupt physical change. It is important in this functioning mode that the implementation will be individualised. How much protection should be given and how much responsibility the child can take varies from one child to the next. The child has the right to be protected from any infringement that can cause chronic disease or can put him or her at physical risk (e.g. wars or civil strife, disease and other hazards).

   – A child that already has an illness or is injured should be compensated in terms of safety.

III. Rights in the *Social* domain

1. *The expressive mode of the social subsystem: e.g. social standing.* The child has the right to express him- or herself as a social being, to be heard in a group situation, and to exercise his or her leadership capabilities.

   – A child who is deprived or suffers from lack of social status among his or her peers should receive skilful encouragement in order to develop his or her abilities to lead and influence others, within the limits of his or her abilities.

2. *The adaptive mode of the social subsystem: e.g. learning social roles.* The child has the right to fair interactions with various social institutions and authorities, in accordance with his or her abilities and stage of development, i.e. the prevention of abuse from police officers and from courts during legal transactions, and the right to due process with regard to social and legal responsibilities, the right to learn and become adjusted to the playing of social roles in school and in similar frameworks, the right to learn how to handle rights and to take responsibilities.

- Children who are unable to deal with social institutions or who cannot play age-appropriate social roles should be given special guidance. Their inability should be compensated for through adequate representation which places the child interests as a priority.

3. *The integrative mode of the social subsystem*: *e.g. intimate relationships*. The child has the right to live in circumstances which enable him or her to develop and maintain intimate relationships of love and affection with both parents. Relationships with peers, based on mutual interests, should be promoted. The child should be able to harmonise the various social roles assigned to him.

   - If a child shows symptoms of distress related to this functioning mode, measures should be taken to alleviate the condition and to assure a loving atmosphere for the child, with capacities to establish satisfying human contacts.

4. *The conservative mode of the social subsystem*: *e.g. a sense of belonging*. The child has the right to belong to a stable network of social relations, and to be part of a community. These relations and this community should contribute to the development of a sense of belonging. The child should be protected from abrupt or hazardous changes in his or her social environment.

   - In cases where the child is subjected to severe social dislocation, measures should be taken to alleviate this condition, including the possibility of placing the child in a community where he or she will feel a sense of belonging.

IV. Rights in the *Cultural* domain

1. *The expressive mode of the cultural subsystem*: *e.g. emergence of opinions*. The child has the right to develop his or her value orientation in an optimal way and to freely express his opinions and value preferences, as they are formed. The child should be given adequate opportunities to learn to express his views.

   - Schools should allow pupils to protest against certain policies of politicians.

2. *The adaptive mode of the cultural subsystem*: *e.g. cultural contacts*. The child has the right to be exposed to diverse values and opinions in his or her society at a suitable pace, and to meet other cultures in order to understand and measure his own values against theirs.

– The child has the right to education and to instruments of communication such as books and the mass-media, which will enhance his or her understanding, tolerance and the possibility of critical thought.

3. *The integrative mode of the cultural subsystem*: *e.g. the search for consistency*. The child and young person should be treated with patience and tolerance as he or she attempts to sort out values and to orientate him- or herself within a cultural coherent system.

– When a child is torn between different values, he or she should be protected from value conflicts (e.g. between two parents).

4. *The conservative mode of the cultural subsystem*: *e.g. cultural foundations*. If possible a child should have the right to develop an affinity with a culture that is enriching, which will equip him or her with moral standards, and which will give him or her the feeling of belonging to a cultural value system.

– For children devoid of any value standards, a suitable humanistic framework should be provided to help alleviate this situation.

Bibliography

1. Sources

1A. Archives

Amsterdam, the Netherlands

- International Institute of Social History (Internationaal Instituut voor Sociale Geschiedenis)
- International Archives of the Women's Movement (Internationaal Archief voor de Vrouwenbeweging, IAV)

Geneva, Switzerland

- Bibliothèque Publique et Universitaire
- Journal de Genève
- Tribune de Genève
- United Nations Library: Historical Collections and League of Nations Archives

Ithaca, New York, U.S.A.

- Cornell University (Department of Manuscripts and University Archives): *The William R. George and George Junior Republic Papers*

Jerusalem, Israel

- Yad Vashem (The Holocaust Martyrs and Heroes Remembrance Authority)

Kibbutz Lohamei Haghetaot, Israel

- (Ghetto Fighters House Museum): *The Janusz Korczak Archives*

London, U.K.

- The Save the Children Fund
- University of London Institute of Education: *New Education Fellowship Papers*
- London Borough of Lewisham: *The Boys and Girls Industrial Homes – Forest Hill*

New York City, U.S.A.

- The New York Public Library (Rare Books and Manuscripts Division)
- UNICEF, United Nations Children's Fund (History Project)
- United Nations

Paris, France

- Musée de Radio France

St. Louis, Missouri, U.S.A.

- St. Louis Post Dispatch

Stockholm, Sweden

- The Royal Library – National Library of Sweden (Kungl. Biblioteket)

Washington, D.C., U.S.A.

- National Archives: *Children's Bureau Papers* and *the Pan American Union Papers*

West Branch, Iowa, U.S.A.

- Herbert Hoover Presidential Library

1B. Collected Oral History Material

Interviews with former pupils and former staff members of Janusz Korczak, (taped and in possession of the author):

- Sarah Bierman (Sonia Strojmanowa)
- Itzhak Berger
- Roman Bertison
- Iona Bocian
- Dora Borberg
- Jehuda Cahana
- Edward Cole (Edek)
- Izaak Celniker
- Miriam Caspi (Surka Ajzenberg)
- Ignacy Chukerman
- Anna Dembinski (Analzia Flajszakier)
- Adam Dembinski
- Hannah Ehrlich
- Jacques (Jakobek) Dodiuk
- Henryk Favel (Fajwlowicz)
- Ella and Janina Fridman
- Erna Friedman
- Smuel Gogol
- Abram Hurman
- Avraham Hamer

- Simone Kowal
- Slawika Anita Korman
- C. Langsam-Bonhart
- Billa Lewin (Mejrowicz)
- Pola Lebman
- Klara Maajan (Klara Münzberg)
- G. Mandelblatt
- Rose Miller (Roza Ajzenstein)
- Szlomo Nadel
- Sara Nadiv (Salena Zaleman)
- Rozia (Rözka) Natiw
- Severyn Nutkiewicz
- Szmuel (Smulek) Nissenbaum
- Ada Poznanska-Hagari
- Pola Rosenblat (Lamm)
- Dwora (Dworcza) Rozenman
- Cylia Rubinstein-Pojliszev
- Israel (Srulek) Schwarzberg
- Genia Schadron
- Arie Sadè
- Ichak (Izak) Skalka
- Sam Stein (Seweryn Kampynsky)
- M. Toller (Szklarz)
- Michael Tyler
- Israel Zyngman
- anonymous
- anonymous

Interviews with former pupils and co-workers of other self-government experiments

- Monick (Moshé) Lipman, *former pupil of Nasz UL orphanage in Poland*
- Ytzhak Luden, *former pupil of the Medem Sanatorium in Poland*
- Dr. Erich (Ezra) Steinitz, *former teacher of the Odenwaldschule*

Other Important Interviews

- Nigel Cantwell, *founder of Defence for Children International*
- Prof. Howard Cohen, *one of the representatives of the Children's Liberation Movement*
- Dr. Haim H. Cohn, *former member of the Human Rights Commission of the U.N.*
- Janet Fink, *Attorney for the Juvenile Rights Division of the Legal Aid Society in New York, N.Y., U.S.A.*
- Dr. Menachem Horovitz, *former Ombudsman for Children of the Jerusalem Council on Children and Youth*
- Prof. J.C.H. Hudig, *Retired Juvenile Court Judge in the Netherlands*
- Gwen James, *of the Voice for the Child in Care, London, U.K.*
- Jacques Jansen, *of the Ministry of Justice in the Netherlands*
- Dr. Dan Mulock Houwer, *former Secretary-General of the International Union for Child Welfare*
- Mark Soler, *director of the Youth Law Center in San Francisco, Calif., U.S.A.*
- Prof. Albert J. Solnit, *Child Study Center, Yale University*
- Elissavet Stamatopoulou-Robbins, *Chief, Centre for Human Rights, United Nations*
- V. Tarzie Vittachi, *former Deputy Executive Director for External Relations of the United Nations Children's Fund, UNICEF*
- James Weill, *of the Children's Defense Fund in Washington, D.C., U.S.A.*

Bibliography

- Monique van der Zouw (lawyer) and Karien Smits (educator) of the *Children's Law Shop in Amsterdam*

1C. Reports

Boyden, Jo and Hudson, Andy
 Children: Rights and Responsibilities, London, November 1985, The Minority Rights Group
Catley-Carson, Margaret
 The role and responsibilities of adult leaders in securing children's rights, The Non-Governmental Organisations Committee on UNICEF, 1980, NGO-Forum, New York, April 15, 1988
Charren, P. and Hulsizer, C.
 Television, Children and the Constitutional Bicentennial, *A Report by Action for Children's Television*, 1986
Children's Defense Fund (CDF)
 A Children's Defense Budget 1987 1986; *A Children's Defense Budget* 1988, 1987; *A Children's Defense Budget* 1989, Washington D.C., 1988
Children's Defense Fund (CDF)
 Children Out of School in America, Washington D.C., 1974
Defence for Children
 The first year, Geneva, July 1980
Defence for Children International (DCI)
 Secretary General's Report to the General Assembly, Geneva, September 6, 1982
Defence for Children International (DCI)
 Report on the Activities of the International Secretariat by the Secretary General, Geneva, July 1984
Defence for Children International (DCI)
 Extraordinary International General Assembly, Xalapa, Mexico, April 3–5, 1986
Defence for Children International *(DCI)*
 DCI in 1986, Activity Report of the International Secretariat, Geneva, March 1987
Defence for Children International (DCI)
 Activity Report 1989, International Secretariat, Geneva, 1990
Doek, J.E.
 Kinderarbeid en Ontwikkelingssamenwerking, Amsterdam, July 1987, Vrije Universiteit, Rapport in opdracht van Het Ministerie van Buitenlandse Zaken, Directoraat-Generaal Internationale Samenwerking
Donahue, Phil
 Can you sue your parents? Cincinnati, Ohio, 1988, Multimedia Entertainment Inc., Transcript No. 031588
Gholam Kibria, K.F.M.
 Rights of Children in a Changing Society: The Case of Botswana, Geneva, 1987, Defence for Children International (DCI), Proceedings of Seminars Held on the Rights of Children and Sale and Trafficking of Children in Botswana
Independent Commission on International Humanitarian Issues
 and Rädda Barnen (Swedish Save the Children) *International Symposium on the Protection of Children*, Amman, Jordan (*November* 1984) New York/Stockholm, 1985
Independent Commission on International Humanitarian Issues
 Street-children, A Growing Tragedy, Report presented by Susanna Agnelli, London, 1986, Weidenfeld and Nicolson
International Lawyers' Committee for Family Reunification
 Communication to the Organization of African Unity and the African Commission on Human

and Peoples Rights: *The Legal Rights of Ethiopia's Jewish Community to Emigration and Family Reunification*, Washington, April 1988

Inter-Parliamentary Union
Summary Records of the LXXXIst Inter-Parliamentary Conference, Budapest, March 13-18, 1989, Geneva, 1989

Joint Commission on the Mental Health of Children
Crisis in child mental health, New York, 1970, Harper and Row

Joseph, Stephen, C.
The common challenge to Humanity: *AIDS and Children and the Implications for a Global Future*, Keynote address to the 1988 Non-Governmental Organisations Committee on UNICEF Forum 'Children's Rights an Agenda for Action, April 15, 1988, New York

Kavanaugh, Dorrict, ed.
Listen to us! New York, 1978, Workman Publishing, A Children's Express Report

Knitzer, Jane E.
Mary Lee Allen and Brenda McGowan, editors, *Children Without Homes*: *An Examination of Public Responsibility to Children in Out-of-Home Care*: *Final Report*. Washington, D.C., 1978, Children's Defense Fund (CDF)

Loon, J.H.A. van
Report on Intercountry Adoption, The Hague, 1990, Hague Conference on Private International Law, Prel.Doc. No. 1

Ministerie van Buitenlandse Zaken
Verslag over de Veertiende Algemene Vergadering van de Verenigde Naties, New York, 15 September-12 December 1959, The Hague, 1960, Staatsuitgeverij

Newell, Peter and Rosenbaum, Martin
Taking Children Seriously London, 1991 (about a children's commissioner in the United Kingdom)

Proceedings of the General Education Seminar
Vol. 8, No. 2, Fall 1979, *The Rights of Children*, New York, N.Y., The University Committee on General Education in collaboration with the Center for the Study of Human Rights, Columbia University

Raoul Wallenberg Institute
Children at War, Report from the conference on children at war, Lurd, 1991, Report No. 10

Report of the Royal Commission
on Family and Children's Law, Vancouver, B.C., 1975

Seminar on the Rights of the Child
held in Warsaw, 6-19 August 1963, U.N.Doc.ST/TAO/HR17, 1964

Stein, R., editor
Planning for the needs of children in developing countries, *a report of a round-table conference*, Bellagio, Italy, New York, 1965, United Nations Children's Fund (UNICEF)

Stichting voor het Kind
Kinderombudsman, Werkverslag van een onderzoeksproject, Amsterdam 1982

The Draft Convention on the Rights of the Child:
Informal Consultations Among International Non-Governmental Organisations, *Report on Conclusions*, Defence for Children International (DCI), Geneva, December 1985

UNICEF
Overview, *Children in especially difficult circumstances*, *report for UNICEF's Executive Board*, 1986 session, New York, February 28, 1986, E/ICEF/L.6

UNICEF
Child abuse and neglect in a global perspective, Report prepared for UNICEF's Executive Board, New York, E/ICEF/1986/Crp.4

UNICEF
Working children and street children, Report prepared for UNICEF's Executive Board, New York, 1986, E/ICEF/1986/Crp.3

UNICEF
Children in Situations of Armed Conflict, Report prepared for UNICEF's Executive Board, 1986 session, E/ICEF/1986/Crp.2., March 10, 1986

UNICEF
  The State of the World's Children Reports, 1980–1991, New York/Geneva, UNICEF Division of Information and Public Affairs
Vaughan, Mark, ed.
  Rights of Children, Report of the First National Conference on Children's Rights, held in London on March 11–12, 1972, London, National Council for Civil Liberties
Vittachi, V. Tarzie
  Children's Rights: A Question of Obligations, New York/Geneva, 1988, UNICEF
Whittome, Candy
  The Right to Unite; The Family Reunification Question in the Palestinian Occupied Territories: Law and Practice, Ramallah, 1991, Al-Haq, Occasional paper, No. 8

1D. Journals

Child Welfare
  (published by the Child Welfare League of America), New York, now in Washington, Vol.I-Vol.LXIX
Child Workers in Asia
  (published by the 'child workers in Asia' Organisation in Bangkok, Thailand), 1985–1990
Childright
  (Published by The Children's Legal Centre, London, England) 1983–1990
Children's Legal Rights Journal
  (from the American Bar Association, National Legal Resource Center for Child Advocacy and Protection) 1979–1990
International Child Welfare Review
  (of the International Union for Child Welfare in Geneva), and the *Newsletter of the International Union for Child Welfare*, 1947–1988
International Children's Rights Monitor
  (published by Defence for Children International, DCI, Geneva) 1983–1990
The World's Children
  (The Magazine of the Save the Children Fund, London) 1919–1990
Youth Law News
  (Journal of the National Center for Youth Law, San Francisco, CA), 1970–1990

1E. Original Works

Cohen, Howard
  Equal Rights for Children, Totowa, NJ. 1980, Littlefield
Edelman, Marian Wright
  'On Mounting Effective Child Advocacy', in Proceedings of the American Philosophical Society 1975, 119, Dec.6, pp. 470–478
Farson, Richard
  Birthrights, New York/London, 1974, MacMillan Publishing Comp., Inc./Collier MacMillan Publishers
Holt, John
  Escape from Childhood, New York, 1974, Ballantine Books (a division of Random House)
Hoover, Herbert
  The Memoirs of Herbert Hoover, Years of Adventure, 1874–1920, New York, 1951, The Macmillan Comp.
Jebb, Eglantyne
  International Responsibilities for Child Welfare, Geneva, 1927, Save the Children International Union

Jebb, Eglantyne
Save the Child! (A posthumous essay) London, Weardale Press, 1929
Key, Ellen
The Century of the Child, New York and London, 1909, G.P. Putnam's Sons
Korczak, Janusz
'Forest Hill', in: *Swietlo*, 1912, No. 2, pp. 30–32
Korczak, Janusz
King Matt the First, New York, 1986, Farrar, Straus and Giroux (with an introduction by Bruno Bettelheim), originally published in 1923 in Warsaw as *Król Marcius Pierwszy*
Korczak, Janusz
Selected Works, (edited by Martin Wolins) Warsaw, 1967, published for the National Science Foundation in Washington D.C.
Korczak, Janusz
Ghetto Diary, in: *The Ghetto Years, 1939–1942*, Tel Aviv/New York, 1980, Ghetto Fighters House and Hakibbutz HaMeuchad Publishing House/Holocaust Library
Pridik, Heinrich, ed.
Das Bildungswesen in Sowjetrussland; Vorträge, Leitsätze und Resolutionen der ersten Moskauer allstadtlichen Konferenz der kulturell-aufklärenden Organisationen (*Mosko-Prolet'kult*) *vom 23–28 Febr. 1918* Annaberg i Erzgeb., 1921, Neuropädagogischer Verlag

Selected Secondary Literature

2A. Monographs and Chapters in Books

Adams, Paul;
Berg, Leila; Berger, Nan; Duane, Michael; Neill A.S.; Ollendorf, Robert *Children's Rights: Toward the Liberation of the Child*, New York, N.Y., 1971, Praeger Publishers
Agostinelli, Maria Enrica
On Wings of Love: The United Nations Declaration of the Rights of the Child, New York, 1979, Collins
Aiken, William and La Folette, Hugh, eds.
Whose Child? Children's Rights, Parental Authority and State Power, Totowa, N.J., 1980, Rowman and Littlefield
Alkema, E.A.
Studies over Europese Grondrechten, Deventer, 1978, Kluwer, doctoral dissertation
Alston, Philip and Tomasevski, Katarina
The Right to Food, Dordrecht/Utrecht, 1984, Martinus Nijhoff/SIM, Stichting Studie en Informatiecentrum Mensenrechten
Allen, Anita Lafrance
Rights, Children and Education, Ann Arbor, Mich., 1979, The University of Michigan, doctoral dissertation
Andrews, Lori B.
Medical Genetics, A Legal Frontier, Chicago, 1987, American Bar Foundation
Anweiler, Oscar
Geschichte der Schule und Pädagogik in Russland, vom Ende des Zarenreiches bis zum Beginn der Stalin-Aera, Berlin, 1964, Ost-Europa Institut, Berlin
Ariès, Philippe
l'Enfant et la vie familiale sous l'ancien régime, Paris, 1960, published in English as *Centuries of Childhood, A Social History of Family Life*, New York, 1962, Vintage Books
Bakan, D.
'Adolescence in America: From idea to social fact', in: Kagan, J. and Coles, R. (eds.), *Twelve to sixteen: Early Adolescence*, New York, 1971, Norton

Berlin, Isaiah
Two Concepts of Liberty, Oxford, 1958, Oxford University Press and Clarendon Press, pp. 7–15
Black, Maggie
The Children and the Nations; The Story of UNICEF, Sydney, Australia/New York, U.S.A., 1986, PIC/UNICEF
Boulding, Elise
'Children's Rights' in Abdul Aziz, Said, ed. *Human Rights and World Order*, New Brunswick, N.J., 1978, Transaction Books
Boulding, Elise
Children's Rights and the Wheel of Life, New Brunswick, N.J., 1979, Transaction Books
Bremner, Robert H.
Children and Youth in America, A Documentary History, Vol.III, 1933–1973, Cambridge, Mass., 1974, Harvard University Press
Cairns, David
Quality of Life; Assessment for Haemodialysis Patients: an application of a systemic Life Quality Model, Sydney, 1990, School of Behavioural Sciences, Macquarie University (Australia), doctoral dissertation
Cohen, Morris L.; Lee, Luke T. and Stepan, Jan
The Rights of the Child: A Classification Plan, A Guide to the Compilation and Review of Laws Affecting the Rights of the Child in Each Country in Observance of the International Year of the Child, Medford, Mass., 1987 Law and Population Programme, The Fletcher School of Law and Diplomacy, Law and Population Monograph Series No. 46
Crompton, M.
Respecting Children, London, 1980, Edward Arnold
Dasberg, Lea
'What is a child and what are its rights?' in: Verhellen, E. and Spiesschaert, F., eds. *Ombudswork for Children*, Louvain, 1988, Acco Publishers
Dasberg, Lea
Grootbrengen door kleinhouden, als historisch verschijnsel, Meppel, 1975, Boom
Davis, Samuel M. and Schwartz, Mortimer D.
Children's Rights and the Law, Lexington, 1987, Lexington Books/D.C. Heath and Comp.
Dearden, R.F.
'Autonomy and education', in: Dearden, R.F., Hirst, P.H., and Peters, R.S., *Education and Reason*, London, 1975, pp. 58–75, Routledge and Kegan Paul (originally published in 1972 as Part III of *Education and the development of reason*)
Deci, Edward L
The Psychology of Self-Determination, Lexington, Mass., 1980, Lexington Books
Deci, Edward L.; Ryan, Richard M.
Intrinsic Motivation and Self-Determination in Human Behavior, New York and London, 1985, Plenum
Dell, Floyd
Women as World Builders, Chicago, 1913, Forbes and Comp.
DeMause, Lloyd, ed.
The History of Childhood, London, 1974, Souvenir Press
Dingwall, Robert; Eekelaar, John and Murray, Topsy
The protection of children – State intervention and family life, Oxford, 1983, Basil Blackwell
Dingwall, Robert; Eekelaar, John, M. and Murray, Topsy
Childhood as a Social Problem: A Survey of the History of Legal Regulation, Oxford, 1982, Centre for Socio-Legal Studies
Empey, Lamar T.
The Future of Childhood and Juvenile Justice, Charlottesville, 1979, University Press of Virginia
Ennew, Judith and Milne, Brian

The Next Generation, Lives of Third World Children, London, 1989, Red Books
Fine, Melvin J.
Parents vs. Children, Making the relationship work, Englewood Cliffs, N.J., 1979, Prentice-Hall, Inc.
Foster, Antoinnette M.
An examination and analysis of the changes in concept of children's rights as reflected in court decisions on child welfare, education, and juvenile court procedures between 1859 *and the present*, Storrs, Connecticut, 1978, The University of Connecticut (can be obtained from University Microfilms International 300 N.Zeeb Road, Ann Arbor, Michigan 48106, U.S.A.)
Franklin, Bob, ed.
The Rights of Children, London, 1986, Basil Blackwell
Freeman, Kathleen
If Any Man Build, The History of Save the Children, London, 1965, Hodder and Stoughton
Freeman, Michael D.A.
The Rights and Wrongs of Children, London and Dover N.H., 1983, Frances Pinter Publishers
Fuller, Edward
The Rights of the Child; A Chapter in Social History, London 1951, Victor Gollancz Ltd.
Fuller, Edward
She Championed Children, London 1956, Save the Children Fund
Gaylin, Willard; Glasser, Ira; Marcus, Steven and Rochman, David
Doing Good: The Limits of Benevolence, New York, 1978, Pantheon Books
Gaylin, Willard and Macklin, Ruth, eds.
Who Speaks for the Child? The Problems of Proxy Convent, New York/London, 1982, Plenum Press
Gerzon, Mark
A childhood for every child: the politics of parenthood, New York, 1973, Outerbridge and Lazard
Goldstein, Joseph; Freud, Anna and Solnit, Albert J.
Beyond the Best Interests of the Child, New York, 1973, MacMillan Publishing Group
Goldstein, Joseph; Freud, Anna and Solnit, Albert J.
Before the Best Interests of the Child, New York, 1986, MacMillan Publishing Group
Goldstein, Joseph; Freud, Anna and Solnit, Albert J.
In the Best Interests of the Child, New York, 1986, MacMillan Publishing Group
Goulet, Denis
The Cruel Choice, A New Concept in the Theory of Development, New York, 1971, Atheneum
Gross, Beatrice and Gross, Ronald, eds.
The children's rights movement – overcoming the oppression of young people, Garden City, N.Y., 1977, Andros Books
Guggenheim, Martin and Sussman, Hans
The Rights of Young People, New York, 1985, Bantam Books
Hallowes, Frances, S.
The Rights of Children in Spirit, Mind and Body Thoughts for Parents, 1986, S.W. Partridge and Comp.
Hart, 't, Willem Anne
Ellen Key, Leyden 1948, State University Leyden, doctoral dissertation
Hartmann, Francis X.
From Children to Citizens, Vol.II, The Role of the Juvenile Court, London, New York, Berlin, 1987, Springer Verlag
Haubrich, Vernon F. and Apple, Michael W., eds.
Schooling and the Rights of Children, Berkeley, Calif., 1975, McCutchan Publ. Comp.
Hayles, M., ed.
Changing Childhood, Publishing Co-operative, London, 1979
Hellinckx, W. and Pauwels, J.
Orthopedagogische Ontwikkelingen in de Kinderbescherming; Leven en Werk van Dr. D.Q.R. Mulock Houwer, Louvain/Amersfoort, 1984, Acco

Henning, James S.
The Rights of Children, Legal and Psychological Perspectives, Springfield, Ill., 1982, Charles C. Thomas Publishers
Houlgate, Laurence D.
The Child and the State: A Normative Theory of Juvenile Rights, Baltimore 1980, John Hopkins University Press
Jansen, W.
Ellen Key en Hare, Paedagogische Idealen, Utrecht, 1905, C.H.E. Breyer
Jenkins, Iredell
Social Order and the Limits of Law, a theoretical essay, Princeton, New Jersey, 1980, Princeton University Press
Keniston, Kennet and the Carnegie Council on Children
All our Children, New York, 1977, Harcourt, Brace, Jovanovich, Inc.
King, Michael, ed.
Childhood, Welfare and Justice, London, 1981, Batsford Academic and Educational Ltd.
Koocher, Gerald, ed.
Children's Rights and the Mental Health Professions, New York/London/Sydney/Toronto, 1977, John Wiley & Sons
Krill, Françoise and Mayer, Michel
'Symposium Croix-Rouge et Croissant-Rouge Protection de l'enfant – rôle de la Croix-Rouge, le 13 Septembre, 1985)', in: *International Institute of Humanitarian Law Yearbook* 1985, San Remo, 1986, Villa Nobel
Kurzweil, Zwi Erich
Vorläufer Progressiver Erziehung, Ratingen/Kastellaun/Dusseldorf, 1974, A. Henn Verlag
Langen, Miek de
Recht voor Jeugdigen, Alphen aan den Rijn, 1973, Samson Uitgeverij
Langen, M. de; Graaf, J.H. de; and Kunneman, F.B.M.
Kinderen en Recht, Deventer/Arnhem, 1989, Gouda and Quint BV and Kluwer; Wetenschappelijke Reeks, Faculteit der Rechtsgeleerdheid, Universiteit van Amsterdam
Lax, Elisabeth; Kirchhoff, Hella and Beiner, Friedrich
'Die Rechte des Kindes im Spiegel der Kinderbücher Korczaks', in: Beiner, F. ed., *Janusz Korczak, Zeugnisse einer lebendigen Pädagogik*, Heinsberg, 1982
Lewin, Aleksander
Système Moderne de l'éducation et la patrimoine des pédagogues-novateurs: J. Korczak, A. Makarenko and C. Freinet, Warsaw, 1976, Institut des Recherches Pédagogiques
Lifton, Betty Jean
The King of Children, A Biography of Janusz Korczak, New York, 1988, Farrar, Straus and Giroux
Lomasky, Loren E.
Persons, Rights, and the Moral Community, Oxford, 1987, Oxford University Press
Maslow, Abraham
Motivation and Psychology, New York, 1954, Harper
Melton, Gary B.
Children's Concepts and Their Right, Boston, 1979, Boston University Graduate School, doctoral dissertation
Melton, Gary B.
'Teaching Children About Their Rights', in: Henning, James, S., ed., *The Rights of Children, Legal and Psychological Perspectives*, Springfield, Ill., 1982, Charles C. Thomas Publisher
Melton, Gary B.; Koocher, G.P. and Saks, M.
Children's Competence to Consent, New York, 1983, Plenum Press
Melton, Gary B.
Child Advocacy: Psychological Issues and Interventions, New York, 1983, Plenum Press
Melton, Gary B.
Reforming the law; impact of child development research, New York/London, 1987, The Guildford Press

Minow, Martha
   'The Public Duties of Families and Children', in: Hartmann, Francis, X., *The Role of the Juvenile Court*, Berlin/New York, 1987, Springer Verlag
Mnookin, Robert H.
   Child, Family and State, Boston, 1978, Little, Brown and Comp.
Mnookin, Robert H., ed.
   In the Interest of Children Advocacy; Advocacy, Law Reform and Public Policy, New York, 1985, W.F. Freeman and Comp.
Morris, David and McAlpin, Michelle B.
   Measuring the Condition of India's Poor, The Physical Quality of Live Index,New Delhi, 1982, Promilla and Comp. Publishers
Mortkowicz-Olczakowa, Hanna
   Janusz Korczak, Artzt und Pädagoge, Weimar, 1961, Munich and Salzburg, 1967, Anton Pustet Verlag, in English: *Mister Doctor, The Life of Janusz Korczak*, London, 1965
Mukherjee, Ramkrishna
   The Quality of Life, Valuation in Social Research, New Delhi/Newbury Park/London, 1989, Sage Publications
Nisbet, Robert
   History of The Idea of Progress, New York, 1980, Basic Books Inc.
Nyström-Hamilton, Louise
   Ellen Key: Her Live and Work, New York, 1930, Putnam
Pappas, Anna Mamalakis
   Law and the Status of the Child, New York, 1979, UNITAR
Piaget, Jean, and Ingelder, B.
   The growth of logical thinking from childhood to adolescence, New York, 1958, Basic Books
Piziali, Patricia Anne
   A historical study of the origin and current status of child advocacy concepts with particular attention to the contributions of Janusz Korczak, Washington D.C., 1981, The Faculty of the Graduate School of Education and Human Development of the George Washington University, doctoral dissertation
Platt, Anthony M.
   The Child Savers, The Invention of Delinquency, Chicago and London, 1969, The University of Chicago Press
Plattner, Denise and Swinarski, Christophe
   'La Protection Juridique de l'enfant victime civile des conflits armés' in: *International Institute of Humanitarian Law Yearbook* 1984, San Remo, 1985, Villa Nobel
Pollock, Linda, A.
   Forgotten Children: Parent-Child Relations 1500–1900, Cambridge, U.K., 1983, Cambridge University Press
Pringle, Mia Kellmer
   The needs of children, London, 1980, Hutchinson
Pye, Anthony Ian
   A Philosophy of Children's Rights, New York City, 1980, Columbia University, Graduate School of Arts and Sciences, doctoral dissertation
Reppuci, Dickon N.; Weithorn, Lois, A.; Mulvey, Edward P. and Monahan, John
   Children, Mental Health and the Law, Beverly Hills/London/New Delhi/1984, Sage Publications
Ressler, Everett, M.; Boothby, Neil and Steinbock, Daniel J.
   Unaccompanied Children, Care and Protection in Wars, Natural Disasters and Refugee Movements, New York and Oxford, 1988, Oxford University Press
Rothman, David
   Conscience and Convenience, Boston, 1980, Little, Brown and Comp.
Sachs, Christina J.R.
   'Children's Rights', in: J.W. Bridge, Lasok, D., Perrot, D.L., and Plender, R.O., *Fundamental Rights*, London, 1973, Sweet and Maxwell

Scharsch, A.
Images of Childhood: An Illustrated Social History, New York, 1979
Scheibe, Wolfgang
Die Reformpädagogische Bewegung 1900–1932, Weinheim 1969
Senn, Milton J.E. and Solnit, Albert J.
Problems in Child Behavior and Development, Philadelphia, 1968, Lea and Febiger
Shah, P.M. and Cantwell, W.
Child Labour: A Threat to Health and Development, Geneva, 1985, Defence for Children International (DCI), (second revised edition)
Short, James F.
'Social Contexts of Child Rights and Delinquency', in: Empey, LaMar T., ed., *The Future of Childhood and Juvenile Justice*, Charlottesville, 1979, University Press of Virginia
Shye, Samuel
'Nonmetric Multivariate Models for Behavioral Action Systems', in: Canter, David, ed., *Facet Theory, Approaches to Social Research*, New York/Berlin, 1985, Springer Verlag
Shye, Samuel
'Human Life Quality: An Action System', in: Shye, Samuel, *Multiple Scaling, The Theory and Application of Partial Order Scalogram Analysis*, Amsterdam/New York/Oxford, 1985, North-Holland Publ.Comp.
Sicault, George, ed.
The Needs of Children, A Study of the Needs of Children in the Developing Countries based on reports by six Agencies of the United Nations, New York, 1963, published for UNICEF by The Free Press of Glencoe and MacMillan
Solnit, Albert J.
Children's rights and needs in the light of new research, Jerusalem, 1986, The National Council of Jewish Women and the Institute of Innovation and Education of the Hebrew University (The First Milton and Eleanor Fromer Lecture on Early Childhood Education)
Spiegelman, Judith M.
We Are the Children, A celebration of UNICEF's first forty years, Boston/New York, 1986, The Atlantic Monthly Press
Tanner, S.M.
'The trend towards earlier physical maturity', in: Meade, J.E. and Parkes, A.S., eds. *Biological Aspects of Social Problems*, New York, 1965
Thane, Pat
'Childhood in History', in: King, Michael, ed., *Childhood, Welfare and Justice*, London, 1981, Batsford Academic and Educational Ltd.
Tomasevski, Katarina, ed.
Children in Adult Prisons, London, 1986, Frances Pinter
Tuck, Richard
Natural Rights Theories: Their Origin and Development, Cambridge 1979, Cambridge University Press
Vardin, Patricia A., and Brody, Ilene N., eds.
Children's Rights: Contemporary Perspectives, New York, 1978, Columbia University, Teachers College Press
Verhellen, E. and Spiesschaert, F., eds.
Ombudswork for Children, Louvain, 1988, Acco Publishers
Verhellen, E.; Spiesschaert, F. and Cattrijse, L., eds.
Rechten van kinderen, een tekstbundel van de Rijks Universiteit Gent naar aanleiding van de UNO Conventie voor de Rechten van het kind, Antwerp, 1989, Kluwer Rechtswetenschappen
Walvin, James
A Child's World. A Social History of English Childhood 1800–1914, Harmondsworth, Middlesex, 1982, Penguin Books Ltd.
Westman, Jack C.
Child Advocacy New Professional Roles for Helping Families, New York and London, 1979, The Free Press

Wilkerson, Albert, ed.
 The Rights of Children: Emergent Concepts in Law and Society, Philadelphia 1973, Temple University Press
Wilson, John P.
 The Rights of Adolescents in the Mental Health System, Lexington, MA, 1978, D.C. Heath and Comp.
Wringe, Colin A.
 Children's Rights: A Philosophical Study, London, 1981, Routledge and Kegan Paul
Zaharoff, Howard George
 Interests, Rights and Choices: An Examination of the Child's Entitlement to Freedom, The John Hopkins University, 1979, doctoral dissertation
Zelizer, Viviana A.
 Pricing the priceless child: The changing social value of children, New York 1985, Basic Books
Zimring, F.E.
 The changing world of legal adolescence, New York, 1982, Free Press

2B. Selected Articles and Papers presented at Conferences

Abella, Rosalie Silberman
 The critical century: the rights of women and children from 1882–1982, in: Gazette, 1984, 18(1): 40–53
Allen, N.F.
 'The parental right to possession of a child', 1986, in Liverpool L. Rev., 8:97–129
Alston, Philip
 'The New Convention on the Rights of the Child', Australian Journal of Early Childhood, 1989, 14, 1060
Arthur, L.G.
 'Should children be as equal as people'? in: North Dakota Law Review, 1968:204–221
Atkin, W.R.
 Parents and children: Mrs. Gillick in the House of Lords, in: New Zealand L.J., 1986: 90–93
Bainham, Andrew
 The balance of power in family decisions, in: Camb.L.J., 1986, 45:262–284
Barnes, Earl
 'Study of Children's Rights as seen by themselves', in: The Paedologist,1900, Vol.2, No. 3, November: 142–144
Baumrind, Diana
 'Reciprocal Rights and Responsibilities in Parent-Child Relations', in The Journal of Social Issues, 1978,34,2, Spring: 179–196
Beck, C.
 'Rights of Children: A Trust Model', in Fordham Law Review, 40, 1978: 669
Beck, Rochelle
 'The White House Conferences and Children: An Historical Perspective' in: Harvard Educational Review, Vol. 43, No. 4, November 1973: 656
Becker, W.
 Weichendes Elternrecht, wachsendes Kindesrecht, in: Recht der Jugend und das Bildungswesen, 1970, 18, 12: 364
Bennett, Walter Jr. and McDonald, Laughlin
 'Rights of Children', in: The Family Co-ordinator, 1977, 26, 4, Oct.: 333–337
Bennett, Walter Jr.
 'A critique of the emerging Convention on the Rights of the Child', in: Cornell International Law Journal, 1987, 20: 1–64

Besharov, Douglas J.
  'Right versus Rights: The Dilemma of Child Protection' in: *Public Welfare*, 1985, 43, 2, Spring: 19–27
Bikson, Tora K.
  'The Status of Children's Intellectual Rights' in: *The Journal of Social Issues*, 1978, 34, 2, Spring: 69–86
Boli-Bennett, John and Meyer, John W.
  'The Ideology of Childhood and the State: Rules distinguishing children in national constitutions 1870–1970', in: *American Sociological Review*, 1978, Vol. 43, December: 797–812
Boulding, Elise
  'Children's Rights', *Society*, 1977, Vol. 15, No. 1, Nov./Dec.: 39–43
Bricker, S.
  'Children's rights: A movement in search of a meaning', in: *University of Richmond Law Review*, 1979, 13: 661–693
Burt, Robert A.
  'Developing Constitutional Rights Of, In, and For Children' in: *Law and Contemporary Problems*, 1975, 39, 3. Summer,: 118–143
Cantwell, Nigel
  'Children's Rights in an Adult Society', in: *Future*, 1986, No. 18–19
Cantwell, Nigel
  'Universalité des droits de l'enfant', in: *Médecine et Enfance*, (Paris) March, 1986, No. 3
Casullo, Catherina
  'The U.N. Declaration of the Rights of the Child', in: *U.N. Secretariat News*, 15 April 1985, Vol.XL; No. 1: 11–12
Cerda, Jaime Sergio
  'The Draft Convention on the Rights of the Child: New Rights' in: *Human Rights Quarterly* 1990, 12: 115–119
Chanlett, Eliska and Morier, G.M.
  'Declaration of the Rights of the Child' in: *International Child Welfare Review*, 1986, Vol.XXII, No. 1
Chisholm, Barbara
  'Children's rights', in: *Perception – a Canadian Journal of Social Comment*, 1977, November/-December, 1: 22–27
Clyde, Margaret
  'Children's Rights – Are They Wrong?' in: *Australian Child and Family Welfare*, 1980, Spring, Vol. 5, No. 3: 11–14
Cohen, Cynthia Price
  'The Human Rights of Children', in: 12, *Capital University Law Review*, 1983
Cohen, Cynthia Price
  'Elasticity of Obligation and the Drafting of the Convention on the Rights of the Child', in: 3, *Connecticut Journal of International Law*, 1987, 71
Cohen, Cynthia Price
  'United Nations Convention on the Rights of the Child – Introductory Note', in: *The Review; For the Rule of Law* (International Commission of Jurists), 1990, No. 44, June: 36–42
Cohen, Cynthia Price
  'Role of Non-Governmental Organisations in the Drafting of the Convention on the Rights of the Child', in: *Human Rights Quarterly*, 1990, Vol. 12, No. 1
Cohen, Cynthia Price and Naimark, Hedwin
  'The United Nations Convention on the Rights of the Child: Individual Rights Concepts and their Significance for Social Scientists' in: *American Psychologist*, 1991, Vol. 46, No. 2
Corbin, Arthur L.
  'Legal Analysis and Terminology' in: *Yale Law Journal*, 1919–1920, Vol.XXIX: 163–173
Coughlin, B.J.
  'The rights of Children' in: *Child Welfare*, 1968, 47, No. 3: 133

Crouch, R.E.
'An essay on the critical and judicial reception of Beyond the Best Interests of the Child', in: *Family Law Quarterly*, 1979, 49, 13

DeMause, Lloyd
'The Evolution of Childhood', in: *History of Childhood Quarterly*, 1973–1974, 1,: 503,507

Edelman, M.W.
'Who is for children?' in *American Psychologist*, 1981, 36: 109–117

Edison, I.
'The rights of the world's children' in: *Child Welfare*, 1961, 40, No. 5

Eekelaar, John, M.
'What are Parental Rights?' in: *Law Quarterly Review*, 1973, 89: 210–234

Eekelaar, John, M.
'Parents and Children: rights, responsibilities and needs', in: *Adoption and Fostering*, 1983, No. 2: 7–9

Eekelaar, John, M.
'The emergence of children's rights', in: *Oxford J. Leg. Stud.*, 1986, 6: 161–182

Feshbach, Norma Deitch and Feshbach, Seymour
'Toward an Historical, Social and Developmental Perspective on Children's Rights' in: *The Journal of Social Issues*, 1978, 34, 2, Spring: 1–7

Fink, Joel and Sponseller, Doris
'Practising for Child Advocacy,' in: *Young Children*, 1977, Vol. 32, No. 3,: 49–54

Foreman, Lynne
'An Alternative to the Concept of Children's Rights' in: *Australian Child and Family Welfare*, 1976, February, No. 1: 16–21

Forer, L.G.
'The rights of children: The legal vacuum', in: *American Bar Association Journal*, 1969, 55: 1151–1155

Forer, L.G.
'The rights of children', in *Young Children*, 1972, 27: 332–339

Fox, Sanford
'Juvenile Justice Reform: An historical perspective' in: *Stanford Law Review*, 1970, 22: 1187–1239

Freeman, K.
'Declaration on the rights of the child of Geneva' in: *World's Children*, 1961, 41, No. 2

Freeman, Michael, D.A.
'The Rights of Children in the International Year of the Child' in: *Current Legal Problems*, 1980, 1

Freeman, M.D.A.
'The Rights of Children When They Do "Wrong"' in: *British Journal of Criminology*, 1981, 21, 3, July: 210–299

Gramam, Janet
'Saviour to the World's Children', in: *The World's Children*, 1979, March: 9–11

Grant, Gerald
'Children's Rights and Adult Confusions' in: *The Public Interest*, 1982, 69, Fall: 83–99

Greenberger, E. and Sorensen, A.
'Toward a concept of psychosocial maturity' in: *Journal of Youth and Adolescence*, 1974, 3: 329–358

Geiser, R.
'The Rights of Children', in: *Hastings Law Journal*, 28, 1977

Hafen, Bruce C.
'Children's Liberation and the New Egalitarianism: Some Reservations about Abandoning Youth to Their "Rights"', in: *Brigham Young University Law Review*, 1976: 605–658

Hafen, Bruce C.
'Puberty, privacy, and protection: the risks of children's rights'; does the movement toward

children's "rights" contain the seeds of destruction for the family?' in: *American Bar Association Journal*, 1977, 63: 1383
Hafen, Bruce C.
'Exploring Test Cases in Child Advocacy', in: *Harvard Law Review*, 1986: 100, 435, 446
Hammarberg, Thomas
'The U.N. Convention on the Rights of the Child – and How 'to Make it Work', in: *Human Rights Quarterly*, 1990, 12: 97–105
Hawker, M.
'Children have rights too', in: *Community Care*, 1983, January 6: 13
Haydon, Graham
'Political theory and the child: problems of the individualist tradition', in: *Political Studies*, 1979, XXCII, September 3
Henkin, Louis
'Rights: American and Human', in: *Columbia Law Review*, 1979, April, Vol. 79, No. 3
Hohfeld, Wesley N.
'Some Fundamental Legal Conceptions as Applied in Judicial Reasoning', *Yale Law Journal*, 1917, 16, 23
Hutton, Patrick H.
'The History of Mentalities: the New Map of Cultural History', in: *History and Theory*, 1981, Vol.XX
Jones, Joan M. and McNeely, R.L.
'Children's Rights in Historical Perspective' in: *Social Development Issues*, 1981, 5, 1, Spring: 9–26, (Magazine published by the University of Iowa, School of Social Work)
Jupp, Michael
'The Human Rights of Children', in: *International Health News*, 1987, Vol. 8, No. 1, January
Katz, Sanford, N.; Schroeder, William, A. and
Sidman, Lawrence, R., 'Emancipating our Children – Coming of Legal Age in America', in *Family Law Quarterly*, 1973, Fall, Vol.VII, No. 3: 211–241
Kemba, Walter J.
'Legal Theory and Hohfeld's Analysis of a Legal Right', in: *The Juridical Review*, 1974, Part 3, December
Klein, F.
'Das Recht auf Erziehung als gesellschaftliche Forderung', in: *Jugendwohl*, Vol. 52, 19/1, No. 7–8: 253–267
Kohlberg, L. and Gilligan, C.
'The adolescent as a philosopher: The discovery of the self in a postconventional world', in: *Daedalus*, 1971, 100: 1051–1086
Konopka, Gisela
'The needs and responsibilities of youth', in: *Child Welfare*, 1976, 55(3), March: 173–182
Landerer, Arthur
'The Rights of Children in America – The Differing Perceptions', in: *Poly Law Review*, 1979, Vol. 5, No. 1: 19–28
Langen, M. de, and Sassenburg, J.M.
'De betekenis van mensenrechten voor kinderen', in Nederlandse Juristen Comité voor Mensenrechten, (Dutch Section of the International Commission of Jurists), *Mensenrechten en Personen – en Familierecht*, Leyden, 1986, Stichting NJCM – Boekerij: 37–63
Langen, Miek de
'Recht voor Kinderen', in: *Jeugd en Samenleving*, 1988, 18, No. 7/8: 395–402
Lejeune, R.
'Eglantyne Jebb, A Life Devoted to the Service of Children in distress', in: *International Child Welfare Review*, No. 58, Sept. 1983: 55–58
Lejeune, R.
'Towards a European Convention on the Rights of the Child', in: *Council of Europe Forum*, 1984, I

Mabbutt, Fred R.
'Juveniles, Mental Hospital Commitment and Civil Rights: The Case of Parham v. J.R.', *Journal of Family Law*, 1980–1981, 19, 1: 27–64

MacCormick, Neil
Children's Rights: A test-Case for Theories of Right', in: *Archiv für Rechts- und Sozial-Philosophie*, 1976, 62: 305–317

Margolin, C.R.
'Salvation versus Liberatikon: The Movement for Children's Rights in a Historical Context', in: *Social Problems*, 1978, 25, 4, April: 441–452

Marks, Raymond F.
'Detours on the Road to Maturity: A view of the legal conception of growing up and letting go', in: *Law and Contemporary Problems*, 1975, Vol. 39, No. 3, Summer: 78–92

Melton, Gary B.
'Children's right to treatment', in *Journal of Clinical Child Psychology*, 1978, 7: 200–202

Melton, Gary B.
'Children's concepts of their rights', in *Journal of Clinical Child Psychology*, 1980, 9: 186–190

Melton, Gary B.
'Children's rights: Where are the children?' in: *American Journal of Orthopsychiatry*, 1982, 52: 530–538

Melton, Gary B.
'Toward "personhood" for adolescents: Autonomy and privacy as values in public policy', in: *American Psychologist*, 1983, 38: 99–103

Melton, Gary B.
'Legal Regulation of Adolescent Abortion', in: *American Psychologist*, 1987, January, Vol. 42: 79–82

Melton, Gary B.
'If the status of adolescents is to change, so must youth services' in: *Division of Child, Youth, and Family Services Newsletter*, 1987, Spring: 13–14

Melton, Gary B.
'The clashing of symbols: Prelude to child and family policy', in: *American Psychologist*, 1987, 42: 345–354

Miljeteig-Olssen, Per
'Advocacy of Children's Rights – the Convention as more than a Legal Document', in: *Human Rights Quarterly*, 1990, 12: 148–155

Minow, Martha
'Rights for the next generation: a feminist approach to children's rights', in: *Harvard Women's Law Journal*, Spring 1986, 9: 1–24

Minow, Martha
'Interpreting Rights: An Essay for Robert Cover', in: *The Yale Law Journal*, July 1987, No. 8, Vol. 96: 1860–1915

Minow, Martha
'Are Rights for Children? Constitutional Bicentennial Symposium: The "Rights Revolution"', in: *Am. Bar Found. Research Journal*, Winter 1987, Vol. I: 203–223

Mnookin, Robert H., and Coons, J.E.
'Toward a theory of children's rights', in: *Harvard Law Bulletin*, 1977, Vol.28, No. 3: 18–22

Mnookin, Robert. H.
'Children's rights: Beyond kiddie libbers and child savers', in: *Journal of Clinical Child Psychology, Fall* 1978, 7: 163–167

Modell, J.; Furstenberg, F. Jr. and Herschberg, T.
'Social Change and Transitions to Adulthood in Historical Perspective', in: *Journal of Family History*, 1976, 1: 7–33

Morton, Miriam, and Aleksin, Anatolii, 'Pravo na detstvo'
(Right to Childhood), in: *Literaturnaya Gazeta* (Russian), 1979, 51, 18, May 1,3 (English Abstract)

Morton, T. and Dubanoski, R.A.
  'Children's Rights: Attitudes and Perceptions', in *Educational Perspectives*, 1980, 19, 4: 24–27
O'Neill, Onora
  'Children's Rights and Children's Lives', in: *Ethics*, 1988, 98, April: 445–463
Olson, Dennis A.
  'The Swedish ban on corporal punishment', in: *Brigham Young U.L. Rev.*, 1984: 447–456
Peiris, G.L.
  'The Gillick case: parental authority, teenage independence and public policy,' in: *Current Leg. Probs.*, 1987, 40: 93–122
Pfohl, Stephen J.
  'The "Discovery" of Child Abuse', in *Social Problems*, 1077, 24 February: 310–23
Pilpel, Harriet F.
  "Minors" Rights to Medical Care', in *Albany Law Review*, 1972, 36.3: 462–487
Plattner, Denise
  'Protection of Children in International Humanitarian Law', in: *International Review of the Red Cross*, 1988, May-June: 1–13
Radin, Max A.
  'A Restatement of Hohfeld', in: *Harvard Law Review*, 1938, Vol. 51:1, reprinted in *Readings of Jurisprudence*, 1938, Indianapolis, Jerome Hall
Reid, Ira A. de
  'The Midcentury White House Conference on Children and Youth', in *Child Welfare*, 1951, July, Vol.XXX, No. 7: 3–6
Robert, P.
  'Historique du droit des Mineurs ou la Conquête de l'Autonomie à travers l'Histoire', in: *Rééducation*, 1968, 23, 07/08, No. 203
Rogers, Carl M. and Wrightsman, Lawrence S.
  'Attitudes toward Children's Rights: Nurturance or Self-Determination?', in: *Journal of Social Issues*, 1978, Vol. 34, No. 2: 59–67
Ross, A.O.
  'The Rights of Children as Psychotherapy Patients, *Paper presented at the American Psychological Association Meeting*, New Orleans, Louisiana, September 1974
Sassenburg, J.M.
  'Evolutie van recht voor jeugdigen', in: *WPNR* (*Weekblad voor Privaatrecht, Notariaat en Registratie*), 1985, 22–29 June, No. 5746, Vol. 116: 477–482
Scarre, G.
  'Children and Paternalism', in: *Philosophy*, 1980, 55
Schrag, Francis
  'Rights Over Children', in *Journal of Value Inquiry*, 1973, 7, 2: 96–105
Sheleff, Leon S.
  'Paternalism and the Young', in: *Children and Youth Services Review*, 1984, 6, 4: 267–283
Shore, Milton F.
  'Legislation, Advocacy, and the Rights of Children and Youth', in: *American Psychologist*, 1979, 34, 10, Oct.: 1017–1019
Shye, S.
  'The Systemic Life Quality Model: A Basis for Urban Renewal Evaluation', in: *Social Indicators Research*, 1989, 21: 343–378
Singer, Eva
  'Selected Bibliography on the Protection of Children's Rights', in *Nordic Journal of International Law*, 1989, vol. 58, pp. 110–123
Singer, Sandra
  'The Protection of Children during Armed Conflict Situations', in: *International Review of the Red Cross*, 1986, May-June
Solnit, Albert J.

'Children, Parents and the State', in: 52, *American Journal of Orthopsychiatry*, 1982, 495: 501–504
Stier, Serena
'Children's Rights and Society's Duties', in: *The Journal of Social Issues*, 1978, 34, 2, Spring: 46–58
Stocker, Hans A.
'Verstärkung der Kinderrechte im Jahr des Kindes: über die Problematik einer UN-Kinderkonvention, in: *Vereinten Nationen*, Zeitschrift für die Vereinten Nationen und ihre Sonderorganisationen, 1979, 27: 90–4
Stone, Olive M.
'Warsaw Conference on the Legal Protection of the Rights of Children,' in: *Alberta Law Review*, 1979, 17, 4: 555–562
Sutton, Thomas L.
'Human Rights and Children', in: *Educational Theory*, 1978, 28, 2: 102–110
Takanishi, Ruby
'Childhood as a Social Issue: Historical Roots of Contemporary Child Advocacy Movements', in: *The Journal of Social Issues*, 1978, 34, 2, Spring: 8–28
Tapp, J.L. and Melton, G.B.
'Preparing children for decision making: Implications of legal socialization research', in: Melton, Gary B., Koocher, G.P. and Saks, M.H. (eds.), in: *Children's competence to consent*, 1983, New York, Plenum Press
Teitelbaum, Lee E.
'Foreword: The Meaning of Rights to Children', in *New Mexico Law Review*, Summer 1980, Vol. 10: 235–253
Tribe, Laurence H.
'Childhood, Suspect Classifications and Conclusive Presumptions: Three Linked Riddles', in: *Law and Contemporary Problems*, Summer 1975, 39, 3: 8–37
Turner, Jill
'Children, Not Cattle', in: *New Society*, 1978, August, 25: 402–403
Veerman, Philip, E.
'Het Weeshuis van Korczak, een oase in Warschau', in: *Sjow, Tijdschrift voor Jeugdbescherming en Jeugdwelzijn*, 1983, No. 1/2, Vol. 11: 38–42
Veerman, Philip, E.
'With a Cold Objective Eye and a Warm Heart; The Work of Child Welfare Pioneer Dan Mulock Houwer' in: *Youth Aliyah Bulletin*, 1985, December: 72–73
Veerman, Philip, E.
'The Rights of the Child today and in the time of Janusz Korczak', *Paper presented at the International Conference on the Training of Educators*, June 20, 1985. A microfiche copy can be ordered through ERIC (Clearinghouse on Elementary and Early Childhood Education in Urbana, Illinois, U.S.A.)
Veerman, Philip, E.
Is Compulsory Education a Right? Paper presented at the *Second International Congress on Psychiatry, Law and Ethics*, Israel, February, 16–21, 1986
Veerman, Philip, E.
'Janusz Korczak and the rights of the child', in *Concern* (Magazine of the National Children's Bureau, London) 1987, Spring, No. 62: 7–9
Veerman, Philip, E.
'In the Shadow of Janusz Korczak; The Story of Stefania Wilczynska', in: *The Melton Journal*, Spring 1990, No. 23: 8–9
Verdross, Alfred
'Fundamental Human Rights: The Journey of an Idea', in: *Human Rights*, 1979, 8:3, :20–23
Vos, Jaap F.
'De 1918–Onderwijswet in de U.S.S.R.: een kort hoofdstuk over de vrijwording van het onderwijs' in: *INFO, Informatiebladen van de Afdeling Onderwijskunde van de Rijksuniversit-*

eit te Groningen, 1970, Vol.I, No. 4: 146–157
Vyver, Johan van der
'The Concept of Human Rights: Its History and Meaning', in: *Acta Juridica*, 1979: 10–32
Wald, Michael D.
'Children's Rights: A Framework for Analysis', in: *Univ. of California at Davis Law Review*, 1979, Vol. 12: 256–281
Watson, David
'Do Children Have Rights?' in: *Philosophical Journal*, 1976, 13, 2,: 89–99
Weekblad
(van het Nederlands Genootschap van Leraren), Editors of; 'Prof. Dr. J. Wemelsfelder bepleit: Rechten van Scholieren vastleggen in een Statuut', in: *Weekblad*, 1977, No. 18, December 8: 689–681
Weisberg, D. Kelly
'Evolution of the concept of the rights of the child in the western world', in: the *Review: for the rule of law, the International Commission of Jurists*, 1978, December: 43–51
Wellman, Carl
'The Growth of Children's Rights', in: *Archive für Rechts- und Sozial Philosophie, ARSP*, 1984, Vol. 73: 441–453
Wilson, Adrian
'The Infancy of the History of Childhood: An Appraisal of Philippe Ariès', in: *History and Theory*, 1980, Vol.XIX, No. 2
Welson, Gillian
'The White Flame', in: *World's Children*, 1976, September
Wolkind, S.N. and Rutter, Michael
'Children who have been "in care'; An epidemiological study', in: *Journal of Child Psychology and Psychiatry*, 1973, 14: 97–105
Wong, B.
'Children's Rights: 'A Contemporary historical perspective', in: *Educational Perspectives*, 1980, 19, 3: 3–7
Worsfold, V.L.
'A Philosophical Justification for Children's Rights', in: *Harvard Educational Review*, 1974, 44, No. 1, February, 142–157
Yudof, Mark A.
'The Dilemma of Children's Autonomy', in: *Policy Analysis*, 1976, 2:3: 387–407
Zuckerman, Michael, 'Children's Rights – The Failure of Reform', in *Policy Analysis*, 1976, 2, 3,: 371–385

3B. Cases

Baumgartner v. City of Long Beach
No. 547482 Los Angeles County Superior Court, Stipulated Judgment and Permanent Injunction filed Feb.13, 1987
Bellotti versus Baird
443 U.S. 622, 1979
Brown versus Board of Education
347 U.S. 483, 1954
Campbell and Cosans v. U.K.
1982, 4 ECHR 293
Gillick versus Norfolk W. and Wisbech A.H.A.
1985, 3 All E.R., 402 (H.L.). and the Weekly Law Reports, 1 November 1985,:831–875
Ginsberg versus New York
U.S., Vol. 390, No. 47, 1968,:629–675

G.L. versus Zumwalt
  564, F. supp. at 1030, and 77-0242-CV-W-3, W.D. May 2, 1979
Hazelwood School District, et al., petitioners
  versus Cathy Kuhlmeier, et al., in: the United States Law Week, 1.12.1988,:4079-4087
Hunt versus County of Los Angeles
  in: ABA Juvenile and child Welfare Law Reporter, October 1986, Vol.V, No. 8, pp. 112-113
In re Gault
  387 U.S. 1, 1967
Joseph Dennis Zepeda versus Louis Roul Zepeda
  190 North Eastern Reporter, 2nd series,:849-859
Kritzik versus Kritzik
  21 Wis. 2 d 442, 124 N.W. 2d 581, 1963
Jon Nielsen versus Denmark
  European Court, Judgment of 28 November 1988, Series A, No. 129
Nick O. v. Terhune
  No.CIV S-89-0755-RAR-JFM US District Court, Eastern District of California, Stipulated and Order Filed Feb.13, 1990
Parham versus J.R.
  442 U.S., 584, 1979
Paula and Alexandre Marckx versus Belgium
  ECHR, 13 June 1979
Prince versus Commonwealth of Massachusetts
  321 U.S. 158, 1944
Procarnik versus Cillo
  97, N.J., 478 A.2d.755, 763, 1984
Tinker versus Des Moines School District
  393 U.S. 503, 515, 1969
Turpin versus Sortini
  31 Cal. 3d,220, 643,:2d, 954, 965, 182, Cal. Rptr.337, 1982
Wisconsin versus Yoder
  406 U.S. 205, 1972.

About the Author

Philip E. Veerman (born in The Netherlands in 1948) has been involved in child welfare since 1970.

In 1972, he started a project in The Netherlands for small therapeutic family group homes (as an alternative for large institutions), and subsequently worked for the Child Psychiatry Department of Rotterdam Academic Hospital. Here he helped to start therapeutic foster family care in the Rotterdam region.

From 1979 to 1985 he worked with children with school/learning problems at the Psychological Special Educational Institute, Amsterdam (PPI Amsterdam). He founded an organisation for exchange of information between the child welfare field and the education field (Stichting Wisselwerking).

In 1982 he founded the Janusz Korczak Stichting in The Netherlands to encourage the study of this Polish-Jewish educator.

Since 1988, he has been living in Israel where he founded the Israel Section of Defence for Children International (DCI).

He is one of the founders of the *International Journal of Children's Rights*, which will appear in 1993, and co-editor of *The Ideologies of Children's Rights* (Nijhoff, 1992).

Index of Subjects

Abduction, Child (–) – 193, 204, 224, 245, 269, 345
Abortion – 165–166, 185–186, 212, 220(68), 256, 294, 404
Abuse (of children) – 6, 198, 256, 262
  (the concept) – 196
  abuse of the child's integrity – 204
  criminal liability – 274(10)
  protection from (–) – see in the rights' index
Adolescence – 254, 438
  (the concept) – 3
  adolescents, rights of (–) – 318–319, 399
  to Self-Determination – 133
  carrying responsibilities – 189, 283
  see also under: Youth, Juveniles
Adoption – 184, 197–198, 341, 344–345, 378–379
  aim of (–) – 344
  adopted Children – legal status as part of the adoptive family – 344
  adopted children, needs of (–)
    to know his background – 344
  adopted children, rights of (–)
    to have a legal representative – 343
    to have a name and nationality – 343
    to have the persons responsible for the adoption professionally trained – 343
  best interests of the child as a paramount consideration – 343
  Intercountry (–) – 126, 132(62), 197–198, 344–345
    conditions to (–) – 344–345
    considering the child's cultural and religious background and interests – 345
  Obstacles on the way to (–) – 270
    Objections to adoptions in General by

    Islamic Law – 341
  Right to (–) – see in the rights' index
  Sale of children for purpose of (–) – 178, 197–198, 221(115)
Adults – 497
  differences from children – 3
  duties toward children – 292–295
    to inform the children about their rights – 292
Advisory Center for Education (London) – 288, 306
African Children
  rights of (–) – 271–273
African Network of the Prevention and Protection Against Child Abuse and Neglect (ANPPCAN) – 271, 280
Age
  as base to granting rights – 136–137, 303
  definition of a minor – 17–18
  minimum (–)
    for admission to employment – 178, 187, 231, 314–317, 321
    at nights – 327
    exceptions – 315–316
    in relation with age of completing compulsory education – 315
    to employment at sea – 314, 315
    to employment in agriculture – 315
    to employment in artistic performances – 316
    to employment in industry – 25, 311–314
      exceptions – 311–314
    to employment in light work – 316
    to employment in mining – 315
    where there may be danger to the minors health – 316, 327
  for driving – 139

Subject Index 627

for marriage – 186–187
for recruiting into armed forces – 206–207, 229(238)
of majority – 187
significance of (–) – 8
AIDS, children born with (–) – 80, 397
Alcoholism – 234
American Child Health Association – 231
American International Institute for the protection of Childhood (now: Inter-American Institute for the Child) – 244
Amman Symposium on Protection of Children – 260
Amnesty International – 126–127
Apartheid, condemning (–) – 273
Arab Children
  rights of (–) – 260–263
Armed Conflicts
  children participating in (–) – 205–207
    age limit – see under: Age
    recruiting children – 205–207, 229(238)
    voluntary participation – 206, 229(238)
  danger zones – 238–241
  Internal and international (–) – 207
  needs of children in (–) – 155, 198, 216, 237–242, 256
    defense areas – 238–240
    economic needs and security – 242
    food – 242. see also under: Food
    homes in wartime – 238–240
    interaction with society – 242
    medical services – 242
    physical safety – 238–242
    play and recreation – 242
  results of children being in (–) – 91, 237 241
  rights of children in (–) – 158, 177–178, 198, 205, 228(233), 237–242
Association for Free Education (U.S.S.R.) – 282
Autonomy
  (the concept) – 18, 32
  Children's (–) – 18, 330–331
    in schools – 306(12)
  personal (–) – 18–19, 24–25
  value of (–) – 19

Best interests
  of the child – 58, 125, 171, 177, 187, 188, 196, 198, 335, 342, 343, 378(88), 387
    as paramount consideration – 171, 182, 187–188, 278(70), 343–344

of the family – 334
Bhopa Statement on Child Labour in India – 373(20)
Breast Feeding – 213
BRIS (Sweden) – 115

Canadian Council for Children and Youth – 143
Censorship – 135–136, 195–196, 404
Child
  (the concept) – 3, 5, 133, 167, 176, 185, 186–187, 207, 261, 322, 398
  as an individual in his or her own right – 293, 330–331, 334, 363
  as a unique individual – 335
  as a subject of rights and not an object of rights – 396–398
  child advocacy – 113, 255
    the concept – 393(177)
    duties of the advocate – 393(177)
  child raising – 7
  child-rearing modes – 6
Child Agent – 142, 147–148
Child Welfare League of America (CWLA) – 29
Childhood
  (the concept) – 3–10, 12, 315, 395
  as a separate status – 8, 10
  image of (–) – xi, 3–10, 398
Children
  abandoned (–) – 342
  as an objective and not as means or property – 277(70), 282, 334, 363
  illegitimate (–) and born out of wedlock – 219(54), 273, 302, 327, 344
    rights of (–)
      not to be discriminated – 163–165, 167, 169, 182, 222(131)
      to inherit from both parents – 376(56)
      to their father's name – 376(56)
  in Israel, rights of (–) – 263–267
  indigenous (–) – 196, 203, 227(216), 219
  mentally ill (–)
    services for (–) – 359
  of aliens to different countries – 327
  responsibilities of (–) – 177, 203
  unborn (–), rights of (–) – 186, 189–191, 278(75), 323. See in the Rights' index (Right to life), and also under: Abortion vulnerability of (–) – 185
Children's Bureau (U.K.) – 232, 233, 239, 274, 275, 338
Children's Defense Fund (U.K.) – 123–124

Children's Legal Center (U.K.) – xi, 299–304
Children's Liberation Movement – 18, 20, 63–64, 133–152, 397, 402
Children's Parliament – 96. see also under: Self-government
Children's rights
  (the concept) – 30, 167, 255, 398
  against parents – 53–54
  amount of (–) over time – 8
  binding also individuals – 168, 178
  'Child Right Comparative Matrix' (of Patricia Piziali) – 96
  conceptualization of (–) by children – 39, 405–406
  cultures' attitudes toward (–) – 9
  demand for (–) – 31
  exercise of (–) – 164
  generally – 4
  importance of (–) – 40
  in emergency situations – 155, 157–158, 177–178, 267, 269. see also under: Armed Conflicts
  in international legislation
    imposition of obligations on Individuals – 187
  in relation to human rights – 26
  in the third world – 406–408
  models used to analyze (–)
    Shye's – 39–55
    Rogers & Wrightsman's – 50–53
    Wald's – 50, 53–54
  public awareness to (–) – 247–248
Children's duties and obligations – 328
  rendering filial services to their parents – 331
Class action suits – 120–121
Commissioner for children
  in New Zealand – 119
  in Norway – 114–115, 130(39)
  see also: Ombudsman
Communication
  as condition to the child's maturity – 82–83
  continual dialogue with the child, importance of (–) – 284
Complaints procedures for children in care – 346
Conventions
  (the concept) – 27–28, 181
  accession to (–) – 27
  regional, need for (–) – 271, 273
Court, children's (–) – 99–100. see also under: Self-government

Curiosity
  encouraging (–) – 251
  importance of (–) – 83
Custody, disputes
  considerations in solving of (–) – 329
  the court
    authorities of (–) – 334
    proceedings, characteristic – 329
    responsibility of (–) – 333
  see also: Divorce

Declarations
  (the concept) – 27–28
  on the rights of the child (functions, types) – 153, 181
Defense for Children International (DCI) – 15, 124–127, 179, 183, 200, 209
Development (of children) – 5, 6, 7
  'developmental line' – 64
  developmental-psychological phases as base to rights – 136–137
  intellectual development – 367
  linkage to development of the State – 250
  psychological development of the child – 360, 367
  right to (–) – see in the rights' index
Disability (the concept) – 16–17
Discipline
  classroom's (–) – 282
  importance of – 248–249
  self (–) versus external (–) – 81
Discrimination – 40
  between adults and children – 133, 137, 143, 252, 363
  between children themselves – 134, 162, 252
Diseases, children's – 190
Divorce
  needs of children in divorce proceedings
    special protection to their welfare – 334
  obligations of parents in divorce actions
    not to degrade each other in front of the children – 335, 336
  rights of children in divorce actions
    not to be a source of arguments between the parents – 336
    to day by day love, care, discipline and protection of the parent having custody of the children – 334
    to equality, relating to other children – 335
  in labor – 178

Drugs
  to experience regular and consistent contact with both parents – 335
  to express love for each parent – 336
  to honest answers to questions about the changing family relationships – 336
  to know the non-custodian parent – 334
  to know that the parents decision to divorce was not the responsibility of the child – 336
  to periodical review of custodial arrangements and child support order –335
Drugs
  children's right to use (–) – see in the Rights' index
  protection of children from the use of – 204, 216
  use of (–) by children – 270
Duty
  (the concept) 14–16
  positive (–) against negative (–) – 20
  the word (–) as an instrument to persuasion – 23

Education
  (–) as a mean to self-realization – 266
  (–) as women's task – 76
  adjustment of school to the pupil – 301
  aims of (–) – 18–19, 30, 50, 81, 83, 176–177, 180, 202, 235–236, 247, 248, 251, 261, 262, 266, 268, 286, 321, 361
  attendance at school – 202
  basing the system of (–) on the needs of the children – 285–286
  compulsory education – 18, 135, 140, 164, 175–177, 186, 202, 286, 319, 332, 376(54)
    fixing of (–), considering minimum age for admission to work – 319
  content of (–) – 158, 179–180, 235–236, 246, 250–252, 305(7)
  cost of (–) – 268
  dialogue in (–) – 216
  early childhood (–) – 263–267
  educators
    (–) and pupils relationships – 99
    (–) no-right to interfere with the development of the child – 81
    Code of Ethics for Teachers – 118
    equal rights to the (–) and to the pupils – 103
    obligations of (–)

  due process in disciplinary hearings – 332
  respect for the child – 104, 202
  rights of (–) – 287–288
  effects of (–) – 18
  equal opportunities in (–) – 285, 286
  free (–) – 166, 175–177, 202, 279(77)
  freedom of (–) and freedom from (–) – see in the Rights' index
  full time schooling – 285, 376(54)
  fundamental (–) – 175
  home (–) – 140–141
  in war times – 240
  individualized (–) – 283
  kindergarten – 176, 235, 266
  Korczak's approach to (–) – 95–103
  nursery schools – 235
  physical punishment in schools – 149(17), 202, 288, 301. see also under: Punishment
  political (–) – 297
  primary (–) – 176, 202, 313
  real life and (–) – 137
  right for (–) – see in the rights' index
  rights of children in schools – 255, 273–274, 276(58)
  safety and welfare in school – 235
  secondary (–) – 176, 202
  self-education – 135
  self-government of youth in school – see under: Self-government
  sex (–) – 49–50, 150(27), 200, 303
  social (–) – 297
  technical (–) – 176
  training schools – see under: Juvenile
  vocational (–) – 176, 214, 283, 319, 321, 361
'Effective Functioning' (as base to evaluate children's rights) – 64–65, 396
Enforcement of children's rights – 165–166, 258, 317, 329, 364
  Declarations vs. Conventions – 181
  enforcing labor laws – 309–310
Equal Opportunity Fund (EOF) – 263–265
Evaluation
  of the capacities of the child – 189, 195, 291
Evolution
  (the concept) – 7
  evolutionism – 77
  social (–) – 8
Exploitation (of children) – 204–205
  economic and social (–) – 203

Exploitation (of children) (Continued)
  protection from (–) – see in the Rights' index
  sexual exploitation – 204–205

Family
  (–) breakdown, dealing with – 302–303
  (–) court systems – 302–303, 332–335. see also under: Divorce
  (–) life – 244–245, 253, 265
    in war-time – 240–241
  (–) planning – 79, 200, 256
  (–) Reunification – 192–193, 198, 302
  (–)'s positive influence on the personality's development – 162
  as an entity – 161
  changes in it's role and strength – 4, 5, 262
  extended (–) – 273
  limitations of (–) – 232
  outside intervention – 173–174
    conditions for (–) – 274(10)
  responsibility of the (–) – 185, 261, 265
    safeguarding against social handicaps – 236
  rural families – 233, 237
  separation of the child from (–) – 173–174, 188, 197–198, 257
    contact of child with the natural family – 265
    criminal liability for illegal (–) – 345
    special care and protection to children deprived of their families - 196–198, 213–214
Fight the Famine Council – 88
Food
  (–) blockade – 87–91, 92(3)
  Children's Right to Food – see under Rights, Specific, Not to be Hungry
Forest Hill Industrial Homes – 93, 105
Foster Care
  children in (–)
    (the concept) – 338
    rights of (–)
      to an independent visitor – 347
      to be able to appeal
        against a care order – 347
        for the discharge of a care order – 347
      to be nurtured by foster parents who have been selected to meet their individual needs – 338–339
      to be placed with a family of their own race – 303
      to be prepared for the life after the placement – 351, 379(118), 381(126)
      to contact with his own family – 348, 381(126)
      to continued support – 351, 381(126)
      to continuity of health care, medical treatment and education – 350, 381(126)
      to equality relating to non-foster children – 340, 347, 350, 379(118), 380(126), 381(126)
      to have a legal independent solicitor and legal advice – 338, 347, 348, 380(126)
      to have access to files and records of the child – 348, 379(118), 380(126)
      to have the foster placement reviewed every six months – 347, 348
      to help in accepting the fact that the biological parents don't take care of them – 338
      to information on the legislation under which they have come into care and how they can be discharged from care – 380(126)
      to know what punishments may or may not be used – 349, 380(126)
      to participate in their own case conferences and reviews of placement – 301, 348, 380(126)
      to preserve his identity and self esteem – 348, 349, 350
      to privacy – 349, 379(118), 380(126)
      to security of the placement – 348–349, 380(126)
      to see relatives as frequently as parties concerned wish to do so – 349, 380(126)
      to take part in the normal activities of their age group – 350, 379(118)
      (see also p. 379–386)
  placement in (–) – 234, 341, 344
    involvement in the decision making process – 344
    of minority children – 350
    regular periodic evaluation of the (–) – 184, 201, 335, 347, 348
    right to (–) – see in the Rights' Incompetence – 17

Subject Index

index the best interests of the child as a paramount consideration – 343
Freedom
  (the concept) – 18
  (–) Of speech – see under Rights, Specific, Freedom of speech
  (–) to against – from – 19

Genocide – 25, 166
Grandmothers of the Plaza de Mayo – 192
Guardianship
  (the concept) – 201
  (–) disputes – 75
  aims – 334
  child's right to choose his own guardian – see in the Rights' index
  children as guardians of children – 101
  considerations of the guardian
    best interests of the child as paramount consideration – 187, 196
  guardian ad litem – 335
  guardian-child relationship, problems in (–) – 115
  guardian's obligations – 196
    to demand the child's rights – 48, 171
    to ensure that wishes and feelings of the child about decisions which affect him should be given due consideration – 301
  guardian's rights
    freedom from intervention by the state – 188

Handicapped Children – 158
  asset to society – 236
  reasons for becoming (–) – 360
    armed conflicts – 91
    harmful employment – 240
    parents' venereal diseases – 79
  rights of (–) – 172–173, 198–199, 236, 249–250, 278(70)
  social handicap – 48–49
  treatment and services for (–) – 121, 158, 226(198), 279(78), 301–302
Health (of children) – 46, 199, 213, 234, 235, 245, 246, 251, 360, 361
  free (–) services – 166
  hygienic surrounding – 213
  information on hygiene and good (–) – 231, 269
  services – 199, 200, 241, 242, 269, 282

Homeless Children – 158, 174, 196–197, 214–216, 302
Hospital, children in (–)
  dangers of the dislocation from the environment – 355
  importance of recreational education – 358
  rights of children in hospital
    to be able to wear their own clothes. – 356
    to be treated with tact and understanding – 356
    to continuation in education – 357
    to enjoy care of appropriately trained staff – 356
    to express all their fears – 356
    to have their parents with them all the time – 355
    to information appropriate to their age and understanding – 355–356
    to information on their condition and treatment – 358
    to personal possession – 356
    to play – 358
      together with children from the same developmental stage – 356
    to privacy – 356
    to protection from unnecessary medical treatment – 356, 358
    to recreation – 357
    to responsive design – 356–357
  separation from the parents – 354–355
  Welfare of Children in Hospital Report ('Platt Report') – 355

Illiteracy – 214, 281
Immunity – 16–17
Implementation, of Children's rights – 165–166, 180, 188–189, 212, 230, 258, 270, 278(70), 302, 332, 338, 362
  of the Charter on the Rights and Welfare of the African Child – 273
  of international agreements on trafficking – 324
  of President Hoover's Conference on Child Health and Protection – 233
  of the U.N. Convention on the Rights of the Child – 208–209
Imprisonment (of children)
  conditions – 120–121, 125–126, 131(61), 365
  life (–) – 205
  rights of the detained child – 30, 126, 205

317

Interests (of children) – xii, 205, 330–331. see also under: Best Interests of The Child
International Association for Child Welfare – 218(35)
International Baby Food Action Network (IBFAN) – 30
International Catholic Child Bureau – 124, 165, 173, 177, 219
International Committee of the Red Cross – 91, 156, 205, 206
International Culture Center for Youth – 265
International Federation of Educative Communities – 328, 343
International Forum for Child Welfare (IFCW) – 218(35)
International Movement for Children's Rights – see under Defense for Children International (DCI)
International Playground Association – 369–372
International Union for Child Welfare (IUCW) – 120, 159, 160, 164, 169, 216(2), 217(4), 218(35), 229(236), 270, 271
International Union of Socialist Youth Organizations – 318

Jerusalem Council for Children and Youth – 117
Joint Commission on the Mental Health of Children (U.S.A.) – 255, 359–362
Jurisdiction – 187, 224
Juvenile
(–) delinquency – 157–158, 162, 173, 176, 276(43), 284, 513
reasons to (–) – 248–249
reducing (–) – 247–249, 322, 327
rights of delinquent juveniles – 278(70). see also under: Juveniles, in closed institutions, rights of
special treatment for delinquent children – 173, 278(70)
in war-time – 240–241
(–) in closed institutions / training schools, rights of (–) basic rights should not be lost – 352
freedom of appearance – 352, 353
to clothing – 352
to counselling to members of their faith by authorized representatives of religious denominations – 353
to development of self-esteem and individuality – 353
to discriminate themselves from others with particular item of jewelry – 353
to receive money sent to them – 354
to send and receive mail without censorship – 353
(–) justice – 207–208, 278(70), 403
juvenile court proceedings – 330
legal aid for minors – 208
(see also under – youth, adolescence)

'Kids Alive' – 149(16)

Labor, child (–) – 138, 150(46), 166, 178, 246, 258, 309–319, 332
(the concept) – 316
(–) in a foreign country – 309–310
(–) in war-time – 240
as an international problem – 311
criminal liability – 221(112), 274(10), 317
dangers in – 203–204, 221(112), 262, 271, 310, 316–317
discrimination, of immigrants' children – 271, 298, 302
employment (the concept) – 316
exploitation of children in labor – 315, 332
family factories – 311, 316
industrial employment – 25
International labor Conference (1919) – 311–314
International labor Conference (1973) – 314–317
labor legislation
enforcing – 309–310
international – 309–317
labor rights – see in the Rights' index
light work, (the concept) – 316
migrant workers – 322, 512
minimum age – see under: Age
night work – see under: Labor, restrictions or prohibitions on
pedagogical value of labor – 283
registration of, and regular reports on, child labor – 316–317
relationship between the young worker and his employer – 302
restrictions and/or prohibitions on
maximum working hours – 310, 322
night work – 310–311, 313–317, 319
work which might harm the child –

underground work (mines, etc.) – 319
working mothers
  prohibition of work after birth – 311
  right to a benefit sufficient for their maintenance and that of thei child in satisfactory hygienic conditions – 311
Law
  (–) Shops for Children – 121–123
  Code of Law (Codex) of Dom Sierot – 99–102
  Islamic Law ('sharia') – 273, 341, 342
  Jewish Law – 31
  Natural law – 24
Liability, (the concept) – 16–17
Liberty
  civil liberties – 26
  opposite interests – 20
  positive (–) against negative (–) – 20
Life
  right to life – see in the Rights' index
  wrongful (–) – 79–80, 84(27), 397
Lobbying for Children – 123–124
Love
  (the concept) – 76
  right for (–) – see in the Rights' index

Malnutrition (of children) – 213, 231, 233, 245
Maltreatment (of children), (the concept) – 196
Mannerheim League for Child Welfare (Finland) – 115
Marriage
  (–) and love – 75–76
  goal of (–) – 77
  minimum age for (–) – see under: Age
Media
  affecting the child's development – 195–196
  harmful public exposure to children in (–) – 278(70)
  protecting the child from the (–) – 195–196
Minor
  (the concept) – 186
  'emancipated (–)' – 17, 18, 331, 332
  incidence of the U.S. Constitution on minors – 20
Minority – 196, 203
  children as (–) – 294, 331
  rights of (–) – 260
    to preserve it's distinctive culture – 26
    to proper education – 256

Mortality
  Child (–) – 87–88, 189–191, 199–200, 211–212, 225(164), 234, 269
  Mother (–) – 234
Mother Care for Children in Hospital (U.K.) – 355. see also under National Association for the Welfare of Children in Hospital
Mozambican Children, rights of (–) – 267–269

National Action for Foster Children Committee (U.S.A.) – 338–339
National Association for the Welfare of Children in Hospital (NAWCH) (U.K.) – 355–357
National Association of Young People in Care (U.K.) – 346–347
National Children's Bureau (London, U.K.) – 346, 379(118, 123)
National Council for the Child (Israel) – 130, 264–265
Needs
  (the concept) – 58, 65(10), 286
  (–) of children – 96, 157, 232, 235, 247–248, 261, 301, 302, 350, 356
    as base to children's rights – 57–65, 396
      'Needs' approach vs. 'Quality of life' approach – 62–63
    basic needs – 198, 294, 360–361
    contradictions between different (–) – 286, 344
    developmental (–) – 57, 245–246
    educational (–) – 265
    for care and guidance of adults – 53–54, 76
    continuity of care – 188
    for continuing loving care and guidance – 335, 339
    for (adequate) diet – 245
    for free space – 293
    for loving care – 362
    for physical safety – 70(55)
    for protection from the danger of harming themselves – 290
    for self-confidence – 293
    for self-determination – 63–64, 133
    for special care and protection – 167, 170, 173, 185–186, 277(70)
    for trust in others – 339
    in different ages – 138
    psychological (–) – 261, 335, 367
    social (–) – 261–262, 335
  parenthood – 236

spiritual (–) – 261–262
UNICEF 'Basic Needs Strategy' – see under: United Nations International Children's Emergency Fund
categories of (–)
  Goulet – 59
  Vittachi – 59–60
criteria to designate (–) – 63
lists of (–)
  Dalkey's 38 needs/characteristics – 68(39)
  Galtung and Wirak's list of Basic Needs – 68(42)
Neglect (of children) – 3, 6
(the concept) – 196
right to protection from (–) – see in the Rights' index
New Education Fellowship – 285–287
New Education Movement (Reformpadagogik) – 75–83, 281–282
New York State Youth Commission – 247–250, 275–276, 460
New York State Division for Youth – 352–354
Non-Governmental Organizations' Working Group for the United Nations Convention on the Rights of the Child – 126
Nurturance Orientation – 50–53

Ombudsman for children – 113, 352, 354
  Functions and Goals of work – 114–120
  in Austria – 119
  in Canada (Ontario; British Columbia) – 116–117
  in Costa Rica – 117
  in Finland – 115
  in Germany (Westphalia) – 119
  in Israel – 117–118
  in the Netherlands – 130(39)
  in South Australia – 119
  in Sweden – 115
  in U. K. – 130(39)
  independence of (–) – 411(36)
  (see also under Commissioner for Children)
Opportunities
  (the concept) – 298
  (–) for children – 243–247
    disadvantages compared to rights – 244
    equal (–) to girls and boys – 213
    for spiritual and moral development – 369

to learn – 214
to play – 50, 177, 252, 369
to recreation – 50, 177, 246, 369
Orphans – 214, 342, 352
  Association for Help to Orphans – 98
  Dom Sierot (Janusz Korczak's house of orphans) – 93, 97–104
  rights of (–) – 158, 174

Parents
(–) love to their children – 7
(–) no-rights
  to abuse or neglect their children – 54
(–) rights – 189, 273, 287–289, 295, 358
  freedom from intervention by the state – 188
  in Jewish Law – 31
  to determine
    the education the child will receive – 176
    religious education – 173
    the school the child will go to – 54
    to educate the child to their belief – 194–195
    the medical care the child will receive – 54, 403
  to do family planning – 256
  to their children's income – 148, 331
  to withhold information about sex 49–50
considerations of (–)
  the child's best interests as paramount consideration – 187, 196
fathers
  children as possession of (–) – 33
mothers
  right to special care and protection – 172–173
  pre-natal and post-natal care – 234, 278(75), 326, 363
  protection from trauma during the birth process – 363
  separating the child from his/her mother – 173–175
parent-child relationship – 6–7, 195, 255, 331, 403
  de facto Parent – 339
  state intervention – 232–233
parental authority vs. rights of the child – 189
parental consent, requirement for (–) – 331

Slavery, Child (–) – 158, 198

Subject Index

responsibilities and obligations of (–) – 76, 93, 157, 163, 168, 173, 187, 189, 196, 232–233, 273, 282, 326, 329–331
   to ensure that wishes and feelings of the children about decisions which affect them should be given due consideration – 301
   to protect the child from abuse, neglect and exploitation – 178
   to take care of the child's welfare – 164
   to use access to genetic information to evaluate the probabilities of transmitting hereditary diseases – 363
  separation of child from (–) – 192–193, 327
  restrictions on (–) – 192–193
  training and guidance (–) – 200, 233, 236, 306(22), 363
Parliament, children's (–) – see under: Self-government
Paternalism – 50–53, 143, 296, 404
  objections to (–) – 95–96
  reasons for (–) – 331
  results of (–) – 350
Periodic Review Of Placement – 184, 200, 201, 227. see also under: Foster Care; Residental Care
Play
  importance of (–) to the child's development – 369–371
  right to (–) – see in the Rights' index
Pornography
  child (–) – 204
  affect of (–) on children – 150(28)
Power (the concept) – 16–17
Prejudice, against children – 293, 338
Privilege (the concept) – 14–15
Prolet'cult' movement – 281–285
Prostitution, Child (–) – 158, 204, 235, 270, 324, 325, 376(47)
Protocol (the concept) – 28
Puberty (the concept) – 3
Punishment – 284
  capital (–) – 205, 212
  corporal (–) – 179, 117, 202, 277(58), 288, 291, 293, 301, 401–402

'Quality of Life' – 39, 40–41, 57, 303
  'Quality of life' approach vs. 'needs' approach – 62–63
  ways to research (–) – 62

Radda Barnen – 91, 115, 200, 207, 228(235), 260
Realization, of Children's rights international co-operation for (–) – 185, 199
Refugee children – 191–192, 198, 216, 285. see also under: right to nationality, in the rights' index
Rehabilitative Care – 207
Residential care
  examples of good (–) – 93–111
  industrial schools – 105(4)
  regular evaluation of placement in (–) – 184, 201
Rights
  (the concept) – 13–15, 22–23, 24, 30, 31, 33(53)
  (the word, as an instrument to persuasion) – 23
  active (–) against passive (–) – 19–20, 21, 32
  base of (–) – 134–137, 261, 341–342. see also under: Age; Development; 'Effective Functioning'; Needs
  'hard' (–) against 'soft' (–) – 23
  no-(–) – 14, 54
  positive (–) against negative (–) – 19–20, 46
  privilege (–) – 14–15
  purpose of (–) – 50
  (see also the Rights' index)

Save the Children Fund – 88–91, 155, 217, 396
Save the Children International Union – 91, 155–156, 159, 217(15), 218(35)
Scandinavian School of Legal Realism – 23–24
self-determination – 39
  right to (–) – see in the Rights' index
self-determination orientation – 50–53
Self-government – 136
  (–) systems for children
    Dom Sierot's self-government – 101, 102, 110(59)
    Geheeb's 'New School' in Hessen (Odenwaldschule) – 103
    George Junior Republic – 103
    Medem Sanatorium – 103
    socio-educational system in residential care – 103
  children's right to self-government – see in the Rights' index

Socialist Youth International – 155, 319
Standards (as codes of conduct) – 28–30
Status
  legal status of children – 164, 282, 295, 332, 352, 365
  social status of children – 94–95, 96, 256, 266, 289, 331, 365, 399
State obligations and responsibilities concerning children – 163, 164, 168, 282, 330
  considerations of the state
    the child's best interests as pre-eminent consideration – 187
  Parens Patriae principle – 174
  to assist
    families – 257, 262
      large families – 175
    in war-time – 240–241
    schools in the training of youth – 237
  to enable family reunification – 192–193
  to ensure
    appropriate standard of living – 201
    re-integration of a child whose rights are violated – 184, 207
  to establish independent complaints' procedures for all institutions which cater for children – 301
  to implement and enforce children's rights – 188–189, 284
  to prevent child abduction – 193
  to provide
    care – 187
    protection – 170
      to the life of the child – 190
      from abuse, neglect and exploitation – 178, 196
      from discrimination – 187
    welfare – 164, 172, 174
  to respect parents'/Families'/guardians' rights and duties – 189, 195, 213
'Stop the Murder of Children on the Road' Group (the Netherlands) – 149(16)
STOPP (Society of Teachers opposed to Physical Punishment, U.K.) – 149(17), 288
Street Children – 197, 406, 410, 411
Swedish Children's Right Committee – 115
'Systemic Quality of Life Model' – 39–55, 63, 64, 79, 95, 395–400
  graphic representation of (–) – 44
  subsystems – Cultural; Personality; Physical; Social (explanation of) – 40–50, 70–72
  modes – Expressive; Adaptive; Integrative; Conservative (explanation of) – 41–50, 70–72

Torture – 205, 270. see also in the Rights' index, Freedom from torture
'Traditional Practices' – 185, 200, 227, 269, 273
Trafficing – 178–179, 197–198, 204
  criminal liability – 324–325
  international cooperation regarding (–) – 323–324
  responsibility for co-ordination of information relative to (–) – 324
  stopping (–) – 324

United Nations International Children's Emergency Fund (UNICEF) – 58, 60–62, 66(24), 165, 182–184, 189–191, 208, 210–211, 216, 223(136), 225(162), 379, 399
  Basic Needs Strategy – 60–62

War – see under: Armed Conflicts
Welfare
  (–) legislation – 21
  (–) rights – see in the Rights' index
  (–) state – 25
  children's (–) – 155–156, 159, 161, 168, 184, 216, 228(233), 230(253), 233, 235, 240, 249, 255, 265, 325, 342
    as base for the protection on (–) – 341–342
  family's (–) – 342
White House Conference on Children (1919) – 231, 258
White House Conference on Child Health and Protection (1930) – 220(68), 231–237, 240, 274(16)
White House Conference on Children (1970) – 57, 254–258
White House Conference on Children and Youth (1950) – 250–253
White House Conference on Youth (1971) – 259–260
World Summit for Children (30.9.90) – 209–216, 395, 399, 400

Year
  International (–) of the Child (1979) – 124, 181, 186, 265, 292, 297, 370
  International Youth (–) (1985) – 295, 307(30)
Young workers International – 318

Youth
  (the concept (–) – 3, 298, 320
  (rights of –) – 259–260, 295–299, 300–301, 319–323, 363–366
  working (–)
    protecting the health of (–)
      compulsory medical examination
        before admission to employment – 319
        periodically – 321
      prohibition of types of works – 309–323
    rights of (–) – 318–323
      concerning continuation schools – 318, 319
        continuity and stability in work relations – 319
      absences (army service, etc.) – 322
      holiday periods – 318
      income rates – 318
      equality in income rates – 322
      industrial training – 318
      migrant workers – 322
      paid educational leave – 321
      prohibition of night work – 318
      social insurance – 322
      working hours – 318
'Youth Land' – 8
Youth Law Center, San Francisco – 120–121
Youth Liberation Program (by Ann Arbor Michigan U.S.A.) – 133
youth unemployment – 298
Youth Suffrage Movement – 143

Index of Children's Rights

CATEGORIES OF RIGHTS

civil – 25–26, 27, 33(50), 303, 329
constitutional – 22–23
cultural – 25–26, 175
economic – 25–26
freedom – 26–27
human – 24–25, 26, 57
labor – 60, 138, 309–323
legal – 22–23
material (vs. non-material) – 182
moral – 22–23

natural – 23, 24–25, 294
ownership – 26
participation – 184
political – 23, 25–26, 33(50), 136, 142–148, 246–247, 262
psychological – 366–369
rhetorical – 23
social – 23, 25–27
welfare – 21, 23, 54

SPECIFIC RIGHTS

Freedom – 259, 265, 278(70)

Freedom of
  association – 26, 194, 195, 284, 289–290, 321
  belief – 252
  culture – 26
  conscience – 26, 45, 182, 194–195
  employment – 26, 321
  expression – 46, 47, 54, 96, 136, 146, 189, 194, 267, 276(58), 283, 298, 368, 398, 399
  education – 133, 140–141, 145, 146, 283, 286–287, 290–291
  incarceration with adult offenders – 365
  movement – 26, 139, 146, 262, 290, 291
  religion – 26, 45, 182, 194–195
  speech – 20, 25, 26, 46, 404
  thought – 26, 45, 182, 194–195, 283

Freedom from
  arbitrary arrest, detention and expulsion – 25–26, 45, 205
  education – 137
  fear of psychological and physical harm of abuse – 368
  indoctrination – 135, 283, 290
  interference in personal life – 26, 46, 195
  intervention – 20
  legal disabilities – 332
  parental control/guidance – 53–54
  physical punishment – 135, 301
  pollution of air, water and food – 364
  religion – 276(58)
  torture – 24, 25, 205, 270
  violence – 269, 277(58), 291

Right not to
  be a child – 140

Right not to (Continued)
  be born – 79–80
  be exploited – 158, 266
  be submitted to initiation rites, premature marriage or bride-price – 269
  be treated as guilty before conviction – 26
  express oneself – 96
  live – 79–80
  work – 291

Right to
  access to books – 289
  access to toys – 289
  affection – 248, 289, 329, 342, 367, 368
  an effective assessment of his/her capabilities – 276(58)
  apply for separate representation in family proceedings – 304
  ask questions – 83, 94, 96
  be a child during childhood – 8, 257, 363, 397
  be a subject – 266
  be able to sue and be sued in his/her own name – 303, 330
  be adopted – 184
  be born
    be well born – 234
    healthy – 256, 360
    wanted – 84(20)
  be different – 257, 282
  be elected – 26, 143, 296
  be first to receive protection and relief
    in all circumstances – 177–178.
    in emergency situations – 269, 278(70)
  be loved – 173–174
  be naughty – 81
  be oneself – 95, 251, 262, 329, 363
  be raised in the faith of his/her parents – 173
  be regarded as a person – 330, 479
  be registered immediately after birth – 191–192
  be treated as an individual in his/her own right – 293, 330–331
  be wanted – 256, 360
  'belong' to a neighborhood of people – 339, 481
  benefit from scientific progress – 26
  benefit from the principle according to which the best interests of the child is the prime consideration – 278(70), 279(78)

  choose and/or dismiss his/her educators – 282, 365
  choose its own parents wisely – 75–83, 157, 360, 363
  choose one's guardian – 139, 146
  clothing – 259, 286
  comradeship – 236
  consistent parental control and expectations – 364
  continuous loving care – 361
  continuous nurturing care – 364
  development – 23, 43, 46, 83, 157, 170, 173–175, 191, 249, 251–253, 257, 265, 278(70), 334, 335, 350, 369
    to development in health – 46, 172
  drive – 139, 146
  due process – 276(58), 278(70), 279(78), 332
  to fair treatment from all in authority – 330, 331, 377
  earn a livelihood – 158
  economic power – 136, 145
  economic security – 173–174, 342
  (adequate) economic support – 335
  education – 14, 15, 21, 26, 50, 175–177, 201–202, 211, 248, 252–253, 255, 262, 268, 278(70), 288, 329–330, 340, 369
    to control his/her learning – 301, 140, 146, 290
    to educate oneself – 135, 145
    to family education – 268, 278(70)
    to free education – 279(77)
    to full time schooling – 285
    to individualized education – 283
    to relevant education – 365
    to religious education – 166, 173, 177, 248, 286, 353
    to sex education – 303
  emancipate from the parent-right relationship – 331–332
  enforce one's rights – 260
  equality – 26
    between children and adults – 53–54, 283, 291, 329
    between different children – 91, 161, 166, 167, 168–170, 179–180, 187, 213, 237, 266, 267, 277(70), 282, 285, 286, 290, 299, 338, 340
  excursions outside the home – 289
  explore the environment – 45
  express fears – 356
  express his/her views in all matters affecting him/her 46–47, 184, 189, 193–194, 257, 283, 290

to be heard and listened to – 330–331
about environmental decisions – 302
fair payment for labor – 26
fair trial – 26
family life – 193, 261, 265, 268, 270, 338, 343, 480
family reunification – 193
food – 45, 60–62, 157, 172, 242, 259, 262, 286, 288, 398, 399
foster care – 184, 338
free time – 262
full realization of his/her potential – 257, 279(77), 286, 299, 361, 369
grow – 265
    to grow in a family were there is family stability – 261
    to grow in the parental home – 174, 278(70), 342
    to grow up nurtured – 256–257, 398
guidance
    to guidance by parents – 248
    to religious guidance – 248
have abortion – 54
    to information on birth control – 255
have feelings – 81
have a lawyer – 54, 330, 332, 338, 343, 403
have a name – 47, 48, 171, 191–192, 266, 267, 278(70), 343
have a nationality – 48–49, 171, 191–192, 266, 278(70), 343–345
have secrets – 47, 95
have social mechanisms developed to enforce one's rights – 258
health
    to a healthy environment – 364
    to adequate health care – 53
his/her own death – 95
a home
    to adequate housing – 53, 172, 265–265, 302, 304, 364
    to alternative home environments – 135, 144, 214
    to a clean house – 262
    to convalescent homes and holiday homes – 327
    to a decent home – 248, 259
    to public housing – 21
identity – 185, 266, 368
    to preserve one identity – 192, 202–203, 268, 303
    to a (positive) social identity – 363
income
    to a guaranteed/minimum income – 138, 139, 146, 298–299, 319, 331
    to keep his own earnings – 331
independence – 298, 368
individuality – 330, 479
information – 135, 144, 268
    about their bodies – 364
    appropriate to his age and understanding – 355–356
    to access to appropriate information – 195–196, 303
    to files (education-, medical-, social service-, etc.) – 303–304, 348
justice – 135
know his/her rights – 291
leave his/her parents – 282
leave home – 139, 303
legal protection and redress – 365
leisure – 203, 299
    to leisure facilities – 299
liberty – 303, 402
life – 165, 167, 189–191
    to full and decent life – 199
live – 6, 24, 25, 166
    to live in peace – 180
love – 256, 265, 266, 268, 270, 278(70), 288, 329, 367, 368
    to be conceived and born in true love – 75–76
marry – 322, 329
medical services – 157, 182, 199–200, 231, 234, 242, 245, 255, 262, 269, 278(75), 282, 285, 286, 304, 327, 331. see also in Subjects' index, under – Hospital
    to free medical services – 172, 199–200
    moral security – 342
mother's milk – 35(94)
nourishment – 265, 365
opportunity – 298
(good) parenting experiance – 364
participate in any activity that is not harmful to the physical and spiritual development of the child himself – 283
participate in cultural and artistic activities – 26, 203
    participate in the political process – 136, 283, 365
place oneself in voluntary care – 303
play – 50, 177, 203, 242, 257, 262, 268, 357, 363, 369–372, 392–393, 400, 402
    to playgrounds and playrooms – 289, 327
political power – 296, 300–301
preserve and cultivate ethnic and cultural

heritages – 259
privacy – 26, 47, 95, 195, 235, 266, 277(58), 278(70), 289, 290, 349, 354, 356
property – 95, 138, 146, 266, 278(70), 332
protection – 265–266, 278(70)
   from abuse, neglect and exploitation, physical or mental, by adults – 53, 54, 162, 178, 221(111), 253, 262, 278(70), 279(78), 289–290
   from excessive claims – 290
   from harmful public exposure
     in communication Media – 278(70), 279(78)
     in court proceedings (child who suffered bodily harm or property damage) – 278(70)
   from labor that endanger the child – 236, 249, 302, 262, 278(70), 279(78)
   from social exploitation – 290
   from the consequences of any inadequacies in his/her their homes or backgrounds – 290
   from unfair commercial dealings – 278(70), 279(78)
   of one's personality – 234
   of one's scientific, literary and artistic work – 26
   of their on very lives – 241
publish his/her opinions – 290
read – 262
reasonably limited working hours – 26
rebel – 257
receive care and protection of a mother who survived the ordeal of childhood – 234
receive care and treatment through facilities which keep the child as closely as possible within their normal social setting – 362
receive good adult example – 249
receive help in his/her growth – 340
recreation – 45, 50, 172, 177, 235, 240, 242, 243, 245, 249, 327, 358
remain silent – 403
representation – 365
respect – 83, 93–105, 170, 195, 202, 205, 256, 278(70), 291, 397
   as a unique human being – 339
   from society to one's parent – 289
(legal and financial) responsibility – 140, 146

responsive design – 134–135, 235, 301, 302
(adequate) rest – 245
safety – 249
   to physical safety – 70(55), 268, 299, 364
satisfying inter-personal relationship – 369
self-determination – 63–64, 133–148, 202, 257, 283, 296–297, 298, 301, 304, 330, 338, 340, 347
self-expression – 267, 287, 293
self-government (to govern themselves) – 110(72)
sexual freedom – 135, 139, 145, 146
(write and) sign contracts – 54, 136, 332
(adequate) sleep – 289, 294
social power – 298
social security – 171, 172, 201, 262, 278(70, 72), 322
social services – 26, 365
sound preparation to life – 363
space (to play, to explore) – 289, 327
special care, consideration and protection
   in the administration of law and justice – 266, 332
   to be interrogated by a suitably trained person and not a member of the police force (child who suffered bodily harm or property damage) – 278(70), 279(78)
sport – 262, 268
a standard of living
   to an appropriate standard of living – 201, 262, 302
   to a minimal standard of living – 26
survival – 62, 189–191
   to survive the present day – 95
(spiritual and moral) training – 233–234
tranquility – 289
understand how to exercise his/her rights – 296–297
understanding – 234, 248, 265, 266, 368
use contraceptives – 54, 256
use drugs – 139–140
vote – 26, 136, 138, 143, 145–147, 296, 299–301, 304, 347
welfare – 54, 172, 248, 256, 481
   to child welfare services – 340
work – 138, 145, 146, 150(46), 249, 262, 273–274, 283, 291, 298, 299
youth services – 299

Index of Names

Abbott Grace – 232, 234, 274(11; 13), 275(21), 312, 373(15)
Abu-Rabia Aref – 12(32)
Ackermane – 371, 393(188)
Adair F. L. – 234, 239, 240, 275(22, 31)
Adams Paul – 149(3)
Ador Gustave – 156
Alden Percy – 91, 92(23)
Alkema Evert A. – 27, 34(85; 86)
Allen Mel – 137, 150(39), 151(62)
Alston Philip – 186, 224(147), 229(242)
Altmeyer A. J. – 162
Ambjornsson Ronny – 83(7), 84(14)
Anderson Lauren – 35(90)
Andrews Lori B. – 85(29)
Angelo Bonnie – 230(252)
Anweiler Oskar – 84(18), 281, 282, 285, 305(5; 6; 10), 306(13)
Apostel L. – 57, 65(1)
Apple Michael W. – 11(19, 31)
Aries Philip – 3–6, 8, 9, 10(3)
Armstrong Louise – 227(224)
Austin Dennis – 378(88)
Ayusava Iwao Frederick – 39, 372(2)

Backer Fru Anna – 376(51; 53)
Bandura A. – 249, 276(46)
Bardman Bertram – 31(8)
Barrat C. J. A. – 166
Baldick Robert – 3, 4, 10(3)
Baldrey Keith – 129(28)
Barnes Earl – 409(24)
Baron K. – 12(32)
Barry H. – 12(32)
Basyn M. – 175, 179
Baumrind Dianna – 152(96)
Beck Rochelle – 255, 274(6), 276(53)

Beiner F. – 56(27), 106(21)
Bellerate Bruno – 109(36)
Bengtsson Arvid – 393(181)
Ben-Hador Avraham – 118, 130(37)
Bennett Walter H. Jr. – 196, 223(137), 226(185)
Benyamini Kalman – 152(77)
Bequele Assefa – 315, 375(26)
Berg Leila – 133, 149(3), 288–289
Berger Nan – 149(3)
Berlin Irving N. – 23, 34, 256, 258, 276(53)
Berlin Isaiah – 20, 33(42–45)
Berro Robert – 244
Bettelheim Bruno – 110(72)
Bevan H. K. – 35(97)
Bhutto Benazir – 209
Biederman Amalia – 264, 277(69)
Bin Talal Hasan, Crown Prince of Jordan – 260–261
Black Maggie – 66(24)
Bladergroen Wilhelmina J. – 371, 393(186)
Blaine Daniel D. – 12(32)
Board Joseph B. – 55(9)
Boli-Bennett John – 56(36)
Bondfield Margaret – 312
Boothby Neil – 34(87), 269, 279(84)
Boudewijn, King of Belgium – 186
Boven, van, Theodoor C. – 26, 34(81)
Bowan M. J. – 223(137)
Bowlby John – 387
Boyd William – 306(17; 19)
Brassard M. R. – 393(180)
Bratholm Anders – 114, 127(5)
Braun A. Linda – 275(42)
Breckinridge de Acosta Aida – 273(1)
Bremner Robert H. – 274, 276(48)
Bridel Renee – 204, 228(225)
Brodie-Olles Marion – 230(249)

Bruce Glacier Katharine – 92(13)
Bruijn-Luckers, de M. L. C. C. – 186, 224(149)
Bunsen de – 218(22)
Burston Bradly – 151(77)
Burt Robert A. – 33(54)
Bush George, president of U.S.A. – 212, 230(253)
Butler R. A. – 285

Cabot Fredrick P. – 275(24)
Campbell Grace – 401
Campbell Tom – 33(41; 42)
Cantwell Nigel – 124, 131(57; 59; 62), 183, 222(130; 134), 224(138)
Capire Claude – 217(10)
Carlsson Bo – 115
Carlsson Ingvar – 209
Casullo Catherina – 167, 174, 178, 179 (64; 93; 110; 118), 220(64), 222(118)
Catterall D. Calvin – 367, 392(169; 170; 173; 174), 393(175)
Cattrijse L. – 12(34)
Cerda Jaime Sergio – 224(139)
Chadwick Marion – 91
Chanlett Eliska – 218(18)
Charnow Jack – 230(256)
Cheng – 168, (70)
Chiba A. – 370, 371, 393(183)
Child L. – 12(32)
Chrisholm Barbara – xi, xii(3)
Chukerman Ignacy – 101, 109(52)
Ciselet Georgette – 165
Clark G. A. – 379(117)
Clark M. P. – 409(23)
Clark K. B. – 409(23)
Clarke John – 8–9, 11(24)
Clerck De Jacques – 220(57) – 220(57)
Cleveland Harian – 61, 67(29)
Clouzot Etienne – 155–156
Cohen Cynthia Price – 181, 222(122; 123)
Cohen Howard – 134, 141–143, 146–148, 151(65–68), 152(97), 397
Cohen Morris L. – 56(36)
Cohen M. I. – 407, 411(33)
Cohn Haim H. – 48, 164, 169, 171, 174, 224(140)
Cohn Ilene – 279(81)
Coles Robert – 212
Collins D. Kenneth – 357–359, 388(140)
Corbin Arthur – 31(6), 32
Cornaz-Besson Jacqueline – 109(37)
Cosans Jane – 401
Cottle Thomas I. (or J ?) – 149, 276

Coughlin W. P. – 151(61)
Cuellar Javier Perez de – 182
Cuk Jochevet – 102, 110(63)
Cukierman Ignacy – 102, 109

Dale Michael J. – 46, 56(24)
Dalkey Norman C. – 63, 67(38; 39)
Danois Jacques – 85(31)
Darwin Charles – 5, 77
Dasberg Lea – 5, 8, 10, 11(11, 21)
Davison Jenny – 355, 387(135)
Dawid Jadwiga – 98
Dawid Jan Wladyslaw – 98
Dayan Rachel – 263
Dearden R. F. – 18–19, 32(36; 37)
Deci Edward L. – 64, 70(47; 49; 50)
Delevinge Malcolm – 412
Dell Floyd – 83(5)
DeMause Lloyd – 6, 7, 8, 9, 10, 11(13)
Demos John – 12(35)
Denzin Norman K. – 106(6), 149(6)
Detrick Sharon – 223(137)
Diemer-Lindeboom F. T. – 48, 177
Dietz Gerhard – 111(73)
Dijk van P. – 153, 170, 220(79)
Ditli Maria Tereza – 229(239)
Dodiuk Jacques (Jakobek) – 101, 109(53)
Doek J. E. – 315–316, 375(27)
Dominedo Francisko Maria – 164, 165
Donahue Phil – 411(34)
Donnelly Jack – 34(79)
Dorfman Anne – 131(47)
Dowling C. Lee – 275(43)
Drapers Jan – 391(156)
Duane Michael – 149(3)
Dubanoski Richard A. – 12(32)
Durand Andre – 154, 156, 217
Dworkin R. – 32(33)
Dyck Van David – 110(69)
Dyck Van Roxa – 110(69)

Ebigbo Peter O. – 280(90)
Eckhardt Christopher – 19
Edelman Marian Wright – 123, 131(53), 391(158)
Edwards C. Paul – 232, 274(9)
Edwards Newton – 11(22)
Eekelaar John M. – 32(21), 287, 306(21), 409(17)
Elkind D. – 64, 70(53)
Ellis Wiliam J. – 275(23)
Ennew Judith – 197, 226(190), 267, 268, 279(82; 83)
Erikson G. – 201, 227(208),

Erikson Erik H. – 48
Escudero Pedro – 245
Euler Rigmor Von – 115

Falkowska Mria Bronikowska – 99, 105(1)
Falska Maria – 99
Farson Richard – 63, 70(45), 110(72), 133–137, 141–152, 397
Faubion James – 12(36)
Feinberg I. – 22, 34(57)
Feshbach Norma Deitch – 57, 65
Feshbach Seymour – 57, 65
Finely John – 232, 274
Finkelnohr David – 224(227)
Fisher Dana – 208
Flekkoy Malfrid Grude – 114–115, 127(4; 7; 9; 10)
Foerster Wilhelm Friedrich – 81–82, 85(36)
Folks Homer – 234, 274(20)
Foss Laurence – 70(56)
Foster Antoinnette M. – 405, 409(21)
Foster Henry H. – 328–332, 377(60; 62–82)
Foucault Michel – 18, 32(34)
Fox Sanford J. – 183, 222(133)
Fox Vivian C. – 11(20)
Franklin Bob – 143, 152(78), 296, 307(35)
Freed Doris Jonas – 328–332, 377(58; 61; 63; 70; 78; 82)
Freeman Bonnie Cook – 11(19)
Freeman Michael D. A. – 31(4; 5), 32(33), 50, 53–54, 56(34; 41; 44; 48), 409(17)
Freiberg Selma – 59, 65(14)
Freivet C. – 106(16)
Freud Anna – 17, 32, 64, 70(51), 188, 224(155; 157)
Freud-Loewenstein Sophie – 11(22)
Friedman Lawrence M. – 21, 33(46; 47; 49; 50; 52)
Froese Leonhard – 292–295
Frost Shimon – 100, 109(50)
Fruchtbaum Harold – 66(24)
Fuller Edward – 88, 92(11; 14; 19; 25), 157–158, 217(6; 15), 218 (23; 27–29; 31)

Galtung Johan – 63, 68(40), 70(42)
Garbarino James – 393(180)
Gee E. Gordon – 33(40)
Geheeb Paul – 103
George William R. – 103, 110(69)
Germain R. – 393(180)
Gerzon Mark – 149(3)
Ghai Dharam – 67(27; 28)
Ghandi Mahatma – 60

Gibson Ian – 401, 408(1)
Gilinsky Luba – 110(70)
Gilligan C. – 410(28)
Gillis John R. – 9, 11(27)
Gmeiner Hermann – 226(191)
Goble George W. – 16–17, 32(22; 23; 27)
Goldszmit Jozef – 105(1)
Goldstein Josef – 17, 32(31), 188, 224(155; 157)
Goldstein Stephen R. – 28, 30(1), 33(40)
Goodman Paul – 149(3)
Gortario de Salinas Carlos – 209
Gortzen Rene – 110(72), 144, 152(93)
Gottlieb David – 133, 149(6)
Goulet Dennis – 59–60, 62, 66(16), 67(33)
Graaf J. H. de – 223(137)
Graham Janet – 92(13)
Grant James P. – 209, 211, 229(247),
Grant Nigel – 282, 305(11)
Green C. Fredrick – 338
Green Reginald Herbold – 67
Guggenheim Martin – 32(32)
Guttman E. – 393(180)
Guyer Malvin J. – 410

Habash Awni – 226
Haeckel Ernst – 83(13)
Hagari-Poznanska Ada – 110(62)
Hagerstrom Axel – 23, 34
Hakim M. – 172
Hall Michael I. – 131(49)
Hallowes Frances S. – 79, 84(25)
Hammarberg Thomas – 208
Hansen W. Robert – 332–333, 377(84), 378(89)
Harris P. J. – 223(137)
Harris William – 131(52)
Harrison Carl – 105(4)
Harrison Saul I. – 410(29)
Hart 't Willem Anne – 75, 83(1), 84(19)
Hart Stuart N. – 367–368, 392(171), 393(176; 180)
Hartmann T. – 56(36)
Hartung Frank E. K. – 59, 65(15)
Hassel Ian – 119
Haubrich Vernon F. – 11(19, 31)
Hegar Rebecca L. – 378(98)
Hellinckx W. – 110(68)
Henkin Louis – 24, 25, 34(68; 76), 151(64)
Hennessy Patrick – 212
Henning James S. – 12(32)
Heringa Aalt W. – 27, 34(84)
Herman Kahn – 39
Hesford Chris – 50, 56(33)

Name Index

Hess Stephen – 254, 276(50; 54)
Heywood J. S. – 274(10)
Hoare Samuel – 164, 167–169, 174, 175, 179, 220(66)
Hodges Lucy – 130(39)
Hofmann Paul – 165, 166, 220(58)
Hohfeld Wesley N. – 13–14, 17, 21, 23, 31(5; 7; 11), 54, 159
Holly Douglas – 281, 305(8)
Holt John Caldwell – 18, 110(72), 133, 137–152, 397
Hoover Herbert, president of U.S.A. – 87, 91(1), 231–237, 250, 273(1; 3), 274(7; 8)
Horio T. – 280(91)
Horne Les – 116–117, 129(23; 25)
Horovitz Menachem – 47, 56(28), 117–118, 130(34; 35)
Hotopf W. H. N. – 65(7)
Hoyles M. – 10(5)
Hunt Herold – 305(3)
Hunter Ian – 134, 143, 152(84; 86)
Hutton Patrick H. – 4, 10(5), 11(12)

Illich Ivan – 18, 32(35)
Illick Joseph E. – 7, 11(16)
Inhelder B. – 409(27)
Itkin-Arzylewicz Regina – 104, 111(76)

Jackson Brian – 288, 306(26)
Jackson Robert – 66(24)
Jansen Jacques – 225(160), 341, 343–345, 378(99; 106; 110), 379(113)
Jansen W. – 78, 83(10), 84(24)
Jatziv Reuven – 109(39)
Jebb Eglantyne – 87–92, 155, 157–159, 217(3; 6; 15), 218(21; 25; 29; 32), 396
Jenkins Iredell – 22, 23, 34
Jha M. – 170, 172
Jobling Megan – 149(15)
Johansson S. – 63, 70(44)
Johns P. Donald – 332–333
Johnston P. – 152(90)
Johnston R. F. – 128(17)
Josef Stephen C. – 80, 85(30)
Julian Williams – 221(108)
Jupp Michael – 229(237)
Juvigny M. – 164, 174, (50)

Kadman Yitzhak – 264–266, 279(78; 79)
Kagan Jerome – 70(46)
Kagitcibasi Cigdem – 12(33)
Kahn Gerard – 106(23)
Kahn Herman – 39, 55(5)
Kahn Alfred J. – 113, 127(1)

Kahtchadourian Haig – 57–58, 65(6)
Kamba Walter K. – 13, 17, 32(25)
Kamerman Sheila B. – 127(1)
Kartashkin Vladimir – 33(36), 34(74)
Kasteren, van, Ineke – 35(94)
Katkin Daniel – 149
Katz Sanford N. – 32(32)
Kelk Doug – 129(27)
Keller Helen – 227(202)
Kelly B. John – 378(92)
Kelsen Hans – 13
Kamba Walter – 31(6), 32(25)
Kempinski-Hurowitz Chava – 104, 111(77)
Kent George – 230(253)
Kerschensteiner Georg – 283
Key Ellen – 75–85, 93, 156, 256, 360, 363, 395, 397
Kimml Anton – 318, 375(33)
Kinnock Neil – 297
Kirchhoff Hella – 56(27)
Kittani M. – 219(54)
Kloosterboer Karin – 123, 131(51)
Kluger Richard – 409(23)
Koenings Sharon L. – 33(40)
Kohlberg Lawrence – 64, 70(54), 393(178), 410(28)
Kohler Mary Conway – 255–257, 276(53), 277(59; 61)
Koocher Gerald – 369, 393(182)
Korczak Janusz – 47, 56(25; 26), 83, 93–111, 397
Kowal Simona – 101, 109(54)
Krauze Harry D. – 377(56)
Krill Francoise – 205–206, 228(232; 234)
Kruithof Bernard – 3, 10(1)
Kuijer Guus – 144
Kulawiec Edwin P. – 108(35)
Kurzweil Zwi Erich – 97, 108(29), 110(71)

Landau Barbara – 403, 409(14)
Landelius Hakan – 277(66)
Lane Allen – 10(5)
Langerman Aahron – 130(35)
Langen M. C. de – 113, 127(3), 404, 409(15)
Lax Elisabeth – 47, 56(27)
Lee Luke T. – 56(36)
Leer van Oscar – 117
Lejeune Rene – 217
Lengborn Thorbjorn – 77, 84(16)
Lenin V. I. – 282
Lenroot Katherine F. – 232, 244, 274(12; 14), 275(25; 33; 36; 39)
Leonard George B. – 149(6)

Leonhard Froese – 306(27)
Lerman Paul – 149
LeRoy Ladurie Emmanuel – 7, 11(15)
LeShan Edna J. – 8, 11(22)
Lestor Joan – 304, 307
Levitt Louis – 35(90)
Levine George – 149(10)
Lewin Aleksander – 105(1), 106(16)
Lewis Amalia – 403, 408(9)
Lewis Ralph – 67
Lifton Betty Jean – 96, 107(27), 108(28)
Lindsay Mike – 130(39)
Lipshitz Feiga – 110(66)
Lloyd of Hampstead, Lord – 31(5)
Lomasky Loren E. – 16, 32(19)
Longford Michael D. – 131(41)
Loon J. H. A. van – 379(116)
Lopatka Adam – 182
Lowe Boutelle Ellsworth – 372(3)
Luden Yizhak – 110(70)
Luke T. Lee – 84(20)
Lucker-Babel Marie-Francoise – 341–345, 378(101; 108;), 379(112; 114)

MacCormack Geoffrey – 23, 34(64)
MacDermid Alan – 307(45)
MacDermot Niall – 130(40)
MacKenzie – 156
Malitza M. – 177, 178, 221(107)
Mallen G. – 156
Mallot Bruce – 338
Mandelblatt G. – 102, 110(60)
Makarenko A. – 106(16)
Maslow Avraham – 59, 62, 67(35)
Masarweh Nabil – 277(63)
Matheson Wilhelm – 114, 127(5)
Mazzolini da Prierio Silvestro – 32(39)
McAlpin Michelle B. – 55(8)
McGowan Brenda G. – 127(1)
Melton Gary B. – 11, 12(36), 32(30), 39, 55(7), 131(42), 405, 409(25), 410(31)
Merzan Ida – 98, 109(43)
Metze Marcel – 128(8)
Meyer John W. – 56(36)
Meyer Peter B. – 149
Middleton N. – 106(4)
Miller Laurance – 306(20)
Milne Brian – 268, 279(83)
Minow Martha – 22, 34(58; 60), 56(36)
Mitra M. – 174–175
Mnookin Robert H. – 144, 152(89; 96)
Moerman Joseph (Canon) – 124
Molander Helena – 128(12)
Moll Hans – 131(51)

Montessori Maria – 83
More Hannah – xi, xii(1)
Morier G. M. – 218(18)
Morris David – 55(8)
Morris William – 77
Morsink Johannes – 34(73)
Mortkowicz-Olczakowa Hanna – 101, 102, 109(57), 110(61)
Morton T. L. – 12(32)
Mosey Chris – 128(16)
Moshman David – 194, 226(177)
Motta Giuseppe – 156
Mubarak Hosni – 209
Mukherjee Ramkrishna – 62–63, 67(36), 70(43)
Mulder Mauk – 16, 32(20)
Mulock Houwer D. Q. R. – 103, 110(68)
Mulroney Brian – 209
Murray Henry A. – 58, 65(10)
Murzi Tarra – 178
Mushlin Michael B. – 35(90)
Musschenga A. W. – 55

Nadel Szlomo – 103, 110(67)
Nagera H. – 387(133)
Naherny Patricia K. – 9, 11(31)
Nahmias Shlomo – 31(9)
Naimark Hedwin – 181, 222(123)
Nearing Scott – 305
Nedbailo M. – 172
Neill A. S. – 133, 149(3)
Newerly Igor – 99, 109(49)
Nganbu Kaheya – 80
Nilsson Nic – 393(189)
Nisbet Robert – 7, 8, 11(17)
Nixon Richard M., president of U.S.A. – 276, 338, 392(173)
Noonan Tim – 320, 375(42)
Noordman Jan – 3, 10(1)
Noi Bilha – 130(36)
North Jeanne-Marie – 230(252)
Nystrom-Hamilton Louise – 83(2)

Ober Steven L. – 33(40)
Ogden John – 347, 379(124)
Olivecrona Karel – 23, 34
Ollendorff Robert – 133, 149(3; 4)
Olson Dennis A. – 408(7)
Olson Rachel – 151(63)
Orlova Nina V. – 306(12)
Otto Berthold – 82–83, 85(37)
Overholt William J. – 39, 55(5)
Owen Stephen – 117
Ozawa Martha W. – 227(209)

Page Raissa – 379(117)
Palme Olaf – 40
Parent Marie – 35(94)
Parfitt Brent – 117
Parmor, Lord – 89
Parsons Talcott – 8
Pascale Boucaud – 279(88)
Pauwels J. – 110(68)
Pennink E. – 149(2)
Perez de Cuellar Javier – 182
Perl Peter – 131(46)
Perry Carol – 363
Pestalozzi J. H. – 98, 109(38)
Peters Alexander – 131(48)
Pfeil Alfred – 218(17)
Piaget Jean – 64, 70(52), 409(27)
Piziali Patricia Anne – 96, 107(24; 26)
Plant Roger – 60, 66(21)
Plotkin Ronit – 110(65)
Plumb I. H. – 10(5)
Pollock Linda A. – 9, 11(25)
Popta Van W. M. – 110(71)
Poublon Guus – 123, 131(51)
Prafitt Brent – 129(26)
Pridik Heinrich – 284, 305

Quijano M. – 221(103)

Rabus W. G. – 207, 229(238; 240)
Rachid Rosalind – 35(94)
Radin Max A. – 14, 31(11)
Rand Lester – 60
Rauche Elnekave helen – 130(33)
Rauschenbusch Walter – 33
Rawls John – 13, 31(3)
Rawson Wyatt – 306(17; 19)
Reed T. M. – 152(89)
Remba N. – 104, (75)
Ressler Everett M. – 34(87)
Reagan Ronald, president of U.S.A. – 362
Ribble Margaret – 58, 65(13)
Richard A. – 12(32)
Richards M.P.M. – 188, 224(156)
Rieveschl Jan L. – 410(29)
Rimmerfors M. – 178
Robb Edward Ellis – 274(19)
Robert H. – 274(18)
Robert P. – 32(33)
Robertson James – 387(132)
Robertson Joyce – 387(132)
Robinson E. E. – 232, 274(9)
Rodham H. – 30, 35(96)
Rogers Carl M. – 50–53, 56(36; 37)
Ronstrom Anita – 128(16)

Roosevelt Theodore, president of U.S.A. – 258
Rooy, de, Piet – 3, 10(1), 77, 83(12)
Rosario Jose – 9, 11
Rosenbaum Martin – 300, 304, 307(43; 50)
Rosenne Shabtai – 223(137)
Ross Catherine I. – 23, 33
Rothenberg Kenneth – 70(56)
Rothman David I. – 11(30)
Rousseau Jean Jacques – 98
Rutter Michael H. – 361–362, 391(156)
Ryan Richard M. – 64, 70(47; 50), 128(9)

Sachs Shimon – 110(65)
Sackij S. T. – 305(7)
Sadat Jehan – 263
Sade Arie – 101, (55)
Salgo Ludwig – 188, 224(154), 229(246)
Salomon Alice – 91, 92(26)
Saltz Irwin – 80, 85(29)
Samaan George – 35(95)
Sandel Michael – 16, 32(17)
Sanders-Woudstra J. A. R. – 41, 55(15)
Sapozhnikov M. – 164, 172, 174, 175, 179
Schafer Walter – 110(71)
Schalkwijk van – 162
Scheibe Wolfgang – 83, 85(39)
Schofield Michael – 49, 56(31)
Schroeder William A. – 32(32)
Seeley J. – 393(180)
Senn Milton J. E. – 58, 65(8)
Shamgar-Handelman Lea – 187, 224(151)
Shaw Bernard – 88
Sheffer Susannah – 138, 141, 150(41)
Shkolnicl Arlene – 32
Shore Milton F. – 366, 392(166)
Shorter – 9
Shroeder William A. – 32
Shue Henry – 20, 33(41)
Shye Samuel – 39–54, 55(2–4; 12; 13; 16; 19; 20; 23; 35) 64, 70, 71, 72(57; 73, 95, 234, 275(40), 286, 395–396, 398
Sidman Lawrence R. – 32(32)
Siegel (mrs ICFTU) – 176, (102)
Sikkink Kathryn – 35(93)
Silbert James D. – 351–354, 386(127; 129)
Singer Sandra – 181, 222(124), 229(239)
Skalka Ichak (Izak) – 101, 110(59)
Skolneck Arlene – 32(29)
Smillie Robert – 89
Smith Adam – 7
Snik – 144, (92)
Soler Mark – 120–121, 131(43; 46)

Solnit Albert J. – 17, 32, 58, 65(8), 188, 224(155; 157)
Soltman Mike – 34(65)
Spencer Herbert – 77
Spiesschaert F. – 12(34)
Sprauce Jacob – 338, 378
Standing E. M. – 85(38)
Stanley Allesandra – 230(251)
Stansby Friedman Janet – 403, 408(11)
Steenhoff Helga Frideborg Maria (Frida) – 84(21)
Steinbock Daniel J. – 34(87)
Steinitz Erich (Ezra) – 110(71)
Stenberg Marten – 115, 128(13)
Stepan Jan – 56(36)
Stone Lawrence – 5, 9, 10(9)
Strubbe Wim – 356, 387(136)
Suphamonghom – 171
Sussman Alan – 32(32), 351–354, 386(127; 129), 387
Swan van der Jose – 132(64)
Swepston Lee – 375(28)
Synder David – 67
Szalazakowa Alicja – 108(33), 109(47)

Takanishi Ruby – 11(26)
Teram E. – 201, 227(208)
Teitelbaum Lee E. – 32(19)
Thedin Nils – 230(256)
Thomas D. R. – 12(32)
Tinker John – 19
Tinker Mary Beth – 19
Tomasevski Katarina – 126, 131(60)
Toniolo – 323
Torgersen Viggo Trond – 114
Traore Moussa – 209
Tribe Laurence H. – 8, 11(23)
Truman Harry S., president of U.S.A. – 250–253, 267
Tuck Richard – 32(39)
Tuttle Lisa – 376(49)

Underhill E. – 226(196)
Ussel Van Jos – 49, 56(32)

Vajaki Julia – 92(16)
Veerman Philip E. – 31(14), 34(75), 106(4), 109(38), 225(172), 230(249), 278(72), 391(156; 157)
Venttsel Konstantin – 305(7)
Verhellen Eugeen – 10, 12(34), 149(2)
Verlag Ernst Klett – 110(71)
Vink Bart – 373(23)
Viquez Jimenez Mario A. - 117

Vittachi V. Tarzie – 11, 11(14), 46, 56(22), 59, 60, 66(18; 20), 144
Vollmar Georg – 77
Voorhoeve, H. W. A. – 190, 225(163)
Vos Jaap F. – 305(1), 306(12)

Wald Michael D. – 50, 53, 54, 55(1), 56(36; 46; 47)
Walkate Jaap – 341
Wallace James – 295–297, 307
Wallace Russel Alfred – 77
Wallerstein Judith – 378(92)
Wallis Elizabeth – 306(24)
Walters F. P. – 156, 218(19)
Walters R. H. – 249, 276(46)
Walton Ron – 346
Wasilkowska Zofia – 170
Watson J. B. – 58
Watt Richard – 99, 109(45)
Weardale, Lord – 91, 92(24)
Weil Simone – 15, 31(15)
Weill James D. – 123, 131(55), 227(204)
Weisberg D. Kelly – 181, 222(125)
Welson Gillian – 88, 92(16)
Werner George – 156, 217(4; 8; 11), 318, (32)
Weston Burns H. – 34
Whiddington Prudence – 117, 129(25)
White Leslie – 8
Wickbom Ulla – 66(24)
Widmayer Ruth – 305(3)
Wigmore Hazel – 288, 292, 306(25)
Wilbur Lyman Ray – 232, 233, 274(8; 9)
Wilby Peter – 408(2)
Wilczynska Stefania (Stefa) – 98–104, 109(41; 44)
Willem Anne – 83(1), 84(19)
William E. – 110(69)
Williams Juan – 409(22)
Wilson W., president of U.S.A. – 231, 273(5)
Wilson Adrian – 4, 5, 10(4, 6, 8)
Wilson Thomas W. – 61, 67(29)
Winfred E. Bain – 8, 11(22)
Winnicott Donald – 355
Wirak Anders – 63, 68(40), 70(42)
Wolfensberger Wolf – 226(198)
Woloszyn Stefan – 97, 108(30)
Wong B. – 10
Worner Yochanan – 55(4)
Worsfold V. L. – 31(4)
Wright Charles – 391(160)
Wrightsman Lawrence S. – 50–53, 56(36; 37)

Wringe, Colin A. – 22, 31(8), 33(53; 55)

Yolga M. – 173, 221(106)
Young Robert – 22, 34(56)
Young Natalie – 363
Yudof Mark C. – 4, 5, 10(7)

Yukanthor Pingpeang (princess) – 166

Zelizer Viviana A. – 85(29)
Zimring Franklin E. – 404, 409(18)
Zucker Dedi – 119, 130(38)
Zweig Stephen – 79, 84(26)

Index of cases

U.S.

Baumgratner vs. City of Long Beach – 121, 131
Bellotti vs. Baird – 404, 409
Brown vs. Board of Education – 405, 406, 409
G. L. vs. Zumwalt – 28, 35
Ginsberg vs. New York – 404, 409
Hazelwood School District et al., petitioners vs. Cathy Kuhlmeier et al. – 404, 409
Hunt vs. County of Los Angeles – 120
In re Gault – 402–403, 408

Joseph Dennis Zepeda vs. Louis Roul Zepeda – 84
Kritzik vs. Kritzik – 333–334
Nick O. vs. Terhune – 121
Parham vs. J. R. – 403–404, 408–409
Plessy vs. Ferguson – 405
Procarnik vs. Cillo – 79, 84
Tinker vs. Des Moines Independent Community School District – 19–20, 33, 46, 404– 405, 409
Turpin vs. Sortini – 80, 85

U.K.

Gillick vs. West Nurfolk & Wisbech A. H. A. – 404, 409

European

Campbell & Cosanas vs. U.K. – 401, 408
Jon Nielsen vs. Denmark – 403–404

Index of Documents

I.L.O.

Convention No. 5 fixing the Minimum Age for Admission of Children to Industrial Employment (1919) – 25, 311–314, 327, 416–419
  Draft International Convention respecting the Prohibition of Night Work of Young Persons Employed in Industrial Occupations (never adopted) – 311
Convention No. 6 concerning the Night Work of Young Persons Employed in Industry (1919) – 311–314, 327, 420–423
Convention No. 33 concerning Minimum Age for Admission to Employment (1932) – 315
Convention No. 59 concerning Minimum Age for Admission to Employment (1937) – 315
Convention No. 60 concerning Minimum Age for Admission to Employment (1937) – 315
Convention No. 138 concerning Minimum Age for Admission to Employment (1973) – 27, 314–317, 484–492
(for a list of other relevant ILO Conventions see – p. 373(25))

United Nations

Beijing Rules – 208, 229(241)
Convention on the Rights of the Child (1989) – 28, 45, 46–47, 48, 126, 153, 181–209, 211, 212, 271–273, 342, 398–399, 553–573
  Polish draft proposals – 183, 188, 194, 195, 222(122)
Declaration of General and Special Rights of the Mentally Retarded – 198, 226(200)
Declaration on the Promotion Among Young of the Ideals of Peace, Mutual Respect and Understanding Between People (1965) – 230(255)
Declaration relating to Foster Placement and Adoption (1986) – 341–345, 378, 379, 540–544
Declaration on the Rights of the Child (1959) – 45, 46, 47–48, 54, 57, 96, 159–180, 181–182, 185, 186, 198, 222, 265, 266, 342, 367, 398, 465–467
Declaration on the Rights of the Mentally Retarded Persons – 198, 226(200; 201)
International Code for the Marketing of Substitute Mothermilk (by the World Health Organization – WHO, 1981) – 29, 35
International Covenant on Civil and Political Rights – 26, 35, 185, 195, 224(152)
International Covenant on Economic, Social and Cultural Rights – 26, 35, 185, 201, 204–205, 224(152)

Rules on the Protection of Juveniles
  Deprived of Liberty (1990) – 30, 35(95),
  126, 131(61)

Universal Declaration of Human Rights
  (1948) – 20, 24, 34(72), 48, 57, 162–163,
  167, 168, 169, 170, 171, 173, 175, 341

Hague Conference on Private International Law

Convention on the Civil Aspects of
  International Child Abduction (1980) –
  225(173)
Convention on Jurisdiction, Applicable

Law and Recognition of Decrees
  Relating an Adoption – 345
draft Convention on Adoption – 198, 345

League of Nations

Declaration of Geneva (1924) – 45, 91,
  96–97, 155–159, 161, 162, 164, 168, 178,
  216(1), 217(4; 16), 218(16), 396, 398, 447

Regional

Charter on the Rights and Welfare of the
  African Child (1990) – 271–273,
  280(90–93), 579–597
Charter on the Rights of the Arab Child
  (by the League of Arab States) – 260–
  263, 517–526
Declaration of Opportunities for Children –
  243–247, 457–459
European Charter for Children in Hospital
  – 388(140)
European Charter on the Rights of Patients
  – 357–359

European Convention on Human Rights –
  271, 401, 404
European Convention for the Protection of
  the Rights of the Child (proposal) – 270,
  279
European Convention on Recognition
  and Enforcement of Decision Concerning
  Custody of Children and Restoration of
  Custody of Children (Council of Europe,
  1980) – 225
Latin American Charter on the Rights of
  the Child – 280(94)

Other International Agreements

Convention on the Prevention and
  Punishment of the Crime of Genocide
  (1948) – 25, 166
Geneva Conventions on International
  Humanitarian Law – 185, 207, 228(233)
International Agreement for the
  Suppression of the White Slave Trade –
  376(43)
International Agreement for the
  Suppression of the White Slave Traffic

(1904) – 323–324, 376(45), 424–426
International Convention for the
  Suppression of the Traffic in Women and
  Children (1921) – 324, 376(45), 432–434
International Convention for the
  Suppression of the White Slave Traffic
  (1910) – 324, 376(45), 427–431
World Declaration on the Survival,
  Protection and Development of Children
  (1990) – 209–216, 574

Document Index 653

NATIONAL

Canada

Canadian Charter of Rights and
 Freedoms – 143
Charter for the Rights of the Child in
 Ontario (by Johnston R. F., not
 accepted) – 128(17)
Child and Family Service Act of 1984–
 115–117
Foster Care: Proposed Standards and
 Guidelines for Agencies Placing Children
 (by the Ontario Ministry of Community
 and Social Services, 1981) – 35

France

Code Napoleon – 377(56)

Japan

Children's Charter – 254, 280(91), 463–464

Mozambique

Declaration of the Rights of the
 Mozambican Children (1979) – 267–269,
 279, 499–500

The Netherlands

Law of Income Support Benefits (A.B.W.)
 – 21

U.K.

British Nationality Act of 1981 – 302
Children's Charter of 1898 – 274(10)

Education Act of 1870 – 105(4)
Education Act of 1986– 301

U.S.

Bill of Rights for the Handicapped Child
 (President Hoover's White House
 Conference on Child Health and
 Protection, 1930) – 236, 275, 449
Bill of Rights for Juveniles (by the New
 York State Division for Youth) – 351–
 354, 482–483
Children's Charter (President Hoover's
 White House Conference on Child
 Health and Protection, 1930) – 220(68),

231–237, 250, 273–274, 445–448
Children's Charter in Wartime (by the United States Department of Labor, Children's Bureau, 1942) – 237–242, 399, 450–455
Children's Rights (White House Conference on Children and Youth, 1970) – 254–258, 473
Constitution of the U.S. – 20, 25, 259
CWLA (Child Welfare League of America) –
  Standards for Adoption Service – 35
  Standards for Child Welfare Institutions – 35
  Standards for Child Protective Service – 35
  Standards for Day Care Service – 35
  Standards for Foster Family Care of the Child – 28–29, 35
  Standards for Group Home Services for Children – 35
  Standards for Homemaker Service for Children – 35
  Standards for Residential Centers for Children – 35
  Standards for Services for Unmarried Parents – 35
Declaration of Independence of the United States – xi, 259
Pledge to Children (Mid-century White House Conference on Children and Youth) – 250–254, 267, 461–462
Rights of the Child (by the Joint Commission on Mental Health of Children) – 359–362, 470
Rights of Youth (White House Conference on Youth, 1971) – 259– 260, 474–475
Standards for Foster Family Systems for Public Agencies (by APWA – American Public Welfare Association, 1979) – 29, 35

PRIVATE SUGGESTIONS BY ORGANIZATIONS OR INDIVIDUALS

Belgian Charter Child in Hospital – 357
Bill of Rights For Children (Proposed by Henry Foster and Doris Freed, 1972) – 328–332, 376–377, 479
Bill of Rights of Children in Divorce Actions (by the family court judges of Milwaukee) – 332–335, 339, 468
Bill of Rights of Children in Divorce Actions (by the staff of the Dane county family court counselling services in Madison) – 334, 335–336, 469
Bill of Rights for Children in Psychotherapy (by Mr. Koocher) – 393
Bill of Rights for Foster Children (1973) – 338–340, 480–481
Charter for Children in Hospital (by the National Association for the Welfare of Children in Hospital – NAWCH, 1984) – 355–357, 516
Charter of Children's Rights (draft, by the British magazine 'Where,' 1971) – 287–292, 306, 307, 476–478
Charter Dutch National Association "Kind en Ziekenhuis" (1985) – 387(139)
Charter of Rights for Children in Care (by the London Boroughs Children's Regional Planning Committee, 1986) – 346–351, 531– 539
Charter of Rights for Children in Care (adopted in Kingston- upon-Thames, 1986) – 379(126)
Charter for Children in Hospital (First European Conference 'Children in Hospital,' 1988) – 357–359, 390(145)
Charter of Rights of Residents – 346
Charter of Rights for Young People in Care (1977) – 346, 379(118)
Charter of Rights for Young People in Care (draft, by the National Association of Young People in Care, 1978) – 381(126)
Charter for Young People (by the Labor Party, London, 1985) – 297–300, 307, 530
Children's Bill of Rights (by EOF) – 263–264, 277(70)
Children's Bill of Rights (by the New York State Youth Commission) – 247–250, 275–276, 460
Children's Charter (by the International Council of Women, 1922) – 325–328, 439– 443
Children's Charter for the Post-War World (by the New Education Fellowship) – 220(78), 285–287, 306, 456
Children and Young People's Charter (by Joan Lestor, 1990) – 304, 305, 307(52, 53)

Children and Youth Bill of Rights (by the National Association for Social Workers) – 363–366, 493–496
Declaration of the Psychological Rights of the Child – 366–369, 498
Tentative Declaration of the Psychological Rights of the Child – 392(172), 393(179)
Declaration of the Rights of the Adolescent (1922) – 155, 318–319
Declaration of the Rights of the Adolescent (Programme of Immediate Demands, by the Young Workers International and the International Union of Socialist Youth Organizations) – 318, 319, 375(36), 438
Declaration of the Rights of the Child (proposed by the Prolet'cult,' Moscow 1918) – 281–285, 305, 306, 399, 435–437
Declaration on the Rights of the Child, based on the 'Systemic Quality of Life Model' – 65, 400, 598–603
Declaration of the Rights of the Child in Israel (1989) – 263– 267, 552
Declaration of the Rights of Death Blind Persons – 198, 226(202)
FICE Malmo-Declaration – 343, 378(105)
Janusz Korczak's Declaration of the Rights of the Child
of Patricia Piziali) – 96, 107(26)
of Betty Jean Lifton) – 96, 107(27)
Malta Declaration of the Child's Right to Play – 369–372, 393, 501–503
Manifesto for Children of the Children's Legal Center (London, 1987) – 299–304, 307, 545–551
Rights of Juveniles Confined in Training Schools (by Silbert and Sussman) – 386(129)
Ten Commandments for Adults – 292– 295, 306, 307, 399, 497
Youth Charter (by ICFTU) – 319–323, 375, 504–515
Youth Charter Act Proposed by James Wallace, M.P. (1985) – 295–297, 307, 527–529

International Studies in Human Rights

1. B. G. Ramcharan (ed.): *International Law and Fact-finding in the Field of Human Rights.* 1982 ISBN 90-247-3042-2
2. B. G. Ramcharan: *Humanitarian Good Offices in International Law.* The Good Offices of the United Nations Secretary-General in the Field of Human Rights. 1983
 ISBN 90-247-2805-3
3. B. G. Ramcharan (ed.): *The Right to Life in International Law.* 1985
 ISBN 90-247-3074-0
4. P. Alston and K. Tomaševski (eds.): *The Right to Food.* 1984 ISBN 90-247-3087-2
5. A. Bloed and P. van Dijk (eds.): *Essays on Human Rights in the Helsinki Process.* 1985
 ISBN 90-247-3211-5
6. K. Törnudd: *Finland and the International Norms of Human Rights.* 1986
 ISBN 90-247-3257-3
7. H. Thoolen and B. Verstappen: *Human Rights Missions.* A Study of the Fact-finding Practice of Non-governmental Organizations. 1986 ISBN 90-247-3364-2
8. H. Hannum: *The Right to Leave and Return in International Law and Practice.* 1987
 ISBN 90-247-3445-2
9. J. H. Burgers and H. Danelius: *The United Nations Convention against Torture.* A Handbook on the Convention against Torture and Other Cruel, Inhuman or Degrading Treatment or Punishment. 1988 ISBN 90-247-3609-9
10. D. A. Martin (ed.): *The New Asylum Seekers: Refugee Law in the 1980s.* The Ninth Sokol Colloquium on International Law. 1988 ISBN 90-247-3730-3
11. C. M. Quiroga: *The Battle of Human Rights.* Gross, Systematic Violations and the Inter-American System. 1988 ISBN 90-247-3687-0
12. L. A. Rehof and C. Gulmann (eds.): *Human Rights in Domestic Law and Development Assistance Policies of the Nordic Countries.* 1989 ISBN 90-247-3743-5
13. B. G. Ramcharan: *The Concept and Present Status of International Protection of Human Rights.* Forty Years After the Universal Declaration. 1989
 ISBN 90-247-3759-1
14. A. D. Byre and B. Y. Byfield (eds.): *International Human Rights Law in the Commonwealth Caribbean.* 1991 ISBN 90-247-3785-0
15. N. Lerner: *Groups Rights and Discrimination in International Law.* 1991
 ISBN 0-7923-0853-0
16. S. Shetreet (ed.): *Free Speech and National Security.* 1991 ISBN 0-7923-1030-6
17. G. Gilbert: *Aspects of Extradition Law.* 1991 ISBN 0-7923-1162-0
18. P.E. Veerman: *The Rights of the Child and the Changing Image of Childhood.* 1991
 ISBN 0-7923-1250-3
19. M. Delmas-Marty (ed.): *The European Convention for the Protection of Human Rights.* International Protection versus National Restrictions. 1991 ISBN 0-7923-1283-X

International Studies in Human Rights

20. A. Bloed and P. van Dijk (eds.): *The Human Dimension of the Helsinki Process.* The Vienna Follow-up Meeting and its Aftermath. 1991   ISBN 0-7923-1337-2
21. L.S. Sunga: *Individual Responsibility in International Law for Serious Human Rights Violations.* 1992   ISBN 0-7923-1453-0
22. S. Frankowski and D. Shelton (eds.): *Preventive Detention.* A Comparative and International Law Perspective. 1992   ISBN 0-7923-1465-4

This series is designed to shed light on current legal and political aspects of process and organization in the field of human rights.

MARTINUS NIJHOFF PUBLISHERS – DORDRECHT / BOSTON / LONDON